The Boer War

The Boer War

Martin Bossenbroek

Translated by Yvette Rosenberg

New York • Oakland • London

First published in 2012 by Athenaeum – Polak & Van Gennep, Singel 262, 1016 AC Amsterdam, Netherlands

First published in English by Jacana Media (Pty) Ltd in 2015

First Seven Stories Press edition January 2018.

Text © Martin Bossenbroek 2012
Translated into English by Yvette Rosenberg

This book is published with the support of the Dutch Foundation for Literature.

Nederlands
letterenfonds
dutch foundation
for literature

Seven Stories Press
140 Watts Street
New York, NY 10013
www.sevenstories.com

Library of Congress Cataloging-in-Publication Data

Names: Bossenbroek, M. P., author. | Rosenberg, Yvette, translator.
Title: The Boer War / Martin Bossenbroek ; translated by Yvette Rosenberg.
Other titles: Boerenoorlog. English.
Description: Seven Stories Press first edition. | New York ; Oakland : Seven Stories Press, 2017.
Identifiers: LCCN 2017001137 (print) | LCCN 2017002436 (ebook) | ISBN 9781609807474 (hardcover) | ISBN 9781609807481 (Ebook)
Subjects: LCSH: South African War, 1899-1902. | Leyds, Willem Johannes, 1859-1940. | Churchill, Winston, 1874-1965. | Reitz, Deneys, 1882-1944.
Classification: LCC DT1896 B6713 2017 (print) | LCC DT1896 (ebook) | DDC
    968.048--dc23
LC record available at https://lccn.loc.gov/2017001137

Printed in the USA.

9 8 7 6 5 4 3 2 1

Contents

Part III – Death and destruction
June 1900 – May 1902

Epilogue – Winners and losers
Bloemfontein, 6 July 2012

Prologue
Heritage Day
Bloemfontein, 24 September 2011

If there is any place where the memory of the Boer War is kept alive, it is in Bloemfontein, the seat of South Africa's Supreme Court of Appeal. This is where both the National Party and the African National Congress (ANC) were conceived, though there is little to see that recalls either of those historic events. But the city does have a worthy memorial to the war fought by the former Boer republics of the Transvaal and the Orange Free State against Great Britain in 1899–1902. It consists of a monument and a museum standing side by side in a large park.

Understandably, no one wants to remember Bloemfontein as the place where the seeds of the reviled apartheid system were sown. In 1914, however, it saw the establishment of the National Party, which came to power in 1948 with an official policy of racial segregation. The embodiment of white supremacy is not something to be commemorated or inscribed in stone.

The founding of the ANC is a different matter. Originally the South African Native National Congress, the ANC was established on 8 January 1912, two years before the National Party, in a small church near the railway station in Fort Street. It took power from the white regime in 1994 and has governed the country ever since. The church in which it first saw the light of day is now a liberation heritage site. Like Nelson Mandela's prison cell on Robben Island, it has become a cultural and historical memorial to African nationalism.

At least, that was the plan, but it hasn't yet materialised. For years, no one had given the building a second glance. It was only recently rediscovered in the run-up to the ANC's centennial celebrations. The problem, however, is that the church is currently being used for a different purpose. It is a panel-beating workshop and appears to be doing a good trade. The yard is littered with car wrecks and waste. Time is running out. The owner knows what his property is worth, but in spite of that ANC spokesmen are confident that he'll be moving out soon and that the building will be restored to its original state by 8 January 2012.[1]

Time isn't an issue in Monument Road, just a few kilometres away. The two structures dedicated to the Boer War have stood there for decades.

The Bauhaus-style museum dates from 1931. The monument is a towering obelisk, 35 metres tall. Unveiled in 1913, it is nearly as old as the ANC.

The park they stand in is an oasis of peace, with manicured lawns and rustling trees. Even so, it has a boom at the entrance and observes opening hours. Time seems to have stood still. A stroll through the grounds strengthens this impression. The entire park is a memorial site, in 1950s style, just as it was meant to be. There are statues, guns and railway carriages, a wall of remembrance and a group of sculptures at the foot of the obelisk, all telling the story of the struggle and suffering of the Boer nation in their Second War of Liberation. For that is what they themselves called the war they fought against the British after an earlier conflict in 1880–81.

It is the story of two insignificant Boer republics forced into war by the imperialist superpower Great Britain. Surprised and exasperated by their successful resistance, first in conventional combat and later in a protracted guerrilla war, the British commanders resorted to a campaign of terror against the civilian population. As a result, the Boers became victims of persecution as well as heroes. This is the narrative the park conveys.

Three sculptures symbolise different stages of the war. *Farewell 11-10-1899* represents a militant young Boer leaving for the front at the outbreak of war. *The Exile* depicts a man and his grandson at the railing of a ship, representing the thousands of Boer prisoners of war whom the British sent to camps overseas. *The Diehard 31 May 1902* illustrates the plight of the surviving commandos at the end of the war. It shows a battle-weary Boer on an emaciated horse, exhausted from years of hardship and deprivation, but with head held high.

These are the memories preserved here. It is the story of David and Goliath, except that this David was forced to surrender under the pressure of unendurable suffering. This is expressed on the circular plinth on which the column rests. An inscription between the sculptures and the plaques reads: 'This National Monument has been erected in commemoration of the 26,370 women and children who died in the concentration camps as well as other women and children who succumbed elsewhere as a result of the war of 1899–1902. Unveiled on 16th December 1913.'

Visitors today might be misled by the inscription. Since the Second World War the term 'concentration camps' has been associated with the Nazis' systematic murder of the Jews, but that is not what it meant in 1913. In the light of what we know today, it would be more accurate to call the British camps 'internment camps', because that is what they were. And they were massive.

Commander-in-Chief Lord Roberts and his successor, Lord Kitchener, hoped that removing the civilian population from the war zone would force the Boer commandos to surrender. Some 115,000 people, mostly women and children, were rounded up and incarcerated in appalling conditions, where almost a quarter of them, mainly children, perished. The population of the two Boer republics was decimated.

The National Women's Memorial—its official name—depicts the suffering of the Boer nation, and shows why the Boers were unable to keep up the fight. But it also alludes to heroism: the monument is dedicated to 'our heroines and beloved children'. Beneath the inscription is a quotation from the Lord's Prayer, 'Thy will be done', four words that encapsulate the Boers' unwavering belief in divine predestination. Five tombs that were later incorporated into the monument also allude to heroism and martyrdom. Here lie the remains of Emily Hobhouse, the British activist who exposed the cruelty and injustice of the camps, along with those of the president of the Orange Free State, Marthinus Steyn, the ultimate diehard, and his wife Tibbie. Beside them are the graves of the commandos' spiritual mentor, 'Father' Kestell, and the legendary Boer general Christiaan de Wet.[2]

This romantic image of the Boers as tragic heroes will be familiar to an older generation of Dutch readers. It lingered on in the collective memory of the Dutch long after the Second World War. Those who grew up with books by L. Penning will recall works like *De verkenner van Christiaan de Wet* (Christiaan de Wet's Scout), one of five volumes in the famous Wessels series, originally published between 1900 and 1904 and reprinted until the 1970s. The Boers in Penning's books were tough, intrepid pioneers, people who feared God but didn't flinch in the face of 'bloodthirsty kaffirs' or 'wild animals'. Men with beards. With a psalm on their lips and a loaded rifle in their hands, they threw themselves into battle defending a righteous cause against a numerically superior force of treacherous Rednecks. Generations of Dutch youngsters revelled in the unequal but heroic struggle. Good against evil. The Boer War.

The adventures of Penning's protagonists, Field Cornet Louis Wessels and his trusty companion Blikoortje were an empathetic blend of fact and fiction. Penning had never actually seen the world he was describing, but neither had his German contemporary Karl May, who created Winnetou and Old Shatterhand without having set foot in the Wild West. Penning, however, had access to reams of documentation. When he started his Wessels series the whole of the Netherlands was riveted by the unfolding story of the Boers. Everyone supported the liberation struggle of their two beleaguered republics and followed their progress day by day. Information was readily available in the early stages, before communications with the Transvaal and the Orange Free State were severed, and there were eyewitness reports in abundance for Penning to consult.

The entire European continent sided with the Boers, but nowhere was their support more emotionally charged than in the Netherlands, where the war rekindled the nation's awareness of its blood ties with the Boers. Until the late nineteenth century, the Dutch had barely given a thought to their cousins on the faraway southern tip of Africa. Most of the Boers, or Afrikaners, were descendants of Dutch colonists who had settled there after Jan van Riebeeck's arrival at the Cape in 1652. The Dutch back in Europe, rather than feeling any affinity with them, were disdainful of their archaic ideas and lifestyle.

All of that changed dramatically when the Boers rose up successfully against British rule—first in 1880–81 and subsequently in the war that began on 11 October 1899 and lasted longer than anyone had expected. Suddenly the Dutch discovered their ties with the Boers, descendants of the same heroic tribe, with the same ancient blood flowing through their veins. The Boers were embraced like prodigal sons, all the more passionately to make up for lost time. Their fond welcome into the family circle created bonds of solidarity. Every right-minded Dutchman identified with their valiant struggle, from young Queen Wilhelmina down to her lowliest subject, from the Protestant centre of the country to the Catholic south and the liberal north. The Dutch began to dream of a new Netherlands under the Southern Cross.

The rise of militant nationalism in the Netherlands around the turn of the century strengthened this sense of shared identity. After decades of struggle, the Dutch colonial army had finally managed to bring the East Indies archipelago under control. Lombok and Atjeh had recently become names spoken of with pride instead of shame, and soon afterwards they started appearing as street names in the Netherlands. The Netherlands' success in the East Indies was infectious and fostered a taste for more. In this context, the Boers' armed conflict in the name of a 'righteous' cause won admiration and support. Alongside Indonesian neighbourhoods, 'Transvaal' neighbourhoods now sprang up in many Dutch cities, with streets named after 'Oom' (Uncle) Paul Kruger, Louis Botha and many others, including of course Steyn and De Wet.

But there was one crucial difference. In the East Indies the Dutch were in a position to act independently, which they did—with an iron fist. Within a few years Dutch rule was firmly established throughout the archipelago. There, they could rightly speak of 'our East Indies'. But South Africa was a different matter. From the start, they had applauded from the sidelines but not actually taken part. The glory they were basking in wasn't their own. The Dutch were quick to offer their services as volunteers, or support the Boer cause in other ways, but as a country the Netherlands was powerless. It was unwilling—because of the East Indies—to incur the wrath of Great Britain, which still ruled the seven seas.

When the tide of war turned against the Boers their defeat was inevitable. Nothing and no one could prevent it. Even the Great Powers balked at the thought of antagonising almighty Britain. The effect was sobering. The dream was over. The Netherlands' infatuation with the Boers fizzled out as abruptly as it had flared up. After the war, a small core of faithful supporters continued to take an interest in the fortunes of the Boers, but for the Dutch as a whole they slipped back into the mists of history. The Boer heroes lived on only in adventure stories for boys and in street names, except for those that have since been renamed to honour a new generation, like Steve Biko and Nelson Mandela.[3]

Although the memorial park in Bloemfontein may look like a relic of bygone times, the museum itself has a surprise in store. Here, time has moved on, at least in some parts of the building. The first sign of this is startling. Two objects dominate the entrance hall. One is an original harmonium, once the pride of every Boer home, around which the family would gather for their daily psalms. It was also a familiar feature of the living rooms of orthodox Dutch Protestants well into the twentieth century. Directly above the harmonium is its incongruous counterpart in modern domestic life: a wide-screen television set, with a slide presentation of what the museum has to offer. A sudden glimpse into the modern age.

For anything more of this kind, the visitor has to be patient. The route starts off in exhibition halls named after well-known Boer leaders—Steyn and De Wet, Kruger, Botha, and Koos de la Rey, 'the lion of the Western Transvaal'—which still appear to be in their original state. The room on 'concentration camps' is named after Emily Hobhouse, corresponding to the scheme outdoors. So far, nothing new. The same applies to the display, where the maxim seems to be the more the better. The inscriptions are in Afrikaans and English. The strains of Bach accompany us from room to room. The whole arrangement is a wonderful time capsule of the 1950s.

Then at last comes the surprise: the Sol Plaatje Room, named after the only black South African known to have kept a diary of the Boer War, in Mafeking during the siege by the Boers. Plaatje was also one of the founding members of the ANC in 1912. He was a good choice as the symbol of a historical truth which only came to light in the 1980s. The Boer War may have started as a white man's war, but it wasn't only whites who were involved in the hostilities. The indigenous African and coloured populations (in South Africa, the term 'coloured' became a way to classify people of mixed-race descent), along with immigrants from British India, were also caught up in the conflict, actively and passively, as participants and as victims. As it progressed, the war increasingly became a struggle between the Boers, the British *and* the African and coloured communities.

This discovery was revealed in 1983 in a book by Peter Warwick. *Black People and the South African War 1899–1902* was an eye-opener. Warwick describes how the African and coloured communities were caught up in the war, which he consequently renamed the South African War.

In the first place, Warwick explains, the Boer commandos employed between 7000 and 9000 African and coloured servants to ride with them, known in Afrikaans as *agterryers*. The British, too, used unarmed Africans and coloureds to perform chores of all kinds. In the guerrilla stage of the war the number of blacks employed by the Boers fell dramatically, while their counterparts on the British side increased at the same rate. Moreover, the British started engaging large numbers of African and coloured paramilitaries as couriers, scouts and guards. They also started arming them and deploying them in active combat. Towards the end of the war an estimated 30,000 armed blacks were in British service. To put this in perspective, the entire British army comprised roughly 250,000 men. The number of Boer commandos who were still active had declined from 60,000 to 15,000.

Besides those in the service of the Boers or the British, a growing number of non-whites were drawn into the war as members of chiefdoms or nations allied to one of the two parties to the conflict—more accurately, the British. In the early days, notably during the siege of Mafeking, the Boers occasionally enlisted the help of their allies, the Rapulana Barolong, but that was the sum of it. The British, however, began to rely more heavily on armed support from Africans and coloureds. Initially they recruited only from the territories bordering on the Transvaal and Orange Free State—Bechuanaland, Griqualand, Basutoland and Zululand—but gradually they cast their net further, to the Boer republics themselves, recruiting notably among the Kgatla and the Pedi in the north-west and east of the Transvaal.

Though hostility between the Boers and the black population escalated in the course of the war, the two also had something in common. On Kitchener's orders, African and coloured families who were not active in the British war effort were systematically removed from the operational arena. Like Boer women and children, they were confined to (segregated) internment camps. As it happens, the same number of Africans and coloureds—115,000—were incarcerated in the same inhumane conditions and with the same appalling mortality rate. And again, most fatalities occurred among children. Although the official death toll was 14,000, Warwick says the real number must have exceeded 20,000.[4]

The exhibition in the Sol Plaatje Room is based on Warwick's findings. This is not the only room in which the museum has moved with the times, at least to some extent. A small outbuilding houses an education centre where information about the Boer War is woven into the national history of the new, multiracial South Africa. Schoolchildren learn the story behind the Afrikaner 'Sarie Marais', but they also learn about the tragic fate suffered by black as well as white children in the internment camps. And that in three languages: Afrikaans, English and isiZulu (after English, South Africa's second lingua franca).

It is an 'inclusive' retrospective of the Boer War, in contrast to the Afrikaner narrative in the rest of the museum and its grounds. The combination takes getting used to, but apparently these things really can coexist in the new South Africa. It is an extraordinary combination, which gives the memorial site in Monument Road the feel of an archaeological dig. Except that here the successive layers of soil, instead of being on top of one another, occur randomly throughout the site.

Boer War commemoration as an archaeological dig would probably explain the insistent involvement of ANC dignitaries in the centenary events in 1999–2002. The new discovery they held up for inspection was the suffering of the population as a whole. The idea of the Boer War as a collective experience tied in nicely with the prevailing ideal of South Africa as a rainbow nation. Nelson Mandela's presidency aimed at national reconciliation. Thabo Mbeki, his successor from June 1999, followed this through during the commemoration of the Boer War.

At the official launch of the commemoration in Brandfort, near Bloemfontein, on 9 October 1999, in the presence of the Duke of Kent, Mbeki honoured all those whom 'the tides of history' had swept into 'a bitter, costly and protracted war . . . Afrikaners, British, Africans, Coloureds, Australians, Canadians and New Zealanders'. Such a war must never be allowed to happen again, Mbeki urged. While paying tribute to the heroism of all who had been involved at the time, he appealed to his audience to dream of new heroes and heroines, 'who will be the architects of a non-racial, a peaceful and prosperous South Africa'.

Mbeki's vice-president, the current president Jacob Zuma, also styled himself as a messenger of reconciliation. A day later he spoke in Mafikeng—the original, now restored name of Mafeking—about Sol Plaatje and his diary, which for once looked at the war from a 'unique black perspective'. But he also spoke about 'our historical responsibility to reconcile and heal those old wounds'. Zuma called for blacks and whites to combine their different versions of the story to form 'a comprehensive narrative'. Because 'distressing as our past may be, it is a shared past that excludes no South African'. To express this inclusive view, Zuma too coined a new name: the Anglo-Boer South African War.[5]

To judge by the event at the museum today, the new name didn't catch on. It is Saturday 24 September 2011, Heritage Day in South Africa. To mark the occasion, the museum has organised a special morning dedicated to the 110th anniversary of the Anglo-Boer War—in Afrikaans, the Anglo-Boereoorlog—the name by which the war has always been known.

The museum is less consistent as far as its own name is concerned. It uses its original name, the War Museum of the Boer Republics, interchangeably with its official name, the Anglo-Boer War Museum. This no longer surprises anyone, any more than the 'archaeological' aspects of the programme do. A lecture on the (Anglo-) Boer War as 'the first media war' was sandwiched between educational films about the Women's Monument and the museum itself. Then came an anthology of war memoirs. The morning ended with the unveiling of an installation by the Johannesburg artist Willem Boshoff.

It is difficult to relate Boshoff's work to any of those other 'layers of soil'. It represents the suffering of the Boers, but not theirs alone. It is clearly not meant to be inclusive or reconciliatory. Quite the contrary, it is an expression of anger and grief, a scathing indictment in the name of the thousands of children—black, white and coloured—who suffered and died in the British internment camps. Boshoff holds Queen Victoria formally responsible for it and observes that neither she nor her four successors have ever apologised for what he considers a war crime. The title of the installation, *32,000 Darling Little Nuisances*, refers to the estimated number of children who died in the camps; 'darling little nuisances' is a phrase Queen Victoria once used herself. The work juxtaposes life-sized portraits of the five monarchs with the names of the 1432 children who were interned in Bethulie, one of the most notorious camps of all.

After the ceremony, 60-year-old Boshoff is happy to talk about his work. With his powerful physique and long beard he looks like a real Afrikaner, which he is, one with a hippie streak. Bethulie was situated near his grandfather's farm. Two of the children who died there had the same name as his. Like the rest of his family, he has been scarred by the war. At the same time, he denounces extremist right-wing movements, such as the Afrikaner Weerstandsbeweging, which exploit the history of the camps for propaganda purposes. A committed pacifist, Boshoff was a conscientious objector to military conscription under the apartheid regime. He lives, as he says, by humanitarian principles and the dictates of his conscience.

Boshoff sees a correspondence between the Boer War and the rise of reactionary conservatism among Afrikaners in the twentieth century, the nation's overreaction, he believes, to anxieties about being reduced to a marginal existence, perhaps being destroyed. The collective trauma of the war generated movements like the National Party, which aimed to protect Afrikaner culture and uncompromisingly appropriate power, only to seek the ultimate illusion of security in the 'disastrous system of apartheid'.[6]

This kind of rationale is nothing new. The hypothesis has been proposed by academics and others. The presumed causal relationship between the war and the apartheid system is one of the five main themes in the historiographical discourse on the Boer War.

The first of these themes is the war as an atypical climax to British imperialism. The Scramble for Africa (1880–1914) went hand in hand with the violent oppression of the indigenous populations of almost the entire continent by the armies of the European powers. The Boer War was the only major conflict between white adversaries. Its scale can be deduced from the financial cost to Great Britain. In October 1899 the British government believed £10 million would see it through; by May 1902 it had cost £217 million. To put this in perspective, that was 12 per cent of Britain's gross national product in 1900. This massive expenditure prompted a flurry of research to establish why London had decided to start the war. The answers range from economic and political to psychological and geostrategic motives—with the balance ultimately coming down on the side of the politicians in Whitehall rather than the bankers in the City.[7]

The second theme examines the political and military links, whether direct or indirect, between the Boer War and the First World War. Widespread sympathy for the Boers on the European continent prompted Great Britain to review its strategic position in relation to emerging economic and military superpowers such as the United States and Germany. Its traditional policy of 'splendid isolation' was no longer effective, so Britain sought alliances instead. This led to a construct of diplomatic dominoes which, in the summer of 1914, threatened to collapse. As for the military aspect, the first stage of conventional warfare in the Boer War revealed the senseless slaughter that results from massive frontal attacks against an entrenched adversary.[8]

In another respect too, the Boer War was a precursor of what military conflicts would be like in the future. Never before had the media played such an important role in war. Never before had they been represented in such numbers. An estimated 200 correspondents were sent to the war zone, mostly from Great Britain, but also from other parts of the British Empire and the United States. Steamships, steam trains and, most importantly, an extensive telegraph network made it possible to travel and disseminate news with little delay. Besides journalists and other eyewitnesses, there were also artists, photographers and film-makers who played a part in shaping opinions and attitudes around the world. Given the mass of available material, European and American public opinion became the pawn in a full-blown propaganda war between the two sides, which sometimes reached the same frenzied pitch as the war on the battlefield.[9]

The fourth theme—the catastrophic impact of the second phase of the war on the civilian populations of the two Boer republics—has already been discussed in the preceding pages. Around 230,000 whites and non-whites were incarcerated; 46,000 are known to have died. In addition, the British troops left a trail of systematic destruction as they swept through the Transvaal and the Orange Free State. Hence the guerrilla phase of the Boer War foreshadowed the devastation caused by all-out warfare as in the Second World War.[10]

The fifth and final theme is the one Willem Boshoff touched on: the possibility of a causal relationship between the Boer War and the surge of white nationalism, culminating in the apartheid ideology. Much has been written on this subject, but the last word has not been said. The same applies to its corollary: the development of an *anti*-apartheid movement. After all, the emergence of black nationalism cannot be examined without taking account of the Boer War. The hopes that black leaders had pinned on a British victory were shattered during the peace talks. The aftermath of war brought even greater disillusionment. To their bitter frustration, the non-white population, with a nod from the British administration, ended up with probably even fewer constitutional rights than they had possessed before. The ANC, like the National Party, didn't come out of nowhere.[11]

This last factor is by far the most relevant today and therefore attracts most social and academic interest. All the more reason to return to this in the Epilogue.

But first, as President Zuma has urged, the whole story must be told. This sounds more self-evident than it is. Few, if any, books offer a complete account. A number expressly aim to do so and some almost succeed. Broadly speaking, there are two approaches. Some writers tell the story from the perspective of the British protagonists, in both Great Britain and South Africa, others from that of the Boer leaders. The most successful accounts present the two points of view alternately as well as that of the non-white population.[12]

But what these works have in common, no matter how informative or revealing some of them are, is that they omit one important frame of reference. The story of the Boer War has never been told from the Dutch point of view. What is missing is a vital link in the chain of cause and effect. The Dutch played a crucial part in the prelude to the war and throughout the actual conflict, not just in practical terms because of the input of Dutch actors in key positions but—no less importantly—because of the psychological aspect of the ties between the Dutch and the Boers. It is true that the Netherlands' infatuation with the Boers may not have impelled the Dutch to take a strong political stand, but emotionally the venerable motherland was a rock and anchor for the Boer cause in Europe. This was felt not only in the Transvaal and the Orange Free State but also in Great Britain. It resounds in the words of the British prime minister, Lord Salisbury, who remarked on the eve of the war that in South Africa 'we, not the Dutch, are Boss'.[13]

The part played by the Netherlands, particularly in the period leading up to the hostilities, is one aspect of the Boer War that has largely been overlooked, even in recent Dutch publications. It received attention in older works such as P.J. van Winter's history of the Netherlands-South African Railway Company, and rightly so given the strategic importance of the railway network built and run by the company. But since the Second World War, nothing more has been said about it. Subsequent histories concerning the ties between the Netherlands and South Africa have focused mainly on their bonds of kinship, language and religion.[14]

This book is the first to tell the story of the Boer War from the Dutch point of view as well. But of course it goes further than that. To tell the *full* story, it weaves this new angle into the bigger picture. As a result, the narrative perspective shifts back and forth throughout the book, from Boer to Briton and, where relevant, to the Dutch.

It highlights three individuals whose accounts of the period encapsulate the three main narratives of the time, and who themselves have personified those narratives up to the present day. The Boer War made them larger than life and they make the war more real through their journals, correspondence and reports, and later through their memoirs and reflections. They are the Dutch lawyer Willem Leyds, the British war correspondent Winston Churchill, and the Boer commando Deneys Reitz, three young men at the start of their careers, each fighting a just cause and each convinced that right was on his side. There are pictures of them close together at the Anglo-Boer War Museum in Bloemfontein. In real life their thinking and experiences were miles apart. Their story begins in June 1884 in the Amstel Hotel in Amsterdam.

SOUTH AFRICA
1884 – 1899

GERMAN

SOUTH WEST

AFRICA

ATLANTIC OCEAN

BECHU
(British Prot

BRIT

BECHUANALAN

GRIQ
LAN
WEST

Orange *(Gariep)*

Port
Nolloth

Concordia

Orange

Hopeto

CAPE

De Aar

Beaufort West

C

CAPE TOWN

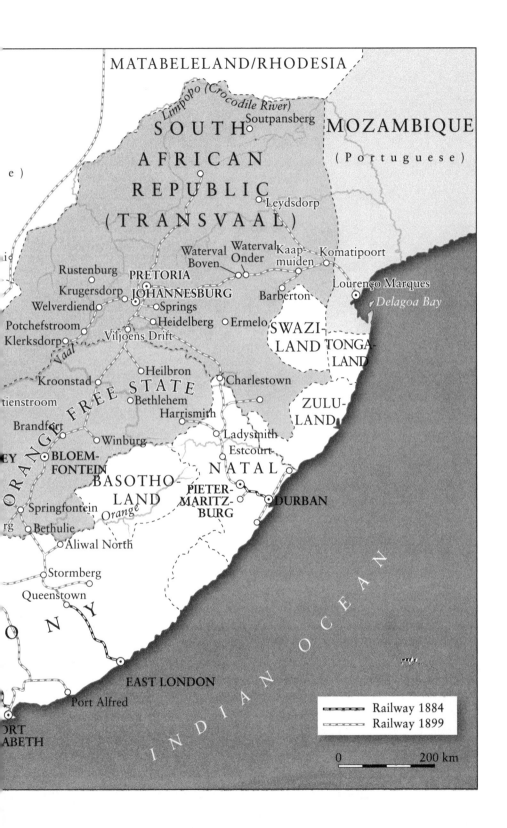

MATABELELAND/RHODESIA

Limpopo (Crocodile River)

S O U T H

A F R I C A N

R E P U B L I C

(T R A N S V A A L)

Soutpansberg

MOZAMBIQUE

(P o r t u g u e s e)

Leydsdorp

Waterval Boven
Waterval Onder
Kaap-muiden
Komatipoort

Rustenburg
Krugersdorp
PRETORIA
JOHANNESBURG
Barberton
Lourenço Marques
Delagoa Bay

Welverdiend
Springs

Potchefstroom
Heidelberg
Ermelo
SWAZI-LAND
TONGA-LAND

Klerksdorp
Viljoens Drift

Vaal

Heilbron
Charlestown

Kroonstad
S T A T E

tienstroom
Bethlehem
ZULU-LAND

Brandfort
Harrismith

O R A N G E   F R E E

Winburg
Ladysmith

EY
BLOEM-FONTEIN
Estcourt

Springfontein
BASOTHO-LAND

Orange
PIETER-MARITZ-BURG
NATAL

rg
Bethulie
DURBAN

Aliwal North

Stormberg

Queenstown

O N Y

EAST LONDON

Port Alfred

RT
ABETH

I N D I A N   O C E A N

| | Railway 1884 |
| | Railway 1899 |

0   200 km

PART I
For a good cause
June 1884—October 1899

Willem Leyds

An extraordinary meeting
Amsterdam, June 1884

It was an offer he could easily have refused. A PhD cum laude, barely 25 years old, the protégé of distinguished academics at Amsterdam's celebrated faculty of law, Willem Leyds could take his pick: the judiciary in the East Indies, a chair at Groningen University, or a position with the Nederlandsche Bank. He could choose any career he wanted.

Then why would he accept such a bizarre proposal? State attorney in the Transvaal? That was the last thing he could have imagined. A country populated by zealous Calvinist cattle farmers, a state not much older than himself, it had little to offer a liberal-minded lawyer. Not to mention the inhospitable cultural climate of the South African highveld. Leyds was not only an academic, but also a gifted artist. He played the cello in a string quartet, read Homer and socialised with the intelligentsia. And now the Transvaal, 'that intellectual desert', in the words of his fiancée Louise Roeff.

Any doubts he may have had were confirmed when he met the man who had made the proposal. Paul Kruger had impressed him with his physical stature, his dark eyes and sonorous voice, his self-assured directness. But the sound came from another world, an echo from the past. The president of the Transvaal was an Afrikaner through and through, a man of the Word, the gun and the wide open savannas. He was also patently unconcerned with his appearance. Leyds, on the other hand, was a handsome young man, groomed to the tips of his stylish moustache. The lumbering grubbiness of the Boer leader, going on 60, filled the luxurious suite of the Amstel Hotel where they had arranged to meet.

For Leyds the contrast was too sharp, the distance too great and the decision too radical. A few hours later he graciously declined the honour. But Kruger wasn't a man to take no for an answer. He persuaded him to reconsider the offer. That was on Thursday 12 June 1884, the day after Leyds's graduation. Two days later, the president of the Transvaal would be leaving Amsterdam. Well, why not? Leyds decided to have another word with his mentor Nicolaas Pierson.[1]

Leyds's reservations were understandable. The Netherlands wasn't sure how to deal with the Boers. They had won admiration for their successful

1

resistance to British colonial rule, but they had only become heroes recently, in December 1880. Who could tell whether the glory would last?

They had been ignored and forgotten for decades. After the British formally gained control over the Cape Colony in 1806, the white colonists there gradually faded into oblivion. That was the case in the Netherlands too, where most of their forefathers had been born. In the 1850s, when the Boers cast off the shackles of British rule and established the independent republics of the Transvaal (officially the South African Republic) and the Orange Free State, the Dutch responded with an indifferent nod. The ties of kinship had gradually weakened, or been swept under the carpet.

The few reports about the Boers that slipped through were generally unflattering. They were said to be lazy, stupid, sanctimonious and, worst of all, they mistreated 'the poor Kaffirs'. Well, it is true that the Boers practised an Old Testament kind of racism, slavery and all, with no sense of shame. On the contrary, they deliberately frustrated the efforts of missionaries who tried to convert the black population to Christianity. So it was mainly the missionary societies that were critical of the Boers and turned public opinion against them, first in Britain and later in the rest of Europe as well. The most incriminating evidence was revealed to the Netherlands by the clergyman Pierre Huet in 1869. Huet had been a missionary for 12 years and had written at length about the plundering, murder and other atrocities committed by the Boers.

In the 1870s, their already bruised reputation came in for another battering. At first it looked as if Thomas Burgers, president of the Transvaal, would help turn the tide of public opinion in their favour. In 1875, he travelled through Europe lobbying support for several ambitious development projects. He made a favourable impression in the Netherlands, at least in liberal circles. Not only did he manage to establish diplomatic ties, he also secured a loan to build a railway from the Transvaal to the Indian Ocean. In addition, he was presented with a national anthem to take home. It was written by the poet Catharina van Rees and opened with the words 'Do you know that brave nation of heroes?' But it is doubtful that Burgers sang along merrily after returning to the Transvaal. It was soon clear that the Boers had lost confidence in him. The loan and the railway project had come to nothing, and the population was divided as a result. Two years later the British stepped in and brought an end to the independence of the South African Republic, virtually without lifting a finger. On 12 April 1877, the Union Jack was hoisted on the government building in Pretoria.[2]

Few tears were shed in the Netherlands. The universities of Utrecht, Amsterdam and Leiden protested against the unconstitutional annexation by Britain, but there was no hint of sympathy for the Boers. Their own fault, according to the liberals, they shouldn't have turned against Burgers. Their own fault, echoed Albert Kuyper and his orthodox Protestants, united in the Anti-Revolutionary Party. They shouldn't have backed Burgers in the first place.

The miracle only occurred in December 1880, when the Boers took up arms to overthrow British rule and succeeded in a matter of days. As if by magic, the black sheep of the family were completely transformed in the eyes of the Dutch public. They were suddenly resurrected as long-lost brethren, members of the same glorious tribe of Hollanders, with the same heroic blood in their veins. Simple souls perhaps, but sensible and at worst just a little more conservative than they were used to in the Netherlands. But then, who wouldn't be, in darkest Africa?

This sudden metamorphosis wasn't the work of just anybody. Behind it was the worthy intellectual elite, who not only reflected on the Boers' amazing rehabilitation but were also the first who were willing to take action. Well, action? Addresses, leaflets, editorial comments, solidarity meetings, fundraising, that sort of thing. Still, this total reversal of public opinion was nothing short of spectacular. And behind it were eminent academics.

The initiative was taken by Pieter Harting, a celebrated professor of pharmacology, anatomy, zoology and geology, to name but a few of his specialities, and as such one of the last natural science polymaths at the University of Utrecht. On 23 December 1880, he published a petition 'To the People of England' in the *Utrechtsch Provinciaal en Stedelijk Dagblad*. It was an appeal in the name of justice, on behalf of the people of the Transvaal, 'the sons of our forefathers', and it soon rallied support. A fortnight later, with 6082 signatures, the petition was presented to Queen Victoria. Of the signatories 81 were Harting's peers—81 out of a total of 180 professors in the whole of the Netherlands.

Add to this the hundreds of church ministers, officers, mayors and members of municipal councils, the provincial executives and the States-General who had also signed the appeal, and the conclusion must be that it was the learned elite in the Netherlands who took up the cause of the far less well-educated Boers. It couldn't have been a feeling of affinity, it was something more like nationalistic projection. Indeed, Harting's initiative marked the beginning of a period in which the Dutch embraced with growing enthusiasm an increasingly focused dream of a Great Netherlands, kindled by their conquest of the East Indies archipelago and their vicarious pride in the success of their Boer kinsmen in South Africa. The true fires of nationalism were to flare up towards the turn of the century, but in the meantime this was quite a blaze.

Harting, as we have seen, took one of the leading roles in this movement. After the success of his petition, he embarked on another project and founded the Supreme Committee in Support of the Interests of the Transvaal Boers. Its members were a select group from Utrecht, all of them liberal-minded professors, except one. Gerard Beelaerts van Blokland, a senior official at the Ministry of Justice, a man who had longstanding ties with South Africa, also joined the group. He was an orthodox Protestant and became a member of the Anti-Revolutionary Party shortly afterwards.

As its name suggests, the Utrecht Supreme Committee was not the only committee of its kind, but it was the most circumspect, as Harting and his followers expressly limited their efforts in support of the Boer cause to 'any permissible, i.e. peaceful, means compatible with the neutrality of our fatherland'. They would do nothing that might offend the British government or public opinion, and wanted no part in the wild schemes that local committees in other towns were concocting, like forming a voluntary corps, or collaborating with Irish nationalists.

Their reservations caused some irritation, particularly in Amsterdam. The Amsterdam Committee for the Transvaal, likewise founded in January 1881, was a more heterogeneous group. Besides liberals, its members included conservatives, radicals and anti-revolutionaries. Among the latter was the Anti-Revolutionary Party leader Kuyper, who was also editor-in-chief of *De Standaard* and professor of theology at the Vrije Universiteit, which had been inaugurated three months earlier. The Amsterdam group took a firmer stand and was more outspoken in its views, which appealed to Kuyper. It was evident, for instance, in their resolve to focus their activities primarily on providing humanitarian aid for victims of the war—those on the Boer side, needless to say. Kuyper attacked the Red Cross for refusing to take sides and support only one of the adversaries. He said it was a 'neutrality that would lead to injustice'.

But these differences within the pro-Boer movement paled into insignificance when it turned out that the Boers were capable of defeating the British on their own. On 27 February 1881, they delivered the final blow on Majuba Hill, a name that would jar in British ears for many years to come. At that point the Utrecht and Amsterdam committees decided to join forces and did so on 12 May. The inaugural meeting of the Dutch South African Association (Nederlandsch Zuid-Afrikaansche Vereeniging) took place in Utrecht. Harting became its honorary chairman by a unanimous vote, and spoke movingly about 'the duties imposed by ties of blood'.

It was a significant merger—the association exists to this day—but one of its most unusual features failed to survive the first year. It turned out that the Liberals and the Anti-Revolutionaries were not natural allies after all. Kuyper believed that the close religious ties between the orthodox Protestant community and the Boers created an affinity that went beyond the ties of kinship. But his exclusionary ideas found no support in the Dutch South African Association. In the summer of 1882 he resigned from the board along with Paul Fabius and Frans Lion Cachet. In the same year Cachet published a history of the Transvalers infused with the principles of the Anti-Revolutionary Party, as we see from passages like the following: 'Three months earlier, the side that seemed hopeless against the might of Britain humbly placed its trust in God. That trust was not betrayed. The Republic was liberated.'[3]

The freedom the Transvalers enjoyed was only relative at that point. The war had ended with a bang but the peace that followed was still inconclusive. The Pretoria Convention, signed on 3 August 1881, was open to interpretation, mainly because it contained ambiguities which the British negotiators had deliberately included on Prime Minister William Gladstone's instructions. In one and the same sentence, the Transvaal gained 'complete self-determination' while remaining subject to the 'suzerainty of Her Majesty', namely Queen Victoria. No one knew exactly what the latter phrase implied other than that it radically curtailed the Boer republic's freedom, notably in its dealings with other states. In Britain it served to maintain the illusion of ultimate control. The Boers contested the clause for precisely that reason. They finally signed the agreement in exchange for an undertaking that the British government would amend it, if there was any practical reason for doing so.[4]

And of course there was, at least as far as the Boers were concerned. In 1883 they decided to send a delegation to London to negotiate amendments to the Convention. Kruger, who had been elected president at the beginning of that year, led the delegation and was accompanied by a general and a dominee, Nicolaas Smit and Stephanus du Toit. Besides London, they were also going to the European mainland, essentially with the same purpose that had sent Burgers to the Continent in 1875. However different Kruger may have been from his predecessor, he was just as eager to develop the Transvaal. He recognised the need for a national bank to reorganise the government's finances and a rail link to the sea, both under Transvaal control. He also needed a new state attorney. Until recently, the position had been held by the theologian Pieter Jorissen, who had arrived from the Netherlands soon after Burgers, but was found to be too weak in jurisprudence—and too liberal in theology. He was dismissed rather unceremoniously. What Kruger wanted now was a qualified lawyer to manage the expansion of the bureaucracy, ideally someone of orthodox Protestant stock.

With that in mind the delegation set off for Europe. They were received graciously in London in November 1883. Lord Derby, the secretary of state for the colonies in Gladstone's Cabinet, was willing to reconsider the question of suzerainty, providing the Boers would be flexible in the matter of their south-western border. They were reluctant but ultimately agreed and the atmosphere at the negotiating table remained amicable. Kruger was granted an audience with Queen Victoria and took the opportunity to demonstrate the niceties of drinking hot coffee from the saucer. He also consented to the terms of the agreement. The word 'suzerainty' disappeared from the London Convention. The only allusion to it was in article 4, which required the South African Republic to obtain the consent of the British government before entering into an agreement with 'any State or Nation other than the Orange Free State', or 'with any Native Tribe to the east or west'. The document was signed on 27 February 1884, three years to the day after the Battle of Majuba.[5]

So as far as the first stage of their European mission was concerned, Kruger and his team had reason to be pleased. And they were adequately prepared for what was to follow. Before leaving London they had met with dignitaries from the Netherlands. Beelaerts van Blokland acted as their legal adviser in the negotiations with Lord Derby. Well satisfied, they promptly offered him the position of state attorney. But the Anti-Revolutionary nobleman had recently been elected to the lower house of the Dutch parliament and chose to remain in that office. He did, however, accept an appointment as special envoy of the South African Republic in Europe.

Kuyper also put in an appearance in London. With the help of Du Toit he tried to counter the allegations of the missionary John Mackenzie and others, who had accused the Boers of failing to honour their 'divine obligation towards Indians, Blacks, Kaffirs and any other race or nation of colour, or any follower of Christ, or any peace-loving persons'. This prompted a lengthy address to the members of the Anti-Slavery Society and the Aborigines Protection Society, which, in Du Toit's opinion, was not unsuccessful.[6]

Of a more material nature was the visit to London by the Amsterdam representatives of high finance. Led by Willem Mees and Nicolaas Pierson, the president and the director of the Nederlandsche Bank respectively, they discussed with the delegation the prospect of a national bank and a railway such as they had in mind. There was good news and bad news.

According to the bankers, the international money market didn't yet have sufficient confidence in the Transvaal economy to extend a bank loan. On the other hand, they believed that a stock market launch of a railway would be feasible. The arrangements could be worked out in detail in Amsterdam.

So all the spadework had been done by the time Kruger, Du Toit and Smit arrived in the Netherlands. Their spirits were raised even further by the warm welcome they received. From the moment they set foot on land in Rotterdam on 29 February 1884 they were given one heart-warming reception after another. In The Hague they appeared on the balcony of the Hotel des Indes to greet the public. In Amsterdam they were serenaded as they drove through the streets from Central Station. This went on for weeks on end. Their programme included a tour not only of the three largest cities but also of Leiden, Utrecht, Amersfoort, Arnhem, Kampen, Groningen and Den Briel.

It was spontaneous, exuberant enthusiasm which, paradoxically, stemmed partly from disunity within the pro-Boer movement. The solidarity of three years earlier had crumbled. Kuyper and his Anti-Revolutionary following had left in 1882 to go their own way. Besides the Dutch South African Association there was now an emigration committee, a standing committee, a joint committee and an organising committee, all jostling to give the Transvaal delegation a special reception, with dignitaries from among their own ranks. As a result, Kruger, in any event, met half of the *haut monde* of the Netherlands, starting with King Willem III and Queen Emma. Government ministers, members of parliament, members of the Council of State, military and judicial authorities, a line-up of professors from Utrecht, Amsterdam and Leiden, diplomats, members of the provincial executives, mayors and municipal executives—every self-respecting senior official wanted to meet Oom Paul in person.[7]

Though they basked in the glory, Kruger, Du Toit and Smit hadn't lost sight of the actual purpose of their mission. They had come to the Continent to get themselves a national bank, a railway line and a state attorney. Mees and Pierson had already intimated in London that their hopes of a bank were too ambitious, but there were still two more things they were determined to accomplish during their visit.

For that they needed to be in Amsterdam. Between receptions and ceremonies they met with representatives of the financial world. A meeting with two engineers, Johannes Groll and David Maarschalk, looked promising. Both were interested in the idea of a railway in the Transvaal. They had made their mark in the Netherlands-East Indies Railway Company in Java as engineers as well as organisers and financiers. With legal advice from Jacob Moltzer, the head of Amsterdam's law faculty, they drafted a concession for the construction and operation of a railway from Pretoria to the port of Lourenço Marques on the Indian Ocean. The last stretch of the route ran through the Portuguese colony of Mozambique, which meant that the project hinged on securing Portugal's cooperation. A provisional agreement, subject to that condition, was signed on 16 April 1884.

A day later the Transvaal delegation travelled to Lisbon, again accompanied by Beelaerts van Blokland and this time with Maarschalk as well. A nasty surprise awaited them. The Portuguese government had already awarded a concession for the section of the railway through its territory to an American businessman, Edward McMurdo. And McMurdo, it turned out, was determined to exploit his asset to the full. It seemed to the Transvaal–Dutch group that he had acquired his rights specifically with the intention of selling them to the highest bidder. The only way to avoid being caught up in that kind of speculation was to find an alternative route, besides McMurdo's. It couldn't be another railway line, his concession precluded that, but what about a tram? The Portuguese government approved and gave them permission for a tram 'operated by animal traction', in other words, a horse-drawn tram.

It wasn't quite what they had in mind. Back in Amsterdam the Transvaal delegation had to pull out all the stops so as not to lose their investors. It was only Groll and Maarschalk's faith in the enterprise that kept the railway project afloat. On 24 May 1884 the concession was signed, paving the way for the Netherlands-South African Railway Company. Now they could only wait and see whether 'the investing public' would be sufficiently interested to raise the 15 million guilders they needed.[8]

There was still the outstanding matter of a state attorney. They had sounded out a few reputable lawyers, both Protestant and liberal, but nothing had come of it. One of the candidates was Professor Moltzer, who had made an excellent impression in the negotiations for the railway concession. But he was no more willing than anyone else to give up a secure position for an uncertain existence in the backwaters of the Transvaal. The Boers' callous treatment of Jorissen, the previous Dutch incumbent, did nothing to help matters either. Time was running out. At the beginning of June 1884, on Beelaerts van Blokland's advice, Kruger began to consider looking for someone younger. He asked whether Moltzer could recommend anyone.

Moltzer had the answer at his fingertips. Talented, energetic, but also earnest and reliable, someone with a keen sense of responsibility. There was only one person who fitted the bill: the young doctoral candidate

Willem Leyds, who was under the supervision of his close colleague, the law professor Gerard van Hamel. But there was no time to be lost. From 7 to 10 June the Transvaal delegation would be in Berlin for an audience with Kaiser Wilhelm I and Chancellor Bismarck. They were scheduled to leave the Netherlands on 14 June. Leyds's graduation would take place on 11 June. That left only the last three days of the delegation's visit to make the necessary arrangements. Moltzer set up an appointment.[9]

As described above, Kruger met Leyds at the Amstel Hotel and offered him the position of state attorney in the Transvaal. Leyds declined, but at Kruger's insistence he agreed to reconsider the offer, and then sought his mentor Pierson's advice.

As one of his lecturers, Pierson knew Leyds's qualities and assets. As director of the Nederlandsche Bank, he had offered him a position himself. But now he took a different line. He emphasised the importance of developing the Transvaal, homeland of their own flesh and blood, and the importance of the Netherlands' input in the railway project, in which both he and Moltzer had a personal stake. He spoke about the opportunity for Leyds to gain valuable professional experience and the generous remuneration attached to the appointment: an annual income of £1000 sterling a year—even a government minister didn't earn more. And he promised to keep the job at the Nederlandsche Bank open.

These were compelling arguments, which persuaded Leyds to review his position—and sweetened the pill for his fiancée. Only two obstacles remained, one spiritual, the other material.

Leyds discussed the first with Kruger at their next meeting at the Amstel Hotel. He believed in God but, he confided, he wasn't really a churchgoer. Would that be a problem? Kruger considered this carefully, 'drew deeply on his pipe' and replied that it needn't stand in the way as long as the state attorney fulfilled his obligations.

The second matter related to Leyds's fears of being dismissed the way Jorissen had been. That wasn't the kind of subject to raise with Kruger, but Moltzer came to his rescue and together with Leyds drew up a watertight contract. On the first day of every month, a twelfth of his £1000 stipend would be paid out in gold. Leyds would receive £200 in advance to cover his travel expenses to Pretoria. The appointment would be for three years and if 'Mr W.J. Leyds was not re-appointed on at least the same terms', he would be entitled to an 'immediate payment of £1000'. All in all, this offered sufficient security.

Kruger wasn't overjoyed with the contract Moltzer presented, a gesture he regarded as a sign of distrust. But, well, it was the morning of Saturday

14 June 1884, the time of his departure was drawing near, there wasn't much choice. Return to the Transvaal without a state attorney? Muttering, he signed the document.

Leyds signed too—for three years—so he thought.[10]

For thou are dust

Pretoria, October 1884

It was a relief to arrive at their destination after the arduous journey. 'Pretoria has made quite a favourable impression on us,' Louise Leyds wrote to her family back home, 'it nestles in the mountains and from the outside the houses look cheerful and friendly; most of them have a veranda with roses or ivy, and gardens around them.' Willem went so far as to call it 'a little paradise'. The couple stayed at the European Hotel, but Louise had already set her sights on a house 'which, from the outside, has stolen my heart'. Willem was to be sworn in on Monday 6 October and they had the weekend before them to recover from the gruelling trip.[11]

The past months had been hectic. The contract that Willem had signed in spite of everything, their wedding in Amsterdam and the honeymoon in England followed by preparations for their departure, and finally boarding the steamship *Trojan*. The voyage was not one they wished to repeat. The weather had let them down. It had been cold and rainy, even around the equator; the ship tossed and rolled 'in a most peculiar fashion'. Louise was seasick all the way, rarely left the cabin, and when she finally felt like eating, the food was disappointing. It was 'an English table, of course', so 'by definition inedible', but 'the way it was prepared surprised even Louise. I say even Louise', for after all she had lived in England for several years and was not unaccustomed to it.

Willem had found diversion in the company of other passengers. Those who made the strongest impression on him were the members of a 'German expedition to Angra Pequena', a village on the coast of South West Africa, present-day Namibia. It was Leyds's first experience of international politics. The German Chancellor Bismarck had never cared much for colonies, but this summer he experienced a change of heart. The expedition on board the *Trojan* was a 'completely private venture undertaken by the Bremen millionaire-merchant Lüderitz', who had 'purchased large tracts of land from the natives there' and would now enjoy official protection. 'So Angra is the first German colony,' Leyds observed, more or less correctly—Togo and Cameroon had been declared German protectorates only a few weeks earlier. Leyds thus witnessed at first hand the arrival of an important new player on the southern African scene.[12]

The *Trojan* sailed into Cape Town a day behind schedule, because of the inclement weather. As a result, Willem and Louise Leyds missed the connecting mail train and were obliged to spend a few days at the foot of Table Mountain. Their sudden exposure to the alien environment came as a shock. Louise in particular, not at her best after the voyage, was aghast. 'We stood there on shore in the dazzling sun, engulfed by black, yellow, brown etc. people. We Amsterdammers complain about the Jews being brash, heavens! Glory to Amsterdam! Jews are positively meek compared to these people, and what's more, there are so few of them.' And then the streets, or what passed for them. 'I think Capetonians would do better to tear down that barren rock and use it to pave the streets of Cape Town. They really are in a dreadful state. When it rains, they're thick with mud and when one of the *many strong* winds blows, we are enveloped in thick clouds of dust.'[13]

The couple had no regrets about leaving Cape Town. On Tuesday 23 September, they took the train to the north, unprepared for the lunar landscape that awaited them. In a letter to Moltzer, Willem summed up the journey in a single word, 'frightful'. Louise wrote to a friend in the East Indies about the 'desert' they had travelled through. 'No bush, no tree, no water, no bird or insect to be seen, nothing but heaps of stone. And every hour a little station, a few houses, sometimes just one. Terribly monotonous.' And that for 40 hours with 55 stops in between, up to De Aar, roughly halfway on the 1600-kilometre journey to Pretoria. The regular train line stopped at De Aar. Rails had been laid as far as Kranskuijl, but for that one had to transfer to an open goods carriage: two benches with a canvas sheet overhead.

The line ended in Kranskuijl. The next leg of the journey, up to Kimberley, was by stagecoach. 'Rather amusing', Louise reflected later, which, considering the occupants of the vehicle, attests to a remarkable sense of humour. The luggage was piled high on the roof and fastened with rope to the back and sides of the coach. In front were two coachmen and three passengers; a fourth lay on the roof, on top of the luggage. Crammed inside were two women, three mothers with babies, four children and one 'incredibly fat, heavy, large man'. And, of course, Mr and Mrs Leyds.

On the journey the ten horses were 'whipped incessantly' and 'the passengers lurched from side to side'. At times the carriage 'balanced precariously on two wheels as if it was uncertain which way to go'. No wonder the horses had to be changed every three hours. The temperature too went from one extreme to another. 'We were hot during the day, very cold in the evenings and especially at night, particularly when we were travelling at speed.' Fortunately, as time went by, there was more to see.

'The landscape improved slightly, now there were not only bushes but also dry grass' and occasionally a large termite nest. Near Beaconsfield, on the outskirts of Kimberley, they passed close to 'the kaffirs' tents'. Louise was appalled. 'Filthy and so small!'

Their arrival in Kimberley was an experience, if only because of the fanfare that greeted every stagecoach. It was a typical boom town built out of nothing after the spectacular discovery of diamonds in 1871. Since then, mining operations had left a deep scar on the landscape. The Big Hole brought prosperity to a great many people, but as usual the bounty was distributed inequitably: fortunes for the magnates, good money for the intermediaries, peanuts for the predominantly black miners.

To Louise Leyds it was 'an abomination. The whole town consists of nothing but fortune-hunters and scum, people who want to get rich quickly and without any effort.' She wanted to see the famous Big Hole with her own eyes, but as they approached it they were suddenly surrounded by 'a swarm of coloured [mixed-race] people . . . They were wild and rude to each other and inspected us with great curiosity.' So the party beat a hasty retreat. Fortunately there was a hotel 'that would pass muster even in Amsterdam', with lovely furniture 'and white servants'. It was more pleasant there than outdoors. As in Cape Town, the streets were unpaved and the wind, even stronger, filled the air with 'red dust. We were constantly walking in a solid cloud of dust. The wind swept up dust in front of us, behind us, all over the show.'

From Kimberley it was still about 500 kilometres to Pretoria. That meant at least another three days by stagecoach, a far smaller one this time and 'truly, even worse than dreadful. The Kimberley carriage was luxurious by comparison.' They could see the road beneath them through the wide gaps between the floor planks. And there was nothing to stop the dust coming in. They suffered most during the first part of the journey, through the Orange Free State. Things improved after crossing the Vaal River, the border to which the Transvaal owes its name, especially after they had reached Potchefstroom. There was more vegetation and less dust.

Their arrival in Pretoria made up for it all. It was just unfortunate that it had already grown dark 'because [the town] nestles snugly between the hills'. But this they only saw the following day, Friday 3 October, ten days after their departure from Cape Town. Here, in any case, was an abundance of water 'bubbling up from a spring'. And, happily, lots of vegetation, weeping willows in particular, 'that grow rapidly; in 15 years one has a large shady tree'. In the centre was 'a large square with outspanned oxwagons belonging to the farmers who come to Pretoria for the sacramental supper of *Nagmaal*; they travel and sleep in those wagons.' The sight of them turned Louise's thoughts to their own huge trunks, which were being transported by oxwagons like these. That would certainly take time. Even so, she had 'already grown accustomed to everything here. Only the kaffirs are rather strange. Some of them walk through town quite naked, with nothing more than a woollen blanket or an animal skin wrapped around them.'[14]

These letters in which Willem and Louise Leyds describe their first impressions of South Africa are beautiful and evocative. Louise at least was an observant correspondent with an eye for telling detail. Her reports would have given her family and friends a vivid idea of the culture shock the couple must have experienced when they suddenly found themselves travelling through that distant, dusty, alien world. Readers today may be shocked in a different way, by their unabashed belief in white superiority. Whatever compromises the Leydses may have had to make in adapting to the primitive living conditions in the Transvaal, they were not uncomfortable with the Boers' confidence in their supremacy over the black population.

But there were still challenges in abundance. For Willem they mainly had to do with his working conditions. They were 'rather disorganised', to put it mildly, as he wrote to Moltzer at the end of his first week. To start with, 'my arrival was not exactly festive'. Kruger had apparently not read his letter from Cape Town 'and no one was there to welcome us'. It was only on the following morning that General Smit went round to the European Hotel to greet them. Leyds nevertheless went to introduce himself to the members of the Volksraad, the supreme legislative body.

Work began in earnest on Monday morning, after he had taken his oath of office. As usual, he wanted to study the files as soon as he could, but it wasn't so simple. 'The laws here! Enough of them, to be sure. But they keep passing new legislation without giving a thought to the old. It causes endless confusion and contradiction. Just imagine, there isn't even a complete set of *Government Gazettes* in my office.' Nor did he find any Blue Books, the official British government publications that were 'indispensable' to 'anyone like myself, to whom everything is unfamiliar'. When his request to purchase them was turned down, he promptly ordered a set 'for myself' and paid for them out of his own pocket. In short, there was 'enough for me to do. A consistent body of law is of great importance here. I shall of course direct my efforts to that end.'[15]

From this it transpires that the state attorney was responsible for far more than instituting prosecutions and heading the judicial system. This wouldn't have occupied much of his workday, as crime hadn't yet become a serious problem in the Transvaal. He could easily manage the police force and the prison system as well. Far more time-consuming was his function as legal adviser 'on matters of every kind, more than you can imagine. They regard me as a walking encyclopaedia they can and may consult by looking up any random word.' 'They' referred in the first place to the state president, Kruger, who was also chair of the Executive Council, which further comprised the commander-in-chief, the minister of native affairs, the state secretary, the minutes secretary and two members with voting rights but no specific function. The members of the Volksraad could make use of his services as well, as could 'every public servant'. Add to this his involvement in decision-making processes in the Executive Council and it is no exaggeration to say that Leyds's position was equivalent to that of a minister of justice.

It entailed a great deal of work. His days in Pretoria started early and ended late. In the first week he attended four evening meetings and still took work home afterwards. On top of it all, the climate made everyone 'lethargic. After a while, just walking, taking a stroll seems to become almost impossible. The most time one can spend on intellectual activity seems to be five hours a day, if one doesn't want to suffer adverse effects. Many people here are already overworked. But I can't possibly manage in five hours.' His average working day was going to be two or three times as long.[16]

Besides 'time and climate', Leyds had to deal with enemies of flesh and blood right from the start. In his orientation interview with Chief Justice John Kotzé, the dismissal of the former state attorney happened to be mentioned in passing. Leyds remarked that he had no comment on the ins and outs of the matter, but he was critical of the way they had gone about it. Jorissen had been dismissed without being given an opportunity to defend himself. This wasn't the proper procedure, according to Leyds, who only heard after the meeting that 'Kotzé himself was the moving spirit behind the intrigue'. Relations between the two men never recovered.

The same applied to Leyds's relationship with Du Toit, one of the members of the Transvaal delegation in Europe. He too had been instrumental in Jorissen's dismissal, but in his case there was another, more compelling reason for the friction. In 1880, Du Toit had been one of the founders of the Afrikaner Bond, a political organisation in the Cape Colony which sought a merger with the other British colony, Natal, as well as the independent republics of the Orange Free State and the Transvaal. Its aim was to establish 'an Afrikaner union for all who considered Africa their home, in the interests of a United South Africa'. Kruger was initially sympathetic to this emergent Afrikaner nationalism, as may be concluded from Du Toit's appointment as minister of education in the Transvaal.

But the first cracks in Du Toit's position of trust appeared soon after the delegation returned from Europe. He had dealt with a delicate border issue without consulting anyone else and, according to Leyds, meddled in various matters which had nothing to do with education and were beyond his brief. 'He neglected his own department, was always in the Exec. Council, whether wanted or not, airing his views on everything and more.' Even more harmful for his position was the fact that Du Toit was becoming increasingly explicit about his commitment to Afrikaner unity, which he considered more important than the independence of the South African Republic. This was expressed, for example, by his promotion of their preferred language, Afrikaans, to the detriment of Dutch, official language of the Transvaal.

On this issue the president's views were diametrically opposed to Du Toit's. The Transvaal's independence was far more important to him than Afrikaner unity. The only book he ever read, and always carried with him, was the Bible—the official Dutch version, needless to say. And rather than trust what he considered anglicised Afrikaners in the Cape Colony, he increasingly recruited staff from the Netherlands, his new state attorney to begin with. After his clash with Kruger, Du Toit launched his own newspaper, *De Republikein*, which frequently attacked Leyds and others from the Netherlands.

Hence, soon after his arrival in Pretoria, Leyds was confronted with the divisions in Transvaal society. Fortunately he was quick to grasp this kind of situation and at the end of his first working week he urged Moltzer to be discreet. 'Please think twice before divulging information that comes from me. You know how quickly small talk finds its way back to Africa. A trifle could do me a lot of harm.' Those were wise words. As a newcomer in the Boer community Leyds was vulnerable, because of his nationality, his liberal outlook and his youthful appearance. Every self-respecting Boer had a beard. Leyds was aware of this—he had started growing one even before Kimberley—but that still didn't make him a real Boer. It would take far more than that, a commitment to the Boers' faith most of all.[17]

And that would have presented a new set of problems. Religion, like nationalism and language, was one of the dividing issues within the Transvaal community. As few as they were, the Boers were quick to make distinctions on religious grounds. The British Blue Books that Leyds consulted put the population of 'the Transvaal territory' in the late 1870s at little more than 32,000—adult male—'Europeans of Dutch origin' and around 5000 'Europeans of non-Dutch origin'. These figures pale into

16

insignificance compared with the 770,000 'Kaffirs'. Still, there were enough Boers to sustain three Christian denominations. All three were Protestant and more or less reflected the schisms that had occurred in the Netherlands in the nineteenth century. So there was a Nederduitsch Hervormde Kerk, a Nederduitsch Gereformeerde Kerk and a Gereformeerde Kerk, each with its own buildings, ministers and rites.

The last of the three was the smallest, newest and most conservative. But more importantly, it was the church Kruger belonged to. In 1859 he had been a member of the first group that broke away to establish a Vrije Gereformeerde Gemeente, consistent with the canons of Dordrecht of 1618–19. This was Calvinism in its most orthodox form, espousing a belief in predestination and divine intervention in the personal life of every human being by an omnipotent God. The Bible, especially the Old Testament, was the only reliable authority for the faithful, who sang only psalms, not 'secular' songs, during worship. They considered themselves the new people of Israel, a Chosen Nation, with the Transvaal as their Promised Land.

The outside world, however, regarded them—and Kruger—as ultraconservative and uncouth. Leyds seems to have been indifferent to the perceived shortcomings attributed to the man he was employed to serve. His letters in the first few months were about his heavy workload, his primitive working conditions or Du Toit's intrigues. There wasn't a bad word about Kruger as a person. In fact there was an unexpected compliment after Leyds had attended a church service. 'We sang Psalm 25 verse 8. The President read it out. I have to say it was splendid. Rarely have I heard anyone recite so beautifully.'[18]

Hunger for land

Veertienstroom, January 1885

Leyds's baptism by fire in the world of diplomacy put his stamina to the test. In January 1885 Kruger decided that the situation on the south-west border of the Transvaal needed his personal attention. He wanted his state attorney to accompany him to the disputed territory to attend to the finer points of law; high-ranking British officials were also involved. It was hard work in spartan conditions, with 'always meat' that smelt foul and 'never vegetables, bread that's mostly rock hard' and 'always something they pass off as coffee'. This was diplomacy out in the bush.

Kruger was in his element. The highveld, the wide open spaces on either side of the Vaal: this was his natural habitat. He had shot his first lion here, at the age of 14, led his first military commando at 17 and lost his left thumb when his rifle exploded. In peacetime he had built farms and churches, grazed cattle, sheep and horses, hunted elephant and rhinoceros. In their many clashes with black adversaries he had always led the way into battle. Once the personification of strength, at 60 he still cut a powerful figure, with scars as badges of honour.

For Leyds, just six months in office, the whole experience was new. Though he had been born in the East Indies and was no stranger to the outdoors, playing on a veranda under the watchful eye of his *babu* was something entirely different. A city-dweller, he was a nobody (in spite of the beard he grew from time to time) in the presence of this man of the earth. Physically, he had never been a weakling. At school he had excelled not only academically but also at gymnastics. At university he had studied music but learned fencing and marksmanship as well. And here on the highveld he furnished proof of his sound constitution. It wasn't easy 'but I shouldn't think a little draught will do me too much harm', he wrote to Louise.[19]

Kruger and Leyds were to meet their British adversaries at the end of January in the far south-west of the Transvaal. The place can best be described as a tongue of land surrounded by three political entities, the Boer Republic of the Orange Free State to the east, the British Cape Colony to the south and Bechuanaland to the west. Bechuanaland was at the centre of the dispute. It was not yet a state in the European sense. As long as anyone could remember, it had been inhabited by Khoikhoi and

Bantu speakers dispersed among several rival empires. Some years earlier a few small groups of *trekboers* had left the Transvaal to settle there, by their own account at the request of two of the warring chiefs, Moswete in the north and Mosweu in the south. In return, the white colonists claimed autonomy over the land they lived on, which in 1882 and 1883 they declared the republics of Goshen and Stellaland respectively.

The new mini-states were a thorn in the side of the British. London regarded any expansion of Transvaal territory to the west as a threat to its own strategic position. It would enable the Boers to block the only open trade route to the north and continue unimpeded to push through to the west, perhaps all the way to the Atlantic coast. Decisive action was called for. The London Convention, signed in 1884, provided an opportunity to establish the south-west border of the Transvaal. Three months later the British reached an agreement with two other black chiefs in the region, Montshioa and Mankuroane, whereby the entire southern part of Bechuanaland, down to the Molopo River, became a British Protectorate. As from May 1884 that territory was officially called British Bechuanaland.

That seemed to spell the end of Goshen and Stellaland. But Stephanus du Toit had other ideas. Assigned to Goshen as special commissioner, he announced in September of that year that the Transvaal would give 'its protection' to both Moswete and Montshioa. In other words, the tiny Boer Republic of Goshen was suddenly annexed to its big brother. At a ceremony to mark the transition, Du Toit had the Transvaal flag hoisted in the capital, Rooi-Grond, 'without having received instructions to that effect,' Leyds noted with disapproval. More than that, when word reached Pretoria, Du Toit was given immediate orders 'not to do so, and if he already had, to lower the flag'.

But the damage had been done. The British protested to the Transvaal government in the strongest terms. This was after all a double violation of the London Convention: unilateral territorial expansion and entering into an agreement with African chiefs without the consent of the British. It was all the more serious, because in the meantime Germany had formally entered the southern African arena in August 1884 with its protectorate over Angra Pequena and its surroundings. A willingness to compromise apparently wasn't one of the qualities required of the British negotiators who were sent to meet Kruger and Leyds in January 1885.

The team was led by Lieutenant-General Charles 'Jerusalem' Warren. The nickname had nothing to do with Warren's piety but alluded to his involvement in important excavations in Palestine—Warren was a professional archaeologist as well. Apart from that, he was as arrogant and stubborn as only a British senior officer can be. Fifteen years later he flaunted these qualities again in the Battle of Spion Kop, one of the most devastating British defeats in the Boer War. It didn't come to an armed conflict in Bechuanaland but that wasn't due to Sir Charles. He was itching to teach the 'Republics of Robbers' a lesson one way or another. For that contingency he had brought with him 4000 troops and a 'Native corps'. Non-whites bearing arms, according to Leyds, 'caused many to shake their heads', that is, many Boers.

They were already shaking their heads over John Mackenzie, the second member of the British delegation. To the Boers he was the personification of slander, the missionary possessed by the devil, who for years had accused them of racism, murder, homicide and exploitation. To supporters of the London Missionary Society, he was a hero who performed a sacred mission among the Africans and used political means to promote their rights at the same time. Earlier, he had made life difficult for the Transvaal delegation in London by turning public opinion against them. Back in South Africa, he was appointed to serve as the first deputy commissioner in the new Protectorate of British Bechuanaland. That didn't last long. He turned out to be less competent as an administrator than a preacher, but Warren insisted that he attend the talks with the Boers.

The third member of the delegation was someone Warren would rather have done without, but he had no choice. Cecil Rhodes, aged 31, had made a fortune and a name for himself in Kimberley and Cape Town. He was destined for even greater wealth and fame, and would eventually achieve the ultimate honour of giving his name to the new state of Rhodesia, since renamed Zimbabwe. In January 1885, Rhodes was a member of parliament in the Cape Colony and Mackenzie's successor as deputy commissioner. Warren thought him far too reasonable. Leyds saw him as someone he could do business with. 'Rhodes has honoured our agreement to the letter, unlike Warren.' After the meeting Kruger was sure he would be seeing more of 'this young man' in the future.

And he was right. In the end the Boers would curse the ground Rhodes walked on, but that was only later. In the tents in Veertienstroom and Blignautspont where they met the three British negotiators, Warren was the hardest nut to crack. They didn't succeed. His troops were a valuable trump and he knew he could count on the support of the high commissioner, Sir Hercules Robinson, in Cape Town and the secretary for the colonies, Lord Derby, in London. Warren wouldn't budge an inch. There were lesser issues they managed to trade off, such as accusations of cattle theft, from both sides, by the pro-British Mankuroane and the Boers' ally Mosweu. But as far as the border was concerned, they made no progress at all. Neither Kruger's razor-sharp arguments nor all of Leyds's shrewdness could change that. 'Just what a statesman wants,' he wrote to Louise, 'especially when he's defending a weak case.' And that's what it was. There was simply no way to save Goshen and Stellaland, not on legal grounds and not by force.

The outcome was that the British upgraded the southern part of Bechuanaland from a protectorate to a Crown colony, governed from Cape Town. The territory above the Molopo River became a new British protectorate. The British had secured their corridor to the north and pre-empted the Transvaal's expansion to the west.

Leyds returned to Pretoria in poor health. The tainted meat had got to him.[20]

What happened in Bechuanaland in 1884 and 1885 was nothing new under the southern African sun. Since the 1820s the region had seen a proliferation of new states, accompanied by the inevitable clashes between expanding white and black empires. The stakes were control of land, human labour, cattle, trade and strategic positions. Land for pasturage and agriculture, or mining. Labour to do the hard work, or conquer new territory. Cattle for subsistence and as symbols of wealth. Trade to make money, buy arms and win prestige. Strategic positions to protect whatever one already possessed and to acquire what one still wanted. Power, fame, wealth, status: these were the personal aspirations. And they were combined with a spirit of enterprise, a desire for freedom, religious zeal and patriotism. What had begun as a patchwork of informal settlements developed in the course of the nineteenth century into large competing territories with firmly demarcated frontiers.

The process can best be understood by looking at two points on the map, one in the south-west and the other in the east. In demographic terms it was about an expanding white population core in the Cape Colony and a dynamic black power centre in what is now KwaZulu-Natal.

The south-west coastal area around Cape Town was the point from which white colonists fanned out to other parts of the country. In the early nineteenth century, this territory was inhabited by two rival groups. The Dutch-speaking community claimed the right of first arrival. They had been there since Jan van Riebeeck established a refreshment station in 1652. Although they had subsequently produced offspring with German and French immigrants and non-white slaves, they had maintained their allegiance to their predominantly Dutch roots and the faith of their seventeenth-century forefathers. The second group were white colonists of British descent. They had come in the wake of the British troops who had

21

taken the Cape Colony from the Netherlands, first from 1795 to 1802 and then permanently in 1806. The English-speaking newcomers had become increasingly dominant, partly by implementing a targeted immigration policy. They upheld the values and principles of the Enlightenment and considered themselves the heirs of a superior culture—to the indignation of the descendants of the Dutch.

These two groups of white colonists in the Cape were also in competition with a number of indigenous communities. They can be divided into three main categories based on origin and language. The oldest inhabitants were the Bushmen, or San, who lived in small groups as hunters and gatherers. Over the years they were driven deeper into mountainous terrain or semi-desert regions such as the Karoo. The second group were the Khoikhoi, a nomadic people who, with their cattle, sheep and goats, roamed vast tracts of land, covering most of the western half of present-day South Africa. The white colonists called them Hottentots, imitating the sound of their language to Dutch ears. The last group differed from the first two in lifestyle and skin colour. The Bantu were cattle and crop famers and darker in appearance than the San or Khoikhoi. They fell into three sub-categories, according to their territorial dispersal. The Damara and the Ovambo lived in the north-west, the Tswana and Sotho on the highveld in the interior, while the largest groups, the Xhosa, the Swazi and the Zulu, occupied the eastern strip from north to south.

In reality the distinctions between the various groups were less clear-cut than this description suggests. Besides being rivals, the different groups also had other forms of contact. The Griqua, for example, originated from intermarriages and sexual relations between European colonists and Khoikhoi. They were recognised as a distinct subgroup by the early nineteenth century. It must be said, however, that intimate relations between whites and members of other groups were rarely consensual. Violence in general was rife. In the eastern part of the Cape Colony, first the Dutch and later the British colonists clashed with the Xhosa so many times that the 'border wars' were assigned numbers. By 1818 they had reached the fifth.

But all of this was still in the area south of the Orange River, or Gariep in the language of the Khoikhoi. The Orange is the longest river in South Africa and runs from the Drakensberg to the Atlantic Ocean, covering a distance of more than 1800 kilometres. The most militant black resistance to white expansionism emerged in the area east of the Drakensberg in the 1820s.

Shaka, the king of that territory, ruthlessly laid the foundations of the legendary Zulu kingdom in Natal. His regiments, or impis, sowed death and destruction along the entire coast of the Indian Ocean. His rivals scattered in all directions and wherever they had taken refuge proceeded to build their own empires, in turn generating new flows of migration. Mzilikazi headed west, crossed the Drakensberg and continued to the basin of the Vaal River on the highveld, where he established the Ndebele kingdom. Moshoeshoe settled in an impenetrable fortress in the high mountains of Basutoland, now Lesotho. In 1828 Shaka was assassinated by his brother Dingane, but the fearsome military prowess of the Zulu kingdom remained a force to be reckoned with.[21]

The white colonists of predominantly Dutch descent who trekked north from the Cape Colony in the 1830s experienced all this at first hand. The term Afrikaner was already in use, but when they established a permanent settlement the Dutch colonists were called Boers. Collectively this group of pioneers was known as Trekkers or, among themselves, Voortrekkers. They migrated in a bid to regain their independence, escape the yoke of the British, stake out pastures wherever their oxwagons might take them and keep their coloured servants subordinate, just as they had always done in the past. That was their idea of independence. They left in waves, ultimately about 15,000 people in all, men, women and children, on a Great Trek that branched out in several directions. Some crossed the Orange River, some continued further and crossed the Vaal, while others headed east, crossed the Drakensberg and ended up in Natal.

That last group ran into Dingane in February 1838. The encounter was horrific. Their invitation to Dingane's quarters ended in a bloodbath, with hundreds of casualties among the Trekker families and their Khoikhoi servants. In December the Boers got their revenge. At the Ncome River their rifles and laager (a circular configuration of wagons joined together) proved a deadly combination. Out of 10,000 Zulu warriors armed with assegais, 3000 lost their lives. Only four of the Boers were wounded, among them their leader, Andries Pretorius. They renamed the Ncome 'Blood River' and declared 16 December Dingane's Day. The Zulu king fled north and was removed from the throne. The Boers established the Republic of Natalia, with Pietermaritzburg as its capital.

In the Transvaal the confrontation between the white newcomers and the established black rulers ended in much the same way. Here it was Mzilikazi who sent his impis to attack the Trekkers, one of whom was the 12-year-old Paul Kruger. And again the assegai proved no match for the rifle and laager. Moreover, the Boers received support from their allies, the Griqua and the Tswana. When they attacked Mzilikazi's flank, he and his Ndebele followers fled north, beyond the Limpopo River.

The success of the Great Trek stirred the British to action as well. They were concerned about the young Boer republic in Natal. The change in the status quo in the region was a risk to the security of the British trading post of Port Natal on the Indian Ocean, known today as Durban. The situation caused consternation in the Cape Colony and even more so in England. If there was one aspect of the South African power game that the government in London considered important, it was the safety of sea routes to Asia, particularly to British India. Halfway ports such as Cape Town and Port Natal played a vital part in that strategic plan. That was why they dispatched the Royal Navy frigate, the *Southampton*, with sufficient reinforcements on board to conquer Natal. The territory was annexed in 1843 and became a British colony.

British rule again—that was a bitter pill for most of the Boers in Natal. Led by Andries Pretorius, they moved on, or rather back west, and crossed the Drakensberg again, finally to settle on the highveld between the Orange River and the Vaal. But even there they remained in the grip of the British. Once again the British argued that the Trekkers were a threat to the prevailing balance of power. The government in Cape Town was anxious to avoid unrest along its colonial frontiers, so in 1848 the Boers' new domain was annexed as well. It was called the Orange River Sovereignty.

The annexation didn't have the desired effect. The British administration reluctantly became embroiled in local conflicts between the Boers and the Sotho under Moshoeshoe; the region was still troubled and it was costing a lot of money. The British didn't have the military resources to deal with the problem, as they were soon tied up in yet another border war—the eighth—with the Xhosa (1850–53). Retreat was the only way out. They left the highveld to the Voortrekkers. To Pretorius the Sand River Convention of 1852 felt like a personal atonement. Great Britain recognised the autonomy of the area north of the Vaal, which became the South African Republic, unofficially known as the Transvaal. In 1854 the Bloemfontein Convention established the same rights for the territory between the Orange and the Vaal. The Orange River Sovereignty became the Orange Free State.[22]

The British resigned themselves to the situation until the 1870s and left the South African Republic and the Orange Free State in peace. There were still fewer than 30,000 Boers living there, in relative isolation. Their only connection to the civilised world was the trail of their wagon wheels to the south. The Boer republics were nominally independent, but in terms of political state-building and economic growth they lagged far behind the Cape Colony. If necessary, the British thought, they could always take them over.

When diamonds were discovered they proved to be right. The whole power game changed dramatically. So far, expansion had been driven by the quest for grazing or agricultural land, or strategic security. As of 1867, there was a new and supremely powerful incentive: the craving for minerals. Diamonds had been discovered around the confluence of the Vaal and the Orange, first near Hopetown and subsequently in other places in the area. In 1870 and 1871, they were found in dazzling profusion on and around Colesberg Kopje, where miners discovered four volcanic pipes of molten lava containing diamonds, near the surface. A month later, thousands of delirious prospectors were digging on hundreds of parcels of land. Their chaotic, rapidly expanding encampment was called New Rush. The name was appropriate. In 1873, with a population of 13,000 whites and 30,000 blacks, New Rush was South Africa's second largest city, after Cape Town. Colesberg Kopje disappeared from the face of the earth. It was excavated hundreds of metres deep and transformed into an immense crater. This was the Big Hole that Willem and Louise Leyds had looked forward to seeing on their journey to Pretoria.

The diamond-mining industry had a tremendous impact. A dynamic city emerged out of nothing in the midst of a rural community, all because of a single activity: large-scale and increasingly industrialised mining. The diamond fields boosted the Cape's economy and attracted tens of thousands of migrant labourers, which again altered the balance of political power.

The diamonds were discovered in the vicinity of disputed territorial borders. There were claims pending from the Transvaal, the Orange Free State and Griqualand West, a territory that had been allocated to the Griqua people in the 1830s. In the chaos and anarchy resulting from the sudden influx of thousands of fortune-hunters, Nicolaas Waterboer, 'captain' of the Griqua, turned to the British for help. Not in vain. In October 1871 the governor of the Cape Colony, Sir Henry Barkly, without waiting for approval from London, declared Griqualand West a British Crown colony. At the same time, he officially established its border with the Orange Free State, carefully drawing it ever so slightly east of the diamond fields. The two Boer republics protested, but were unable to support their claims. In July 1873, New Rush was renamed Kimberley after the incumbent British secretary of state for the colonies. The point was made.[23]

Barkly's successor, Lord Carnarvon, continued to make every effort to annex the territory, now with support from London. The new Disraeli government had explicitly imperialist ambitions. Lord Carnarvon's ideal for South Africa was a confederation, such as he had created in Canada.

The Boers could object as much as they liked. They had also grumbled about the diamond fields being incorporated into the Cape Colony, only to resign themselves to the situation subsequently. There was also Burgers, the president of the Transvaal since 1872, who was hatching a plan which the British weren't happy with. He wanted to end the South African Republic's isolation, in the first place by building a railway to the sea at Delagoa Bay in the Portuguese colony of Mozambique. On a journey through Europe he had managed to secure diplomatic and financial support for that purpose. The idea conflicted with Lord Carnarvon's dream of a united South Africa. He needed a pretext to annex the Transvaal, and now one presented itself.

In 1876, a Boer attack against Sekhukhune, king of the Pedi in the eastern Transvaal, had ended badly. Burgers was held responsible, as he was for the financial bankruptcy his projects had led to. The Boers were divided and incapacitated as a result. Lord Carnarvon saw his chance. Twenty-five mounted police officers from Natal under the command of Theophilus Shepstone were all it took to put an end to 25 years of independence. The Transvaal was annexed on 12 April 1877.

This easy victory put the British in a winning mood. The new high commissioner, Sir Bartle Frere, who had just arrived in Cape Town, was a hard-core imperialist like Lord Carnarvon but far less patient. He saw the remaining independent black kingdoms as the main obstacle in the way of his plans for federation and decided to take them on, one by one. British troops defeated the Xhosa in the ninth—and last—border war. Next, they quelled a series of 'uprisings' in various parts of the region, including Griqualand East and West. At this point Bartle Frere felt it was time for a final showdown with the Zulu, whose kingdom he considered the biggest threat to British supremacy in South Africa.

Since the 1830s, the Zulu kingdom had diminished in size, but its military prowess was still fearsome. The implicit declaration of war that Bartle Frere sent King Cetshwayo in December 1878 took considerable courage. Stupidity, many said, when the first battle ended in disaster. On 22 January 1879, a contingent of British troops was overwhelmed by 20,000 Zulu warriors at Isandhlwana. More than 1000 men were lost on both sides. It was the most crushing defeat in Britain's entire colonial history.

Such a humiliation could not go unavenged. The British raised reinforcements as quickly as possible and appointed a new commander. General Sir Garnet Wolseley had gained a reputation in India, Russia, China, Canada and West Africa. He was a living legend, 'our only general', according to the British press. But the Zulu War was over even before he arrived. His predecessor, Lord Chelmsford, was determined to settle the score for Isandhlwana himself and he succeeded in doing so at the very last minute. On 4 July 1879 he led a decisive attack on the royal capital at Ulundi. It was now up to Wolseley to decide on the future of the Zulu empire. Wolseley was ruthless. Cetshwayo was taken prisoner and his empire divided into a patchwork of 13 territories. The mighty Zulu kingdom ceased to exist.

In the same year Wolseley made a clean sweep in the eastern Transvaal. With a superior force of regular and other troops, including some 8000 Swazi, he defeated the Pedi and captured their king, Sekhukhune, putting an end to all organised armed resistance from the African population. The British were lord and master of the whole of South Africa. They could proceed to create a confederation.

But that was not to be, firstly because of a change of guard in the British camp. In April 1880, Prime Minister Disraeli was succeeded by William Gladstone, who opposed colonial expansion. Lord Carnarvon disappeared from the London scene, Bartle Frere was recalled from Cape Town and Wolseley's presence was needed at another flashpoint, this time in Egypt.

The disappearance of these diehard imperialists opened up new avenues for the Boers, although this wasn't evident at first. They were divided and overwhelmed by Shepstone's coup in April 1877, but they had never resigned themselves to the annexation. Twice, their representatives, among them Paul Kruger, had pleaded their cause in London, but to no avail. Gladstone was expected to be more sympathetic. In June 1880, when Gladstone made it known that he wasn't prepared to change course, the Boers lost hope of a peaceful solution. Thanks to Chelmsford and Wolseley, they had been delivered from the Zulu and the Pedi, their most formidable black adversaries. Now there were only the British themselves to deal with. Under the command of Kruger, Piet Joubert and Marthinus Pretorius, the Boers prepared for war. At a huge gathering in Paardekraal this triumvirate restored the republic. On 20 December 1880, it became clear that they were in earnest.

The first real contest between the Boer and the British forces took place near Bronkhorstspruit, 50 kilometres east of Pretoria. It was a memorable occasion. The two rival white communities in South Africa had been waging wars for decades, but so far their encounters had always been against black opponents, rifles against assegais. Among themselves, it had never gone beyond posturing. Never before had they challenged each other in battle. Now for the first time, it was white against white, rifle against rifle.

The British had the most difficulty with this situation. Their officers couldn't bring themselves to see the Boers as a real adversary. Buffoons, they thought, in those corduroy trousers and floppy hats. It brought out the worst of their legendary arrogance, and they ended up making elementary tactical errors. It had happened to Colonel Philip Anstruther at Bronkhorstspruit and to Major-General Sir George Pomeroy Colley, three times over at Laing's Nek, Ingogo and finally Majuba Hill on 27 February 1881. That last, decisive battle took the lives of 92 Britons, including Colley, and left 134 wounded. The Boers suffered one fatality and five wounded.

Their losses were smaller than at Isandhlwana, but the humiliation was no less bitter. Queen Victoria and the Conservative Opposition demanded revenge. Now, however, it was clear that it did matter—very much—who was in government. Gladstone was anxious to prevent the conflict from spreading to the rest of southern Africa and decided to cut his losses. As a result, the campaign was limited to four battles, waged in a little over two months. The Boers gained a conclusive victory at what later came to be known as the First Boer or Anglo-Boer War.[24]

Restoring peace was far more difficult. It took the Boers another three years, and Kruger a third visit to London, to rid themselves of formal British suzerainty. In return, under the London Convention, they would agree to fixed borders. On that point Gladstone was adamant, as Kruger and Leyds discovered in Bechuanaland in January 1885. The South African Republic had regained its independence internally, but it would be unable to expand any further, so it seemed.

Gold

Johannesburg, January 1887

The family in Amsterdam must have been astounded. What was all this about gold in the Transvaal? At the beginning of August 1886, Louise Leyds wrote that she and Willem were thinking about 'going to the Barberton goldfields, where there is a lot of excitement at the moment'. In late September she again mentioned Barberton, 350 kilometres east of Pretoria, not far from the Mozambique border. She described it as 'the centre of the goldfields', which had been 'transformed from a small town into a city in the space of just a few months'. Four months later it transpired that the journey had taken them somewhere completely different. 'We went on a wonderful excursion to the goldfields,' she said in a letter dated Friday 4 February 1887. 'We went in our own horse-driven coach' and 'arrived on the Witwatersrand around eleven o'clock'. Witwatersrand? Wasn't that an escarpment south of Pretoria, no more than 50 kilometres away? Where exactly *was* this gold?[25]

It wasn't only outsiders who were puzzled. The experts, too, had a lot to think about when it came to the Transvaal's mineral resources. Everyone had known for decades that there were gold deposits in the ground—the samples found in many parts of the area looked promising. The only question was how to extract it profitably.

Some saw mountains of gold in every shimmering riverbed, but time and again the geological facts shattered their illusions. That is, until 1883, when a commercially viable artery was discovered in De Kaap, a valley in the eastern Transvaal. More deposits were found in 1884, followed a year later by the spectacular discovery of the Sheba Reef. All in all, it was enough to trigger a massive gold rush and inevitably a boom town—Barberton—to go with it. What had happened after the discovery of diamonds in Kimberley in 1871 was now being repeated here. In no time at all, a bustling city rose from the ground, built on the hopes and dreams of thousands of fortune-seekers. Barberton had it all: offices, shops, bars, hotels, clubs, music halls, brothels and of course a stock exchange, where speculators traded frantically from dawn to dusk, hoping for even more fabulous discoveries.

Kimberley and London traded with the same fervour. On the London

Stock Exchange the price of shares in the Barberton gold mines went through the roof, increasing a hundredfold. Mining companies with nothing but a glossy prospectus to offer had no trouble raising share capital. It was pure speculation, a calculated risk and nothing to do with production. As we know, this can go terribly wrong, and indeed it did. It was soon clear that investors had been living in cloud cuckoo land and the Barberton bubble burst with a vengeance. Only five out of thousands of claims ultimately developed into viable mines. The rest vanished into thin air, along with the fortunes that had been invested in them. Transvaal gold had turned out to be an extremely risky investment.

That was one of the reasons why technical and financial experts became more cautious when new deposits were discovered on the Witwatersrand in the course of 1886. The other reason was related to the unusual nature of the gold on the Rand, as the escarpment was generally called. It didn't occur in clumps or as threads of ore in quartz crystals, but was buried in a subterranean channel, mostly in low concentrations. This disadvantage was, however, more than compensated for by the sheer magnitude of the goldfield. It covered a vast stretch of land, 200 kilometres long, scores of kilometres wide and in parts four kilometres deep.

The full extent was obviously unknown at the time, and even where the reef emerged at the surface it wasn't always recognised for what it was. The famous American mining engineer Gardner Williams made a blunder he was never allowed to forget. After a ten-day reconnaissance of all the gold-bearing sites known at the time, Gardner announced, 'If I rode over these reefs in America I would not get off my horse to look at them. In my opinion they are not worth Hell room.' And there he was, standing on the largest reserve of gold in the world.[26]

Besides the sceptics, there were others, including engineers and investors, who were prepared to stake their lives on the Rand's potential. Here, as in Barberton, the diamond magnates of Kimberley stepped into the limelight. J.B. Robinson, originally from the Cape Colony, was a notoriously tough businessman. Though up to his neck in debt, he arrived on the Rand in July 1886 with enough capital to buy up huge parcels of land, laying the foundations for an untold fortune. His financier, Alfred Beit, born in Hamburg and educated in Amsterdam, had emerged in Kimberley as the wealthiest and most astute diamond merchant of them all. He and his two German colleagues, Julius Wernher and Hermann Eckstein, had started out in the employ of Jules Porgès & Cie, an international dealer based in Paris. Its founder, too, born as Yehuda Porgès in Vienna and raised in Prague, had abandoned the city of lights a decade earlier in favour of the city of diamonds. And now he had set his sights on the fledgling city of gold.

The company wouldn't have been complete without Cecil Rhodes and his partner Charles Rudd. Rhodes was known in Kimberley as a man who bought everything from everyone or, rather, the man who bought everything *and* everyone. Diamonds, pumping equipment, horses, competitors, it was all the same to him. The one principle he did uphold was that of consolidation—providing he was at the helm. He had achieved success by wheeling and dealing. With financial support from the Rothschilds, he was determined to put the jewel in the crown of his career: a total monopoly of diamonds for the business he had founded, the De Beers Mining Company, named after the brothers from whom he had bought the land. He had already brought in Beit, and in 1888 the last serious rival followed. This was the clownish but shrewd Barney Barnato, born in London as Barnet Isaacs, who haggled but in the end was seduced by Rhodes's offer of membership of the Kimberley Club, a seat in the parliament of the Cape Colony and 7000 shares in the newly established De Beers Consolidated Mines, 'the richest, the greatest, and the most powerful company the world has ever seen'. Barnato used the millions he made from that deal to invest in the Rand.[27]

This, then, was the select and already fabulously wealthy consortium that laid the foundations for organised gold mining on the Witwatersrand. They started off cautiously, given the recent fiasco in Barberton, but with enough conviction to unleash another gold rush and see the rise of another boom town—on the highveld, 1800 metres above sea level, and this time for good. In October 1886, a patch of land known as the Randjeslaagte was reserved to accommodate the huge influx of fortune-hunters. It was called Johannesburg. No one remembers why.[28]

Three months later, when Willem and Louise Leyds came to see the mining camp, it was 'a bustling village, already so large that you couldn't get from one end to the other on foot. Of course, everything is still quite primitive. One sees e.g. a house of thatch and clay being built in a single day. There are signboards saying Standard Bank or Transvaal Hotel etc.' There was also a wooden building, 'the mine commissioner's office, which houses the post office as well'. Three months later, in April 1887, it had been transformed. 'It's amazing how quickly places like Johannesburg are being built,' Louise wrote to her family. 'Six months ago it was still a barren piece of land.' They had seen only 'tents and clay huts' and 'now it's a sprawling town with lots of buildings and new ones going up all the time'.[29]

And that was only the beginning. Right from the start there was no shortage of capital or labour on the Rand, but mining had to be industrialised and this demanded careful planning. Dynamite was needed to blast the rock, wood to support shafts and coal to fire the steam engines that drove the drills and stamping mills. The pulverised ore was washed over mercury-coated copper sheets, causing the fine particles of gold to form an amalgam with the mercury. The particles were then separated by heating and what remained was pure gold. The technical process wasn't particularly complicated but the logistics of getting the raw materials and equipment to the site were time-consuming. Once the operation was up and running, in the course of 1888, Johannesburg began to boom.

There was just one last hurdle. It turned out that the gold ore found beneath a depth of 60 or 70 metres was mixed with pyrite, the 'fool's gold' that every miner dreaded. Mercury was of no use at all. As a result, the growth of the gold-mining industry and the influx of immigrants stagnated after 1890. But no time was lost in seeking a solution and it came in the form of potassium cyanide, which produced the necessary chemical reaction. The technique was developed in Glasgow, and tested and applied soon afterwards by Wernher, Beit & Co., the successor of Jules Porgès & Cie. And in fact it was far more effective than the old method. Potassium cyanide extracted the gold residue that mercury left behind. In 1892, confidence was restored and the streets were again teeming with newcomers. Nothing stood in the way of Johannesburg's expansion, not in South Africa, nor anywhere in the world. By 1896, a decade after it was founded, Johannesburg had a population of 100,000. More than 40,000 were African immigrants from all corners of the southern African subcontinent. They performed the physical, unskilled labour, above and below ground. There were also 5000 coloureds and over 50,000 whites, who took the semi-skilled jobs, providing technical, administrative or financial services. Only 6000 of them were born in the Transvaal. Two-thirds were English-speaking, from the Cape Colony and Great Britain; the remainder were a hotchpotch from all parts of the globe: Russian Jews, Germans, Hollanders. The vast majority of them were single young men. Bars, gambling halls and brothels did a roaring trade. Johannesburg had evolved into a hybrid between Monte Carlo and Sodom and Gomorrah.[30]

The town was like Kimberley, which was in a sense the 'mother city'. Yet there were marked differences between the two, attributable to different mining techniques and the respective market values of gold and diamonds. In Kimberley's early days, mining was random and indiscriminate, with countless operators holding claims to parcels of ground of various sizes. Diamonds came out of the ground as a more or less finished product. Those who performed the labour could easily pocket the stones and sell them for their own profit. As the market value of diamonds is determined by demand and supply, the mine operators soon realised they could only keep the selling price at a reasonable level through some form of regulation, mainly by limiting production and supervising their workforce more closely. That was why people like Rhodes wanted to consolidate right from the start. They were helped along by the technological and organisational demands of deep mining. They helped themselves too by imposing increasingly rigorous and ultimately drastic controls. Black miners were subjected to a strip search at the end of the working day. Nose, mouth, armpits, navel, anus, every orifice and every part of the body where diamonds could be concealed was scrutinised. Wounds, potentially self-inflicted, received special attention. A week before their contracts expired, miners were confined to a 'detention house', where their hands were shackled and their faeces inspected. If their bowel movements were irregular, they were given laxatives. The object of course was to retrieve any stones they may have ingested. Something like a production line had even been devised to expedite the procedure. Sewage from the latrines passed through several layers of gauze, ranging from coarse to fine, to sort the excreted gems.[31]

It wasn't high-tech, but it was symptomatic of the mine bosses' obsessive efficiency. It took 17 years to transform the chaos of Kimberley's early days into a slick monopoly. From 1888, De Beers dominated the world trade in diamonds.

Johannesburg's development was influenced by a different set of factors. From the start, gold mining on the Rand was dependent on raw materials and machinery, in other words, capital and organisation. If for this reason only, land and mining concessions weren't awarded piecemeal as they were in Kimberley—and labourers couldn't make off with the end product. It was the diamond magnates from Kimberley who took the lead in forming what were ultimately ten or so mining syndicates, thus achieving fame and fortune as gold barons into the bargain. Johannesburg's iconic Corner House, with Hermann Eckstein in the saddle, epitomised the power of the Randlords. But the concentration of power never culminated in a monopoly, mainly because of the way gold derives its value. Like diamonds, it is used for jewellery and has various industrial applications, but its principal economic function is to serve as security for the global monetary system. Consigned to the vaults of national banks, gold isn't subject to the simple market mechanism of demand and supply, which means that monopolies cannot manipulate its price. The only guaranteed way for the mining industry to increase profits is to reduce costs.

Of course, there was another fundamental difference between the two cities, namely their geographical location. The British had drawn

Kimberley within the borders of the Cape Colony. Johannesburg was in the heart of the Boer republic of the Transvaal, between Potchefstroom, the former capital, and Pretoria, its successor. The contrast between the two couldn't have been greater. A nineteenth-century industrial variant of a new Babylon emerged out of nothing in the middle of the grassy pastures of the highveld, an outpost of international big business, where Mammon had taken the place of the Protestant God. Paul Kruger called Johannesburg the city of the devil.[32]

Even so, the laws of the Transvaal had to be enforced in Johannesburg, like anywhere else. This meant considerably more work for Willem Leyds. He was an attorney not only at the Supreme Court in Pretoria, but also at what were known as circuit courts. As a result of mass immigration to the goldfields, magistrates were spending more of their time in the De Kaap Valley and more still on the Rand. Added to that, a completely new police apparatus had to be formed in Barberton and Johannesburg, including mounted police forces and an intelligence agency.[33]

The nature of the magistrates' work was changing as well, from routine misdemeanours like cattle theft to more complex offences. Leyds had a taste of what was to come in the course of 1886, in the case of the *State* vs *Alois Nellmapius*. This was a controversial matter, mainly because it involved conflicts of interest up to the highest level. It put Leyds's professional competence as well as his integrity to the test.

Nellmapius was a Hungarian businessman who had been active in the Transvaal since 1873. He had outstanding connections in the highest circles and was a close friend of Kruger's. This brought several lucrative contracts his way, including one for the manufacture of gunpowder. But as director of the gunpowder factory he had run into trouble. His superiors in London accused him of using company funds for his personal benefit and laid charges against him in Pretoria. Leyds believed there were sufficient grounds to prosecute Nellmapius—with the consent of the judiciary but to the chagrin of the political authorities.

The dispute escalated. The Executive Council, including President Kruger, was opposed to the case being brought to court. State Secretary Willem Bok, himself a member of the gunpowder factory's supervisory board, urged that 'Mr Nellmapius's friends must be kept on our side'. Many gave in to the pressure, but Leyds held his ground because, as he said, 'it was simply my duty'. He won the case, which was heard in late September 1886, and Nellmapius ended up behind bars.

But not for long. He was released a few days later on the authority of the Executive Council. The judicial authorities and the business world were outraged. 'What assurance would one have in future if a judgment can simply be overturned?' Chief Justice Kotzé immediately had Nellmapius rearrested. The knives were drawn. The Executive Council protested and wanted to discipline Kotzé. Although Kotzé was no friend of Leyds, in Leyds's opinion he was in the right. He appealed for lenience on Kotzé's behalf but failed to persuade Kruger. Until one night at a quarter to four, when there was a knock on the Leydses' door. Their astonishment resounded in the letter Louise wrote home the following morning. 'It really *was* the President.' Kruger had evidently come round to Leyds's way of thinking. 'They sat talking in the living room until half past five. W. wrote another letter.' But Louise had other things to worry about. 'In the meantime I lay in bed fretting about my carpet and chairs, because, you know, it's not only wise words that come out of Oom Paul's mouth, but a spray of saliva too. I was pleasantly surprised that the chairs were spared.'

The politicians won in the end. But thanks to Leyds, Kotzé was able to back down without losing face. Nellmapius was pardoned. The incident tarnished the Transvaal's reputation for upholding the rule of law, but the state attorney came out with flying colours. Leyds had shouldered his responsibility and acquitted himself with integrity. He no longer needed to wear a beard to win respect. He expressed his pride to his father-in-law. 'N's conviction was a huge triumph for me and, between you and me, it has enhanced my prestige.'[34]

The Nellmapius affair played an important role in Leyds's decision about his own future. In early April 1886, he and Louise had opened a bottle of champagne to celebrate the completion of the first half of his contract period. They were missing Holland, more than ever perhaps after the loss of their first son at the age of only five months. By the end of the year, however, there was no longer any question of them returning to the Netherlands. The Nellmapius affair could well have become a breaking point. Leyds might have thrown in the towel out of contempt for the Boer leaders' nepotism. But he didn't. Nor was his relationship with wheeler-dealer Kruger irreparably harmed. At 27, Leyds was still a youngster by Transvaal standards, but he had proved his mettle in a politically sensitive post. He had taken an independent stand, diametrically opposed to the president's, and been vindicated by Kruger's meek apology in the middle of the night. Leyds must have found this sufficiently gratifying both professionally and personally, to turn a blind eye to the Boers' all too obvious shortcomings.[35]

It would be no exaggeration to say that by the end of 1886, Leyds had been won over to the Boer cause. This emerges firstly from his reaction to two royal distinctions conferred on him in November, one by the Portuguese government, the other by Great Britain. He accepted the knighthood from Portugal without reservation. From then on, he was entitled to wear the decorations of a Knight of the Royal Order of Our Lady of the Immaculate Conception of Vila Viçosa. But he declined a knighthood as Commander of the Most Distinguished Order of Saint Michael and Saint George, a distinction of equivalent rank, just as Kruger had turned down the Great Cross in the same Order. Unlike the president of the Orange Free State, Johannes Brand, they refused to compromise themselves for the sake of a British medal. Considering all they would have to endure in their dealings with the United Kingdom in the future, the titles 'Sir Paul' and 'Sir William' would have left a bitter taste in the mouth.[36]

Even more compelling evidence of Leyds's enhanced prestige and his solidarity with the Boer cause came in December 1886. The setting was Paardekraal, just west of the fledgling Johannesburg. This was where the signal had been given for an armed uprising against the British in December 1880. A four-day festival held there a year later to commemorate the event had attracted huge crowds. The 12,000 Boers who attended enjoyed a programme of entertainments as well as a pious homily. Kruger delivered a stirring speech about God's mysterious ways: the victory at Blood River in 1838, the expulsion of the Ndebele from the Transvaal after independence in 1852, the return to freedom earlier that year. All of this, according to Kruger, bore witness to the Lord's abiding benevolence. The Boers, he believed, were a chosen people. The gathering had all the hallmarks of an invented tradition, culminating in the celebration of Dingane's Day on 16 December.[37]

Five years later, in December 1886, thousands of Boers and their families converged on Paardekraal once more for another incongruous mix of market, entertainment and worship. Willem and Louise Leyds were there as well. Louise was amazed at the number of oxwagons—11,000 and more—the 'city of tents', as sprawling as Pretoria, the stone monument and the stage in the centre. This time, too, there was 'much fun and festivity'. Most of all, Louise enjoyed the fireworks, the shooting gallery and the band. Her only complaint was 'the complete absence of certain indispensable facilities, which was particularly inconvenient because so many people were present'. Willem was preoccupied with weightier matters. He had the honour of addressing the gathering, which he did with genuine empathy. As if born and bred on the highveld, he spoke of the many tribulations 'our people' have endured. 'For that we give thanks to the Almighty.' All their 'adversaries among people, among animals and in nature' had given the Boers the opportunity to prove their worth. Moreover, the experience had been edifying. 'All of this was an instrument in God's hands. It was uplifting.' The Boer leaders in particular, he believed, had been chastened by their perpetual 'struggle for freedom and justice . . . Beset by peril and firmly committed to the rights of this nation and this Republic, with God's help they have learned the lessons of experience.'[38]

The bridge had been crossed. Willem Leyds had taken sides, at a remarkable time and in a remarkable place. The symbolism was obvious. Paardekraal and Johannesburg, December 1886. Two tented camps, less than 25 kilometres apart. Two cities bustling with life and energy, yet the difference couldn't have been greater. Paardekraal epitomised the old Transvaal, where they honoured tradition, erected cairns to commemorate a cherished past, praised the Lord for the afflictions He had sent to try them, amused themselves with Bengal fireworks and departed by oxwagon a few days later, each to his own and to his own remote farmstead. See you in five years' time! And hopefully nothing will have changed.

In Johannesburg, a new Transvaal was shooting up at a furious pace. Here, everyone's gaze was fixed on the future. They were just waiting for the dynamite, coal and steam machines to arrive. The mountains of gold they had been dreaming of were finally there, and the whole world was jostling to share in the bounty. It just kept on growing. Canvas, reed and clay were replaced with wood, iron and stone. Liquor flowed in abundance, women were available for money. And this in the very same state. It couldn't last. The two worlds were bound to collide.

The first more or less official clash between old and new occurred two months later, in February 1887. President Kruger was visiting Johannesburg to see for himself and form his own impression of the newcomers to his territory. He wasn't pleased. He was given a warm reception, that wasn't the problem, but he was also presented with a long list of demands: a daily postal service, a local council, a special court for concession disputes, lower taxes and representation in the Volksraad. The president snapped back. This was all too fast. There was only one law in the Transvaal and everyone had to obey it, he warned. That applied to Johannesburg too. Change takes time. One has to consider things carefully.[39]

At least he knew he could count on the support of his state attorney for some time to come. It was clear that Leyds had found his place at the president's side. And the other way round: everyone was satisfied with his work. In July 1887, the Volksraad had approved the Executive Council's proposal to extend Leyds's contract, which was due to expire on 6 October. Or, more accurately, renew it, because the contract Leyds had originally drawn up with Moltzer's help entitled him to an extra lump-sum payment of £1000. Now that the contract had expired and he was entering into new terms of service, the bonus was promptly paid out. 'It's not a fortune,' he observed realistically, and indeed it paled into insignificance beside the riches a Cecil Rhodes or an Alfred Beit had amassed by the same tender age. But still, it was 'a tidy sum and I'm more than pleased with it'.[40]

Concessions

Pretoria, June 1887

So far it had been a good winter for Willem and Louise Leyds. Since April they had been living in a large new house in the market square, with eight rooms and 'a veranda with grapes' at the back. In May they had been blessed with another child, Louis, a 'nice chubby' little boy with 'a small delicate face'. And early June brought good news from Amsterdam. They had finally found a way to fund the longed-for railway to the Indian Ocean. At least, the company that would arrange funding was in the process of being established. On 21 June 1887, more than three years after the concession had been awarded, the deed establishing the Netherlands-South African Railway Company was signed. And Leyds became the government commissioner.[41]

This appointment, along with his renewed contract as state attorney, was proof of the confidence the Boer leaders had in him, Kruger in particular. To the president, the railway line to Lourenço Marques was more than just a project. It was part of the 'Great Cause', a matter of life and death. Kruger was determined that the Transvaal should have its own link to the open sea and ideally its own harbour as well. Without them the Boer republic could forget about any further independent development, especially after the discovery of gold on the Rand, on which so many covetous eyes were now focused.

The government commissioner of the company in charge of this lifeline would bear a heavy responsibility. Leyds was an understandable, if not obvious, choice for that position. From the moment he set foot in the Transvaal, he had worked towards implementing the plans for a railway—out of a sense of duty towards Kruger—and out of loyalty to his mentors Moltzer and Pierson, who themselves had a stake in the enterprise—but it served his own interest as well. Leyds had also come to see the railway as a lifeline. He opened his heart in a letter to Moltzer. He wanted to demonstrate that people 'actually *could* expect something of Holland', or rather, 'of *me*, representing Holland'. That would 'infinitely strengthen my position'. This indeed proved to be true, now that the Netherlands-South African Railway Company was a fact. Leyds gained prestige in Amsterdam as well as Pretoria. Moltzer assured him that it was 'thanks to your persistence that we still have the Dutch concession'. And Kruger's gratitude was evident from the prestigious appointment which, one might add, brought in a nice little extra. As government commissioner Leyds received £250 on top of his annual salary of £1000.[42]

Even so, in retrospect it might have been better not to accept the post. There was a price to pay for the benefits, and that was his reputation for absolute integrity. Only nine months earlier, in the case against Nellmapius, Leyds had distinguished himself by taking an independent stand and proving himself to be a man of principle. In all the Boers' intrigues and nepotism—from which Kruger was not excluded—he had stood out as a beacon of integrity. And it was that perception of him as impartial, a man impervious to corruption, that was compromised by his appointment as government commissioner of the railway company. The two functions were incompatible. He couldn't represent the company's interests and monitor its affairs at the same time without losing people's confidence. Leyds's attempt to do so exposed him to slurs in the local and overseas press, like the mouthpiece of the Randlords that Percy FitzPatrick edited, which later scoffed that the set-up was a scam, all of it planned in advance. The 'gentlemen in Holland' who had recommended him for the position of state attorney in 1884 were the same people who had been awarded the railway concession and arranged his posting to the Transvaal 'as the agent of the concessionaires in order to protect and advance their interests, although at the same time in the service of the Republic'.[43]

Leyds was no longer in a position to debunk conspiracy theories of that kind. In that respect, too, he had taken sides. He had committed himself to Kruger's dream, to the interests of his Amsterdam network and to the Boers' way of conducting politics. In his own mind he was still committed exclusively to the interests of the Transvaal and the Netherlands, which he considered compatible, but in the eyes of the world he had lost his innocence. He had become part of the system, and from then on the whiff of suspicion that surrounded conflicts of interest clung to him as well. Because it's not unfair to say that this had become one of the hallmarks of Transvaal politics. However scrupulous the Boers may have been in religious matters, they were lax in political affairs. Or maybe it was just the young republic's lack of experience. Seizing land from hostile African chiefdoms, using it to graze cattle, sheep and horses and then defending it against British invaders didn't amount to building a state. That took far more: trade, industry, communications, infrastructure; in short, economic activity. And those didn't simply happen by themselves; they had to be built up and organised. But where to start?

Kruger found the answer in the economic model advocated in the early 1880s by—unsurprisingly—Nellmapius. The formula was simple: restrict imports and promote exports. Attract foreign entrepreneurs with capital, who would produce the basics, such as clothing, leather, flour and sugar. Give them concessions and other privileges and protect them with high import duties. That would stimulate exports and bring money in, instead of the other way round. It wasn't an innovative theory—it recalled the mercantilism of earlier centuries and ran counter to the nineteenth-century principle of free trade—but this was probably the very reason that Kruger embraced it.

In October 1881, Nellmapius was rewarded with the two monopolies he had applied for, one for producing sugar from maize and beet, the other for distilling alcohol. Eighteen months later, Kruger, himself a teetotaller, personally attended the opening of Nellmapius's brandy distillery to toast the new venture with a glass of milk. Intemperance couldn't be condoned, but a shot after a hard day's work wouldn't do any harm, and this first factory in the Transvaal—prosaically called the First Factory—received his wholehearted blessing.

Many others followed Nellmapius's example, attracted by the favourable terms of the concession system. There were huge interests at stake: factories to produce paper, soap, matches and rope; buildings for markets and abattoirs; the infrastructure for and the delivery of water, gas and electricity. And before long, the most lucrative concession of all, at least potentially: parcels of land, first in and around Barberton, subsequently on the Rand, with rights to mine gold. Then everything that the mining industry entailed: the extraction of coal and iron, the transportation of raw materials and machinery, the supply of gunpowder and dynamite.[44]

The concession for gunpowder and dynamite was initially awarded to Nellmapius. Later, towards the end of 1887, after Nellmapius's infamous court case, it was transferred to Eduard Lippert. But the sector seemed to be jinxed. A few years later Lippert was also involved in a concession scandal and with him, once again, the entire political elite—with Kruger in the lead. It showed how vulnerable the system was to fraud. The multitude of government contracts attracted not only genuine entrepreneurs, but also swindlers and speculators out to make a quick profit. Moreover, the agents responsible for awarding concessions knew little about government finances. There was no independent oversight, no control mechanism, no clear distinction between the public and private domains. Rumours of nepotism, bribery and abuse of power were soon rife, and there was more than a grain of truth to them. The concession system was wide open to corruption.[45]

Leyds wasn't in favour of it, either. As a rule he was 'opposed to concessions, or more specifically, monopolies'. He felt they 'harmed rather than benefited a country. Instead of promoting a country's industry, they have the opposite effect. In my opinion, we should be aiming at free trade and free industry.' However, 'there are exceptions to every rule, and that is the case here, too. There are matters which only the State can deal with, which it cannot leave to private individuals, and in these the State should have a monopoly.' He was referring to matters that impinge on the security of the state, like firearms, gunpowder and dynamite. And, of course, railways.[46]

The implication was, however, that conflicts of interest were inherent in a venture like the Netherlands-South African Railway Company. Even during the lengthy and arduous process of establishing it, the justification for its existence had been called into question. By 1884, the Dutch concessionaires had failed to raise even a fraction of the share capital they needed. Thereafter they faced one setback after another. The driving forces behind the venture, Groll and Maarschalk, died early on in the process. The American speculator McMurdo, who held the concession for the Portuguese stretch of the line, continued to be obstructive. The Volksraad became increasingly critical. Most worrying of all was the growing competition on three different fronts. To the south-west, the south and the south-east, steady progress was being made with the construction of a railway to the Transvaal. In 1884, Willem and Louise Leyds had travelled by stagecoach to complete the last 200 kilometres of their journey from Cape Town to Kimberley; a year later the first locomotive steamed triumphantly into the city of diamonds. In the same year, branch lines of the southern railway from the ports of East London and Port Elizabeth were extended up to the border of the Orange Free State. And a year later, the south-eastern line, starting in Durban, had already reached Ladysmith.

The three new concessionaires of the future Netherlands-South African Railway Company, Rudolf van den Wall Bake, Jacob Cluysenaer and Johannes Groll Jr, had nothing of the kind to show. The project only gained momentum with the spectacular discoveries of gold, which boosted the Transvaal's economic prospects and consequently the company's anticipated profitability. Prospective investors gradually gained confidence. In March 1886, urged by Leyds—through Moltzer—the Amsterdam banker Adriaan de Marez Oyens took the initiative to raise a 500,000-guilder loan to the Transvaal. The loan succeeded, Leyds got the credit and Kruger the funds he needed to convert the old loans and lay pipes to supply water to the goldfields.

This was encouraging and it came just in time to reassure the president that he was still backing the right horse: a line to Lourenço Marques built and run by a Dutch company. Kruger, in the meantime, disheartened by the sluggish development of the project, had briefly entertained the idea of a link to the rail networks in the Cape Colony and Natal. But with the discovery of gold and the promise of a loan, he soon abandoned the notion. He returned to his original plan and pursued it with dogged determination, refusing to submit to the fierce opposition of the Executive Council, or the demands of Johannesburg's gold diggers, who were lobbying for a rail link to their mother city of Kimberley. The only compromise Kruger was prepared to make in the decisive meeting of the Volksraad was to set a time limit—September 1887—for the establishment of the Dutch company.

The deadline was met in June, with time to spare, but only with a great deal of outside help. More than two million guilders was needed as start-up capital. Dutch financiers put up only 581,000 guilders; the bulk, once again, came from De Marez Oyens. A further 891,000 guilders came from two German institutions, the Berliner Handels-Gesellschaft and the bankers Robert Warschauer & Co. The remaining balance of 600,000 guilders was pledged on behalf of the South African Republic by Kruger in person. On the face of it, this seemed strange. A year earlier he had been happy with a loan of 500,000 guilders from Amsterdam, and in May 1887 he returned 600,000 guilders to help finance a Dutch railway company. The explanation lay in the four-letter word 'gold'.

The Rand's unprecedented mineral wealth functioned as a flywheel for the economy of the Transvaal, in which respect Nellmapius had been unable to help Kruger. To be fair, however, it was thanks to all the concessions that the state treasury, like everyone else, was now profiting directly and lavishly from the business boom. In 1886, government revenue was less than £200,000; in 1887 it tripled. There was enough left over to invest in Kruger's great dream. The fact that the two directors of the Netherlands-South African Railway Company, Van den Wall Bake and Cluysenaer, were Dutch wasn't a problem. A board of directors made up of four Dutch and three German bankers, fine. Kruger made do with two government commissioners, Beelaerts van Blokland, the special envoy in the Netherlands, and Leyds in the Transvaal. Anything, as long as that railway was built.[47]

Kruger is unlikely to have known Goethe's *Faust*, in which the protagonist sells his soul to the devil. The only book he read was the Bible, though even that contains passages that must have given him pause for thought. Three of the four Gospels of the New Testament—Matthew, Mark and Luke—include the story of Jesus casting out devils. The Pharisees knew for certain after the miracle: 'He casteth out devils through Beelzebub chief of the devils.' It takes little imagination to see the parallels, not to mention the—let's say, coincidental—connection between the city's name and the fourth evangelist, Johannes in Dutch.

To Kruger, Johannesburg was a city of sin, where people worshipped Mammon, not God. Yet he had no qualms about benefiting from the rock—the devil's gold—from which it was built. The symbolism even acquired a tangible form. Gold was also found at Paardekraal, the dedicated memorial of the Boer past. In 1887, a settlement developed here which was named—ironically, however well intended—Krugersdorp, after the president. Psychologically, it all seems difficult to reconcile. Nor would Kruger have taken heart from Jesus's reply to the Pharisees: 'And Jesus knew their thoughts, and said unto them, Every Kingdom divided against itself is brought to desolation; and a house divided against itself falleth.'[48]

Be that as it may, this wasn't the way things looked in 1887. On the contrary, the entire country was flourishing because of the gold and the future looked bright. At the beginning of 1888, Louise Leyds boasted to her family in the Netherlands, 'One might compare the Transvaal to an ugly girl who suddenly gets rich and is courted by suitors who showed no interest in her before. The Cape is as insipid as can be. Everyone's leaving and streaming in here. In Pretoria houses are sprouting like mushrooms and still there's a shortage. Across from us, there used to be a shack, but now they're building a lovely house.' The apotheosis of the building boom in Pretoria was the new government building in Church Square, of which Kruger had laid the first stone in May 1889. Three magnificent storeys in the neo-Renaissance style. Leyds could hardly wait. 'I've promised my staff a dinner party once we move in. I'll be happy to leave the dump we're in now, where we have draughts but no air, dust but no space, not to mention moths, woodworm and rats.'[49]

In contrast to all this activity and progress, the railway company had made little headway. A team of five Dutch engineers was sent out as soon as it was officially established in June 1887. In November they started surveying at the eastern end of the line, near the Mozambique border, which proved an unfortunate choice. They arrived at the height of the summer, when malaria is rife and the heat unbearable, especially for Dutchmen unaccustomed to the climate. Two men succumbed soon after starting work, a third resigned and fled. Six months later, when director Cluysenaer arrived in the Transvaal to make a fresh start, he received a piece of bad news. The negotiations with McMurdo's company regarding tariff agreements were still deadlocked. To keep up the pressure,

Kruger—it must have been painful for him—decided to suspend work on the eastern line.

Fortunately for the railway company, there was an alternative. Though relatively minor and less dramatic, it was of inestimable importance to get a foot in the door. It was about transporting coal, vital to industrial gold mining, to Johannesburg. Some time earlier, mainly on Leyds's advice, Isaac Lewis and Sammy Marks had been refused a concession for a 'coal line' from the south on the grounds that it would pre-empt 'an extension of the railway line through the Orange Free State to the Vaal River'. And, after all, it was 'the Government's policy to build the line from the north to the south'. But there were still two more applications, from Thomas Tancred, the contractor for the Portuguese stretch of the eastern line, and from Lippert of the dynamite monopoly. Both were interested in a link with the coal mines west of Johannesburg. To this, Cluysenaer added an application for a short railway line, more like a tram line, to Boksburg in the east. Coalfields had recently been discovered there, but not all of them had yet been claimed—which Cluysenaer promptly proceeded to do.

The three applications came before the Volksraad in July 1888. There was a heated debate. Kruger's partiality towards the Netherlands-South African Railway Company was widely known and he came under attack. Several members accused him of favouring the Dutch. Seething with irritation, he recited Leyds's patient explanations and in the end managed to win majority support. Construction work began in January 1889. The line was barely 27 kilometres long, but it got the company under way, and managing the railway and the coal mine proved both profitable and instructive.[50]

In July 1888, a new opportunity came Leyds's way. State Secretary Bok's term of office was due to lapse at the end of the year. Though he was eligible for re-election, Kruger proposed Leyds as a rival candidate. The Volksraad adopted the motion and chose Leyds by 18 votes to 12. Honoured as he was, Leyds had two reservations. He didn't meet the age requirement—the state secretary had to be at least 30—and he would only be eligible on 1 May 1889. In addition, he thought it unreasonable for a more senior position to be less well paid than the one he already held. Earlier that year, his salary as state attorney had been raised to £1200 (excluding his fee as government commissioner of the railway company), whereas the state secretary was still earning only £1000.

Many members of the Volksraad were shocked by Leyds's request for a salary increase, and by his age. Most of them had thought he was older. The debate was postponed until the following session, which gave Kruger time to iron things out. Bok's term of office was extended by a few months and Leyds replaced him as state secretary on 2 May 1889. A month later the Volksraad agreed to raise his salary to £1200. He was strongly advised, however, to grow his beard again, as he had done five years earlier, when he first arrived in the Transvaal.

It can rightly be called a lightning career. At 25 Leyds had parachuted into a foreign country as state attorney and, not yet 30, he had been elected state secretary by a clear majority. He was the second man in the political hierarchy, working directly under and in close collaboration with the president. As he himself described his position, 'There are no set limits to the office of state secretary. The system here is strongly centralised. Ultimately, everything ends up with the government (i.e. the president and the state secretary) which may in some cases refer to the Executive Council. All documents intended for the government are addressed to the state secretary, who also signs all government correspondence and minutes.'[51]

It was a demanding job with a lot of responsibility, which he had to tackle alone for the first few months. In mid-May 1889, Louise, little Louis and baby Willemine, who was born at the beginning of February, went to the Netherlands to spend a few months with their family. They had vaguely arranged that Willem would try to fetch them at the end of the year, but there were a few obstacles in the way. There were several matters Kruger was unable or unwilling to handle without him, and some that Leyds wanted to attend to personally.

Most of them were about linking the Transvaal to the outside world, in other words, railways and harbours. Early in March 1889, Kruger and Leyds had held talks in Potchefstroom with a delegation from the Orange Free State headed by the new president, F.W. Reitz. Three treaties were concluded, with far-reaching consequences. First, a railway agreement, in which Reitz promised that without the Transvaal's consent the lines from the Cape Colony and Natal would go no further than Bloemfontein and Harrismith. Kruger reciprocated: without prior approval from the Orange Free State, they would not build a link to the outside world other than to the east, or the south—in other words, to Lourenço Marques or the Free State—and not 'round about' to Kimberley. The second treaty was a trade and friendship agreement, while the third established a political and military alliance, which paved the way for a joint struggle against Britain a decade later. The provision in question read: 'The South African Republic and the Orange Free State hereby enter into a mutual alliance and declare themselves willing to assist one another with all force and means, should the independence of either of the two States be threatened or undermined from outside.'[52]

In the short term the railways convention had the most far-reaching implications. It was clear that the 'British' lines were again making headway and that the 'race to the Rand' had not yet been won. An unexpected stroke of good luck came in late June 1889, when the Portuguese government rallied and showed its more efficient side. In spite of pressure from the British, Lisbon decided to withdraw McMurdo's concession on the grounds that he had failed to meet the agreed deadline. So the way was clear again. Beelaerts van Blokland immediately resumed talks about a tariff agreement, now directly with the Portuguese authorities. Pending the outcome, just as had happened a year earlier, the Volksraad discussed another local matter concerning the railway. In July 1889, it was about the stretch between Pretoria and Johannesburg, and again there were three applications, including one from the Netherlands-South African Railway Company and one from 'that wretched Lippert'. This time Kruger and Leyds were unable to get their way. It mattered little that none of the applications was granted and that a proposal to extend the Rand tram by a total of 81 kilometres—to Krugersdorp in the west and Springs in the east—was adopted without any problem. For Kruger personally there was pleasant news as well. The Volksraad approved an increase of his salary from £2000 to £8000 a year.[53]

This seemed a good time for Leyds to discuss his leave with the president. But Kruger turned the conversation to the subject of the eastern frontier. Two territories to the south of Mozambique, Swaziland and Tsongaland, had no international status. Kruger was in favour of annexing them. That would give the Transvaal an independent link to the sea and its own harbour, Kosi Bay. Leyds wasn't enthusiastic. Kosi Bay had less potential than Delagoa Bay. In the meantime, however, a Transvaal delegation had gone there to negotiate with the British. Kruger wanted his state secretary close at hand in case anything came of it, though he might have known that the British would never let the Transvaal have a harbour of their own. They were simply keeping him dangling.

That was one of the drawbacks of Leyds's new position. Before long he discovered another: bribery, whether subtle or not. In July 1889, for instance, he received a concession proposal accompanied by a personal letter with a £10 cheque tucked inside. He was furious. He wrote to Louise, 'I received another insulting letter today from a chap who wanted to bribe me. I'll send you a copy of it and of my reply. I won't write it today because I'm still too upset. What bothers me most is that, after five years of honest work, I haven't managed to convince everyone that I am a man who cannot be bribed.' He would just have to live with it. Having accepted the appointment as government commissioner of the railway company, he found the odds were stacked against him. To some, being partisan meant being open to bribery.

There were advantages, too, such as tributes that boosted his ego. Many of those came his way in the course of his political career, but the first was something special. About 300 kilometres north of Barberton, known for the first gold rush, another promising artery was found. This was to become the Selati goldfield. The settlement that developed there, Leydsdorp, was named after him. Leyds was quite proud of it, he told Louise. 'I'm curious to know how the village named after me will develop. Of course, there's a bit of vanity there, but then everyone has their foibles. I certainly feel my name should continue to be associated with this country, with the gold industry in particular.'[54]

He probably didn't mean it like that, but the symbolism is unmistakable. After Krugersdorp, now Leydsdorp, surrounded by goldfields. No ideals without compromises, huge compromises. Fight the devil with his own gold. Mix personal interests with the interests of the state. All for the 'Great Cause'.

On 19 September 1889, Leyds received a telegram from Beelaerts van Blokland saying that the tariff agreement with Portugal was in place. The moratorium on the construction of the eastern line was cancelled on the spot and the railway company could go ahead. Leyds was keener than ever to take a break. He wanted 'to get away because it would do me good, physically and mentally'. What if he were to combine his visit to Europe with business meetings, but still keep it officially a private trip? Kruger relented and gave his consent on 8 October. Three weeks later Leyds boarded the *Grantully Castle* in Cape Town.[55]

Boers and Hollanders, love and hate

Amsterdam, November 1889

They hadn't seen each other for six months and Louise was longing to have her husband all to herself. 'When you get here you must spend time with me, and not keep rushing off to all those people,' she implored. With her, and with the children, of course. Louis 'is starting to talk' and he would 'absolutely fall in love' with little Willemine, 'so contented and sweet with her dark eyes'. Willem had also looked forward to being reunited with his family, but he knew beforehand that he wouldn't be able to devote himself solely to them. He had been granted leave only on condition that his trip would serve a political purpose as well.[56]

That is, harbours and railways. He arrived in Amsterdam in mid-November, and in early December he was expected in Lisbon. Since the Portuguese had withdrawn McMurdo's concession six months earlier, all sorts of wild schemes had been doing the rounds concerning the critically strategic southern coast of Mozambique. Not only in London and Cape Town, but in Pretoria too. Even so, the deep harbour of Delagoa Bay had far more going for it than Kosi Bay with its sandbanks. Perhaps it would still be possible to work something out with the Portuguese?

Arrangements were soon made for Leyds to visit Lisbon, 'secretly', so that the Portuguese government would have 'less trouble with pressure from Britain'. The news inevitably leaked, but by then Leyds already knew what he wanted to know. It was clear that the more unconventional plans stood no chance. 'The Portuguese are afraid of being driven into the sea,' he reported to Kruger. They were against the idea of selling a strip of land in Mozambique to the Transvaal to provide a corridor to the sea. The same applied to the railway company having its own cargo depot in the harbour of Lourenço Marques. His conclusion was that Portugal 'needs to be reassured about our intentions; that they understand that we want to work with them, not against them'. The message he himself conveyed in Lisbon was that the Transvaal government would consider it 'a hostile act' if special privileges were given to 'others', for which read 'Britain'.[57]

This wasn't Leyds's only mission in Europe. After Portugal he visited France and Belgium in the vain hope of arousing their interest in establishing a Transvaal steamship company. In the Netherlands he had mainly matters pertaining to the railway to discuss, not only with old acquaintances like Beelaerts van Blokland and Moltzer, but also with the railway company's new executive board. He had met a few of its members before: financier De Marez Oyens to start with, and directors Van den Wall Bake and Gerrit Middelberg, the latter having succeeded Cluysenaer on 1 January 1890.

Leyds also wanted to find out what the Dutch thought of the Transvaal. At the time of his departure, more than five years earlier, the Boers were held in high regard. Their successful war of independence against the British was still fresh in people's minds. In February 1884, Kruger, Smit and Du Toit had been given a hero's welcome throughout the country, although the acclaim they received was unfortunately not matched by anything more substantial. People waved flags in abundance, but not chequebooks. Leyds soon realised that little had changed. Pompous speeches about kinship, but no funds when it came to investing in the South African Republic. The spectacular discoveries of gold had made almost no impression at all.

In that respect, the difficulty he experienced in raising funds for the railway company spoke volumes. Amsterdam's high finance preferred to invest their capital in the Dutch East Indies, where they held the strings in their own trusted hands and where the government gave the business sector all the legroom it needed. Compared with that tropical entrepreneurs' paradise, the risks and returns in the Boer republic were far more difficult to calculate. There was relatively little Dutch economic activity in the Transvaal apart from the Netherlands-South African Railway Company and two financial institutions, the Netherlands Bank and Credit Union of South Africa (Nederlandsche Bank en Credietvereeniging voor Zuid-Afrika) and the Pretoria Mortgage Company (Pretoria Hypotheek-Maatschappij), and this wasn't going to change.[58]

It was no different with the public. The Dutch South African Association made numerous efforts to promote emigration to the Transvaal, but they proved futile. The supply didn't match the demand. Employment was available only for certain occupations such as teachers, civil servants and church ministers. The motherland had little to offer in the way of skilled labour for the mining industry, the Transvaal's major growth sector, and no substantial mining enterprise existed in the Netherlands to recruit and train people locally. The importance of this last factor was evident from the—again exceptional—example of the railway company. The Dutch had no special reputation in the field of railway construction, yet the company managed to recruit more than half its workforce in the Netherlands.[59]

So the Netherlands hadn't achieved much in the way of strengthening its relations with the South African Republic over the previous five years.

But they continued to dream about the Transvaal. Their Afrikaner 'cousins' still held a romantic attraction, however fanciful, in the nationalistic imagination of the Dutch intellectual elite, united, or rather, fragmented as they were in a range of pro-Boer associations. Their infatuation with the Boers may not have been blind, but it was at best short-sighted. The Boers' difficult relationship with modern times looked better through rose-coloured spectacles. And few people in the Netherlands were even aware of the schisms and animosities that divided them.

An interesting example emerged from Du Toit's visit to the Netherlands in early October 1889, more than a month before Leyds returned to his native soil. It was a rather strange situation. Du Toit had come to discuss the possibility of establishing a university in the Transvaal, a mission for which he wasn't ideally suited. He had been a co-founder of the Afrikaner Bond, and fiercely resented the Dutch influence in the Transvaal. He was also one of Leyds's harshest critics. The only reason Kruger had chosen him was his supposed good relationship with the Anti-Revolutionary Party leader, Kuyper, founder of the Vrije Universiteit. Yet it was Kuyper, of all people, who stalled, while the board of the Dutch South African Association welcomed Du Toit with open arms. There was a festive reception complete with carriage, garlands and national anthem.

Louise Leyds, who was also in Amsterdam but not at the reception, considered it 'an absolute scandal'. Bristling with indignation, she fulminated to Willem that 'their display of respect for that man, who has flung so much mud at us Hollanders, reveals a lack of all sense of national honour'. And to think De Marez Oyens was involved in organising it! She went so far as to raise the matter in person with the secretary of the Dutch South African Association, the Amsterdam professor of philosophy Bellaar Spruyt, at the home of Moltzer, who—'thank God'—hadn't been present at the reception. Louise could just picture Du Toit 'alone in his room afterwards, holding his sides with laughter and thinking "those good old Hollanders—you can kick them around as much as you like and they'll still lick your hand"'.[60]

A bit melodramatic, perhaps, but Louise Leyds's outrage is easy to understand. Not long before, Willem himself had referred to Du Toit as 'that damned hypocrite'. He was stung to think that Du Toit had received such hospitality in the Netherlands from the very people he regarded as his allies. That was also the most important lesson he learned after five years' absence from his fatherland. The attitude in the Netherlands towards the Boers and their republic could best be summed up as: maintain cordial relations but steer clear of business. Over the previous few years Leyds had moved in exactly the opposite direction. His commitment to the Boer cause had deepened, but his personal relations with the Boer leaders had remained cool and critical.[61]

Nor did they improve when Leyds and his family returned to Pretoria in March 1890. He was confronted soon afterwards with a personal attack by P.J. Scherpenseel, with D.H. Schmüll as an unwitting accomplice. The two men had been eligible for appointment as consuls of the South African Republic in Belgium and the Netherlands respectively, but their hopes had gone up in smoke—Beelaerts van Blokland had dismissed them as not up to standard—and Scherpenseel wanted to settle the score. Moreover, he was the representative of a Franco-Belgian railway syndicate angling for concessions in the Transvaal, that is, a rival of the Netherlands-South African Railway Company. Reason enough to take it out on Leyds. The weapon was a letter from Leyds himself. Written in 1886, it was addressed to Schmüll, who had forwarded a copy to Scherpenseel. At the time, Leyds had still been on close terms with Schmüll, and preoccupied with the Nellmapius affair. He had been frank in his views about the Boer leaders, notably General Smit and the vice-president, Commandant-General Piet Joubert. 'Be wary about trusting General Smit,' he wrote, and 'the reason for Piet Joubert's conduct is his jealousy of the President. Back then he was a serious contender for the presidency and it hurts every time he has to say "President" to someone else. On top of that, he has a deep-seated hatred of Hollanders.'

Those weren't nice things to say about one's colleagues, and when the letter found its way to the *Transvaal Advertiser* Leyds was in trouble. The Volksraad received memorandums demanding a thorough investigation, the press speculated about his imminent resignation, and an angry Kruger demanded an explanation. Leyds was obliged to offer a written apology to the two aggrieved generals and to Kruger himself. He did so in all humility. 'It was 1886 at the time and it is now 1890. In the intervening period I have come to know both General Smit and General Joubert better. I have had the privilege of working with them on a daily basis and I deeply regret having spoken of them in that spirit and in those terms. Whatever decision might be taken, I hope in any event that it will be in the interests of this Republic, which for years I have served to the best of my ability and which I have come to love so deeply.'

Kruger, Smit and Joubert accepted the apology. The threat to Leyds's political career had passed. The Volksraad continued to grumble, but Kruger rose firmly to his defence. As a Christian he had forgiven Leyds and he appealed to the honourable members to do the same. Everyone makes a mistake once in a while.[62]

Forgiven he was, but the letter was never forgotten. Leyds's critics were quick to invoke it whenever anti-Dutch sentiment flared up. As state secretary, he was after all the undisputed figurehead of the Dutch in the Transvaal and therefore the perfect target for those who disliked the Dutch. There were more of them than the Boer-lovers in the Netherlands realised. What upset people most was the 'haughtiness' of the Dutch— Willem and Louise Leyds not being exempt. Their disdain for the unsophisticated Boers was obvious. They refused to speak Afrikaans, attended church infrequently, if at all, and socialised only with their own kind. As a result, and in spite of their good intentions, the Boers and the Dutch remained strangers to one another and never became true compatriots. The resentment was strongest among Kruger's conservative, devout Calvinist following. In less orthodox circles, united around Vice-President Joubert, the grievances against the Dutch related mainly to the disproportionately influential position they allegedly occupied under Paul Kruger. The argument was that they took jobs away from no less talented candidates from the Transvaal, the Orange Free State and the Cape, and so undermined the Afrikaner quest for unity. There were several reasons for this antipathy towards the Dutch in Johannesburg and its surroundings. The predominantly English-speaking and pro-British immigrants in the gold-mining industry saw them as Kruger's inner circle, the clique responsible for their continuing status as second-class citizens, foreigners, or Uitlanders, as the Boers called them.[63]

All things considered, this probably gave undue credit to the Dutch in the Transvaal. In the first place, there were relatively few of them. On the other hand, they were strongly represented in certain fields, in education, the church and, most prominently, in government service, especially in senior positions. Between 15 and 20 per cent of civil servants in the state secretariat and the education department were Dutch-speaking. It was mainly their high visibility in key administrative positions, Leyds being the most obvious example, that gave the impression of a Dutch power bloc in Pretoria.[64]

Plus of course that supreme Dutch bulwark, the Netherlands-South African Railway Company. If there was one institution that fed into anti-Dutch sentiment, it was the railway company, which was gradually gathering momentum. None of that changed with the inauguration of the Rand tram in March 1890, or the appointment of its new director. Gerrit Middelberg, an experienced engineer educated in Germany and England, was a devout Calvinist and a regular churchgoer. He was good at dealing with people, in the boardroom or on the work floor. The right man in the right place. Yet even he was unable to improve the company's image.

This was partly due to the large contingent of Hollanders on his staff whose standards of moral propriety differed from those of the Boers. But then piety and abstinence weren't high on the list of qualifications for recruitment in the Netherlands. Behind it all, however, was economic and political rivalry. The company held one of the most coveted concessions in the entire Transvaal and it had been a bone of contention for years. The Cape Colony and Natal wanted to extend their own government lines to the north and then complete the line in the Transvaal. Tariffs were left to the whims of a monopolist, and the Uitlanders on the Rand were unable to do anything about it. And everyone knew that the company enjoyed the patronage of Kruger—and of course Leyds. The president pinned all his hopes on the railway company, which was to become the most powerful instrument in his quest for an independent link to the sea. The railway to the Indian Ocean would be the lifeblood of the Transvaal, the engine for independent development, free from Britain, unconnected to the struggle for Afrikaner unity and beyond the grasp of the Randlords. The railway company was in every respect a political venture.[65]

It was therefore also the pawn in a political struggle, with all the give and take this entails, as became apparent in the course of 1890. The company came under fire again around the same time as the personal attack on Leyds. It was no coincidence that Vice-President Joubert was at the forefront. In two lengthy open letters he raised questions about the company's operations. Kruger realised that something had to be done. To some extent the criticism was justified. They would have to make a concession of some kind to take the wind out of the opposition's sails.

Together with Leyds, Kruger summoned Middelberg to discuss amendments to the railway concession. The matter was resolved after a couple of weeks of hard talks and telegraphs to and from Amsterdam. On the one hand, the outcome imposed restrictions on the company. The Republic was given more say in the fixing of tariffs and routes, and the deadline for completing the eastern line was brought forward to 31 December 1894. In addition, the company had to accept that there would also be a southern line, from Pretoria via Johannesburg to the Vaal River, where it would connect with the 'Cape' line coming from Bloemfontein. Finally, the Netherlands-South African Railway Company lost its preferential rights on all local lines. By way of compensation it acquired exclusive rights to all mainline links to other countries, which of course included the Transvaal section of the southern line. The eastern line would also get another branch, this one going to Barberton.

The new concession was a gamble for both parties. For the Netherlands-South African Railway Company it entailed far greater entrepreneurial risks. More kilometres of railway line had to be laid within a shorter period of time. The government in turn staked its key political objective: Johannesburg had to be linked to Lourenço Marques before being linked to any ports in the Cape Colony. The payoff for both was that the political storm died down. The parliamentary debate on the amended draft concession took its usual course. A special parliamentary commission pored over the proposal at Kruger's home, where the 'old president' bombarded its members with arguments, intimidation and abuse until they gave in and agreed to his demands. On 25 June 1890, the Volksraad passed the amended concession as it stood.[66]

It was less easy for Kruger to impose his will on the world outside Pretoria. In late 1890, the international financial world was facing a crisis, which continued into 1892. Credit was hard to come by throughout that period. Investors were holding onto their money. This was a major setback for a railway company that needed large sums of working capital to lay extra kilometres of track in a shorter period of time. At the same time the gold-mining industry on the Rand had the pyrite problem to deal with. Mercury turned out to be ineffective for extracting gold below a certain depth. The first laboratory tests using potassium cyanide as a substitute were promising, but it took time to adapt the production process. In 1890 and 1891 the revenue was substantially lower than expected, which meant that the Transvaal was in difficulty as well. With its main source of income declining, it couldn't afford to keep up its extravagant spending of the past few years.

But Kruger was slow to grasp all the implications. As if the problems with the railway weren't enough, in July 1891 he allowed himself to be talked into a new adventure by the French Baron Eugène Oppenheim—the Selati railway running from the eastern line near the border with Mozambique to the Selati goldfields. He even allowed Oppenheim to look for backers in Europe on behalf of the Republic. Leyds was strongly opposed. Although the line would open up his eponymous Leydsdorp, his misgivings outweighed his vanity. Through Beelaerts van Blokland he had Oppenheim investigated and discovered he was 'peddling government loans' left, right and centre and in the process 'irreparably damaging our country's credit rating'. Kruger was furious with Leyds when he heard about it. The Oppenheim episode led to one of the fiercest clashes between the two men. Leyds wrote to Beelaerts van Blokland about the matter some time later. 'Once, after a terrible scene, I was on the verge of handing in my resignation.' But he didn't do so and in the end got his way. Oppenheim was given to understand that he was to put an end to his shady dealings.[67]

Their financial woes would have to be solved in some other way. The railway company was in serious trouble. The most pressing problems were dealt with by obtaining loans, but the company hadn't managed to secure the long-term loans it urgently needed. It was November 1891 and its funds were running out. How was it to proceed?

Rhodes & Company

Pretoria, July 1892

The reprieve came from an unexpected quarter. Anyone who might have predicted in November 1891 that the railway company would be rescued by Rhodes, Robinson and Rothschild would have been declared insane. But just over six months later that's exactly what happened. The Netherlands-South African Railway Company, the most important vehicle of Kruger's vision of independence, was kept alive by British investors. It doesn't sound logical and at the time it came as a shock.

It started with an act of desperation by chief engineer W. Verwey, in Middelberg's absence the company's top man in Pretoria. In early December 1891, a telegram from Amsterdam with bad financial news reduced him to 'a state of insomnia' in which he saw no option but to turn to the Cape Colony. By his own account, it was 'to save the honour of the enterprise and of myself'. The idea in itself wasn't so bad. The Cape Colony had an obvious interest in the completion of the southern line. At the same time, there was someone influential in Cape Town who was known to be unsympathetic towards Kruger.

Cecil Rhodes hadn't been idle since his first meetings with Kruger and Leyds at Veertienstroom and Blignautspont in January 1885. In 1888 he forced a merger with his last competitor in Kimberley, resulting in a diamond monopoly for De Beers Consolidated Mines. In 1889, he and his usual business partners incorporated the British South Africa Company (BSAC) under a royal charter, which gave it almost sovereign rights over a vast territory to the north of the Transvaal. In 1890, with the support of Jan Hofmeyr and his Afrikaner Bond, he became premier of the Cape Colony. Hence Rhodes held three very different key positions—speaking of conflicts of interest, Leyds was a novice by comparison—but in each of those capacities he was passionately committed to the expansion of the British Empire. His dream encompassed the entire continent of Africa. His stalking ground was the whole of southern Africa.[68]

In Rhodes's ideal of a federal South Africa under British rule there was no place for an unmanageable Boer republic striving for independence, especially not since it had become the economic hub of the region. The Rand's gold had turned everything on its head. The Transvaal could no longer be ignored, circumvented or isolated. It was a factor to be reckoned with. The gold mines were already in the hands of like-minded magnates. If Rhodes could now gain control of its links to the outside world as well, he would have the Transvaal in the palm of his hand. Kruger's concession in 1890, agreeing to the construction of a southern line, had been an important first step in that direction. Cape Town and the Colony's other ports, Port Elizabeth and East London, would get their railway links to Johannesburg— at least if the railway company kept to its contractual obligations for the construction of the Transvaal stretch—and not go bankrupt in the meantime.

That would of course be another option for Rhodes: the railway company insolvent and swept away, the path clear for a new, preferably British, company. But there was also something to be said for consenting to Verwey's request and helping the railway company out of its financial quagmire. There were actually three reasons in favour of doing so.

First, there was another contender, Natal. It was also a British colony, that much was true, but, like the Cape Colony, it had its own administrative responsibilities, its own economic policies and its own harbour. Durban was 300 kilometres closer to Johannesburg than East London, the Cape Colony's closest port. Moreover, the railway line from Durban already went as far as the Transvaal border, and Natal had eagerly been currying favour with Kruger. If the railway company went bankrupt, Kruger might choose a connection with Durban, rather than a link to the Cape line.

The second reason was that, besides the southern line, Rhodes had another iron in the fire, or at least that is what he believed. A man of no small ambition, he had in mind to buy the last, Portuguese stretch of the eastern line, and take Lourenço Marques into the bargain. The Portuguese were strapped for cash. In the City of London Rhodes found sufficient capital and enthusiasm for this spectacular takeover, which would rein in the Transvaal once and for all. To make the investment pay off, however, there would have to be an eastern line.

There was a third reason, too. With the railway company in a weaker position, it would probably be possible to make further demands, for example about the operation of the southern line. All things considered, the chances were good. As a result, the Cape commissioner for public works, James Sivewright, received permission to negotiate with Verwey. Amsterdam was also in favour. The talks were fairly brief. On 10 December 1891 Sivewright and Verwey reached an agreement. The Cape Colony would provide construction funds of at least £300,000—the final total came to £550,000. In return, the Cape railway company would receive not only bonds in the Netherlands-South African Railway Company, but also the right to maintain the service on the southern line—in the Transvaal itself—until the eastern line was completed.

It was a bitter pill for the Netherlands-South African Railway Company to swallow and a disappointment for Kruger and Leyds, but there was little choice. And that was only the beginning. The funds from the Cape Colony were intended for the southern line. The longer eastern line would need far more working capital. In February 1892, with blood, sweat and tears, the railway company managed to prise loose an additional 600,000-guilder loan from Dutch and German bankers. The Transvaal government, however, had nowhere to turn other than to one of the Randlords, J.B. Robinson, for a loan of £100,000 to increase its share in the company.

These were still only drops in the ocean. Many more times those amounts were needed and a capital investment of that magnitude could only come from Europe. Both the governors of the railway company and the Transvaal government—represented by the director of the National Bank, W. Knappe—went to see what the prospects were. A few months later Knappe came back with the first bite. It had come from the heart of the City of London, no less, from the eminent Rothschild family. This, again, was not what one would have expected, but the explanation is simple.

The bank had a considerable interest in Kimberley and Johannesburg; it worked in close collaboration with Rhodes and knew all there was to know about economic developments in the region—including, of course, on the Rand. In the spring of 1892, thanks to potassium cyanide, the gold-mining industry had recovered completely and was anticipating another spectacular boom. The Rothschilds were sufficiently confident to give the South African Republic the substantial loan it wanted—£2,500,000— on condition of 'the money being spent exclusively within the limits of the Republic'. That clause had been discreetly proposed by Rhodes. The Transvaal was obviously not meant to use the money to whisk Lourenço Marques from under his nose.

Nor did that happen. Pretoria spent almost the entire amount on shares in and loans to the railway company. In order to do so, Kruger and Leyds had to get the approval of the Volksraad. The Rothschild loan was on the agenda for late June 1892, but three weeks before that date they faced their first test, Leyds in particular.

His term of office as state secretary was drawing to an end and at the beginning of June the Volksraad voted on the possibility of re-electing him. It was more than just a formality. Scores of memorandums had come in, strongly critical of Leyds, both personally and about his work. His detractors recalled the comments of two years earlier, after the exposure of his letter to Schmüll. The main issues were again his failure to attend church and his 'Dutch' way of doing things, but this time, more importantly, the conflict of interests inherent in his roles as state secretary and government commissioner of the railway company. Leyds had no option but to resign as commissioner, which put an end to the debate once and for all. He was re-elected state secretary by 20 votes to three. The motion regarding the Rothschild loan still required the usual bullying and coaxing, but in the end it went through intact. In early July 1892 the contract was published in the Transvaal *Government Gazette*. Both Leyds and the railway company could move on.[69]

Rhodes also moved on, tirelessly. He had so much to do, and so little time. Diamonds, gold, political power—not bad for half a lifetime, for a man who was not yet 40. But he wanted more, much more—more railways and another harbour, but most of all, more land, infinitely more land to fulfil his boundless dreams. The satirical magazine *Punch* illustrated him full-length as a modern Colossus of Rhodes, the giant of classical antiquity straddling Africa 'from Cape to Cairo': a telegraph system, a railway and then casual annexation. 'I would annex the planets if I could,' he famously said. By comparison, a mere continent wasn't all that ambitious.

So, to the north, deeper into the interior. Bechuanaland, wrangled into the orbit of British rule in 1885, was only a stepping stone. Rhodes had set his sights on the territory beyond it, the endless savanna north of the Limpopo River, where the biblical land of Ophir was said to have been; King Solomon's mines, too, in the north-eastern region known as Mashonaland. Fortune-seekers dreamed of the wealth waiting to be amassed there. By comparison, the Rand paled into insignificance. Rhodes was impatient to take possession of the country. There was only one problem—actually two.

Firstly, the territory happened to be inhabited. The Ndebele had been living there since the late 1830s, when the Voortrekkers drove them out of the Transvaal. King Mzilikazi had been succeeded by his son Lobengula. From the royal capital in Bulawayo he ruled in name over a territory which roughly corresponds to present-day Zimbabwe. His authority was more or less recognised by the other peoples living there, among them the Shona. Lobengula was a sight to behold, according to his white visitors, and there were quite a few of them. Rhodes bombarded him with envoys, all of whom returned with vivid descriptions of a cruel but charming tyrant, 'very much like a wild beast', but with 'a very pleasant smile', and in all his obesity 'every inch a king'. Some returned with a signed agreement as well, and that of course is what Rhodes was after. The coveted document was obtained in October 1888 by his trusted business partner, Charles Rudd. In exchange for a thousand Martini-Henry rifles with ammunition, a steamboat on the Zambezi River and a monthly stipend of £100, Lobengula relinquished full and exclusive rights to all the mineral resources in his country. Legally, the contract was full of holes, but that didn't bother Rhodes. He had obtained the concession he wanted and, a year later, a royal charter for his British South Africa Company, which gave him sovereign rights in Matabeleland and Mashonaland.[70]

That was one problem solved. The other involved the Boers. At the age of 16, Kruger had helped drive Mzilikazi from the Transvaal, which in his view created a lasting bond between him and the Ndebele. He was bound by the provisions of the Convention of London of 1884 on the eastern and western frontiers of the Transvaal, but the agreement said nothing about the northern frontier. So Kruger considered himself free to enter into treaties with the Ndebele as he pleased. And so he did. In 1887 Pieter Grobler, on behalf of the South African Republic, signed a peace and friendship agreement with Lobengula. Hence Kruger, too, possessed a document which he believed gave him certain rights—and entitled him to some form of compensation when 'consul' Grobler was murdered near the Bechuanaland border in July 1888. Kruger was convinced that Rhodes was behind his death. The matter was settled by payment of compensation to Grobler's widow, but the legal principle remained unresolved. Who had the oldest rights or the strongest claim to the land north of the Limpopo?

In January 1890, rumours began to circulate that a group of Boers in the Transvaal were preparing to embark on an old-fashioned trek to Mashonaland. The situation threatened to escalate. The new high commissioner, Sir Henry Loch, who had just arrived in the Cape, insisted that Kruger put an end to the expedition. After a difficult start, Kruger had built up a good relationship with Sir Henry's predecessor, Sir Hercules Robinson, and he hoped to achieve the same with Sir Henry. He invited him to attend a personal meeting. Rhodes was welcome too. Leyds had recently returned from his leave in Europe and would accompany Kruger.

The meeting was held in the same place where five years earlier Kruger and Leyds had been involved in the unsuccessful negotiations over Goshen and Stellaland. This time the talks would go down in history as the Conference of Blignautspont. The name suggests rather more than what it actually was. The Berlin Conference, held from November 1884 to February 1885 at which Western diplomats carved up the continent of Africa, now *that* was a real conference. The meeting held at Blignautspont on 12 and 13 March 1890 was simply a gathering of four white men in a tent in a tiny spot on the veld. The Scramble for Africa in miniature. Conspicuously absent were the black leaders over whose fortunes they were deciding: King Lobengula of Matabeleland and Mashonaland, King Ngwane V—also known as Bhunu—of Swaziland, and the chiefs Sambane and Mbikiza of Tsongaland.

Their fates were bound together by an idea which Kruger had expressed some time earlier and which he was hoping to formalise at Blignautspont. He was prepared to relinquish all claims north of the Limpopo, in exchange for Britain's agreement to give the Transvaal a free hand in Swaziland and Tsongaland, including Kosi Bay. This went too far for Loch. With his striking long, grey beard he could be mistaken for a Boer leader, but he spoke the language of the cricket pitch not the bush. Leyds described him as 'a pleasant but quick-tempered man with a jingoistic streak', who relied too heavily on 'information from subordinates who loathe us'.[71] Loch's counter-proposal came in the form of a ready-made draft convention with less favourable—and non-negotiable—terms for the Transvaal.

Kruger was put out by Loch's unwillingness to compromise and said he would have to consult the Executive Council and the Volksraad. As a result, nothing was signed at Blignautspont. After months of haggling, the two parties finally reached an agreement on 2 August 1890. Leyds had always had reservations and was still not in favour of the deal, but that was the price Kruger was prepared to pay for an independent railway line and harbour. Under the convention, the Transvaal waived all rights to Matabeleland and Mashonaland, and agreed to the British colonial railway system being extended up to its borders. In return, Britain recognised the validity of all the concessions the Boers had acquired in Swaziland, which was to be administered jointly. The Transvaal also gained the right—and this was Kruger's main objective—to buy a strip of land in Swaziland and Tsongaland, just wide enough to build a railway line and a harbour. An extra condition was that after buying the land, the Transvaal would join the customs union between the British colonies and the Orange Free State.[72]

Everyone got something out of the deal. Rhodes was able to go ahead with his British South Africa Company. In July 1890, even before the convention was signed, he sent a troop of pioneers—including a large number of 'youngsters of the la-di-da class'—to the promised land of gold in the north. Rhodes knew that would go down well back home. In mid-September they arrived at their destination, a hill in Mashonaland. They named it Fort Salisbury, after the British prime minister, hoisted the Union Jack, said three hurrahs for Queen Victoria, and so the territory was annexed. But unhappily for Rhodes and his pioneers, the fortunes they had dreamed of were nowhere to be found. Lord Randolph Churchill, an influential Conservative politician and shareholder in the BSAC, came specially from London to see for himself, but was forced to conclude that 'Mashonaland . . . is neither Arcadia nor an El Dorado'.

The ground contained little of value, so there was nothing to do but either share out the land above it or sell it to the highest bidder. Rhodes had minions for everything and this, he decided, was a job for 'Doctor Jim'. Leander Starr Jameson was a Scot by birth, a physician by profession and an adventurer by vocation. He was stubborn to the point of being reckless, a man after Rhodes's heart. He did what was expected of him: he put an end to the Ndebele problem. Lobengula tried to avoid a conflict, sent letters and envoys to Queen Victoria, and managed to ward off his downfall for a couple of years. But in November 1893 his time ran out. Jameson provided the pretext and executed the sentence, with a little over a thousand men armed with state-of-the-art Maxim machine guns. The Ndebeles' spears and even their Martini-Henry rifles were a poor match. Lobengula fled from Bulawayo and committed suicide. Matabeleland became Rhodesia and its old name was soon forgotten.[73]

A whole country named after you. That was even more than Kruger had achieved. The convention of August 1890 gave the Transvaal joint control over Swaziland and a conditional right to a corridor through which they could build a railway to Kosi Bay in Tsongaland. There was still a lot to discuss—not so much with the Swazis and Tsongas: they would have to wait and see what happened—but mainly with the British colonial authorities in Cape Town and London. The talks dragged on for years. Sir Henry Loch was the hardest nut to crack. In the end it was Lord Ripon, secretary of state for the colonies, who acceded to the Boers' demands. In November 1893, Swaziland effectively came under the control of the Transvaal and in December 1894 it was annexed. Young King Ngwane V could only resign himself to the fact. Kruger gained a feather in his cap. The gateway to the coast was open at last and an independent harbour seemed within reach.

How much greater the disappointment when that gateway was barricaded almost immediately afterwards, courtesy of Sir Henry. He would soon be leaving as high commissioner but he still had another unpleasant surprise in store, like the time he and Kruger had first met, in Blignautspont five years earlier. On this occasion Sir Henry insisted on the speedy annexation of adjacent lands in the Tsonga, Sambane and Mbikiza territories. Lord Ripon considered this an appropriate parting gift. On 16 March 1895 Tsongaland was formally annexed. After all the expectations Britain had been raising, Leyds noted bitterly, it had now erected 'this wall, which cut Swaziland off from the sea, and therefore kept the South African Republic landlocked as well'.[74]

Now everything hinged on the eastern line. After the Rothschild loan of July 1892, money was no longer the biggest problem and no problem at all when the financial markets in Amsterdam and Berlin rallied in November, yielding another loan of 31 million guilders, paid out directly to the Netherlands-South African Railway Company. It enabled the company to pull out the stops and forge ahead. A good thing too, because there were enough problems on other fronts, technical, logistical and, most importantly, personnel. Director Middelberg and Verwey's successor, the chief engineer Breuning, had their hands full. Looming over them was the rapidly completed southern line, which came into service on 1 January 1893. Pretoria and Johannesburg now had direct links to Cape Town.

Politically, too, the eastern line was still a headache for the Transvaal government. The 'Dutch' railway as well as everything related to it was at the centre of a tough campaign in the run-up to the presidential elections of February 1893. Vice-President Piet Joubert had stood against Kruger twice in the past, in 1883 and 1888, but this time his chances looked good. It was a neck-and-neck race. It took all Kruger's political weight and powers of persuasion—foul play too, according to his defeated rival—to win by a narrow margin of 7911 to 7246 votes. Kruger's position was apparently not unassailable.

That was something he and Leyds would have to bear in mind, especially in their dealings abroad. From a diplomatic point of view, the eastern line had been a thorny issue right from the start. It was a Dutch railway financed by German and British capital, running from a British city on Transvaal territory to a Portuguese harbour. There was also the formidable Colossus of Rhodes to contend with, their neighbour to the south, west and north, who was determined to gain control of the Portuguese end of the railway line and become their neighbour to the east as well. Operating from a narrow local power base, Leyds had to perform an intricate balancing act. Though no longer government commissioner, he was still the Transvaal government's railways man.

As all communications with the railway company and its overseas stakeholders were conducted through the state secretary's office, the company's ups and downs were chronicled in Leyds's official and personal correspondence. Those documents reveal that in the spring of 1893 Leyds was also unhappy with the company, particularly its management. To begin with, he had expected more appreciation for the loan the Transvaal government had wrested from Rothschild on its behalf. But after securing a capital loan in its own right in November 1892, the company spent months quibbling over the terms of the Rothschild loan. Moreover, Leyds felt it was time to transfer its headquarters from Amsterdam to Pretoria. That would make it more effective and put an end to a situation in which management only looked after their European shareholders. Leyds felt that the company should be supporting the national interests of the Transvaal as well. For a while he contemplated a totally different structure: a nationalised enterprise pooled with the British colonial railway companies. But he soon abandoned the idea. By the second half of 1893 relations were back to normal. A compromise was reached as to where the headquarters should be based. Van den Wall Bake would continue to operate from Amsterdam, but Middelberg, who had been commuting between Europe and South Africa, would settle in Pretoria indefinitely, as from the beginning of 1894.[75]

Leyds made it clear that he had to balance different interests. The economic importance of the railway company still played a role, but the political interests of the Transvaal weighed more heavily. Those considerations also had diplomatic implications, as he revealed when a third party, Natal, joined the 'race to the Rand'.

The agreement between the Transvaal and the Cape Colony had only strengthened the other British colony's determination to establish a direct link between Durban and Johannesburg. Natal redoubled its efforts to extend its own railway line, which went as far as Charlestown, on the border, warning that it would otherwise have to consider a connection to the Cape line. That couldn't be ruled out. There was already a line from Ladysmith in Natal to Harrismith in the Orange Free State, and it wouldn't be difficult to extend it. The Transvaal would suffer as a result. It wouldn't benefit from an economic merger between the two British colonies, as it would in the case of their respective competitors. Kruger and Leyds ultimately considered this more important than the anticipated loss of revenue on the eastern line. They decided to give in to the pressure from Natal. The Volksraad consented. The agreement was concluded in February 1894. The Transvaal would have a third rail link extending beyond its frontiers, this time to Durban in the south-east.

There was still a lot to be ironed out with the Netherlands-South African Railway Company, of course, which was dismayed at the arrival of a new competitor. The only consolation was that it would ultimately be running this line as well. But outside parties that were directly or indirectly involved—Natal itself, the Orange Free State and Portugal— would also have to be informed. Each was given its own tailor-made version of the story: that the Transvaal simply had no choice, and that the other two lines wouldn't suffer as a result. Leyds had the honour of explaining the situation, both locally and in Lisbon, and he did so with admirable diplomacy. On his European trip he also made a flying visit to Berlin, in January 1894. This turned out to be a good move. He was received by the young Kaiser Wilhelm II, who was deeply impressed by the whole enterprise. By the time the eastern line was nearing completion, in September 1894, everyone was pleased with the Transvaal's three-way system.

Everyone? Cecil Rhodes lived by his own rules. That same month the newspapers announced that he had bought Lourenço Marques. Rumours to that effect had circulated before, but now it seemed there was indeed something afoot. At the same time, King Gungunhana of Gaza, the territory near the border between Mozambique and the newly founded Rhodesia, was preparing to attack the port. In addition, the British consul in Lourenço Marques was allowing sailors to land there. That surely couldn't be a coincidence? It looked suspiciously like a hostile takeover. Lourenço Marques and Pretoria sent anxious telegrams. From Berlin the Kaiser ordered three warships to make for Delagoa Bay.[76]

Lifeline

Lourenço Marques, July 1895

It turned out to be a false alarm. In any event, the British insisted that their intentions were honourable. Leyds had his own thoughts on the matter, but noted with satisfaction that they had tied themselves into a diplomatic knot vis-à-vis Berlin. That was all to the good of the Transvaal. A new player had appeared on the scene, which even 'Mighty England' would have to deal with. Kruger had been pinning his hopes on ascendant Germany, and now the time seemed ripe to strengthen his ties with his powerful ally.

Kaiser Wilhelm II needed little encouragement. He had dispensed with the 'old pilot' Bismarck some time before and taken the helm himself. He was pompous and impulsive, at his best when set on a collision course. 'Willy', along with half the crowned heads of Europe, was related to Queen Victoria, her grandson in fact, but for him water was thicker than blood: the water of the seven seas (let there be no mistake), over which the Royal Navy had ruled long enough. He wanted a fleet of his own, a 'place in the sun' for Germany and a leading role on the international political stage for himself. Southern Africa looked like a good place to start.

Pretoria read the signs with relief. Leyds had remarked on the kaiser's interest in their affairs when he visited Berlin in January 1894. He had been graciously received at the annual *Ordensfest*. 'The Emperor addressed me twice, the Empress once,' he noted with satisfaction. He was to convey the emperor's regards to President Kruger and his good wishes for 'the speedy completion of the Delagoa railway'. The iron was hot and the official inauguration of the eastern line was a good time to strike. It was an opportunity, Leyds suggested to the Volksraad, 'to make a political showing' by inviting 'Germany and Holland to be represented by a warship in Delagoa Bay'. As far as he was concerned, France was welcome too, although its relations with Germany under Wilhelm II were strained. In the end they decided to invite only the countries from which funds had been invested in the railway. These included Britain and the host country, Portugal. In their presence the German warship would have even more impact, Leyds explained to Beelaerts van Blokland: 'a demonstration is not without political significance for us.'[77]

The invitations were sent out in July 1894. The celebrations would take place a year later. It could have been sooner—the eastern line came into service on 1 January 1895—but that was the middle of summer, unbearably hot in Lourenço Marques and therefore unwise with so many dignitaries attending. In any case, it left more time for the preparations. The arrangement suited Leyds, who had to organise the event, on top of his usual duties. He considered it one of his tasks to inform the Republic's new allies about the Transvaal's constitutional status. The most important point was Britain's claim to suzerainty. In Leyds's opinion, this had come to an end with the London Convention of 1884. But that infernal word was still being bandied about in British government circles. He sent several memorandums with official documentation to Berlin to persuade at least the German government that the Transvaal was correct about its constitutional status. For a wider public he published a watered-down version in the *Kölnische Zeitung*.

In his own peculiar way, Kruger also took steps to strengthen his country's ties with Germany, particularly its head of state. Wilhelm's belligerent response to the threat of a British takeover of Lourenço Marques had done the old Boer warrior some good. A few months later, on 27 January 1895, Kruger took advantage of the emperor's birthday to reciprocate. At a dinner in Pretoria, hosted by the French consul Franz von Herff, he toasted the emperor and then proceeded with a typical Kruger-style allegory. He cast the Transvaal as a child that had outgrown its clothes but received no new ones from Britain. Germany, however, understood that the Transvaal was growing and needed a bigger size, for which the youngster was deeply grateful. The tale, inspired by the Bible, won Kruger, via Beelaerts van Blokland, a telegram of thanks from the emperor and the assurance of his 'enduring support'.[78]

The cordial relationship between the two heads of state was reaffirmed during the celebrations from 8 to 10 July 1895. The official guests, local and foreign, met up in Pretoria and from there went east in gaily decorated trains. They travelled 560 kilometres through the highveld, the lowveld, and then the crowning moment: the sea, Lourenço Marques. It was a glorious triumph for Kruger. His dream had come true at last. Right from the start of his presidency in 1883 he had fought for this one 'great cause'. His predecessor, Burgers, had stalled; he had persevered. It had been exhausting, many had lost faith, but there it was, the sea, the Indian Ocean, his salvation. The Transvaal finally had a lifeline to the outside world—with a German warship parading in the harbour. Awaiting him on board was a congratulatory telegram from the kaiser. It was intended, Von Herff assured Leyds, 'to affirm that Germany would never allow Delagoa Bay to fall into British hands'.[79]

It was 'a great success by and large', as Leyds concluded in an 'appraisal' of the festivities. It was his victory too, a reward for his perseverance. Personally, however, he wasn't in the best of spirits. He had been working too hard, had felt unwell for some time, and his family's health wasn't all it should be either. Louise had been suffering from 'frightful headaches' and had gone to Durban for a few months to recuperate. As a result of her absence Willem had missed the first two days of the celebrations, 'because my son was unwell and the doctor advised me not to leave town'. Louise fortunately made a speedy recovery and Leyds was able to travel to Lourenço Marques on the last day of the festivities, just in time to accompany Kruger on a visit to the Dutch frigate, the *Koningin Wilhelmina*. It wasn't an unqualified success. Formal and decorous, Leyds was offended by the officers' slovenly appearance. They were 'in full dress uniform, of course, but some of them hadn't shaved! The stubble on the President's face, which has embarrassed me so often on occasions like this, will never bother me again!' By comparison 'the British governors, admiral and officers were . . . infinitely better turned out.'[80]

But still, personal vexations aside, the eastern line, which was now operational, was doing exceptionally well financially. As of 1 January 1895 the Transvaal had its coveted railway to the sea, and all the advantages that went with it. The political benefits were having a link to the outside world that wasn't controlled by the meddlesome British, and a European ally that seemed willing and able to restrain them.

Economically, the line gave the Transvaal government more room to manoeuvre as far as its administration was concerned and the railway company more freedom in managing its commercial affairs. Besides the eastern line, the contract with the Cape railway company gave Middelberg and his colleagues responsibility for the southern line as well, with immediate effect. The Netherlands-South African Railway Company's profits skyrocketed. Its closing balance of around 2.5 million guilders at the end of 1894 was clearly going to increase in 1895, and, indeed, the turnover at the end of the year came to almost 20 million guilders, with 4.5 million guilders' profit.

That was a huge sum of money. And from the Transvaal's point of view, the best part of it was that under the terms of the railway concession, 85 per cent of the net profit, 3.9 million guilders, went to the government—not counting the dividend it was entitled to as the principal shareholder. It had taken more than a decade, but now that the trains were finally running, the wait had been well worthwhile. The company was a phenomenal source of revenue for the Transvaal's treasury.[81]

Politically, economically and financially, the eastern line gave the South African Republic more room to breathe, and its leaders, notably the president and state secretary, a huge psychological boost. For years Kruger and Leyds had been maligned for their obstinacy and for favouring the Dutch, but now at last they were vindicated. An independent link to the sea, in trusted hands—that was what they had aimed for and the whole of the Transvaal was reaping the benefits.

Well, the whole of the Transvaal? There was still that exotic enclave 50 kilometres south of the capital. A tented camp in 1886, a city with a population of 100,000 less than a decade later, Johannesburg was an emerging metropolis. There were different ways of looking at it. In the eyes of Lady Sarah Wilson, Lord Randolph Churchill's sister, it was 'a wonderful town'. Its bustling streets, the restless eyes, the breathless rush, all reminded her of the City of London. To South Africa's first female intellectual, Olive Schreiner, it was 'a great, fiendish, hell of a city', an empty shell of corruption, with its palatial mansions, brothels and gambling halls.[82] And these were women of the world. To the average Boer, Johannesburg was a different planet altogether, with an atmosphere unfit to sustain human life.

On his first visit to Johannesburg, in February 1887, Kruger disliked the city and its gold diggers. He returned a few times afterwards, but never enjoyed it. In March 1890 he had an unpleasant experience on his way to a meeting with Sir Henry Loch at Blignautspont. It was during the pyrite crisis and the city, normally bursting with confidence, was on edge. A hostile crowd had gathered and, while waiting for Kruger to arrive, they tore down and trampled the red, white, blue and green flag of the Transvaal to the strains of 'Rule Britannia' and 'God Save the Queen'. A less courageous man might have been apprehensive. Kruger turned the incident into a parable. The demonstrators reminded him of a baboon he had once kept, he told Sir Henry later at Blignautspont. The creature loved him and allowed no one else to touch it. Then one day it burned its tail in a campfire and turned on him. The people of Johannesburg behaved in the same way. They had burned their fingers speculating and were now taking it out on Paul Kruger.

He didn't say what became of the baboon. But it was soon clear that Johannesburg would never rise in his esteem. Exclusion and curtailment of rights were the only measures he could come up with to control what he regarded as a horde of shifty intruders. Until then, newcomers to the Transvaal had been eligible for naturalisation after five years' residence and on payment of £25. Adult males were then also entitled to vote in presidential and parliamentary elections. It must be said that this applied only to whites. In the Transvaal, unlike the Cape Colony, civil rights were not accorded to blacks, no matter whether they were locals or immigrants. Nor, for that matter, were they accorded to coloureds or Asians. As Leyds explained to the young activist Mohandas Gandhi, 'though the culture of a Brahmin is on a totally different plane, the Kaffirs would not understand that difference. For them it is an easy division: blacks and whites.'[83]

In 1890 Kruger felt it was time to start classifying the different groups that made up the white population as well. The term Uitlander, or foreigner, had already become generally accepted, but for future newcomers acceptance as citizens would take longer. The waiting time to acquire citizenship and voting rights was increased to 14 years and the voting age to 40. To soften the blow, the Uitlanders would be able to vote for their own, separate parliament after four years. This new body would be competent to deal with a range of economic issues, but not with strategic matters such as currency, banking, taxation, concessions or railways. Johannesburg would not receive its own municipal council. Its inhabitants would have to settle for a health committee, instituted in 1887, in which Dutch was the official language. The South African Republic Police (commonly known as the Zarps), a force established specifically for the goldfields, was administered from Pretoria. It recruited only burghers—people with citizenship rights—many of them landless Boers, or *bywoners*, 'who had sought their fortune in Johannesburg without success'.

In August 1892 the Uitlanders responded by establishing the Transvaal National Union, chaired by the advocate Charles Leonard. Addressing the public at the inauguration, he asked, 'Who made the Transvaal?' Who had made the economic boom possible? The answer was not unexpected. 'We! Yet we are regarded as birds of passage, and because they were here before us, we have no rights.' The National Union intended to change that. Year after year they submitted petitions bearing thousands of signatures to Pretoria, all to no avail. The only response was a summons sent in May 1894 to a number of Uitlanders—of British, Dutch and German descent—to join a punitive expedition against an African chief in the north-east of the Transvaal. Five British 'conscripts' refused. They were arrested, sentenced and escorted by armed guards to the battlefield in the Zoutpansberg district.

The National Union cast them as martyrs for the cause. No vote, no conscription. The British, including the government in London, were outraged. The secretary for the colonies, Lord Ripon, sent the high commissioner, Sir Henry Loch, to Pretoria to discuss the matter. His arrival exposed Kruger to an experience even more mortifying than the incident in Johannesburg four years earlier. In his own capital, the Boers' ultimate citadel, the old president was made to witness the welcome extended to Sir Henry at the station by an enthusiastic throng cheering for Queen and Country. That alone was distressing, but worse was still to come on the way to his hotel. Someone in the crowd hurled a Union Jack into the president's carriage. Kruger thrashed about with his cane, but wasn't able to remove the flag draped over his shoulders. And this time, he could think of no anecdote to ease his embarrassment.

The symbolism spoke volumes, but the matter itself was settled amicably. In the meantime, London had requested that British citizens be exempted from commando service. Leyds was in favour of this, mainly because it would involve changing the London Convention, which he could present to the British government as a trade-off for an 'amendment to other provisions'—article 4, in particular, which was the basis for the British claim to suzerainty. The Volksraad agreed. In future, residents who did not possess civil rights would be allowed to buy off their obligation to serve in the army.[84]

But that did not address the Uitlanders' main grievance. They were still disadvantaged when it came to political rights, whereas they were the driving force behind the Republic's economy. This applied to workers in the gold-mining industry and equally to their employers, the Randlords—or at least that was the view of the Randlords. They too had established an organisation, the exclusive Chamber of Mines, with Kruger as its honorary—and ever absent—president. The first active president was Hermann Eckstein of Corner House. All the large mining companies were represented. Their grievances against Kruger and Leyds were confined to only one aspect of official policies, but it happened to be the cornerstone: economic protectionism and especially that lousy concession system. For everything they needed in order to extract gold, the mine barons came up against unassailable monopolies, licences and tariffs—for labour, water, food, wood, chemicals, tools, machinery and, most of all, coal, dynamite and rail transport. They had to get Pretoria's approval for the lot. The Rand was at the mercy of the tight network of the friends, family and business associates around Kruger and his Hollanders. For everything they acquired, the mining companies felt—and were often able to prove—that they were paying more than they would in a free market.

The abuses inherent in the system were illustrated by the dynamite dispute, which flared up intermittently over a number of years. Towards the end of 1887 Eduard Lippert had taken over the explosives monopoly from Nellmapius. The concession was for manufacturing dynamite, but not importing it. However, it came to light in 1892 that Lippert's South

African Company for Explosive Substances was importing not the raw materials for explosives but the ready-made end product, which he then sold to the mining companies at a 200 per cent profit. It was a scandal. Kruger and Leyds took the full blast and the concession was withdrawn. But it was not the end of Lippert. A new concession was issued in 1894, after endless consultations in the Volksraad. The Chamber of Mines applied for the concession, but so did Lippert, and to everyone's amazement, he won it. The South African Company for Explosive Substances opened its doors again, with a 15-year monopoly on the manufacture of dynamite, gunpowder and munitions. What only emerged subsequently, and sparked off another scandal a few years later, was that Lippert had done a deal with one of the biggest dynamite producers in the world, the Nobel Trust Dynamite Company, now a German–British concern. Once again the Randlords had been taken for a ride.[85]

The next head-on collision between the interests of the Transvaal state and the commercial interests of the Rand came soon afterwards. This time it wasn't only between Pretoria and Johannesburg. Cape Town was also involved. Technically, that is where the instigator was. John Laing, Sivewright's successor as commissioner for public works under Rhodes, triggered a tariff war with the Netherlands-South African Railway Company in January 1895.

For two years the southern line, run by the Cape, had been the only rail link with the Rand, which of course brought economic advantages. On 1 January 1895 the eastern line came into service, administered by the Netherlands-South African Railway Company, which also took over the management of the 78-kilometre Transvaal section of the southern line. The same would happen with the south-eastern line, which was expected to be completed before the end of the year. The tables would then be turned. The railway company would be holding all the trumps, with the added advantage that the eastern and south-eastern lines were strategically in the strongest position. Johannesburg was 630 rail kilometres from Lourenço Marques and 770 from Durban. The three ports in the Cape Colony—East London, Port Elizabeth and Cape Town—were further away, 1070, 1150 and 1630 kilometres respectively. Laing thought of two ways to prevent the Cape line from being forced out of business by the competition. They could either negotiate a fixed market share—such as half of all rail transport to the Rand—or lower their tariffs.

The railway company wasn't interested in a fifty-fifty deal. In any case, according to the director, Middelberg, the Capetonians were no longer in a position to make demands. Van den Wall Bake, in Amsterdam, agreed. 'We need to shift our focus and not let the British take the decisions.

Making money is secondary to that, but the two will have to go hand in hand if both competitors believe that we're trying to lay down the law.' After years of being browbeaten, the directors of the railway company had finally gained the upper hand. They refused to offer more than a third share for each line.[86]

When the talks broke down, Laing tried the alternative scenario of lowering tariffs. He didn't have to wait long for an answer from the railway company: a tariff increase on the Transvaal section of the southern line, at least for goods coming from overseas. Now things were getting serious. The next move looked like a step backwards. From then on, goods coming from the Cape Colony were transferred to old-fashioned oxwagons when they reached the Transvaal border. From there, they could cross the Vaal at two fords (or drifts as they are called in South Africa)—Viljoen's Drift and Sand Drift—and continue to the Rand. Scores of them every day. It was a time-consuming but effective enough manoeuvre for Middelberg to insist that the Transvaal government take counter-measures. Kruger was in favour and Leyds backed him. In late August Kruger announced that the drifts on the Vaal would be closed to overseas goods as from 1 October 1895.

That was the start of the 'drifts crisis'. Cape Town protested vehemently and so did Johannesburg, whose umpteenth application for voting rights for the Uitlanders had just been turned down. For Rhodes this was reason enough for another attempt to form a power bloc against the obstructive Boers—this time with force. After his turbulent visit to Pretoria in May 1894, Sir Henry Loch had hatched a plot which involved an uprising among the Uitlanders, followed by an invasion by British colonial troops. He had even submitted the idea as a formal proposal to London, but the secretary for the colonies, Lord Ripon, had dismissed it as being too risky.

By August 1895 the cast had changed. Sir Henry had been replaced by his predecessor, Sir Hercules Robinson, then in his seventies and in poor health. Rhodes could expect little of him and had nothing to fear from him. Lord Ripon, on the other hand, had made way for a new breed of politician after the elections.

As far as background was concerned, Joseph Chamberlain was something of an outsider in a Cabinet in which the prime minister and foreign secretary, Lord Salisbury, had surrounded himself with Conservative aristocrats from his own circle—and his own family. 'Joe' Chamberlain came from industrial Birmingham. A self-made entrepreneur who had made a fortune by manufacturing screws, he went into politics filled with ambition. First as mayor, then as a member of parliament and still a confirmed Liberal, he had opposed Gladstone's plans for Irish self-determination and joined the Liberal Unionists. He was a firm believer in the organic unity of the United Kingdom and, by extension, in the lofty mission of the British Empire. Given his view of the world, Chamberlain's move to join Salisbury's Conservative government was not illogical.

Chamberlain was the first British secretary for the colonies with a coherent imperialist ideology. He believed 'the British race is the greatest of the governing races that the world has ever seen'. And that brought with it the obligation to act with honour. Overseas territorial expansion alone wasn't enough. 'It is the duty of a landlord to develop his estate.' That was music to Rhodes's ears. Moreover, Chamberlain was a man of action. His first decision as state secretary was to renovate the drab Colonial Office. Carpets, wallpaper, furniture and especially charts and globes, everything had to be new, including electricity instead of gaslight. A switch to modern times.

That was good news for Rhodes and very bad news for the Boers. Rhodes had challenged the closure of the drifts, which he claimed was a violation of the London Convention. Article 13 denied the Transvaal the right to accord different treatment to goods 'coming from any part of Her Majesty's dominions'. Chamberlain took the same line and put Pretoria in a spot. If Kruger failed to reopen the drifts, a British colonial expedition would see to it. To make the point clear, troopships en route to British India were rerouted and ordered to make for Cape Town. The railway tariff dispute was about to erupt into a real war.

Leyds, surprisingly, was prepared to take the risk. He felt that giving in would be 'a sign of weakness'. Kruger saw things differently. He decided on a tactical retreat. The drifts were opened in early November 1895. The fight over tariffs had not been resolved, but the prospect of a military confrontation between the British and the Boers had been averted—for the time being.[87]

Leyds's stance should not be taken for belligerence. He had underestimated the seriousness of the situation. In the second half of 1895 his judgment was clouded and he seemed to be out of touch with reality. It had been a tough year, with uneven results. He had put a lot of energy into the preparations for the festivities in Lourenço Marques. There were the difficulties of acquiring protectorate rights over Swaziland, and then in March the damper of the British annexation of Tsongaland. On the positive side, the eastern line had come into service, and there had been the conspicuous display of support from their powerful new ally, Germany. Yet it seems to have been precisely those triumphs that gave him a rose-tinted view of the Transvaal's influence in economic and diplomatic affairs. Kruger had the same problem, but he soon came to his senses when Chamberlain forced him to show his hand. Right up to November Leyds kept telegraphing Pretoria, trying to persuade Kruger not to give in.

That in itself reveals one of the reasons for Leyds's distorted view of reality. At the time of the 'drifts crisis' he was not at his post, but in Natal for talks about the railways—with hosts who were more sympathetic to the Transvaal's point of view than that of the Cape Colony. So Leyds obviously didn't have all the information that would have reached him in Pretoria. As a result, he interpreted the matter from a purely legal perspective—he believed the closure of the drifts was *not* in violation of the London Convention—and underestimated the international political dimension.[88]

But that wasn't the only reason. His physical and mental state was also a factor. Leyds was exhausted and exasperated. Early in 1895 he had complained about this to his mentor and friend Moltzer. It wasn't only Louise and Louis who had health problems; he, too, was under the weather. First, a 'prolonged bout of parrot disease (that's what the Portuguese call diarrhoea)' and after that his 'throat wouldn't come right'. He knew the cause. 'It's because of my condition in general; I need to get fitter and rest for a while. I feel I need it. I've worked hard from childhood, without rest, mostly on Sundays as well, often twenty hours a day.' He was also getting more irritated with Kruger. 'The older he gets, the worse it is. He's turning deaf, slow-witted, bossier than ever (if that's possible) and more cantankerous and ill-mannered towards the public, especially foreigners . . . He has this typical Afrikaner quirk of misplacing trust and distrust, and mixing them up in the most amazing way, and it's getting worse.' Leyds had 'to navigate my way through everything, but it isn't easy or pleasant . . . Sometimes I just want to get away from it all. Heavens, what a miserable job.'[89]

His mood did not improve. In July 1895 he was embarrassed by Kruger's behaviour at the celebrations in Lourenço Marques. He quarrelled with him over the visit to Lippert's new dynamite factory and clashed over the awarding of a coal concession. He began to have serious doubts about staying on in the Transvaal. Moltzer had just exchanged his chair in Amsterdam for a seat in the Council of State, and Leyds toyed with the idea of trying to get Moltzer's old job. By the time he reached a decision and heard that Moltzer wanted to propose him as a candidate, the opportunity had passed. Louise had this to say, 'If you don't go to Holland, I would write and tell M. [Moltzer] what you really consider best for yourself. If you find your work inspiring and enjoy it in spite of the mundane side of it, I would certainly stay here. If not, and you want something different, I would write and tell M. so at least some people in Holland know what you're looking for. This professorship may have led to a political career in Holland. But if no one knows about your circumstances, nothing will happen and they'll leave you here with your ideals.'[90]

The point was clear and Leyds was persuaded to be more resolute about putting himself first, if it came to that. It did, in early November 1895. After the railway business he spent a few days' holiday in Durban, where Louise had been since July, but his health didn't improve. He sent two telegrams, one shortly after the other, to H. van Boeschoten, his deputy in Pretoria. In the first he asked the Executive Council for leave. 'To my regret, my throat is worse instead of better and I must have treatment for my laryngitis immediately and go to Europe without delay.' The second telegram was worded more strongly. 'Doctor says postponement treatment irresponsible. Condition not life-threatening but could deprive use of throat permanently. Doctor says treatment in Africa possible but recommends specialised attention in Europe also better for rest, environment, etc. I hope President, etc. will approve.' And finally, 'If I don't get leave, I'll have to resign.'[91]

It never came to that. On 10 November 1895, he wrote to tell Moltzer that he had booked a passage on the *Dunottar Castle*, which would be sailing from Cape Town in two weeks' time. He went alone. 'You can imagine how much I would have liked to bring Louise with me, and how reluctant she was to let me go alone. But then the children and their governess would have had to come as well, and I can't afford it. This unfortunate trip is already costing me enough. Well, as long as I get better.'

He was counting on Dr Fränkel, a famous specialist in Berlin. After a pleasant crossing and a brief stop in Amsterdam 'to see the family', he went on to Germany. His first visit to the physician, on 18 December, lifted his spirits. 'Consultation favourable, recovery definite.' He wrote to Moltzer a week later, on Christmas Day, to say the treatment was producing results. 'And there I was, stuck with it in Africa, where no one was able to do a thing about it. It made life sour. The injections, ointments and electric therapy I'm getting now seem so simple' that he wondered whether it had been necessary to go to so much expense in the first place. 'When I see the palace that Fritz Fränkel lives in, I quake to think of my wallet.' And he missed his family. 'It's lonely here. People are kind, but that doesn't make up for being without my wife and children.' He felt it most at the Christmas dinner he had been to that evening, which was 'really a family occasion' and which had left him feeling 'like a fish out of water'.[92]

By New Year's Eve the mood had passed. Melancholy had given way to full-blown panic. On 31 December 1895 Leyds received news that 'the troops of the Chartered Co have taken Rustenburg'. A British invasion in the Transvaal—surely that was not possible? He immediately sent 'cable after cable to Pretoria', but no answer came back. 'The British have probably intercepted my telegrams.' Nothing to do but send a letter. Desperate for news, he wrote to Louise: 'Where are you? What's happening to you? . . . If only you and the children had come with me!'[93]

To arms

Berlin, January 1896

It would be 'easier than Matabeleland', Rhodes assured him. That was all the encouragement Jameson needed. Doctor Jim was always ready for a challenge, and two years had passed since the expedition against Lobengula. It was time for a new venture, now with a touch of chivalry. Countrymen in danger: 'Thousands of unarmed men, women and children of our race . . . at the mercy of well-armed Boers.' That's what was said in the letter he had been given by the conspirators in Johannesburg. He would fill in the date when the time came. The melodramatic appeal spurred his men to action. Four hundred mounted police from Rhodesia, a hundred volunteers from the Cape Colony and another hundred coloured auxiliaries; six Maxim machine guns, three pieces of artillery. It was not an impressive force, but, according to Jameson, big enough. The Boers' so-called military prowess was 'the biggest bubble of the century'. On the night of Sunday 29 December 1895 Jameson gave the sign to proceed. The raiders struck camp in Pitsani in Bechuanaland and crossed the border— heading for one of the biggest fiascos in colonial history.

The Jameson Raid was badly planned and poorly executed. It was the brainchild of Sir Henry Loch. An Uitlander uprising in Johannesburg, an invading force coming to their aid, and the high commissioner, acting as mediator, to manoeuvre the Transvaal towards a general election in which the Uitlanders could vote. Exit Kruger. Rhodes developed the plan in the summer of 1895. His business partner Alfred Beit donated funds, Sir Hercules Robinson consented with quaking knees and Chamberlain obtained exactly the right amount of information to officially know nothing about it. *The Times* agreed to launch a propaganda campaign. The British South Africa Company was assigned a strip of land near the border in Bechuanaland to station a police force, which was passed off as security guards for the railway construction site. The uprising in Johannesburg would be organised by Charles Leonard, chairman of the Transvaal National Union, Lionel Phillips, Hermann Eckstein's successor as president of the Chamber of Mines, the American engineer John Hays Hammond, the mine owner George Farrar and Rhodes's brother Frank, a former cavalry officer. Weapons were smuggled into the city and hidden in the gold mines.

The plan had two flaws. The first was the assumption that everyone involved had the same goal in mind, which wasn't the case. The second was that an Uitlander uprising was bound to occur sooner or later. But things turned out differently.

Rhodes still had his vision of a single South African federation ultimately under British rule. But Chamberlain would settle for nothing less than the establishment of direct imperial control. And Johannesburg wasn't the mutinous tinderbox that Rhodes and Jameson had thought it to be. There was a certain amount of dissatisfaction in the city, but no revolutionary fire flared up in the streets. According to the journalist Francis Younghusband, the people of Johannesburg weren't the type. Their only concern, he said, was to make money. This was certainly true of some of the Randlords. J.B. Robinson, Barney Barnato and others, mainly of German extraction, were firmly on Kruger's side. In the course of December 1895 even the conspirators were clawing their way back. They fell out with Rhodes over the flag, which was supposed to suggest something revolutionary, but they insisted on the Transvaal *Vierkleur*. They wanted reforms, nothing more. No British flag over Johannesburg, Hammond proclaimed in public.

At the end of December they informed Rhodes that 'the polo tournament'—the code name for the uprising—would have to be postponed. At the same time Rhodes received a telegram from London urging him to act without delay. The British government was going to have its hands full with a confrontation with the United States—a border conflict between British Guiana and Venezuela had escalated. Chamberlain thought it best to go ahead right away; otherwise they would have to postpone everything for at least two years. Another factor was that a journalist from *The Times*, Flora Shaw, had heard that the Transvaal secretary of state, Willem Leyds, was in London, on his way to Berlin. She was an admirer of Rhodes, fully aware of the plot, and she decided to interview Leyds. The meeting confirmed her suspicions. There was nothing at all the matter with Leyds. It was just a bit too obvious, the way he was sucking those throat lozenges. She had figured him out. He was on his way to the Continent to conduct an 'anti-Rhodes' campaign. His throat complaint was a 'diplomatic illness'. All the more reason to get moving.[94]

No one could accuse Cecil Rhodes of being indecisive, but this time he was at a loss to know how to handle the conflicting messages from London and Johannesburg. All he could come up with were a few half-hearted telegrams, which left Jameson enough scope to take the decision himself—as he did with reckless abandon. He had rustled up only 500 of the 1500 armed troops they had planned, but Doctor Jim wasn't the kind to let anything stand in his way. Hadn't he once bragged, 'I could drive them out of the Transvaal with five hundred men armed with sjamboks'?

Four days later it was clear who was wielding the whip. Kruger had known about the raid by 30 December. Jameson's men had cut the telegraph lines, but not those to Pretoria. Hundreds of Boers were armed and ready within a few hours. The uprising in Johannesburg didn't materialise. The Boer commandants were able to focus their attention on the invaders. On New Year's Day 1896 they drove them back—in Krugersdorp, appropriately enough. A day later the raiders surrendered at Doornkop. Jameson's 'rescue mission' landed him in a Pretoria jail.[95]

Leyds sighed with relief. The good news had reached Berlin that same day. He could stop worrying about his wife and children. He was still having trouble with his telegrams, but he knew from other sources 'that Pretoria (which is probably where you are) has not been affected, that the British troops have been defeated and Jameson, White and Willoughby are in jail in Pretoria'.

As he was already in Berlin, he might be able to make himself useful. Not that Flora Shaw was right. Leyds had really come to Europe to save his voice. But Dr Fränkel's treatment was working and this was a political windfall. Rhodes and Jameson had done the Boer republic a favour. 'The entire continent is on our side,' Leyds remarked. He would be a fool not to take advantage of it. 'The whole of Germany is over the moon, rich and poor, powerful and lowly. The papers are full of it.' It gave him new energy. 'I'm doing all I can to turn the whole of Europe against Britain. I'm working like a dog . . . Yesterday I went to the Chancellor. The day before, the Duke of Mecklenburg came round to the hotel to congratulate me. And so forth.'

For its part, the German government took advantage of Leyds's presence. The foreign minister, Marshall von Bieberstein, asked Leyds 'whether we would be able to do it alone and get the better of Jameson without help from outside'. Leyds's affirmative reply resulted in the congratulatory telegram that Kaiser Wilhelm sent Kruger on 3 January 1896. The telegram was only one in a recent exchange of cordialities between the two heads of state. It caused a diplomatic stir because of the remark that the Boers had succeeded in repelling the attack 'without requesting assistance from friendly powers'. Three days later Leyds was received in audience. In response to his thanks for the emperor's unequivocal support, he was assured that 'if things had gone differently, he would have ordered troops from the German frigate, which was in L.M. [Lourenço Marques] at the time, to "boot" Jameson out of the Transvaal'.

His militant language was infectious. Leyds advised Pretoria not to be lenient towards the insurgents. 'You have the sympathy and support of governments as well as the public, as long as you stand firm . . . At least one of the prisoners' heads must roll.'[96]

Besides political backing, the Boers also had the approval of the business world in Germany. Leyds was particularly pleased with the spontaneous support of an old acquaintance. 'The most committed of them all is Lippert. He and his wife have come specially from Hamburg and they're staying here in the same hotel.' All the trouble Leyds had been through with Lippert over dynamite and railway issues in recent years was forgotten. 'It's truly from the heart. It's a matter of sentiment, not a calculated move.' They had a lot to talk about. A Franco-German telegraph link with southern Africa to break the British monopoly. Their own mail service to Europe. And, of course, reinforcements for the Transvaal's defences. The Boers needed modern weapons to defend themselves against any future attack. Lippert was the right person for that. He dealt in all kinds of explosives and had useful connections in the arms industry.[97]

Leyds left Germany in mid-February 1896 feeling satisfied. His throat had been treated successfully—it cost him 1000 marks in the end—he had received diplomatic support at the highest level and established business connections that might come in useful. The only disappointment was that he hadn't managed to find support for the international conference he had proposed. Germany and Russia seemed to be in favour, but the Executive Council hadn't backed him. Joubert and Chief Justice Kotzé thought it too risky, and Kruger was reluctant to force the issue. Leyds regretted 'that Pretoria did not give me a free hand. The Great Powers were ready to guarantee the independence and neutrality of the Republic along the same lines as Belgium and Switzerland.'[98]

On the positive side, there was the immense personal gratification of meeting with Otto von Bismarck, 80 years old and leading a quiet life on his estate, Friedrichsruhe. 'It was an interesting day for me, one of the highlights of my life,' he wrote to Louise. 'My first impression was *very* old. But he perked up as we went on, over breakfast and especially after a few glasses of champagne.' And once he did, there was no stopping him. Leyds was surprised by the unusually high pitch of his voice, and by his lack of reserve. The empress and her ladies-in-waiting and German colonial politics were the main targets of his sharp tongue, but the British bore the real brunt of it. You couldn't trust them further than you could throw them, the former chancellor warned. One could get along with an Englishman socially, but as soon as they went into politics they hung their conscience next to their umbrella on the coat rack. That was an intriguing characterisation from the architect of realpolitik. Leyds must have been mindful of it when he stopped off in London on his way home to pay a brief courtesy call on Joe Chamberlain.[99]

At the end of March 1896 Leyds was back in Pretoria. His wife and children were fine, apart from Louise's and Louis's usual health problems. All was well with the president too. He had kept his nerve during the raid and a sense of proportion afterwards. Though many Boers were clamouring for revenge, against the raiders, against the conspirators, against the whole of Johannesburg, Kruger relied on his shrewd political judgment. Strategic generosity was what was needed, he explained to the other Boer leaders. Extradite Jameson and his men to Britain and let them stand trial there, before the eyes of a sceptical world. He managed to persuade them, as he did about the best way to deal with the conspirators in Johannesburg.

At the beginning of the raid the conspirators had set up a Reform Committee with scores of others, in the hope of still achieving something by political means. Once again, this turned out to be a mistake. Virtually all of them were arrested and tried. One or two, such as Leonard, got away. The saddlebags belonging to Jameson and his raiders contained more than enough incriminating evidence to hang them: telegrams, codebooks and a copy of the dramatic letter. Five of the conspirators—Phillips, Hammond, Farrar, Frank Rhodes and the secretary of the Reform Committee, Percy FitzPatrick—were sentenced to death. Others received prison sentences and fines. The death sentences sparked off a heated debate in the Executive Council. Kruger argued in favour of making a grand gesture—good for public relations—towards the condemned men. Leyds, who had meanwhile joined in the discussion, was categorically against any remission. Just for once, he found his fiercest opponent, General Joubert, on his side. Kruger pushed the compromise through in stages. First, the death penalty was commuted to 15 years' imprisonment and, after that, fines. All in all, the conspirators paid £200,000. They were reimbursed by Rhodes and Beit. The two super-rich financiers could easily afford it. In the end, the Jameson Raid cost them twice as much—each.[100]

It was an illuminating lesson in leadership from the 70-year-old Kruger. Relentless in battle, merciful in victory. Everyone took sides with Oom Paul. All the doubts about his judgment evaporated, the charges of nepotism and cronyism faded away. His boorishness became just one of those things. Only for a while, but the effect was startling. After the hearing, all the evidence was recorded in a Green Book, which identified

Rhodes and Jameson as the main culprits and hinted at the complicity of the British government. The Boers were drawn together in resolute unanimity and a shared aversion to the British.

In shared adversity, too. In 1896, as if the devil had taken a hand, nature conspired against them as well: drought, locusts, famine and then rinderpest on top of it all. It looks like all the plagues of Egypt, Leyds wrote to the Duke of Mecklenburg in May. 'It was the ancient Egyptians' good fortune that there were no British in those days,' he added. But the Boers remained stoical. Leyds could not have known at the time what devastation this first outbreak of African cattle plague would wreak. The epidemic wiped out about two and a half million head of cattle, an estimated 80 to 90 per cent of the entire herd in the southern African subcontinent. Sheep, pigs and goats were also susceptible to the virus, as were gnu, kudu and antelope in the wild. The unmitigated suffering of the cattle farmers, black and white, was heartbreaking. The epidemic also had a calamitous impact on society as a whole. In spite of the new railway, the oxwagon was then still by far the most common form of transport.[101]

The one glimmer of light—in poignant contrast—was the flourishing state of the Republic's finances. As if to widen the chasm between the pastoral and industrial worlds that coexisted in the Transvaal, business was booming on the Rand in 1896. No rinderpest tragedy, not so much as a scar after the botched coup d'état. Just fortunes being made from gold. The railway company and the Transvaal's treasury were reaping huge profits. The railway company's turnover soared from 20 to 36 million guilders and its profit from 4.5 to 10.5 million. This was thanks to the insatiable demand for coal and the flow of goods that came via the eastern and south-eastern lines, not instead of but as well as the southern line. By contract 85 per cent, nearly 9 million guilders of the 10.5 million guilders' worth of profit went straight to the state. As a result, the Transvaal government's revenue that year came to an unprecedented £3.9 million, or 47 million guilders.

Politicians and government employees benefited personally as well. Salaries in the civil service rose significantly. Leyds's annual income, for instance—after an increase from £1200 to £1650 in 1889—went up to £2300 in one go.[102]

Forty-seven million Dutch guilders. That was an immense sum of money, equal to 80 million German marks or 100 million French francs. In Germany and France one could buy a whole lot of rifles and cannons for that. And that is exactly what the Transvaal government did. At the time of the Jameson Raid it transpired that many of the civilians who were called up for military service did not possess suitable weapons. Commandant-General Joubert had rushed off to order batches of rifles wherever he could find them. But these would not be enough for the inevitable 'next time'. The Executive Council decided that, as a precaution, every able-bodied man should be equipped with a modern firearm at government expense. Huge supplies of rifles and ammunition were brought in within a few months; even duplicates. Money wasn't a problem. First, 30,000 Martini-Henry rifles, because Joubert was accustomed to them. Then 37,000 Mausers and 20 million cartridges, when tests showed they were actually superior. Light, solid, easy to handle, suitable for rapid fire, good short-range performance, small lightweight bullets, smokeless powder: modern and state-of-the-art. A few years later this last feature proved its worth many times over.

Fortifications were built or reinforced in strategic places and the artillery was brought up to standard. Before the Jameson Raid the arsenal consisted of fewer than 20 guns. A series of orders in Germany and France—Krupp and Creusot cannon of various calibres—brought the total to 80. Plus 34 Maxim machine guns. All supplied with ample ammunition. Hardware would not be the problem next time around.[103]

There was still the threat from within. The Executive Council wanted better protection on that side too. This meant tougher legislation and more police control. A new Press Act was introduced to start with. For years, Kruger and Leyds had battled with opposition newspapers such as *Land en Volk* and *The Star*. The new law banned the publication of anonymous contributions or articles that were deemed either morally offensive, a threat to peace and stability, libellous, or likely to incite violence. And it was the president alone who decided. Another two new pieces of legislation, the Aliens Act and the Extradition Act, widened the government's powers to bar or deport undesirable immigrants. The Boers dug in and sharpened their claws.

At least, as far as the British were concerned. All Afrikanerdom was outraged over the raid and came to the rescue. In the February 1896 presidential elections in the Orange Free State, the Afrikaner candidate, Marthinus Steyn, won with an overwhelming majority from the opposition, which stood for closer affiliation with the Cape Colony. Steyn was a lawyer educated in Leiden and London. In theory he had a choice between two directions. In practice he made no secret of his solidarity with the Transvaal Boers. The contract with the Cape railway was cancelled, and the railway service in the Free State came under his administration. The Volksraad in Bloemfontein promised military aid if the need arose. The Volksraad in Pretoria made this reciprocal. In March 1897 the closer ties between the two Boer republics were consolidated by a political alliance.

It was a welcome boost and brought with it significantly more firepower. The Orange Free State possessed another 12,000 Martini-Henrys, 12,000 Mausers, 24 cannon and three machine guns.[104]

The shock was just as great in the Cape Colony. Jan Hofmeyr and his Afrikaner Bond felt betrayed and withdrew their support for Rhodes. He had made his position impossible and should resign as prime minister. The Cape parliament subsequently published a Blue Book, which came to basically the same conclusion as the Transvaal's Green Book: the Colossus had 'directed and controlled the combination'.

That wasn't all. Rhodes also had reason to fear for the future of the country named after him. Chamberlain was concerned about his own political career and threatened to cancel the charter of the British South Africa Company. Rhodes saw blackmail as the only way out. He had enough telegrams from Chamberlain to prove that he had prior knowledge of the raid. He also had a good lawyer, who discreetly conveyed the message. That took care of the BSAC's future—and Chamberlain's at the same time.[105]

But not Rhodesia's, not yet. Jameson had taken most of Rhodesia's police troops for his raid on the Transvaal. After their defeat and imprisonment, the whole of that huge territory had to make do with only 60 white policemen. Independently of each other, the Ndebele and the Shona arrived at the same conclusion. The BSAC's pioneers had driven them from their land, stolen most of their cattle and condemned them to hard labour. And Rhodesia, like the Transvaal, was plagued by drought, locusts and rinderpest. This was their chance. They hadn't handed in their weapons, but had hidden them away. They rose up, both using the same means—attacking remote farms, trading posts and settlements and killing or wounding a total of 500 people, roughly ten per cent of the white population.

Their tactics horrified the survivors, but probably saved their colony. Massive, direct attacks on the virtually undefended administrative centres of Bulawayo and Fort Salisbury would have done far more harm. As things were, the BSAC had time to bring in auxiliaries from the Cape Colony and Natal. Rhodes led the campaign. It was one endless retaliation. 'You should kill all you can, as it serves as a lesson to them when they talk things over at their fires at night.' His instructions were carried out to the letter. Thousands of Ndebele and Shona were wiped out: ten thousand, according to some estimates. Olive Schreiner wrote about the incident in *Trooper Peter Halket of Mashonaland*, an indictment of the ruthless and indiscriminate colonial war. She had once believed in Rhodes; this was her revenge. In 1897 order was restored in white Rhodesia.[106]

The Jameson Raid sent ripples through Europe as well, but the response was less clear cut than in southern Africa. The initial response was unequivocal, in political circles and among the public. Fury at the violation of the Transvaal's autonomy, relief at the Boers' successful resistance, sniggers over the botched raid. That was the general attitude on the European continent. It was felt most keenly by Britain's fiercest rivals, Germany and France, and by the Netherlands, with its blood ties to the Boers.

In Britain things were more complicated. There was indignation there too, especially over the mining magnates and their cynical power games. The raid lent credence to the nascent hypothesis of a critical observer, John Hobson. In *Imperialism* (1902) he would argue that imperialism was driven by the City of London and its international offshoots. Not everyone went as far as Hobson, but many felt uncomfortable about the situation. It wasn't right. At the same time, however, it was hard to suppress a glow of national pride. At least those men had guts. Doctor Jim actually *did* something. The 'rescue letter' inspired the poet laureate Alfred Austin to write about 'girls in the gold-reef city, there are mothers and children too . . . So what can a brave man do?' No wonder the raiders had heeded the call.[107]

The British public's ambivalence vanished in a puff of smoke after Kaiser Wilhelm's telegram to Kruger. His forthright promise of military support for the Transvaal was a flagrant insult, a sign of German aggression. All their outrage was now directed at Berlin. 'It is considered very unfriendly towards this country,' Queen Victoria told her grandson. The serious newspapers endorsed her view, the popular press screamed it out. Germans were harassed in London's docks, in shops and in bars. In music halls, actors dressed up as Jameson's 'troopers' sang ominously, 'We don't want to fight but by Jingo if we do, we've got the ships, we've got the men, we've got the money too.'

It therefore isn't surprising that the raiders received relatively mild sentences in June 1896. The main suspects, Jameson and his second-in-charge, Willoughby, got 15 months' imprisonment. Jameson didn't even complete his sentence. He became ill, was granted a remission and then was released before the end of the year.

Chamberlain got off scot-free. A parliamentary investigation in which he was questioned, along with the others who were directly involved—Rhodes, Beit, Jameson, Phillips and Leonard—ended with nothing more than a cunningly worded statement. The incriminating telegrams weren't submitted to the commission. But they *were* submitted to Lord Salisbury, along with Chamberlain's resignation. However, the prime minister wasn't prepared to lose his most popular minister. He refused his resignation and became complicit in the cover-up, including the deal with Rhodes. The investigating commission concluded that Chamberlain and his staff were above reproach. Salisbury's Liberal predecessor, Lord Rosebery, took a different view: 'I have never read a document at once so shameful and so absurd.'[108]

Be that as it may, as from July 1896 Chamberlain had a free hand as regards the Transvaal. Rhodes had tried, unsuccessfully, to achieve his aims by force. Chamberlain opted for the patient diplomatic art of pulling and prodding, running the show not via Cape Town but directly from London. His opening move was to extend an invitation to President Kruger. A personal meeting in the English capital might help to restore their trust, he suggested. They could discuss matters like the Transvaal's security and South Africa's economic development. That would be fine, Pretoria replied, but they would also discuss replacing the London Convention with a new agreement, minus article 4. That wasn't exactly what Chamberlain had in mind. But he'd be happy to talk about the Uitlanders' grievances. This diplomatic sparring went on for a couple of months. Kruger said more or less nothing; Leyds rendered it in watertight legal terms.

It didn't make them any more popular in Whitehall. In an internal memorandum Chamberlain described Kruger as 'an ignorant, dirty, cunning and obstinate man who has known how to feather his own nest and to enrich all his family and dependants'. Leyds he didn't trust at all, with his so-called health problems and his intrigues in Berlin. He wasn't the only one in London who didn't trust him. When Lippert visited the City in June 1896 he encountered less animosity towards the Germans than towards 'Dr Leyds'. According to his business associates, Leyds was known in London as 'the snake in the grass'. So strong was the feeling against him that a banker friend confided in Lippert, 'Give us up Dr Leyds, and we will give up Rhodes.'[109]

If Leyds had been given a say in the matter, his critics would have had their way. His ailment returned with a vengeance in the South African winter of 1896. In the middle of August he turned to Moltzer in despair. 'I'm worried about the future, mainly because of my throat condition.' He had been optimistic after his treatment in Berlin, but now he was sure that 'if I continue to live in this environment and with the assistance available to me here, I will lose my voice permanently. You can imagine what that would mean to me, I, who have no independent means.' His wife and son weren't in the best of health either. 'Louise cannot spend another summer here.

The heat gives her headaches; they must *not* recur.' And Louis couldn't bear 'either the heat or the winter months. He is ill every June and July; you know those months are bad for the health here. This year he had bronchitis first and after that a typhus-like fever.'

Leyds saw only one solution. It was time to leave Africa and return to Europe. Moltzer was in a position to help him. During his last visit they had discussed the inadequacies of the Transvaal's diplomatic representation to the Great Powers. Beelaerts van Blokland did the best he could to act on the Transvaal's behalf, but because of his parliamentary obligations it was always from The Hague. There really should be embassies in Berlin, Paris, London and Lisbon. Leyds would be the right man for the job. He had countered by saying, 'I can't leave the Boers in the lurch', but now, realising 'that my health will put me out of action', this argument was no longer valid. 'It is *imperative* that I look after myself; I can't sacrifice my voice for my work.' He asked his 'best friend' Moltzer to write to Kruger, adding, 'it would be good to point out—without mentioning a figure—that representatives of the Republic must be paid *well* because, as is customary all over the world, there are expenses they cannot avoid incurring'.

Moltzer didn't waste time. Within a few weeks he wrote a long, carefully worded letter to Kruger, saying exactly what Leyds had asked him to. He also gave it a personal touch to drive the message home. 'I myself had to give up my position last year as Professor at the University of Amsterdam, as a result of a voice and throat complaint, and unfortunately I know from experience how debilitating excessive strain on the vocal chords can be. But, with sincere gratitude, I can also tell you from experience about the wonderful kindness shown to me when the Government of my country—alerted by a faithful friend of mine—prevented my health from being destroyed prematurely by entrusting me with the senior position I hold now.'[110]

It was perfectly clear. The Transvaal needed good diplomatic representatives to promote its interests. In his present position Leyds was in danger of working himself to a standstill. He could, however, use his talents to serve the Boer cause as an envoy to Europe.

Kruger wasn't overjoyed. He didn't want to lose his trusted state secretary. He would think it over. In the meantime Willem and Louise Leyds took one decision at least: their children, now nine and seven years old, were going back to the Netherlands. Louise went with them to settle them in and make arrangement for their schooling. At Christmas she gave a farewell party. At the beginning of January 1897 Willem saw his wife and children off in Lourenço Marques.

It was hard on Leyds. To make matters worse, he was having a difficult time at work. Chief Justice Kotzé raised a fundamental question in connection with a court case concerning mining rights: who had the last word when it came to legislation in the Transvaal? Up to then it had been the Volksraad, but now Kotzé wanted to give the Supreme Court the right to veto all new legislation to ensure that it was constitutional. His proposal led to an out-and-out power struggle between the political and judicial authorities. This crisis at the heart of the South African Republic affected more than just Leyds's work. It disturbed him on a personal level as well. The other four Supreme Court judges backed Kotzé. Even 'Ameshoff, who owes his position to me, has dealt the State a blow which . . . is nothing short of criminal'. Because that's what upset Leyds the most. He felt that Kotzé and his henchmen were jeopardising the entire judicial system purely to further their own political ambitions and out of 'personal vanity'. And just when the Transvaal was in trouble. 'Merely raising this matter is a triumph for the British,' he remarked bitterly. It suggests 'that we need reforms to guarantee legal certainty for persons and property'.

In response, the politicians proposed legislation whereby decisions taken by the Volksraad would be binding on 'every court of law'. In a decisive meeting Leyds delivered an uncharacteristically long speech, advocating the primacy of the Volksraad. The motion was passed. The president was authorised to dismiss members of the judiciary who were not prepared to abide by the decision.

It didn't come to that, at least not at that stage, but for Leyds it was the last straw. 'I have more or less decided not to continue as State Sec.,' he noted in mid-February 1897, in the diary he kept for his wife. He agreed on a scenario with Kruger. If he was re-elected at the end of May, he would 'leave for Europe immediately afterwards, for health reasons'. The president would then try to arrange the matter of diplomatic representation with the Volksraad 'and discuss it with Beelaerts, because we mustn't go over his head'. To be on the safe side he proposed an alternative scenario, in the strictest confidence, to Middelberg, director of the Netherlands-South African Railway Company, who agreed to consider appointing Leyds 'as adviser, for something in the region of £1000'. So once Leyds returned to Europe he would have two options. 'What I do', he wrote to Louise in his diary, 'depends on many different factors: money, position as commissioner, railway company, etc., you etc.'[111]

Diamond Jubilee

London, May 1897

The life of a diplomat in Europe had its good side. Two days after landing in Plymouth on 16 April 1897, Leyds travelled on to the Netherlands. First to The Hague, to his wife and children, who were doing well. Visits to friends and relatives, a few business meetings in Amsterdam, and then the whole of May spent between London and Paris. In London he had many useful talks with interesting people. Nothing was better than personal contact.

Even Chamberlain had thawed. Their last meeting, more than a year earlier, had been little more than a formal exchange of greetings. Now, the British secretary for the colonies took time to have a frank discussion. Apparently Leyds made a good impression on him. Chamberlain introduced him to fellow politicians as 'the ablest representative' of the South African Republic, and made sure that invitations poured in. In June it was Queen Victoria's sixtieth jubilee and the whole of London was celebrating. Leyds had already reserved three good places—for himself, Louise and her sister—to watch the Jubilee Procession on 22 June. Now he was offered three tickets for the Naval Review on the 26th, with a personal note from Chamberlain: 'It will be a fair sight and will I am sure interest you.'[112]

This was the scenario Leyds had arranged with Kruger, except that he started on his journey two months earlier than planned. As fate would have it, Beelaerts van Blokland died unexpectedly on 14 March 1897. The South African Republic no longer had a diplomatic representative in Europe. President Kruger was in Bloemfontein at the time to sign the political treaty with the Orange Free State. Three days later he telegraphed Leyds, instructing him to 'prepare for the journey'. His assignment was wide-ranging. Sound out the mood in Europe, among the public and the governments with which the Transvaal had relations. And then make recommendations about improving the image of the South African Republic.[113]

Its image did need improving. The Jameson Raid had taken place more than a year earlier. On the European continent indignation had been replaced by alarm, which is to say, among shareholders in the gold mines. After being convicted in Pretoria and Cape Town, Rhodes had been officially cleared and was now hustling in London, where he and Chamberlain were doing their best to undermine confidence in the Transvaal government: Rhodes, as always, by buying whatever he needed, in this case newspaper reports about the Boers' supposed reign of terror over the gold mines, and Chamberlain by putting more pressure on Kruger. In early March 1897 he had two dispatches drawn up. One accused the Boer republic of systematically violating the London Convention. For instance, he said, Pretoria had signed the Geneva Convention—for the protection of soldiers wounded in battle—without informing the British government. It had also negotiated treaties with the Orange Free State and Portugal. The second dispatch demanded the immediate repeal of the Transvaal's Aliens Act. In mid-April the British representative in Pretoria, William Conyngham Greene, handed the two dispatches to Kruger in person, with the implicit threat that a large fleet of British ships was on its way to South Africa.

Leyds arrived in England around the same time, unaware of the dispatches. A few days later he received a telegram about them from his deputy in Pretoria, Van Boeschoten. He couldn't make head or tail of Van Boeschoten's message. The actual text of the dispatches came just under a week later. As a result, he decided to change his plans, and informed Pretoria of this at the end of April. The original idea was that he would present himself as an envoy in various capital cities. He had his diplomatic credentials, but he would have to travel and do 'the whole round . . . official receptions and other solemnities'. In view of the dispatches, he felt it would be better not to give up his position as 'state secretary at large', and to spend as much time as possible in London. 'People don't know me and they've got the wrong idea. They think I'm deliberately avoiding London out of hostility. They think I'll go plotting and playing up to Germany and France, and if I go there now, they'll use that to stir up the worst sentiments of the English by talking about German intrigues etc. At the moment I believe I can be of most use in London.' With that idea in mind, he had moved into the apartment of Montagu White, the Transvaal consul in London, for four months. It was a good base from which to meet as many people as possible. He began right away. 'Next week I'll be having lunch with friend and foe.'[114]

Leyds wanted to talk to prominent lawyers as well as politicians. In his professional opinion, there was nothing legally wrong with the recent legislation in the Transvaal, or the treaty with the Orange Free State. But his case would be stronger if he could get internationally respected legal experts to endorse it. Tobias Asser, who had been one of his mentors in Amsterdam, had already agreed to look into the matter, as had the Utrecht jurist Jan de Louter. For obvious reasons Leyds also wanted confirmation from an Englishman. He succeeded. John Westlake, the top British authority on international law, was prepared to examine the documents. And through Westlake, Leyds came into contact with his French counterpart, Edouard Clunet.

Unfortunately, the learned gentlemen did not all agree. Asser's advice wasn't much help. Leyds should try to find precedents, he suggested. By way of explanation, Leyds mentioned that Asser's wife was seriously ill and Asser himself 'very down'. In De Louter's opinion the treaty between the Transvaal and the Orange Free State was consistent with the letter but not the spirit of the London Convention. Clunet concluded that the Transvaal was free to enter into any agreements it wanted with the Orange Free State, including this treaty, which gave citizens of the Orange Free State unrestricted admission to the Transvaal. Westlake saw things differently. According to him, it implied that Britain was entitled to claim the same right for its citizens. Also, he maintained that the Aliens Act was not in conflict with the London Convention, but the Extradition Act was. This was not the unanimous expert opinion Leyds had wanted, but at least he was no longer empty-handed.[115]

In the meantime Leyds had expressed his views loud and clear on another contentious issue, the Uitlanders. Soon after arriving in Plymouth he had been interviewed by the French newspaper *Le Temps*. He prepared his case well. To begin with, he said, the Transvaal's mining legislation could stand comparison with that in other countries. Taxes and import duties for the mining industry had been lowered, along with the cost of telegraphs, thanks to a subsidy from the Transvaal government. According to Leyds, the price of coal and dynamite—the biggest bone of contention—was open to debate. But, he reminded them, these were relatively small costs. The average monthly gold yield on the Rand was worth at least £800,000. And coal cost the mine owners little more than £30,000 a month. Less than four per cent. You could hardly call that a deterrent. Finally, Leyds said that even the Uitlanders' grievances could be solved. As long as that handful of financiers and imperialists who were bent on war didn't keep stoking them up.[116]

These were unusually strong statements for Leyds to make in public and they drew a lot of attention. Apparently he wasn't intending to keep a low profile in Europe. As a prelude to the talks he was planning, the interview didn't do any harm. It aroused people's interest. In his three weeks in London—late April to 19 May 1897, interrupted by a few days in Paris—he managed to speak to many leading politicians. Not to the prime minister and foreign secretary, Lord Salisbury himself, but to his cousin, Arthur Balfour, leader of the House of Commons and 'an extraordinary man', along with Salisbury's son-in-law, Lord Selborne, the under-secretary at the Colonial Office, and influential parliamentarians such as Herbert Asquith and Henry Labouchère, who was also the publisher of the controversial weekly journal *Truth*. He also had meetings with Sir Henry Loch, the former high commissioner to South Africa, and the businessman Sir Charles Tennant, 'one of the richest men in England', who had money in 'the dynamite business'. He had to decline an invitation to dine with Lord and Lady Rothschild because he already had commitments in Paris.[117]

But the most important meeting was the one with Chamberlain. Leyds received the official invitation on 10 May, a few days after the Volksraad in Pretoria had decided to repeal the Aliens Act. It had done so at the insistence of the Executive Council on the pretext of complaints from neighbouring states. Chamberlain's invitation explicitly mentioned this conciliatory gesture on the part of the Transvaal government, which made it possible for them to discuss their differences on an amicable footing. Informally to start with, that seemed best. Would lunch at two o'clock the following Saturday, 15 May, be convenient?[118]

It was. Afterwards, Leyds sent a detailed report to Van Boeschoten. Pretoria soon knew that the talks had not been 'hostile' and became 'more cordial towards the end'. Under-Secretary Lord Selborne had also been present, but Chamberlain did most of the talking. He started by stating his intentions. 'Britain has a paramount interest in S.A. which it intends to defend at all costs. As far as the Convention [of London] is concerned, Britain cannot allow any departure from it. It will adhere to it stringently and if necessary go to war for it. On this point we cannot accept arbitration.' Having emphasised that the matter was not negotiable, Chamberlain went into more detail. The matters he had raised in his dispatches were 'not of great importance'. It was everything taken together that had led him to conclude that the Transvaal was trying to sidestep the Convention. That wasn't only the view of the ministry but also of the public in general. Then there was the legal interpretation of the Convention. 'I understand you and I have been given different legal advice.' Chamberlain realised that 'one can seek the opinion of this or that lawyer on any matter, as one wishes'. But he was now citing 'the opinion of lawyers of the Crown' and they came to a different conclusion.

Then there was also 'the Uitlander question'. The Transvaal government insisted that it was an internal affair, but Chamberlain argued that it concerned British subjects. He had the right to defend them, just as he would if they were in France, for instance. Did Leyds realise how many complaints he had received? 'You cannot imagine the position we are in at the moment, the British public in Africa and here, the floods of letters we have been receiving with complaints against you (at least 90 out of 100 to go to war).' A year earlier, Kruger had declined to travel to England to discuss the matter personally. Would it be an idea 'for President Kruger to authorise you to discuss the Uitlanders' grievances with me and decide in consultation how they can be resolved'?

In reply, Leyds promptly denied that Pretoria had any intention of violating the London Convention. The Executive Council and the Volksraad were totally unaware that the Transvaal's signing of the Geneva Convention, for example, could harm Britain's interests. After all, Britain had signed it too. Moreover, there was a precedent—Leyds and his private secretary, F.A. van der Hoeven, had heeded Asser's advice. 'Namely, we signed the Universal Postal Union Treaty, just as you did, and you did not object.' Leyds felt that this argument in particular hit its mark. Chamberlain and Selborne 'made a gesture suggesting there was something to be said for it'.

Chamberlain was also open-minded about the disputed legislation. The Aliens Act had been scrapped and the Extradition Act and the Press Act were 'in themselves not breaches' of the London Convention. It was more that they opened the way for the Transvaal government to commit violations. In other words, 'if you deport criminals or prostitutes, I shall say nothing about it, but I shall speak out if for political reasons you deport any person who has done nothing.' Leyds was pleased with this last statement; it kept the door open. For the time being, he warned Pretoria, apply the legislation in question only to those two categories: criminals and prostitutes.

Finally, there was the question of Leyds being authorised to confer about the Uitlanders' grievances. It was not something he could discuss with Kruger or the Executive Council by telegram. He told Chamberlain 'it could not even be done by letter, but would necessitate my return to Africa'. Mr Chamberlain 'said he understood'. It seemed to him that the British secretary for the colonies 'was willing to approach matters in a spirit of friendship'.[119]

Chamberlain's attitude towards Leyds in the following days strengthened that impression. He introduced him to Sir William Harcourt, leader of the Liberal Opposition, and spoke in glowing terms about his 'education and experience'. Leyds was optimistic too. 'I'm happy', he wrote to Van Boeschoten, 'that the resentment that distressed me when I arrived here has abated, because it came from friend as well as foe. As you know, the market has gone up hugely. I played a major part in that.' He had good reason to be satisfied with what he had accomplished.[120]

And then there were the celebrations to look forward to, first the Jubilee Procession on 22 June, followed by the Naval Review on the 26th. The Royal Navy would certainly be impressive. Just to be on the safe side, he decided to check which ship he had been assigned to. He didn't want to find himself in the company of all the 'colonial prime ministers'.[121]

His diligence paid off. Discreet enquiries revealed that it would not be diplomats on board the flagship *Wildfire*, but indeed the prime ministers of the British colonies. The scales fell from Leyds's eyes. It had all been a sham: Chamberlain feigning kindness. An invitation to the Aldershot Review, a reception with the Prince and Princess of Wales, an invitation to Chamberlain's home in Birmingham, and on top of it the cunning ploy of a letter from his wife, Mary, to Louise. All of it was contrived only to compromise Leyds as the South African Republic's representative. Thank heavens he had looked into things. If he'd fallen for it, his days 'as a republican statesman' would have been over. He resolved to steer clear of Chamberlain as much as possible in future.[122]

It was too late to get out of the Jubilee Procession, but he soon thought up an excuse for the Naval Review. Besides Moltzer and Asser, another of his mentors had made it to the top. Pierson was finance minister and chairman of the Dutch Council of Ministers. Leyds arranged an invitation for another flagship, this time the flagship of the Dutch navy. 'Please don't trouble yourself any more,' he wrote to Chamberlain. This was an invitation he obviously couldn't refuse. Old friends of his would be on board. And in the days before the review he had commitments in Paris and Berlin.[123]

The latter was true. In Paris he had appointments with the foreign minister, Gabriel Hanotaux, and the president, Félix Faure. His talk with the president was mainly about the Transvaal's diplomatic representation. Faure was strongly in favour of a single envoy, especially for France. With Hanotaux he discussed other affairs, mainly the 'vast amounts of French capital' invested in the Transvaal gold mines. 'The Parisians', Leyds had noted earlier, 'are even more firmly convinced than the British that the Boers are deliberately working against the interests of the mines . . . I am making every possible effort to change that view.' This was apparently what Hanotaux needed. He had been urging the French government to do all they could for the mining industry. It would be an issue in the French elections in November, and 'in the meanwhile you've got time to get something done; those were more or less his words. He didn't mean them as a threat, but as friendly advice; though when you read them, they do sound a bit like that.'[124]

Leyds had his own thoughts about the concerns of the French shareholders. He felt they had 'allowed themselves to be conned. They allowed themselves to be fooled into thinking bad mines were good, and they allowed land where there isn't a grain of gold to be palmed off as gold mines.' And now they thought that 'the shares would go up to their former value, if only our Government wanted them to. They got that idea from the British. It's time they understood that it's not possible, that they've been conned *but not by us*; that there are companies that cannot be saved even if we were to supply them with dynamite and transport everything by rail completely free of charge.'[125]

There was also good news for Leyds in Paris. It came from Pretoria. On 27 May 1897 he heard that he had been re-elected as state secretary, again. The result gave him an extra boost. He had won 19 of the 25 votes in the Volksraad, five went to Abraham Fischer, a candidate he had recommended, and one to Herman Coster. Leyds saw his election and particularly the percentages as 'a signal to Britain and a victory for myself . . . especially since I wasn't there in person and therefore wouldn't have been able to do anything'.[126]

Over Whitsun the Leyds family spent a few days together in The Hague. The children were doing 'extremely well', but Leyds soon had to move on. To Berlin, where he hadn't been since his return to Europe. Much had changed since his last visit, more than a year earlier. Here, too, support for the Boer cause had declined considerably. An audience with the kaiser was no longer on the cards, but he was received by the old chancellor, Chlodwig zu Hohenlohe-Schillingsfürst. 'The tone was very friendly but there's nothing much to report,' he telegraphed to Pretoria. As in France, this was because German financiers were worried about their investments in the Transvaal gold mines, which were running at a loss. From the consul in Frankfurt, Leyds learned that they totalled about £15 to £20 million, 'for southern and western Germany alone'. Here, too, accusing fingers were pointing at Pretoria. 'They've been told that the situation would get better if the government were more forthcoming in certain matters.'[127]

So it was not support that Leyds received on the European continent. It was criticism and a demand for greater compliance with the wishes of the mining industry—and its European shareholders. Rightly or wrongly, this made no difference to the way people perceived things, he realised. What it came down to was winning the support of the public—and consequently their governments—for the Boer cause. A press campaign to challenge

Rhodes's slurs and Chamberlain's manipulations. But that was more than the incumbent of the Transvaal's diplomatic and consular service could cope with. 'It's a pity I can't quadruplicate myself,' he lamented in a personal letter to Van Boeschoten, 'it's a pity I'm not based in one place. It's a pity I haven't got staff.' When he returned to Pretoria, he would advise the Executive Council to do something about it.[128]

But first that dodgy fortnight in London. How should he react to Chamberlain's double-dealings? While still in Berlin he had received worrying news from Pretoria about British troop reinforcements on the borders of the Transvaal. He was asked to obtain 'certainty' that 'no one has aggressive intentions towards us'. Leyds decided to tell Chamberlain frankly and honestly about the consternation in the Transvaal. Pretoria wanted peace, he wrote, and would appreciate a reassuring gesture from the British side.[129]

Chamberlain feigned surprise, and threw the ball back. For the past 18 months Pretoria had been busy organising reinforcements and laying in huge supplies of weapons and ammunition, he replied. That could only be seen as preparation for an armed confrontation with 'the Paramount Power'. So in his opinion it was only logical for Britain to react. He added charmingly that Leyds was still welcome on board the British flagship for the Naval Review. He could imagine that Leyds would prefer the company of his compatriots, but then he would miss something special, because 'the foreign ships of war will be stationary and will not go down the line'.[130]

What a hypocrite. Leyds would have to mind his step. Even photographers asking to take pictures of him were part of the ruse to frame him. When he enquired, they said it was for some 'hall of famous men of the Empire, etc.'. At the Jubilee Procession on 22 June, he wasn't able to avoid Chamberlain. After the pageant the Chamberlains approached Leyds and his wife and invited them to the Colonial Office. Over lunch there, Chamberlain again urged him to 'get permission to negotiate with him', because he couldn't 'discuss the same matter with two different people at the same time'. Leyds kept him at arm's length as far as possible and not only at the Naval Review. He often had to say he was 'out of town', but there were also times when he spoke his mind. He made no secret, for instance, about not wanting to meet the Prince of Wales 'because he shakes hands with Rhodes in public'.

For Leyds that was a kind of litmus test. If the main culprit behind the Jameson Raid was still a member of the Privy Council—Queen Victoria's highest political advisory body—'how can our people believe in the British Government's good faith?' He personally had little confidence left in them. Even the members of the Opposition he had spoken to, their leader, Sir William Harcourt, first and foremost, 'couldn't care less about us'. They defended the Boer cause not 'in the interests of justice, but for the benefit of the party'. Back in Paris at the beginning of July, he drew his conclusions. 'We cannot count on support in England.' The English were 'despised more and more around the world'. And they were well aware of it, with the result that they were 'closing ranks more than they would otherwise; after all, an Englishman is still an Englishman, even if he's in the Opposition'.

Leyds saw the Jubilee festivities in the same light. The whole celebration was meant 'to arouse the patriotism of the English'. In that it succeeded, mainly because of the Naval Review, which was 'splendid', he had to admit. But he was less impressed by the Jubilee Procession. It was nothing more than 'a parade of soldiers'. The British wanted to 'prove, or delude the world and themselves into believing, that they're not just *any* power with any army'. Except that they didn't succeed at all. In this respect, Leyds considered the parade 'a *testimonium paupertatis*'.[131]

He believed that 'Britain would not easily resort to war'. The mood in the country was less militant than when he had arrived three months earlier. He saw no immediate danger of a British invasion of the Transvaal, although it was important not to relax 'all vigilance, care and precautions. In relation to Britain, that would be unwise, always and in all circumstances.'[132]

Leyds only discovered how true those words were shortly before he went back to South Africa. He spent the last weeks with his family in The Hague, recovering from all the stress. Early in August 1897, a week before he was due to sail, Chamberlain came up with a nasty surprise. Actually, a double surprise, just as one would expect of him. First he publicly announced that the British government would not punish Cecil Rhodes. Then he proclaimed in the Commons that the London Convention was an agreement 'between the suzerain and the subordinate power'.[133]

A parting of ways

Pretoria, February 1898

'And the President's foul temper on top of it all.' Leyds was distraught. 'It's sad to see what old age is doing to him. He's losing his integrity.' He had been unable to write about it 'for several hours . . . I was trembling from suppressed indignation and rage.' Kruger 'has no compunction about telling stupid, barefaced lies. It doesn't trouble him in the least, as long as he gets what he wants.'

The president and the state secretary had clashed in the past, but this time there were no holds barred. Leyds was badly shaken, even a day later when he wrote to Louise. The row was sparked off by the most recent of a series of slanderous newspaper articles. Leyds was accustomed to insults and slurs, particularly from a sleazy opposition paper like *Land en Volk*. Now they had raked up the old canard about him being an atheist. Leyds had just shrugged it off, but Kruger insisted on having an official denial from Leyds published in the paper. Otherwise, he added, the Volksraad might be difficult about Leyds's diplomatic appointment.

Normally he could control his feelings, but this time Leyds exploded. Did the president think he was going to Europe for his own pleasure? If the Volksraad didn't trust him after all those years he had dedicated to the Boer cause, they would just have to vote against him. In any event, he refused to write anything for 'a malicious rag like *Land en Volk* . . . which would twist things or hush them up and then trot them out again later, whether I deny them or not'. Kruger wouldn't budge. The end of the story was that he got someone else to write the denial.[134]

Leyds's anger gradually subsided, but he still had trouble dealing with Kruger. Oom Paul to his people, a tyrant to everyone around him. Kruger had never been the most civil of men and he became more difficult with age. But he was the undisputed leader of the Boers, after all, especially after the Jameson Raid. In early February 1898, at the age of 72, he was re-elected as president for the fourth time. The results said it all: almost 13,000 votes, more than twice as many as his rivals Schalk Burger and the 'eternal loser' Joubert put together.

Reassured by his support from the Boer population, Kruger continued on the same political course. Chief Judge Kotzé lost his job and no more concessions went to the Rand barons or Uitlanders. Burger had been more sympathetic to their demands. He was chairman of the industrial commission made up of government officials and members of the Chamber of Mines. The commission had been looking into the needs of the mining industry since April 1897, and three months later made far-reaching recommendations to the Transvaal government: break the dynamite monopoly, lower the prices of coal and dynamite, nationalise the Netherlands-South African Railway Company and facilitate the recruitment of cheap black labour.

After Leyds's return from Europe early in September 1897, the Volksraad debated the industrial commission's report. Ending the dynamite monopoly was too big a step for Kruger, but he was willing to adopt some of the other recommendations, at least to some extent. The price of dynamite went down, as did several of the railway company tariffs, the latter to the tune of £200,000 a year. He saw no benefit in nationalising the company overnight. It would cost an estimated £7 or £8 million and the government lacked the resources to run an enterprise of that magnitude. At Leyds's suggestion it was decided to take over the company in stages by buying up shares until the company automatically became a state enterprise. The government also helped to expand the labour reserve for the mining industry. In October 1897, Leyds signed an agreement with the Portuguese governor, allowing the recruitment of labour from Mozambique.[135]

It was more than nothing, but less than the industrial commission had recommended. The opposition wasn't happy, but as far as Leyds was concerned, they could take it or leave it. After Kruger's re-election he was mainly preoccupied with two issues: a suitable response to Chamberlain's suzerainty claim, and preparations for his posting overseas.

Chamberlain didn't stop at his address to the House of Commons. More than two months later, on 16 October 1897, he had repeated Britain's claim to suzerainty in a letter to the Transvaal government. Leyds had been brooding over a response ever since. At the end of March 1898, he was ready. He wrote about it to Louise, who had gone ahead to their children in the Netherlands. He had made 'a wonderful discovery in some old documents', he announced proudly, which would 'trash' Chamberlain's case. He was meticulous about the wording. The drafts he received from his assistants were never good enough. 'I want this dispatch to reveal, here and there, *my* own thoughts and hand.'[136]

It did. The letter he sent to Chamberlain on 16 April 1898 on behalf of the Transvaal government opened with a detailed account of the events leading up to the signing of the London Convention. Unlike the preceding Pretoria Convention (1881), the London document did not contain the word 'suzerain'. It had been removed deliberately, Leyds argued. That was apparent if one compared the texts and it was also clear from oral and written testimonies. The British signatory, Sir Hercules Robinson, then high commissioner and now known as Lord Rosmead, had conceded this explicitly in a newspaper interview. That was Leyds's 'wonderful discovery'. Since then, moreover, Great Britain and the South African Republic had exchanged consular representatives. That was only possible between independent states, and the same applied to the settlement of disputes by arbitration. The latter had once been invoked over a provision of the London Convention. The dispute concerned the 'coolie question', whether or not Asians from the British colonies enjoyed rights of residence, among other things the right to render services. The arbitrator—the Supreme Court of the Orange Free State—had ruled in favour of the Transvaal and the British government had respected its judgment. These were powerful arguments. Convinced that his case was airtight, Leyds sent copies of Chamberlain's letter and his own reply to the governments of the Netherlands, Germany, France, Portugal, Switzerland and the United States.[137]

The final arrangements for Leyds's appointment as diplomatic envoy were being made around the same time. After his experience in 1897, he had initially appealed for a larger diplomatic service, with agents in London, Paris, Berlin and Lisbon. Kruger and the rest of the Executive Council considered this too expensive. They would keep it to a single envoy, with offices in each of the four capital cities, plus The Hague and Brussels. The consulates there would remain open, as would the ones in London, Amsterdam and Frankfurt. All of this for a total of £15,000 a year, which included £4000 for the envoy's salary. He would also get an allowance for business trips, six weeks' annual leave and a trip to Pretoria for consultations once a year, or every two years. Leyds chose Brussels as his base. He preferred it to The Hague because he couldn't stand all 'that gossip, those snide remarks! About clothes, about everything.'[138]

Behind closed doors, the Executive Council approved Leyds's appointment in April 1898. But there were still two small matters to resolve. Not only had the rumour about Leyds's atheism continued to circulate, but fingers were being pointed at him for another reason as well. It was alleged that he had received £500 from the dynamite company: in short, a bribe. It was best for him and for the government as a whole to clear his name before he resigned as state secretary and started work as the country's envoy. This time Leyds was prepared to issue a formal denial. He was charged with bribery and acquitted by the Supreme Court. He furnished the Executive Council with proof that he had been christened in Magelang, Java, and was a registered member of the Nederduitsch Hervormde Kerk in Pretoria. On 20 May 1898, Willem Johannes Leyds was officially appointed special envoy and minister plenipotentiary of the South African Republic.[139]

Kruger's re-election was bad news for Cape Town. Sir Alfred Milner, the new high commissioner, had seen enough of him. Another five years of Boer dictatorship and the Transvaal would be ruined for good. Worse than that, 'the richest spot on earth' would drag the rest of the southern African subcontinent down; it would drift away from the British Empire. It was already 'the weakest link in the Imperial chain'. What had happened in America was imminent here. No dominion under the British flag, but an independent state. Not a Canada, but a United States of South Africa. What had become of Chamberlain's Grand Scheme or their shared belief in the superiority of the British race? His conclusion was straightforward. 'The waiting game' didn't work. Something had to change, for better or worse.

Absolute dedication to the British Empire: to that he owed his appointment as high commissioner in South Africa and governor of the Cape Colony. Alfred Milner was driven by a fanatical, almost zealous nationalism. Overcompensating for his German background, critics said. His grandmother was German, he had been born in Hesse and raised in Baden-Württemberg. But everything came together in Oxford. He got his education and found his vocation there: a knowledge of the classics, political acumen, social commitment and imperialist ideals. He was a brilliant student in all subjects. After a few years in journalism, as editor of the *Pall Mall Gazette,* Milner gained his first experience in colonial administration in Egypt. He spent three years there as minister of finance. At the end of his term he enumerated the blessings of British administration in *England and Egypt.* The book was an instant success. It established his reputation as a writer and administrator but, most of all, as an imperialist in heart and soul. Back in England Milner occupied a senior position at the ministry of finance. In 1894 he became a Companion of the Order of the Bath and in 1895 Knight Commander in the same order. This was appropriate for his new position. Sir Hercules was succeeded by Sir Alfred. He arrived in Cape Town in May 1897.

Milner allowed himself time to grow accustomed to his role. Not that he was patient—on the contrary—but these were Chamberlain's orders. The Jameson Raid had stirred up a lot of bad blood among the Afrikaners in the Cape Colony. Milner had to avoid acting in haste, like Rhodes. 'Wait and see' was his watchword for the time being, and hope that the internal opposition to Kruger would gather momentum. In the meantime he travelled in order to get to know the country and its people and to decide on the best way to proceed.

After Kruger's re-election he was ready. In a personal letter he sent Chamberlain in late February 1898, Milner proposed giving Kruger two options: either reforms in the Transvaal or war. With the old tyrant at the helm in Pretoria, reform was not going to happen. The Boers quarrelled among themselves, but over jobs and contracts, not political issues. There was nothing to do but prepare for a crisis: step up the pressure systematically and not be distracted by details. During the drifts crisis of 1895 they had found that threats of violence yielded results. Kruger had considered backing down and making concessions. The same would happen this time as well. If not, then war. It couldn't last long and there was no doubt the British would win.[140]

It meant that everyone on the British side would have to close ranks. Henry Binns, the governor of Natal, found himself in trouble for sending Kruger a congratulatory telegram after his re-election. How could he? The point now was to separate the wheat from the chaff. It wasn't so much between 'the English and the Dutch' as between supporters and opponents of the despotic regime in Pretoria. It was time for everyone living in the Cape Colony and Natal to take sides 'as loyal citizens of a free British Community'.

The message was clear, and Milner emphasised it in public three weeks later. On 3 March 1898 he delivered a speech in Graaff-Reinet, a town about 600 kilometres north-east of Cape Town, at the opening of a new railway line. His audience comprised mainly Afrikaners and he addressed himself to them, in terms that left nothing to the imagination. They were living in the Cape Colony, in peace and prosperity, enjoying all the fruits of British colonial rule: freedom, justice, equality and self-government. Those were precisely the conditions that did not exist in the South African Republic. In spite of that, there were many Cape Afrikaners who sympathised with their clansmen in the Transvaal. Sympathy he could understand. But anyone who put the independence of the Boer republic above the honour and interests of their own country, no. In Milner's view, they were betraying their own flag. If they truly wanted a peaceful solution for the whole of South Africa, they should try to influence Pretoria to introduce reforms, to make the Transvaal government more open to change.[141]

Milner's words were not subtle. Everyone, friend and foe, knew what he was driving at. He had spent almost a year checking out the lie of the land. Now he took a position. He was forcing every white South African to make a choice: for or against the enlightened British regime, for or against Kruger's dictatorship. Those were the only options.

Milner's Graaff-Reinet speech had the effect of polarising the two parties, and the situation worsened a few days later when a familiar face reappeared on the scene. An interview in the *Cape Times* and a public appearance at the Good Hope Hall on 12 March 1898 removed any doubt. Cecil Rhodes was back in town. The Jameson Raid and the uprisings in Rhodesia had dulled the Colossus's sheen, but he hadn't fallen from his pedestal. Elections for the Cape parliament were due in September 1898, and he was aiming for the premiership again. His political programme was still basically the same, and so was his campaign strategy. He still had enough money to buy supporters and pay off his adversaries. He still had his vision of a federation of the whole of southern Africa, united under the Union Jack. Except that this time he was targeting a different group of voters. The Jameson Raid had severed his ties with Jan Hofmeyr and his Afrikaner Bond. Rhodes had traded them in for a more natural ally, the South African League. Founded in May 1896, it was the new hub for British nationalists in South Africa. Besides the Cape Colony and Natal, it also had a branch in the Transvaal. In the motherland it was called the South African Association.

So Rhodes was back in the political arena, this time openly as the champion of 'jingoism'. It was also Rhodes who coined the memorable slogan 'Equal rights for every civilised man south of the Zambezi'. It must have raised his opponents' hackles. It wasn't just money he flung around, but also old-fashioned mud. His election campaign was dirty and a cliff-hanger all the way through. The result came as a surprise. Rhodes didn't win. By a small margin the victory went to the South Africa Party, led by William Schreiner. With the support of the Afrikaner Bond, Schreiner became the new prime minister.

Politically, he was a moderate. Like his sister Olive, the writer, Schreiner had once been an admirer of Rhodes, but the Jameson Raid was the breaking point for him too. He considered himself a loyal subject of Queen Victoria, but at the same time an advocate of the Boer republics' right to decide their own future. That wasn't what Milner and Rhodes wanted to hear. They would have to find a way to deal with him.[142]

Leyds's transfer from the backwaters of Boer society to the rarefied world of diplomacy was a big step in his life. On the one hand it was a relief. Coming from a respectable, bourgeois background, he was offended by the lack of refinement and decorum in the Transvaal. He had never grown accustomed to it and never wanted to. A sense of proportion and respect for authority were hard to find in Pretoria. The Boer cause had become important to him, but the Boers themselves were a different matter. For 14 years he had lived among them, shared their hopes and their fears, but never had he become one of them. As dedicated as he was, he remained an outsider.

Leyds was a vain man, proud of his accomplishments and privileges. He enjoyed wearing his decorations at the opening of the Volksraad and on other official occasions. As state attorney he had received a Portuguese knighthood and, as state secretary, honours from the Netherlands, Belgium, Germany and France. *Land en Volk* called him 'the man with the medals'. Like any diplomat, he wore a uniform, somewhat 'festooned with gilt' by his predecessor, Beelaerts van Blokland. But then this wasn't inappropriate for an envoy of the world's biggest producer of gold.[143]

There was also a downside to his life as a diplomat. In the nineteenth century, the diplomatic corps was a bastion of aristocracy and old money. Men of lowlier birth weren't welcomed with open arms. Even worse, he represented a nouveau riche on the international scene, an insignificant Boer republic which, on top of it, was at loggerheads with the most powerful nation on earth. All in all, he was not well placed to make his entrée into the courts of Europe. He was an outsider there, too. The difference was that this time he actually wanted to belong.

But it wasn't that easy. It took half a year to present his credentials. Leyds put it down to 'fate', which wasn't 'kind to me'. But it had at least as much to do with diplomatic sensitivities in the various capitals. He realised this when he first presented his credentials in Paris. He was received by President Faure at the Elysée Palace on 8 July 1898. Diplomatic protocol was observed, including his arrival in a coach with a guard of honour of cuirassiers. But when he subsequently paid his courtesy calls on other diplomats in Paris, the British closed the door in his face. On Lord Salisbury's instructions, the ambassador, Sir Edward Monson, avoided an official meeting with him.

This was a taste of what Leyds could expect all over the Continent. London did not officially challenge his accreditation, but British diplomats were advised to avoid formal contact with him. This unofficial boycott affected the way other governments treated him, the Netherlands less than some others. In early August, Queen Regent Emma and young Princess Wilhelmina, the future queen, received him at Soestdijk Palace, observing the rules of diplomatic etiquette. But elsewhere the atmosphere was strained. Kaiser Wilhelm II and King Leopold II of Belgium made a point of keeping him waiting. Also under British pressure, Tsar Nicholas of Russia decided not to invite the Transvaal—or the Orange Free State—

to the International Peace Conference, which was held, at his initiative, in The Hague in 1899.[144]

Leyds had to do something about the journalists as well as the diplomats. He soon realised that 'the mood in Europe, especially France, is hostile towards the Republic'. He knew who was behind it: Milner and Rhodes. They were far away, but their tentacles reached all the way to the French press. Through the South African Association in London they filled newspaper pages with half-truths about the Transvaal, outright lies about Kruger and fabrications about him. *Le Figaro*, *La Liberté*, *Le Matin*. All of them could be bought, for heaps of money; but that was no problem for the mining magnates from Kimberley and Johannesburg.

For Leyds it was a very serious problem. He wasn't in a position to repay them in kind. It would cost thousands of pounds. 'The Republic cannot afford to spend as much to defend itself as its enemies spend to attack it.' But something had to be done 'to tell people the truth'. A press office in Paris, to begin with. 'The most reliable person and one I believe would be suitable for the job' was the French journalist E. Roels. For £1000 a month, Roels collected cuttings from scores of newspapers— French, German, British, Portuguese and even Russian—and launched a pro-Boer campaign. The other side had a great deal more money, but it was for a good cause and that was also worth something. 'It's a contest between money and justice.'[145]

Justice for the Boer cause. That was still the ideal Leyds was pursuing. His goal remained unchanged, but the kind of life he was dedicating to it was totally different. It was refined, civilised, extrovert, with more variety and pageantry. And of course it gave more opportunity to travel. As envoy-at-large, he was constantly on the move, visiting one capital after another. Towards the end of the year, he began to suffer from 'the fatigue caused by excessive travel and work. The distances here in Europe are considerable too.'

But there was more to come. He still had to present his credentials in Lisbon and St Petersburg. In late November 1898 he travelled to Lisbon, where he was received first by King Carlos, subsequently in another palace by Queen Amélie, and finally by the queen mother, Maria Pia, who lived in Cascais. The train journey to Cascais was an experience he would never forget. To enjoy the view he went to sit outdoors on the balcony of the lounge car, where his eyes were suddenly 'filled with grit'. He attended the audience regardless—with tears streaming down his cheeks—but back in Lisbon he needed 'two surgical interventions to relieve me of my load of coal'. Blinded by coal soot on a train journey. *Land en Volk* would have relished the symbolism.

He never made it to St Petersburg. He hadn't been keen to go in the first place. 'It must be bitterly cold in Russia,' he wrote to Pretoria on 16 December 1898. 'I'm not looking forward to the journey for that reason, and I hope I get through it all right as far as my health is concerned.' To be on the safe side he went to see his doctor anyway. That put an end to the trip. He was 'absolutely' forbidden to go to St Petersburg. The old complaints had come back. 'My nose and throat . . . need immediate attention, daily.' He had been told off for 'not coming sooner. But how could I? I rush from city to city and when I get there I hardly have time to breathe.' Fortunately the Russian government was sympathetic. The second secretary of the mission, Van der Hoeven, whose mother was a member of the Russian aristocracy, was authorised to present his credentials to Tsar Nicholas II. At the end of December 1898, Leyds was accredited as an envoy of the South African Republic in Russia as well.[146]

Chamberlain wasn't pleased. Leyds hadn't made a bad impression on him when they had met at the Diamond Jubilee in the summer of 1897. Even Lord Selborne, the colonial under-secretary, had a good word for him. Leyds was sociable, he thought, intelligent and pleasant-looking. And Chamberlain had admired his 'shrewd evasions' at the time of the Naval Review. At least Leyds wasn't a backward Boer.

But that made him all the more dangerous. The Colonial Office's South Africa expert, Fred Graham, had made this very point to his minister. Leyds was known to be totally unreliable, he reported. He was considered their most dangerous opponent. That was more important than the man's personal charm, Selborne agreed. 'All British South Africa . . . are united in believing him to be *the* enemy.' True or not, what mattered was what people thought. The Transvaal's new envoy in Europe, with his 'Hollander policy', was seen as the Boers' evil genius. They had to keep that idea alive and nurture it.[147]

The Colonial Office and the Foreign Office kept Leyds under surveillance, observing his every move with suspicion. They had instructions to make his life difficult and tarnish his reputation in the press. Not officially, because that would be counterproductive. Objecting to his accreditation would embarrass the British government, Lord Salisbury wrote to Chamberlain. It would raise questions in the capitals of Europe and, before you knew it, that wretched arbitration business would raise its ugly head again. A disastrous scenario. Next, they would also be challenging Britain's suzerainty over the Transvaal.[148]

That was the last thing Salisbury or Chamberlain wanted. Britain was making good progress with its colonial ambitions. In the summer of 1898, they would actually be sitting at the negotiation table with Germany to stake their claims in southern Africa. This had come about because of Portugal's ongoing financial problems. The Portuguese had turned to London to secure a loan, offering the revenue from their colonies as security. Berlin had got wind of this and proposed talks. The British government had agreed. The two countries had discussed the matter—without Portugal—and then proceeded to negotiate in earnest. Their talks culminated in a British–German treaty, signed on 30 August 1898.

It had far-reaching implications. If there was to be a loan, they would extend it jointly. As security, Britain claimed the revenues from central Angola and Mozambique south of the Zambezi—including Delagoa Bay. The Germans would get the proceeds from the rest. If Portugal failed to recover financially, they would divide its colonial territories between themselves according to the same formula. This arrangement was a strategic coup for Britain, regardless of how things turned out for Portugal. At least Germany was out of the running for Delagoa Bay. It made no difference that Portugal managed to save its colonies by taking a loan in Paris: they had pre-empted an alliance between Germany and the Transvaal.[149]

This wasn't their only successful manoeuvre. A new opportunity soon presented itself, this time in North Africa, where the age-old colonial rivalry between Britain and France was building up and threatening to erupt into a violent confrontation. The British imperialists' vision of the Union Jack spanning the continent from the Cape to Cairo was incompatible with the French colonial party's dream of the tricolour flying over Africa, from the Niger to the Nile. At some point the north-south and east-west lines would inevitably intersect. This happened at Fashoda, on the upper reaches of the Nile in present-day southern Sudan, in September 1898.

The main local protagonists were Major Jean-Baptiste Marchand and Lord Kitchener of Khartoum, two unevenly matched forces. Marchand limped in with barely a hundred men at the end of a gruelling two-year tramp through the African jungle. Meanwhile, Kitchener had arrived with a victorious army, straight from the city where he had defeated the formidable Sudanese Mahdi, and whose name he was subsequently entitled to use. If it had come to a battle, there was no doubt who would have won. But it never reached that point. The hostilities went no further than Marchand hoisting the French tricolour and Kitchener the Egyptian flag under protest. The conflict was thus taken to the level at which it belonged, that of international power politics.

In London, Lord Salisbury and Chamberlain confidently picked up the gauntlet. Their opposite number in Paris was Théophile Delcassé, the foreign minister, who was no less certain than they that his claims were justified, and no less driven by imperialist zeal. The big difference lay in the trumps the two sides could and were actually prepared to play. In that respect the game was just as unequal as Fashoda had been. Politically, Salisbury and Chamberlain were firmly in power, safe in the knowledge that their backs were covered by the recent treaty with Germany, and that they outnumbered their opponents in the region. Delcassé was in the middle of a political crisis. He received no support from his Russian ally, and was powerless to change the military balance of power. It was true that France had a far bigger army than Britain, but how could you get your soldiers to Africa as long as Britannia ruled the waves? There was nothing to do but pass. On 3 November 1898 Delcassé instructed Marchand to call the whole thing off.[150]

Britain was doing well on all colonial fronts. Chamberlain had every reason to gloat. France had been cut off from North Africa. Agreements with Germany had been bought off with Portuguese territory. Britain held sway over southern Africa. Now there were just the Boers. There was still a memorandum from Pretoria from six months earlier. Probably some nit-picking over that suzerainty business, and it was undoubtedly Leyds's doing. It still had to be dealt with. Chamberlain's staff had advised him not to respond to any of the points it raised, especially not the question of arbitration. Ignore it, they said, and rather insist on some issue that was open to debate; that always gets them flustered. It was 15 December 1898. Chamberlain began to dictate.

Last chances

Atlantic Ocean, January 1899

Reconciliation. A plan to keep the peace. Resolve the differences between Pretoria and Johannesburg. Hold talks in a spirit of mutual understanding. Make concessions. It wouldn't be easy but it was certainly worth the try. War would destroy everything. It was a question of getting the right people and doing the right things in the right order. He had an idea.

Willem Leyds didn't waste his time on trivialities during the voyage from Southampton to Cape Town. War or peace, the future of South Africa, the survival of the Transvaal as an independent state. He was on his way to Pretoria to report his findings in Europe after his first six months as the Transvaal's official agent. He had plenty to think about, and at sea everything fell into place. There could only be one conclusion. No matter how fiercely he defended the Boer cause, the problem could not be solved by diplomatic exchanges or press campaigns. The problem was in the Transvaal itself. It lay in the conflict with the Randlords and the Uitlanders.

Only when that was resolved would there be a reasonable chance of winning the support of the gold-mining shareholders, the politicians and public opinion in the European countries that mattered—France, Germany and Russia. Only then would the Boers be in a position to cast themselves as the injured party, driven into a corner by Britain's lust for power. As long as the conflict persisted, people would continue to believe that the Boers were in part to blame, that they blackmailed the mine owners and discriminated against their employees. Diplomacy and public relations could not move mountains.

On 28 January 1899, Leyds was back in Pretoria, where he had lived and worked for almost 14 years. Little had changed in the past six months except for the incumbents of two key positions. When Leyds became an envoy, his position as state secretary was taken over by the former president of the Orange Free State, F.W. Reitz, with whom Kruger had sought closer ties of friendship in 1889. Reitz had been obliged to resign for health reasons, but he had since recovered and was keen to continue his political career in the Transvaal. The young Jan Smuts was the new state attorney, on the brink of a long and dazzling career. Both men had been born in the Cape Colony and had studied law in Britain, from where

111

they returned with their fanatical Afrikaner nationalism intact. Sons of the soil with knowledge of the world—it showed in all they did. Self-assured, erudite Boers with an easy commanding presence, a quality Leyds the Hollander had never managed to cultivate. Together with the old president they formed the new leadership in Pretoria, spanning three generations: Kruger was already 73, Reitz 54 and Smuts 28 years old.

All three agreed with Leyds's ideas about reconciliation with Johannesburg and the intermediary he had in mind: Eduard Lippert, cousin of Alfred Beit, the uncrowned king of the Rand. Lippert was also the nuisance from the days of the railway and dynamite affairs, but after the Jameson Raid and the support he'd given Leyds in Germany, he had become a trusted friend. He presented the opening bid to representatives of the mining industry in late February 1899. The Transvaal government was offering to make substantial concessions on three points: it would amend the terms of the dynamite monopoly, relax the rules on the enfranchisement of Uitlanders and appoint a 'treasurer' to put the state's financial affairs in order. In return, Pretoria wanted the mine owners to stop the press from agitating against the government, and to distance themselves from the South African League.

It was a genuine attempt to negotiate a deal. At first the prospects looked good. A number of Randlords were sufficiently interested to consider further talks—and put forward serious counter-proposals. Kruger emphasised his honourable intentions in three reconciliatory speeches, in Heidelberg (18 March), Rustenburg (27 March) and Johannesburg (1 April). If it had come to an agreement, he would have been honoured for this spectacular Great Deal. And Leyds, the man behind it, might have gone down in history as Willem the Conciliator.

But that was not to be. Honesty has to come from both sides. At least one of their negotiating partners was not playing the game. Percy FitzPatrick had been one of the Johannesburg conspirators sentenced for complicity in the Jameson Raid, first to death, then to imprisonment and in the end to a fine. The remissions had not appeased him. He still harboured a grudge against the Boer regime and against Kruger and Leyds in particular. The mere fact that he had been chosen to liaise on the mine owners' behalf gave pause for thought. Even so, the Boer leaders gave him the benefit of the doubt.

Smuts had several confidential meetings with him, unaware that FitzPatrick's real intention was to sabotage the talks. In close consultation with his superiors in London, Beit and Wernher, and the British representative in Pretoria, Conyngham Greene—and through him with the high commissioner in Cape Town, Sir Alfred Milner—FitzPatrick brought the episode to an abrupt end in late March 1899. He leaked the outcome of the secret talks to English-language newspapers in Johannesburg, Cape Town and London—with the expected results. At the beginning of April everything was out in the open, and anyone who had stuck out their neck went back on their word. The Great Deal had fizzled out, the opportunity to reach an internal solution between Pretoria and Johannesburg had passed. This was driven home by a petition drawn up by the South African League around the same time. Addressed to Queen Victoria, it was an appeal signed by 21,000 Uitlanders for measures to improve their legal status in the Transvaal.[151]

Leyds wasn't around to witness the failure of his initiative. He had left Pretoria on 24 March 1899 to resume his life in Europe. He had a superficial encounter with Milner in Cape Town—the two men exchanged pleasantries, not a word about politics—and he completed a last chore. Chamberlain's dispatch of 15 December 1898 on the question of suzerainty still needed a reply. Kruger and Reitz had asked Leyds to deal with it. He was, after all, their expert in that field. He hadn't managed to work on it in Pretoria. Only in Cape Town was he able to give it his full attention. He sent his draft to Pretoria at the very last minute, before embarking for Europe on 30 March.

All the talk on board the *Carisbrooke Castle* was about the looming war and the rapidly fading chance of peace. Most of the British passengers feared that war was inevitable. It would also have 'the support of the entire British nation'. Leyds found their conversation depressing. Two months earlier, on the voyage out, he had been optimistic. This time the waves broke against the ship's hull like ominous portents. 'It is clear that after the Fashoda Incident and its coalition with Germany, Britain considers itself master of the whole world.'[152]

Sir Alfred Milner was pleasantly surprised. Radical reforms in Pretoria, including recognition of British paramountcy in the whole of southern Africa—either that or war. This was what he had demanded in his Graaff-Reinet speech, more than a year earlier. He had been preparing himself for it ever since, and growing more and more impatient. Reconciliation between the Boers and the Randlords, disregarding Britain's imperial claims, would have been a disaster, he felt. So he was pleased when FitzPatrick torpedoed the Great Deal. Add to that the Uitlanders' widely supported petition to Queen Victoria and it was obvious: this was a golden opportunity to mobilise public opinion in Britain and put pressure on Chamberlain to take action.

They mustn't throw away another opportunity. That had happened a few months earlier around Christmas 1898, when the Uitlanders had first appealed to the British head of state. It had been in response to the death of an English boilermaker, Tom Edgar. He had been shot in his own home by a Johannesburg policeman who had come to arrest him. The authorities maintained it was self-defence. To the British community it was murder, committed by one of the despicable 'Zarps'. A Tom Edgar Relief Committee was set up with help from the South African League, and thousands of Uitlanders demonstrated in the streets. They called for a hearing of the policeman, who was out on bail, better protection against random actions by the police, and more political rights. Those demands were set out in a petition, which was presented to Her Majesty's representative in Cape Town a few days later.

Milner was in London for talks at the time. The reaction of his deputy, Lieutenant-General Sir William Butler, commander-in-chief of the British troops in South Africa, came as a shock. Butler was sympathetic to the Boers, that much was known, and he had little time for the Uitlanders. That was no secret either. But no one had expected him to refuse the petition—as he did. Moreover, he informed Chamberlain that it was 'all a prepared business', fabricated by the South African League, whom he considered the 'direct descendants' of the raiders and reformers of 1895. Butler was sure that Rhodes was behind it.

But he was wrong about that. It was FitzPatrick—in the wings—who had orchestrated it. Milner probably forgave him for the mistake when he got back to Cape Town. But what he didn't forgive was Butler's refusal to accept the petition. It was an unspeakable act of defiance, which Milner called 'out-Krugering Kruger'. It was a flagrant and inexcusable breach of his carefully planned policies. If it were up to him, Butler would have been stripped of his command. And in time, he actually was. Six months later, Butler was forced to resign.

Milner didn't have to wait that long for another chance to correct Butler's error. At the end of March 1899, he received the second petition from the Uitlanders, which was potentially explosive, as he knew from his experience as a journalist for the *Pall Mall Gazette*. If it was used properly, the voting issue could swell into a 'stirring battle cry' in Britain itself—that's where it had to happen.

Milner had already taken care of public opinion in South Africa. He was on good terms with the editor-in-chief of the *Cape Times* and had the support of two Transvaal newspapers owned by Wernher, Beit & Co. *The Star* had been the leading English-language newspaper on the Rand for years, and in March it had been joined by the *Transvaal Leader*. Both papers had been instrumental in stirring up complaints from the

Uitlanders, which they did with renewed vigour when the negotiations between Pretoria and Johannesburg fell through. The chief editor of *The Star*, William Monypenny, played a prominent role. He had come from Fleet Street specially to add a toxic finishing touch to the rabble-rousing and to work as correspondent for *The Times* in England.

Things were going well in Johannesburg as far as Milner was concerned. FitzPatrick and Monypenny were the perfect firebrands to keep stoking the flame of nationalism. Now the spark needed to catch in London, which was more of a problem. The Uitlanders' second petition attracted attention and support, in government circles and from the public, but it failed to provoke the conflagration Milner had been hoping for. To his annoyance South Africa disappeared from the front pages in the course of April. What should he do? Too much pressure on Chamberlain would be counterproductive, he had seen that. There was nothing for it but to steel himself and wait for another opportunity.

It came a couple of weeks later. Chamberlain made the opening move. He needed a hot-blooded statement from the high commissioner for the Blue Book he was having compiled about the latest developments in the Transvaal. That he could get. But Milner put extra work into it and added 'some vitriol' of his own. The result is known as the 'Helot Dispatch'. The Boers, Milner wrote, were reducing thousands of British subjects to slavery, like the helots of ancient Sparta. Their appeals to the British government had been futile. What were they waiting for? 'The case for intervention is overwhelming', he concluded. The regime in Pretoria had nothing to offer except malicious lies about Britain's intentions.

Milner realised perfectly well it was a gamble. By the same token, Chamberlain might have felt pressured by the urgency of his tone. Or the explicit call for intervention might raise objections in the Cabinet. This time he didn't have to wait long. On 9 May 1899, he received a telegram saying, 'The despatch is approved. We have adopted your suggestion.' That was wonderful news. Chamberlain was in agreement and, by the looks of it, Lord Salisbury too. Whitehall agreed to immediate intervention: peaceful intervention for the time being, but one thing leads to another. Milner was sure that when the Blue Book was published, his Helot Dispatch would jolt the British public out of their complacency.

The only pity was that pacifists were suddenly starting to crawl out of the woodwork. First, Prime Minister Schreiner and Jan Hofmeyr in the Cape Colony, followed by President Steyn in the Orange Free State. They insisted on a personal meeting with Kruger. Milner was against it, but with the world looking on, he could hardly refuse. Chamberlain thought it a good idea. The publication of the Blue Book was postponed for the time being.

On 31 May 1899, Milner reported at the place Steyn had proposed for the meeting, the railway station in Bloemfontein. He came not to negotiate but to issue an ultimatum: full electoral rights for all Uitlanders after five years' residence, with immediate and retroactive effect, and seven representatives in the Volksraad. His only fear was that Kruger, the sly old fox, would actually concede—and start haggling afterwards. That would put Milner back to square one. He would have to start building up the tension all over again. His best hope was that the Bloemfontein Conference would fail.

It did. Kruger had not come to the talks in the capital of the Orange Free State with high expectations, but he did observe the rules of the game. Concessions and compromises. On the third day, for instance, he produced a carefully prepared reform bill, like a rabbit out of a hat. Five seats in the Volksraad for the gold-mining districts and voting rights for Uitlanders within variable time frames: within two to seven years, depending on how long they had been in the Transvaal.

Relative to the population demographics, this was a substantial concession. According to the most recent census, published in the *State Almanac for the South African Republic* of 1899, the electorate—adult male Boers—comprised fewer than 30,000 voters. The total white population in the Transvaal had grown to almost ten times that number: 290,000 men, women and children. The statistics further included a coloured population of 600,000. Of the white population in Johannesburg and its immediate surroundings, over 50,000 were male Uitlanders. Once they were armed with voting rights, there were more than enough of them to significantly impact the political balance of power in the Transvaal.[153]

Kruger's offer came close to meeting Milner's demands. Promisingly close, thought Chamberlain, who promptly congratulated Milner by telegram. Dangerously close, thought Milner, who raised countless objections and warned Chamberlain that the talks were on the brink of collapse. The reaction from London—keep going, 'Boers do not understand quick decisions'—reached him too late. On 5 June 1899 Milner walked out of the conference, free to return to his original plan and provoke a head-on confrontation.[154]

Joe Chamberlain spent a long time dithering. He agreed with his high commissioner in South Africa that they would have to bring Kruger to his knees. But so much the better if they could achieve this by diplomatic means. It wouldn't need to come to an armed struggle as long as the old Boer leader accepted Britain's terms: equal rights for the Uitlanders. They had made such an issue of it that they couldn't back down without losing face. But the most contentious issue was British supremacy in South Africa. This was something Kruger would have to acknowledge, one way or another, officially and in practice.

That is why Chamberlain was troubled by Pretoria's reply to his letter of 15 December 1898 on the question of suzerainty. It was dated 9 May 1899 and had presumably been written by someone other than Leyds—Leyds had left Pretoria at the end of March. The hair-splitting in some of the legal passages was still obviously his work, but one sentence was unusually hard-hitting. It argued that the Transvaal's right to self-determination was not based on the London Convention of 1884, but was simply a right in itself. Leyds had never expressed himself with such self-confidence—well, presumption in fact. Milner was taken aback. Chamberlain also considered the Transvaal's claim to full sovereign status unacceptable. He saw it as a threat to 'our position as the paramount power in South Africa'.[155]

This would certainly justify tightening the diplomatic thumbscrews on the Boer republic. But war? Chamberlain hadn't reached that point in June 1899. Milner's haste to break off the talks with Kruger in Bloemfontein had alarmed him and the entire staff of the Colonial Office—with the exception of the under-secretary, Lord Selborne, Milner's rock and anchor through thick and thin. Moreover, if it came to an armed confrontation, Chamberlain would be dependent on the War Ministry for troops—and that was more than just a formal obstacle. Lord Lansdowne headed a decaying and hopelessly divided department, which was blasé about the military threat posed by the Boers. They had made no preparations of any significance.

The country as a whole was not yet fired up for war. Newspapers like *The Times* and the *Morning Post* beat the drum for the Uitlanders as best they could. On Milner's advice Percy FitzPatrick published a hawkish book, *The Transvaal from Within*, which became the bestseller of the summer season. But there were other opinions as well. The Blue Book, which incorporated the Helot Dispatch, was not enough to get the fires burning. There were murmurs of scepticism and dismay. The satirical weekly magazine *Punch* showed a very different 'South African helot': well fed, with a heavy gold chain standing for wealth not slavery, stylish clothes and a jewelled tie pin. 'Such a man may be many things, but a helot he is not.'[156]

For a while the threat of war seemed to have passed. In mid-July 1899, Pretoria agreed to more concessions than Kruger had already proposed in

117

Bloemfontein. A new law gave the Uitlanders six seats in the Volksraad and voting rights after seven years, with retroactive effect. This prompted Chamberlain to congratulate Milner—again. It prompted Milner to warn his minister—again—to watch out for the traps and pitfalls in the Boers' proposal. He also had a counter-proposal. A joint (British–Transvaal) commission of inquiry to look into the franchise issue from all angles.

Selborne agreed immediately, which helped to get Chamberlain 'back on the old right tack'. On 28 July 1899, in the only House of Commons session that dealt with South Africa that year, he was far less enthusiastic about the latest reforms in Pretoria. It wasn't about getting voting rights two years earlier or later, he said. It wasn't about the petty details. A special committee—he had learned from Milner's advice—would be in a better position to judge all of that. No, this was about something more fundamental. It was about 'the power and authority of the British Empire . . . It is the question of our predominance.' This was a clear statement and it persuaded both the government and opposition parties. Parliament was satisfied and went into recess. The Cabinet members went off to their summer residences, Chamberlain to Highbury, his country estate in Birmingham, to devote himself to his orchids. The proposal to set up a joint commission of inquiry was put to the Transvaal government.

Three weeks later, on 19 August 1899, a reply came from Pretoria. They saw a joint commission as an infringement of the Transvaal's autonomy and rejected the proposal on those grounds. But Kruger came up with a new offer which, on the face of it, seemed extraordinary. Voting rights for the Uitlanders after five years, with retroactive force, and ten seats for the Rand in a Volksraad that would be enlarged to a total of 36 members. That was even more than Milner had asked for in Bloemfontein. But there was one string attached. In return the British government would have to renounce its claims to suzerainty and stop meddling in the Transvaal's internal affairs.

It seemed like a final offer, a last concession—and it was. But that made no difference to the way it was received in Cape Town and London. The authorities there reacted exactly the way they had on previous occasions. Milner rejected the offer out of hand as yet another ploy by the Boer leader, an inadequate concession that failed to take account of Britain's status 'as the Paramount Power in South Africa'. Chamberlain needed a few more days. In his initial reaction he called it 'a complete climb down' on Kruger's part and told Lord Salisbury that the crisis had been warded off. But on 24 August it turned out that he had changed his mind after hearing Milner's arguments. And this time, there would be no turning back. Now, he conveyed a very different message to the prime minister and the secretary for war, Lord Lansdowne. He said the Boers would have to clarify their offer and withdraw their conditions, which were totally unacceptable. If they failed to do so within a week to ten days, they were presumably not interested in peace. In that event, Britain would immediately dispatch an expeditionary force of 10,000 men. Two days later Chamberlain ran out of patience. In a speech delivered from the lawns of Highbury Hall, he repeated his warning to Kruger. He said the president of the Transvaal had set impossible conditions and was withholding the details of his reform proposals. Things couldn't continue like this. 'The sands are running down in the glass.'[157]

The threat was clear. But Kruger made no further concessions. On the contrary, he withdrew his second offer and left the question of a joint commission open. Too half-hearted, in Chamberlain's opinion. On his instructions, Lord Salisbury summoned the Cabinet members back to London.

The Cabinet convened on 8 September 1899. Chamberlain presented a memorandum, summarising his standpoint once again. The Uitlanders were being treated as 'an inferior race, little better than Kaffirs or Indians'. Great Britain's position was being jeopardised in South Africa, as was its prestige in its colonies and the rest of the world. The president of the Transvaal was unwilling to accede to the justified demands of the British government. They had no choice but to bare their teeth. Chamberlain assured the honourable members that this did not necessarily mean war. Kruger had the reputation of being a man who would 'bluff up to the cannon's mouth and then capitulate'. An expeditionary force of 10,000 men would persuade him that they were in earnest. This would probably make him give up.

Not all the ministers agreed with Chamberlain's point of view and certainly not with his aggressive tone, but his last argument—Kruger's notorious posturing—won them over. The Cabinet agreed to the immediate dispatch of an expeditionary force. Once it arrived in Natal, probably at the beginning of October, they would issue an ultimatum.

The prime minister, Lord Salisbury, had the last word. He was sombre. He didn't believe that Kruger would back down. He had no doubt they were heading for war, for Britain possibly the biggest since the Crimean War. He bitterly regretted it, especially as the stakes were so low, 'all for people whom we despise and for territory which will bring no power to England'. But there was no other choice. He knew that South Africa was strategically too important to the British Empire. Some time earlier, he had expressed these thoughts to his son-in-law Lord Selborne, the under-secretary for the colonies: 'The real point to be made good to South Africa is that we, not the Dutch, are Boss.'[158]

Paul Kruger stood firm: no more concessions. Chamberlain wanted war: that much was obvious from his doom-laden speech of 26 August. And the same message was there, in as many words, in the letter he wrote two days later. For months Kruger had done everything in his power to meet Britain's demands. This was the result. Kruger no longer believed in Britain's good faith. 'It is our country you want,' he had snapped back at Milner on the last day of their talks in Bloemfontein in early June. It was now two months later, 2 September 1899, and he had been proved right. More than that, it was not only Milner; 'Camberlen' too wanted to incorporate the Transvaal in the British Empire. There was no doubt in Kruger's mind. No matter how much the Boers in the Cape Colony and the Orange Free State pleaded for further negotiations, he no longer believed anything could come of it. He had done enough listening. Schreiner and Hofmeyr, Steyn and his right-hand man, Abraham Fischer, and of course his own state secretary and state attorney, Reitz and Smuts—all of them had given him well-intentioned advice, but look where it had led.

It had all started with the Great Deal, in early April. It was the capitalists who had sabotaged it, there was no denying that, but it had also been naive to trust FitzPatrick. Moreover, the reply to Chamberlain's suzerainty letter, in early May, had been carelessly worded. Leyds had prepared a draft, in his usual meticulous style, but Reitz—or Smuts, he wasn't sure which—had added those passages about the Transvaal's inherent rights as an independent state under international law. They had struck the wrong chord with Milner and Chamberlain, and Reitz had been forced to back down in their further communications.

To say nothing of the frustrating voting rights they had talked him into conceding—completely against his will. First, his proposal to Milner at the Bloemfontein Conference in early June. Then the reform bill that the Volksraad passed in mid-July. Finally, the last offer of 19 August, making even more concessions than Milner had asked for. And the outcome? Threats from Chamberlain. The more Kruger conceded, the more the British demanded. What more could he do? Young Boers were clamouring to drive the British into the sea. Friendly governments urged discretion. A decision had to be taken. There would be war.

The Rand had already drawn that conclusion. In the first six months of 1899 the gold mines had produced record yields, but in the South African winter of that year Johannesburg and its surrounds found themselves facing a reverse gold rush. In August it was almost an exodus. Tens of thousands of black miners were laid off. An even greater number of Uitlanders were looking for somewhere else to go. In September there was utter panic. A stampede of miners, craftsmen, barkeepers and prostitutes. Anyone lucky enough to squeeze into a train, an oxwagon or any other vehicle fled to the Cape Colony or Natal. By late September most of the gold mines had shut down. Johannesburg became just another quiet, provincial town.[159]

In Pretoria, too, everyone was preparing to leave—for the front. Reitz and Smuts agreed with Kruger. There was no way to avoid a war, certainly not after the Cabinet meeting of 8 September 1899, when the British decided to send out an expeditionary force. It would take a month for the troops to reach South Africa. They had to put the time to good use. Smuts hastily worked out a plan. He was in favour of a surprise attack. The Boers were by far in the majority. If they invaded Natal without delay, they could easily push through to Durban and seize the artillery and munitions they found there, thus depriving the British of their nearest supply port. In all likelihood the Afrikaners in the Cape Colony would join in and fight with them. With a third Boer republic against them, the British would have a hard time of it. And France, Russia and Germany wouldn't hesitate to take advantage of the situation.[160]

The plan didn't sound unreasonable, but Smuts never had the opportunity to see it in action. The Orange Free State, President Steyn to be exact, wasn't ready to take the step. He still believed in a peaceful solution and kept offering suggestions. Kruger dutifully considered them. He thought it a waste of time, but he was unwilling to antagonise his ally by launching an attack on his own. As a result, he spent weeks waiting for Bloemfontein.

Smuts was too fired up to wait. To occupy himself usefully in the meantime, he started writing a historical pamphlet, with the help of Jacob de Villiers Roos. *A Century of Wrong* was an impassioned protest against 'our oppression and persecution during the past hundred years'. It was meant to rally Afrikaners throughout the country, in the two British colonies as well as the two Boer republics, to resist 'an unjust and hated Government 7000 miles away'. The Boers were the heroes, the British the villains. The piece was rhetorical and demagogic, even by nineteenth-century standards.

It portrayed the British as hypocrites motivated by 'a spirit of annexation and plunder which has at all times characterised its dealings with our people'. They had a 'morbid love of the natives', which wasn't *that* so much as 'hatred and contempt of the Boer'. After the discovery of the republic's mineral wealth, they had harnessed their old insidious policies to the new forces of capitalism and drawn a 'cordon of beasts of plunder and birds of prey . . . around this poor doomed people'.

In spite of their 'great sacrifices . . . and the many vicissitudes' they had endured, the Boers possessed 'a dignity which reminds the world of a greater and more painful example of suffering'. They had pursued their 'pilgrimage of martyrdom throughout South Africa, until every portion of that unhappy country has been painted red with the blood, not so much of men capable of resistance as with that of our murdered and defenceless women and children'. Through it all they had clung to 'the Righteousness which . . . proceeds according to eternal laws, unmoved by human pride and ambition'.

The last chapter sounded like a reply to the Helot Dispatch. Milner was from Oxford, Smuts from Cambridge and at least as well versed in the classics. He likened Britain, which was conveying 'troops from every corner of the globe in order to smash this little handful of people', to the Persian king Xerxes 'with his millions against little Greece'. And the Boers, of course, were the Spartans, Leonidas 'with his 300 men when they advanced unflinchingly at Thermopylae against Xerxes and his myriads'. And 'whether the result be Victory or Death, Liberty will assuredly rise in South Africa like the sun from out of the mists of the morning, just as Freedom dawned over the United States of America a little more than a century ago. Then from the Zambezi to Simon's Bay it will be "Africa for the Africander".'[161]

By 28 September 1899 Kruger had grown tired of waiting. A few days earlier he had heard that the British expeditionary force would be followed by a complete army corps. The Transvaal mobilised. On 2 October the Orange Free State did the same. Even Steyn saw no way out.

Willem Leyds felt uncomfortable. He was doing the best he could for the Boer cause, but he was miles away. His business was diplomacy and public relations; he was no longer involved with policy. He travelled back and forth between Brussels, The Hague, Paris and Amsterdam, and occasionally Berlin. It was useful, he got things done, but still. 'I wish I were in Pretoria,' he wrote to two of his confidants in the Transvaal in mid-August 1899. 'I believe in all modesty that I could be of some use.' The government consulted him frequently, his telegraph bills were high, but 'one can say far more in person than by cable from a distance'.[162]

Not only by way of encouragement. Leyds was also critical of his successors in Pretoria. They kept vacillating, he felt. They were either too assertive or too submissive. The best example was their reply to

Chamberlain's suzerainty letter. All his hard work had been ruined by the rash sentence they had added to it, and Chamberlain was quick to exploit his advantage. Leyds was also critical of the tone of the voting rights proposals. The wording was extremely important, he said. It sounded as if the concessions had been extracted with a knife at someone's throat. The British didn't like that kind of thing. What's more, Pretoria's indecisiveness made his job as an envoy more difficult. He wasn't informed promptly about new developments, and his instructions were often unclear.

But so be it. It was questionable whether his presence in Pretoria would really have made any difference, as it was now obvious that Milner and Chamberlain were intent on war. Beit, too, for that matter—because Leyds kept a sharp eye on things from his observation post in Europe. 'Everyone with a financial interest in South Africa dances to the tune of Wernher, Beit & Co.,' he said. They were so powerful that 'no one can stand up to them, and to avoid being boycotted they do whatever Beit wants (Wernher is less overbearing) and Beit in turn takes his orders from Chamberlain'.[163]

From reports like this, it seems Leyds was probably more useful in Europe than he would have been in the Transvaal—on the one hand, by keeping Pretoria up to date about the mood in the European capitals, in centres of government and financial circles and among the general public, on the other hand, by supporting the Transvaal and improving its image. He picked up the thread of the pro-Boer campaign he had launched in 1898. It was vitally important. After a visit to Paris in late April 1899, he noted that 'the press have launched another campaign against the Republic'. He had to be vigilant and make sure he exposed all their half-truths and slurs. They targeted him personally as well. The *Financial Times,* for example, reported that he had made money from illicit dealings in gold during his term as state secretary. It was a shot in the dark, but it was hard to disprove. You could deny false allegations, but you couldn't erase them from people's minds.[164]

Some of Leyds's duties were in the public eye, but most of his work took place behind closed doors. His diplomatic activities ranged from finding suitable state investors and organising the Transvaal's entry to the Paris World Fair in 1900, to mediating (this was a sensitive matter) to secure the release of a munitions transport under embargo in Lourenço Marques.

It was a consignment of Mausers and more than three and a half million cartridges, en route from German Weapons and Munitions to Pretoria. In the past few years several arms transports had been sent via Mozambique, but for no apparent reason the Portuguese authorities suddenly started to raise objections—under pressure from Britain, the Transvaal government believed. In mid-August Leyds was instructed to go to Lisbon post-haste to put pressure on the Portuguese from his side as well. He was also advised to inform the German government. After all, the goods came from Germany and were being transported on a German vessel, the *Reichstag*. Leyds followed this advice, although not quite to the letter. He didn't actually go to Lisbon, but handed the Portuguese envoy in Brussels a memorandum of protest and then concentrated on applying pressure indirectly. This he did with help not only from Berlin, but also Paris, because France would soon be shipping arms—two large Creusot guns—along the same route. They would be labelled 'machinery' but, even so, it was better for the French to know about these developments—and use their influence with Portugal. At the end of August the port authorities in Lourenço Marques released the consignment of rifles and munitions.[165]

Thanks to Germany and France. But Pretoria shouldn't be under any illusions, Leyds warned more than once. This time it had been purely in their own interests. If pressed, neither would side against Britain. His telegrams were absolutely explicit. On 3 August 1899 he said, 'if it comes to a war, Germany and France will be cordial towards us and might express that openly, but they won't give us any real support'. His message of 25 September read, 'Germany will do nothing. France would gladly make things difficult for Britain, but one can't depend on them. They're unpredictable. However, the general consensus is that Russia might intervene in Asia.'[166]

Russia might well see a war between Great Britain and the Transvaal as an opportunity to pursue its own interests. Whatever the case, no one expected Tsar Nicholas II to do anything out of conviction. Under pressure from Britain he hadn't invited the Transvaal or the Orange Free State to the Peace Conference held in The Hague from mid-May to the end of July 1899. Leyds had avoided The Hague throughout that period. 'I'm in a rather tight spot,' he had said.[167]

But he was gratified to see that the exclusion of the two Boer republics had unleashed a storm of protest in the Netherlands, in the press and in parliament. That was reassuring in itself, although the criticism was targeted, unfairly, at the foreign minister, Willem de Beaufort. Abraham Kuyper, the leader of the Anti-Revolutionary Party, went so far as to hold the minister personally responsible for the snub against 'the two Dutch commonwealths' and accused him of 'unforgivable weakness'. Leyds knew better. It had all been arranged beforehand. De Beaufort had only two options: conference or no conference, in The Hague or anywhere else.

Leyds also knew that all the fuss in the Netherlands had no impact on the rest of the world, least of all in Britain. In the spring, the Dutch

Women's Association had presented a petition with 200,000 signatures to Tsar Nicholas II, endorsing his peace initiative. In August the Dutch South African Association had collected 140,000 signatures in support of an impassioned appeal on behalf of the Boers, addressed 'To the People of Great Britain'. The petitions were received politely, but at this stage they carried no weight at all. They were well-meant but irrelevant.[168]

Leyds had reached this conclusion a few months earlier, after a similar campaign in the Transvaal that actually *could* have made a difference. A petition to Queen Victoria from 21,000 Uitlanders in late March 1899 was followed two months later by a second petition from 23,000—dissenting—Uitlanders. The text read, 'We disagree with the sentiments and opinions expressed in the memorial [the first petition to Queen Victoria] because we know that life and property are as safe and secure in the S.A. Republic as in any part of the civilized world.' The signatories, unlike the South African League, stood firmly behind the government of the Transvaal. It was clear that the immigrant community on the Rand was sharply divided over the Kruger regime.

Pretoria made sure the British government was aware of the second petition, and sent copies to Berlin, Paris, The Hague and Washington as well. But after that—perhaps even more surprising than the petition itself—nothing at all happened. There was no response whatsoever, although the earlier appeal to Queen Victoria resounded in the British press for a long time afterwards. Leyds had got the message. The time for public petitions had passed. It all came down to power politics.[169]

This point of view was reflected in an extraordinary correspondence that Leyds conducted from mid-July to the end of September 1899. It started with a letter from his old mentor and friend Moltzer, who was a member of the Dutch Council of State and still deeply concerned with the fate of the Boers. Was there anything the Dutch government could do to prevent a war with England? If so, he would take it up at once with Prime Minister Nicolaas Pierson, whom Leyds knew well.

Leyds thought there was. He made a suggestion but it fell flat with his other teacher. The idea was an urgent appeal from the Dutch Queen Wilhelmina—'a young girl on the threshold of her career'—to Queen Victoria—'an older woman nearing the end of her life'—but Pierson thought it too much of a gamble. He wasn't prepared to risk 'compromising the Queen'. He also made it clear—on behalf of the foreign minister De Beaufort, as well—that nothing could be expected from 'the Dutch Government as such'. Like everyone else, the Netherlands was too dependent on mighty Britain, not least because of the vulnerable Dutch East Indies.[170]

The correspondence might have ended there had Pierson not offered to take action in a personal capacity. He was close friends with George Goschen, First Lord of the Admiralty and thus a member of the Salisbury government. He suggested that a personal letter might help to change the British Cabinet's standpoint, from the inside. The Dutch prime minister respected the British and believed they were open to reason. In fact he was known to be 'an anglophile and admitted it himself'. He made no secret of his conviction that the Transvaal 'should have pursued a liberal policy' far earlier and should have moved towards 'admitting the British on the same terms as the Dutch'. If Leyds approved, Pierson was prepared to have a word with Goschen.

Leyds was not in favour but thanked him politely for the offer. What followed was a rather schizophrenic exchange of letters between the two men. On the one side Pierson, who reported to Leyds about his increasingly hopeful contacts with Goschen. From this Pierson had concluded that 'there is a strong pacifist trend in the British Cabinet'. On the other side Leyds, who observed academic decorum by addressing Pierson as 'Learned Professor', only to tell him, with indecorous bluntness, what he thought of his optimism. On 22 August 1899 he wrote, 'You still believe in the possibility of winning Goschen over. I don't.' Pierson kept on writing, nevertheless, to Goschen as well as Leyds. On 26 September he wrote again about 'a pacifist movement in the British Cabinet'. The Transvaal shouldn't allow its understandable mistrust of Britain to stand in the way of concessions, he argued. Bilingualism could actually work. Take the Belgian parliament, for example.[171]

His words fell on deaf ears. Fifteen years earlier Pierson had managed to persuade an ambivalent young lawyer to seek his fortune in South Africa, dwelling on the excellent prospects that awaited him as state attorney. Now he was trying to convince a sceptical statesman that concessions were the answer, elaborating on the opportunities for peace that were still open in London. His efforts were to no avail. Leyds no longer believed in it. Nor did he have any confidence left in the British Cabinet. It was time to get things over and done with.

That's what he told Pretoria. He wrote to Reitz on 6 October, 'The whole of Europe is wondering why the Boers don't start the war, after telling or rather asking the British to withdraw their troops. Everyone thinks it's suicide to wait for a large British force to arrive in Natal.' On 9 October he mentioned Europe's bewilderment again. A day later, on Kruger's 74th birthday, Leyds received the telegram he had long been expecting. The Boers had issued their ultimatum. The war would begin the following day.[172]

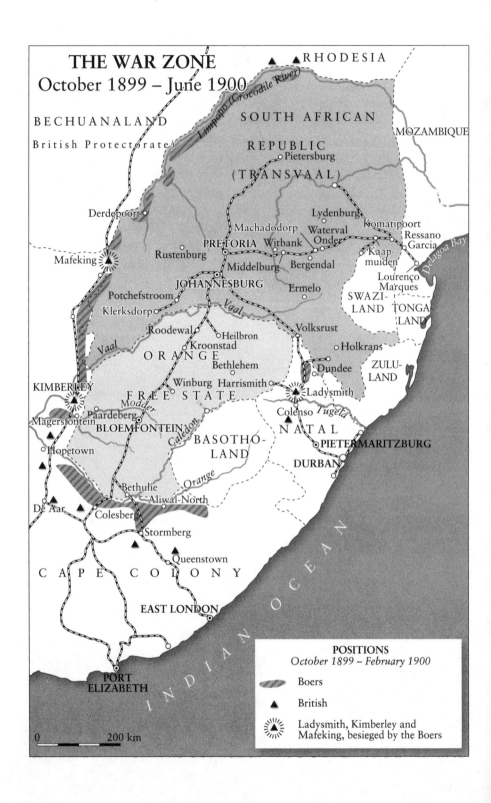

THE WAR ZONE
October 1899 – June 1900

RHODESIA

BECHUANALAND
British Protectorate

SOUTH AFRICAN

MOZAMBIQUE

REPUBLIC

Pietersburg

(TRANSVAAL)

Derdepoort

Lydenburg
Machadodorp Waterval Komatipoort
PRETORIA Witbank Onder Ressano
Rustenburg Garcia
Mafeking Middelburg Bergendal Kaap-
muiden
JOHANNESBURG Lourenço
Ermelo Marques
Potchefstroom SWAZI-
Klerksdorp LAND TONGA-
Vaal LAND
Roodewal Heilbron Volksrust
Kroonstad Holkrans
ORANGE Bethlehem
Vaal ZULU-
FREE STATE Dundee LAND
KIMBERLEY Winburg Harrismith
Modder Ladysmith
Paardeberg Colenso Tugela
Magersfontein BLOEMFONTEIN NATAL
Caledon PIETERMARITZBURG
Hopetown BASOTHO-
LAND DURBAN

Bethulie Orange
Aliwal-North
De Aar Colesberg
Stormberg
Queenstown

CAPE COLONY

INDIAN OCEAN

EAST LONDON

PORT
ELIZABETH

0   200 km

POSITIONS
October 1899 – February 1900

Boers

British

Ladysmith, Kimberley and
Mafeking, besieged by the Boers

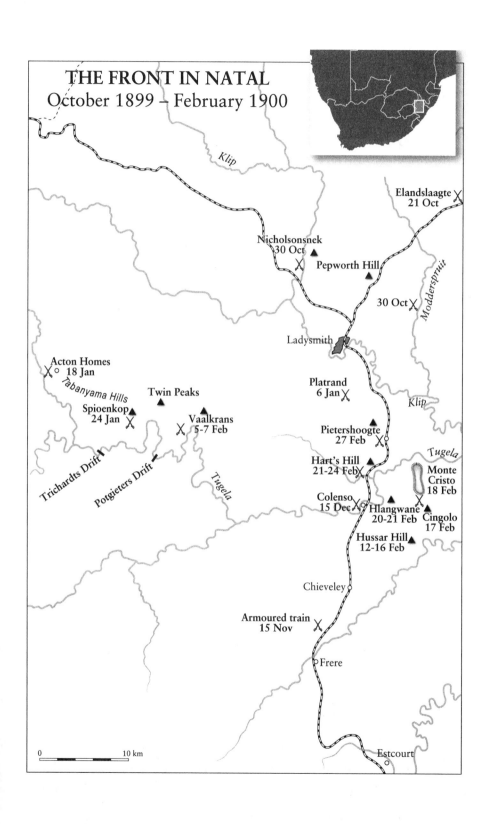

THE FRONT IN NATAL
October 1899 – February 1900

Klip

Elandslaagte ✗
21 Oct

Nicholsonsnek
30 Oct ▲
✗ Pepworth Hill ▲

Moddurspruit

30 Oct ✗

Ladysmith

Acton Homes
✗ ○ 18 Jan

Tabanyama Hills

Platrand
6 Jan ✗

Klip

Twin Peaks ▲

Spioenkop ▲
24 Jan ✗

Vaalkrans
✗ ▲ 5-7 Feb

Pietershoogte ▲
27 Feb ✗ ○

Tugela

Hart's Hill ▲
21-24 Feb ✗

Monte
Cristo ▲
18 Feb

Trichardts Drift ▮

Potgieters Drift

Tugela

Colenso ○
15 Dec ✗ ○ Hlangwane ▲
20-21 Feb Cingolo ▲
17 Feb

Hussar Hill ▲
12-16 Feb

Chieveley ○

Armoured train ✗
15 Nov

○ Frere

0   10 km

Estcourt
○

PART II
Like a boys' adventure story

October 1899—June 1900

Winston Churchill

Rule, Britannia!

Southampton, 14 October 1899

Many people, especially in the upper echelons of the army, thought Winston Churchill was nothing but a publicity-seeker and medal-chaser, with his lisp, his wisecracks, his pretentious newspaper articles and his extravagant American mother, whose high-society friends had helped him from one prestigious job to the next. Churchill saw things differently. He knew in his heart that he was destined for something more exalted, or at least more exciting, and there was no time to lose. His father, Lord Randolph, had died young, and he wouldn't live long either, so he believed. To accomplish what fate had in store for him he would have to make his mark soon, distinguish himself, gain a reputation and excel in a political career that in his father's case had been so tragically cut short.

That was why, not yet 25, he had travelled half the world looking for action, the more dangerous the better. He had come under fire from Cuban guerrillas, narrowly escaped the swords of the Pathans on the north-west frontier of British India, and in the Battle of Omdurman in Sudan had experienced the thrill of a cavalry charge against a superior force of Mahdi fighters. All without even a scratch. What he did gain, however, was a reputation as a writer. He had combined his military duties—as second lieutenant in the 4th Hussars—with freelance assignments as a war correspondent for newspapers like the *Daily Graphic,* the *Daily Telegraph* and the *Morning Post.* He had also written a successful book, *The Story of the Malakand Field Force,* recounting his war-time experiences in British India. Two more books, *The River War* about the campaign in Sudan and the novel *Savrola,* were about to be published.

In May 1899 Churchill decided it was time to leave the army and turn his skills to a career in politics. In the mill town of Oldham, near Manchester, he was one of two Conservative candidates who stood for election to the House of Commons. However, they lost to their Liberal opponents and Churchill's thoughts turned to an alternative that would consolidate his reputation and bring in a bit of cash.

An opportunity came his way before long. War was looming over South Africa, that was obvious by September, and every self-respecting British newspaper wanted its own reporter on the spot. Churchill could take his pick. The *Morning Post* was offering £250 a month—a generous sum for a war correspondent—with a contract for at least four months, plus expenses. He could also keep the copyrights, which would come in useful if he ever wanted to use the material for a book. There was someone special in his life, but lacking his mother's amorous temperament, he didn't take long to choose between Pamela Plowden and a new adventure in South Africa. On Saturday 14 October 1899 Churchill stood on the quay at Southampton, ready to embark on the *Dunottar Castle*.[1]

It was the best start one could imagine for an ambitious reporter. In Southampton Churchill witnessed one of the classical opening scenes in the British Empire's rich military history. The commander embarks, the expeditionary force sets off for battlefields at the far ends of the earth. The famous general stands surrounded by his staff officers, men in uniform are mobbed by a doting crowd. Half of Southampton had come to see them off. Daredevils climbed onto the roofs of railway carriages and clambered up the cranes. There was also something new on the quay and, later, on board. The American Mutoscope and Biograph Company was sending out a party of cinematographers to record the battlefields on film. Churchill had thought of that too, but his business associate had let him down. He would just have to rely on his writing. Fortunately his writing skills were good enough, and in any case images couldn't be sent by telegraph.

It took all day for everyone to embark. There were military personnel, civilians, passengers and journalists, heaps of suitcases and trunks, an amazing array of weaponry, horses, polo mallets and bicycles. The commander's special train pulled in at four o'clock sharp. The crowd on the quay roared with excitement. There he was, the man who was going to teach the Boers a lesson: General Sir Redvers Buller VC. He wasn't in uniform, but with his towering stature, long black coat, grey Bismarck moustache and set jaw, he was an awe-inspiring figure. From the gangplank he delivered a few solemn words of farewell. The crowd responded with patriotic zeal, 'Rule, Britannia!', 'God save the Queen', 'For he's a jolly good fellow', and cries of encouragement, 'Give it to the Boers!' and 'Remember Majuba!'

Buller probably didn't want to be reminded of Majuba. He had been in South Africa in February 1881 and witnessed that humiliating British defeat. It had left him with great respect for the Boer commandos' military prowess. He didn't believe this expedition would be as straightforward as many were predicting, and he cringed at the brash 'Home for Christmas!', which those on board and their well-wishers on the quay were calling out to each other.[2]

Buller knew South Africa all too well. He had fought not only the Boers but the Xhosa and Zulu, too, the latter more successfully. He had won his

Victoria Cross at the Battle of Hlobane in Zululand in 1879. And he had been on military expeditions in West Africa, Egypt and China. He had earned his spurs on the battlefield. But that was a long time ago. He hadn't seen active service outside Great Britain since 1886. In the mid-1890s he could have been appointed commander-in-chief, but he'd been passed over and given command of Aldershot, the home base of the 1st (and only) British Army Corps. It was to that position and his earlier war experience that he owed his commission, at the age of almost 60, as commander of all the troops in South Africa. He was succeeding Lieutenant-General Sir William Butler, who had been compelled to resign in August at the insistence of the high commissioner, Sir Alfred Milner.

This could have been an opportunity for him to distinguish himself again in the only way that really mattered to a Victorian general: by leading a victorious campaign against a worthy adversary. But Buller didn't expect it to be easy. There hadn't been time to prepare properly. He was also frustrated at having been excluded when the operation was being planned. In previous overseas expeditions, commanders had been consulted on matters of strategy and the composition of the expeditionary force. But Buller hadn't even been able to appoint his own adjutants. He just had to wait and see what came out of the talks—months of bickering actually— between the war secretary, Lord Lansdowne, and the commander-in-chief, Field Marshal Lord Wolseley.

Since June 1899 Wolseley had been urging Lansdowne to send 10,000 men to the Cape Colony and Natal as quickly as possible, and to mobilise the 1st Army Corps—47,000 men, including reserves—so they would be ready to leave as soon as they were needed. But Lansdowne thought it too early and too expensive. As long as it wasn't certain that there actually would be a war, as long as the secretary for the colonies, Joe Chamberlain, hadn't taken a decision, he felt there was no need to rush. It was also reassuring for Lansdowne to know that his opinion was shared by the local commanding officer in Natal. That's where the Boers were most likely to invade, if it did come to a war. The commander in question, Major-General Sir William Penn Symons, had decided a few days after arriving in Durban—where he was transferred from British India—that 2000 troops would be enough to defend the whole of Natal. Well, make it 5000, he said after thinking it over, but more wouldn't be necessary.

Wolseley, however, had more faith in the judgment of another major-general, one who didn't fire his opinions off like salvos, but based them on facts and figures. Sir John Ardagh, the head of intelligence at the War Office, had a higher regard than Symons for the Boers' military capability. He believed their own side would need many times more troops. The problem was that the 'Military Notes on the Dutch Republics', which had been compiled under Ardagh's supervision, were inconsistent and left room for interpretation. Lansdowne went for the loopholes. He glossed over the disturbing figures and smugly drew Wolseley's attention to the passages that suited his purpose.

Buller wasn't so keen to hear Ardagh's advice either, though for different reasons. He returned the 'Military Notes' by courier, with a message saying he 'already knew everything about South Africa'. He said much the same in a letter he wrote in early September and sent directly to Lord Salisbury—bypassing Lord Lansdowne. He complained about their not having made adequate preparations, which he believed could have serious consequences, and the fact that he, the commander, hadn't been given a say in the planning. Passing over Lord Lansdowne did little to improve Buller's already awkward relationship with the war secretary, but for the time being it didn't affect his commission.

It was hard to say whether the letter made any impression on Lord Salisbury. In any event, it didn't show. And luck was on Buller's side. His letter had arrived the day before the Cabinet meeting of 8 September 1899, when Chamberlain proposed to send an expeditionary force of 10,000 men to South Africa.[3] The other ministers agreed to the proposal, including Lansdowne and Salisbury, which was good news for Wolseley and Buller. At last they had something to do. It wasn't the serious business they had been hoping for, but at least it was a start.

Even this relatively small contingent of troops wasn't easy to raise. One of the problems was the old clan rivalry that was endemic in the British army. There were two competing factions, the 'African' and the 'Indian' rings. Wolseley headed the 'Africans', while the 'Indians', known as Roberts's army, were led by Field Marshal Lord Roberts of Kandahar, who had returned to the United Kingdom a few years earlier as the highest-ranking military officer in Ireland.

It was agreed that British India would provide the 10,000 reinforcements, but the authorities in Calcutta were compelled to reduce the number to 5500 because of unrest on their north-west border. The remainder had to be rustled up elsewhere: a regiment from Malta, a battalion from Alexandria, a brigade from Crete. All were expected to arrive in Durban in mid-October. At that stage, Natal would have a total British force of 15,000 troops, including the units already stationed there. According to Wolseley, this was more than enough to defend the colony against a Boer invasion, especially under an experienced commander like Buller. Lansdowne decided otherwise. At first he had thought Symons could handle the situation on his own. But at Wolseley's insistence he appointed a new commander for Natal, not an 'African', but the 'Indian' Lieutenant-General Sir George White. He, too, had won a Victoria Cross, and countless medals besides, but Chamberlain thought him too set in his ways and, at 64, too old. Lansdowne took no notice. As adjutants White chose two friends, colonels Ian Hamilton and Sir Henry Rawlinson. On 16 September 1899 they left for South Africa.

Buller was strongly against this arrangement. He had already challenged Wolseley's claim that 15,000 men would be enough to defend Natal against an attack. And in any case, the commander-in-chief's strategy was completely wrong. He had insisted to Lansdowne that the Biggarsberg, north of Ladysmith, would be a suitable defence line. According to Buller, that was a serious mistake. He believed the only good defence position was on the Tugela, south of Ladysmith. Moreover, he had insisted to Lansdowne in a heated discussion and subsequently in a personal letter that they would need far more reinforcements to hold off the Boers.

Lansdowne wasn't interested. He thought Buller 'talked Boer'. It was a good thing they hadn't consulted him before appointing White and his adjutants. Perhaps Buller and White should have discussed the strategy beforehand. But that's the way it was. How bad could it be? According to Symons and Wolseley, White had enough troops to prevent a Boer invasion. They could always dispatch the 1st Army Corps later.

In late September the British Cabinet came to the conclusion that the Boers were indeed likely to attack. Orders to mobilise were given in early October, when the Transvaal and the Orange Free State called their burghers to arms. With reserves included, the 1st Army Corps comprised 47,551 officers and men, equipped with 122 pieces of artillery. All in all there were three infantry divisions, a cavalry division, eleven field hospitals, a railway team, pontoniers and two observation balloons.

Buller got his way in the end, but by then he was afraid it was too late. He was concerned about the telegrams that had been coming in, from which he learned that the commanders in Natal had ignored his urgent, repeated warning, 'Do not go north of the Tugela.' Immediately after landing in Durban, White had proceeded to Ladysmith to establish his headquarters there. Symons had left Ladysmith a few days later, heading not south, but further north, in the direction of the Transvaal border. He and his 4000-strong brigade had crossed the Biggarsberg and set up camp in Dundee.

This was the situation on 9 October 1899, when the Boers issued their ultimatum. Their demands were clear. All British troops on the Transvaal borders were to withdraw. The reinforcements the British had sent to South Africa over the preceding few months were to leave. Those en route were to turn back. Disputes would be settled by arbitration. The South African Republic would regard any failure to meet these four demands by five o'clock on the afternoon of 11 October as a formal declaration of war.

The response from London was rapturous. 'They have done it!' Chamberlain crowed. Now they could stop squabbling over the wording of their own ultimatum. Lord Salisbury was relieved that he wouldn't have to keep explaining things to the British public. Lord Lansdowne sent his congratulations to Chamberlain and assured him that 'my soldiers are in ecstasies'. There was only that lone voice in Aldershot. Buller's forebodings continued to haunt him. He still had misgivings on the afternoon of Saturday 14 October when he boarded the *Dunottar Castle* in Southampton, no matter how eagerly the crowd cheered him on. The words went round and round in his head. 'Do not go north of the Tugela. Do not go north of the Tugela.'⁴

The slight, boyish-looking reporter with ginger hair watched him embark and decided to talk to him as soon as he got the chance. It was presumptuous, of course, but that's what Churchill was like. He came from an elite aristocratic family. His late father, Lord Randolph, had been a prominent and well-connected, somewhat controversial Conservative politician. His mother, the still desirable Lady Randolph, née Jennie Jerome, had her own coterie of friends, amorous or otherwise. From childhood Churchill had moved confidently—too much so, some thought—in these privileged circles. He was quick to make new friends, and nurtured his friendships carefully.

From the moment he knew he was going to South Africa he had put his time to good use. He had contacted all his acquaintances, starting at the top, and things had worked out well. Chamberlain, an old friend of his father's, was busy preparing for war, but nevertheless made time to receive him at home. They spoke frankly and at length about how the war would turn out. Churchill left with a valuable—and shrewdly worded—letter of recommendation, addressed to none less than the high commissioner in Cape Town. Chamberlain introduced 'the son of an old friend' to Sir Alfred Milner as 'a very clever young man'. He was said to be pushy, but Chamberlain thought this was rather an extreme view.

It wasn't the only letter of recommendation Churchill received for Milner. After dining together, the under-secretary for war, George Wyndham, also took the trouble to compliment his sharp and 'unprejudiced' mind. Wyndham was generous with information as well as praise. He told Churchill openly that he was less optimistic than his minister, Lord Lansdowne, or the commander-in-chief, Lord Wolseley.

The Boers were armed to the teeth, he warned, and with their new heavy artillery they were in a position to deal the British troops a severe blow.

Two letters of recommendation from eminent British politicians to the highest commander in South Africa made for an auspicious start, but they were rather one-sided for a journalist, Churchill thought. He also needed testimonials from people from different backgrounds and with different connections in the country. Again, he found what he was looking for among his father's circle of friends. One was the wealthy and powerful mining magnate Alfred Beit, a business associate of Cecil Rhodes and one of the sponsors of the Jameson Raid as well as a string of anti-Boer press campaigns. Through Beit Churchill obtained five more letters of recommendation addressed to various people, Englishmen and Afrikaners, with connections in the mining sector and South African politics.[5]

It goes without saying that these luminaries commended Churchill not only on the strength of his background, but also because he shared their imperialist aspirations. Make no mistake, Churchill held the Victorian belief that British rule was a godsend to all humankind, including those who were fighting it with all their might. As for the conflict with the Boers, he had written about that in early 1896, shortly after the Jameson Raid, in an unpublished memorandum called 'Our Account with the Boers'. He clarified his position—no half measures, vital British interests, the Uitlanders' political rights, and if necessary, 'ruthless' action—and concluded that 'for the sake of our Empire, for the sake of our honour, for the sake of the race, we must fight the Boers'. Meaning, first subjugate them and then magnanimously allow them to enjoy the blessings of the British Empire.

At the time of his departure for South Africa, Churchill can best be described—in twenty-first-century terms—as an informally screened, ideologically approved, embedded war correspondent, with sterling connections and added employment benefits that would be the envy of any reporter today. He had his own retainer, Thomas Walden, who had accompanied Lord Randolph on many of his travels, including a journey to Mashonaland in 1891. In short, he was a seasoned traveller and, as such, had laid in provisions: 18 bottles of whiskey, 24 bottles of wine, six bottles of port, six each of vermouth and eau de vie, and 12 flasks of lemon juice.[6]

These supplies helped to make the voyage bearable. Compared with the sailing ships of the old days, which used to spend months at sea, the *Dunottar Castle* travelled at lightning speed. Even so, the passage from Southampton to Cape Town took a good two weeks. To Churchill, that was 'a large chunk of the nineteenth century'. In addition, rough seas made him nauseous and for the first few days seasickness kept him from writing or any other activity. When the weather improved, after Madeira—nothing to write about there—boredom set in. He had hoped to exchange a few words with Buller and his staff officers, but little came of it. The general was cordial to everyone, even the journalists. He allowed the Americans to film him strolling casually on deck, but he kept his innermost thoughts to himself. Even Churchill was unable to prise anything out of him. Churchill's first report for the *Morning Post,* dated 26 October 1899, reflected his growing impatience. A modern sea voyage was wretched. It was 'torture' for him to be deprived of news for more than 14 days, especially with a war just getting under way. Out of sheer frustration he amused himself with daydreams, from Kruger conquering Cape Town to White or Symons marching on Pretoria.

The voyagers got their first hint of the true state of affairs in the war zone on 29 October, just one day before they sailed into Cape Town. The message wasn't entirely clear. On the deck of a homeward-bound steamer that passed them less than 200 metres away was a blackboard which announced in white letters, 'Boers defeated. Three battles. Penn Symons killed.' This sounded contradictory. Or perhaps not? Churchill knew how impulsive Symons could be—he had been with him in British India—and knew he would always lead the way into battle. The death of a British general, shocking as it was, didn't rule out the possibility of a British victory. Three in fact, if they could trust their information. The Boers had been defeated. As long as it didn't mean the war was all over. Otherwise, they could just turn round and go home.

Speculation was rife and the atmosphere grew increasingly sombre. Only Buller, true to form, kept his thoughts to himself. After a few minutes one of his adjutants made an attempt to strike up a conversation. 'It looks as if it will be over, sir.' At which the commander broke his silence for the first time on the voyage and grumbled, 'I dare say there will be enough left to give us a fight outside Pretoria.' His words had a miraculous effect. As if the oracle had spoken, the glad tidings passed from mouth to mouth. The mood on board lifted instantly. Sir Redvers says there will still be enough to fight about![7]

War on four fronts

Cape Town, 31 October 1899

The ship's arrival in Cape Town was as festive as its departure from Southampton. An excited crowd had come to welcome the new commander-in-chief in spite of the driving rain early that Tuesday morning. The boom of a gun salute filled the air, the film cameras were running, the streets were gaily decorated. But here, too, Buller concealed his thoughts as he waved cheerily from an open landau at the well-wishers lining the streets on his way to Government House. He had an appointment with the high commissioner at ten o'clock.

The first confidential telegrams had been delivered to him as soon as the *Dunottar Castle* docked the previous evening. They confirmed his fears. The news was up-to-the-minute and grim. He heard the tragic details later, from Milner. Boer commandos had swarmed in all directions, to the north towards Rhodesia, and to the west, where they had attacked and surrounded the main British border towns, Mafeking and Kimberley. In the south-east they had invaded Natal, from the Transvaal as well as the Orange Free State. What had happened there was exactly what Buller had feared. White had been unable to hold his positions north of the Tugela.

The British had been victorious at Talana—where Symons was fatally wounded—and Elandslaagte, as Buller knew from the message on the passing ship. But after that, things had gone badly wrong at Modderspruit and Nicholson's Nek. On the very day of Buller's arrival, Monday 30 October, they had suffered two crushing defeats. White and his remaining troops had been forced to retreat to Ladysmith and were in danger of being surrounded. The British press later called it Mournful Monday.

The high commissioner had more bad news. An even greater disaster was looming, far closer than Natal, here in the Cape Colony, right under his nose. Milner was afraid that the Afrikaners, encouraged by their clansmen's successes, would rebel in support. Commandos were also said to be massing on the southern border of the Orange Free State, preparing to invade the Cape. The consequences were too frightful to contemplate.

Buller couldn't imagine a worse start. He would obviously have to change his strategy. The original idea had been straightforward: as soon as possible the whole of the 1st Army Corps would mount a frontal attack at the heart of the Boer republics. They would simply charge straight through the centre. In the present circumstances, that would be dangerous, at least for the British soldiers in the towns under siege. Cecil Rhodes had already sent a furious telegram from Kimberley, complaining about the lack of reinforcements. White had blundered, but did everyone in Ladysmith, and probably the whole of Natal, have to suffer for it? Then there was the uprising in the Cape Colony that Milner was so worried about. What was Buller to do? Should he back just one horse, and, if so, which one? Or hedge his bets? He needed more time to decide.[8]

Winston Churchill had no trouble reaching a decision, but then his options were relatively simple. A war correspondent's place was on the front and it was clear that the main action would be in Natal—Ladysmith to be more precise. Even without confidential telegrams he soon realised just how serious the situation was. Late on Monday evening, as soon as the *Dunottar Castle* docked, he read all the local newspapers and spoke to everyone he could think of. The following day he was received by the high commissioner, again thanks to Chamberlain's and Wyndham's letters of recommendation. Milner discussed his concerns with the fledgling reporter almost as frankly as with the famous general, withholding only the shocking details of Modderspruit and Nicholson's Nek. As a result of the meeting, Churchill was able to write—and dispatch—a lengthy report for the *Morning Post*.

The article was up to the minute and peppered with the kind of lively detail that characterised Churchill's style. He wrote at length about the high casualty rate among British officers in the first weeks of the war. Besides Symons, there were several others he knew, men he had met during his military adventures in British India, Sudan or—a few, like Lieutenant Reggie Barnes—in Cuba. He was scathing about the Liberal Opposition in his own country. He felt it was dangerous to have postponed sending reinforcements because of the Peace Party's anti-war campaign, and held 'these humanitarian gentlemen' personally responsible for the huge loss of human life. He expressed equally strong views on the future course of the war, predicting 'a fierce, certainly bloody, possibly prolonged struggle'. Churchill was determined to be in the forefront, with his eye on an award for journalism, but, no less importantly, in pursuit of his imperialistic ideals. 'We are at war with the pen as well as the sword.'

There was no time to lose. He could have returned to the *Dunottar Castle* before it sailed on to Durban, but he decided this would take too long. There was a quicker way that would save him a couple of days. He could take the train to East London, from there an overnight boat to Durban, and cover the last stretch again by train. He left Cape Town that evening, accompanied by his retainer, Thomas Walden, and two other reporters, John Atkins of the *Manchester Guardian* and Alister Campbell of *Laffan's News Agency*. It was still Tuesday 31 October. Churchill set off for Ladysmith.[9]

And to think the news could have been even worse. If the Boers had carried out the daring raid that Jan Smuts had proposed, Natal would probably have been lost and the uprising in the Cape Colony a fact. The Transvaal's young state attorney had given a graphic description of the plan of campaign in his memorandum of early September 1899. He felt that the military leaders of the two Boer republics should work out a joint plan as quickly as possible for 'a combined attack on Natal'. The key was to push through to Durban before British reinforcements arrived, and seize the munitions and supplies they found there. A successful raid would boost morale. It would spur the Afrikaners in the Cape Colony to action, and Great Britain would then have a third Boer republic to deal with. The European powers would be only too happy to take advantage of Britain's predicament. He hinted broadly at the possibility of 'instigating a widespread rebellion in India with Russia's help'.[10]

In retrospect, it is easy to dismiss Smuts's enthusiasm for the 'offensive method' as science fiction, particularly the political consequences he expected. But at the time, the scenario was not unrealistic. And from a strategic point of view it made sense. Before the arrival of their first 10,000 reinforcements, the British in South Africa had far fewer troops than the Boers. So the question is, why wasn't Smuts's plan carried out? There are four closely linked reasons. The first two had to do with specific individuals, the last two were more fundamental in nature.

The first and simplest reason is that Smuts's plan depended on a joint war plan, and no such thing existed. This was mainly due to President Steyn of the Orange Free State. He too had a young lawyer on his side, Barry Hertzog, who also favoured a surprise attack on Natal. Steyn, however, was against it, still hoping for a peaceful solution. By the time he was ready to mobilise the Free State troops, on 2 October, the 10,000 British servicemen had already arrived in Durban.

Even then, with a sound war plan, they would have stood a good chance of occupying Natal. But there was no plan at all, not even in Pretoria. According to those in the know, one must have existed, but if it did, it was so secret that even a century of archive research has brought nothing to light. No plan, perhaps, but they did have an objective: the British troops massed just over the border had to be defeated, repulsed or isolated. Exactly how they would do that depended on the progress of the war. The Transvaal military leaders hadn't arranged anything with their counterparts in Bloemfontein either. By 11 October Marthinus Prinsloo, the leader of the Free State forces on the Natal border, still had little idea of what was expected of him. At five past two—barely three hours before the British ultimatum expired—he sent a revealing telegram to the Transvaal commandant-general, Piet Joubert: 'The men have taken up position; awaiting instructions.'[11]

Prinsloo's attitude exemplifies the second reason: the military leaders in the Boer republics were unwilling and unable to plan and carry out a coordinated assault on Durban. This was true in particular of the commander-in-chief. Joubert, at 68, had been resting on the laurels he had won in the past, in clashes with African chieftains but mainly during the Boers' first encounter with the British, 18 years earlier. Since then he had been more involved in politics, as Paul Kruger's vice-president—and four times his rival for the presidency. This was evident in his strategy, which was political rather than military. He pictured the new confrontation against the British as a replay of Majuba, perhaps on a bigger scale: deal a few good blows just over the borders, break through their defences, and wait and see what happened, in the hope that the British would be sufficiently intimidated to negotiate. This was why he had taken command of the troops in Natal. Piet Joubert was a cautious man, who believed that defence was the best form of attack.

He wasn't the only Boer leader to hold this view. Defensive warfare—a third and more structural reason why the Boers failed to attack—was in their blood, particularly for the older generation. It sounds strange for a nation of pioneers, descendants of the Voortrekkers, who had fought for every inch of their territory, but it isn't hard to understand. In their many confrontations with African adversaries they had always preferred to operate from a laager, a circular formation of wagons which provided a primitive but effective form of forward defence. Their first military conflict with the British (1880–81) had also been a defensive war, with a primarily political objective. They were thus accustomed to defensive warfare, which was in any event more compatible with their moral values. Pretoria's argument was that this war had been forced on them by Britain's expansionist aspirations. The Boers were simply defending themselves; they weren't out to conquer anyone else's land; at least, not land belonging to whites.

But even if the military leaders of the Boer republics *had* decided to carry out Smuts's plan and attack Durban, they would still have had a serious handicap. This is the fourth and last reason. The forces the Boers raised were very different from a professional standing army trained and equipped to execute a long-range strategy. Except for the artillery, it was a civilian militia made up of men aged 16 to 60, comprising a force of around 60,000 in the Transvaal and Orange Free State combined. To avoid disrupting the economy, they were called up only when they were needed, in varying strengths but rarely all of them simultaneously.

As a result it was difficult to organise a coordinated and therefore logistically complex offensive. There was also the fact that the Boers weren't comfortable with hierarchical structures and discipline. There was a commandant-general in the Transvaal but no equivalent rank in the Orange Free State, where President Steyn effectively fulfilled that role. There were Transvaal adjutant-generals, Piet Cronjé and Jan Kock, and a Free State commander-in-chief, the Marthinus Prinsloo mentioned earlier. Next in rank were combat generals, who led two or more regional commandos. The military units, varying in strength from 300 to 3000 men, were headed by commandants, and were subdivided into smaller sections led by field cornets and adjutant field cornets.

Although the force ostensibly had a command structure, it was riddled with religious and political differences, between 'Kruger men' and 'Joubert men', for instance. Moreover, most burghers had difficulty reconciling a system of military rank with their view of themselves as equals. There was good reason why no one except the artillery wore a uniform, or why officers all the way up to the commandant-general were elected by their 'subordinates'. It was the rule rather than the exception for decisions taken by superiors to be debated and sometimes overturned or ignored. Even in combat, every Boer was first and foremost his own man.[12]

All this explains why the Boer flags weren't flying over the Indian Ocean by the time the British commander, Buller, landed in Cape Town. It is also why he was rightly concerned about British prospects. At the same time, in the first two weeks of the war the strategic weakness of the Boers' mode of combat—their defensive strategies and their freedom to act independently—turned out to be their tactical strength. In direct combat, after a faltering start, their armed civilians proved superior to Britain's professional soldiers. And this seemed to be more than just a matter of luck.

Firstly, the Boers still were numerically superior. At the start of the war the Transvaal and the Orange Free State had 35,000 men active on the four fronts, against 25,000 British troops. They were more evenly matched in Natal—17,500 Boers to 16,000 Britons—but Natal was also where the British suffered their worst defeats. The only logical conclusion was that a Brit was no match for a Boer.

What it came down to was the Boer's horse and rifle. Every man owned a horse. He was an infantryman and a cavalryman in one, and therefore infinitely more mobile. Not in actual combat, when the horses were out of range in the care of *agterryers*—the 7000 to 9000 African and coloured servants who accompanied the Boer troops—but before, after and in the intervals between exchanges of fire, the Boers were able to move rapidly and surprise the enemy from unexpected positions. In these situations their independence was an asset.

So too was the fact that every Boer possessed a rifle—and not just any rifle, but the most advanced rapid-firing weapon the European arms industry had to offer at the end of the nineteenth century. After the Jameson Raid the Transvaal government had imported huge consignments of weapons—through the efforts of Willem Leyds, who was recuperating in Germany at the time—and Bloemfontein had followed their example. As a result, the Boer republics now had an arsenal of 45,000 Martini-Henry rifles and, far more importantly, the same number of Mausers—more than enough to arm all their mobilised civilians. The Mausers in particular suited the Boers' style of combat. They were relatively light, easy to use and accurate over a long range. The bullets were small, light, fast and quick to load. Even a small number of marksmen could sustain a barrage of fire, while their smokeless gunpowder ensured that the Boers, entrenched or sheltered behind rocks one or two kilometres away, remained undetected. The British soldiers complained that they were fighting 'an invisible enemy' and literally didn't know which way to turn.

Not only were the Boers' personal weapons the most modern in the world, but their artillery was also the best that gold could buy. Most of it was new and in perfect condition. They had small Lee-Metford and large Vickers-Maxim machine guns, known as pom-poms because of the sound they made, Krupp field artillery, and, to crown it all, four 155-mm Creusot guns. These formidable Long Toms were actually fortress guns, but the Boers used them on the battlefield as well, this being another example of their forward defence. The railway network, which had been nationalised at the outbreak of war, came in useful for transporting their matériel. To install their artillery in the field, ideally on a hilltop, they used oxwagons. All this effort paid off, as the Long Toms had a reach of ten kilometres, twice that of the British Howitzer and Armstrong field guns.

The Boers were thus superior in number, mobility and firing power. They were also familiar with the terrain and accustomed to the climate. Both were important advantages, as the land was rugged and hilly, at any rate in Natal, while the spring brought heavy downpours, chilly nights and, on clear days, blistering sun, from which there was little shelter.[13]

The differences between the Boers and their British adversaries couldn't have been greater, strategically, tactically, operationally and in culture.

One was a professional army, hierarchical, disciplined and organised, sticklers for traditions. Their biggest concession to modern times was a change of uniform, from bull's-eye red to camouflage khaki. Their officers were class-conscious aristocrats, polo fans, warhorses, who had earned their spurs in colonial campaigns against indigenous adversaries. In battle they were self-assured, their strategic reflex was the classical offensive, which had been drummed into them at Aldershot: first, the artillery bombardment, then the infantry charge in close formation, bayonets fixed on rifles, and finally the cavalry charge to round up the fleeing enemy. The rank and file were expected to obey commands—fire salvos, attack, withdraw—not to think or act on their own initiative.[14]

All this was food for thought for anyone who was passionately concerned about the fortunes of the British troops. Churchill had all the time he needed to absorb his impressions. The train journey from Cape Town to East London would take at least three days, perhaps longer because of the war. The first stretch, to De Aar, crossed the same barren, hill-studded Karoo landscape that Willem and Louise Leyds had found so tedious 15 years earlier.[15] Churchill wasn't impressed either. 'The scenery would depress the most buoyant spirits . . . Wherefore was this miserable land of stone and scrub created?' The news he picked up in Beaufort West on the way did little to improve his mood. On Mournful Monday the Boers had taken 1200 British prisoners.

His own experiences made matters even worse. The railway line from De Aar to Stormberg, the next sizeable station on the way to East London, ran along the Orange Free State border. It was the only front where the Boers hadn't yet mounted a large-scale assault, but everyone believed an attack was imminent. Rumours about advancing Boer commandos were confirmed when Churchill and his fellow passengers arrived in Stormberg. For the time being, their train would be the last to come from De Aar. Stormberg had been hurriedly evacuated, like every other village in the area. Churchill thought this was sensible, but it made him uneasy. Even the train sounded different. All the way to East London, he kept hearing the wheels on the tracks saying 'retreat, retreat, retreat'.

He wrote a gloomy but resolute letter to his mother. 'We have greatly underestimated the military strength and spirit of the Boers.' He doubted that a single army corps would be enough. It would certainly be a tough, bloody struggle, he said, with at least 10,000 to 12,000 casualties. But Britain would win in the end, he was sure, just as he was sure about his own destiny. 'I shall believe I am to be preserved for future things.' These words were prophetic in every way.

147

There was another shock to come, but even that left him undaunted. In East London they found a ship bound for Durban. Storms and seasickness turned the voyage into an ordeal for Churchill but he recovered soon after landing in Durban at midnight on Saturday 4 November. Early on Sunday morning he went to the hospital ship *Sumatra*, hoping to find some old friends. There were a few, among them Reggie Barnes, his travel companion in Cuba, and, at a later stage, a member of his prize-winning polo team from the 4th Hussars in India. Churchill flinched at the sight of him. Barnes had been wounded in the thigh and his leg was 'absolutely coal black from hip to toe'. Churchill feared the worst. But it wasn't gangrene, the doctor assured him, just a massive bruise.

Barnes had been shot in 'our brilliant little victory at Elandslaagte Station', which for a while had raised British hopes of being able to halt the Boer advance. He told Churchill about their changing fortunes during the battle and their breakthrough in the middle of a thunderstorm which had obscured the Boers' vision. To Churchill's delight, the final attack had been led by Ian Hamilton, another friend from India, who had since worked his way up to the rank of brigadier-general. The thrill of the victory hadn't lasted long. Hamilton, too, had been compelled to retreat in the end and was now under siege in Ladysmith with the rest of the British troops. All the more reason for Churchill to get there as soon as possible. The latest news from Durban was that Ladysmith was no longer accessible, but he was going to give it a try, anyway, confident that 'Ian Hamilton would look after me and give me a good show'.[16]

Elandslaagte would certainly have fallen into Churchill's category of 'good shows', except for its bitter aftertaste. On 21 October 1899 a memorable battle was fought there, along the railway line between Ladysmith and Dundee. It ended in tragedy for everyone involved, including the British victors.

The battle as such seemed to confirm the merits of the time-honoured Aldershot strategy. Major-General John French, leading a cavalry of 1300 men and 550 artillerymen with 18 guns, and Hamilton, with his 1600-strong infantry, kept to the rules of the book: artillery, infantry, cavalry. The only difference was that Hamilton's formation was less compact than the manual prescribed. This time the formula worked. At the end of the afternoon, after the bombardment, they carried out the charge, with bayonets on their rifles and the battle-cry 'Majuba!' on their lips. With the weather on their side, the Imperial Light Horse—in this instance on foot—along with the experienced infantrymen of the 1st Devonshire Regiment, the 1st Manchester Regiment and the 2nd Gordon

Highlanders, flushed the Boers out of their positions. Some fled, others waved white handkerchiefs, but out of the blue a group of about 50 mounted a fierce counterattack. The initial confusion among the British soon gave way to outrage at having been deceived by a bogus surrender. The advance was resumed with a vengeance and culminated in a furious cavalry charge. Again and again, three times in all, the 5th Lancers and the 5th Dragoon Guards, brandishing lances and sabres, swept mercilessly through the fleeing Boers. When they counted their casualties that evening, the British discovered what they had paid for their victory: 52 dead and 213 wounded. And this for a position which Lieutenant-General White ordered his men to abandon shortly afterwards.

The Boers incurred even heavier losses at Elandslaagte: 46 dead, including Adjutant-General Jan Kock, who had led the contentious counterattack, 105 wounded and captured, and another 180 who had surrendered. All told, this amounted to 340 of the 800 Boers who had gone into battle. There was a reason for it—Kock had advanced dangerously far into enemy territory, where his men were outnumbered by four to one—but even so, the losses were unprecedented and the defeat was shocking. More shocking still were the tactics the British had resorted to. For the Boers, shooting each other was as far as one could go. Bayonets, sabres and lances were beyond the pale. One could expect that kind of thing from uncivilised black warriors, but whites weren't supposed to skewer each other to death. They were appalled at the British cavalry's massacre of fleeing Boers, including the wounded and men who had already surrendered. The battle at Elandslaagte drove home a hard lesson once more: steer clear of the British and, if they come too close, move on and take new positions.[17]

The lesson came too late for the Hollander Corps, one of the Boer army's units. It had been formed by the Dutch community less than a month earlier, on 22 September 1899. These were people who lived and worked in the Transvaal, who had offered their services as volunteers, just like the Germans, Irish, Scandinavians, French, Italians and Austrians. About 2000 foreigners were deployed in their own units. The driving force behind the Hollander Corps was Herman Coster, a young lawyer from Leiden, who in 1895 had followed in Willem Leyds's footsteps to become the state attorney of the Transvaal. But he hadn't held out for long. Within two years Kruger's quirks were more than he could bear. Coster resigned but remained in Pretoria. Four hundred and fifty of his compatriots and a handful of Belgians joined the corps. The majority, being either unfit or ineligible for active service, were deployed for surveillance. The rest, about 150 men, were sent to the front in Natal in early October, having had little opportunity to train beforehand. They had the misfortune of being assigned to the group led by the arrogant Kock. Elandslaagte was their baptism by fire. It was also the last resting place for eight of them, including Coster. Another 54 Hollanders, some of them wounded, fell into the hands of the British. The remainder were subsequently redeployed in other commandos. The Hollander Corps ceased to exist as an independent unit.[18]

The name Elandslaagte had a bitter undertone in Britain, the Netherlands and the Boer republics in particular. And in Germany too, because among the casualties were 30 men from the German commando, which was also disbanded after the battle.

For Churchill, however, Elandslaagte was 'our little victory', with a heroic role for his friend Ian Hamilton, who undoubtedly had more dashing exploits to tell him about the next time they met. It was only 200 kilometres to Ladysmith. The first stretch was uneventful, from Durban to Pietermaritzburg, the capital of Natal. On arrival, the reporters discovered that the regular train service had been suspended. They could hire a train, which they promptly did. After all, their employers were paying. For a few hours they enjoyed the illusion that they might still manage to reach their destination, but the bubble burst when they were held up at a small station. Further ahead, near Colenso, the Boers had blocked the rail bridge over the Tugela and no more trains could get through. Ladysmith was effectively surrounded. Their long journey had come to an end.

The station was in Estcourt. The reporters installed themselves in tents in the marshalling yard. While his man, Thomas Walden, attended to their trunks and chests, Churchill went off to inspect the surroundings. Estcourt was one of those small country towns where there was nothing to do. It consisted of two streets and 300 low houses made from brick and corrugated iron, nestling in a valley surrounded by green hills. What came to mind first was that it would be a hard place to defend. And behind the hills? It was only 70 kilometres to Ladysmith. Churchill was sure there must be a way to get there.[19]

A hail of bullets

Chieveley, 15 November 1899

An armoured train: even the name was strange. It was the epitome of nineteenth-century progress clad in medieval armour, a train that resembled a latter-day knight errant. And though it looked impressive, as Churchill had told his readers in the *Morning Post* a few days earlier, 'nothing is more vulnerable and helpless'. If just one bridge were blown up, it would all be over for the train and its occupants. Unable to proceed, the steel-plated monster would be at the mercy of the enemy. And the fate of the inferior specimen in which the expedition was now leaving Estcourt would be so much the worse. There was no roof to its trucks, no shutters to its loopholes, and no weapon apart from an antiquated naval gun. The soldiers called it 'Wilson's death trap'.

Churchill had no idea who Wilson was, but the nickname said it all. The two reporters sharing his tent had wisely decided to stay put when he woke them at five that morning. One of them—Leo Amery of *The Times,* an old school friend from Harrow, who also happened to be in Estcourt—said it was raining too hard. The other, John Atkins, who had travelled with Churchill from Cape Town, put it more bluntly. He was paid to report on the war, he replied from his bunk, not risk ending up in the hands of the enemy. Churchill took his point, but set off nevertheless. The evening before, he had given his word to Captain Aylmer Haldane, another acquaintance he had run into here. Haldane had helped him secure a post in the Malakand Field Force in India, which Churchill had written about with considerable success. This was a chance to return the favour. Moreover, as a war correspondent it was his job to gather as much news as he could. There was a third reason too, no worse than any other—'I was eager for trouble'.

And trouble would certainly come, though it may not have seemed so at the start. All went well for the first few kilometres. At the head of the train was a truck carrying the naval gun, manned by four sailors. Behind it were two armoured carriages with Dublin Fusiliers, followed by the locomotive and the coal tender. Then came two more armoured carriages, with troops from the Durban Light Infantry and a team of mechanics, and at the rear a truck with tools and equipment. There were 120 men in total, all under Haldane's command. Churchill stood beside his friend in the carriage with the Irish, and scanned the surroundings with his field glasses. At six thirty they pulled into Frere station, where a Natal Police patrol reported that no Boers had been spotted.

Should they continue to the next stop at Chieveley? It was higher up and would afford a better view. Haldane's orders from Colonel Charles Long, the garrison commander in Estcourt, were to proceed as far as they could and try to reach Colenso. The green, hilly countryside looked peaceful. They decided to continue their journey.[20]

Reconnaissance expeditions by armoured train were a daily chore for the troops in Estcourt. The soldiers saw them as a form of discipline, the war correspondents thought them absurd, but Long stood his ground, even though a single mounted patrol could obtain more information than the lumbering, clattering colossus. He stuck to routine, as if to prove that he wasn't going to change his ways on account of the Boers.

Churchill had already spent about ten days in Estcourt and was growing impatient. On his arrival he had been met with good news from London. His recent book, *The River War*, about Kitchener's campaign in Sudan, had received good reviews, and this was a chance to consolidate his reputation. He had spread the word that he was offering a generous reward to anyone who would escort him through the Boer lines to Ladysmith. A couple of military guides had shown some interest, but nothing came of it. Their superiors thought it ridiculous for them 'to lead a bloody war correspondent into Ladysmith'.

In the circumstances, any distraction was welcome. Churchill had been on similar missions before, once on horseback with the entire garrison and once in the same armoured train. On that occasion they had gone all the way to Colenso, edging their way at a snail's pace on the last stretch of the journey. Five hundred metres from the town the commanding officer—not Haldane this time—had disembarked with a sergeant to inspect the area on foot. And of course Churchill had joined them. They found Colenso deserted. It was even smaller than Estcourt and had apparently been 'ransacked and plundered by the Boers and the Kaffirs'. The streets were littered with people's possessions and several houses had been burned down. A dead horse lay in the middle of the road, its stiff legs extended in the air. A straggler at the end of the street waved a white rag on a stick. 'But no Dutchmen were to be seen.' The rails had been torn up and broken telegraph wires trailed over the ground. The damage could be repaired, however, and the bridge over the Tugela was still intact. The Boers had apparently been meaning to use it themselves, Churchill concluded. The men spent only a short time in Colenso and returned at full speed, trying to identify what they saw on the way: 'Black dots on the horizon?' 'Perhaps, but definitely not Boers. They're still too far away.'

But that had been a week earlier. On Wednesday 15 November they knew there were Boers in the area. The question was, where? The train was approaching Chieveley, when Churchill spotted them. A hundred men on horseback were galloping towards them. They were now about a kilometre and a half from the tracks. At the station, Haldane had sent a telegram to Estcourt, saying they had arrived in Chieveley safely and that there were Boers in the vicinity. Long's instructions came at once. They were to return to Frere and follow developments from there.

The engine driver was pleased, and the train set off in the direction from which it had come. The truck carrying Churchill, Haldane and the naval gun was now at the rear. Churchill climbed onto a box to gain a better vantage point. A few kilometres on, as they rounded a bend, they realised they had run into trouble. The Boers were waiting for them on a craggy ridge, 500 metres away. Out of the blue 'three wheeled things' appeared on the crest of the hill. A few blinding flashes, an eerie silence, and then all hell broke loose. A cloud of white smoke erupted overhead. Churchill leapt for cover. Hailstones hammered the metal plating. He had come under fire before, in Cuba. He had stood face to face with men wielding sabres at Tirah and Omdurman. But this was completely different. They were being pounded by rapid fire and shrapnel from hundreds of Mausers, a Maxim machine gun and two field guns. They had no option but to carry on. The driver gave steam.[21]

The Dublin Fusiliers had faced the Boers' firepower before. They had achieved a hard-fought victory at Talana Hill, only to suffer a humiliating defeat on Mournful Monday. At Modderspruit on 30 October they had endured shellfire for hours, before retreating in disarray to Ladysmith. The Gordon Highlanders and the English regiments had fared no better, but that did little to soothe the Irish Fusiliers' injured pride. The only consolation for the common soldiers was that the blame for the debacle would be borne by their bungling officers.

Lieutenant-General Sir George White was the main culprit. From the start his actions in northern Natal had been erratic. He kept vacillating between two extremes. First, there had been his reckless decision to ambush the Boers north of the Tugela and, later, after his first minor victories at Talana Hill and Elandslaagte, the fretful dithering and overhasty withdrawal of his troops to Ladysmith. There, he had recovered his composure and decided to stage a decisive confrontation. That's what the textbooks said and that's what he was intending to do.

For days he had been sending out reconnaissance patrols, even using an observation balloon, so he knew exactly where the Boer positions were. They were dispersed over a broad front on the hills north-east of Ladysmith, roughly in the form of a horseshoe. The main force, led by Joubert, was in the centre, on Pepworth Hill, and that was where White intended to concentrate his attack. The old advance-and-assault routine would be carried out by the infantry brigade, which had been successful under Ian Hamilton at Elandslaagte, with support from the artillery and cavalry. And this time, White himself would be in command. On the right flank Colonel Geoffrey Grimwood would lead a second brigade similar in kind. They would circle around Long Hill, drive out the Boers and attack Pepworth Hill from the south-east. And if the Boers tried to flee from the two-pronged attack, they could expect a nasty surprise. In the meantime, the Royal Irish Fusiliers and the Gloucestershire Regiment, under the command of Lieutenant-Colonel F.R.C. Carleton, would be at Nicholson's Nek to intercept the fleeing Boers.

The plan was insane, as most of his staff officers agreed. The Boers were still some distance away, they argued, hiding out in the hills. Wouldn't it be wiser to wait until they were closer to Ladysmith? But White was determined to deliver a knock-down blow. He had more men than Joubert—12,000 compared with his 7500—and three times as many guns—60 to Joubert's 20. He was also keen on the idea of an ambush at Nicholson's Nek, which one of his staff officers, Major W. Adye, had proposed. White took the final decision on Sunday 29 October, after the last reconnaissance. Monday was the moment of truth. On Sunday night the troops moved into position. At eleven o'clock Carleton led his column north, in the direction of Nicholson's Nek. The two brigades set off shortly afterwards. Grimwood headed for Long Hill in the east, White and Hamilton made for Pepworth Hill in the north-east.

The Boers had no idea what was coming, but Joubert, cautious as ever, had had second thoughts about their forward position on Long Hill. On Sunday evening, after the British reconnaissance balloon had completed its mission, he ordered the Lydenburg Commando under General Schalk Burger to clear the hill and take positions on the opposite bank of the Modderspruit. At the same time, he was informed that 400 officers of the South African Mounted Police, known as Zarps, had arrived from Johannesburg. Joubert sent them to Nicholson's Nek to reinforce the western flank of his 'horseshoe'. A third stroke of luck was the arrival of the Long Tom, the heaviest-calibre gun in the Boers' arsenal. It took 22 mules and hundreds of men to haul it up Pepworth Hill. But there it stood at last, installed on the base that Lieutenant-Colonel S.P.E. Trichardt of the State Artillery had prepared for it.

The advantages of these three circumstances became apparent on Monday morning. By daylight, around five o'clock, Grimwood discovered that his march through the night had brought him to an abandoned position. His men did come under fire, but not from Long Hill. It was the Long Tom bombarding them from Pepworth Hill. At the same time, they were being battered by heavy artillery and gunfire from the east and had to direct their efforts in that direction. Their strategy was in shreds. Instead of supporting the assault on Pepworth Hill, Grimwood himself needed assistance. White and Hamilton came to the rescue, but as a result both British brigades found themselves in different positions from those they had expected. Their carefully coordinated combat plan for artillery, infantry and cavalry had come apart at the seams. Each unit was left to improvise and fend for itself, and in this respect the British—both officers and men—were no match for their adversaries. At half past eleven White gave his men the order to retreat. They fled in disarray under pitiless fire from the advancing Boers. The battle at Modderspruit, the first major encounter between the two sides, ended in a crushing defeat for the British.

The disaster unfolding at Nicholson's Nek at the same time only added to their humiliation. The troubles there had started earlier, at two o'clock in the morning. Carleton's column, comprising 950 infantrymen and 150 artillerymen with mountain guns, was making slower progress than they had expected and had lost hope of reaching Nicholson's Nek before sunrise. Carleton and Adye, who had joined the expedition to witness his plan in action, decided instead to take positions on Cayingubo Hill, nearby. But fate intervened. For one reason or another, pandemonium broke out. Some said it was caused by falling stones, others by the sound of gunshot; no one really knew. In any event, the mules carrying the munitions and mountain guns suddenly bolted and scrambled downhill in the dark. Scores of men were trampled underfoot; some were dragged along by the animals; many fled. It looked as if the mission had come to an end, but Carleton and Adye weren't ready to give up. They restored order and assigned their remaining troops to the south side of Cayingubo Hill, to lie in wait for Boers on the retreat.

They didn't have to wait long. The Boers soon appeared, but they weren't retreating. Three of their units had heard the commotion on the hill. At daybreak, a division of the Pretoria Commando, led by Piet Zeederberg, opened fire from the south-east. Approaching from the opposite side, the northern slope of the Cayingubo—which wasn't visible from the British position—were 300 Free Staters of the Heilbron

Commando. For their acting commandant, Christiaan de Wet, this was a re-enactment of Majuba. He had been there, 18 years earlier, and the scenario was exactly the same. Yet again, the British had left one slope unguarded, allowing the Boers to advance, crawling through the tall grass and sheltering behind the outcrops of rock that covered the hill. Around eight o'clock, the Free Staters received reinforcements from the Zarps, led by Commandant G.M.J. van Dam. The British troops on the southern slope were surrounded.

The Boers were in no hurry. They continued to climb the hill at a leisurely pace, knowing that heat and fatigue would take their toll. At eleven o'clock the front units of the Gloucesters began to retreat. Half an hour later, Carleton saw flashes of light coming from a spot near the British headquarters. It was a heliogram from White, in Morse code. He was instructing them to 'retire as opportunity offers', but they didn't stand a chance. They were hemmed in and their supply of ammunition was almost depleted. At a quarter past one, a few white flags appeared, and the Boers emerged from their shelters. Carleton and Adye surrendered. The remaining Gloucesters and Royal Irish Fusiliers—the 840 men who had not fled or been killed or wounded—were taken prisoner.

The British sustained far heavier casualties than the Boers at Nicholson's Nek as well as Modderspruit. The two clashes together are known as the Battle of Ladysmith. All in all, on Monday 30 October, the Boers lost 16 dead and 75 wounded. The British losses amounted to 106 dead, 374 wounded, and 1284 captured.

But the outcome could have been far worse. If the commandant-general, Joubert, had listened to his younger officers, the British press might have had to think up an epithet even more dismal than Mournful Monday. Commanding officers like De Wet and Louis Botha—Botha had replaced the ailing Lukas Meyer at the eastern end of the Boer horseshoe—were eager to give chase to the British troops fleeing to Ladysmith. But Joubert wouldn't allow it. His men were exhausted, he said, and he wouldn't risk throwing away the victory. In any case, he felt it was 'unchristian to pursue an enemy on the run'. De Wet could only watch from the heights as the plain filled with demoralised British soldiers. He gave vent to his frustration. As if Joubert were at his side, he hissed, 'Go, your horsemen, go! Go, your horsemen.'[22]

Thus the Dublin Fusiliers at Modderspruit were spared the humiliation that befell the Royal Irish Fusiliers at Nicholson's Nek. The wholesale surrender of British troops caused dismay in military circles and beyond, even more than the high toll in casualties. Churchill was outraged and expressed his views in the *Morning Post*. He wrote a personal letter to the adjutant-general, Sir Evelyn Wood—another old family friend—demanding that the officers responsible be punished.[23]

But five days later, on 15 November, it was Churchill himself who was under fire from the Boers. He was taking cover with the Dublin Fusiliers and Captain Haldane in an armoured train that was gathering speed as it hurtled downhill. Slow down, he thought to himself, convinced that the Boers would have blocked the line up ahead. He was just turning to Haldane to suggest that someone should warn the driver, when the train crashed. It came to an abrupt halt, as if it had hit a brick wall, hurling the men in all directions. After recovering from the shock, Churchill returned to his box. He had little time to inspect the damage to the front of the train. Bullets whistled past his ears and clattered like hailstones against the steel armour. He ducked down again and conferred with Haldane. None of the Dubliners or sailors were injured. If the gunners could return the Boer fire with their rifles and the naval gun, he would go out to investigate. Haldane agreed.

Protected by the train and crouching low, Churchill made his way to the front of the train as swiftly as he could. The engine and the tender were still on the line, but the three cars in front of them had derailed. It had only taken a single rock to do the job. The front truck containing equipment for repairs had uncoupled and overturned on the embankment. The two carriages behind it, carrying the Durban Light Infantry and the labourers, were badly damaged. One lay on its side, the other was wedged across the track, half on and half off the rails.

As Churchill drew level with the locomotive, a shell burst overhead. He was unharmed, but the driver was injured by a shard. He stormed out of his cab in a rage, his face bleeding. He was a civilian, he protested, he wasn't getting paid to be shot at. He took shelter behind the overturned cars and refused to budge. Realising that there could be no escape without the driver, Churchill used all his powers of persuasion to calm him down. If he—the man's name was Charles Wagner—remained at his post, Churchill assured him, he would receive a medal for 'distinguished gallantry' in action. The ploy was successful. Wagner wiped the blood from his face and went back to the locomotive. The Durban Light Infantrymen had been flung out of their carriage, but most of them could still hold a rifle and fire it. Churchill returned to the rear of the train. He had a plan.

Churchill never stopped to reflect that he was a civilian too, a correspondent dispatched to report on the war, not take part in it. Under enemy fire, he conducted himself like the officer he had once been, and instinctively assumed command. Even Haldane seems to have accepted Churchill's authority when he explained his plan. The Dubliners and the

Durban Light Infantry gunners would keep the Boers at a distance while Churchill used the locomotive to remove the wreckage from the line. They had the expertise and equipment, so it wouldn't be too difficult. The only problem was that many of the labourers had fled, leaving their equipment scattered on the ground. There was also the unrelenting attack from the Boers to deal with. Their own gun had been damaged beyond repair. Undeterred, Churchill went ahead with the help of the engine driver, who meekly followed his orders.

First, they uncoupled the truck that was lying on its side and pushed it off the rails. The carriage was more of a problem. Using steam and sheer physical power—nine men volunteered to face the Boers' barrage of fire—they managed to move it, too. Well, almost. There was just enough room for the tender to pass, but the locomotive was too wide to get through. The driver struggled to clear a passage, taking care not to derail the engine in the process. They finally succeeded more than an hour later, after 11 or 12 attempts. After they managed to lift the carriage a few inches off the ground, the engine tilted precariously to the right, but inched through, with a grating screech of steel on steel.

Estcourt was now within reach—in any event, for the locomotive. To Churchill's dismay, the coupling between the engine and the carriage behind it gave way at the crucial moment. It would be too risky to try to force the engine past the obstruction a second time, and if they were to push the cars up to the engine, the men would be exposed to the Boers' line of fire. The only option was to transport the wounded—more than 40 at that stage—in the engine and the tender and have everyone else run alongside the train. There was a small hamlet near Frere station, 800 metres further along. They might be able to take shelter there while the engine continued to Estcourt to fetch reinforcements.

Fearing that their prey was about to escape, the Boer gunners redoubled their efforts. The engine driver put on steam. The men running alongside struggled to keep pace and many of them, including Haldane, were left behind. As the locomotive approached the houses, Churchill leapt off to assist the stragglers, after instructing Wagner to press on and get the wounded to safety in Estcourt. He then returned on foot along the railway line, passing through a cleft in a hill, unaware that most of the men he was going back to help had already surrendered.

Two figures in civilian clothes suddenly appeared a hundred metres ahead of him. At first, Churchill thought they were British railway workers. But he was wrong—they were Boers and they were armed. Churchill spun around and fled. He heard the thud of bullets left and right, felt one of them graze his hand, but he continued to run and managed to scramble up the railway embankment. There was a brief respite, then shock, when he realised that another disaster was looming on the crest of the hill. A horseman was galloping towards him across the tracks, a tall, dark figure with his rifle trained on him. Churchill weighed up the odds. He knew how to shoot and—war correspondent or not—he was carrying a Mauser pistol. He had shot to kill before, in Tirah and Omdurman. He felt for his holster, but the pistol was gone. Slowly, he raised his hands.[24]

The rules of warfare

Pretoria, 18 November 1899

His arrival at Pretoria station was ghastly. On the way, walking through Natal and during the train ride, Churchill had almost come to like the Boers. They had been inquisitive and trusting, had gathered around him, offered him coffee and cigars, bandaged his wounded hand and plied him with questions. 'So they were not cruel men, these enemy,' he had noted with some surprise, having expected to meet with hostility and humiliation. But it felt different here on the platform of the station in Pretoria. In those three days in captivity, he had come to respect and even sympathise with the simple, kind-hearted burghers who were making their way to the front to defend home and hearth. Here, however, he sensed animosity—and corruption. These were the profiteers, the fat cats who got others to do their dirty work. Unsavoury types, Portuguese, Dutch, all scum. Ugly women, too, in threadbare clothes, who stood in the hot sun glaring at the British for a good 20 minutes.

A battery of cameras recorded their shame: prisoners at the mercy of the enemy, compelled to submit and obey. A few days earlier he had scoffed at the officers who had been so quick to surrender. Then he had done so himself. It was the ultimate humiliation. Policemen in white helmets—called Zarps, he was told—herded them into rows: himself, Haldane, the 50 men from the Dublin Fusiliers and the Durban Light Infantry. Couldn't they stop sneering? 'Now for the first time since my capture I hated the enemy.'

His fame meant nothing here. At first he had been placed with the soldiers. Haldane had put in a word for him. Churchill belongs with the officers, he protested—not because he had acted like an officer on the train (it was wiser not to mention that)—but because he was a war correspondent and, moreover, the son of a lord. Your aristocrats mean nothing to us, they snapped back. Haldane spoke to a field cornet, with more success. A few minutes later, Churchill rejoined the two officers. The conditions under which the two groups were detained were vastly different. Soldiers were assigned to the racecourse, already congested with 2000 men, while officers were housed in a former school building, now used as a prison. There were already about 60 men there.

Churchill had mixed feelings about them, but at least they were all

British. Their quarters were reasonably comfortable, and they were treated exceptionally well. Even so, he wanted nothing more than to be free as soon as possible. At the time of his capture he had invoked his status as a journalist. He was a civilian, he had insisted, and should be released—though he didn't really have a leg to stand on, as he realised himself. He was wearing an army jacket of sorts, and had taken part in active combat, a leading role in fact. A military tribunal could have had him executed there and then. Moreover, he had reason to be grateful to the Boer who had captured him, Field Cornet Sarel Oosthuizen—although Churchill claimed to his dying day that it was Louis Botha in person. On his way to prison, he had suddenly remembered the two clips of Mauser bullets in his pocket. They were 'soft-nosed bullets', in other words dum-dums. Just having them in his possession was a serious offence. He managed to drop one round on the ground without being noticed, but he was caught with the second. 'What have you got there?' the dark horseman asked in English. Churchill feigned innocence and opened his hand. 'What is it? I picked it up.' He got away with it. The man took the clip, inspected it and tossed it away without saying another word.

The Boer leaders he spoke to weren't intending to release him. The state attorney, Jan Smuts, was in Commandant-General Joubert's tent when Joubert took the decision. Smuts's advice was clear. On the train Churchill had conducted himself like a soldier, and what a soldier! The story of his heroic exploits had spread like wildfire. So there was nothing to do but detain him. Joubert agreed. He also had unpleasant memories of Churchill's father, Lord Randolph, who had travelled through southern Africa eight years earlier and spoken disparagingly about the Boer regime. Even after Churchill had arrived in Pretoria by train, Joubert sent a telegram to the authorities there, instructing them '*not* to release the son of Lord Churchill' as long as the two countries were still at war.

The upshot was that they turned down Churchill's formal request for recognition of his civilian status. President Paul Kruger would probably have approved it, but he wasn't prepared to override Joubert. So Churchill remained in prison. As a British prisoner of war he was short of nothing except his freedom. They slept six to a room, but in warm weather they were allowed to spend the night outdoors on the veranda, with only a flimsy iron fence separating them from the street. Their mess committee supplemented the prison rations they received daily, and they could buy anything else they wanted, except firearms, from the local shop. Churchill traded his prison-issue mustard-yellow overalls for a dark tweed suit. Prisoners could also communicate freely with the outside world, by telegram or letter, and they were allowed to receive visitors. And

Churchill could continue to send his dispatches to the *Morning Post*, as usual. The prison governors treated them well, too. The deputy director, J.W.B. Gunning, 'an amiable little Hollander', went out of his way to make them as comfortable as possible, even borrowing books for them from the national library. Churchill formed a friendship with one of the governors, Louis de Souza, a Transvaler of Portuguese descent, who was also secretary of the war ministry and second only to Joubert in rank. The two men corresponded and De Souza visited Churchill frequently. Over a bottle of whiskey he smuggled into the prison in a basket of fruit, they reflected on the outcome of the conflict for both sides, poring over charts of the theatre of war. Adversaries, but gentlemen.

As for visitors, Churchill couldn't complain. The American consul Charles Macrum, whom his mother had contacted through friends and acquaintances, called to see how he was getting along. Other war correspondents came to interview him. The under-secretary for foreign affairs, Pieter Grobler, spent time with him as well, reflecting on the causes of the war. Churchill was in demand because of his family background as well as his new-found fame. It was just what he had always wanted, but what good was it here in prison? He hated being confined, however comfortable the conditions. The fences, the guards, the regulations—the humiliation was unbearable. He was determined to get out, and he kept trying.

He wrote letter after letter to the Transvaal government, asking them to review his case. He persuaded Haldane to testify on his behalf. On his birthday, 30 November, he wrote a long letter to the Prince of Wales, another of his mother's friends. It was on the pretext of commending the bravery of Charles Wagner, the driver of the armoured train, but he made a point of noting that he himself had been present strictly as a 'non-combatant'. That last statement was presumably intended for the benefit of the Transvaal censors, as was his praise for the Boers' kindness, courage and compassion. He wrote a second letter that day, to another of his mother's admirers, the American entrepreneur and politician Bourke Cockran, with whom he had struck up a friendship on his journey to Cuba. Here he expressed his feelings more candidly. 'I am 25 today—it is terrible to think how little time remains.'[25]

Impatient, ashamed and disappointed by the lack of good news, Churchill continued to languish in prison. There was nothing uplifting for a British patriot to report as far as the war was concerned, though of course all the news that filtered through from the four fronts reflected the Boers' point of view. And for all his usual complacency, even he was shaken.

He had felt miserable that first night in custody, cold and wet in a shed somewhere in Natal. Unable to sleep, he had heard the Boers singing their evening psalm. Worse than shellfire, he thought, 'It struck the fear of God into me.' What if the war was unjust and the heavens had turned against them? What if the Boers were actually better men than they were? He could see it all before him: Ladysmith, Mafeking and Kimberley fallen, the garrison in Estcourt wiped out, intervention by foreign powers, South Africa lost. 'That would be the beginning of the end.'

The sun rose the following morning and dispelled his gloom. On the way to Pretoria, Churchill used his skills as a journalist to record his own experiences. He wrote in detail about his lively conversations with his prison guards, giving readers of the *Morning Post* an impression of the thoughts and sentiments of ordinary Boers. On the culprits, for instance, 'You know it's those damned capitalists and Jews who have caused the war.' And on the controversial cavalry charge at Elandslaagte, 'We have heard that your Lancers speared our wounded.' But most revealing for newspaper readers in the late nineteenth century—and certainly for readers today—was what Churchill heard from a certain Spaarwater, a Transvaal Boer from the Ermelo district. He struck Churchill as a mild, soft-spoken man until the subject turned to freedom. That was something they enjoyed in the Transvaal and the Orange Free State, Spaarwater remarked, but life in Natal and the Cape Colony was 'not free'. There, the natives could do what they liked. 'Well, is it right that a dirty Kaffir should walk on the pavement—without a pass too?' That's what they do in your British colonies. Equal! Free! Not a bit . . . *We* know how to treat Kaffirs in *this* country . . . We educate 'em with a stick . . . They were put here by the God Almighty to work for us. We'll stand no damned nonsense from them.' Churchill made no reply.

His other conversations with the enemy, in the persons of De Souza and Grobler, were more sophisticated. But the unscrupulous Transvaal press was getting him down. *De Volksstem*, for instance, had published a stream of depressing reports about fictitious Boer victories and British cowardice. All lies and propaganda, no question about that, but he didn't have access to reliable information and it preyed on his mind. There was the story of General Koos de la Rey, who had captured another armoured train on the western front and discovered a cache of dum-dums; the one about the 'surrender' of the besieged garrison at Mafeking followed by a bayonet attack that night; the endless griping about the cavalry charge at Elandslaagte; more dum-dum bullets found after the battle at Rietfontein; General Kock wounded and left behind on the battlefield at Elandslaagte, stripped of everything he owned, even his clothes. It was all nonsense, of course, or grossly exaggerated, but it left Churchill feeling uneasy.

The most controversial reports in the Transvaal papers were allegations about the deployment of African and coloured auxiliary troops. The British commanders in Mafeking and Kimberley were said to be forcing Africans to engage in combat, contrary to the unwritten agreement between the opposing parties that this was to be a white man's war. Most shocking of all was the incident in the village of Derdepoort in the western Transvaal, near the Bechuanaland border. On 25 November a Boer laager in the area had been raided by a group of Kgatla led by Segale, the half-brother of their chief, Lentshwe, who was apparently armed and supported by British troops. They had massacred half the population and then fled to Bechuanaland, taking several Boer women and children with them. What was Churchill to think of it all?[26]

Willem Leyds knew exactly what to think about Derdepoort, about Elandslaagte, the dum-dum bullets and that unspeakable incident with the white flag. He had no doubt that it was all true. Right from the start, the British military censors had prevented him from telegraphing Pretoria directly, but through various channels and of course by mail he had received quite a few reliable reports of atrocities committed by British troops. On 26 October 1899 he had issued a press release from his office in Brussels, saying, 'the British are arming local coloured people and deploying them in active combat against the Boers.' As the South African Republic's official representative, he had protested in the strongest terms—he didn't need any special authorisation from his government to do so—against 'this criminal and despicable act . . . which places the lives of the entire white population of South Africa in jeopardy'.

Nor did he stop there. British soldiers were behaving 'like true barbarians' on the battlefield, he wrote to the Russian envoy in Brussels, N. de Giers, in early December. The evidence was pouring in. They were slaughtering disarmed adversaries as if they were on a boar hunt, robbing the dead and wounded of wedding rings and other possessions, carrying out military operations under the ruse of a white flag, and using dum-dum bullets and grenades containing lyddite. All were violations of the rules of warfare laid down in the Geneva Convention of 1864 and reaffirmed at the International Peace Conference in The Hague just a few months earlier. The British were flouting international agreements off the battlefield as well. They were buying huge numbers of horses and mules for their troops in South Africa wherever they could lay their hands on them, including officially neutral countries like Italy and Spain.

Leyds had an ulterior motive for conveying this urgent message to his Russian counterpart in Brussels. Tsar Nicholas II had personally instructed De Giers to keep him informed of developments in the war. Leyds knew this, and through the envoy addressed himself almost directly to the head of state who was the most likely to do something in response. Unlike his wife, Queen Victoria's granddaughter, Nicholas II was firmly on the side of the Boers. He seemed open to the idea of an anti-British initiative and would act alone if it came to that, with the support of the Russian military authorities and public opinion. But the foreign minister, Count N.V. Muraviev, and the rest of the Cabinet had reservations. They weren't against collaborating in a Franco-German initiative, but felt that unilateral action, like massing troops on the Afghanistan border, would be too great a risk for the Russian government.[27]

Staking his bets on the whims of an autocratic emperor was a long shot, as Leyds knew. He had tried it before with Kaiser Wilhelm II after the Jameson Raid. But he didn't have much choice. After the Anglo-German accord of August 1898, which divided up bankrupt Portugal's colonial territories, nothing much could be expected of Berlin, and even less after the Kaiser and his wife paid a family visit to Windsor Castle in late November 1899, accompanied by their foreign minister, Bernhard von Bülow. If it had been up to Chamberlain, the visit would have paved the way for closer ties between the two countries and ideally with the United States as well. But that was a step too far for the Germans. After the war broke out anti-British sentiment, stoked by the pro-expansionist Pan-German League, had flared up in the German press and infected public opinion. Wilhelm II and Von Bülow would commit to nothing more than strict neutrality as far as the war in South Africa was concerned. In exchange, Germany would receive concessions from Britain in other parts of the world to further its own imperialistic ambitions, which included, with growing urgency, the acquisition of a fleet of its own.

Paris was equally reluctant to take measures of any consequence. The French public were as keenly interested in the war as the Germans and Russians. They rejoiced at the Boers' successes and jeered at the British defeats, but Fashoda had tied their hands. If the French government did anything at all, it was in the realm of quiet diplomacy. The best example of this was handed to Leyds personally on 4 November 1899 by a senior official of the French ministry of foreign affairs. It was a document drawn up in consultation with, perhaps even by, the minister, Delcassé, in person. Delcassé had high expectations of this *Appeal to the Nations Represented at the Hague Conference*, an urgent petition to the British government on behalf of 'the conscience of the world' to stop annihilating a civilised nation. Delcassé thought it best to remain on the sidelines. He wanted Leyds to disseminate the document and rally support in as many countries as possible, with a view to stepping up international pressure on London.[28]

Initially, Leyds approved of the idea. The petition addressed 'British philanthropists', not 'the British financial world', and called on them to endorse 'the principles of arbitration'. This tied in with his work as an envoy, and it had also been explicitly incorporated in the Boers' ultimatum of 9 October. He instructed his consular staff to arrange for the document to be translated and disseminated with as many signatures as possible.

This was easier said than done. Getting the wording right in the various translations was a nightmare. The more signatories there were, the more difficult it was to edit the texts. The thorniest problems, surprisingly, arose in the Netherlands. Since 29 October 1899 a press office in Dordrecht had been assisting Leyds with his propaganda campaigns. In charge of it was H.J. Kiewiet de Jonge, a teacher at the local high school and secretary of the Algemeen Nederlandsch Verbond, or General Dutch Alliance, which had been founded after the Jameson Raid, in the summer of 1896. Unlike the Dutch South African Association, the Alliance targeted the Dutch-speaking community, which included Flanders. After the outbreak of the war it had also become more active and more vocal than the Association. Its offer to provide 'a well-equipped press office' serves to illustrate this point. Leyds already had a press office in Paris but he welcomed this extra opportunity to have 'information in the Dutch-African spirit translated and published in sympathetic newspapers'.[29]

Kiewiet de Jonge went to work straight away. He published a Dutch edition of Jan Smuts's diatribe, *A Century of Wrong*, which had been sent to Leyds from Pretoria, and had it translated into French and German. With the same enthusiasm, he arranged for the *Appeal* to be circulated. Kiewiet de Jonge had translated it into Dutch himself and presented the result to prominent members of the General Dutch Alliance, at which point things started going wrong. Everyone had something to say. Some were critical of the legal terminology, but most importantly they objected to the way the message came across, and especially to its emphasis on arbitration. To Leyds's surprise, the mood in the Netherlands was 'more militant' than anywhere else. 'In fact, no one wants to hear about ending the war, whether by arbitration or otherwise . . . After all, it's going so well, why not keep going and drive the British into the sea? That's the general attitude in Holland.'

It was a fair observation. The whole of Europe sympathised with the Boers—'the whole Continent is on our side,' Leyds had observed with satisfaction when hostilities broke out—but the Dutch were the most supportive of all. Rich and poor, Protestant and Catholic, across the whole political spectrum, academics, journalists and shopkeepers, everyone was passionately involved in the fate of their blood brothers in Africa.

After the Dutch colonial army's recent display of strength in the East Indies—in Lombok in 1894 and Atjeh in 1898—the country was caught up in a frenzy of militant nationalism. The Boers' successes seemed like a sequel, like something they had accomplished themselves. The Dutch were organising public petitions, solidarity projects, fundraising campaigns and ambulances. Many were volunteering to go out and fight. Even Leyds was fired up. As soon as the war started he had written to Pretoria, saying, 'I wish to assure His Excellency [President Kruger] that I am entirely at his service. I hate being here in Europe and am willing to come and give my life at a moment's notice.'

It never actually came to this, any more than all the emotional drumbeating in Europe led to political action. The Dutch government, especially the foreign minister, De Beaufort, kept a cool head and, in the interest of peaceful enjoyment of their possessions in the Dutch East Indies, remained strictly neutral. Leyds also recovered his composure and continued to look for a solution in some form of mediation. Rejecting that option now, he explained to his mentor and confidant Moltzer, would be doing the same as Britain had done before the war, 'when it refused arbitration or mediation, because it believed it was the stronger of the two parties'. But, he lamented in the same letter, given that so many of their respected fellow countrymen favoured that course, he was thinking of 'abandoning' the 'Petition' altogether.[30]

That left diplomacy as the only way forward. Leyds had to admit there was little to choose from when it came to candidates for mediation. In fact, there were only two, apart from the Russian tsar. One was near at hand. He knew that the young Dutch queen, Wilhelmina, was fervently committed to the Boer cause. Earlier, in July 1899, he had intimated to Prime Minister Pierson and De Beaufort that she might get somewhere with the elderly British queen. They had dismissed the idea, but Wilhelmina had nevertheless taken it upon herself to write a letter to Victoria, appealing to her 'well-known feeling of humanity and magnanimity . . . to stop this war'. It hadn't achieved anything. Queen Victoria had thrown the ball back: if Kruger had been reasonable, there wouldn't have been a war in the first place. Leyds didn't know about Wilhelmina's single-handed intercession. But in December she indicated that she would be willing 'to mediate between the two, alone or with others, now or at any convenient time in the future'. A personal appeal to the German emperor? The answer depended on her constitutional powers. Leyds would have to wait and see.[31]

The second candidate for mediation was far away, across the Atlantic Ocean. To be honest, Leyds had little faith in the American president, William McKinley. Britain had sided with the United States in the Spanish-American War of 1898, in fact if not on paper, and Leyds thought that Washington might be willing to reciprocate. And though most Americans seemed to support the Boers, they weren't as keyed up about the war as the Europeans. As a result, the American government had considerably more room to manoeuvre. This applied in particular to the secretary of state, John Hay, to whom McKinley had delegated much of the decision-making about the conflict. The situation didn't bode well. Hay was a self-professed anglophile, who believed in the superiority of the Anglo-American way of life. But because 'Pretoria was still hoping the United States would mediate', Leyds did what was expected of him. He arranged for the Transvaal's consul-general in London, Montagu White, to be transferred to Washington, and proposed that the Orange Free State's consul-general in The Hague, Hendrik Muller, should go there as well. But, like many of his compatriots, he felt the time wasn't ripe for mediation. 'In view of our favourable prospects at the moment, I would be disinclined towards any form of intervention.'[32] So White went to the United States alone.

That left only the anti-war movement in the British Empire itself. In this respect the dominions could be written off. Canada, Australia and New Zealand had sided with the motherland and were in the process of sending their own contingents to reinforce the British troops in South Africa. Ireland was trickier. There were Irish troops fighting on both sides—the Dublin Fusiliers and the Royal Irish Fusiliers with the British, the Irish Brigade with the Boers—which exacerbated the already troubled relationship between the two parts of the United Kingdom. Riots broke out in Dublin, but they were contained: the Irish had no links to the anti-war movement in England.

And that movement was substantial. Its adherents included church and social-democratic organisations, independent Liberal politicians, academics, journalists and business people, represented by groups like the South African Conciliation Committee. The secretary of the committee's women's division, Emily Hobhouse, was later to play a significant role in the war. At this stage, however, the most prominent anti-war protester was the controversial journalist William Stead. He was as deeply committed to British imperialism as to world peace, and believed that the two went hand in hand. In late September 1899, after returning from the International Peace Conference in The Hague, he had published a manifesto called *Shall I Slay My Brother Boer? An Appeal to the Conscience of Britain*. It was an indictment of the impending war, 'this great crime', which would cost thousands of lives and produce nothing but 'another and more distant Dutch Ireland'. Stead continued to protest. He founded his own Stop the War Committee and published a weekly journal, *War Against War in South Africa.*

Leyds found in him a welcome ally in his pro-Boer campaign. Stead wrote the preface to the English edition of *A Century of Wrong* and voiced his support for the 'Petition'. Their collaboration, however, entailed risks for both parties. Leyds's association with the peace activist would close doors he would rather keep open, while Stead's contact with the Transvaal envoy put his own reputation for independence at risk. So anxious was he to safeguard his credibility that he wouldn't allow Leyds to reimburse him for a postage stamp. This was just the kind of thing the 'Jingo papers' would pounce on and regurgitate as 'distributing thousands of pounds for the corruption of the Press'.[33]

As far as mud-slinging was concerned, nothing had changed since the outbreak of war. In the British press Leyds was still a liar and slanderer. But the balance of power had shifted. Leyds now held the winning hand in the propaganda war on the European continent, like the Boers on the battlefield itself. Even so, 'Jingo journalism' in Britain had become more strident than ever. Protests by Stead and his followers were no more than a whisper in a raging storm of nationalism, one that was growing even more militant now that there was something to fight for. Challenging the South African Conciliation Committee were numerous pro-war groups, like the Imperial South African Association (formerly the South African Association), the Primrose League and the Empire League. The war against the Boers was the talk of Britain, in boardrooms and drawing rooms, in public houses and music halls. There was actually something at stake. Victories inspired popular songs, defeats were lamented in poems, dramatic events thrilled audiences who saw them enacted on film. As in Pretoria, accusations and recriminations were dished out left, right and centre. Whatever *De Volksstem* flung at the British, *The Times* flung back at the Boers. Fraudulent use of the white flag, theft from the dead and wounded, the plundering of occupied villages, the deployment of black auxiliary forces. Here, the Boers were the transgressors. The British were fighting a horde of unscrupulous barbarians. The Boers were no good.

Fortunately, 'our Boys' were showing them what true heroism was all about—like Winston Churchill, whose name had been on everyone's lips since that farce—for that's all it really was—with the armoured train near Chieveley. The wounded soldiers who had made their way back to Estcourt in the damaged locomotive had nothing but praise for his gallantry and presence of mind. And to think he was only there as a war correspondent.

The story had done the rounds in no time, in Britain as well as South Africa, helped along by Churchill's colleagues Leo Amery and John Atkins and his old retainer, Thomas Walden. Walden had sent Lady Randolph a letter, which was subsequently published in the *Morning Post*. Churchill had regrettably been captured, Walden wrote to say, but he was fairly certain that he hadn't been wounded. 'Every officer in Estcourt thinks Mr C. and the engine-driver will get the V.C.,' he announced proudly, adding that 'the driver says he was as cool as anything and worked like a nigger, and how he escaped he doesn't know, as about fifty shells hit the engine. Everyone in Maritzburg is talking about Mr Churchill.'[34]

What better publicity for a young man burning with political ambition, who wanted nothing more than to be a celebrity. The only trouble was that Churchill couldn't take advantage of it. He was still imprisoned in Pretoria. It was already December 1899 and nothing had come of his requests to the Transvaal authorities for a discharge on the grounds of his civilian status. On 8 December he tried a different tack. He sent De Souza another letter, to be forwarded to Joubert, using his word of honour as ammunition. 'If I am released I will give any parole that may be required not to serve against the Republican forces or to give any information affecting the military situation.'

Surprisingly enough, this letter prompted Joubert to think things over again. A few days later it turned out that he had indeed changed his mind. On 12 December he sent a telegram to the state secretary, Reitz, giving his consent to Churchill's release in exchange for his word that he would return to Europe and give a true account of his experiences as a prisoner of war in the Transvaal. But he added a postscript which reveals his misgivings. 'Will he tell the truth? He probably has something of his father's nature.'

Joubert's suspicions were warranted, but not for the reason he thought. In the meantime, Churchill had grown increasingly impatient. Instead of waiting for a reply, he devoted his ingenuity and energy to finding some other way to regain his freedom. From the very moment of his capture he had been trying to think of ways to break out. Once in prison, he and a couple of young officers and soldiers had hatched a sensational plan. They weren't simply going to escape; they were going to overpower the guards, free the 2000 non-commissioned officers and soldiers on the racecourse, occupy Pretoria, abduct Kruger and the rest of the Transvaal government, and broker an honourable peace. It was a hare-brained scheme, the kind of melodrama that Churchill relished, but the senior British officers put an end to it.

In that case, he'd have to settle for something less ambitious. He knew Captain Haldane was hatching a plan in cahoots with a fellow inmate, a sergeant-major who had passed himself off as a lieutenant. The impostor was A. Brockie of the Imperial Light Horse. The partnership suited Haldane. Brockie knew the country and spoke Afrikaans as well as an African language, which would be an asset on their journey to the Mozambique border, 450 kilometres away. Churchill wanted to join them, but they turned him down. To make their escape it was important for them not to be missed for several hours. There were no roll calls in their prison. Churchill, however, was something of a celebrity and his absence would be noticed at once. So they said, rather not. But Churchill persisted. Mindful of his heroic exploits on the ambushed train, Haldane found it difficult to refuse him. In the end he relented and won Brockie's consent as well. It was an extra risk, but so what? The three of them would escape together.

The plan began to take shape on 9 December. It was fairly straightforward, but timing was of the essence. A latrine shed stood at the far end of the yard, near the iron fence. Hidden inside it, unseen by their guards, they would wait for the right opportunity. Early evening would be best, a few moments when the sentries were distracted. They would sprint to the iron fence, scale it as quickly as possible—from there they would be in full view—then drop down into the garden of the abandoned house next door. There, Haldane would reveal the rest of the plan.

They set the date for the evening of Monday 11 December. Churchill was nervous but he nevertheless wrote a farewell note to De Souza, intending to leave it on his bed. He must have gloated over passages like 'I have decided to escape from your custody' and 'regretting that I am unable to bid you a more ceremonious or a personal farewell'. In any event, it helped to relieve the tension. When evening fell, Haldane, Brockie and Churchill were ready to go, but it all came to nothing. A sentry stationed beside the shed refused to budge and the plan had to be postponed.

The following evening—Joubert's consent to Churchill's release had already arrived in Pretoria, but hadn't yet reached the state secretary's desk—it looked as if their escape would be foiled again. The sentry was back in the same place. The three would-be fugitives grew restless and started pacing back and forth between the veranda and the shed. Suddenly Churchill saw his chance. He was alone in the shack, when the sentry strolled away to talk to a comrade. This was a golden opportunity. It was too dangerous to fetch the others, so he decided to go first; they could follow later. It was now or never. He dashed to the fence, hoisted himself up, hesitated, lowered himself again, then clambered to the top. Now! His jacket caught on the ironwork and in a flash he saw the glow of a sentry's cigarette, not 15 metres away. He tugged at his jacket, pulled himself free and dropped lightly into the garden below.[35]

The abandoned mine

Witbank, 15 December 1899

The rats weren't the worst part of it. They made off with Churchill's candles and occasionally scurried over him, startling him out of his sleep. But what he couldn't stand was being cooped up underground with nothing to do, alone and bored to tears. How long had he been here? Was it one day? Two? He had lost all sense of time. It seemed interminable. When the mine manager, John Howard, returned, he would explain that he wanted to be on his way. With food, a pistol, an escort and if possible a horse he'd be able to cover the last stretch to the border. After all, he had managed to get this far on his own. From what Howard had told him, the Boers believed he was still hiding out in Pretoria, though in fact he had left the first evening. He had been lucky, for sure, incredibly lucky. But then he always was.

Looking back, it was strange to think how he'd sauntered out of Pretoria, like someone taking an evening stroll. The truth is that he'd been scared to death. Fear had gripped him from the moment he climbed over the prison fence and landed in the garden next door. He'd spent more than an hour there, crouching in the bushes, waiting for his two companions. He'd even exchanged a few whispered words with Haldane on the other side of the fence. Haldane and Brockie had decided not to risk it. The sentries seemed to sense something was up and were more vigilant than usual—though it hadn't occurred to them to investigate outside the grounds. If Churchill couldn't return without being caught, he should continue alone. That was Haldane's advice.

It wasn't ideal. Churchill spoke neither Afrikaans nor an African language, he had no map and no compass. His companions were going to bring those, along with some biltong and a few opium tablets, the all-purpose painkiller. All he had with him was cash—a decent amount, £75 to be exact—and four bars of chocolate. The house they had believed to be unoccupied was teeming with people. But climbing back over the fence would be idiotic. No, he would continue on his way and hope that his luck would hold.

He put on the hat a fellow inmate had given him, straightened his clothes, smoothed his trousers, stepped out of the bushes and ambled to the gate. He made a point of passing close to the window, trying to look as if he had every right to be there. Out in the street he caught sight of a guard, less than five metres from where he stood. He turned his face away, fought back the panic and the urge to run, and strolled casually into the bustling street. No one even noticed the young man in a dark suit, humming softly to himself.

By the time he reached the outskirts of the city he had worked out a plan. The railway line to Lourenço Marques was his best bet. Nearing a small station, he managed to clamber onto a goods train and hide in a heap of empty coal sacks. At least that would get him out of Pretoria and, what's more, he was heading in the right direction. The next morning, just before dawn, he jumped off the train. He had no idea where he was, but he found a pool of water, quenched his thirst and spent the rest of the day in hiding. When darkness fell, he looked for a suitable place to repeat the procedure of the day before. He found the perfect spot on an incline where the tracks rounded a bend. The train would be forced to slow down.

Churchill's luck seemed to have run out. He waited for hours, but there was no sign of a train. Around midnight he gave up and started walking along the tracks. This would get him at least ten, 15 kilometres further. It was hard going. He had to keep making detours to dodge a station here, a house there, sentry posts on every bridge. The moon was full and, to avoid detection, he had to scramble through reeds and wade through water. He couldn't keep it up much longer. Suddenly he saw campfires in the distance. A kraal, he thought, and decided to try his luck. He had heard that the Africans disliked the Boers, and his English banknotes would probably help too. As he drew closer, he realised he had been mistaken. The fires were ovens, the kraal was a coal mine. He must be on the outskirts of the mining district of Witbank and Middelburg.

This discovery put everything in a different light. In Pretoria he had been told that a few Englishmen had stayed on here to keep the mines running until they could start extracting coal again. But how was he going to find them? There were a few houses nearby, one made of brick. Should he take the risk and knock on the door? He felt for his money. He could promise far more, a thousand pounds, if that's what it took. It was half past two in the morning. The alternative was to keep trudging through the open veld. Churchill walked up to the house and knocked on the door.

It worked like magic—as if the knock had restored his legendary good luck. The tall man who appeared in the doorway was John Howard, the manager of the Transvaal and Delagoa Bay Collieries, a fellow countryman and someone who was willing to help. Churchill had chanced on the only house for miles around where he would not be turned over to the authorities. Howard assured him that 'we are all British here, and we will see you through'. He was true to his word. He offered Churchill whiskey and roast lamb while he went to confer with his colleagues. To remain there and continue working they had been obliged to take an oath of neutrality. Helping a fugitive would put them at risk, but all four—Howard's secretary, an engineer from Lancashire and two Scottish miners—agreed at once. For the time being, Churchill could take refuge in the mine. They gave him a mattress, blankets, candles, a bottle of whiskey and a box of cigars. And good wishes from the engineer, Daniel Dewsnap, who, by coincidence, came from Oldham, the constituency in which Churchill had unsuccessfully stood for parliament six months earlier. 'When you go to Oldham again, lad, they'll all vote for you. Good luck!'[36]

He had scaled a fence, strolled out of Pretoria, hopped on a train, stolen past sentry posts and, with the help of generous compatriots, found a sanctuary in the bowels of a coal mine. So far, Churchill's escape had been a great adventure, borne along by chance and incredibly good luck. And its protagonist was a daring young man with faith in himself and his extraordinary destiny.

But the story of Churchill's escape is more than a series of colourful anecdotes. It raises the question of what it meant for the Transvaal—and to a lesser extent the Orange Free State—to be a country at war for the first time. It wasn't about organised violence as such. Military campaigns, on a larger or smaller scale, were nothing new to the Boers. But apart from their few brief confrontations with the British in 1880–81 and the Jameson Raid in early 1896, they had always been conducted against indigenous adversaries, on or within their borders. And they had generally come to a predictable—successful—end, without seriously disrupting the country's political or economic life. The present war with Great Britain was of a different magnitude and a totally different order. The largest and most powerful empire on earth had resolved to bring the Boer republics to their knees and was directing all its military, economic and human resources to that end. For the Boers the threat was internal as well. This applied in particular to the two branches of industry that were of crucial economic and military importance to the republics, namely the railways and the mining sector. The mines employed huge numbers of British citizens. How were the Boer authorities to deal with them?

As far as the railways were concerned, the solution was fairly straightforward. The only direct line through the Orange Free State—the southern line and its few branches—was already run by the state and was therefore not an immediate security problem. In the Transvaal, the Dutch-owned Netherlands-South African Railway Company—a source of pride as well as a headache to Kruger and Leyds—had acquired a virtual monopoly in the years before the war and was operating on all trunk lines. Only the local line from Pretoria to Pietersburg in the north was still in the hands of a British company. When, on the grounds of the company's neutrality, its director refused to make the line available to the military authorities, he and his British staff were deported and the line was taken over by the Netherlands-South African Railway Company. The same happened to lines in Natal and the Cape Colony, which the advancing Boers required for military purposes.

At this stage the company's principal function was to support the war effort. Kruger and Leyds had much to be proud of. The concession awarded to the company in August 1884, which they had subsequently fought to retain, proved to be a long-term investment with the best possible return. Since 1895 the company had been a massive contributor to the Transvaal treasury. After the Jameson Raid it had played an important part in building up the Republic's substantial arsenal. And now, its new director since late 1898, J.A. Kretschmar van Veen, was dedicating its facilities and services to the Transvaal's war effort.

He was obliged to do so under article 22 of the concession, which provided that 'in times of war or in the event of internal unrest the Government may take control of the railway and everything required to operate it, for defence purposes or in the interests of public order, and may wholly or partly suspend regular traffic, subject to payment of compensation to the concessionary'. On 29 September 1899 the Volksraad had decided to invoke that provision. From then on, the Netherlands-South African Railway Company came under the control of the military authorities and functioned as the Boer forces' railways division. It provided transport for Boer commandos, British prisoners of war, war casualties, horses, mules, oxen, wagons, guns, munitions and supplies of every kind. The company's staff also repaired and guarded bridges and crossings in Natal and the Cape Colony that retreating British troops had destroyed. In addition, its management offered favourable terms to any of its employees who wanted to join the Hollander Corps or any of the Boer commandos.

But Kretschmar van Veen did far more than was formally required by article 22, and even that, he felt, wasn't sufficient. He saw the concession as more than just a business contract. It represented the trust placed in him by the Transvaal government. 'We have a moral obligation in all circumstances to merit that trust . . . We are a Dutch company and we are in business to make money, but what we possess is a Transvaal railway. The first can be neutral, the second cannot.' Inspired by his belief, he also put the company's central workshop in Pretoria at the army's disposal. There, besides building hospital trains they also cast horseshoes, produced munitions and even repaired and assembled artillery, complete with mounts.[37]

This kind of loyalty and commitment obviously couldn't be expected of the mining industry. The most vehement opponents of the Kruger regime were to be found in and around Johannesburg: the mine owners, frustrated by the oppressive monopolies, and the Uitlanders, deprived of political rights. One didn't need to agree with the British Liberal parliamentarian James Duckworth—'If the Rand had been a potato field, there would have been no war'—to appreciate the extent of the gold industry's impact on the Transvaal, if only on its demographics and its social and cultural life. Because of it Johannesburg had evolved into a dynamic centre of business and finance. It was the fastest-growing city in the world, where population figures rose and fell to the rhythm of the stock market, where life itself was in a rush. English was the lingua franca, the majority of the white population originated from and maintained ties with Great Britain, while many had links with Cape Town and London. In short, the enemy.

This was a serious problem for the Boer leaders. Johannesburg was a breeding ground for conspirators, a potential fifth column, within 50 kilometres of Pretoria. Deporting them all would cripple the goldfields and deprive the Boers of the revenue they needed to fight the war. Leaving them where they were would be a considerable security risk.

By and large, the problem resolved itself. As from June 1899 it was clear that people were apprehensive and many were starting to leave the mining areas. Political tensions were mounting—the talks between Milner and Kruger in Bloemfontein collapsed early that month—and everyone could see they were preparing for war. A large fort was being built on the crest of Hospital Hill, in central Johannesburg, and at this point it was nearing completion. It formed part of the fortifications the government had decided to build after the Jameson Raid. The fort was intended as a defence against attacks from outside, but it also served—intentionally—as a warning to the local population. Unfortunately, it was more effective in that respect than the authorities had expected. Rumours spread like wildfire among the Uitlanders. The Boers were going to bomb the mines from the fort. They were going to send foreigners to the front to form a human shield. They were going to stand by while unemployed black miners plundered the city. They were going to starve them to death.

These anxieties triggered a migration. September saw an exodus, early October a frenzied flight, in goods wagons filled to the gunnels. The Boer leaders in Pretoria tried in vain to stem the flow. Even they didn't want the entire population to run off, especially not the educated, white working community. They assured the mine owners there was nothing to fear as long as the mines continued to operate. For most, this came too late. Even the promise of generous bonuses for experienced personnel fell on deaf ears. Mines closed down, one after the other. Between June and mid-October 1899 an estimated 100,000 whites and as many Africans, coloureds and Asians left the Rand.

The mining areas didn't die out completely. About 20,000 whites and 15,000 Africans stayed on, just enough to keep at least a few mines running, which was exactly what the Transvaal government wanted. Towards the end of September the Executive Council, with the Volksraad's approval, passed a number of resolutions in anticipation of a state of emergency. Mine owners who wanted to continue operating were obliged to obtain work permits for their employees. Mine workers had to take an oath of obedience and good conduct. Gold yields were to be handed over to the government in Pretoria for safekeeping. The government would mint and supply sufficient coins to cover the mine owners' costs and would refund the balance when the war ended. Mines that suspended production could be taken over by the state, either temporarily or permanently. A Peace and Order Commission was installed, chaired by the commissioner of peace D.E. Schutte. Alcohol was prohibited, travel permits became mandatory. British citizens without a work or residence permit were deported.[38]

In early October, with the war imminent, the Transvaal government compiled an inventory of abandoned mines. There were 66 in all. How could they make the most profit with the smallest possible workforce? When war broke out, they soon reached a decision. The three most promising mines, the Robinson, the Bonanza and the Ferreira Deep, were taken over by the state right away. The Rose Deep followed in November. The eight privately owned mines that continued to operate were placed under the supervision of an inspector.

Even before the war broke out, Pretoria had introduced a far more direct method to supplement its gold reserve, namely confiscation. On 2 October, by order of the state attorney, Jan Smuts, a consignment of gold worth more than £400,000, en route by train from Johannesburg to Cape Town, was intercepted at the Transvaal border. A week later Smuts sent police officers to empty the gold vaults of Johannesburg's banks. As of 11 October goods and services of all kinds could be requisitioned. The state-controlled gold mines flourished as a result. The Boers seized dynamite, potassium cyanide and whatever else they needed. They extracted gold only from the layers of rock containing the highest concentrations, with no thought for the prospects of the mining industry in future. They slashed the wages of the black workforce.

All these measures were permissible under the state of emergency. Labour was declared one of the services that could be lawfully requisitioned. It was to be deployed according to new regulations based on nationality, education and skin colour. Burghers were called up for commando service on the front. Uitlanders who wanted to remain in the Transvaal were obliged to obtain work permits; those with special skills were awarded bonuses. This largesse was something the black miners couldn't even dream of. For them the approaching war meant loss of income, an uncertain future and expulsion from the Transvaal; the war itself brought the prospect of forced labour. The thousands of Africans who found themselves without work or food after the mass closure of mines in September and early October received no assistance from their former employers. Many of them had been recruited from the coastal regions of Mozambique, Zululand and Natal, and were left to make their own way home. They needed special passes to travel, but with their numbers steadily increasing they became a threat to public order. The authorities responded by relaxing controls, bundling them into goods trucks and shunting them off in droves. If there wasn't space for them in the trains to Lourenço Marques, they were sent south.

Trains were being deployed for military transports and many of these miners were unable to travel at all. In early October, an estimated 7000 men from Zululand found themselves stranded in Johannesburg. Rather than leave them waiting for trains to become available, John Marwick of the Native Affairs Department in Natal obtained permission from the authorities to escort them home on foot. The men set off in an orderly column, 30 abreast, singing traditional Zulu songs. They covered more than 50 kilometres a day. Initially they were provided with food and places to rest. Seven days after leaving Johannesburg they limped into northern Natal, famished and exhausted, only to face another ordeal. They were intercepted by Boer fighters, who commandeered a few hundred men to haul their guns up a hill. Only once they had done so were they able to complete their march home.

Those who undertook the journey had only this one experience of forced labour. The men left behind were subjected to it every day of the whole war. They could either keep their jobs on the mines, mostly working longer hours for less pay, or, like all other Africans in the Transvaal, work on the land or as servants of the Boer commandos.[39]

Although the authorities in Pretoria enforced rigorous security measures in vital sectors like the railways and the mining industry, these precautions didn't extend to their surveillance of British prisoners of war. Churchill's escape from prison, daring as it may have been, was made possible by an amateurish prison regime. Scaling a fence was hardly a Houdini-like feat. The authorities hadn't reckoned on such large numbers of prisoners and had underestimated their determination. Churchill's escape turned the whole of Pretoria upside down.

As Haldane and Brockie had anticipated, his disappearance was discovered early the following morning, causing a great deal of commotion. No one could figure out how he had done it and speculation was rife. Some said he'd escaped in a rubbish bin, or disguised as a woman; he was lying low somewhere in town, or had he already been recaptured in Waterval Boven? Homes were searched, a couple of Zarps were sent to the front in disgrace, a few 'suspect' Englishmen were thrown out of the country. The Boer leaders felt betrayed, Commandant-General Joubert most of all. He had sent his telegram approving Churchill's release only days before. The affair should be made public, he insisted to the state secretary, Reitz, 'to show the world what a villain he is'. A photograph of the fugitive, along with a personal description, was pasted on the wall of the government building. Beside it was a 'Dead or Alive' poster. Churchill had a price of £25 on his head.

Prison security was tightened, more sentries were employed, some to patrol the garden next door. Alcohol was prohibited, sleeping on the veranda became a thing of the past, no more newspapers for inmates, and roll call twice a day. It was especially hard on Haldane and Brockie, whose hopes of escaping had gone up in smoke. Churchill's impatience had led to a great deal of frustration in the prison and beyond, and the incident was never forgotten. The legend that he had broken his word and betrayed his friends was an understandable emotional reaction, but it wasn't actually true. Even so, it hounded Churchill for the rest of his life.[40]

Churchill himself was oblivious to all the upheaval. He had other things on his mind in his underground lair. He felt claustrophobic and hated being confined again, this time on his own, in total darkness and in a silence broken only by an unnerving pitter-patter. Howard listened sympathetically when Churchill told him this during his next visit, and on the night of Friday 15 December he escorted him to the surface. A stroll on the veld and a breath of fresh air lifted Churchill's spirits. Howard realised it would be better for his health and state of mind to remain above ground. At the back of the mine office was an unused storage room. It would be reasonably safe.

And so it was, for as long as it lasted. But at some stage he would have to move on. Churchill still believed he would manage with a horse, a pistol, an escort and some food, but Howard disagreed. He proposed an alternative which he had already discussed with a local merchant, Charles Burnham, another Englishman who was prepared to take risks to help a fellow countryman. Burnham was about to send a consignment of wool to Lourenço Marques for shipment abroad. There was enough to fill a couple of railway wagons, with sufficient space left over for Churchill to hide among the bales. This was the plan.

It took a couple of days to make the arrangements. On the night of Monday 18 December they were ready. The wool had been loaded and covered with sailcloth, and a space had been cleared for Churchill on the floor of one of the wagons. He packed a loaf of bread, a melon, two roast chickens, three flasks of cold tea, some whiskey and a pistol—but no cigars, for obvious reasons. They expected the journey to take 16 hours at most, although in wartime one always had to be prepared for delays. At the last minute, Burnham decided to accompany Churchill, just to be on the safe side.

It turned out to be a good move. The journey was not as uneventful as they had hoped. In Witbank, soon after they set off, Burnham parted with a couple of 'Christmas gifts' to have the wagons coupled to an ongoing passenger train. A few generous shots of whiskey persuaded the guard to cooperate. He used the same ruse in Waterval Onder, where—after a whole night's wait—their wagons were joined to another train. And in Kaapmuiden, the last station before the Mozambique border, Burnham managed to prevent a Boer commando from searching Churchill's wagon. This time, it was coffee that did the trick. After that, crossing the border at Komatipoort was easy. The customs officer allowed the consignment to pass without being inspected, but the Portuguese authorities were more difficult. They demanded that the wagons be uncoupled from the passenger train, which held them up for several hours, until the next goods train arrived.

All that time—it was already Thursday 21 December—the wagons had been in Portuguese territory, but Churchill was still on edge. He thought he heard people speaking Dutch and was desperate not to be caught at the last minute. He only calmed down when the train set off again and arrived at the next station. Through a chink in the wall he saw Portuguese uniforms and a signboard indicating that they had arrived in Ressano Garcia. Once they had passed the station, he gave vent to his excitement. He peered out, emerged from the sailcloth and sang, roared, crowed with delight. Free at last. He drew his pistol and fired two, three shots in the air.[41]

A warm welcome

Durban, 23 December 1899

The local newspaper, the *Natal Mercury*, was short of good news. Disappointment following the Black Week disaster hung like a cloud over the town. The British troops had suffered crushing defeats on three fronts. In a single week three distinguished generals had fallen into disgrace: on 10 December Sir William Gatacre at Stormberg on the southern front; on 11 December Lord Methuen at Magersfontein on the western border of the Orange Free State; and on 15 December the commander-in-chief, Sir Redvers Buller, at Colenso, here in Natal, less than 200 kilometres from Durban. It had been a week of shame and humiliation, with almost 3000 British soldiers killed, wounded or captured. The numbers were staggering—almost ten times as many as on the Boer side.

The *Natal Mercury* and the whole of Durban were desperate for something to lift their spirits. The news about the spectacular escape of the *Morning Post*'s young war correspondent came as a godsend, and he was now on his way here. That very afternoon, Saturday 23 December, Winston Churchill would be arriving in Durban, the headlines announced, on board the *Induna*, the weekly mail steamship from Lourenço Marques. By one o'clock a rapturous crowd had gathered on the quay. Among them was a large contingent of Uitlanders who had left the Johannesburg area to settle in Durban. The ships in the harbour were decorated with flags. When the *Induna* sailed in, around four o'clock, at least a thousand people were waiting to welcome the hero. In the absence of a free berth, the *Induna* moored alongside two other vessels. Everyone went wild and people swarmed over the decks. The most determined of them bounded over to Churchill and lifted him onto their shoulders. He barely had time to nod at the dignitaries queuing up to greet him as he was taken to the quay, where the crowd demanded a speech.

Standing on a box, hands on his hips, the cowboy hat from Lourenço Marques clasped lightly in his hand, Churchill addressed his ecstatic admirers. The impression he made was more militant and more self-assured than the photograph suggests. 'No matter what the difficulties, no matter what the dangers . . . we shall be successful in the end.' The Boers, 'these reactionary Republics that menace our peace', would be defeated, 'because our cause is a just and right one, because we strike for equal rights for every white man in South Africa and because we are representing the forces of civilization and progress'.

This was the rallying cry they had been waiting for. They wouldn't let him go. He was installed in a rickshaw and paraded to the town hall, while the crowd continued to swell. A flat wagon had been placed in front of the building to serve as a platform. Whether he wanted to or not, he would have to deliver another speech. No one had to twist his arm. After the crowd's spontaneous rendition of 'Rule, Britannia!', Churchill rose to speak. Again, effortlessly, he struck the perfect note of nationalistic pride. 'We are now in the region of war, and in this war we have not yet arrived at the half-way house.' But the outcome would be triumphant, he assured them. 'Under the old Union Jack there will be an era of peace, purity, liberty, equality, and good government in South Africa.' The 'loyal and devoted colonists of Natal' could depend on it.

Finally inside the town hall, Churchill had a chance to catch his breath. He received a handful of congratulatory telegrams from the local commanding officer. He regaled journalists with the story of his escape, carefully omitting details that might incriminate Howard or Burnham or any of the others who had helped him. Then he went outdoors again. The crowd was still euphoric and kept cheering. Churchill posed for photographs, then announced that he wanted to get back as soon as possible. Back to the front. A rickshaw festooned with British flags was waiting for him. This time it took him to the railway station where the 17.40 to Pietermaritzburg was ready to depart. Churchill had his own coupé. Well-wishers flocked to the platform to wave him off. The train shuddered into motion, the last hoorahs, the last goodbyes, handkerchiefs fluttering, and off he went. Churchill had spent one hundred minutes in Durban. He settled back in his seat. He had plenty of time to read a month's supply of newspapers.[42]

The contrast couldn't have been greater. Churchill was exhilarated by his successful escape and his overwhelming reception in Durban, but he was also distressed about the catastrophes that had befallen the British forces. The shameful details of the fiascos at Stormberg, Magersfontein and Colenso differed, but the reasons for the three defeats were essentially the same: over-confident commanders, an inflexible strategy, underestimation of the adversary's capability, unfamiliarity with the terrain, poor coordination, an inability to improvise. It seemed as if British officers took pride in making the same mistakes over and over again. Even Buller, for all his experience in South Africa, had lost his touch. Colenso was his personal Majuba. He came out of it a broken man, his career in shreds.

Three days after the defeat, on 18 December, he had been relieved of his command and replaced by Field Marshal Lord Roberts, the leader of the 'Indian ring' in the British army.

His downfall fitted into a pattern. From the start Buller had felt he had no control over his own war. While he was still in England, the war secretary, Lord Lansdowne, had given him little say in the preparations. At the same time, Buller's urgent warnings against taking positions north of the Tugela had been cast to the winds. To make things worse, they had suffered both defeats on the very day he set foot in Cape Town. And Milner only had more bad news. Mafeking and Kimberley were under siege as well, and Milner himself feared an Afrikaner uprising in the Cape Colony.

In these circumstances, in early November, Buller felt it would be unwise to follow his original plan. At one stage it had all seemed so straightforward. The idea was to take his entire 1st Army Corps of 47,000 men and steamroll his way to the north, over the highveld to Bloemfontein, Johannesburg and Pretoria. He mulled it over for a few more days, but then abandoned the plan altogether. It would be irresponsible. Instead, he decided to divide his forces. Milner had recommended two detachments, which would enable them to defend the Cape Colony and relieve the sieges of Kimberley and Mafeking at the same time, but Buller opted for three. Unlike the high commissioner, he wasn't prepared to give up White, Ladysmith and, as a result, perhaps the whole of Natal.

What is more, he would go to the eastern front himself with more than half his corps—that is, half once all his units had arrived. He knew that part of the country well. He loved its rolling green hills. He would be able to force the decision. He instructed Lieutenant-General Lord Methuen to proceed west with 11,000 men to relieve Kimberley. Major-General Sir William Gatacre would repel the Boer commandos who had invaded the Cape Colony from the Orange Free State. Gatacre had 3000 men as well as support from the cavalry units under Major-General French, who had narrowly escaped from the besieged Ladysmith. It took a few weeks to organise the detachments, ensuring that suitable command structures were in place and that the units were evenly balanced. Then, of course, the entire logistical operation still had to be planned. On 21 November Methuen crossed the Orange River, and a day later Buller set off for Natal.[43]

Methuen wasted no time. 'I shall breakfast in Kimberley on Monday,' he bragged in a telegram to the commanding officer of the embattled Kimberley, Lieutenant-Colonel R.G. Kekewich. In other words, it wouldn't take more than a week. His first encounters with the Boers boosted his confidence even further. Advancing along the railway line, he defeated them at Belmont on 23 November, at Graspan two days later, and at Modder River on 28 November. They were hard-fought victories, it must be said, especially the last, where Methuen himself was wounded. All in all, the British incurred heavy casualties: 140 dead and 780 wounded, far more than the 50 dead, 140 wounded and 90 captured on the side of the Free State and Transvaal forces. But Methuen had managed to flush the Boers from their positions on three occasions, and there was only one more obstacle on the way to Kimberley. He felt this compensated for his heavy losses. And he saw no reason at all to change his strategy: first, his artillery fire against the enemy positions, then the frontal infantry attack, and finally the cavalry pursuit.

The Boers, on the other hand, did change their strategy, notably the kind of positions they chose. They had always preferred positions on the slopes or crest of a hill or mountain. But the Transvaal field general, Koos de la Rey, had learned from experience at Modder River that there might be a better alternative. An entrenched position at the foot of a hill, for instance, would give them the advantage of a horizontal and therefore more effective line of fire over British infantry storming towards them. He proposed trying this more systematically with the next line of defence—the last before Kimberley—near Magersfontein. The Transvaal adjutant-general, Piet Cronjé, dismissed the idea as a dangerous gimmick, but President Steyn of the Orange Free State, who had come to the front, was impressed. De la Rey could go ahead. He ordered his 8000 troops to dig trenches in a sweeping half-moon formation over an eight-kilometre front, around the forward slope and two sides of Magersfontein Hill. In front of them he erected a barbed-wire fence. Now they would wait for the British to attack.

They came in the same formation as always, but this time with an overwhelming force. Methuen had increased his troops to 15,000 men. On Sunday 10 December Boer sharpshooters in decoy positions on the crest of the hill held off the British scouts. Believing that the Boers were dispersed over the slopes as usual, Methuen ordered an all-out artillery bombardment. For more than two hours his 33 guns transformed Magersfontein and the surrounding heights into a blazing inferno which surely no one could have survived. This was the moment to storm the Boer positions. Shortly after midnight—it was now 11 December—the Highland Brigade, led by Major-General Andy Wauchope, began its advance, with other units following on either side. By dawn they were to be in position for a frontal attack on Magersfontein Hill. They got there in time. At first light they were about to cover the last few hundred metres to the hill.

The Boers, safely entrenched, were ready as well. The ferocious bombardment of the previous day had claimed only three casualties. Now their time had come. The Highlanders, at close range and in their conspicuous green kilts, were an easy target. The Boers unleashed a relentless barrage of gunfire. The elite Scottish troops fell by the dozen, Wauchope among them. Those who were lucky managed to protect themselves by lying flat on the ground. Those who were wise remained there all day in the burning sun, enduring hunger, thirst, ants, flies and sunstroke, rather than face a certain bullet. The battle around them was more evenly matched. Both sides were frenzied. The Scandinavian Volunteer Corps, holding a forward position on the Boer side, incurred the heaviest casualties. British infantrymen managed to penetrate parts of the Boer lines, only to be driven back subsequently. By afternoon it was over. The retreat had begun even before Methuen gave the signal. Only the unfortunate Highlanders, too close to the Boers to escape, were compelled to wait until nightfall. The British losses came to 210 dead and 740 wounded, missing or captured, the vast majority of them from the Highland Brigade. On the Boer side 90 were killed and 185 wounded.[44]

The British defeat at Magersfontein was all the more bitter because things had gone badly the previous day as well, on 10 December, at Stormberg, the railway junction on the line between De Aar and East London. Five weeks earlier Churchill had travelled on the last train to get through. Since then, 2000 Free State commandos led by Jan Olivier had occupied the Stormberg valley. Sir William Gatacre was determined to drive them out. Like Lord Methuen, he was counting on the surprise effect of an attack by night. The evening before, at nine o'clock, he and his column of 3000 men had set off from nearby Molteno. As at Magersfontein, it was the attacking force that was taken by surprise, and again because they were unfamiliar with the terrain. The column lost its way and the disoriented troops wandered around aimlessly in the dark. As it turned out, they ended up close to the Boer commandos on the Kissieberg, precisely where they were heading, except that they had come from the opposite direction and had no idea where they were.

They soon found out. The Boers, having just sat down to breakfast, were pleasantly surprised. They couldn't believe their eyes. The British troops had unwittingly walked straight into their trap. From their positions on the hillside they could pick them off one by one. But there were still the Royal Irish Rifles and the Northumberland Fusiliers to contend with. Once they had recovered from the shock, they began to storm the crest, but boulders near the top blocked their way. Close to exhaustion after their ordeal in the night, they took cover to await reinforcement. When help arrived, it only made matters worse. The British artillerymen firing on Kissieberg were blinded by the rising sun and failed to realise that their missiles were raining down on their own men. Their infantrymen on the hill had only one thought: get down as quickly as possible. Those who couldn't took shelter behind the boulders. Eventually Gatacre had to concede that the situation was hopeless. He called a retreat at half past five, just over an hour after the fighting had begun. But as soon as they started their descent, the British troops were attacked from the opposite side by commandos under Esaias Grobler, the Free State chief commander on the spot. In all the commotion Gatacre had 'forgotten' that his order to withdraw hadn't reached the contingent at the rear. After waiting in vain for hours, the 600 officers and men on the slopes of the Kissieberg were forced to surrender. Casualties on the British side came to 28 dead, 60 wounded and 634 captured. The Boers lost eight dead and 26 wounded.[45]

After the debacles at Stormberg and Magersfontein, Buller had a lot to put right in Natal. From Estcourt and Chieveley, both familiar to Churchill, he made preparations for the relief of Ladysmith. The whole situation was worrying. By mid-December his force had grown to 19,500 men. He also had 44 guns and 18 machine guns, but before him lay the Tugela. It was a turbulent, meandering river which could only be crossed at a few unreliable drifts. And the railway bridge at Colenso—still intact a month earlier, when Churchill had joined the reconnaissance in the armoured train—had since been blown up. The real problem, however, was the positions the Boers had taken on the opposite bank of the river. Buller could see their strongholds on the hills on the north bank. They were mainly concentrated around the railway line he had been depending on to get his troops and supplies closer to Ladysmith. They had obviously been waiting for him here, so he couldn't take them by surprise; skirting around them, moving away from the railway line, was too dangerous. It would have to happen here.

The Boers across the Tugela *did* have a surprise in store. Firstly, they had a new commander, a man of a different calibre from Piet Joubert. The commandant-general had fallen from his horse and was unable to remain active on the front. On 30 November 37-year-old Louis Botha assumed command of the troops at the Tugela. At Modderspruit he had made a favourable impression as acting commandant. Here, at Colenso, he was about to demonstrate his brilliance as a tactician.

Botha's force was greatly outnumbered by Buller's. He had 3000 men with five pieces of artillery, and a few kilometres to the west another 1500 men to cover his right flank. Even so, Botha had absolute confidence in the strength of his position. Like De la Rey at Magersfontein, he had chosen flat terrain rather than hillside positions, as close to the river as possible. The strongholds Buller had seen on the heights were deliberately intended to mislead him. In reality, the Boers were entrenched in the mud over a ten-kilometre front on the north bank. Their positions were well camouflaged and fortified with sandbags.

The only weak spot in the Boer line was its far left flank at Hlangwane Hill, where the Tugela took a sharp bend to the north. When the commandos who were first sent there fled in panic on 13 December, President Kruger had to intervene in person, or at least by way of three peremptory telegrams. 'Do not surrender the summit across the river, or all hope will be lost. Fear God, not the enemy . . . Fight in the name of the Lord and trust Providence to guide you and lead you to victory.' The message helped. On 14 December Botha replied that as a result of Kruger's words 'our fears have been overtaken by courage'.

It was just in time. For the previous two days the British artillery had been pounding the hills north of the Tugela, and that night the Boers saw a multitude of small lights flickering in the British camp. Buller was obviously preparing for an all-out attack. His war machine went into action at a quarter past five the following morning, Friday 15 December. First a battering from the powerful naval gun at the rear, then the infantry divisions advanced over a broad front. At Colenso itself they were preceded—an element of surprise after all—by Colonel Long with 12 field guns and six small naval guns. For two days the Boers had managed to keep their gunpowder dry—and their positions secret—and they continued to do so until Botha gave the signal. Once the British infantry units reached the south bank of the Tugela and Long had ranged his guns neatly in the vicinity of Colenso, then, and only then, did Botha give the command to open fire, first with the largest of the Boers guns, then the remaining four. This was what his men had been waiting for. They discharged a volley of Mauser bullets, at far closer range than the British had expected. It came as a complete surprise: vicious fire from an invisible enemy and nowhere to hide. British soldiers fell to the ground left, right and centre, slain, wounded or in sheer terror. Their artillery also took a beating. Long himself was wounded, and at seven o'clock the survivors retreated. They took their wounded and their small naval guns, but were forced to abandon their 12 fifteen-pounders.

Half an hour later Buller withdrew other units from untenable positions and in the course of the morning he ordered a general retreat. He called for volunteers to rescue the remaining guns. One of the men who came forward was Lieutenant Frederick Roberts, the field marshal's only son. They managed to retrieve two of the guns, but ten were left behind. Seven of the men were recommended for a Victoria Cross, including Lieutenant Roberts. But the award came posthumously. Roberts was one of 143 killed on the British side, along with 756 wounded and 240 missing. The Boers lost eight dead and 30 wounded, took 38 prisoners, and captured ten guns in perfect working order, as well as a good supply of ammunition. All told, Black Week cost the British 2800 men, killed, wounded or captured, compared with 350 Boers. It was a total humiliation.[46]

The only good news Churchill came across in his pile of newspapers was about the three towns besieged by the Boers. Mafeking, Kimberley and Ladysmith were still holding out. Glimmers of hope turned into blinding spotlights in the British press. The Boers had destroyed their telegraph lines, but the towns were able to communicate with the outside world by means of heliograms and with the help of African and coloured couriers who managed to slip through the Boer lines. The local commanders— White in Ladysmith, Kekewich in Kimberley and Colonel Robert Baden-Powell in Mafeking—were thus informed about the liberating armies' delay. Conversely, the outside world received news about the plight of the beleaguered civilians and soldiers.

After the British defeats on the battlefield, their ordeals—bombardments, starvation, infectious diseases—assumed epic proportions. The three towns were of special interest to those who followed the news in Natal, the Cape Colony and Britain, as there was at least one well-known personality in each of them. 'Doctor Jim' Jameson, who had carried out the controversial raid, was in Ladysmith. Cecil Rhodes, the architect and sponsor of the raid, was in Kimberley, the city of diamonds, which he, as the kingpin of De Beers Consolidated Mines, regarded more or less as his personal property. Mafeking's celebrities came from the ranks of the titled and well-to-do. There was Baden-Powell, who made a name for himself during the siege and later as a pioneer of the international Scout movement, and his two staff officers, both with noteworthy family connections. Major Lord Edward Cecil was the son of Lord Salisbury, the British prime minister; Lieutenant Gordon Wilson was married to Lady Sarah, Lord Randolph Churchill's youngest sister. In other words, Lady Sarah Wilson was Winston Churchill's aunt. She was a fellow journalist as well, reporting on the war in South Africa for another English newspaper, the *Daily Mail*. They had even more in common. Lady Sarah had also been imprisoned by the Boers, in her case—rightly—for espionage. She regained her freedom around the same time as her nephew, though not through her own doing. The Boers agreed to release her in exchange for Baden-Powell's undertaking to extradite a certain Petrus Viljoen, a horse thief with whom they still had a score to settle. In any event, Lady Sarah was able to join her husband in Mafeking in time for Christmas. By smuggling out dispatches she kept readers of the *Daily Mail* informed about daily life in the besieged town. Winston Churchill's interest in her was purely professional. Personally, he couldn't care: he was not particularly fond of his aunt. During his time as a military cadet at Sandhurst she had once accused him of 'thievish practices'—and only because he had tried to sell a pair of surplus field glasses. 'Such a liar that woman is,' he had fulminated to his mother. He had kept out of her way ever since.[47]

But the sieges of Mafeking, Kimberley and Ladysmith were interesting enough, personal anecdotes aside. There were similarities in the way events unfolded in the three embattled towns, just as there had been in the battles at Magersfontein, Stormberg and Colenso. The most surprising characteristic was a complete reversal of roles. Here, the Boers were the unsuccessful invaders and the British the victorious defenders. None of the Boer commanders—Piet Joubert at Ladysmith, Piet Cronjé at Mafeking and Christiaan Wessels at Kimberley—had tried to push through right at the start. As a result, their counterparts, White, Baden-Powell and Kekewich, had all the opportunity they needed to organise their defences and improve their reinforcements, trenches and underground hideouts. After an initial burst of momentum, the sieges gradually declined into a state of inertia, broken only by the occasional skirmish. The Boers' artillery fire became predictable and discipline in their camp grew slack.

Again it was clear that the Boers weren't at their best in an offensive position, at least not as far as their older commanders were concerned. Even when they were out to conquer they seemed to retreat into a defensive role. They shrank from frontal attacks to avoid losses. Unlike British generals, they were sparing with their men. Instead, they resorted to the tactics they had always used against the fortified settlements of indigenous adversaries, namely surround them and starve them into submission. And they too dug trenches and erected fortifications. Seen from the air, the three towns under siege must have been a remarkable sight. All three were surrounded by a double ring of defence lines facing each other: the rings of Saturn symbolising defence as a superior tactical concept.

Not that life was easy for the civilians and soldiers in Mafeking, Kimberley and Ladysmith. The bombardments claimed casualties, food was scarce, rations were steadily reduced, and infectious diseases were rampant. But that didn't diminish the perseverance and resourcefulness with which the organised white community defended themselves—or their indifference to the plight of the African and coloured population. For this was also typical of all three sieges: Africans and coloureds paid the highest price.

Mafeking, with a white population of 1500, was located just over the south-western border of the Transvaal. The adjacent and likewise beleaguered 'stadt' of Mafikeng was inhabited by 5000 Tshidi Barolong and 1500 black mine workers who had fled from the Rand. Baden-Powell called on everyone to assist in the town's defence. He increased his regular white troops with locally recruited volunteers to a total of 1200, and armed another 400 Barolong and other Africans and coloureds with rifles. The heavy work on the defence lines was done by black labourers, who were also responsible for vital intelligence work—with occasional help from the odd eccentric like Lady Sarah. African scouts, spies and couriers transmitted information to and from the outside world. Yet their valuable contributions to the defence effort were not rewarded with an equitable share of available food. When rationing was introduced in November 1899, many of them, particularly the refugees from the Rand, were unable to afford even the meagre rations to which they were entitled. As a result, most of the deaths during the siege occurred in Mafikeng.

The Boers likewise employed black labour. They recruited workers among their old allies, the Rapulana Barolong, rivals of the traditionally pro-British Tshidi Barolong. Around 300 men were armed and deployed in the trenches and on the fortifications. Others served as scouts or were sent to raid cattle from the enemy. Before long these raids were their only form of offensive action. Cronjé had started the siege in mid-October with 5500 men, but within a week Koos de la Rey had gone off with 2500 of them, first to Kimberley, then to Modder River. Cronjé himself followed three weeks later. By mid-November there were no more than 1400 Boers around Mafeking, under the command of General Kootjie Snyman. They had three pieces of artillery left, a Long Tom, a Krupp and a Maxim, none of which was put to much use. Once a week, they fell totally silent as the Boers faithfully observed a day of worship. This gave the townspeople and soldiers a chance to relax, with polo for the officers and soccer for everyone else.[48]

In Kimberley too, the number of Boers holding the siege declined significantly. In late October, Wessels still had 7000 men from the Free State and the Transvaal. In November, they countered several attempts by British units trying to break through, making use of their heavy artillery. Kimberley was a coveted prize. It occupied a strategic position and was home to the famous diamond mines, along with their infrastructure and large supplies of dynamite and coal. There was also a psychological factor. The Boers hadn't forgotten the time the British had confiscated the diamond fields in 1871.[49] They also knew that Cecil Rhodes, the bane of their lives, was in town. But none of this was enough to make them change their approach. The countryside around Kimberley is flat and open, offering no natural cover. That alone was a reason for the Boers not to attack. They merely shelled the town from a distance, to little effect. In the heaviest bombardment, on 11 November, they fired around 400 shells. Most of them landed in the Big Hole and only one of the town's inhabitants was killed. Their last direct confrontation was a skirmish on 28 November. After that the Boers turned their attention to Lord Methuen's advancing army. No more than 1500 Free Staters, under the command of General Sarel du Toit, were left around Kimberley. The opportunity to capture the town had passed.

Starving the population was, however, still an option. In the meantime, the town's defence works had been improved and were in excellent condition. With generous help from De Beers there were now forts equipped with searchlights and linked by telephone lines, and a 50-metre watchtower, as good as could be. Kimberley's weak spot was its relatively large population. At the outbreak of war it totalled 50,000, comprising 13,000 whites, 7000 coloureds and 30,000 Africans. On the one hand, this provided Kekewich with large reserves of labour and reinforcements for his regular troops—which he doubled to a total of more than 4500. The downside was the many mouths to feed. Malnutrition was a growing problem and, as in Mafeking, Africans and coloureds bore the brunt of it. They received less of the available—and steadily dwindling—supplies. Attempts were made to reduce their numbers by force. Rhodes took the lead—on his own initiative, so as to undermine the commanding officer, Kekewich. On the night of 6 November he drove 3000 black mine workers out of town, but to no avail: the Boers sent them straight back. Bids to flee—some forced, some voluntary—were more successful. Around 8000 Africans managed to escape from the besieged town. Their departure eased the pressure on the town's food supply, but for many this came too late. By mid-November diseases like typhoid, dysentery and scurvy had become rampant. Hundreds perished, the vast majority of them Africans and coloureds.[50]

The third siege, at Ladysmith, was the largest and most crucial showdown. The railway lines to Durban, the Transvaal and the Orange Free State intersected here, making the town a strategic junction. With a peacetime population of 5500 whites, Ladysmith had initially been the starting point for White's foolhardy expeditions in northern Natal. After Mournful Monday it became a refuge for his 13,500 defeated troops. Added to this was the influx of 2500 African and Indian refugees from the coal-mining district in Natal. By the time it was besieged the town had a total population of 21,500. White had 50 artillery pieces and 18 machine guns to defend them.

At the start of the siege the Boers in the surrounding hills had 10,000 men and 22 guns, including three Long Toms, and five machine guns. Besides Ladysmith's strategic position—it was the key to the Boers' further advance in Natal and their chance to eliminate an entire British army—there was also the lure of spectacular spoils: guns, personal arms and equipment, munitions, food and other supplies. An enterprising Boer leader would have done everything in his power to take the demoralised and disorganised British troops by surprise as quickly as possible. But Piet Joubert wasn't that kind of leader. On that legendary Monday 30 October he had prevented his men from pursuing the fleeing British soldiers, to the frustration of young commanders like De Wet and Botha. In the days that followed, he did nothing to put pressure on the beleaguered troops in Ladysmith. His inertia gave White a chance to recover and organise the town's defence, for example by deploying Africans and Indian refugees to dig foundations for fortifications. In the course of November the Boers launched two half-hearted attacks, but that was all. Joubert rejected a proposal to dig trenches in a zigzag configuration, which would have brought his marksmen to the edge of the town. He considered starvation and grenades the best means of forcing a surrender.

When poor health compelled Joubert to resign as commander on the Natal front in late November, the Boers saw these as the only options. In a council of war held on 2 December their commanders concluded that the opportunity to storm the town had passed. There was also the fact that Buller was approaching with a detachment of the 1st British Army Corps. They had to be stopped at the Tugela. The force around Ladysmith, already diminished by the many Boers who had left of their own accord, was reduced to 3500 men. A few British officers in Ladysmith took the opportunity to organise two breakouts, on the nights of 8 and 9 December, when they managed to put one of the Long Toms out of commission. This did much to boost the morale of the soldiers and townspeople in Ladysmith. Besides the ordeals of bombardments and food shortages, they were also short of clean drinking water. Here, too, they fell prey to typhoid and dysentery. Thousands ended up in the hospital encampment that had been set up on neutral territory, with Joubert's consent, in Intombi, to the south-east of the town. Hundreds of them died.

On 15 December it turned out that help, so close at hand in the form of Buller's army, would take a while longer to arrive. The unfortunate British defeat at Colenso had destroyed all hope that Ladysmith would be liberated any time soon. This was underlined by the disheartening tone of Buller's message. A few days after the fiasco he sent White a heliogram saying he still needed about a month to prepare another attack on the

Boer lines. Would he manage to hold out? If not, Buller advised him to use up as much ammunition as possible and then try to negotiate the best deal he could. In other words, he was to surrender. And above all, he shouldn't forget to burn his secret codebook. There were other messages that betrayed Buller's desperation. It was also evident from the telegram he had sent the war secretary, Lord Lansdowne, the evening after the battle. 'I believe I ought to let Ladysmith go, and occupy good positions for the defence of South Natal, and let time help us.'

This wasn't the kind of attitude that won respect for a commander-in-chief. Nor did White follow Buller's advice. He never had. He steeled himself for the long, hot summer ahead. The Cabinet in London decided it was time to bring out the big guns. Buller was relieved of his duties, and only remained in command of the troops in Natal. Lord Roberts of Kandahar replaced him as commander-in-chief, with Lord Kitchener of Khartoum as chief of staff.[51]

It wasn't fair. Churchill realised that, too. The general who had repeatedly warned them not to go 'north of the Tugela' had been forced to rush to the assistance of another general who had done precisely that, and now he was being made to pay the price. But White wasn't the only one to blame. In Churchill's opinion, Buller had also slipped up a couple of times and they weren't just occasional gaffes. By the looks of it, Sir Redvers was physically and mentally burned out. He wasn't his old self or, rather, he was no longer the dynamic young Buller who had won a Victoria Cross for bravery. In Churchill's view, at 60 he was too old for the job and he lacked the resilience to cope with adversity. He made a revealing remark to his friend Pamela Plowden: 'I cannot begin to criticise—for I should never stop.'

Churchill wisely refrained from sharing these thoughts with readers of the *Morning Post*. He must also have been watching his words when he reported to the British camp on 24 December 1899, after his train journey from Durban and the overnight stop in Pietermaritzburg. The camp was in an area he knew well, the valley between Frere and Chieveley, where the Boers had ambushed the armoured train just over five weeks earlier. His own tent was there too, strangely enough, less than five metres from the spot where he had been captured. 'I came home safely again to the wars,' he noted with satisfaction.

Now it was time to fight. This too went smoothly, thanks to the much-maligned Buller, who sent for him soon after he arrived. The roles in which the two men found themselves had changed dramatically since the last time they had seen each other on the *Dunottar Castle* less than two months earlier. The ageing general had fallen from grace, while the young reporter had emerged as a folk hero. Buller was quick to compliment Churchill on his valiant feat. He listened with interest to his experiences in prison and after his escape. Finally he asked whether there was anything he could do for Churchill. The answer came in a flash: an appointment in one of the many units that were now being formed. That would be perfect. But what about the *Morning Post*? Buller asked. Well, he couldn't get out of the contract, Churchill replied, but he could combine the two—war correspondent *and* soldier—as he had done in British India and Sudan.

Buller needed time to think it over. The War Office had recently clamped down on people holding more than one job—mainly because of the critical articles a certain Winston Churchill had written about Kitchener's campaign in Sudan. Buller paced wordlessly around his room before reaching a decision. Eventually he made up his mind and offered Churchill an appointment as lieutenant in the South African Light Horse, a cavalry regiment of 700 men led by Colonel Julian Byng. He wouldn't be remunerated but he could continue to work for the newspaper. Churchill accepted the offer without a moment's hesitation. The regiment he was assigned to was known as the Cockyolibirds on account of the plume cockades they wore on their hats. Churchill was to report for duty on 2 January 1900. He was a soldier again—and now a soldier with feathers in his cap.[52]

Blind spot

Spion Kop, 24 January 1900

It must have been absolute hell up there. But from a distance it looked idyllic: puffs of white smoke every ten seconds, swirls of brown dust and, in the intervals, small dark figures bustling back and forth. It was like a huge anthill, hazy in the summer heat. Churchill raised his field glasses again. He shivered. Those were people he knew up there on the hill, under a torrent of shells. Not personally, but he knew they were from the Lancashire Brigade, along with 200 men of the Mounted Infantry from Natal. Altogether, there were close on 2000 men, or at least there had been when they climbed up the previous evening. Who knows how many were left? They were being buffeted from all sides—the roar of artillery, the crack of machine-gun fire, Mauser bullets raining down. The Boers were swarming over the heights around them. But where exactly? The artillerymen here on Three Tree Hill, the British base, weren't able to locate them.

Churchill looked at his watch. The fight had been going on all day, nearly nine hours without a moment's respite. When the mist lifted that morning, around seven o'clock, the Boers had opened a barrage of fire. The capture of Spion Kop in the night threatened to breach their defence line north of the Tugela. Their commander, Louis Botha, had obviously seen the danger and was doing all he could to drive the British off the hilltop. He set up a fire-spitting shield all the way from the Tabanyama hills in the north-west, past Green Hill, Conical Hill and Aloe Knoll, to Twin Peaks in the north-east. The Boers had also launched a counterattack from the northern, unprotected slope of Spion Kop. Their front-line riflemen were lying along the edge of the ridge, 20 or 30 metres from the first line of British infantrymen.

It was a man-to-man fight to the death. From his vantage point Churchill saw sparks of light reflecting from bayonets in the bright sunshine. Why didn't Lieutenant-General Sir Charles Warren intervene? He was the commander in charge and he could summon all the reserve battalions he needed. Over the past few hours he could have sent reinforcements to Spion Kop, but why didn't he mount an all-out assault on the Boer lines to ease the pressure on the hilltop? After all, he had requested and obtained reinforcements from Major-General Neville Lyttelton, who was

195

standing by with his battalions a few kilometres to the east. And why didn't Buller do anything? He and his troops were still on Mount Alice, on the south bank of the Tugela. From there they could see the disaster unfolding on Spion Kop. Why didn't he insist that Warren take action? Or do something himself? The theatre of war along the Tugela was surreal. An overwhelming force of British soldiers stood by idly and from a distance watched their comrades fight to the death on a battlefield hardly bigger than a polo ground.

Churchill couldn't bear it any longer. He had to go and see what was happening. Captain R. Brooke of the 7th Hussars accompanied him. They galloped to Spion Kop as fast as they could. It was Wednesday 24 January, the fifth anniversary of his father's death. And he was convinced that he wouldn't see the day out either.[53]

Churchill's premonition about his death came true but only 65 years later. Nevertheless, 24 January 1900 was a day overshadowed by death. After what he had seen on Spion Kop, the horrors of war in British India, Sudan and Cuba paled into insignificance. Until then, his exposure to war in South Africa had been more exciting than disturbing. The armoured train, his capture and escape, and the extraordinary reception in Durban were all incidents he had experienced and written about as one big adventure. Although he was a war correspondent, he hadn't actually been present on Mournful Monday or during Black Week. He had only read about them in the newspapers.

Nothing changed when he returned to active service. The Christmas of 1899 had gone by quietly in Natal and on the other fronts. The only skirmishes had occurred on the western front, one just before and one just after Christmas. On 22 December the Boers had retaliated for the raid against Segale and his Kgatla warriors at Derdepoort just under a month earlier, destroying three settlements and killing scores of Kgatla. On 26 December the British in besieged Mafeking had stormed one of the Boer positions on Game Tree Hill. They were defeated, incurring 25 dead and as many wounded.

In Natal, the lull in hostilities ended on 6 January 1900, interestingly enough because of a Boer raid on Ladysmith. The attack was remarkable on two counts. A real offensive was unusual in itself. But it was also carried out on the orders of the commandant-general, Joubert, who had meanwhile returned to the front. What he did took everyone by surprise. Exhilarated by Botha's victory over Buller at Colenso, just for once he threw caution to the wind. In a war council meeting on 3 January the Boer commandants had planned a diversionary attack on the British positions north of Ladysmith, to be followed up with a real offensive from the south. It would be carried out by Transvaal commandos from Heidelberg, Utrecht, Pretoria and other districts, led by General Schalk Burger, together with forces from various parts of the Free State including Harrismith, Heilbron and Kroonstad, under Commandant-General Marthinus Prinsloo. They would target the Caesar's Camp and Wagon Hill strongholds, both located on a massif the Boers called Platrand. The British commander there was Churchill's old friend, General Ian Hamilton. Shortly after one o'clock on the morning of 6 January the Boers started climbing the two hills. At half past two they were detected. A chaotic exchange of gunfire broke out in the dark of night, and only at daybreak were they able to see what they were doing. Both sides engaged their artillery and the confrontation escalated. It turned into a man-to-man struggle. The Transvaal forces gained ground at Caesar's Camp, the Free State commandos on Wagon Hill, but in neither case was it enough to force a breakthrough. Hamilton organised an efficient defence and deployed his men where they were most needed. In Ladysmith, White soon realised that the offensive in the north was a diversionary tactic and that the real threat came from the south. All day long he sent reinforcements to Platrand. The Boer force was uncoordinated and they lacked an overview of the situation. Burger and Prinsloo failed to give them direction. Left to decide for themselves, many of the commandos chose not to risk the climb uphill, and simply fired over a large distance from safe cover.

The climax came in the middle of a torrential downpour at the end of the afternoon. The Boers made one last, unsuccessful attempt to break through. The British launched a counterattack and towards nightfall, around seven o'clock, they drove the Boers from Wagon Hill and Caesar's Camp. As on several occasions before, the British incurred far higher casualties than the Boers—150 dead and 275 wounded as compared with 65 dead and 125 wounded—but at least they had managed to repel the assault on Ladysmith. The outcome shattered the Boers' morale. They had taken the offensive, but once again failed to follow through. However, it restored the confidence of the British defenders of Ladysmith, in spite of their heavy losses, and strengthened their resolve to fight on.[54]

Twenty-five kilometres further south, between Frere and Chieveley, the men in Buller's camp had no idea what was happening. Churchill had woken up early on that 6 January to the sound of artillery fire in the distance. For hours, they could only speculate. Was it an offensive from the garrison or the overwhelming Boer onslaught they had long been dreading? Around midday a heliogram came through from Ladysmith.

'General attack all sides by Boers—everywhere repulsed—but fight still going on.'

Buller leapt into action. He prepared his entire army as quickly as possible and marched on Colenso in battle formation. Churchill soon realised it wouldn't be a real attack, just a show of force to take the pressure off Ladysmith. If the Boers had diverted troops from the Tugela line for their attack, they would probably send them back at once. His reasoning was correct. It only made a difference of 300 men, but they were men under the command of Louis Botha. Moreover, the show of strength gave the British troops confidence. According to Churchill, it was an awe-inspiring sight, especially at the end of the afternoon, when the naval and field guns opened fire on the Boer positions. Right at that moment, the violent thunderstorm that was raging over Wagon Hill and Caesar's Camp broke here too, creating a magnificent spectacle for the British troops massed on the south bank of the Tugela. As they stood watching in bright sunshine, the north bank of the Tugela was transformed into an eerie tableau. Black clouds gathered over the hill to the roar of thunder and guns, flashes of blue lightning, red muzzle-fire, clouds of yellow-grey smoke and columns of dark brown dust. In Churchill's words, 'We watched the impressive spectacle in safety and the sunlight.'

The only disappointment was that the Boers sat through it all without budging an inch. One of the reasons for the attack on them was to find out where they were, but there was no reaction from across the river. When evening fell, the British returned to their encampment. The retaliation came after dark and took the form of a strange air fight. When the British telegraphist tried to communicate with Ladysmith by using a searchlight to beam a Morse code message onto the clouds, the Boers disrupted it, using the same means.[55]

Judging by Buller's vigorous response to the fighting at Platrand, it looked as if he had recovered from Colenso. Indeed he had, in any event sufficiently to risk crossing the Tugela again. The new commander-in-chief, Lord Roberts, was due to arrive from Cape Town a few days later and Buller had regained his confidence. Another division had been added to his expeditionary army and with a total of more than 25,000 men he was sure he could confront the formidable Boer force on the opposite bank.

He was less happy with the commander of the reinforcements. Officially, Lieutenant-General Sir Charles Warren was his second-in-charge, they were roughly the same age, but there was no love lost between them. Warren had been thrust upon him from London by the commander-in-chief of the forces, Field Marshal Lord Wolseley, to replace him if things went wrong, as Buller—rightly—suspected. Warren's appointment had surprised him, and others as well. Warren had experience of South Africa—Kruger and Leyds had come to know him as a tough negotiator in the talks on Bechuanaland in January 1885[56]—but that had been the end of his active military career. Since then he had held only administrative positions. Some of them had been challenging enough—he had been chief commissioner of Scotland Yard at the time of the Jack the Ripper murders—but that didn't make him a commanding officer. The proof came soon after his arrival in Natal.

Buller had devised a new plan of campaign and, in spite of their difficult relationship, he entrusted Warren with the command of his main force. Some considered this incomprehensible and unwise. Others wondered whether it was a deliberate ploy to trip Warren up. When it was all over, Buller insisted that the assignment really hadn't been all that difficult. The plan was basically to outflank the Boer positions to the west, about 25 kilometres from the railway line and Colenso, in other words upstream. He had selected two points where they could cross the Tugela. There, the British expeditionary force—22,000 men strong (the remaining 3000 were to stay behind at the base camp between Frere and Chieveley)—would form two separate detachments. Buller and a third of his troops would cross the river at Potgieter's Drift and take positions on the heights on the north bank, opposite the Boer positions. Warren and the main force were to cross at Trichardt's Drift, five kilometres to the west. From there they would advance to the north-west, working their way around the Tabanyama hills. This would enable them to pass the Boers unnoticed and attack them from the rear. At that stage, Buller would also come into action, so they would be attacking the Boers from two sides.

The plan might have worked if it had been carried out quickly and efficiently. But this wasn't the case. It took a week, from 11 to 17 January, just to get the expeditionary force to Potgieter's Drift and Trichardt's Drift. The cumbersome supplies they were lugging along with them had held them up. Better safe than sorry, Buller and Warren agreed—they were as one when it came to provisions and equipment. As a result, Churchill, along with the rest of the South African Light Horse assigned to Colonel Lord Dundonald's cavalry brigade, looked on in amazement as an 'almost interminable procession' passed by. How on earth did they expect to take the Boers by surprise? They had brought tents for each and every soldier! Churchill had never seen anything like this in British India or Sudan. There, even officers made do without. And in the meantime, they had given the Boers ample opportunity to strengthen their positions. It was one thing for Buller to look after his soldiers, but, he noted prophetically, 'it is a poor economy to let a soldier live well for three days at the price of killing him on the fourth'.[57]

Lord Dundonald's mounted force showed them how things were done. On 17 January they took their ponies and horses and crossed the Tugela, not over the pontoon bridge that had been built at Trichardt's Drift for the rest of Warren's troops, but a little further on, at Wagon Drift, which was more difficult to ford. The following day, they pressed on to the north-west—the infantry and artillery remained behind—to find out how far the Boers' defence line extended. Their haste paid off. Early that afternoon they reached the western spurs of the Tabanyama range. There, they discovered a group of about 200 Boers heading for the next hilltop, near the Acton Homes farm, to reinforce their right flank. They intercepted them, arrived at the hill first, and opened fire. The ambush caught the Boers off guard. They scattered, took cover or fled. Heavy fighting ensued, which put 57 Boers out of action: ten were killed, 23 wounded and 24 captured, compared with two dead and two wounded on the British side. Their tactical gain was even more important. The ridge they now occupied commanded the route around the Tabanyama hills to the rear of the Boers' defence line. In other words, the way to Ladysmith lay open.

But this wasn't how Warren saw it. He wasn't pleased but furious on receiving the news from Dundonald that evening and the following morning. It was all wrong, according to the manuals on warfare. In Warren's opinion, the cavalry should have remained close to the main force to protect the convoy. Dundonald shouldn't have been indulging in 'semi-independent antics'. And to crown it all he wanted more guns and infantry. Warren had little faith in his plan to take the route around Acton Homes. He felt it was too great a distance for his heavily laden ammunition and supply wagons, and without them he wouldn't dream of sending an infantry division anywhere at all. To prevent Dundonald from pressing on alone, he ordered the wagons made specially for the cavalry to turn back. 'If I let them go, Lord Dundonald will try and go on to Ladysmith.' Warren seems not to have realised just how incongruous that remark was. Be that as it may, he knowingly threw away a perfect opportunity to complete the flanking movement that Buller had planned. Instead of taking the route around the perimeter of the Tabanyama hills, from 20 January he did everything in his power to cut straight across. For four full days he made his men charge ahead, for nothing, culminating in the seizure of Spion Kop on the night of 23 January.

The encounter at Acton Homes made a lasting impression on Churchill. He hadn't fought there but he had witnessed the final stage from a distance, and helped tend the wounded Boers. It was that kind of war. To his own surprise, he was deeply distressed. He confided this to the readers of the *Morning Post*. 'I have often seen dead men, killed in war—thousands at Omdurman—scores elsewhere, black and white, but the Boer dead aroused the most painful emotions.' He couldn't say why. Was it that old field cornet from Heilbron—his name was Mentz, the Boer prisoners had told him—a man with grey hair and sharp features set in an expression of unyielding conviction? A bullet had shattered his left leg. They said he had refused to surrender; he just lay there and kept firing his rifle. He was ashen, he had bled to death. That's how they had found him, with a letter from his wife crumpled in his hand. Or was it the boy beside him, not more than 17, with a bullet through his heart? Or there, further along, 'our own two poor riflemen with their heads smashed like eggshells?' Churchill wasn't easily shaken, but what he saw moved him to a rare lament about the dignity and the horrors of war. 'Ah, horrible war, amazing medley of the glorious and the squalid, the pitiful and the sublime, if modern men of light and leading saw your face closer, simple folk would see it hardly ever.'[58]

At Acton Homes it was the small, personal tragedies that had distressed him. On Spion Kop he was shocked by the sheer scale of the carnage. Late in the afternoon of 24 January he and Captain Brooke arrived at the foot of the hill. A whole village of ambulance tents and wagons had sprung up. Stretcher-bearers from the Natal Indian Ambulance Corps—the body-snatchers, as the soldiers called them—scurried back and forth. Churchill and Brooke tethered their ponies and began to climb. Wounded men came towards them in droves, limping down on their own, leaning on four, maybe five comrades, lying on stretchers, crawling on their knees. Bodies lay everywhere, mutilated by shrapnel. Churchill counted 200 on the way up. They also saw soldiers, shell-shocked and dazed, stumbling blindly downhill. Some cursed and raged, others fell to the ground, numb and exhausted, and fell asleep on the spot. The higher they climbed, the fiercer the rifle and artillery fire. Nearing the crest, they came across the Dorset Regiment, the only battalion still functioning as a combat unit, which had been sent uphill in the course of the day to provide reinforcement.

One of the officers told them what had happened. He described the successful night attack by the Lancashire Brigade under Major-General Edward Woodgate, together with Lieutenant-Colonel Alexander Thorneycroft's Mounted Infantry; the hard rocky surface, in which they had only managed to dig shallow trenches for cover; the alarm early the next morning, when the mist lifted and they discovered they hadn't reached the summit but were instead on a plateau beneath it. There had been no time to correct their mistake. Firing from all sides, the Boers had advanced on them over the northern slope. Woodgate was fatally wounded right at the start. For a while it was unclear who was to assume command. Major-General Talbot Coke was the highest-ranking officer, but he was somewhere uphill. From his headquarters Warren had decided, on Buller's advice, to put Thorneycroft in command, with the provisional rank of brigade general. In the heat of the battle, the message had failed to reach the commanding officers in time, if at all. Some refused to accept Thorneycroft's authority, awed though they were by his bravery. As the catastrophe on the plateau unfolded—Churchill's fellow journalist John Atkins described it later as an 'acre of massacre'—it was Thorneycroft who singlehandedly kept up the fight. Early in the afternoon the first white handkerchiefs appeared over one of the British positions, signalling surrender. The Boers had already started taking prisoners, when Thorneycroft leapt forward, limping on a sprained ankle but roaring like a lion, 'I'm commandant here; take your men back to hell, sir! There's no surrender.'

The troops on the plateau were still holding their ground, Churchill and Brooke were told, but the situation was critical. Hunger, thirst, hellfire from all sides, wounded men whimpering in agony, soldiers taking cover behind the mutilated bodies of their slain comrades. If they could hold out until dark, they still had a chance. Get a large team of sappers up the hill with equipment to dig trenches and build fortifications, weapons to counter the Boer artillery, fresh troops to relieve the exhausted survivors: that's what was needed. Churchill and Brooke had seen and heard enough. It was too dangerous to continue up to the plateau. They decided to report back to Warren.[59]

They returned to Three Tree Hill, distraught by what they had seen on Spion Kop. Churchill's report in the *Morning Post* a few days later suggested that Warren had been interested and listened to them attentively. But there is a different and more plausible version of the story. According to Warren's staff officer, Captain C.B. Levita, Churchill had flown off the handle as soon as he got there, protesting about the lack of support for Thorneycroft and his men. 'For God's sake, Levita, don't let this be a second Majuba Hill.' Levita had sent him on to Warren, to whom he repeated his story in basically the same words. In response, Warren bellowed to Levita, 'Who is this man? Take him away, put him in arrest.' It was then that Levita had heard him out and calmed him down. He had given Churchill to understand that they were indeed intending to send reinforcements under cover of darkness, at least new infantry battalions, a large team of engineers and perhaps some naval guns as well. They just wanted to know what Thorneycroft thought about it. Could Churchill go and find out? He didn't have to think about it for long. But he wanted the request in black and white. He got it, and at half past eight that evening he set off for Spion Kop again with an official dispatch for Thorneycroft.

This time it was in the dark, which didn't make the ascent any easier. The rifle and artillery fire had almost completely died down, but he kept stumbling over wounded men, some on stretchers, some on the bare ground, and some wandering aimlessly, alone or in small groups. Here and there, officers or adjutants had gathered men together to form units ready to fight, but there was nothing they could do in the dark.

Churchill found Thorneycroft where he had expected, on the plateau just beneath the summit. He was slumped on the ground, sapped of all his strength. Around him were the miserable tatters of the proud regiment he had scraped together only the day before. 'My poor boys . . . my poor boys,' he murmured over and over again. The ordeal of a full day under devastating fire had taken its toll. An awe-inspiring figure in normal circumstances, a formidable commander all day, Thorneycroft was now completely crushed. Churchill's reassuring words didn't get through to him. What do you mean, reinforcements? All day he had been hoping Warren or Buller would launch a strong offensive against the Boers and ease the pressure on his own positions, but nothing had come, no word, no news. And now it was too late. He no longer believed in it. Half an hour earlier he had resolved to clear Spion Kop and he wasn't going to change his mind. 'Better six good battalions safely down the hill than a mop-up in the morning.'

Thorneycroft and Churchill descended together. At the foot of the hill they ran into the reinforcements—a long row of sappers with shovels and pickaxes. Their commander had a message for Thorneycroft: the infantry battalions were on their way. By morning they would be entrenched. Thorneycroft waved his cane. He would have none of it. Orders overruled, about turn, march. Churchill accompanied him to Warren's headquarters. The general was asleep when they arrived. Churchill woke him up. Warren took the news calmly. Churchill resigned himself to it, with a touch of subtle sarcasm. 'He was a charming old gentleman. I was genuinely sorry for him. I was also sorry for the army.'[60]

The most painful discovery was still to come. In the fading light it was decided to retreat not only from Spion Kop but also from Twin Peaks, the most north-easterly of the chain of hills. There, towards the end of the afternoon, after a fierce bayonet encounter, a battalion of the King's Royal Rifles had managed to flush the Boers from their positions. Major-General Lyttelton had initiated the action to relieve the pressure on Spion

Kop—at the cost of heavy casualties. It was a success, or at least, it would have been had anyone at Warren's headquarters realised just how much Lyttelton's unsolicited assistance had achieved. But no one did. To their great frustration the battered but victorious Royal Rifles were recalled.

By cruel coincidence for the British, many of the Boers began to leave their positions on and around Spion Kop at almost the same time: some from fatigue, to quench their thirst and still their hunger, but most because they believed they had lost the battle. General Schalk Burger was so disheartened by the British success on Twin Peaks that he had started making his way to Ladysmith with his entire commando and all his weapons. It was only the determination of commanding officers like Daniel Opperman and, most importantly, Louis Botha that prevented a complete exodus from the Boer positions.

They were soon rewarded. Boer scouts who were sent to appraise the damage on the crest of Spion Kop at the crack of dawn the following morning couldn't believe their eyes. The only Britons they found there were dead, wounded or dazed beyond consciousness. They were appalled at the sight of the largest trench, filled to the brim with corpses, but the truth gradually dawned and their horror gave way to jubilation. The British had fled, they had won!

The bizarre ending of the Battle of Spion Kop was an appropriate finale to a 14-day campaign full of blunders, misjudgments and misunderstandings. Buller's plan to skirt the hills via the Upper Tugela wasn't bad in itself, but for tactical, operational and logistical reasons it hadn't been implemented successfully. The problems were largely due to delays and poor coordination, not to mention antipathy, primarily between Buller and Warren. Or, as Churchill put it in the *Morning Post*, with ironic understatement, 'It is an event which . . . redounds to the honour of the soldiers, though not greatly to that of the generals.'

He was more outspoken in another publication. On 25 January Buller decided to call off the campaign and retreat with troops and all, back across the Tugela. This in itself was an onerous, two-day undertaking. To Churchill's astonishment, the Boers made no attempt to stop them. The retreat turned out to be the most efficiently organised part of the entire operation. At the end of it Buller noted with satisfaction that it had all been completed 'without the loss of a man or a pound of stores'. Churchill's conclusion was scathing. 'That was all there was to show for the operations of a whole army corps for sixteen days at a cost of about eighteen hundred casualties.'

The figure he cited came from the official British source and was far lower than the enemy's estimate. According to the Boers, the British casualties on 24 January alone came to some 2000 dead and wounded, the vast majority of them on Spion Kop. That was ten times their own losses. Buller's campaign along the Tugela claimed another 500 to 700 casualties.

By either estimate, the Boer or the British, in terms of casualties Spion Kop was one of the British army's most disastrous defeats in the Boer War. But Churchill was affected more by personal tragedy than nameless numbers. In this case, it was the loss of an old friend from his student days in Harrow, someone he had glimpsed near the pontoon bridge, only the day before. Churchill couldn't remember his name, but he had just arrived and was hoping 'to get a job'. The day after the encounter Churchill heard there was a body at the top of Spion Kop that no one had been able to identify. All there was to go by was a pair of field glasses clenched in his hand, inscribed with the name 'M'Corquodale'. Churchill knew at once. It was him, that was his name, that boy from Harrow. He must have managed to get a place in Thorneycroft's Mounted Infantry. 'Poor gallant young Englishman . . . joined in the evening, shot at dawn.'[61]

Breakthrough

Monte Cristo, 18 February 1900

What a magnificent, sobering sight, one he had never seen here before—
Boers in droves, running as if the devil were at their heels. Churchill
could picture the scene. They had seen Lyttelton's entire infantry division
storming towards them; Dundonald's cavalry brigade was attacking their
flank; and behind them was a deep, fast-running river. Even so, he was
baffled. In the past few weeks he had got to know the Boers as fearless
combatants, entrenched and invisible in unassailable positions. Yet here
they were, fleeing en masse, with no sign of any rearguard action, running
for their lives. It was a strange sight. 'When the Dutchman makes up his
mind to go, he throws all dignity to the winds.'

It was more than two months since Colenso, three and a half weeks
since Spion Kop, Sunday 18 February. And it looked as if Buller had truly
found the secret combination to break through the Boers' defence line on
the Tugela. In the meantime, he had made a third attempt, at Vaal Krantz,
between Colenso and Spion Kop. It had ended exactly as on the first two
occasions, with heavy losses and another mortifying return across the
Tugela. Behind his back his officers called him the Ferryman of the Tugela,
General Charon, Sir Reverse.

Yet interestingly enough, Buller still had the trust of his men. Of course
they complained, endlessly, about their wasted effort and their comrades
who had fallen for nothing. But they also knew that Buller cared about
what happened to them, and that the gaps in their ranks would be filled.
The expeditionary force had kept up its strength of 25,000 men and
even gained firepower when heavy naval guns were added to its artillery.
This inspired confidence, as did the words of their commander, who still
had faith in himself—unlike after Colenso—and kept repeating that this
time he had the key in his hands. The relief of Ladysmith had become
a personal matter for Buller, especially now that Roberts had begun his
campaign, some 500 kilometres to the west. Buller had to succeed and he
would make sure he did. His men were more than willing to believe him.
What the foot soldiers wanted most of all was a chance to take on their
elusive, unseen enemy in an all-out bayonet attack.

Right from the start, the key Buller was talking about had been there
for the taking. The weak spot in the Tugela line was the Boers' left flank,

at the point, just past Colenso, where the river took two right-angled turns, first to the north, then to the east. Because of this Louis Botha had had to extend his defence line up to the south-east bank (Kruger, an old hand at the game, had also insisted on this all the way from Pretoria),[62] first to Hlangwane Hill and from there further east to Green Hill and the linked summits of Monte Cristo and Cingolo. There were not particularly many Boers on the defence line, about 2000 men, but their positions were sufficiently fortified to withstand a British artillery and infantry attack. What Botha hadn't counted on was an unconventional manoeuvre by the British mounted forces.

The cavalry played a crucial part in Buller's new plan of attack. From 12 February Lord Dundonald and his horsemen, among them Churchill and the rest of the South African Light Horse, led a reconnaissance of the terrain east of Colenso. The rest of Buller's army followed two days later, advancing from the base camp between Frere and Chieveley. The infantry took positions opposite Hlangwane, Green Hill and Cingolo; the artillery was mounted on Hussar Hill. But Dundonald's cavalry continued further east, circling around the Boers' left flank. The route was barely passable. The ground was rocky and overgrown with tall grass and dense bush, forcing the men to keep dismounting to cut their way through. This was the natural barrier Botha had been depending on. He was sure the ever-predictable Buller wouldn't risk it. As a result, the Boers up on Cingolo—the furthest outpost of the line, with no more than 100 men— were caught off guard when they were suddenly attacked from the south-east, by Dundonald's mounted troops operating on foot. At the same time, British infantry units were approaching from the south-west. The Boers weren't prepared for an attack from two sides. They abandoned Cingolo and regrouped on the adjacent crest of Monte Cristo.

These events had taken place on 17 February, and the British were ready for more. This was the kind of campaign Churchill loved: the great outdoors, spartan conditions, trotting through the pristine, verdant hills of Natal, reconnoitring, spying, stalking, sniping and being sniped at, sleeping under the stars, rising at the first light of dawn. Water on the fire for coffee—how many mugs would be left undrunk this morning? Perhaps it would be his turn today. Live for the day. 'Existence is never so sweet as when it is at hazard.'

It was easy for Churchill to say this. His luck on the battlefield was legendary. The experience of his brother Jack, a youngster of 19, who had arrived a week earlier, showed how differently things could turn out. Churchill had arranged for him to join the Cockyolibirds as a lieutenant, like himself, in spite of his misgivings both before and afterwards. Nor were they unfounded, as it transpired during the reconnaissance of Hussar Hill on 12 February. The mission had ended in an exchange of fire with the Boers, whose positions were dispersed over the slopes. Both Churchills took part. Winston had often been in combat before, but this was Jack's first time under fire. It was also his last on the battlefield. He took a flesh wound to the leg right at the start. Nothing life-threatening, but it meant a month in the sick bay, his elder brother noted, secretly relieved that he wouldn't need to worry about him for the time being. But it made him reflect on 'the strange caprice which strikes down one man in his first skirmish and protects another time after time'. A fellow journalist, John Atkins, proposed an explanation to make sense of the younger Churchill's misfortune. 'It seemed as though he had paid his brother's debts.'

Almost a week had passed since then. It was now Sunday 18 February and it seemed to be only a matter of time before they broke through the Tugela line. The assault on Monte Cristo had followed the same course as that on Cingolo. Dundonald's cavalry had skirted around the Boer positions and attacked them from the east, their unprotected side. At the same time, the Boers were getting the full blast of the artillery on Hussar Hill and the onslaught of the infantry advancing over a broad front. There was no way they could hold out. They retreated, and by midday Churchill was standing on the summit of Monte Cristo. The panic was still palpable. The Boers had left everything behind in a desperate bid to escape—weapons, supplies, tents. The British soldiers were delighted and shared out the tents, though they balked at the stench inside them. But what did it matter? The sight that met their eyes made up for it all. Boers fleeing down the slopes and in the distance, 12 or 13 kilometres away, Ladysmith, there for the taking. The end was in sight.[63]

A British general who defied the rules of the military manual. This came as a nasty surprise, also to Adjutant-General Piet Cronjé, the Boer commander on the western front. The British outnumbered them even more than in Natal: the army advancing on him from 11 February comprised at least 50,000 men, ten times more than he could raise. But this wasn't the main problem. Most of Cronjé's men were safely entrenched at Magersfontein, where they had resisted a British general with a powerful army once before: Lord Methuen on 11 December. Cronjé was sure this would happen again, that the British infantry would launch its usual attack, with the same result. This time, however, the British general did something completely different. He outflanked the Boer positions, just as Buller was doing in Natal at the same time. First he sent out the cavalry. It was a complete mounted division of 13,000 cavalrymen and mounted infantry, which blazed a trail between the Boer trenches at Magersfontein and the commandos under Christiaan de Wet, about 30 kilometres further along. Before Cronjé realised what was happening, the British had crossed the Modder River. His positions, which had grown into a veritable stronghold, were in danger of being surrounded. Cronjé had to get clear of Magersfontein and find a new defence line as quickly as possible.

The British officer responsible for this unexpected manoeuvre was a field marshal, Lord Roberts of Kandahar, the new commander-in-chief of the British troops in South Africa. He was a small man, known as Bobs, but at 67 one of Britain's most decorated military commanders. Roberts had earned his spurs in British India, starting with the Victoria Cross in 1858. Since then, honours had come pouring in. He had been in South Africa once before, in 1881, after Majuba, then too coming as a saviour in time of need, but by the time he landed the hostilities were over and the opportunity to win more distinctions had passed.

This time it was different, even though his second chance as commander-in-chief in South Africa had started out under an unlucky star. On the day of his appointment, 17 December 1899, he heard that his son had been killed in the Battle of Colenso, but he threw himself into his new mission all the same. He arrived in Cape Town on 10 January 1900. There was no longer a shortage of manpower. Troops had been brought in by the thousand from Britain, the colonies and the dominions, more than enough to reinforce all fronts. For himself, Roberts formed an expeditionary army of 50,000 men, ensuring that he achieved the right balance of forces. Things had to change, he concluded after studying the lost battles. Transport and supplies needed to be organised centrally and more efficiently. Intelligence work had to be improved and, most important of all, they needed many more horses. These were rustled up wherever they could be found, in Europe, America, anywhere in the world. Cavalry and mounted infantry, that was the answer, he believed. They would be mobile and give the Boers the surprise of their lives. Major-General French was instructed to raise a full mounted division.

The preparations were completed in early February 1900. Roberts's plan was not to march through the centre, along the railway line from Cape Town to Bloemfontein, as Buller had initially intended to do and as most of the Boers were expecting, but instead to take the west route, via Kimberley. Cronjé was one of the few to have thought of this. But what he hadn't anticipated was that Roberts would suddenly veer off to the east and invade the Orange Free State. French's overwhelming cavalry advance guard charged north at such speed that Christiaan de Wet and his commandos were too late to stop them. On 15 February French was on the opposite bank of the Modder River and ready to complete his mission, the relief of Kimberley, 20 kilometres to the north. He decided on an old-fashioned cavalry charge. The Boer contingent that Cronjé had hastily dispatched to intercept him at Roodekalkfontein was sent scurrying in all directions. The British pressed on at breakneck speed, hitting Kimberley like a sandstorm. But French had driven his cavalrymen beyond endurance and hundreds of their horses, not yet acclimatised and unaccustomed to the hard ground, collapsed from exhaustion. The triumphant procession reached its destination leaving a trail of death on the highveld.[64]

Even so, Kimberley gave them a warm welcome. After a siege of 123 days the cavalry had arrived at last. The first men rode into town at four in the afternoon of Thursday 15 February, sweating, exhausted and covered in dust. But nothing could stop the prim ladies of Kimberley from dragging them off their horses and hugging them. The official welcome was magnificent. Rhodes entertained French and his staff at a private party at the Sanatorium Hotel, where he brought out his stash of champagne and delicacies. French was won over. He promptly took Rhodes's side in a heated dispute with Kekewich. The garrison commander was dismissed and replaced by one of French's officers.

It was a cruel blow for Kekewich. For months he had led the town's defence and organised the distribution of its steadily dwindling food supplies. Rhodes had been cooperative and obstructive by turns. He had given him access, for instance, to De Beers equipment and labour to build fortifications. And one of his employees, an American mining engineer called George Labram, had amazed everyone with his inventions: a 50-metre observation tower, a gigantic cold-box to preserve meat, a device to supply water from one of the mines, and, best of all, as from 19 January, they had the benefit of a homemade long-range gun, which was christened Long Cecil as a token of thanks to Rhodes.

But Rhodes had also worked against Kekewich, often acting without Kekewich's knowledge or consent, and had sent bulletins that sowed panic in the outside world. More than once he had incited unrest in Kimberley itself. On 7 February the Boers had mounted a Long Tom to counter Long Cecil. It was Silent Susan, the gun that had previously been in Ladysmith, where the British had put it out of action. In the meantime it had been repaired at the workshop of the Netherlands-South African Railway Company in Pretoria and made a comeback in Kimberley, renamed the Jew because of its shortened barrel. The discharges from the heavy ninety-pounder guns caused more alarm among the town's inhabitants than the rifle fire they had been experiencing for months. It also claimed more victims including, ironically, Long Cecil's designer, George Labram.

Rhodes retaliated in his usual style, with a theatrical solo action. Without telling Kekewich, he put up posters on 11 February announcing that he was opening the De Beers mines to serve as shelters. The response was huge. That evening 3000—white—women and children took refuge hundreds of metres underground, huddled together, an eyewitness said, like seagulls on the pinnacle of a rock. And there they remained until the town was liberated four days later. By then, conditions were dangerously unsanitary, but virtually everyone survived. The ordeals they were spared in their underground hideout are reflected in the death toll during the siege of Kimberley: 135 men died in the garrison, 21 civilians as a result of bombardments and far more, around 1500, from malnutrition and disease, mostly in the African and coloured communities.[65]

With Kimberley liberated, Roberts had already achieved his first victory. Now for Buller. After his successes on 17 and 18 February, Ladysmith was there for the taking. The following day it transpired that the Boers had retreated from the south-east bank of the Tugela. The next step was obvious. Deploy the artillery—by this time Buller had over 75 guns—on the occupied hilltops and from there launch an offensive on the Boers' fragmented left flank.

Yet strangely enough, this isn't what Buller did. As if trying to prove that his original plan would work—up from Colenso and straight through the Boer defence line—he brought his troops back from the south-east bank and prepared to attack the crests of Rooikop, Horseshoe Hill and Wynne's Hill to the north and north-west of Colenso.

The Boers perked up. Their disappointment after losing their positions on the south-east bank had prompted Louis Botha to suggest abandoning the Tugela line and, with it, the siege of Ladysmith. They were already discouraged, because their last desperate attempt to bring Ladysmith to its knees seemed likely to fail. The idea had been to build a dam in the Klip River to create a lake, which would eventually overflow and inundate the town below. It was an innovative plan, which they believed could be accomplished with about 30,000 sandbags, to be filled and transported by 500 black labourers. The project got off to a good start in January, but it gradually began to look over-ambitious. On reviewing their calculations, it turned out that they would need far more sandbags, at least 160,000, and that there was too little rain to fill the dam in the foreseeable future. And now Buller was at the Tugela, ready to deliver the final blow.[66]

To their amazement, however, he had abandoned his successful new strategy and was apparently going to make another attempt to squeeze his army through a narrow mountain pass. As Churchill said, quoting a staff officer who wisely chose to remain nameless, 'It will be like being in the Coliseum and shot at by every row of seats.' He was absolutely right. The Boers realised immediately that the obstinate Buller was giving them another chance and took up their positions again. The battle, which started on 21 February and lasted for four days, was a repeat performance. Death-defying British infantry units captured a hill, incurring heavy losses along the way, only to find themselves isolated at the top and under even fiercer fire from the adjacent hill. The sequence was repeated again and again, in different places, each 'a frantic scene of blood and fury'. The battle on Hart's Hill was the most horrendous. A no man's land strewn with dead and wounded men separated the warring parties. The wounded were left untended for days, directly in the line of fire, without food, water or protection from the elements. Looking on from a distance, Churchill was distressed by 'these poor fellows moving about feebly and trying to wiggle themselves into some position of safety'. They reminded him of the wounded Mahdi fighters at Omdurman, 'only these were our own countrymen'.

On Sunday 25 February, Buller decided enough was enough. He proposed a ceasefire to bury the dead and rescue the wounded. Botha formally turned down his request but agreed to a de facto ceasefire. The stretcher-bearers spent the morning doing their work. After days of neglect, the wounded were in a pitiful state. Churchill was shocked at the sight of the dead, 'swollen, blackened, and torn by the terrible wounds of the expansive bullets, now so generally used by the enemy'. Buller took the opportunity to reposition his troops. After all, it wasn't an official ceasefire. The Boers made no attempt to stop him. They watched detachments of the British force withdraw across the Tugela again—they had lost count of the number of times this had happened—and thought they had taught Buller another lesson.

This was true, but Buller had also learned something from all those futile attacks. The key really did lie in the positions they had previously captured and subsequently abandoned on the south-east bank. He had his heavy artillery reinstalled on Hlangwane and Monte Cristo. 'The big guns were getting back on to the big hills,' Churchill noted with satisfaction. The pontoon bridge for the aborted attack was dismantled and then reassembled a few kilometres downstream, closer to the new target, the left flank of the Boer positions at Pietershoogte. All the infantry brigades were clustered around it. There was also an assignment for the Cockyolibirds and the rest of Dundonald's mounted troops, they heard on 26 February. They were to take positions early the next morning on Monte Cristo and Hlangwane, as close to the Tugela as they could get, and from there maintain a constant barrage of fire on the Boer positions across the river, using rifles, Maxim machine guns, field guns, everything they possessed. At long last—his fifth attempt to break through—Buller was finally preparing to engage his complete force: artillery, infantry and cavalry, and all of them simultaneously.

Everything and everyone would be in action. Churchill was looking forward to it. The following day would be the moment of truth on the Tugela: it was now or never. In any event the date, 27 February, was well chosen. Majuba Day. Exactly 19 years earlier the Boers had shattered Britain's military pride. It was time to settle the score.[67]

Showdown on Majuba Day: that was the buzzword on the western front as well. Roberts's unexpected incursion into the Orange Free State, and particularly his cavalry's advance on Kimberley on 15 February, had thrown the Boers into confusion and destroyed all coordination between their ranks. Cronjé and De Wet chose their strategies—each his own.

Right at the start, De Wet showed Roberts how risky an overhasty advance could be. This applied in particular to an expeditionary force as large as Roberts's, which was steadily moving further away from the railway line and would therefore have to rely on traditional modes of transport for supplies. Before the campaign started Roberts had got Kitchener to change the existing arrangement whereby each battalion was responsible for its own provisions. It might seem more flexible, but he and Kitchener agreed that it was inefficient and wasteful. They wanted a single, large supply convoy. And that's what they got. They soon discovered just how vulnerable it was. The day Kimberley was liberated, a large British convoy of oxwagons, which had broken its journey at Waterval Drift to rest the animals, fell into the hands of Christiaan de Wet's commandos. They made off with 180 wagons filled with valuable supplies of food, as well as 2800 oxen—almost a third of the number the British expeditionary army would need for its march to Bloemfontein. As thrilled as they were about the relief of Kimberley, this was a serious setback for Roberts. The options now were either to turn back with a detachment to recapture the convoy, or reduce the rations. Roberts chose the latter—in other words, speed.[68]

On the same day, 15 February, 20 kilometres to the north, Cronjé found himself in the same predicament—and took the other option. His 5000 men couldn't remain in their trenches at Magersfontein. They were in danger of being surrounded and had to strike camp. The question was, what should they take with them? They had been there for months and had built a semi-permanent camp, where even women and children came to visit. Their supplies were stacked on hundreds of oxwagons.

Taking it all would slow them down. Still, Cronjé decided to take as much as possible. He was planning to occupy new positions further to the east and obstruct the British advance to Bloemfontein, and to do so they would need their equipment. That evening, a procession trailing back eight kilometres set off along the north bank of the Modder.

They were spotted early the following morning. Roberts hadn't arrived yet, but Kitchener immediately sent his troops in pursuit of the Boers. His advance units met their rearguard at Klipdrift. An exchange of fire followed, but the Boers were still able to proceed. That night they reached Paardeberg Drift. From there Cronjé sent part of his oxwagon convoy to the south bank of the Modder. That group managed to escape. Cronjé himself, together with his main force and the rest of the convoy, continued along the north bank towards Vendutie Drift. There, on 17 February, he discovered that they were almost completely surrounded—to the west by Lieutenant-General Sir Henry Colville's 9th Infantry Division; to the south, from the opposite bank of the Modder, by Lieutenant-General Thomas Kelly-Kenny's 6th Infantry Division; and to the north and east by the cavalry units French had raised in Kimberley. French's horsemen had intercepted back-up troops under General Naas Ferreira, and now took advantage of the Boers' bewilderment to rob them of 2000 oxen—fair compensation for the cattle De Wet had made off with. There was only one way for Cronjé and his men to escape. They would have to leave their wagons behind and under cover of darkness cross the river to the south bank on foot in the hope of meeting up with De Wet's commandos. At least, this is what Cronjé's commandants advised him to do, but Cronjé decided otherwise. They would entrench themselves on the north bank and fight.

This was exactly what Kitchener wanted. Roberts, suffering from a bad cold, had remained in Jacobsdal and entrusted Kitchener with command of his men during his absence. This was Kitchener's chance to show how the Boers should be dealt with. After the Mahdi fighters at Omdurman he would be able to add the Boers at Paardeberg to his list of notable feats. He would strike at once, now that they were on the defensive, with a full-scale assault from all sides. The divisional generals protested, but he waved their objections aside. On 18 February Kitchener gave the command for the usual onslaught accompanied by artillery fire. Like Methuen, like Buller and a long line of British generals before him, he believed he could simply charge through the Boer positions. But Kitchener was also to learn 'the hard way' about entrenched sharpshooters with modern rapid-firing weapons. The encounter turned into a bloodbath, but then on his side. By nightfall, the British had lost 300 dead and 900 wounded.

This was comparable to Spion Kop in terms of casualties and it damaged Kitchener's reputation permanently. Roberts was distraught and rushed to the front line the following day. They would handle things differently, he decided. The Boers had paid a price, too. The artillery bombardments had destroyed most of their supplies, and virtually all their horses and oxen had been killed or seized. They were stranded. All Roberts had to do was tighten the screws: surround them completely, blast them with his hundred guns, dig trenches to get closer to them, and it would be over in no time at all.

The Boer positions at Paardeberg were indeed hopeless. The British forces on the south bank of the Modder were managing to hold off De Wet, but he thought there was still a way out. Inclement weather prevented him from communicating with Cronjé by heliograph, so on the night of 24 February he instructed the commander of the Boer Scouts Corps, Captain Danie Theron, to slip through the British lines and deliver a message by hand. If Cronjé tried to escape to the south, De Wet would cover him. It was doubtful whether De Wet was in a position to do so, Cronjé knew, but he was prepared to take the chance. His commandants were, however, against it. The unrelenting British bombardments had taken their toll. They were close to exhaustion, they had been drinking water contaminated by corpses, their food smelled of lyddite, they were worn out, they were broken, and on top of it all the rain of the past few days had swollen the river and turned their trenches into mud holes. They weren't interested in trying to escape. They were ready to surrender.

Cronjé managed to hold out for two more days. On the evening of Monday 26 February he held another war council meeting. If they were really determined to capitulate, could they at least wait until after Majuba Day? But his commandants refused. In the meantime, the British troops were within earshot of the Boer trenches. Early the next morning they prepared to mount the decisive attack. At five o'clock Major-General Horace Smith-Dorrien called on the Boers to surrender. White handkerchiefs went up one after another. Cronjé resigned himself to the situation; there was nothing else he could do. At six o'clock he hoisted the white flag. He was escorted to Roberts, who greeted him courteously. 'I am glad to see you. You have made a gallant defence, sir.' More than 4000 men surrendered at Paardeberg that day. The units under De Wet, Ferreira and other Boer commandants in the area moved on. It was the end of the western front. Roberts could march into Bloemfontein.[69]

The good news reached Buller by field telegraph. It was Tuesday 27 February, just before dawn. Roberts had achieved his breakthrough. Now it was Buller's turn. The unique chance to achieve a double success on Majuba Day was in his hands. Another failure would mean the end of his career; he could count on that. By ten o'clock in the morning the pontoon bridge was installed in its new location. From there his infantry brigades, backed by the artillery and cavalry on the south-east bank, would attack Hart's Hill, Spoorwegkop and Pietershoogte. Buller pulled out all the stops. For the first time he took advantage of his numerical superiority; he had four times more men and ten times more guns. The Ferryman of the Tugela was ready to embark on his last crossing.

From his vantage point Churchill had an excellent view of the whole operation. The Cockyolibirds had taken cover behind boulders near the river, and kept up a steady barrage of rifle and machine-gun fire against the Boer positions on the opposite bank. The rest of the cavalry and the artillery batteries higher up did the same. It took a while for them to get going, as far as Churchill was concerned, but the firing gradually built up to 'a capital loud noise, which I think is a most invigorating element in an attack'. The thundering explosions and the volley of covering fire served to unnerve the Boers, but it was the infantrymen who had to do the real work. Churchill saw them fanning out from the pontoon bridge to the hilltops. They advanced slowly, fighting to gain each hill, but this time their actions were coordinated and they were making progress. The Boers lost more ground as the day wore on. At the end of the afternoon they abandoned some of their positions and fled or surrendered. Towards evening their resistance was broken and cheers from the British rang out. They had won the battle at Pietershoogte and broken through here as well. They had taken revenge for Majuba.

This was the sign for Lord Dundonald and his impatient cavalrymen to leave their positions, mount their horses and cross the Tugela in pursuit of the fleeing Boers. However, at the pontoon bridge they found Buller waiting for them in person. He was still uneasy. There might be a counterattack by night and he wasn't prepared to put his cavalry at risk. No pursuit. The disappointed horsemen returned to their camp.

On his way back, Churchill passed a small group of Boer prisoners. They looked like men one might see in a bar, 'very ordinary people, who grinned and chattered without dignity . . . it was difficult to understand what qualities made them such a terrible foe'. He was also taken aback by one of their guards, who was railing against them. 'I never saw such cowards in my life; shoot at you till you come up to them, and then beg for mercy. I'd teach 'em.' He would have bayoneted them there and then, if it had been up to him and his mates, but their officers had intervened. With which remark the man turned to the prisoners and offered them water from his own canteen. The incident left Churchill 'wondering at the opposite and contradictory sides of human nature as shown by Briton as well as Boer'.

The following day, 28 February, the cavalry—and the artillery—were sent across the Tugela. The infantrymen were given a day's rest. They had gained their victory at a loss of 80 dead and more than 400 wounded. The British casualties over the previous two weeks—in the campaign against the Boers' left flank—came to a total of 400 dead and more than 1800 wounded. Buller was intending to push forward on 1 March. He had dispatched reconnaissance patrols to find out whether the Boers had set up a new defence line ahead of Ladysmith and, if so, where.

Churchill took the opportunity to examine the abandoned Boer trenches on Hart's Hill. There, he met a group of soldiers from the East Surrey Regiment, who were more than willing to show him around. 'Come along here, sir; there's a bloke here without a head; took clean off, sir.' Churchill thanked him for his kindness, but he was more interested in the way the trenches had been constructed. They were deep, he could stand upright in them, and they had no real parapet, just a few rocks placed along the edge in front, with small heaps of Mauser ammunition every few metres along. The floor was knee-deep in cartridge cases. One of the officers produced a few dum-dum bullets. They had found boxes full of them, he said, roughly one in five of all the bullets left behind. Churchill responded with a derogatory remark about the dark side of the Boers' character, presumably forgetting that he himself had been carrying dum-dums at the time of his capture.[70]

As the day wore on, more and more evidence emerged that the Boers had not only abandoned the Tugela line, but were retreating from Ladysmith as well. Dundonald's cavalry occasionally encountered resistance, but none of it lasted long. Towards evening a message came from Major Hubert Gough's regiment in the vanguard, saying that the way to Ladysmith lay open. On hearing this, Dundonald decided to ride there himself and invited Churchill to join him. It was an unforgettable experience. Galloping through the countryside in a cool evening breeze, knowing that Ladysmith was just beyond the next hill, perhaps the one after that, one more to go, and there it lay before them. Just before reaching the town they joined Gough's column of Natal Carbineers and Imperial Light Horse which, after 118 days, brought an end to the siege of Ladysmith.

That evening, Churchill had dinner at the headquarters of the garrison commander, White. He was seated next to his old friend Ian Hamilton. It had been a while, but here they were, together again at last. Time for a drink and a good cigar. They had a lot to talk about.[71]

Fever

Ladysmith, 3 March 1900

Not many sons would escort their mother on a tour of a battlefield almost 10,000 kilometres from home, where they had taken part in a life-and-death struggle barely a week earlier. Winston Churchill was that kind of son. Neither he nor his mother gave it a second thought. She was an unconventional woman who did as she pleased, he had never known her to be otherwise, and she happened to be passing that way. Lady Randolph had arrived in Durban towards the end of January 1900 on board the *Maine*, a hospital ship she had chartered in London on behalf of an American women's relief group. Churchill had visited her in Durban some time earlier. Once the hostilities were over, she wanted to see the front where it had all taken place: the reports her elder son had written, the misfortune that had befallen her younger son, who happened to be one of her first patients on the *Maine*.

Churchill obtained a pass for her as if it were the most normal thing in the world. He would have liked to take his friend on the trip as well, but for some unfathomable reason Pamela Plowden had decided to remain in England. Lady Randolph had embarked on her 'sightseeing tour' in early March. She had taken the train to Colenso, and at Chieveley passed close to the derailed trucks of Churchill's first exploit. After that it was a matter of improvising. She crossed the Tugela over a makeshift bridge and then travelled on to Ladysmith in an open railway truck. The journey was slow but it had one big advantage, 'We could see and understand everything with the help of Winston's graphic tongue.' And there was plenty of time for 'Kodaking'. Ladysmith itself was a disappointment: a sweltering, dusty ghost town, houses with shutters over the windows and people slinking warily through the streets. Fortunately Sir Redvers was kind enough to invite her to dinner and offer her a real bed in the convent where he was staying. The following morning Lady Randolph left for Durban and a week later sailed back to England.[72]

The relief group she was working with was one of many spontaneous initiatives organised in the wake of Black Week, in Great Britain and its overseas territories. 'We are not interested in the possibilities of defeat; they do not exist,' 81-year-old Queen Victoria had replied on hearing the bad news. Her subjects throughout the British Empire echoed that view. Many of them also wanted to do something about it. 'War fever' cut across all geographical and social boundaries: from Ottawa to Melbourne and Auckland, from the polo club to the music hall and the beer hall, everyone was eager to help. Thousands of volunteers applied to join one of the newly formed cavalry regiments such as the Imperial Yeomanry in Britain, or the Imperial Light Horse or the South African Light Horse— the Churchill brothers' Cockyolibirds—in the Cape Colony and Natal. It was the same in Canada, Australia and New Zealand. The public flocked to join the contingents their governments had promised to send out. The British Empire was getting ready to hit back.

Those who couldn't or chose not to engage in combat found other ways to help. They organised fundraising drives to support the troops overseas, or joined teams of medics like Lady Randolph's. That was how Arthur Conan Doyle, for instance, a physician by profession, but better known as the creator of Sherlock Holmes, expressed his patriotic sentiments. The Imperial Yeomanry had rejected him because of his age (40) and military experience (none), but he was more than welcome at the privately run field hospital that the philanthropist John Langman was sending out. He set sail for South Africa in February 1900.

Mohandas Gandhi had a shorter distance to travel. He had been living in Natal and working as a lawyer since 1893. But he also had a handicap, namely his race. The military authorities didn't welcome 'sons of Empire' from a different ethnic background, at least not in the beginning. After all, there were limits to imperialistic fervour. At the beginning of the war, in mid-October 1899, Gandhi had offered his services as a token of the loyalty of the local Indian population, but he was scoffed at. 'You Indians know nothing of war,' he was told. Things changed after Mournful Monday, 30 October. Gandhi repeated his offer, which was gratefully accepted. The Natal Indian Ambulance Corps was formed, made up of roughly 1000 stretcher-bearers. They were desperately needed, as evidenced by the sad list of battlefields they served: Colenso, Spion Kop, Vaal Krantz.[73]

These private initiatives were welcome additions to the British army's regular medical services, which by nineteenth-century standards were fairly comprehensive. The Royal Army Medical Corps, established in 1898 after much urging by the British Medical Association, improved the status of military physicians and the quality of their services. But it had little time to prepare for its mission in South Africa. Nor could this have been otherwise. The army had expected to dispatch a relatively small expeditionary force, not the tens of thousands of soldiers who were needed after Black Week. Just the scale of the operation in all respects— manpower, bandages, equipment, transport, everything imaginable— made it difficult to provide adequate medical care for British soldiers.

The wounded were generally the best off, at least if they could be removed from the battlefield reasonably quickly. Depending on the severity of their injuries, they were treated either at a field hospital on the spot or in a facility at some distance from the front. They were attended by skilled surgeons, who could treat most bullet wounds and broken bones, and who possessed ether, chloroform, X-ray equipment and a practised hand to perform amputations. They knew the dangers of infection and how to prevent and treat it.

The same kind of expertise was available to deal with infectious diseases, though these were hard to control. Wounds heal and their treatment ends after a period of nursing, rest and rehabilitation, when the patient has recovered or learned to live with a permanent disability. But infectious diseases are pervasive. It takes discipline to prevent them and a rigorous regime of hygiene to cure them. This is hard to achieve without sufficient fresh food, clean water and medical care.

Ladysmith was a poignant example. After months under siege by the Boers, the local population and the garrison were on the verge of physical exhaustion. Churchill gave the readers of the *Morning Post* an eyewitness account. On 3 March 1900 Buller and his entire force paraded triumphantly through the town. They were worn out from months of fighting, their uniforms were in tatters and their boots and helmets in shreds, but with their proud, tanned faces they resembled 'a procession of lions'. Beside them, the town's inhabitants, the soldiers in particular, were a pitiful sight to behold. Commander White and his staff 'sat on their skeleton horses'. His men had done their best to make themselves presentable, but underneath it all they were pale and gaunt, at least those who were up and about. Some 2000 patients were in the hospital tent camp at Intombi, most of them suffering from typhoid or dysentery. This, too, Churchill shared with his readers. He wrote at length about the emaciated, neglected inmates, shivering with fever and confined in congested and unhygienic quarters. They lacked food, milk, brandy and adequate medical care. Behind the hospital was a 'forest of crosses, marking the graves of six hundred men'.[74]

Sister L.M. Hellemans was appalled by the Intombi camp. It bore no resemblance to their own easily accessible and well-equipped field hospital on Potgieter's farm, which the British advance in early March had forced them to close down. A fastidious nurse from Holland, she had been shocked by the Boers' indifference to hygiene, but never before had she seen such squalor. General Buller in person had prevented her Red Cross team from accompanying the retreating Boers. Here in Intombi, he said, there were 18 Boer prisoners who needed medical attention. Her unit, the Second Dutch Red Cross Ambulance, was to take care of them. Dr J.D. Koster had protested and claimed their right to freedom of movement, but Buller had been adamant. It was rumoured that he suspected them of having done more for the Boers than just provide medical treatment. Hellemans and her colleagues had to resign themselves to the situation.

It was hard to imagine anything filthier or more unsanitary. They were told to pitch their tents on the perimeter of the camp, next to 'the burial place for all detritus, the laundry and other facilities of that kind'—in other words, on 'contaminated ground teeming with typhus bacteria etc.'. The stench was overwhelming and 'the unbearable heat turned that pestilent place into a breeding ground for disease'. But they had no choice. They began to unpack their possessions. British soldiers offered to help but 'they stole whatever they could lay their hands on'. With difficulty, the team managed to have a guard assigned to their quarters, but he ended up denying them access to their own food supplies. They had been confiscated, he said, they would have to get by with food from the canteen. Although their relatively generous supplies were eventually returned, they were still plagued by 'all kinds of crawling and winged creatures'. They were 'a scourge. It was a feat to take a bite of food or a sip of something to drink, without swallowing a fly'. The 18 wounded Boers, on the other hand, were nowhere to be seen.[75]

Complaints to General Buller about their treatment, the unauthorised detention of an official Red Cross unit, eventually bore fruit. Three weeks later the Second Dutch Red Cross Ambulance was escorted to the Boer encampment in the Biggarsberg. From there they returned to Pretoria to be deployed elsewhere, this time on the western front. Where, precisely, had yet to be decided. It depended on the talks between the Transvaal Red Cross, the medical commission appointed by the government in January, and the overseas relief organisations.

Medical care in the Boer camps was clearly inadequate and uncoordinated. The commandos were left to improvise. Even in peacetime it was not a priority in the Boer republics. There were two decent hospitals, one in Pretoria and one in Johannesburg; the rest were small, poorly equipped and not easily accessible. The outbreak of war brought no immediate change. Virtually no preparations were made. Physicians, like all other conscripts, served in the commando of their home district and continued to treat their own patients. The only professional military unit in the Transvaal, the State Artillery, was also the only unit with its own medical team, consisting of a physician, a vet, a pharmacist and 12 male nurses.[76]

It took outside intervention to change the situation. One of the first to offer practical help was the director of the Netherlands-South African Railway Company, Kretschmar van Veen, who offered his company's services to assist in the war effort. This included medical care for the Boer commandos, who were given access to the company's physicians and hospitals. Kretschmar van Veen also donated four fully equipped hospital wagons, which were manufactured at their central workshop in Pretoria. In addition, he played an important part in rallying support in the Netherlands. With the help of his co-directors in Amsterdam and Willem Leyds, the Transvaal's diplomatic representative in Europe, an agreement was reached with the Dutch Red Cross. As a result, a medical team known as the First Dutch Ambulance left for Pretoria on 28 October 1899. A second team, Sister Hellemans's group, left a month later. Two more followed in December 1899, the last being a Russian–Dutch initiative. The Dutch East Indies also sent out one of its ambulances around the same time.

The Netherlands was not the only country to contribute medical equipment and personnel. Fourteen foreign teams—from Germany, Russia, Belgium, Switzerland and Scandinavia—came to the aid of the Transvaal and the Orange Free State. More than 200 physicians, sisters and male nurses arrived with modern equipment and huge supplies of medications, bandages and food, which greatly improved the medical care available to the Boer commandos. Even so, the care on offer was largely piecemeal. The service was too disorganised and working conditions were too primitive for it to be otherwise. Sister Hellemans and her colleagues weren't alone in complaining about the climate, the vermin and the risks of infection. All the overseas aid workers were in the same boat, just as they all met with distrust from the Boers—all those new-fangled ideas about hygiene—and suspicion from the British about their neutrality. In one case these concerns were justified. As soon as they set foot in the Transvaal most members of the 60-strong Irish-American relief team which had left from Chicago in mid-February 1900, shed their Red Cross armbands in favour of rifles and cartridge belts.[77]

All things considered, Willem Leyds had reason to be satisfied with the humanitarian aid that Europe was sending to his adopted country. He had no connection with the Irish-American contingent, despite mutterings to the contrary in the British press. But he was accustomed to this kind of criticism. After all, in Britain he was seen as the evil genius who organised shady deals for the Boers. In early April 1900, when a 16-year-old anarchist fired two bullets at the Prince of Wales in the Brussels-North railway station—without harming him, as it turned out—even the respectable

Lord George Hamilton, the under-secretary for India, remarked that 'Brussels had been the headquarters of that factory of lies of which Mr Leyds was the manager'.[78]

Leyds had a better reputation on the Continent, where he was considered the unrivalled champion of the righteous Boer cause. Since the outbreak of war there had been no need for him to solicit public support. Europe was almost unanimously on the Boers' side. Much of his time was spent dealing with relief groups, solidarity marches, letters from well-wishers and fundraising campaigns, leaving him little opportunity to attend to the hordes of volunteers wanting to join the Boer ranks. They were all referred to Paris, where Johannes Pierson, the consul-general and a cousin of the Dutch prime minister, provided the information they needed. Many of them lost interest when it transpired that Pretoria only wanted volunteers who were willing to travel at their own risk and expense.[79]

With so much wind in their sails, it was disappointing to hear that the British had broken through on two fronts in late February 1900. Leyds realised just how much 'the reports about Cronjé, Kimberley and Ladysmith have affected our friends in Holland'. He took leave for a few days, but only to nurse a bad cold. He didn't consider the situation 'as hopeless as most people think. I still believe that justice will prevail.' Paradoxically, he felt that the military defeats opened up new opportunities.

Firstly, he believed the time was ripe to publish the long-delayed manifesto, *Appeal to the Nations*. As long as the Boers were on a winning streak, many sympathisers in Europe, especially the Dutch, had been opposed to 'mediation and intervention'. That would probably change, Leyds assumed, now that they were on the defensive both in Natal and the western Orange Free State. He was proved to be right, at least as far as the Netherlands was concerned. On 4 March, the *Appeal to the Nations*, signed by 'around 3000 luminaries in the fields of the sciences, arts, commerce and industry', was published in several Dutch newspapers. To his disappointment, it had little effect. The *Appeal* was translated into English, but nothing happened in the countries for which it was mainly intended: Germany, France and Russia. 'No one said anything about it or did anything because of it,' Leyds lamented two months later. 'It has fallen flat.'[80]

What was the reason? Leyds had his own thoughts on the matter. It wasn't so much to do with the *Appeal* as such. The real problem was the lack of communication between Pretoria and its diplomatic representative in Europe, namely himself. They had been unable to telegraph each other since the beginning of the war. Everything was censored by the British. Messages conveyed by more furtive means got through from time to time, but mostly they were dependent on the mail packet steamships, which inevitably meant long delays. Quick consultations in critical situations were simply not possible. Had things been different, he would have been able to save Pretoria and Bloemfontein from a huge political blunder. Because in Leyds's opinion, this was the main reason for the failure of the *Appeal* and, worse still, the undoing of all his efforts to arrange mediation over the previous few months in the best tradition of silent diplomacy. As he had long believed, the Boers' hope lay with the great powers: Russia, Germany, France or the United States. Nothing else would work. Everything was in limbo until the tide of the war turned, in late February. The Great Powers were taking advantage of Britain's preoccupation with South Africa to pursue their own interests. Russia was conducting military exercises in Afghanistan, on the border of British India; France was expanding its influence in Algeria; Germany was dividing up the Samoan islands; and the United States, once a colony itself, was taking its first steps on the path of imperialism in the Philippines. 'The powers can't get themselves to join forces against a common enemy. Their jealousy and distrust of each other are insurmountable.'[81]

But this changed with Britain's military success. The time and energy Leyds had spent cultivating a cordial relationship with his Russian counterpart, De Giers—and through him with Tsar Nicholas II—seemed to be paying off at last. On 3 March 1900 the Russian government took the initiative for joint action. The German foreign minister, Von Bülow, received a proposal to the effect that 'the European governments should apply friendly pressure' to end the bloody war in South Africa. The time was ripe after the British armies' recent successes. 'British patriotism' had been satisfied and any further delay could result in the total destruction of the Boer republics. The idea was that France as well as Germany would support the appeal to Britain in the name of morality and on the grounds of the humanitarian principles of the Hague Peace Conference.[82]

This would have been music to Leyds's ears. It was exactly what he had always wanted. But a few days later, when De Giers told him about the Russian proposal, it was already too late. The proposal had been ruined by another initiative, also conceived on 3 March, but in Pretoria, 10,000 kilometres to the south. This was the brainchild of the commandant-general, Piet Joubert. Disappointed by their military reverses, he had been pressing for a peace agreement since February. At first, President Kruger was receptive to the idea and discussed it in the Executive Council on 3 March. The talks yielded two resolutions: Lord Salisbury would be sent a telegram, and an appeal would be made to the Great Powers. Leyds was not asked his opinion—if that had even have been possible at such short notice—but

Kruger felt obliged to confer with President Steyn of the Orange Free State. He left post-haste for Bloemfontein where on 5 March the two heads of state composed a telegram, which they sent to Lord Salisbury that same day—bypassing Chamberlain, the secretary for the colonies.

The naive wording was disarming, but it had the opposite effect. Invoking 'the blood and tears of thousands who have suffered by this war, and the prospect of complete moral and economic ruin', Kruger and Steyn pleaded for the restoration of peace in South Africa. It was not their intention to set up 'an administration over all of South Africa independent of her Majesty's Government' but 'only to maintain the indisputable independence of both republics as sovereign international states'. However, if the British government wouldn't grant this, there was 'nothing left to us and to our people but to continue on our present course'. In spite of the British Empire's vastly superior power, 'we trust that we will not be forsaken by the God who kindled in our hearts and the hearts of our fathers an inextinguishable love of freedom'.

From Pretoria the state secretary, Reitz, and the state attorney, Smuts, advised them to wait for Salisbury's reply before approaching the other powers, but Kruger and Steyn went their own way. From 9 to 11 March they brought their telegram to Salisbury to the attention of the consular representatives of Russia, Germany, France, the United States, the Netherlands, Belgium, Italy, Austria and Switzerland, in both their capital cities. They also requested the governments of those countries to 'intervene in this conflict in order to prevent any further unnecessary bloodshed in this cruel war'.

A reply from London came by telegram the following day, 12 March. It was icy. Salisbury recalled the arsenal of weapons the Boers had amassed prior to the war. He expressed his outrage at their insulting ultimatum and subsequent incursions into Natal and the Cape Colony. The Boers had forced upon 'the Empire a costly war and the loss of thousands of precious lives'. For Britain to acknowledge the independence of the Boer republics was out of the question.

The message was clear, but Bloemfontein and Pretoria initially failed to grasp its full—disastrous—implications. Reitz and Smuts even started drafting a scathing reply to Salisbury and backed down only when they saw the reactions from other countries. Leyds had understood immediately just how serious it all was. It was a huge disappointment and a blow to him personally. All his efforts and subtle diplomatic manoeuvring had been for nothing. Kruger and Steyn had trampled over his work like two bulls in a china shop. That was the sad truth. They had bungled and dealt themselves a deadly blow.

Every experienced diplomat agreed. De Giers informed them that the Russian initiative had become 'inopportune' after the telegram from the two presidents and 'Lord Salisbury's categorical statements' in reply. The response from the Dutch foreign minister, De Beaufort, was that 'the British Government's resolute statement' ruled out 'any possibility of intervention'. The French foreign minister, Delcassé, felt that any thought of mediating at that stage was 'manifestly futile'. The governments of Germany and the other countries they had written to responded in the same vein. The American government, however, offered its services to London—the only country to do so—only to be told that its help was not needed. The one person who paid no attention to all the diplomatic turmoil was the young Queen Wilhelmina of the Netherlands. She turned to the German emperor in her personal capacity, as she had done six months earlier in her appeal to Queen Victoria. But Wilhelm II was no more sympathetic to Wilhelmina's emotional plea than his grandmother had been. Nothing had changed in the world of diplomacy.[83]

The war continued. Lord Roberts had taken little notice of all the upheaval. He ignored it and went on regardless. On 13 March 1900 the British expeditionary army advanced on Bloemfontein. The previous day, President Steyn and his government had fled to Kroonstad, 200 kilometres further north, now the new capital of the Orange Free State.

Roberts was hoping that Bloemfontein would just be a stopover on his way to Johannesburg and Pretoria, but things turned out differently. His troops had taken a beating. They were unaccustomed to the extreme heat and unpredictable thunderstorms of the highveld summers. The long marches, the heavy fighting and the halving of their rations hadn't made their lives any easier. The soldiers were worn out, they were constantly hungry and the water they had been consuming was suspect. Paardeberg was particularly bad. After their confrontation with Cronjé's commandos, the Modder River was polluted by the corpses of horses and oxen. The men had been warned not to drink from it, but many had done so nevertheless. And they had brought the germs to Bloemfontein. Tens of thousands of exhausted, undernourished and diseased soldiers arriving in a town with 3000 inhabitants was a recipe for disaster. A typhoid epidemic broke out, one more rampant than in beleaguered Ladysmith.

The massive scale of the epidemic was largely due to unreliable supply lines, which was the biggest problem facing Roberts's army. Bloemfontein had the logistical advantage of being on the direct railway line from the Cape Colony, but in wartime its dependence on rail transport was a drawback. The retreating Boers had blown up the main bridges along the supply route and it would take time to repair them. Temporary, makeshift bridges were not designed to carry the heavily laden goods wagons that were needed daily to supply an expeditionary army of 50,000 men. And when transport became available again, there was still the problem of bottlenecks. Everything the troops needed in the way of food, weapons, ammunition, clothing, tents, horses and medical supplies had to be transported along a single track. Military supplies were given priority over supplies for hospitals that were bursting at the seams. Roberts and his chief of staff were taken to task for bringing this logistical disaster upon themselves by insisting on a centralised transport system. Kitchener of Khartoum, who was ultimately responsible for coordinating it all, came to be known as Kitchener of Chaos.[84]

The fact that Roberts's expeditionary army was held up in Bloemfontein suited one man quite well. Winston Churchill, the *Morning Post's* war correspondent and second lieutenant in the South African Light Horse, was always eager for action. The relief of Ladysmith had brought an end to the hostilities in Natal. The Boers had withdrawn to the Drakensberg and Biggarsberg. By the look of things, Buller was planning to give his own men and White's time to recover from the many hardships they had endured. So for the time being, there was no war to be waged or won. It was time to move on to the other front, to see how the last part was playing out there, to witness the march to Pretoria. Ian Hamilton, a friend of Roberts's from British India, had gone there too.

Churchill had no difficulty in obtaining leave from the Cockyolibirds and left Ladysmith on 29 March 1900. The train to Durban took him past the now-empty hospital tent camp. The dead were still buried there, but the patients had been transferred to other hospitals. 'Ghastly Intombi had faded into the past, as a nightmare flies at the dawn of day,' he wrote, not suspecting that there was another nightmare to come. From Durban he took the boat to East London and from there the train to Cape Town. He booked a suite at the Mount Nelson Hotel while awaiting his new accreditation. A mere formality, no doubt. Lord Roberts was an old friend of the family. As a child, Churchill had seen him on many occasions. Moreover, Bobs owed his appointment as commander-in-chief in British India in 1885 to Lord Randolph, who was the state secretary for India in that period. To pass the time Churchill went jackal hunting with the high commissioner, Milner, and grumbled about the gossip he had heard from other guests at the hotel, where 'all the world and his wife are residing—particularly the wife'.

A week later it dawned on him that something was wrong. He decided to ask two old acquaintances in Roberts's staff, Ian Hamilton and another general he had met in British India, William Nicholson. The answer came by telegram. Churchill's unsparing pen had evidently offended both Roberts and Kitchener.

Kitchener's grievance dated back to the Sudan campaign in 1898. Churchill had published an unembellished account of it in *The River War*, criticising the killing of wounded Mahdi fighters after the Battle of Omdurman, and condemning the exhumation and beheading of the Mahdi. 'To destroy what was sacred and holy to them was a wicked act.' Kitchener hadn't forgotten that Churchill held him responsible for both atrocities. By the same token, this applied to Roberts as well. Churchill had subsequently redeemed himself by his heroism on the armoured train, his escape from Pretoria and by taking part in Buller's campaign in Natal. But he had thrown those military triumphs out of the window by publishing his newspaper reports. After the defeat at Spion Kop, for instance, he had written a disparaging article for the *Morning Post* about a sermon by an Anglican chaplain, which didn't measure up to one he had heard in Sudan by the inspired (Roman Catholic) Father Brindle. More than anything else, his little gem, 'whether Rome was again seizing the opportunity which Canterbury disdained', had upset not only the Anglican clergy in Britain, but also the devout Lord Roberts.

The last straw was his contribution to a debate in Ladysmith about the treatment accorded to those in Natal and the Cape Colony—of Dutch as well as British descent—who had sided with the Boers after their invasion. Many Britons were clamouring for revenge against the 'rebels', but Churchill made a public appeal for reconciliation. Vengeance, he wrote in a Natal newspaper, was morally wrong and counterproductive. An eye for an eye, a tooth for a tooth, wouldn't work. It would only alienate the Boers even further. 'We desire a speedy peace and the last thing in the world we want is that this war should enter a guerrilla phase.' His advice was to establish British supremacy in the Transvaal and the Orange Free State, but after that offer forgiveness and refrain from individual reprisals.

This kind of thinking went down badly in Natal and the Cape Colony as well as Britain. His articles expressing similar opinions in the *Morning Post* appeared with a disclaimer from the editors. Roberts and Kitchener weren't in favour of reconciliation either. Hamilton and Nicholson, however, did support Churchill's view. Had they not done so, he could have packed his bags and taken himself back to England. Now, on 11 April, he was finally given permission to accompany and report on Roberts's campaign, but 'only for your father's sake'. On his arrival in Bloemfontein he was also subjected to a sermon by Nicholson—Roberts's military secretary—'against reckless and uncharitable criticism'.[85]

It seemed to help. A few days earlier he had sent an indignant article to the *Morning Post* about Gatacre's dismissal. Gatacre, the general who had lost the battle at Stormberg, had fouled up again and been sent packing from one day to the next—unfairly, in Churchill's opinion. But once in Bloemfontein, Churchill kept his criticism to himself. In his first contribution from there, on 16 April 1900, he outlined the logistical problems without even mentioning Kitchener's name, let alone his new nickname. And Roberts—who was pointedly ignoring him—he described in glowing terms as 'the Queen's greatest subject, the Commander who had in the brief space of a month revolutionised the fortunes of the war, had turned disaster into victory'.

Most interesting of all, especially in the light of his experiences in Ladysmith, was what Churchill omitted to say. In the meantime, the typhoid epidemic in Bloemfontein had grown to frightening proportions. Conditions had deteriorated since 31 March after a joint attack on the waterworks at Sannaspos, carried out by Boer commandos under the brothers Christiaan and Piet de Wet. During Churchill's stay in Bloemfontein 5000 people had been infected and 1000 of them died. But there wasn't a word about it in any of his reports—unlike Arthur Conan Doyle, who was working at Langman's private hospital during the same period and who insisted in several publications that compulsory vaccination could have prevented all those fatalities. At the time, vaccines were provided only on request. Even then, Churchill didn't respond.

The most likely reason is that the subject was too sensitive and he was unwilling to jeopardise his position—or embarrass his patrons Hamilton and Nicholson—by offending Roberts again. Otherwise he would surely have had something to say about Conan Doyle's call for vaccination against typhoid. He had discussed the subject once before, on his voyage to South Africa on the *Dunottar Castle*. On that occasion he had taken a stand against vaccination, because he was not convinced of its efficacy. Instead, he put his faith in 'health and the laws of health'.[86]

Columns on the move

Bloemfontein, 16 April 1900

Churchill hadn't come to Bloemfontein to fritter his time away. Action, march, advance, that was the kind of idiom he wanted to convey in the *Morning Post*. The endless convoys of goods wagons and the daily procession of dark brown body bags were subjects he left for others to write about. He wanted to be on campaign again, accompanying the troops to the highveld. He had no military assignment there, but as a journalist he was impatient to be where the action was.

In that respect, his timing was perfect. In March 1900 the Boers were as good as played out, at least in the Orange Free State; in April they were back in top form. Under the inspiring leadership of the exiled President Steyn and their new chief commandant, Christiaan de Wet, they developed a new and more flexible strategy. They carried out one raid after another in the contested territory south-east of Bloemfontein. British headquarters reacted with astonishment and indignation. It wasn't right. The capital had been occupied; the Orange Free State had lost the war; the Free Staters were supposed to surrender. As Lord Roberts put it in a personal letter to Queen Victoria after the fall of Bloemfontein, 'It seems unlikely that this State will give much more trouble.' That still left the Transvaal, but after the invasion of Pretoria the war wouldn't take long, he predicted. A month later, in mid-April, Roberts still thought the same. There had just been a bit of a delay. Before advancing further north, they would need to deal with a few pockets of resistance in the south-east of the Orange Free State. His generals were growing restless.

Roberts didn't foresee any major obstacles. He had confidence in his plan: firm military action against insurgents, backed up by the power of the written word. That was how he had operated from the start, his tone gradually hardening from conciliatory to threatening. Not for nothing did the Boers speak of Roberts's 'paper bombs'. He issued his first proclamation to the burghers of the Orange Free State on 17 February 1900, a few days before the battle at Paardeberg, calling on them to cease hostilities and assuring those who did that they would not be troubled. His second proclamation of 11 March contained an emphatic warning. He was about to occupy Bloemfontein and promised its inhabitants that those 'staying peacefully at home will not be molested'. But if the British troops encountered resistance, he added ominously, they would have themselves to blame for the consequences.

After the fall of Bloemfontein, Roberts's duplicity became blatantly evident. On the one hand, he put people off their guard by laying on festivities and brass bands. He also launched a bilingual newspaper, *The Friend*, for which he engaged the services of Rudyard Kipling, Poet of the Empire and author of gems like 'Take up the white man's burden'. But at the same time, on 15 March he issued a third proclamation, far more strongly worded than the previous two. It was an infinitely high-calibre paper bomb. Now, he added vindictively, punishment would be meted out to virtually any Boer who had ever pointed a Mauser at a British soldier. Moreover, those who refused to 'lay down their arms and take an oath to abstain from further part in the war' would be arrested and deprived of their property. Those who acquiesced would be given 'safe conduct to their homes'.

Churchill's views on the matter didn't appear in the *Morning Post*. This was another subject he wisely avoided. Given his earlier appeal for reconciliation between Britons and Boers, he must have had reservations about the edict. What he did describe to his readers were the unintended repercussions of Roberts's last proclamation. On returning home, many of the Boers who had laid down their arms and taken the oath were lambasted by their commandants and, in some cases, by their families as well. As a result, 'most of them, from fear or inclination, rejoined their commandos . . . the lately penitent rebels stirred, are stirring'. In this way, Christiaan and his brother Piet de Wet, in particular, managed to raise a substantial army of insurgents. Roberts responded by sending several columns to break the resistance.

As a war correspondent, Churchill could choose which division he wanted to accompany, providing they would have him. He knew at once. It looked as if the critical encounters would take place in the vicinity of Dewetsdorp, about 70 kilometres south-east of Bloemfontein. Among those who were heading there was an Imperial Yeomanry brigade under the command of General John Brabazon. Churchill knew Old Brab well. He was, needless to say, an old friend of the family, and commanding officer of the 4th Hussars, with whom Churchill had begun his military career. Churchill bought a carriage and four horses, and on 17 April put them on the train to Edenburg—there was enough room going south—and from there rode alone to Dewetsdorp, 'across a landscape charged with silent menace'.[87]

One can only guess what Marthinus Steyn thought of Roberts's latest proclamation. It was a disgrace, a gift from heaven. Out of respect for Oom Paul, he had taken part in his peace initiatives, but in his heart he had more faith in fighting than diplomacy. In September 1899 he had been reluctant to go to war, but once hostilities broke out his doubts had evaporated. He visited the fronts, gave encouragement to the dispirited commandos, and emerged as the soul of perseverance, even when the war turned against them in late February 1900. Neither Lord Salisbury's brusque reply to their telegram nor the capture of his capital city by Lord Roberts did anything to weaken his resolve. Roberts's last proclamation of 15 March had given him an opportunity, which he grasped with both hands, to take some kind of action.

On 19 March Steyn responded with two paper projectiles of his own. The first was formal and challenged the legal grounds of Roberts's demands. The Republic of the Orange Free State still existed, he declared, and the government was doing what it had undertaken to do. Every citizen was therefore obliged to perform military service. Anyone who failed to do so or who laid down his weapons 'without being coerced' to do so was guilty of high treason.

His second reply was addressed to the people of the Orange Free State. It was an impassioned appeal to their loyalty. 'Let us not be misled by this cunning ruse . . . The enemy now by fair promises seeks to divide us by offering a reward for disloyalty and cowardice. Could a greater insult be offered than to dissuade us from a sacred duty, thus betraying ourselves, betraying our people, betraying the blood that has already flowed for our land and nation, and betraying our children? . . . The man who has broken his solemn agreements with our people, will he now honour his deceitful promise?' The first promises had already been broken. There had been 'the shameful destruction of property at Jacobsdal, and in Bloemfontein the arrest of citizens who had trusted his proclamation and laid down their arms'. The capital was in the enemy's hands, 'but the battle is not lost. On the contrary, it gives greater reason to fight harder . . . Take courage and be steadfast in your faith. The Lord God shall not suffer His purpose for our nation to be obstructed. Persevere in the struggle. The darkest hour is just before dawn.'

Steyn didn't stop at words. Two days earlier, on 17 March, a joint council of war had been held in Kroonstad, which had far-reaching consequences for the Boers' military tactics—and the subsequent course of the war. The meeting was attended by Kruger and Steyn along with other top brass from both Boer republics, including their highest-ranking military leaders, the Transvaal commandant-general, Joubert, and the Free State's new chief commandant, Christiaan de Wet. With surprising alacrity they agreed on a drastic change of strategy. Even Joubert, the ultimate advocate of defensive warfare, acknowledged the advantages of offensive action as favoured by De Wet, De la Rey and other generals of a younger generation. They would attack, but within limits, in smaller and more mobile units divided into companies of 25 men. They would dispense with their oxwagons and tighten up discipline. The idea was to avoid major confrontations and aim instead for the Achilles' heel of the British army: their long, vulnerable lines of communication.

The only matter the two military commanders disagreed on was a surprising measure De Wet had taken a few days earlier. The British would want time to catch their breath after the capture of Bloemfontein, he reasoned, so he had taken the opportunity to disband his commandos and give them leave to go home. On 25 March they were to reassemble at the railway bridge over the Sand River, north of Bloemfontein. Joubert was aghast. How could he! De Wet admitted he had taken a risk. Perhaps some of them wouldn't come back. But, he thought, his men had spent six months giving the very best of themselves, they were in low spirits after the British successes, discipline was slack, he had to do something. Those who did return would at least be motivated, and he'd rather have 'ten with the will to fight than a hundred dragging their heels'.[88]

De Wet didn't manage to persuade Joubert, but on 25 March he was proved right. All his men returned except those from districts that were effectively occupied by the British. And, indeed, they came with renewed vigour. His decision proved its worth in the successful surprise attack he undertook at Sannaspos on 31 March. Not only did his commandos and those under his brother Piet manage to put Bloemfontein's water supply out of action, but they also seized 80 supply wagons and seven guns and took more than 400 British prisoners. It was a triumph that made a powerful statement: the war was not over, the Boers' new tactics were successful.

De Wet gave a repeat performance a few days later, on 3 April, when he showed up unexpectedly at Mostertshoek, 60 kilometres further south. With an army of re-conscripted burghers and the commandos of generals Stoffel Froneman and A.I. de Villiers, he mounted a surprise attack against a British infantry unit under Captain W.J. McWhinnie. Reinforcements under Major-General Gatacre arrived too late—this was the blunder after Stormberg that proved fatal for Gatacre—and De Wet captured another 450 British prisoners. There was clearly a problem Roberts would have to deal with before advancing on Johannesburg and Pretoria.

Joubert didn't live to see the first fruits of the new tactics. On 27 March, aged 69, he died in Pretoria of peritonitis. Friend and foe paid their respects.

Unaware of the unpleasant surprise De Wet had in store for him, Roberts sent a telegram offering his condolences. Rudyard Kipling honoured him—a bit prematurely—as a steadfast defender of a hopeless cause. 'But subtle, strong, and stubborn, gave his life / To a lost cause, and knew the gift was vain.' In accordance with his last will, Joubert was buried on his farm in Rustfontein. At the railway station President Kruger took leave of his lifelong comrade-in-arms and favourite political rival. He spoke movingly of the old days, the days of the Voortrekkers and their sacred commitment to the Promised Land. He was the last survivor of them all.[89]

It was hard on the old patriarch. Jan Kock had been killed at Elandslaagte, Piet Cronjé captured and banished to St Helena, and now Piet Joubert gone as well. There was no one left of his own generation. He was 74, and the men who were now running the show in the Transvaal were far younger. Schalk Burger, Joubert's successor as vice-president, wasn't yet 50; the new commandant-general, Louis Botha, not even 40; and the state attorney, Smuts, was still in his twenties. State Secretary Reitz, in his mid-fifties, was the oldest, but sometimes so rash that he seemed half his age. He was completely different from his predecessor, Leyds, who, young as he was, had always been so thorough and vigilant. But Leyds was far away and out of reach, isolated in his European observation post.

Kruger's voice was still firm and impressive when he addressed his people, but his eyesight had dimmed, his gait was less steady, and his thinking more often inspired by the teachings of the Old Testament. He spoke not of Roberts or international political relations, but of the strength of the lion and the king of Assyria. His faith remained steadfast, but he was losing touch with the world. He had allowed himself to be talked into the ill-conceived idea of a telegram to Salisbury and had proceeded to push it through, first in his own Executive Council and then past the 30-year-younger president of the Orange Free State. Immediately afterwards, without waiting for a reply from London, they had called on half of Europe to mediate.

As if that wasn't futile enough, Kruger, with Steyn's backing, went a step further. Why not send a delegation to Europe to persuade one or more of the powers to 'intervene or assist'? The choice of delegates was easily made. The chairman representing the two Boer republics was Abraham Fischer, a lawyer and a friend of Steyn's. He was accompanied by Cornelius Wessels, speaker of the Free State Volksraad, and A.D.W. Wolmarans, a member of the Transvaal's Executive Council, with J.M. de Bruijn as secretary. The fact that none of the three delegates had any experience of diplomacy and that only Fischer spoke fluent English and

Dutch—but no German or French—wasn't considered a handicap. All three were given diplomatic credentials and set off in haste for Lourenço Marques. On 13 March 1900 they embarked on the *Kaiser*—an obvious clue to anyone who knew anything about European diplomacy.

Leyds was left to find out about the peace initiative from the newspapers. Even so, he was loyal to this foolhardy mission, as he had been to others in the past. He thought it would be wise to travel ahead to confer with his new colleagues. They met in Milan on 13 April in the presence of Hendrik Muller, the Orange Free State's consul-general in the Netherlands. It was a frustrating experience for Leyds. He took pains to inform the delegation at length about political and diplomatic relations in Europe and the United States. In his opinion—which had recently been confirmed by his well-informed Russian sources—they only stood a chance if they travelled on to Berlin without delay. Tsar Nicholas II was still willing to take some kind of action, but only if he was certain that Germany would cooperate. The French government was holding back so as not to jeopardise the World Exhibition in Paris. No other country, the Netherlands included, was in a position to do anything at all. Kaiser Wilhelm II held the key in his hands. There was no guarantee, but if the three 'suddenly appeared before him . . . like Boers straight from the battlefield' and appealed to 'his conscience and magnanimity', there was a 'chance of moving him, touching a sentimental corner of his heart, stirring his vanity'.

The delegation listened politely, but cast Leyds's advice to the winds. They had already decided to go to the Netherlands first, because of their blood ties with the Dutch, and as Muller strongly supported the idea they proceeded as planned. They arrived in The Hague a few days later and were given a warm reception, but the outcome was what Leyds had expected. Nothing. Prime Minister Pierson was happy to receive them, and their audiences with Queen Wilhelmina and subsequently the Queen Mother, Emma, were cordial and hospitable. But in the talks that really mattered, their official meeting with the foreign minister, De Beaufort, on 26 April, Fischer, Wessels and Wolmarans were unceremoniously fobbed off. De Beaufort had no qualms about the way he dealt with them. Fischer more or less made the grade. He was 'the smartest, much like an Englishman'. But in his diary De Beaufort described Wessels and Wolmarans as 'peasants with the cunning, guile and distrust of their kind, who felt superior because they were the leading and ruling class in their country'. Naturally they knew beforehand 'that the Dutch government would do nothing', but in spite of this they were 'bitterly disappointed when I explained . . . that any step we might take would turn the British public against them and that would only be to their detriment'.

After this disillusioning meeting the delegation decided there was nothing to be gained by staying on in the Netherlands. As their next destination they chose the United States. This, too, Leyds considered a pointless exercise as long as the Republican president, McKinley, and his state secretary, Hay, were in government. But again he gave in to Fischer and his associates. He went so far as to escort them on the first leg of the voyage, from Rotterdam to Boulogne-sur-Mer. On 3 May they embarked on the *Maasdam*. A thousand well-wishers were on the quay to see them off. Their presence at least helped to sweeten the bitter pill they had been made to swallow. They had won the hearts of the Dutch people.[90]

That same day, 2 May 1900, after spending seven weeks in Bloemfontein, Lord Roberts resumed his advance to the north. It had taken a huge effort, but now everything was in place. The men had recovered their strength, their equipment was in order, the gaps in the ranks caused in combat and by the typhus epidemic had been filled, their supplies replenished and—last but not least—the Boer resistance south-east of Bloemfontein had been crushed. More accurately, Christiaan de Wet, who had been prowling around there with some 2500 Boer fighters for the previous few weeks, had been driven away. It had taken ten times as many troops to accomplish this, 25,000 divided into five columns, but step by step they had gained ground. At one point, they had almost surrounded De Wet, but at the very last moment he managed to slip through their fingers—not for the last time.

It hadn't been a major battle, more like a series of intermittent skirmishes, with much manoeuvring back and forth on both sides. This was the kind of action Churchill couldn't resist, even though he was no longer wearing the cockade of black sakabula tail feathers on his hat. On 19 April he arrived in his carriage and reported to Brabazon's brigade, near Dewetsdorp. Old Brab was delighted see him and at once launched into a litany of complaints about his superior, Major-General French, the liberator of Kimberley. It was entertaining enough—Churchill always enjoyed a bit of quality gossip—but he had really come for the action. Two days later he left with the colourful cavalry units under Brabazon's command, among them Montmorency's Scouts with their distinctive death's head insignia. Raymond de Montmorency, after whom the unit was named, had died two months earlier and Angus McNeill was now their commanding officer.

It was the same McNeill whom Churchill lured into an adventure that could have cost him dearly. On a reconnaissance they came upon a group of Boers who were making their way to a koppie two kilometres further on. McNeill asked Brabazon's permission to intercept them. It was granted. 'Mount, mount, mount, Scouts!' he cried, and, to Churchill, 'Come with us, we'll give you a show now—first-class.'

And that it certainly was, at any rate for the objective observer. A thrilling race between 200 Boers and 50 Scouts. Whoever reached the hill first would be able to take cover and fire on the enemy. In full gallop Churchill fell to musing about the triumphant mission he had taken part in at Acton Homes three months earlier, except on that occasion they had had the advantage of surprise. Now the boot was on the other foot. Barbed wire stopped them about a hundred metres from the hill, and they were forced to dismount. A few men were trying to cut through the wire, when suddenly they saw the heads and shoulders of ten or so Boers.

This was nothing at all like Acton Homes. It was Chieveley all over again; the armoured train. 'Grim, hairy, and terrible', and how many more were there behind them? 'Too late,' McNeill shouted, 'back to the other kopje. Gallop!' The Boers opened fire, the Scouts leapt onto their horses and sped off. As Churchill was putting his foot in the stirrup, his horse took fright at the sound of gunfire, bolted, broke loose and galloped away.

There he was again, on foot as at Chieveley, an easy target on the open veld. This time he had his pistol at hand, but what could he hope to achieve against who knows how many Mausers? He turned on his heel and, for the second time in this war, ran for his life. It looked as if his luck had abandoned him. 'Here at last I take it.' The words flashed through his mind. Suddenly, as before, he caught a glimpse of a tall man on a grey horse. Would he be captured again?

Then he caught sight of the skull and crossbones: a Scout. 'Death in Revelation, but life to me.' He called out, 'Give me a stirrup.' The rider slackened his pace, Churchill ran towards him, leapt up behind him and flung his arms around him. He clung to the horse's mane. Bullets whistled past his ears, his hands were covered in blood. The horse had taken a bullet but it continued to run. Four hundred metres, five hundred, the gunfire died down. It looked as if they were going to make it. Churchill heaved a sigh of relief.

The rider didn't. 'My poor horse, oh my poor fucking horse; shot with an explosive bullet. The devils! But their hour will come. Oh, my poor horse.' Churchill tried to console him. 'Never mind, you've saved my life.' But that didn't help. 'Ah, but it's the horse I'm thinking about.' No more was said. They reached the safety of the next koppie. He had escaped again.[91]

Colour

Kroonstad, 12 May 1900

By all accounts it was one of the most beautiful towns in the Orange Free State. But Churchill found Kroonstad a bit disappointing. It was slightly bigger than Winburg, but not half as well kept. Everything was covered by a thick layer of red dust and it was dry as could be. Roberts marched one of his divisions into town, for effect, and then out again. His force had left Bloemfontein nine days earlier, singing 'We are marching to Pretoria'. They had come 200 kilometres since then, nearly halfway. The government of the Orange Free State had been forced to flee again. Let's hope they've got strong legs, Churchill quipped.

He could allow himself to include a frivolous note in his dispatches to the *Morning Post*. They were making progress these days. The bulldozer strategy Buller had dreamed of had been set in motion by Roberts and Kitchener. The British war machine was rolling over a 40-kilometre front through the highveld, on either side of the railway line, a massive, unstoppable procession of guns, men and horses heading for Johannesburg and Pretoria. Roberts was in command, with French's cavalry on his left and Hamilton's heavily armed column on his right. At the same time, two infantry divisions under lieutenants-general Lord Methuen and Sir Archibald Hunter had left Kimberley and were marching north along the railway track to Rhodesia. The peace on the eastern front had now been shattered as well. On 8 May Buller's amply reinforced expeditionary army got under way, making for the Biggarsberg and Drakensberg. As Churchill explained to his readers, the hugely outnumbered Boers had been forced to spread their forces over such a wide area that the British armies were breaking through everywhere 'as an iron bar might smash thin ice, with scarcely any shock'.

In a word, the Boers didn't stand a chance. They were desperately short of men and equipment. Their new strategy would have meant allowing Roberts's forces to proceed unhindered and then cutting him off from his supply lines. This was what Christiaan de Wet had suggested. When he found himself in danger of being surrounded in the vicinity of Dewetsdorp, he had hoped to be able to escape to the south, to the strip of land along the border between the Orange Free State and the Cape Colony. This would put him in a better position to sabotage the vital railway lines. But the other Boer leaders weren't convinced. The Transvalers were reluctant to let the enemy continue their march to Johannesburg and Pretoria. Their new commandant-general, Louis Botha, had come from Natal to lead the defence in person. He considered his options: a Long Tom to counter the British naval guns; burn the veld so that the British in their khaki uniforms would be more visible against the scorched plains. President Steyn agreed with him and recalled De Wet. He would have to join in to block Roberts's advance. Resourceful and enterprising as he was, De Wet did everything he could, but all the Boers' cunning was no match for the sheer magnitude of the British assault, their firepower, their bayonets and now the flanking manoeuvres they had learned after those first insane weeks.

There was too much happening to follow everything closely; even a wide-awake war correspondent couldn't take it all in. Churchill had opted for a position on the right flank, near his favourite general, Ian Hamilton, for obvious reasons. Roberts was still giving him the cold shoulder, and after the few days he had spent with Brabazon, French wanted nothing to do with him either. Hamilton was still decent to him, as always. He had even allowed Churchill's cousin, the Duke of Marlborough, to accompany them. 'Sunny' had been attached to Roberts's staff, along with a Duke of Norfolk and a Duke of Westminster. The British press had quibbled about the number of aristocrats who were being given honorary appointments and Roberts shrewdly decided to dispose of one of them. And so the two cousins found themselves together in Hamilton's column.

They had a marvellous time. They rode in Churchill's carriage from one engagement to the next, enjoying the unspoilt countryside, ultimate freedom, each day bringing a new adventure. A reconnaissance, an ambush, a pursuit, the familiar crack of rifle fire. Nights under the stars. Living off sheep the army carried with them, a few chickens they scrounged along the way and such comforts as they had managed to store in the carriage: 'two feet of the best tinned provisions and alcoholic stimulants London could supply'.

Besides military operations, Churchill wrote about the settlements they passed—mostly disappointing—and the people they met on their way. Some of those encounters were interesting. There was that family living on the large farm near the Sand River who had put them up for the night at Hamilton's request. Four generations of Boers: an elderly man and, for the rest, only women and children. The men and boys, even the youngest of them, had joined the commandos. The family grudgingly offered them the use of a bedroom and the living room. Hamilton's staff installed themselves on the veranda. Churchill took the opportunity to explore the surroundings. There were a dozen children, he noted, black and white, running around together, 'little Kaffirs, the offspring of the servants, playing with the sons and daughters of the house'.

In the living room 'one very curious book' caught his eye. It was a songbook compiled by F.W. Reitz, the former president of the Orange Free State, now the state secretary of the Transvaal. It was a book of patriotic battle hymns, with a few English songs in translation. They were all in Dutch and all intended 'to manufacture a new Dutch nation in South Africa'. Churchill made no effort to conceal his admiration. He regarded this kind of book as 'the foundation stone of a vernacular literature'. The Boers had been struggling for years to develop a culture of their own. With a little more patience, he reflected, a little less preoccupation with themselves, the odd compromise here and there, they would have succeeded without too much trouble. Instead, their obstinacy had brought 'a conquering army to this quiet farm, and scattered the schemers far and wide'.

A few days later—Kroonstad had meanwhile fallen—he had a different kind of unusual meeting. At least, he might have, if Hamilton had had his way. Piet de Wet and his commandos were near Lindley, 80 kilometres east of Kroonstad. De Wet was apparently tired of fighting. On 18 May the brigade general, Robert Broadwood, received an intriguing message. He heard that De Wet was prepared to surrender on condition that he could return to his farm. Broadwood, who had suffered at the hands of the De Wet brothers at Sannaspos six weeks earlier, seized the opportunity. The surrender of a Boer general, the brother of the Free State's chief commander—this was a chance to get his revenge. Hamilton, too, was more than willing to accept De Wet's terms. But to be on the safe side he sent a telegram asking for Roberts's consent. The answer came quickly, and there were no two ways about it. Out of the question. An unconditional surrender or none at all. Hamilton and Broadwood were flabbergasted. Churchill forgot his resolution not to antagonise Roberts. 'I need not say with what astonishment this decision was received.' Exile to St Helena or Ceylon, that wasn't what Piet de Wet had done it for. He chose to keep fighting, as Churchill lamented, 'to our loss in life, honour, and money'.[92]

In the meantime, Sister Hellemans had also succumbed. Like everyone else in the Second Dutch Ambulance, she too 'paid toll to Ladysmith'. In her case it was dysentery. Fortunately she took ill only after reaching Pretoria in early April 1900, at the end of a long, exhausting journey. Now it was her turn to be nursed. There was nothing to do but spend a few weeks resting and recuperating.

By early May she had recovered sufficiently to get back to work. Her colleagues had already gone on ahead. Their new posting was a town called Christiana in the far south-west of the Transvaal. It was near Veertienstroom, where 15 years earlier Willem Leyds had gained his first practical experience of the workings of diplomacy.[93] There was heavy fighting in the area and 'many sick and wounded patients' needed medical attention. The special train that took her to the western front on 7 May was packed with Boer commandos. They arrived in Klerksdorp at midnight and from there she travelled another four days on a 'mule cart' downstream along the Vaal.

In Christiana, Hellemans discovered that the local inn had been converted to serve as a hospital. It was a real building and could accommodate 40 patients. Before the Dutch corps arrived they had been looked after by the Transvaal Red Cross. No lack of dedication, Hellemans thought, but a billiard room where people 'played and smoked immoderately' was no place for the sick and wounded. They had to have separate quarters. The standard of 'cleanliness and tidiness' wasn't satisfactory either. 'A Dutch housewife's hair would stand on end' at the sight of the kitchen. The floor was made from cow dung, which 'turned into porridge when anyone spilt a few drops of water'. In addition, it was dingy and musty, the washing-up water was brown and the dishcloths were revolting. Luckily, the Boer girls who worked there were willing to learn. In no time at all, they were 'polishing and scrubbing, the kitchen looked brighter and our Dutch instincts were assuaged'.

Fortunately, they had assistants to lighten the load. 'Those kaffirs make life much easier.' They did the cleaning and the fetching and carrying—a good thing too, as the actual nursing occupied all their time. Many of the patients in the surgery ward, where Hellemans was assigned, were seriously injured. One Boer had 'eleven wounds, caused by a bomb that went off' and another 'a bullet wound to the right temple, as large as a five-cent coin'. He also had a small swelling on the left side of his forehead and complained of headaches. When they operated they found a bullet, all right, buried five centimetres deep. A week after it was removed the man was up and walking about. He was 'a rare example of how tough the Boers are'.

Hellemans and her team were happy with their work but the British advance soon had an impact on them as well. It grew quieter, which in the circumstances didn't bode well. In the middle of May the Boers began to retreat. This meant they would have to evacuate the patients who were well enough to be moved as quickly as possible to prevent them from falling into the hands of the British. They managed in good time. Brother E. Meuleman took them to Klerksdorp in a special double-decker ambulance. The rest of the Dutch team would follow later.

Now that the Boer commandos had gone, those left behind spent a sleepless night. They assembled their belongings in the hospital grounds where they could keep an eye on them, and took turns looking after their patients. They didn't know who to fear most, 'the advancing British or ... the kaffirs. We were equally afraid of both.' Their worries weren't over when the British actually invaded Christiana—without harming anything or anyone—and subsequently 'abandoned it to its fate' again. There was no garrison, but from now on British law was in force, which meant—so they believed—'the kaffirs' would be free to do as they pleased. The Africans may have been 'a great convenience' under the harsh Boer regime, but under British law they had 'the same rights as a white person'. However, as they were 'not yet civilised, the dramatic change in their status leads to excesses . . . they forget their place and take liberties, and they're cheeky even to those who used to be their superiors'. And when they drank whiskey, which the British gave them 'in abundance . . . they become murderous'.

No wonder the Dutch medics had trouble sleeping that first night. But all went well, and the following morning 'at the breakfast table Doctor P [Pino] congratulated me on the way things had turned out'. There had been some plundering but only from unoccupied buildings. Their fears had proved unfounded. They stopped keeping guard at night and gradually the days grew 'quiet, even monotonous'. When their remaining black servants—most had fled—stepped out of line, Hellemans was merely amused. 'The kitchen-boy was the funniest and the cheekiest.' He even proposed—would you believe!—'to one of the maids', a Boer girl, for heaven's sake.[94]

Colour was one of the main stumbling blocks when the two worlds collided. Boers and Britons held different views on the matter of race, at least in theory. The Boers scoffed at their opponents' professed belief in equality. In God's immutable creation black people were inferior and destined to serve whites. It was fine for black and white children to play together, but as adults their ways parted irrevocably. Relationships between them were sharply defined, in war as in peacetime: master–servant, supervisor–labourer, fighter–*agterryer*.

The British were more ambivalent. They believed in political rights for Uitlanders and some political rights for Africans. But in practice things were more difficult. Zealous as they were in their efforts to convert the Boers to their modern ideas, the British themselves weren't always scrupulous about protecting the interests of their protégés and were inclined to make the same distinctions as the Boers.

This was most clearly evident in and around the three besieged towns, where the heaviest burdens—literally and figuratively—were borne by the black population. The relief of Ladysmith and Kimberley brought no change to that situation. Mafeking had not yet been liberated. This was down for 18 May in Roberts's planning, but before it happened, the Boers mounted a last, desperate offensive.

The initiative was taken by Commandant Sarel Eloff, President Kruger's grandson. From a strategic point of view the attack was meaningless, but Eloff was hoping to achieve a psychological coup. A last-minute success for the Boers at Mafeking would send the burghers a message of hope in troubled times. With 250 volunteers and his grandfather's blessing, Eloff approached the force besieging the town. General Kootjie Snyman approved his plan to launch a surprise attack. He also agreed to provide 500 reinforcements once Eloff had managed to break through the defence.

They went into action on the night of 11 May. It started off well. Eloff and his men pushed through via 'black' Mafikeng and proceeded from there to the garrison on the boundary with 'white' Mafeking. Thirty men under the command of Lieutenant-Colonel C.O. Hore were overpowered and captured. To signal the breakthrough to Snyman, Eloff set fire to a few of the Tshidi Barolong huts. To provoke Baden-Powell he called him to say he had captured his second-in-charge and was on his way into town. But he spoke too soon. Snyman had changed his mind and Eloff's unit fell apart. Eloff himself got no further than the garrison, which was now under attack from all sides—by the British in Mafeking as well as the Barolong in Mafikeng. The battle raged all day. By nightfall Eloff conceded that his situation was hopeless. He released Hore and surrendered, along with more than 100 other volunteers. The Boers' final attempt to capture Mafeking had also ended in humiliation.[95]

Once again this was due to the Tshidi Barolong's valuable contribution to the defence effort right up to the last months of the siege. They had been helpful, if not indispensable, in combat, trench work, espionage, courier assignments, cattle raids. The same was true of their main rivals, the Rapulana Barolong, on the enemy side. Both parties to the conflict knowingly violated their unspoken agreement to wage a 'white man's war', yet kept hurling recriminations at the other. At the start of the siege Piet Cronjé—who was still the commandant at the time—had sent Baden-Powell an accusing letter: 'you have armed Bastards, Fingos and Baralongs against us.' Baden-Powell denied this, saying it was the Boers who were soliciting 'the assistance of armed Natives'. The quarrel was resumed in January. As if he himself didn't depend heavily on his Barolong auxiliaries, Baden-Powell warned Snyman that continuing to deploy armed Africans 'would justify the English in allowing the Basuto to join in the war, in bringing Ghurkha troops from India, in using "dum dum" bullets, and other such acts'.

But both parties carried on as before. Right to the end, blacks as well as whites were involved in the siege of Mafeking, particularly in its defence. That some went hungrier than others was all the more shameful. As from November 1899 everyone was subjected to rationing on Baden-Powell's orders, but Africans and coloureds suffered the most. To save flour, which was needed for 'white' bread, they were forced to switch to oats, which had previously been used as horse feed. The horses were put out to graze, if they hadn't already been served up as meat or soup. In January rations were reduced again. In February they were cancelled for the black miners who had fled from the Rand. Their only recourse was the soup kitchen for broth made from the leftovers of horse, chicken, mule and dog meat. Baden-Powell would have liked to see them leave altogether. They could go to Kanye in Bechuanaland, where the British authorities had stockpiled huge reserves of food. He made one attempt to expel them en masse but subsequently abandoned the idea because the Boers had fired on them mercilessly. Expulsions and escapes on a smaller scale were more successful and brought some relief—at least for those left behind.

Malnutrition reached such proportions in Mafeking, and especially its black neighbourhood, that in April 1900 a plague of locusts was welcomed as an extra source of nutrition. That went for the white population too, according to a telegram from Churchill's aunt, Lady Sarah Wilson, to the family back home. 'Breakfast today, horse sausages; lunch minced mule, curried locusts. All well.'

All well? Not for the town's black inhabitants. They had to make do with less food and an even less palatable diet. Sol Plaatje, a court interpreter and to this day the only black African known to have kept a diary of the Boer War, saw them die of starvation, one by one, right there in the street, 'backwards with a dead thud'. Crazed with hunger, people exhumed dead horses and dogs for food, with all the inevitable consequences. Diseases like diphtheria and typhoid were rampant, in Mafikeng most of all. And this in addition to the estimated 1000 people killed in the Boer bombardments.[96]

The mood was sombre even when relief finally arrived. Perhaps it was just bad timing. Around dinner time on 16 May, Lady Sarah heard a commotion in the market square. She ran out to greet the first cavalrymen trickling in, tired and covered in dust. Their welcome was lukewarm, no cheering crowd, no music. All she saw was 'a score or so begrimed figures' on worn-out horses and a cluster of women around them, weeping with joy. The rest followed in the middle of the night, Colonel Herbert Plumer's columns from the north and Colonel Bryan Mahon's from the south. After spending the whole day in combat against De la Rey's commandos, they had continued on their way. They were exhausted. They fell asleep wherever their horses happened to be standing. After 217 days the siege of Mafeking had come to an end. Lady Sarah stayed up all night nursing the wounded in hospital.

The reaction in Britain was anything but lukewarm. In London and other big cities the news sparked off celebrations such as had never been seen before, more exuberant even than those after the relief of Ladysmith. Jubilant crowds took to the streets, singing, dancing and waving flags. Performances in music halls and theatres were interrupted, newspapers published special editions with exultant headlines. It was a huge outburst of emotion. The nation's humiliation was over; there was a happy ending, with euphoria verging on hysteria. Baden-Powell was the hero incarnate, the personification of the British ideal: dauntless, invincible, dependable, humorous. The festivities went on and on. Mafeking Night became a tradition, and the word 'mafficking' entered the English language.[97]

The Boers still had one trump up their sleeve. At least, that's how the Transvaal state secretary, Reitz, saw things. Not that they could stop Roberts's advance: there was nothing they could do about that but keep fighting and hoping against hope. What they could do, however, was frustrate the British on a spectacular scale and settle their score with the Randlords and the Uitlanders at the same time. Blowing up the gold mines would get back at everyone responsible for dragging the Transvaal into the misery of war. It was nothing more than the revenge of the righteous. Big capital had planted in their midst the burgeoning and divisive organism that was Johannesburg. And it had obstructed them at every turn. Now the situation was hopeless and big capital deserved to go down the drain along with everything else.

Reitz didn't stop at wishful thinking. In February 1900 Pretoria instructed the government mining engineer, John Munnik, to start making preparations. Holes suitable for taking charges of dynamite were drilled into some 25 mines. A project on this scale obviously couldn't be kept secret. The *Standard and Diggers' News* got wind of the scheme and proclaimed it a crime against civilisation and a blot on the good name of the Afrikaner nation. Johannesburg's Peace and Order Commission promptly denounced any such act of random destruction. The state attorney, Smuts, sent the paper a letter denying the charge, but this didn't put an end to the rumours. Nor were they unfounded, because work on the project continued surreptitiously.

In far-off Europe Willem Leyds initially believed that the Transvaal government had no intention of blowing up the mines. Needless to say, the turmoil overseas was causing consternation among shareholders. Unnecessary, Leyds wrote on 11 April 1900 to Paul Leroy-Beaulieu, the president of the Association of French Owners and Shareholders of the Transvaal Gold Mines. That kind of thing simply wasn't in the Boers' nature. They were people who respected property rights. It sounded reassuring, but at that stage Leyds was unaware that a letter from Reitz was on its way to him. It had been sent on 6 March and he received it on 4 May. It said, 'If we are unable to save our country, we are firmly resolved to blow up and destroy the mines and equipment in Johannesburg and elsewhere.'

Leyds was taken aback. He thought it most unwise, but he wasn't in a position to do anything. Pretoria was a different matter. The Transvaal leaders were sharply divided. President Kruger and Smuts supported Reitz's view or, in any event, the idea of using it as a threat. It would be enough, they were sure, to persuade mine owners, shareholders and governments in Europe to put pressure on Great Britain. One man, however, was vehemently opposed. The new commandant-general, Louis Botha, condemned the plan as cowardly and barbaric. He set off for Pretoria as soon as he heard about it. If it was carried out, he warned Kruger, he would summon his men from the front to come to the defence of Johannesburg. This was going a bit far, but it made the point. Kruger gave his word that it wouldn't actually happen.

In Johannesburg itself, meanwhile, distrust between the various communities was mounting by the day. Would the Boers retaliate by blowing up the mines? Were pro-British Uitlanders passing on information to Roberts's advancing army? Would black miners run amok after the fall of the city? Amid this tension, panic broke out when a deafening explosion rocked the city at half past five on the evening of 24 April. Flames rising a hundred metres into the air were followed by a column of white smoke and a toxic green mushroom. In the event, it wasn't the mines but the Begbie munitions factory which was reduced to ashes. The damage was enormous. Human limbs were scattered far and wide. Even before the casualties were counted—12 killed and 30 injured—the perpetrators had been identified. The British Uitlanders, who else? Rumour had it that a tunnel had been dug from an adjacent building. The electric light switch was supposed to have been used as a detonator.

Although nothing was proved, the government immediately carried out reprisals. All British subjects who were still on the Rand were ordered to leave the country. Only technicians who were indispensable, about 100 in all, were allowed to remain. The police commissioner, Schutte, also paid a high price. He had been responsible for securing

246

the foundry. The public prosecutor, Fritz Krause, succeeded him as head of the Peace and Order Commission.

Roberts's troops were awaited with fear and trepidation. On 22 May, after ten days' rest in Kroonstad, they resumed their march to Johannesburg. It was now or never, Reitz decided. He found a willing collaborator in a young judge, the son of General Jan Kock, who had been killed at Elandslaagte. Antonie Kock was shocked by the brutal treatment of his father,[98] and vowed to take revenge. On 23 May he went to Krause with a letter from Reitz, explicitly instructing them to blow up the mines. Kock requisitioned all the transport and equipment he needed. Krause refused. Earlier that day Botha—who knew about Kock's mission and knew that he had Kruger's approval—had given him exactly the opposite instructions. Krause was to protect the mine shafts, the buildings and the machinery at all costs. He warned Kock that he would have him arrested, executed if necessary, if he went ahead with his act of sabotage.

Kock wasn't so easily deterred. That evening, he assembled a group of almost 100 volunteers, mostly Irishmen and Germans, who were prepared to help him. The next day they made their way to the Robinson, one of the mines now under state control. When on arriving there he found a load of crude gold, he assumed—wrongly—that it had been kept aside for the British. He went to Krause's office and told him what he suspected. It wasn't a smart move, because what was Kock doing in the Robinson in the first place? Finding himself in a corner, Kock drew his revolver, but Krause and his assistant, Commandant L.E. van Diggelen, managed to overpower him. He was arrested and sent to prison in Pretoria. The mine police dealt with his 'desperadoes'. The mines were saved.[99]

The war wasn't about gold, as Churchill kept reminding readers of the *Morning Post* and himself. Still, he was distressed by the scene before him. In the distance he saw 'the tall chimneys of the Rand'. Here, right in front of him, were 18 Gordon Highlanders, lined up with blankets over their heads, no boots, dead. Those grey socks saddened him more than anything else. 'There they lay stiff and cold' on the surface of the Reef. Their lives, more precious than all the gold in the world, had been cut short. It wasn't about gold. It was the 'lying foreigners' who said so. But still. He was angry with the horizon, angry with those damned chimneys.

Churchill was overtaken by this bout of melancholy on 30 May 1900, the morning after the battle at Doornkop, a few kilometres west of Johannesburg. Commandos under Louis Botha and Koos de la Rey had taken up positions in one last attempt to block the British advance. Their previous positions, near the Renoster River and on the border near the Vaal, had soon proved untenable. On 28 May Roberts crossed into the Transvaal. A few days earlier he had issued a proclamation whereby the Orange Free State was officially annexed and would be known as the Orange River Colony. Hamilton's army had been sent from the right flank to the left, so that with French's cavalry they could surround Johannesburg from the west. Roberts's main force had followed the railway line and approached the city from the south-east.

Doornkop was a historical place. It was where Jameson and his raiders had surrendered four and a half years earlier. The Boers went into battle fully aware of what was at stake. On their way, they had set fire to the grass. The smoke threw the advancing Britons into confusion. Conspicuous in their khaki uniforms against the blackened earth, they became easy targets for the Mausers. So fierce was the Boers' resistance that Hamilton resorted to the old formula: the frontal infantry assault. French's outflanking manoeuvre, as per his latest instructions, didn't extend far enough. Now it was up to the Highlanders. Churchill was apprehensive. He had witnessed this on several occasions, in Natal. And indeed, the Scots fell by the score—besides the dead, 80 were wounded—but they kept up the fight, with bayonets on their rifles. By evening they had driven the Boers from their positions. The next morning, Wednesday 30 May, it was clear that they had all withdrawn. The way to Johannesburg lay open. Hamilton stationed his men in Florida, on the Rand tram route.

But what did Roberts have in mind? He was many kilometres ahead and they had neither a field telegraph nor a heliograph. So they knew nothing about the agreement Roberts and Krause had reached when discussing Johannesburg's surrender that morning. Krause had agreed not to damage the mines provided the Boer commandos were given 24 hours to effect an orderly retreat. Otherwise there might be civilian casualties. Roberts saw no harm in it—something he would live to regret. He thought it was worth waiting a day to protect the City of Gold.

Hamilton was unaware of this agreement, just as Roberts had no idea how his generals to the west of the city were faring. Early that morning Hamilton had dispatched two couriers, but they had made a detour to the south to circumvent the retreating Boers. They wouldn't reach Roberts before nightfall. Churchill, having recovered from his depression at lunchtime, wanted to send a telegram as well. As usual, he had written his report on the encounter at lightning speed. Now he wanted to get it to London as quickly as possible. He was a war reporter after all, and Doornkop was hot news. He needed to find a telegraph. The one at Roberts's headquarters would be ideal. The shortest route there was through Johannesburg. But how safe was that?

Luck was on his side once again. Two cyclists arrived after lunch. They had come straight from Johannesburg, said one of them, a Frenchman, Monsieur Lautré, who worked at the Langlaagte mine. In any event there were no more Boers there, and probably none, he thought, in the city itself. If the *Morning Post* correspondent wanted to go there, Lautré would escort him with pleasure. Churchill needed no further encouragement. Lautré's companion offered him the use of his bicycle. Hamilton was confident enough to entrust his dispatches for Roberts to the two couriers—well, to Lautré, actually, just to be on the safe side. Churchill changed into inconspicuous clothing, and off they went.

Lautré wanted to avoid the main roads. It meant pedalling harder, but it was safer. In three-quarters of an hour they were at the Langlaagte mine, where they heard that another *Times* correspondent had passed by earlier. A pity, but fortunately he was on horseback. The Boers would have arrested him, Lautré assumed. They continued on to the city. Much of the route was downhill and they arrived in the centre in the early evening, taking the side streets. How good was his French? 'Good enough to deceive a Dutchman,' Churchill replied. Perfect. 'If they stop us, speak French,' Lautré said. 'The French are in good standing in these parts.'

There were a few anxious moments in the market square, at any rate for Churchill. Three armed Boers loomed up in front of them. Lautré remained calm and kept talking. The men passed by, taking no notice of the two cyclists. 'Encore un Boer,' Lautré said airily, and indeed another man approached from the rear and drew up alongside them. He slackened his horse's pace to a walk. Trying to avoid his gaze would have looked suspicious. Churchill sized him up. He took in the rifle on his back and the three cartridge belts slung over his shoulder and fastened around his waist. Their eyes met. 'He had a pale, almost ghastly visage, peering ill-favoured and cruel from beneath a slouch hat with a large white feather.' He shivered. Another of those phantom-like horsemen. The man spurred his horse and disappeared in the gathering dusk. Churchill sighed with relief. Lautré smiled.

They cycled on towards the suburbs on the south-east side of the city, where they expected to run into Roberts's first units, or at least his sentries. But they were able to proceed unimpeded and suddenly found themselves in the middle of a British army encampment. Not Roberts's, which was in Germiston, ten kilometres further on, a couple of officers told Churchill. They would have to cross an open field and at the end of it was a road where they would be able to cycle again. By this time it was pitch dark. Luckily, Lautré knew the area well. On arriving in Germiston, they dined in a hotel and reserved half the billiard table on which to spend the night, if necessary. Churchill sent his own dispatches from the telegraph office. The *Times* reporter hadn't called in. They continued on to Roberts's headquarters a short distance away, and handed Hamilton's dispatches to an orderly. It was ten thirty. Mission accomplished.

The real reward was still to come. A few minutes later, the orderly came outside. 'The Chief wanted to see the messengers.' Churchill wasn't easily impressed, but this was a moment he had long been waiting for. For the first time in this war he stood face to face with Roberts, in the presence of his entire staff. The commander-in-chief was exceptionally cordial. It seemed that all had been forgiven and forgotten. He was pleased with the good news from Hamilton and asked how Churchill and Lautré had managed to cross the centre of Johannesburg. Churchill was sold. 'His eye twinkled. I have never seen a man before with such extraordinary eyes.' They could spew fire, he knew, they could be cold and pitiless, but now they shone—merry, friendly, amused. 'Tell me about the action,' the field marshal said.[100]

Victory

Pretoria, 5 June 1900

Six months earlier, Churchill had slunk out of the Transvaal capital like a thief in the night. Now he was returning without fear or dishonour, as a knight, a liberator. Alongside his cousin, the Duke of Marlborough, he rode into Pretoria with the first British units and set off to find the officers who had been arrested as prisoners of war. They were no longer in the building from which he had escaped. They were said to have been transferred hundreds of kilometres to the east. Although the information wasn't correct, the men had indeed been moved and were now in one of the suburbs, a kilometre away.

Just one more corner, over a stream, and there it was: a long building with a corrugated-iron roof and a barbed-wire fence around the perimeter. They spurred their horses and galloped ahead, Churchill whooping with delight and waving his hat. As they drew up to the fence his former fellow prisoners stared in disbelief. It's Winston! The officers were overjoyed. Marlborough called on the camp commandant to surrender. The 50 armed guards were dumbstruck and meekly surrendered their weapons. An officer of the Dublin Fusiliers produced a British flag from nowhere—a patchwork Union Jack made from a Transvaal *Vierkleur*—and hoisted it amid cries of jubilation.

It was a quarter to nine on the morning of 5 June 1900. For Churchill this was a moment to remember. All those familiar faces, beaming with gratitude. Only Haldane and Brockie were missing. During the move to new premises they had managed to escape after all. Even that couldn't diminish Churchill's triumph. What a splendid return to Pretoria!

The rest of the day was uneventful and dull, especially for a war correspondent. The capital of the Transvaal came under British control with as little ceremony or fuss as Bloemfontein, Kroonstad or Johannesburg. There was no struggle worth mentioning, no shooting, no street fighting, no excitement at all. The Boers had simply handed over their most important cities. There was nothing to write home about, let alone report to his readers. The Boers had removed the artillery from their forts and taken it somewhere east of Pretoria. British troops entered the town quietly, paraded before their commander-in-chief in the main square of the town, lowered the Transvaal flag, raised the Union Jack—this one handmade in silk by Lady Roberts—and that was that. It would have been nice to get a picture of the old president, 'seated on his stoep reading his Bible and smoking a sullen pipe'. But Kruger had left a few days earlier on the train going east to Machadodorp, halfway to the Mozambique border. It was now the capital and the rest of the Transvaal government was there.

It looked as if the Boers had done the same thing in Pretoria as in Johannesburg. They hadn't defended themselves to the bitter end but had simply stalled for time to organise an orderly—and bountiful—retreat. Gold, money, arms, munitions, provisions, share certificates, government records, everything they wanted to keep out of British hands had been rescued in order to be whisked away by train. The Boers had been working towards this right up to the day the British arrived. In the early hours of the morning Churchill looked on in astonishment as two locomotives pulled out of the station. Behind them were ten trucks full of horses, plus one carrying heavily armed Boers. A few British officers tried unsuccessfully to stop the train, though they did manage to intercept three more that were still waiting to leave.

Lord Roberts wasn't bothered. He had now conquered the capital of the second Boer republic as well. In European terms, the war was over. They were just waiting for their adversaries to sign the official surrender. On his arrival in Johannesburg on 31 May he had issued his first proclamation, setting out the conditions on which citizens of the South African Republic could surrender. The terms were the same as those that had been applicable in the Orange Free State since 15 March. A second proclamation followed within days of the fall of Pretoria. Transvalers who swore neutrality would be able to take their cattle out to the winter pastures.

But Roberts had his eye on one Transvaler in particular: the commandant-general, Louis Botha. He had tried by various means— letters, personal messengers, including Mrs Botha—to persuade him to enter into peace talks. The response he had been hoping for came on 7 June. The two men arranged to meet at Zwartkoppies two days later. On 9 June, Roberts was about to set off—he literally had his foot in the stirrup—when a message arrived from Botha. On second thoughts, the commandant-general of the Transvaal had decided to call the meeting off—unless Roberts had something new to offer. He hadn't.[101]

It wasn't just a ploy or an attempt to mislead anyone. The Transvaal leaders didn't know which way to turn. Their defeat at Doornkop on 29 May had been the last straw. It had broken their men's morale: they had lost hope and made off in spite of the heavy penalties for desertion. They just wanted to go home. Discipline had always been a problem among the Boer commandos, but now there was no stopping them—especially when they heard that Kruger and the rest of the government had fled that same day.

The vice-president, Schalk Burger, remained in Pretoria, but not for long. The state attorney, Jan Smuts, was the only official government representative left, and not everyone recognised his authority. The mayor of Pretoria, Piet Potgieter, appointed a Peace and Order Commission, but it failed to live up to its name. Its purpose was to protect the town, but control of public life slipped through its fingers. The townspeople took advantage of the absence of their regular police force—the police had been sent to the front—and on the evening of Wednesday 30 May, black as well as white looters broke into government warehouses and plundered them. The unrest continued in broad daylight. Only when Louis Botha arrived on the scene and imposed martial law was order finally restored.

But he couldn't restore hope. Botha and the other Boer generals were at their wits' end. How could they continue the struggle when their people refused to fight? They could raise 3000, maybe 4000 men against Roberts's superior force, but no more. On 1 June Botha conferred with Koos de la Rey and a few other generals. Their decision was disappointing but they had made up their minds. Perhaps peace was the best option after all; perhaps they should reconcile themselves to surrender after the inevitable fall of Pretoria. This was what they proposed to the president.

They sent a telegram, because Kruger had been in Machadodorp for the previous two days. Being torn away from his familiar surroundings and his ailing wife, Gezina, had done his already battered confidence no good. He gritted his teeth and telegraphed his generals' proposal to Steyn. By this time, Steyn was in his fourth capital, Bethlehem, in the eastern Free State. The Boer War might have ended there and then.

But Steyn was furious. He wasn't interested in peace. He alerted his chief commandant, Christiaan de Wet, and gave Kruger a reply that must have sent sparks through the telegraph wires. What a bunch of cowards, those Transvalers. It was they who had drawn the Free Staters and the Cape Afrikaners into their struggle for independence. And to suggest giving up at this stage! The British army had barely crossed the Vaal. Steyn was speechless. The Orange Free State would fight to the bitter end, he assured Kruger, even if they had to do it alone.

De Wet also replied at once, more gently but just as firmly and with extraordinary sensitivity and tact. He sent Botha a reassuring telegram. 'Brother, I understand Your Excellency's anguish because I have been in the same predicament.' In fact, it must be even worse for Botha, he suggested, now that even 'a rock like President Kruger' was crumbling.

But he had no doubt that he could count on Botha, 'in whom I have the greatest confidence . . . to fight to the last for our cherished independence, a cause which I believe is not hopeless at all'. De Wet knew what he was talking about. After the fall of Bloemfontein, 'almost every one of our burghers went home'. And look at them now, six weeks later, those very same people 'are full of confidence and have been fighting well for the past few days'.

Steyn's brusque reproach and De Wet's shrewd empathy worked like a charm—at any rate with Botha and Smuts, who were sent copies of Steyn's reply. The Free Staters' determination helped them make some difficult choices. The following morning, 2 June, a war council meeting was held in the Volksraad chambers. It was mostly the young commandants, Danie Theron in particular, who wanted to fight on. This, too, helped in deciding on a course of action. After intense talks, they opted to go along with the Orange Free State. No peace talks, no all-or-nothing defence of the capital, but resistance 'to frustrate' the enemy.

Botha deployed his remaining commandos to that end. At the very least they were to delay Roberts's advance so as to give Smuts a chance to salvage as much as he could from Pretoria. They succeeded beyond their expectation. Smuts's greatest accomplishment was retrieving all the government's assets, almost half a million pounds in gold and cash, from the vaults of the National Bank and the Mint. The Mint cooperated in every possible way, but the governors of the bank were less forthcoming. Smuts only gained access to their holdings by resorting to threats of violence. On the afternoon of Monday 4 June he had everything transferred to a special train with an extra contingent of guards. With bombs exploding left and right, the gold train set off to the east. Its valuable cargo would enable the Boers to keep up the fight for a good while to come.

At least, financially. What Botha needed was something to boost his and his men's morale. Roberts made every effort to inveigle him into negotiating. But for Botha—in any event, after the war council meeting of 2 June—this was no longer on the cards. In any case, Roberts's attempts to manipulate him had raised his hackles. Using his wife, would you believe! As if she would compromise herself by trying to persuade him. But, never mind. He played along, all the while working on a plan to put his new-found confidence to good use.

Again, it was Christiaan de Wet who set the example, first by capturing a British convoy of 56 wagons near Swavelkrans on 4 June. The 160 men escorting the convoy surrendered without a word. Three days later De Wet demonstrated even more convincingly just how vulnerable the British supply lines were. With commandants Stoffel Froneman and Lucas

Steenkamp he carried out three attacks on and around Roodewal railway station, 50 kilometres north of Kroonstad. The British had amassed large quantities of munitions, provisions, blankets and clothing, ready to be transported to Pretoria. Some of the goods had already been loaded onto a train. The entire consignment now fell into De Wet's hands. It was far too much to take with them, especially now that they were travelling light in order to remain mobile. He took as much ammunition as he could and buried it on his farm, Roodepoort, a short distance away, for future use. He allowed his men to take whatever they wanted. And, of course, their British prisoners, almost 800 of them, had to be taken along as well. Whatever was left was blown up: the train, the station, the railway tracks, clothing, supplies and the remaining munitions. These made for a thunderous explosion, which left a crater of 30 metres by 18, and six metres deep. The spectacular fireworks could be seen all the way from Kroonstad.[102]

Lord Roberts couldn't deny it: the capture of Pretoria hadn't achieved what he'd expected. The Boers remained undefeated. Behind his back, in the Orange Free State, De Wet was attacking his supply lines. Under his nose, Botha was making a fool of him. If the Transvaal's commandant-general had ever contemplated surrendering in the first place—Roberts had picked up one or two things through the grapevine—then he had obviously changed his mind. Calling off peace talks just like that could mean only one thing: he was going to carry on fighting. In fact, it looked as if Botha was aiming for a major confrontation. Once again, he had sent his remaining troops, about 4000 men with 30 guns, to the Magaliesberg, 25 kilometres east of Pretoria. They would take up their usual positions, forming a broad front on either side of the railway line. Roberts had four times as many troops and 80 guns at the ready. On 11 June he mounted an attack at Diamond Hill—the Boers called it Donkerhoek, 'dark corner'—following the usual procedure: he himself with the infantry in the centre, the cavalry manoeuvring around the enemy on the flanks, French on the left, Hamilton on the right, artillery across the full breadth.

This second-last major confrontation of the Boer War had all the usual ups and downs: promising breakthroughs, imminent counterattacks, tactical shufflings of units and an abrupt ending. For the last time, Churchill—on Hamilton's right of course—gave readers of the *Morning Post* a vivid description of the battlefield complete with colourful anecdotes and heroic exploits. There was Hamilton, who was struck in the left shoulder by shrapnel but fortunately managed to keep fighting; Broadwood, who had two horses shot from under him, one after the other, but 'preserved his usual impassive composure' nevertheless; the Earl of Airlie, who led a daring cavalry charge to relieve an artillery unit, and as a result took 'a heavy bullet through the body, and died almost immediately'.

Churchill also told them about their adversary's extraordinary 'stubbornness and dash'. This was something he hadn't seen in the past few weeks, not since Natal. The British troops gained ground on Hamilton's flank and in the centre, where Botha was leading the Boers' defence, but not enough to achieve a decisive victory. And French's flank ran into serious problems with De la Rey's commandos. After the first day anything could have happened. Things were no different on 12 June. De la Rey gained the upper hand and was preparing to mount a counterattack against French. But Botha was coming under increasing pressure from Hamilton and at the end of the afternoon he was unable to prevent a breakthrough. As a result, they were in danger of being surrounded. By evening he felt it was too big a risk. To De la Rey's regret, he gave the command for a full withdrawal. Although it was a defeat, the battle at Diamond Hill gave the Boers fresh inspiration. They fled 'encouraged and hopeful' ('*vlug in vol moed*'). The Transvaal commandos had followed the Freestaters' example and shown that they could still put up a fight. They had incurred only 30 casualties, dead, wounded and captured. And all their artillery, including a Long Tom on a train truck, was still intact and going with them further east. It was just the kind of morale-booster Botha had hoped for.

For Roberts, the morning of 13 June brought first the surprising news that the Boers had fled, and then the sobering realisation that the war still wasn't over. The Transvalers had held out with unexpected determination. The casualties on his side came to 175 dead and wounded. Moreover, from the Boers' orderly retreat it was clear that they had become more disciplined and better organised. They were already too far away, for instance, to warrant a pursuit. All in all, this meant that the battle had not yet been won. But so be it. At least the area around Pretoria had been cleared of commandos. Now it was time to do something about that nuisance Christiaan de Wet. This was another job for Ian Hamilton's long-suffering brigades, except that now they would be marching off without their war correspondent. Churchill had decided to return to England. Just for the sake of it he had put his implausibly good luck to the test once again. He never wrote about it, but Hamilton took it upon himself to do so.

In the battle at Diamond Hill, Churchill had again spurned his non-combatant status and ventured forward to a point directly under a Boer position. There he had tied his handkerchief to a stick and fearlessly signalled to draw Hamilton's attention to an unexpected route by which he could advance. Hamilton described it as 'an exhibition of conspicuous gallantry', knowing these words could win Churchill a Victoria Cross. The VC couldn't be awarded to a civilian, but it had been a courageous deed and Hamilton felt that Churchill deserved recognition. Neither Roberts nor Kitchener, however, was prepared to make a formal recommendation. That the commander-in-chief had even deigned to speak to the impertinent young reporter after Johannesburg was honour enough. Churchill never mentioned the incident, at least not publicly. His last paragraph in the *Morning Post* was a tribute to Hamilton and his 'gallant column in whose good company I had marched so many miles and seen such successful fights . . . May they all come home safely.'[103]

The day the British marched into Pretoria, 5 June 1900, Leyds was attending an important meeting in Nieuwe Doelenstraat in Amsterdam. There was a matter he had to deal with at the headquarters of Labouchère, Oyens & Co., the bankers who administered the South African Republic's assets in Europe. A few days earlier they had given him the fright of his life. In future, they said, he would need special authorisation from the Transvaal government to access the account. The reason for this was Lord Roberts's proclamation annexing the Orange Free State, followed by the fall of Johannesburg. It looked as if the Transvaal was about to be annexed as well. The bankers wanted some form of guarantee. Did Leyds still represent the rightful owners of the assets?

Coming on top of all the distressing news from the Transvaal, this was an outright disaster. Of course Leyds had no formal authorisation. He had never needed it, and how could he get it now? They had known him for years. Labouchère, Oyens & Co. had always managed the Transvaal's financial affairs in Europe. And now this. 'To find myself without a cent to my name, in a manner of speaking, even for the day-to-day requirements of the many people who depend on me.' It couldn't be true. There was almost 800,000 guilders in the account. Without access to it he could do nothing, and 'all our work in Europe and American was at risk'.

He consulted his lawyers. His trusty advisers Moltzer and Asser also came to his help, and with the backing of this heavy legal artillery he managed to ward off the danger. During the meeting the bankers relented and gave Leyds access to the account. He immediately transferred the funds to several other banks, keeping only the relatively small sum of 25,000 guilders to cover his current costs.[104]

'The Labouchere case has been dealt with,' he telegraphed on 6 June to the delegation travelling through the United States. Fischer, Wessels and Wolmarans were relieved at the news. Their expenses were also paid from the Amsterdam account. And they too had more than enough to worry about. Their mission in the New World was as disappointing as that in the Netherlands. There was no lack of enthusiasm or solidarity, but even less political support than they had found in The Hague. In deference to public opinion they had presented themselves as 'delegates' rather than accredited envoys. Because of that, President McKinley and Secretary Hay had received them informally, but not given them an official reception. It was as cordial as could be, but the upshot was clear from the press conference afterwards. The president expressed an 'earnest desire to see an end to the strife which has caused so much suffering', but saw no option other than 'to persist in the policy of impartial neutrality'.

Diplomatic mission unaccomplished. What to do now? The delegation was divided on this point. On 8 June Leyds received two letters from Washington. In one, Fischer said he was optimistic about public opinion. 'There is more support than I had expected. I believe 90% of the American people are behind us.' If they were to 'make their views known in resolutions, memorandums etc.', McKinley would probably give way. It was an election year after all. The other letter was from Wolmarans. His thinking went in a different direction, or rather, jumped every which way. On the one hand, he asked Leyds to transfer £10,000 to Chicago to be used for propaganda. But at the same time, he urged him to offer protectorate rights over the two Boer republics to France or Russia or both. Leyds should contact the French and Russian envoys without delay.

The two requests put Leyds in an embarrassing position. Firstly, because he had reason to believe that Wolmarans was acting alone. Secondly, because the idea was insane. Or in Leyds's more discreet words, 'His letter may not convey to all the full measure of his intelligence.' Even so, Leyds felt he had no right to refuse the requests. He transferred the money and put the idea of a protectorate to the Russian and French agents in Brussels. 'Not because I think anyone will do anything about it'—it would inevitably lead to war with Britain—but 'only to please Mr Wolmarans'. The reply from St Petersburg and Paris came within a few days. On 12 June Leyds forwarded it to the United States. 'Russia and France convey their sincere regrets, but decline the protectorate.'[105]

Conscientious, that was Willem Leyds in a nutshell. The closer Roberts approached, the more uncertain Leyds was whether anyone was receiving his letters to the Transvaal government and, if so, who and when. But he kept sending them, always by way of Gerard Pott, the consul-general of the two Boer republics in Lourenço Marques. Leyds also kept up with another important task, organising secret arms exports. They were transported along the same route, with a transit stop in the French colony of Madagascar. In May 1900 he sent a substantial consignment comprising 10,000 Mauser cartridges 'concealed in soap'; components for machinery to manufacture cartridges, plus two technicians on a four-month contract; brass cases and percussion caps for rapid-firing artillery 'also packed in bars of soap'; devices to blow up trains, mirrors for electric searchlights, kites for signalling, a field telephone, silk for balloons. He just kept sending it all in the hope that it would end up where it was supposed to.[106]

He could only keep trying. That was the best thing to do. Perhaps he knew better, but he needed something to hold onto and keep his hopes alive. That was also why, on 11 June, he appeared before a Brussels court, to testify as a Crown witness in the Selati case. The affair dated back to 1891, when President Kruger and the Executive Council—against Leyds's advice—concluded a deal with Baron Eugène Oppenheim regarding the construction of a railway line to the Selati goldfields. Over the years it had transpired that the company formed for that purpose was enmeshed in a web of shady financial deals. It had ended up in legal proceedings, including criminal charges against Baron Eugène, his brother Baron Robert and several other directors. Leyds knew more about the case than anyone else and felt obliged to attend the hearing.[107] His effort paid off. Six weeks later, the defendants were sentenced to imprisonment and fines. But all the work it entailed had kept him from attending to another matter of great importance for the Transvaal, one he had been very much involved in.

The Transvaal Pavilion for the World Exhibition in Paris was officially opened on the afternoon of Saturday 9 June. The young Boer republic was being showcased internationally for the first time. Preparations had begun a year earlier, in peacetime. But now of course it was awkward to be exhibiting alongside another—ostentatiously present—participant, with which it was embroiled in a relentless war. And just after their capital had been occupied. The occasion was anything but festive. Pierson, the consul-general, received a few guests and showed them around.

The exhibit was incongruous. The pavilion was divided into three sections. The Transvaal's official presentation in the classicist main building included the usual assortment of photographs and drawings, a statistical display on education and other public services, stuffed animals, local produce and a miniature oxwagon. It all looked idyllic. Nothing alluded to the war. Then there was the grand salon on the first floor. In the centre stood a bust of President Kruger, 'whose features', according to Gustave

Babin of the *Journal des Débats*, 'betray an unwavering and buoyant confidence'. Placed in front of it on behalf of the Parisian proletariat was a bouquet of red, white and blue flowers with green ferns, ribbons in the same colours, and the words *Vive les Boers!*

The theme of the second building was the Transvaal's gold: the source of its prosperity, a socially divisive and destabilising force and, according to many, the cause of the war. But the war itself didn't come into the picture. The display was mainly about gold as an industrial product. A stand had been built to give visitors an impression of the production process. It showed step by step how gold was extracted and processed, and then its spectacular yields and profits. In short, it conveyed an idea of the new, industrial Transvaal—which in reality had been under British control for the preceding ten days.

The third building was different again. It told the story of the old, pastoral and still independent Transvaal, the Boers as people of the land. The exhibit was a faithful replica of a farmhouse, a simple structure with whitewashed walls and a thatched roof, narrow windows and low doors. Inside, it had the living room in the centre, the kitchen behind it, bedrooms and storerooms on either side. A table with a drab cloth, a loaf of bread. A riempie bench and a few old chairs. A couple of flower vases placed on a cabinet, photographs in marbled frames on the walls, a cuckoo clock and, as the centrepiece, a harmonium with a Bible bound in calf leather. In the main bedroom, to the left of the lounge, a bedstead with cotton drapes, a few garments and—the only allusion to the war—the farmer's slouch hat and his rifle. Babin was surprised and impressed. 'It is humble and moving. These, then, are the homes and hearths the brave Boers out there are defending.'[108]

After eight months of war, Churchill still found himself baffled and intrigued by the Boers. Looking back, he reflected in the *Morning Post* that what they were doing was not humanly possible. By way of explanation, he likened the situation to the human body. Considered rationally, Roberts had subdued the enemy. 'We had taken possession of the Rand', the bowels, the source of gold and munitions. 'We had seized the heart at Bloemfontein, the brain at Pretoria.' Most of the rail network, 'the veins and nerves', was in British hands. In other words, the body—the Boers— had been mortally wounded. Yet still it shuddered, the heavily booted left leg in particular, which was still capable of delivering an unexpected and painful blow. Two operations were needed to put an end to it once and for all: one to incapacitate the dangerous limb and one 'to place a strangling grip on the windpipe', the supply route from Lourenço Marques.

The right men for these assignments, he believed, were Ian Hamilton and Redvers Buller, the two generals whose troops he had accompanied for several months. But he wouldn't be there to witness it. His resolve to return to England was firm. 'Politics, Pamela, finances and books all need my attention,' he wrote to his mother on 9 June. His stay in South Africa had been a wonderful experience for him personally. He had got out of it everything he had hoped for: a succession of adventures, fame and even glory, with or without a medal. On his own steam, and not just because of his father's influence, he had made many new friends, some in high places, and managed reasonably well not to make too many enemies. He had firmly established his reputation as a writer. His reports for the *Morning Post* had attracted attention. The first series, from Natal, had been published in book form in early May as *London to Ladysmith via Pretoria*, and it was selling extremely well. As soon as possible he wanted to start editing the second volume, *Ian Hamilton's March*, in order to have it in the shops before his extensive lecture tour through Britain and the United States. This would provide him with a nice little nest egg and allow him to pursue his dream of a career in politics. Hoping to benefit from the success of the war, Salisbury's Conservative government had called elections for later that year. Churchill was going to make another bid for a seat in the House of Commons, once again in the Liberal bastion of Oldham, but this time as a distinguished war veteran.

He had started preparing for his return immediately after the Battle of Diamond Hill. Another surprise awaited him a few hours before his departure from Pretoria. He was busy packing his trunks in his suite at the Transvaal Hotel, when suddenly the manager appeared, with two women behind him. The hotel was full and the manager had a request. But Churchill was no longer listening. One of the women was none other than his aunt, Lady Sarah. What on earth was she doing here? There was no time for embarrassment. Their past differences were forgotten in the surprise of the moment. She embraced him warmly. She had just arrived from Mafeking. Churchill responded like a dutiful nephew, immediately offering to extend his stay for another day to show her around Pretoria. And it went without saying that they were welcome to share his suite.

Of course, he showed her the camp where he and her other nephew, the Duke of Marlborough, had freed the prisoners. At the prison he told her the exciting story of his escape. In the evening he invited her to a farewell dinner with a group of officers. All in all, he made a far better impression on her than he had done in the past. He had changed for the better, she thought. 'Winston . . . had been but a short time . . . with Lord Roberts's force,' but he had managed 'to acquire influence and authority'.

He turned out to be 'most interesting to listen to, and a general favourite'. The following morning she saw him off at Pretoria station.

The very last surprise came on the train journey to Cape Town. A short distance from Kroonstad, just before Koppies, the train stopped abruptly. Churchill got off to see what had happened. Just at that moment a bomb exploded nearby. It was a small one, but a bomb all the same. A hundred metres ahead, in front of the locomotive, the wooden railway bridge was on fire. The train was full of soldiers, all of whom were now emerging from their carriages. But there wasn't an officer in sight. The scene was all too familiar to Churchill. Chieveley, the armoured train—this surely couldn't happen to him again. He sprinted to the locomotive, leapt in and barked orders to the driver. Return to Koppies. It's only five kilometres away and there's a British camp there. Reverse. Sound the steam whistle— while he stood on the running board and ordered the soldiers to return to their seats. Suddenly a few dark figures emerged from the dry riverbed. Boers! Churchill loaded his Mauser pistol. He was no longer a soldier or a war correspondent, and he certainly wasn't going to be captured at the last minute. He fired six, seven shots. The train rumbled into motion, back to Koppies. All he had to do now was organise a carriage and horses.[109]

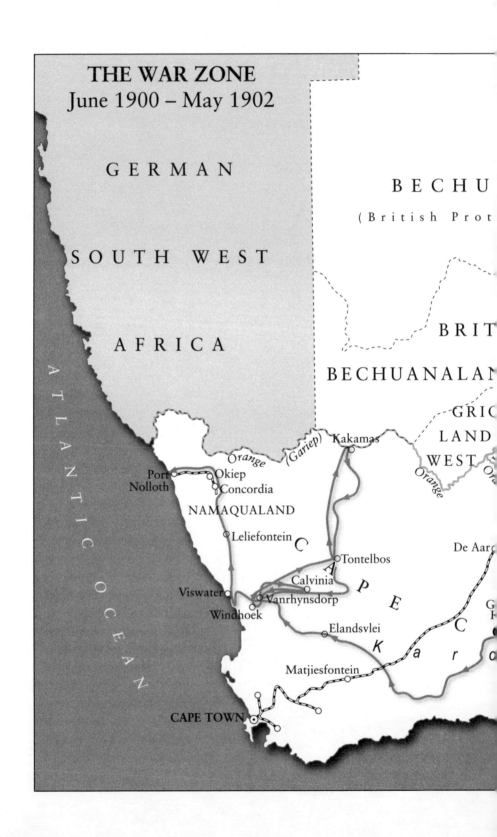

THE WAR ZONE
June 1900 – May 1902

GERMAN

SOUTH WEST

AFRICA

BECHU

(British Prot

BRIT

BECHUANALAN

GRIC
LAND
WEST

ATLANTIC OCEAN

Orange *(Gariep)* Kakamas

Orange Or

Port
Nolloth Okiep

Concordia

NAMAQUALAND

C

Leliefontein

Tontelbos

De Aar

A

P

Calvinia

E

Viswater

Vanrhynsdorp

Windhoek

Elandsvlei

K a r o

G

C

Matjiesfontein

CAPE TOWN

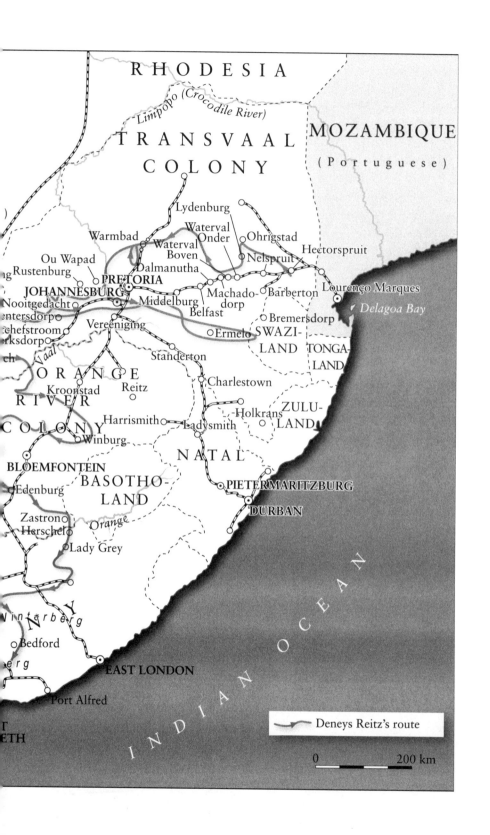

R H O D E S I A

Limpopo (Crocodile River)

T R A N S V A A L

C O L O N Y

MOZAMBIQUE

(P o r t u g u e s e)

Lydenburg

Waterval
Onder

Ohrigstad

Hectorspruit

Warmbad

Waterval
Boven

Ou Wapad

Dalmanutha

Nelspruit

ng Rustenburg

PRETORIA

Machado-
dorp

Barberton

Lourenço Marques

JOHANNESBURG

Middelburg

Belfast

Delagoa Bay

Nooitgedacht

entersdorpo

Vereëniging

Bremersdorp

chefstroom

Ermelo

SWAZI-

ksdorpo

Vaal

Standerton

LAND

TONGA-

ch

O R A N G E

LAND

Kroonstad

Reitz

Charlestown

R I V E R

ZULU-

C O L O N Y

Harrismith

Holkrans

LAND

Winburg

Ladysmith

BLOEMFONTEIN

N A T A L

Edenburg

BASOTHO-
LAND

PIETERMARITZBURG

Zastron

Orange

DURBAN

Herschel

Lady Grey

I N D I A N   O C E A N

Ninterberg

Bedford

erg

EAST LONDON

Port Alfred

ETH

Deneys Reitz's route

0   200 km

PART III

Death and destruction

June 1900—May 1902

Deneys Reitz

Adrift

Pretoria, June 1900

The going was slow. Everyone was heading for Pretoria. The road leading out of Johannesburg was choked with refugees, with their belongings piled onto oxwagons or whatever transport they could find. Impatient Boer fighters on worn-out horses, recently returned from the front, threaded their way through the crowd. 'Going home, the war is over,' they called, for all the world to hear.[1] British soldiers kept an eye on them from a distance and allowed them to proceed. They were all refugees and not worth bothering about.

Deneys Reitz was among them, heading home on his Basuto pony. He picked his way nimbly through the crowd, keeping close to his eldest brother, Hjalmar. Charley, their African servant, followed them. Deneys had lost touch with his two other brothers. They had managed to get Arend on board a goods train in Johannesburg, in the care of a man who had promised to look after him. Deneys could only hope he would be all right. He was already delirious; it could well be typhoid fever. No one knew where Joubert was. It was said that a cavalry regiment had taken his unit by surprise at Koppie Alleen a fortnight earlier. That was the last Deneys had heard of him. He could be dead, for all he knew. All he wanted now was to get home. His father would know what to do. After all, he was the one who had started the war, literally, by signing the ultimatum to the British. Deneys felt miserable.

Things were very different when he had left for Natal eight months before. He was 17, filled with romantic notions and eager to fight. They were going to drive the British into the sea. And he had been given permission to accompany them, taking his own Mauser, even though he had to plead for it. But the experience had shattered his illusions. There was the interminable siege of Ladysmith, which had ultimately achieved nothing; the battle at Spion Kop, where he had witnessed the full horror of war: 'the valiant dead . . . with blow flies in their mouths and nostrils', human remains that looked as if they had been 'through a meat grinder', 'mutilated faces . . . swelling up in the sun'.

These grim images continued to haunt him for a long time to come, but after their withdrawal from Natal he had nevertheless returned to enlist for duty at the front. This time he went to the Orange Free State, his birthplace, which held memories of a happy childhood, although it was hardly a front at all. The campaign had ended in a humiliating defeat. The widely dispersed Boer units hadn't stood a chance against Roberts's superior force. He himself had hardly fought at all. The British had driven them off. Even Koos de la Rey had been powerless to do anything. The same had happened in the Transvaal. The British had wiped them out. Most of the Boer fighters were disillusioned and many had abandoned the struggle. Johannesburg had already fallen and they had no idea what they would find in Pretoria.

It was late, around ten o'clock, when they arrived. They had ridden through the dark streets to their home in the suburb of Sunnyside, only to be bitterly disappointed. The grounds were deserted, the house was empty. They went round to their neighbours, but no one answered their knock. A few houses further on, someone finally appeared at the door. A few brief words— the president and the state secretary had fled; Pretoria would be surrendered to the British the following day—then the door was slammed shut.

They couldn't believe that Kruger and their father had fled, but it was too late to make further enquiries. The brothers forced their way into their home, stabled their weary horses and found some food in the pantry. And after all those bitterly cold nights they had spent in the open they could sleep in their own beds again at last, but it was a dismal homecoming nevertheless. One brother missing, another ill and still making his way home, their house deserted. Their father and stepmother, their younger half-siblings were all gone. No one knew where.

The following morning Hjalmar and Deneys ventured out to see what had happened in their absence. The town was in chaos. There was gunfire, shops and supply depots had been plundered, and disturbing rumours were circulating. The British were evidently heading in their direction. They returned home and were packing their belongings when, to their delight, Joubert suddenly turned up, unharmed. His horse had been killed at Koppie Alleen, but he had escaped on foot and later completed the journey by train. There was no time to celebrate their reunion. The three brothers decided to leave as quickly as possible and head east while they still had a chance. Outside one of the ransacked shops they found a horse, which they requisitioned for Joubert. Charley had to remain behind. 'The poor fellow piteously entreated us to keep him, but we had to harden our hearts.' They could no longer afford the luxury of a servant. Horses and food were hard to come by; the animals they possessed were needed to carry their supplies. Charley was to take blankets and all he wanted from the house. Then their ways parted.

By evening the brothers were about 15 kilometres from Pretoria. They spent the night in the vicinity of the First Factory brandy distillery and at sunrise they discovered that hundreds of other Boer fighters had also sought refuge in the area. But there was no sign of their own military unit, the Afrikander Cavalry Corps. Who they did run into, however, was the state attorney, Jan Smuts, who told them where Kruger and their father had gone. Of course they hadn't fled. They were in Machadodorp, about 250 kilometres further east along the railway line, where they had set up a new capital. From there they would continue to lead the struggle. Louis Botha was already raising a fresh army and Smuts himself was making his way to the western Transvaal to help Koos de la Rey organise the resistance.

This was the best news the brothers had heard in a long time. Joubert decided to head directly for Botha's camp. Hjalmar and Deneys wanted to speak to their father first and hear what he thought of it all. He might also have news of Arend. They set off for Machadodorp.[2]

Lord Roberts wasted no time. As far as he was concerned, the capture of Pretoria on 5 June 1900 had brought the war to an end. This was the harsh reality and the Boers would have to resign themselves to it. He moved into Melrose House, one of the ostentatious new mansions in town, and got down to business. Until then, he had relied on tough military action and proclamations to intimidate his adversaries. Now it was time to introduce penalties to enforce those 'paper bombs'. If the Boer leaders had any sense, they would accept his invitation to sit down and talk. If not, they would have to face the consequences.

He had more or less written off the leaders of the resistance in the Orange Free State, or the Orange River Colony, as it had been renamed on 24 May. There was nothing to be done with them. That much was clear from Steyn's counter-proclamations and Christiaan de Wet's acts of sabotage. On 31 May Roberts acquired additional powers by imposing martial law. A day later, he issued a proclamation with a firm deadline. Anyone who failed to hand in their arms within 14 days, by 15 June, would be deemed—and treated as—a rebel, with all the consequences for their person and property.[3]

At first Roberts still hoped that something would come of his edict, as far as the Transvaal authorities were concerned. At the beginning of June Louis Botha, for one, seemed to be open to reason. Intermediaries, including his wife, Annie, were sent to talk to him. Louis de Souza, the War Department secretary with whom Churchill had become acquainted during his time in prison, went a step further. He sent Botha a letter, purportedly from Roberts, which amounted to nothing less than an outright attempt at bribery. He offered Botha—and De la Rey—exemption from exile, if they surrendered. They would be allowed to remain in South Africa on trust, with an annual stipend of £10,000 each. No one was sure who was behind the offer. Botha couldn't believe that Roberts would stoop so low, but found any attempt to approach him, directly or indirectly, insulting. It strengthened his resolve not to negotiate without a prior guarantee that the South African Republic would retain its independence. Otherwise, the Transvalers, like the Freestaters, would continue to fight. The Battle of Diamond Hill on 11 and 12 June proved they were still capable of doing so.

Roberts was losing patience. He decided to tighten the screws, on everyone. On 16 June 1900 he issued a proclamation for both territories—the fifth proclamation by this time—to deal with the 'small parties of raiders' who were continuing to destroy railway bridges and telegraph lines. They wouldn't be able to do this, he reasoned, without the knowledge and consent of other inhabitants and 'the principal civil residents' in the vicinity. And those in question would be deemed guilty of complicity with immediate effect. Any destruction of public property would be punished by burning down homesteads in the area and imprisoning prominent citizens in the district.

Three days later, Roberts introduced further measures. Proclamation 6 of 19 June added to the existing sanctions a penalty of collective financial liability. The local community would be held to account for any costs resulting from damage to property. In addition, the director of the now militarised railway system was authorised to carry prominent civilians on the trains as hostages.

Roberts decided to set an example right away to show that he meant business. The man who had conducted the most daring raids and caused the greatest damage to the British railway and telegraph lines was, without a doubt, Christiaan de Wet. On 7 June he had carried out a spectacular raid on Roodewal station, not far from his own farm, Roodepoort. There was also the fact that the two-week amnesty Roberts had granted for all Boers under arms in the Orange River Colony on 1 June was about to expire. The next step was obvious. On 15 June Roberts informed his staff officers of his decision. He declared De Wet a rebel and ordered that he be treated accordingly. Proclamation 5 was issued the following day. Roberts demanded that the sanctions announced in it—including the burning down of farmsteads—were seen to be enforced. 'A few examples only will be necessary and let us begin with De Wet's farm.' Lord Methuen was responsible for executing the sentence. On 16 June Roodepoort was reduced to ashes.[4]

This was too close for comfort. By the time it was safe enough for Christiaan de Wet to return to his property, the embers had died, but the sight of it, even from a distance, was heartbreaking. They had destroyed the work of a lifetime. De Wet asked his generals Stoffel Froneman and Piet Fourie to rein in their horses, and proceeded alone. This was the price he had paid. His three eldest sons, Kotie, Izak and Christiaan, were on commando with him; his wife, Cornelia, and their nine other children had been roaming the countryside for months, taking refuge in a laager somewhere along the Vaal. And now his farm and everything he possessed had been razed to the ground. They had used dynamite, as he saw at once, and they had done the job thoroughly. He dismounted, knelt at the grave of his infant daughter, and prayed. Then he rode back to his companions, his face pale and drawn. 'Let's go. There's work to be done.'[5]

Roberts's aim to create a deterrent succeeded, at least partially. The Boers were shaken by the attack on Roodepoort. For those who were still uncommitted, the reprisal against the Free State's commandant-general was a turning point. If even De Wet's farm could go up in flames, nothing was safe; their own homes were also in danger. There was nothing to do but accept the enemy's terms. Thousands of Boer fighters had done so after the British army's double breakthrough on 27 February 1900 and now thousands more followed suit. Between March and July of that year 12,000 to 14,000 Boers—between a fifth and a quarter of the original 60,000 conscripts in the two republics—abandoned the struggle. The impact was huge and, to compound the problem, many of them were wealthy burghers and senior government officials. These were people who had something to lose. Among them were men like General Hendrik Schoeman, a member of the Transvaal Executive Council, and General Andries Cronjé, the younger brother of Piet 'Paardeberg' Cronjé.[6]

But the Roodepoort incident was counterproductive as well. Many Boers were defiant and more determined to fight on. De Wet's example counted for more than Roberts's deterrent. He had sacrificed all for the sake of a free and independent country. More resolute than ever, 'Chrisjan' was going to fight on, to the bitter end if necessary. His attitude enhanced his moral authority and strengthened the resolve of many who had not yet taken the plunge.

Roodepoort became a double-edged symbol. For the defectors, or 'hands-uppers' (*hensoppers*), it exemplified the futility of resistance; for the hardliners, the 'bitter-enders' (*bittereinders*), it confirmed the noble purpose of their cause. But the upshot was that Roberts's draconian measures sowed discord among the Boers, who were compelled to choose sides for or against him. The choice was between returning to their peaceful, rustic way of life, as loyal subjects of the British regime, or being hunted down as rebels. This was the war Roberts declared on every Boer personally. It was a war waged not on the battlefield but in village communities and families, between neighbours, brothers, fathers and sons. A war of conscience.

Pressure from their leaders left them virtually no choice at all. President Steyn's first counter-proclamation, issued on 19 March, made that clear to the burghers of the Orange Free State. His government was, and would continue to be, the only legitimate authority. Evading military service was deemed an act of treason. Roberts's subsequent proclamations of 24 May and 1 June changed nothing as far as he was concerned. On 11 June Steyn hit back with a new counter-proclamation. Roberts's demands, he said, were in violation of international law, 'as the Government of the Orange Free State is still fully functional' and burghers must comply with its orders alone.[7]

After their initial ambivalence, the Transvaal authorities took an equally firm stand. From Machadodorp, on 8 June, President Kruger issued his own counter-proclamation against Roberts's first and second 'Transvaal' proclamations. In substance it was similar to Steyn's. He rejected the validity of the British demands and urged burghers not to be misled 'by their promises and threats'. Swearing an 'oath of loyalty' to the British regime was considered treason. And doing so, he warned them, was no guarantee against being banished to St Helena.

That wasn't the end of it. Reports came in from Botha and other commandants about demoralised burghers. Kruger responded with a series of telegrams, some encouraging, some reproachful, and some an inimitable combination of the two. On 20 June, for instance, he addressed himself directly to those who were still undecided. 'Brothers, brothers, I implore you not to give up hope. Be steadfast and fight in the name of the Lord. Look into your hearts: if you are cowardly and flee, it is because you have ceased to believe in a God in Heaven and have forsaken the Almighty.' But, he assured Sarel Oosthuizen—the 'dark horseman' who had captured Churchill and who now held the rank of general—there was still hope, even if there were only a few left who were prepared to fight. 'I believe it will be the same as in the case of Gideon and his three hundred men: a small band of stalwarts will take it upon themselves to fight the whole battle and the Lord will say unto the beast, so far and no further.'

Along with biblical aphorisms, the telegrams from Machadodorp also contained warnings of earthly retribution. Burghers who abandoned their posts would be 'guilty of murder'. And in districts where the Boers were still in control, those who shirked military service were to be arrested and court-martialled. In addition, their property was to be confiscated, the president added on 24 June. Anyone who took the oath of neutrality was to be prosecuted. In the words of the state secretary, F.W. Reitz, the oath was 'a betrayal of country and nation'.[8]

Long rows of railway carriages constituted the new headquarters of the Transvaal government and its entourage of civil servants who had come from Pretoria. Deneys and Hjalmar Reitz had been travelling for three days, first on horseback as far as Middelburg, where they managed to get a lift on a goods train. They reached the new capital, Machadodorp, early in the morning and found their father in one of the train carriages. They were relieved to see each other again, safe and sound after all those months. And he knew where Arend was: in a Russian field hospital in Waterval Onder, 20 kilometres down the line. Their stepmother and the younger children had gone to Lourenço Marques, and from there sailed to Holland to stay with relatives. The war was far from over, their father continued. The new strategy was working better for the Boers than large-scale confrontations. Look at George Washington! He too had fought for a seemingly lost cause, but triumphed in the end.

Deneys was cheered by his optimism. Still, he couldn't stop worrying about all those burghers who were giving up the fight. But first he wanted to see Arend. From the edge of the escarpment the train clawed its way down the precipitous slope from Waterval Boven to Waterval Onder. It was far warmer in the valley. Arend was in good hands. The Russian nurses said he was improving. His fever had subsided, though the danger hadn't yet passed. Near the hospital they caught a glimpse of Kruger. They knew from their father that he had fled from the bitter cold of the heights. He was sitting in a saloon carriage, 'a lonely, tired man', lost in thought, with a large Bible lying open on the table before him. They didn't presume to approach him.

Back in Machadodorp they took leave of their father and set off to find a commando unit they could join. After collecting their horses in Middelburg, they met up with a contingent of German volunteers, about 60 strong, led by an Austrian, Baron von Goldeck. They were on reconnaissance for Louis Botha, a task that appealed to Deneys and Hjalmar. Botha was assembling a new army and was pleased with the results. Thousands of weaker men had disappeared, but those who remained were 'good fighting men'.

One evening Deneys's old unit turned up. It was the Pretoria commando he had fought with in Natal—or, at least, what was left of it, no more than half, 150 men at most. They had a new field cornet, Max Theunissen, a youngster of 25. Although Deneys had got on well with the Germans, he felt closer to his old comrades and decided to rejoin them. Hjalmar remained with Von Goldeck. Deneys took his roan and the Basuto pony to carry his supplies. Botha had given Theunissen instructions to destroy the railway line between Pretoria and Johannesburg. They were back on familiar territory.

But the fates were against them. The British were guarding the railway and they were unable to get anywhere near it. They nevertheless remained in the area for a while, hoping an opportunity would present itself. A few days later Reitz was told that the Afrikander Cavalry Corps in which he had served in the Orange Free State was also operating in the region. He decided to look up his 'old companions' and have a word with Commandant Malan.

The happy reunion ended in tragedy. While Reitz was talking to his friends, a British column bombarded them with lyddite grenades. The first shells were wide of the mark, but the British artillerymen soon had them in their sights. Malan ordered his men to take cover. Reitz found safety behind a garden wall, while several others sought shelter behind a willow tree. It was a poor position. A shell hit the trunk and exploded on impact. The seven unfortunate men standing there were 'blown to pieces which strewed the ground for thirty yards beyond'. When the British gun stopped firing, 'their remains had to be collected with a shovel, a most sickening spectacle.'

As if that wasn't bad enough, a few minutes later Commandant Malan was also hit. He took a bullet through the throat and died within minutes. Reitz was devastated. He had been considering joining the Afrikander Cavalry, but now abandoned the idea. They seemed to be under an unlucky star.

So he remained with the Pretoria commando. The weeks that followed were uneventful. They lingered around Pretoria and kept an eye on the British troops, sniping at them from time to time. The spell of relative calm gave the Boer leaders an opportunity to reorganise their scattered troops, and the townspeople time to recover. It was mid-July, in the dead of winter.[9]

Piet de Wet had been mulling over the idea for some time. It was 19 July, and that day's encounter at Karroospruit confirmed the conclusion he had reached. He had done all he could, along with Danie Theron, the commandant of the Scouts Corps, but they had been forced to flee from Broadwood's troops. They had been hopelessly outnumbered and hadn't stood a chance. It had been like this all the time lately. There was simply no point. He would have to have a word with his brother.

It is hard to say who was the more stubborn, Christiaan or Piet de

Wet. Perhaps that's why they had always got on so well together. Piet was seven years younger than Christiaan, his favourite elder brother. They came from a family of 14, living in Dewetsdorp in the Orange Free State, a village named after their father. The brothers had farmed together in the Transvaal for a while and shared many memories of the war. They had been in Paardekraal in December 1880, the first time war was declared on the British. They had also helped to win that war, on the slopes of Majuba Hill on 27 February 1881. And their names were linked to the successes of the present war as well, most notably the battles at Nicholson's Nek on 30 October 1899 and Sannaspos on 31 March 1900. They had risen through the ranks at lightning speed; both had become generals in almost no time at all. Christiaan was commander-in-chief of the Free State forces. Piet held the same rank over the men on the 'Cape' front, to the south.

But they reacted differently to Roberts's advance, and this drove a wedge between them. Christiaan wanted to change tactics right away. This was the opportunity he had been waiting for. He would let the British through and attack their communication lines from the rear, taking decisions one at a time as events unfolded, and relying on his instincts. A resourceful, independent thinker with a recalcitrant streak, he found this kind of approach suited him best. Piet preferred tried and trusted methods: shrewdly chosen positions and skilful manoeuvres to intercept the British advance, rather than improvisations and decisions on the spur of the moment. He was a man committed to law and order, a man with respect for private property.

These traits came to the fore in a dispute that dragged on for months between himself and the Transvaal military procurements commission. Shortly before the war, Piet de Wet had supplied them with 100 horses. They had agreed on a price of £20 per head, but De Wet received only £18. He was incensed and even the war did nothing to take his mind off the matter. On 18 March 1900—within days of the fall of Bloemfontein—he sent two furious telegrams to Pretoria, one of them to Kruger himself. It was scandalous. The sale had set him back £200. Did those office clerks actually have the authority to take decisions like that at their own discretion? Who were they to say his horses weren't worth the price they had agreed on? It was the worst kind of injustice: a man who was out fighting, risking his life, while they were simply juggling paper clips in Pretoria.

No one knows how the affair ended, but it showed what kind of man Piet de Wet was. If he believed he was in the right, nothing could persuade him otherwise. And that was his attitude to the war. The closer the British approached, the less convinced he was that it would end well. The Boers had done their best, he more than anyone else, but it hadn't been enough. It was time to face up to the truth. To continue would cost them their land, their possessions, their wives and children. The Boer leaders would have to make the best of it. They owed it to their families. He decided to act. On 18 May he informed Broadwood and Hamilton that he was prepared to surrender on condition that he could return to his farm in Lindley. His proposal was turned down—on Roberts's authority, he was given to understand. They would accept only an unconditional surrender. For him, this was a step too far.

So he continued to fight. Two weeks later, on 31 May, he achieved a brilliant success. Not far from Lindley, he and Commandant Michael Prinsloo—Marthinus's younger brother—captured an entire British battalion. And not just any battalion. It comprised 500 volunteers of the 13th Imperial Yeomanry, including many from wealthy, aristocratic families.

The Lindley affair caused a commotion in Britain, but that didn't raise Piet de Wet's hopes. In early June he decided of his own accord to propose a partial ceasefire to Lord Methuen. Steyn was against it—Roberts too, incidentally—and in a military council meeting on 6 June Piet's elder brother called him to account. It was a serious clash, with Piet in turn accusing Christiaan—along with Steyn and particularly the Transvaal authorities—of misleading the public. The foreign intervention they were promising was a myth. In the meantime, Pretoria had also fallen. Continuing the war would ruin the country, he warned them, with innocent women and children paying the highest price. But his words fell on deaf ears. Worse than that, Christiaan lost his temper and flew into a rage.

At the end of June a more personal quarrel widened the rift between the brothers. Surprisingly, they found themselves embroiled in a squalid contest. Steyn had nominated Christiaan to succeed Naas Ferreira as commandant-general. He hadn't been elected in accordance with the usual procedure, and Piet and two other generals, Marthinus Prinsloo and Jan Olivier, raised objections. Although Steyn saw no need for it, Christiaan decided to call an election to remove any doubt. The outcome was clear: he won 26 votes, Olivier three, Prinsloo two and his brother one.

The implications were self-evident. Piet de Wet left the meeting, disappointed. He took command again, out of a sense of duty, but never moved far from his farm in Lindley. He and his wife, Susanna, had a heart-to-heart talk. She was worried about the British burning down their house as well. What would become of her and their 11 children? Would they end up living like vagabonds, like her sister-in-law Cornelia? The prospect was too awful to contemplate.

After grappling with the problem for several weeks, Piet decided to make one last attempt. On 20 July he visited his elder brother in Blesbokfontein. Did Christiaan still see any chance of being able to continue the struggle? The question alone infuriated him. 'Are you mad?' was his only reply. There was nothing more to be said. Piet returned to his troops and discussed the matter with a few trusted friends. They agreed with him. On 24 July he made enquiries about the terms the British were offering. In reply to one of his men, he said, 'I can't advise you. Each of you must do what you believe best, but I am going home.' On 26 July 1900 he went to Kroonstad to surrender.[10]

Flushing out the foe

Bronkhorstspruit, July 1900

Early one morning Deneys Reitz woke up with a start. One glance into the distance was enough. The British were advancing again. It wasn't a column or a battalion, but a complete army. A cloud of dust obscured the entire western horizon. As far as he could make out, there were more than 30,000 men. The Pretoria commando took positions on koppies a short distance away. Before long the first shells came hissing down in the pale light of dawn. More followed in rapid succession, frighteningly close by. They didn't stand a chance. The only thing to do was break up, fall back and take new positions.

The British were approaching over a broad front on either side of the railway line to Lourenço Marques, and they were quickening their pace. The Boer fighters had no option but to retreat. They fell back from hill to hill, firing the occasional frantic salvo on a unit of scouts and then retreating further. They were too heavily outnumbered, the shellfire was overwhelming. There was no doubt about it: Roberts was determined to cut off the Boers' lifeline.

The speed of the pursuit reminded Reitz of their earlier retreat, in the Orange Free State. They had got to Middelburg, halfway to Machadodorp, within a week. But there was one important difference. This time, the Boers were keeping their spirits up. No one was talking about going home. By all accounts, Botha was intending to fight one last pitched battle, in a carefully chosen spot. After that, like Christiaan de Wet, he would divide his force into 'smaller bands'. That prospect made it easier to endure the humiliation of being constantly on the retreat.

Reitz experienced some frightening moments. Near the hamlet of Belfast, there was such confusion in the dark that he found himself separated from the Pretoria Commando. The following morning his comrades were nowhere to be seen, so he joined a division from the mining village of Boksburg, men he had met once before in Johannesburg. A few days later, they arrived in Dalmanutha, just outside Machadodorp, where they were assigned a new position.

This was where Botha intended to make a last stand, the mountainous area at the edge of the escarpment. To Reitz it seemed the perfect place. He had been here two months earlier, visiting his father, and it was indeed a 'natural fortress'. From the mountains they had an unobstructed view over the plain, and behind them was a precipice offering 'excellent cover for men and horses'. Moreover, the British advance came to a halt at Belfast. For weeks nothing happened. The Boers took advantage of the opportunity to strengthen their defences.

A week later the Pretoria Commando arrived unexpectedly, and, to Deneys's surprise, his two elder brothers were with them. He took leave of the Boksburgers and rejoined his unit, happy to be back with Hjalmar, Joubert and his comrades. He was ready to face the British.[11]

The attack came, but only on 21 August 1900, exactly a month after the British had set off along the eastern line. There were two reasons for their slow progress over the previous few weeks. The first related to another proclamation which Roberts had issued on 17 July. This time it affected the families of Boers who were still on active commando. Many of them, women and children, had fled from their homes to seek refuge in cities like Johannesburg and Pretoria. Poverty-stricken and with no means of support, they were dependent on the British administration. But in Roberts's opinion, it was absurd to be feeding the enemy's families. The Boer insurgents should be providing for their wives and children. So he decided to return them to their care. As from 19 July they would be transferred by train to Van der Merwe, 15 kilometres east of Pretoria.

Botha was shocked by the news. They were talking about hundreds, if not thousands, of women and children for whom he would have to provide food and shelter—in two days' time. He had his hands full regrouping his men. He was still busy protesting about the British burning down farms—and now this. From Machadodorp Kruger advised him first to refuse responsibility for the families and then to demand a ceasefire. In any event, he was to lodge a formal protest against these deplorable measures.

Botha's objections made little impression on Roberts, who callously replied that the British administration couldn't continue to support Boer women and children. Their husbands and fathers were to blame for their plight. It was they who were destroying the railway lines and holding up food supplies. If they stopped committing sabotage, their families would get what they needed. But as long as they persisted, he had no alternative but to send destitute women and children elsewhere. On 19 July more than 400 of them were crammed into open goods trucks and sent to Van der Merwe, where they arrived in the late hours of a bitterly cold winter's night.

Racing against time, Botha had asked General Ben Viljoen to improvise temporary accommodation for them. From there the families were taken to Barberton, in the eastern Transvaal, near the Swaziland border. The arrangements took time and effort, and heightened the anguish of those who knew that their families were involved. And instead of a ceasefire, Botha was facing the prospect of another offensive. On 21 July the British began to advance along the same railway line. It was as much as he could cope with. He had to organise the defence and at the same time prepare to receive another contingent of women and children.

Roberts was threatening to send more. He dismissed Botha's complaint that the families had fled to Johannesburg and Pretoria because their farms had been burned down. The real culprits, he argued, were the bands of roaming insurgents who were inciting civilians to renounce their oath of loyalty and resume the struggle. They were also forcing those families to provide them with food. And in any event, they were still sabotaging the railway line. He therefore saw no reason to stop the deportations. In early August he announced that another batch of 450 women and 1500 children would be transported on the 11th and 13th, this time to Belfast. His only concession was an undertaking to suspend all troop movements until 16 August.

Botha could only resign himself to the situation. The next group of 800 women and children arrived late on the evening of Saturday 11 August, shivering in open cattle trucks. Again Viljoen arranged accommodation until they could be sent on to Barberton. The women had lost none of their fighting spirit. Wearing the Vierkleur on their clothing, they raised their voices to sing the Transvaal anthem as the trains pulled in. They seemed to be coping better than Botha, who expressed his despair in a telegram to Kruger. He was 'tired and overcome by the transports of women and children, because it's clear that the British are using the women as a weapon against us'.[12]

Although Roberts obviously gave no sign, the army's delay actually suited him quite well, because he was anxious—the second reason—to wait for Buller, who was advancing from the south-east with a detachment of his expeditionary army. Roberts thought it wiser for the two forces to mount a joint attack against Botha's 'natural fortress'.

Buller's advance from Natal hadn't been as swift as Roberts's. After his experiences along the Tugela line, he had been especially wary when approaching the Boer positions in the Biggarsberg and Drakensberg mountains. There he had found a new adversary, Chris Botha, Louis's younger brother, and earned himself a new nickname, Sitting Bull. But he had achieved results. Thanks to his thorough reconnaissance of the area and skilful flanking manoeuvres he had managed to overcome both formidable obstacles, incurring surprisingly few casualties in the process.

Buller had crossed the Transvaal border on 1 June. His priority was to repair the south-eastern railway line from Durban to Johannesburg. By 7 July he was able to travel to Pretoria himself to pay his respects to Roberts. The two men had a long history of rivalry—one had been the leader of the 'Indians', the other second-in-charge of the 'Africans'—and in South Africa new wounds had been added to the old. The darkest cloud over their heads was Colenso, where Buller had forfeited his command and Roberts had lost his only son, Freddy. Each of them had reason to blame the other, and so they did. But at this—their first—encounter, they were calm and pragmatic.

At this stage at least, there was one thing they agreed on and that was to answer sabotage with reprisals. Buller felt even more strongly about this than Roberts. As soon as he had entered Transvaal territory—a couple of days before Roberts's Proclamation 5 of 16 June—he had put up posters warning that 'the residents of any locality will be held responsible both in their persons and their property if any danger is done to Railway or telegraph or any violence done to any other of the British forces in the vicinity of their homes'. In early July it was clear that he meant it. Six farms in the Standerton district, where 'a few scattered bandits' had allegedly planned attacks, were demolished on his instructions. One of them was the farm Varkenspruit, the property of none other than Louis Botha.

People said it was sheer coincidence, but Buller's well-targeted reprisal wouldn't have displeased Roberts. Two weeks earlier it had been Roodepoort, this time it was Varkenspruit. Another harsh deterrent. No Transvaler who continued to resist could delude himself by thinking he was safe. Not even their commandant-general, that was the message. Botha protested vehemently, condemning what he called godless, barbaric practices, which had no place in a civilised war. But Roberts had grown accustomed to criticism of this kind, which he fielded with accusations of his own. British troops had been under fire from farms displaying the white flag; Boer commandos were intimidating law-abiding citizens.

He pushed it even further. On 14 August he published a new proclamation, the twelfth. Burghers who had not sworn neutrality would be deemed prisoners of war and could be sent to the camps. Buildings in which 'the enemy' were harboured would be razed to the ground. Boer families who failed to inform British soldiers about the presence of 'hostile elements' would be deemed guilty of complicity.

There was no escape for anyone, which was precisely the object. And certainly no escape for Louis Botha. On 15 August the two British army corps joined forces, a few kilometres south of Belfast, with Roberts's troops approaching from the west and Buller's from the south-east. It was time to deal the final blow.[13]

It was also time for a bit of good luck. Bad news had come in from the western Transvaal a day earlier. De Wet, along with Steyn and some 2000 men, had managed to escape after all. No one could tell Roberts how on earth it could have happened. Everyone pointed a finger at somebody else, Methuen at Kitchener, Kitchener at Hamilton, and Hamilton—well, there wasn't really much he could say. He just happened to be the last in the line of British generals who had allowed the Free State commandant-general to slip through their hands. They had spent a whole month stalking him, from east to west, right across the Orange Free State, across the Vaal to the Magaliesberg mountains. It had been a massive hunt, bigger than anything anyone had seen before, and they had covered a huge distance. They had been at his heels for hundreds of kilometres, with—in successive stages—no fewer than 50,000 men. But they still hadn't caught him.

It had all seemed so promising a while back. In mid-July 1900 the majority of the remaining Free State commandos, including De Wet, had been in the Brandwater valley, on the eastern border, near Basutoland. There were about 8000 Boers, with all their guns, wagons, munitions, horses, oxen and sheep: a fantastic prey. If they remained there, they would have been caught in the trap. The valley was virtually closed off by the horseshoe-shaped ranges of the Witteberg and Roodeberg mountains, and there were only a few accessible passes. And Lieutenant-General Sir Archibald Hunter—a more appropriate surname would be hard to imagine—with 20,000 men was busy blocking and occupying each of them. To the south was Basutoland, hostile territory, which the Boers would avoid at any cost. They would be trapped and, for the British, it would just be a matter of waiting for them to surrender.

But this was where things started going wrong. De Wet had seen the danger and decided to leave the valley, in three groups, moving in different directions. He would head north, with President Steyn, the remaining members of the Free State government and 2000 men. Another 2000 men would make their way to the south-west, led by the general— and dominee—Paul Roux. A third group of 500 men, under General J. Crowther, would go east. The rest, Marthinus Prinsloo's men, would stay behind to defend the mountain passes as long as they could, and then withdraw.

De Wet left at once, on the night of 15 July. He took one of the two northern passes, Slabbert's Nek, with all his commandos, 400 oxwagons and five guns. He had come dangerously close to the camp of one of Hunter's army commanders, Major-General Arthur Paget—less than three kilometres away—but no one had spotted them. This was the first of a series of miraculous escapes.

But Hunter wasn't aware of De Wet's movements at the time. One group of Boers had managed to slip out, so he was told the following day, but, all being well, the rest were still in the Brandwater valley. They were. The other Boer commandants had been less assertive than De Wet. They had dithered about breaking up their laagers, and Prinsloo and Roux had ended up quarrelling as to who was in charge. Putting it to the vote didn't resolve anything. Prinsloo won initially, but the votes that came in later gave Roux the edge. Prinsloo challenged the procedure and insisted on taking command.

It was Hunter who benefited from the dispute. On 24 July, in the depths of winter, with snow on the mountain slopes and in a torrential downpour, he flushed the Boers from their positions on Slabbert's Nek and Retief's Nek, before doing the same, a few days later, on Commando Nek in the south-west and Nauwpoort Nek in the north-east. The British troops swept into the valley from all four sides. The Boers had no way out.

At any rate, this is what Prinsloo believed. He called for a ceasefire. Hunter refused and demanded an unconditional surrender. On 30 July Prinsloo conceded, on behalf of all the Boer commandos. Roux protested, and personally made it known to Hunter. He was the highest-ranking officer, he insisted, not Prinsloo; hence the surrender wasn't legally valid. Hunter heard him out, probably with some amusement at his naivety, and then had him arrested.

But other Boer commandos did see a way out. Some 1500 men under General Piet Fourie escaped through the Golden Gate, the easternmost pass. The rest followed Prinsloo's example. There were so many of them that it took more than a week for them all to hand in their weapons. On 9 August they took stock of the damage. A total of 4314 men had surrendered, even more than at Paardeberg. They were shipped to Ceylon, where they remained for the duration of the war. Their two million Mauser cartridges ended up on a bonfire. The British made better use of their 5500 horses, 4000 sheep and 3000 oxen.[14]

By then, De Wet was hundreds of kilometres and several 'narrow escapes' away. The first reports of the surrender reached him on 2 August. He was appalled. A few days earlier it had been his own brother, Piet, and now Prinsloo, Roux and all those thousands of others. It was 'an abominable murder of the Government, Country and People'. And it upset his plans. He was at the Vaal and had been intending to veer off to the south, in the direction of the Cape Colony. But now that there were so many British troops in the Orange Free State, it would make more sense to head north, into the Transvaal. There was also the consideration that Steyn wanted to confer with Kruger, not by telegraph, but president to president. He could be of some use.

The road north wasn't exactly empty. South of the Vaal 11,000 British troops were advancing with the aim of hemming the Boers in, but even more were lying in wait across the river. There were roughly 18,000 in all, with celebrated commanders like Methuen, Smith-Dorrien, Hamilton and Baden-Powell. And all of them were led by Kitchener personally.

Even so, De Wet managed to pilot them through. They crossed the Vaal at Schoeman's Drift, scrambled over an almost impassable trail to Van Vuurenskloof, rested for a couple of hours at Buffelsdoorn. Then they crossed the railway line at Welverdiend, blowing it up at eight places as they went along, forded the Mooi River, and joined Piet Liebenberg's Transvaal commandos. They veered north outside Ventersdorp, setting fire to the dry grass behind them, and headed for the Magaliesberg. At the last moment they turned eastward. On 14 August they crossed at Olifant's Nek. They had shaken off their pursuers and escaped.

That was the gist of the reports Roberts received from his generals. He had to admit that De Wet deserved his good fortune. No Boer commandant had his men so firmly in hand, wielded the sjambok so unsparingly, drove them so hard to maintain his own breathtaking momentum. No one had better scouts. His diversionary strategies were unrivalled, oxwagons and all. He had been assisted by Transvaal commandos. All of that was true. But it didn't alter the fact that opportunities had been missed, miscalculations made, wrong decisions taken. There had been communication breakdowns, errors, blunders, call them what you like. Whatever the case, they had to do better. He, personally, would be in command against Botha.[15]

This was the response Willem Leyds had been hoping for. Dated The Hague, 1 August 1900, it was a draft statement of protest, an unequivocal objection—legally correct and heartwarmingly scathing—to Roberts's first 'Transvaal' proclamations. Typical of Asser, his friend and former mentor. In Asser's opinion the damage the British had inflicted on civilian property was 'an outright violation of the established rules of international law. Private property, other than the contraband of war, must be respected in war on land.' Article 46 of the Convention with Respect to the Laws and Customs of War on Land, signed at The Hague on 29 July 1899, was perfectly clear on that point. And Britain was one of its signatories. In Roberts's proclamations 'the citizens of the Republic' were deemed 'belligerent parties'. Until a peace settlement was reached or the Republican armed forces were destroyed, the Transvaal would remain under martial law.

Leyds received Asser's reply more than a week later. He was in Berlin on another impossible mission with Fischer, Wessels and Wolmarans. The members of the delegation had returned from America and desperately wanted an audience with Wilhelm II. Leyds had warned them that the kaiser was unlikely to receive them. In Paris, through personal connections, he had managed to arrange an informal interview with President Loubet, but there was no chance of something similar in Berlin. The signals he had picked up previously were decidedly unfavourable. But the three of them wanted to try nevertheless. So off they went to Berlin, only to be snubbed and humiliated. They weren't granted so much as a meeting with a deputy under-secretary, let alone the emperor. Wilhelm bluntly refused to receive them, saying they had nothing of interest to tell him. They should have taken Leyds's advice, he complained, and come to Berlin as soon as they arrived from South Africa, and not gone off to the Netherlands and America first.[16]

On the other hand, Leyds could understand the delegation's motive. They were willing to grasp any opportunity they could, no matter how slight their chance of success. They clung to the faintest glimmer of hope to counter the gloomy reports on the war. The British were now deporting Dutch nationals employed by the Netherlands-South African Railway Company. Including their families, the numbers amounted to 1400 of his compatriots. And the staff of the Dutch ambulances were being sent home, too. The men were even being imprisoned, on charges of aiding and abetting the Boers. News like that made one wish to do something, if only to send a cheering message from faraway Europe.

Leyds had done so himself, in a personal letter to Kruger in mid-June, after the fall of Pretoria. He had poured out his heart. 'My thoughts are with you every day, my honourable State President, and every day I wish I could be close at hand.' He had ended with a hopeful postscript. 'The delegation has telegraphed from America. If we persist a little longer, the American government will be compelled to do something for the Republics.'

He knew they were clutching at straws, but it might give Kruger and the others something to believe in. Otherwise, there were the troubles in China: something of benefit might come out of that. In late June 1900 an uprising in the provinces had spilled over into Peking. The rebels—called Boxers because of their religiously inspired method of fighting—were seeking to curb the growing influence of the West on China. They were murdering foreigners, missionaries in particular, and had laid siege to diplomatic missions in Peking. An international expeditionary force had been raised as quickly as possible, representing all the major Western nations as well as Japan. It was now advancing on the Chinese capital. The British were also involved. With luck, they would need more troops than the 10,000 they had already diverted from British India. And it would probably encourage them to bring a quick end to the war in South Africa.[17]

With such thoughts Leyds did his best to keep his spirits up. He needed to, because after Berlin he and the delegation were about to face another ordeal: St Petersburg. Again, they were unlikely to be granted an imperial audience. On the afternoon of Wednesday 15 August 1900, their train pulled into the station of the Russian capital. They were encouraged by the cheering crowd that had come out to meet them, but that was the only warm welcome they received. It was soon painfully clear that the Russian authorities had had enough of their uninvited guests. Newspapers were ordered not to write about them, and the tsar was away on military exercises, which could take weeks. While waiting for his return, Leyds was received anyway, by the foreign minister, Count V.N. Lamsdorff. He was given full diplomatic honours. Leyds was an officially accredited envoy— the second secretary, Van der Hoeven, had presented his credentials in December 1898[18]—so he was always welcome to speak to the tsar, Lamsdorff assured him. But the members of the delegation? Well, their status wasn't clear, so it was impossible for His Majesty to receive them. Lamsdorff, of course, couldn't either.

This was a bitter pill for Fischer, Wessels and Wolmarans to swallow. Leyds was given an appointment for his audience: two o'clock on the afternoon of Saturday 25 August. In the meantime, they were working on the official letter protesting against Roberts's proclamations. It was almost identical to Asser's draft, but included another emphatic objection to Roberts's subsequent proclamations of 16 and 19 June. Leyds sent the letter to the consul-general in London, H.S.J. Maas, asking him to pass it on to Lord Salisbury, and to have 100 copies printed for the press. 'St Petersbourg, August 18th 1900'—that alone would make the British think twice. It would look as if the tsar were symbolically supporting the protest.

A week later, at the Peterhof Palace, Leyds heard with his own ears what Nicholas II was actually prepared to do. The tsar came straight to the point. Could Leyds explain why the German emperor had made it so obvious that he was turning his back on the Transvaal? 'None of my ambassadors has been able to shed light on it.' Leyds replied tactfully. Only once, he said, had Wilhelm II expressed displeasure with the Boers, and that was when they had ordered guns from France as well as Germany. 'We are the gun manufacturers of the world,' he had chided them. But this couldn't be the problem. The real reason, Leyds suggested tentatively, 'must . . . be sought in his volatile disposition'. This was apparently exactly what the tsar wanted to hear. Wilhelm II's habit of changing his mind was Leyds's only hope, he insisted. 'If you can obtain his assurance that he will not take Britain's side, I would still be prepared to intervene.'

As usual, it was a case of one autocrat shifting responsibility onto another. This was as much as Leyds achieved. That and a request to keep the tsar informed of any developments, through De Giers, his envoy in Brussels. Leyds almost ruined the meeting by making a last plea on the delegation's behalf. It was not appreciated. 'I would only be able to repeat to them what I have told you. And do you think it's pleasant for me, the Emperor of all Russians, to say twice, "I cannot"?'[19]

The first thing Roberts did on arriving in Belfast was turn the plan of attack upside-down. It was Saturday 25 August 1900. Buller, French and the others on the mountain ridge had been shelling the Boer trenches for four days, but there was no sign of a breakthrough. The troops were positioned too closely together, Roberts concluded. They needed to be dispersed in order to thin out Botha's line of defence. He kept Buller on the right, but directed French's cavalry to the left. They would employ their usual outflanking tactic on both sides. In the centre Lieutenant-General Sir Reginald Pole-Carew would keep up the pressure on the Boers.

Roberts's plan worked, though Buller was also entitled to some of the credit. After a day and a half of heavy fighting, he decided not to take the route he had originally planned, but to cut through the centre. From the morning of Monday 27 August he concentrated his firepower from the Bergendal plateau straight onto the railway line. The Boer positions there were held by Zarps, Johannesburg's police officers. They were nobody's favourites, but the bombardment they endured won them a lasting reputation on the battlefield. It was one of the most savage onslaughts of the entire war, on a par with Vaal Krantz and Pietershoogte. The Zarps also held out for hours against the subsequent infantry assault by the Rifle Brigade and the 1st Inniskilling Fusiliers. But in the course of the afternoon, the onslaught became unbearable. Those who could still walk—most of their horses were dead or wounded—beat a retreat. The Boers' defence line had been broken.[20]

That evening Botha took stock of the situation. The British breakthrough in the centre had rendered his position untenable. Not only Buller, but also French and Pole-Carew had gained ground. He was in danger of being surrounded and decided to withdraw his whole army. They had lost the

Battle of Bergendal (the British called it the Battle of Dalmanutha), the last set-piece battle of the war. There was nothing left to do but follow De Wet's example and divide his army into smaller detachments that would be able to operate quickly and independently.

The Transvaal's political leaders were also compelled to retreat further, as fate would have it, at the same time as those of the Orange Free State. President Steyn, along with the rest of his government, arrived at Waterval Onder in the final stage of the battle. He wanted to confer with Kruger and his advisers. The meeting was held on 28 August in Nelspruit, 75 kilometres by rail to the east. It was a memorable occasion. Not only did the Transvaal government officially approve the new methods of war, but both Executive Councils also agreed to a desperate move, proposed by Steyn. The elderly Kruger would be given six months' leave to go to Europe and use his prestige to achieve the goal that had constantly eluded Leyds and the delegation: he would persuade other powers to intervene. In his absence Schalk Burger would deputise as president. Reitz would retain the office of state secretary.[21]

Reitz's three sons, Hjalmar, Joubert and Deneys, had survived the battle at Bergendal. It was sheer good fortune. The Pretoria Commando had been no more than a kilometre and a half from the Zarps and well within the British line of fire. Hjalmar had been wounded just under the eye and Joubert had taken him to the field hospital. Deneys had escaped twice—miraculously—from exploding lyddite shells. The first time, the blast had stunned him. The second time, his horse had saved him. The roan had become entangled in its reins and Deneys had gone to free him. No sooner had he reached the horse than 'a shell burst on the ant heap' he had been sitting on.

In the confusion of their journey back to Nelspruit the brothers had become separated from one another. Halfway there, however, Deneys met his father, who had come in search of them. His father told him what Botha had in mind. He was planning to strike north into the wilds beyond Lydenburg to reorganise the forces in order to carry out guerrilla warfare. They would assemble at Hectorspruit, the second-to-last railway station before the Mozambique border. They agreed to see each other there. The meeting ended in tragedy. The train taking his father back to Nelspruit accidentally 'killed my poor little Basuto pony'. Deneys was overcome with emotion. 'Besides having served me faithfully since the first day of the war, he was an intimate link with our old home life, for he had come with us from the Free State as a foal, and the loss of this loyal companion was a great blow to me.'

There was no time to grieve, as the British had resumed their advance.

The Pretoria Commando decided to return to the highveld by way of a detour and continue fighting closer to their families. Deneys wanted to do the same, but his people were in Hectorspruit. At least, he hoped he would find them there. He took leave of the Pretoria men once again and joined other commandos who were making for Hectorspruit. He reached it a day or two later. His three brothers were already there, Joubert, Hjalmar with a large bandage around his head, and Arend, who had recovered sufficiently to ride his horse again, thanks to the Russian nurses. His father arrived two days later, 'so our family is united again for the first time after several months'.[22]

His own way

Lydenburg, October 1900

A fortnight was as much as Deneys Reitz could endure. He had been fascinated by all the new things he had discovered on the way. From Hectorspruit they had struck north-west, first through the lowveld on either side of the Sabi, where they had seen an abundance of wildlife: herds of zebra and wildebeest, and at night lions prowling around their camps. From there they had crossed the mountains to Ohrigstad. The route had taken them through lush mountain passes and some of the country's rare stretches of pine forest. They had spent a week in Ohrigstad, but an outbreak of malaria spurred them on to Lydenburg, which was on higher ground.

There boredom had soon set in. Kruger had already left Hectorspruit for Lourenço Marques to wait for a ship sailing to Europe. Botha was travelling in the Transvaal, setting up a new commando structure. The government consisted of Schalk Burger and his father, assisted by a few other department heads. There was nothing in Lydenburg to keep Deneys and his brothers occupied, and their enforced idleness made them irritable. Arend was still too weak to leave, but the three others decided to go on commando again. Hjalmar, who had 'a queer bent of his own', went to the eastern Transvaal. Deneys and Joubert chose a different direction. They'd heard that General Christiaan Beyers was organising a force in the area north of Pretoria. He was near Warmbaths, a good 250 kilometres to the west. That's where they would go.

There wasn't much to prepare. They shot a kudu and made biltong, and collected a supply of mealies. These were all the provisions they had. After taking leave of their father, the brothers set off, Deneys on his roan and Joubert on the horse they had recovered from Charley in Pretoria. It was mid-October 1900. They had a long journey ahead of them, through the northern Transvaal bush, 'untenanted save by native tribes and wild animals'.[23]

Officially it was now British territory—at least, according to Lord Roberts. In his view, the victory at Bergendal was decisive enough to allow him to annex the Transvaal with an easy mind. On 1 September 1900 he proclaimed the South African Republic the new Transvaal Colony. Kruger, of course, had responded with a counter-proclamation a few days later, this time from Nelspruit. But he had lost all credibility almost immediately afterwards. His departure for Lourenço Marques was a gift from heaven for Roberts.

'Resignation of Mr S.J.P. Kruger', announced his new proclamation of 14 September, which went on to reveal that the old president had formally resigned. This wasn't entirely true, but that didn't matter much to Roberts. Nor was it true, as he alleged, that Reitz, the state secretary, had left the country, taking the complete archives of the South African Republic. In fact, Reitz was on his way to Lydenburg. Only the part about the archives was true. The Transvaal's official documents were being shipped to Leyds in Europe for safekeeping. But the most important thing, of course, was Kruger's departure. 'His desertion of the Boer cause', the proclamation explained, confirmed that he considered the war hopeless and futile.

To convince the Boers, Roberts summarised his case once again. Nearly 15,000 Boers were prisoners of war. Not a single one of them would be released without a universal, unconditional surrender. Intervention by any foreign power could be ruled out. The British Empire would win the war. By any means whatsoever, he added ominously. 'The war is degenerating, and has degenerated, into operations carried on in an irregular and irresponsible manner by small, and in very many cases, insignificant bodies of men.' Neither the British government nor the British army could turn a blind eye to them. Measures to curb their activities would be ruinous to the country and cause great suffering to the burghers and their families, but they would have to be taken nevertheless. The longer the guerrilla war lasted, the tougher those measures would be.[24]

In other words, more farms and harvests would be razed, more cattle confiscated and destroyed. His announcement wasn't just bluster. From September 1900 the incidence of farm burnings soared, even according to the systematically underestimated official British accounts. Often they were not reprisals for sabotage, but random acts of destruction carried out on the instructions of individual officers, who were receiving increasingly ruthless orders from their superiors.

And those orders frequently came from Roberts himself. One incident in the Krugersdorp district stood out in particular. The community was known to be virulently anti-British. Roberts decided that the Paardekraal Monument was part of the problem. It had been erected on a cairn of stones laid there in December 1880 at Paul Kruger's initiative, as a symbol of resistance to the British regime.[25] As long as the stones remained in place, the Transvaal's independence was secured, or so the 'ignorant Boer farmers' believed. Roberts believed it too, so he had the stones removed. On the night of 16 September they were chipped out, packed in flour bags and sent by train to Johannesburg. From there they were taken to Durban and dumped in the Indian Ocean. Others said they were thrown into the Vaal from the railway bridge at Vereeniging. All the same, Krugersdorp continued to oppose the regime.[26]

Not everyone approved of Roberts's iron-fisted repression. Besides continuous protests from Botha, De Wet and other Boer leaders, there were voices in his own circle raised in objection. Just as there were officers who went more than the extra mile in carrying out Roberts's instructions, so there were others who condemned the savagery of his actions against the civilian population.

Even Milner, the high commissioner, not the most charitable of men, expressed his reservations to Roberts, though perhaps only because the damage was being inflicted on a country that was now in British hands. Milner was more outspoken towards Chamberlain, the colonial secretary. He wasn't against the destruction of farms as a punitive measure, but demolishing entire districts for no purpose other than to render them useless to the enemy was going too far. It was '1) barbarous and 2) ineffectual'. It meant more homeless people swelling the ranks of 'the army of desperadoes roaming the country which it is our object to reduce'. He believed that more could be achieved by winning them over to the British side.[27]

Roberts wasn't too bothered about all the protests and criticism—in any event, not at the beginning. October and November saw a growing number of attacks on property and they were becoming increasingly arbitrary. On one point he did take Milner's advice to heart. More had to be done to secure the loyalty of Boers who were amenable to the British regime. Most importantly, those who had sworn neutrality and surrendered their arms needed special protection. They were caught in the crossfire, sometimes literally. Accommodating them in temporarily unoccupied homes only created new problems. It seemed more practical to house them in camps in the vicinity of British garrisons. They would be safe there and have access to grazing land for their cattle. The first of these 'refugee camps' were set up in Bloemfontein, Kroonstad and Pretoria in September 1900. More were to follow in rapid succession.

One thing led to another. Besides ensuring the safety of the *hensoppers*, the British military administration had another problem to solve, one it had created itself and was making worse by the day. Milner was right about this, too. The wholesale destruction of property had left many Boer families homeless. In July and August Roberts had tried to saddle Botha with the responsibility for the families of his men, but in September he was back to square one. On 13 September 1900, when

British troops reached Barberton, on the Swaziland border, they found all the women and children there, 2800 in all. They had ample supplies of food, but their husbands and fathers, led by Botha, had proceeded north, beyond the reach of the railway. New arrangements had to be made for their families.

And now, thousands more were in the same position. The solution was obvious. Several camps already existed for *hensoppers*; the homeless Boer families could join them. They could kill two birds with one stone. The bitter animosity between the two groups wasn't Roberts's problem. They would have food, they would have shelter (tents), they would be under military supervision, and they would no longer obstruct military operations: these were the main considerations. Roberts wanted to round things off. On 29 September, a few days before his 68th birthday, London had offered him the position of commander-in-chief, the highest-ranking officer in the entire British army, successor to his 'African' rival, Wolseley. It would be a glorious ending to his career. But first, he needed to put things in order in South Africa.[28]

Today was the big day, 1 October 1900. Twenty-five thousand voters would be deciding on Winston Churchill's future as a politician. The election would take roughly a month, and Oldham was one of the first constituencies in the series. There were two seats to be won. Again, like 18 months earlier, Churchill and another Conservative candidate were standing for election against two Liberals, both of whom were currently members of parliament. They stood the best chance, but there was one important difference: the war in South Africa. This was a khaki election, which Salisbury's Cabinet had called in order to benefit from the war sentiment. And Churchill was a war hero. His praises were sung even in music halls:

> You've heard of Winston Churchill,
> This is all I need to say,
> He's the latest and the greatest
> Correspondent of the day.

Sentiments like these set the tone for his campaign in Oldham. He was driven in an open landau to the Theatre Royal, where an excited crowd was waiting to catch a glimpse of him. He gave a dazzling account of his escape from prison and his subsequent adventures, culminating in the episode of his confinement in a coal mine. Never before had he revealed the names of those who had helped him. But now that the mining district of Witbank and Middelburg was in British hands, he could do so without jeopardising their safety. And this was the perfect moment. At his mention of the name Daniel Dewsnap, the engineer from Oldham who had wished him well in the next election, the audience went wild. 'His wife's in the gallery,' someone called, prompting a round of tumultuous applause.[29]

But, for all their enthusiasm, the race in Oldham was not yet won. The Liberal candidates were moderates, neither pro-Boer nor anti-war as such, but critical of the Conservative government's handling of it. Churchill had, of course, tried to capitalise on the differences. In one of his speeches he had lambasted a Liberal member of parliament for consorting with the notorious 'Dr Leyds' in Brussels. That city, he had recalled—and that man, he had insinuated—were noted for their contempt 'for the lives of British nobles'. Everyone knew he was referring to an attempt on the life of the Prince of Wales in the Belgian capital, six months earlier.[30]

Prominent Cabinet members were adopting the same tone. Chamberlain's slogan was 'Every seat lost to the Government is a seat gained to the Boers'. The colonial secretary had come to Oldham in person to support Churchill's campaign. His presence alone had given rise to tension. The hall in which Chamberlain and Churchill were to speak was filled with supporters, but a hostile crowd had been waiting for them at the entrance. Demonstrators hurling insults and abuse had delayed their landau for several minutes. On the evening of the election the final outcome was still uncertain. *The Times* of 2 October reported that Churchill had been defeated again. It published a correction the following day. Each voter could cast two votes and it transpired that Churchill had gained enough 'second' votes to win a seat. He ended with 12,931 votes, 16 fewer than the successful Liberal candidate and 222 more than the other.

A member of parliament! And a lost seat recovered—all the more credit to him. At the Conservative Club Lord Salisbury was one of the first to congratulate him. And Chamberlain in turn asked him to support his campaign in Birmingham. Arthur Balfour, the leader of the Commons and Salisbury's nephew and prospective successor, wanted Churchill with him on the platform in Manchester. Other party bigwigs followed suit. For weeks Churchill appeared at one crowded rally after another, proudly paraded to audiences of 5000, 6000. And he was still only 25 years old. His debut in politics was nothing short of spectacular.

And all thanks to the war in South Africa. It had worked for Churchill. For the Cabinet as a whole things were less clear-cut. At the end of the election month it emerged that the Conservative–Liberal Unionist coalition had consolidated its majority, taking 402 of the 670 seats. In this respect, the Cabinet's decision had proved successful, although it had nine seats fewer than in 1895. The Liberals under Sir Henry Campbell-Bannerman had won six and now had a total of 183 seats. And Labour, for the first time, took two. In overall votes, however, discounting the distortion of the constituency system, the coalition had increased its majority from 49 per cent to 50.3 per cent, with the Liberals down from 45.7 per cent to 44.7 per cent. In other words, it was an outcome that both government and opposition could claim as a victory. The same applied to the main election issue, the war in South Africa and public support for it in Britain.[31]

So the Salisbury government remained in power: this was the most relevant fact for the Boer leaders. Britain's policy wouldn't change. And Kruger had just sailed off to Europe, so for the time being nothing could be expected of him either. It was all up to them and a good plan.

They rarely had a chance to meet and confer, but an opportunity came in late October 1900. Steyn and the rest of the Free State government were returning from their meeting with Kruger in Nelspruit, and made a detour through the northern Transvaal. Botha joined them there and together they travelled on to Cyferfontein, a farm in the Swartrug, about 100 kilometres west of Johannesburg. De la Rey and Smuts had set up their tents there. On 27 October they all came together. De Wet had also been sent an invitation by courier. He was probably on his way.

It was a comfortable place and in the circumstances almost idyllic. The tents stood in the shelter of mimosa trees in bloom. Oranges and naartjies were there for the picking. There was good grazing for the horses, and a lake nearby in which to cool off. The camp had only one disadvantage: the British knew they were there. But what they didn't know was that the Boer leaders were informed about all their plans. Their scouts had been keeping a close watch on the movements of British troops for miles around, and reporting back by heliograph. There was also a telegraph line near the farm and a telegraph office a kilometre further on. Although both had been put out of service, the problem was easy to fix. One of Steyn's men was an experienced telegraphist, originally John Acton, now Jan Eksteen, who was able to intercept all telegraphic communications to and from the British headquarters. So the Boers knew the exact whereabouts of the British columns and their marching orders—and they knew how much time they had for their talks.

In the event, it was more than enough to reach two major decisions. They agreed on a modified version of their original, bold plan of attack, the one Smuts had advocated. They would fight beyond their own borders, on British territory, invade Natal (5000 men under Botha) and the Cape

Colony (De la Rey and De Wet, with 5000 men each), with the ultimate goal of organising the long-anticipated Afrikaner uprising. But this time it would start with a spectacular curtain-raiser: an unexpected combined attack—with 15,000 men—on the gold mines.

All the gold mines. Five months earlier Botha had been dead against such a plan, but circumstances had changed in the meantime. Previously, he had thought it a pointless form of retaliation, nothing more than an act of vandalism. But much had changed since then. Roberts was waging a barbaric war, the Boers had their backs to the wall. Their farms had been destroyed, their wives and children hunted down and incarcerated, their cattle plundered and slaughtered, their harvests burned. A harsher response was justified. In that light, even Botha agreed that the mines were a legitimate military target. Show the Randlords what it felt like to lose everything they possessed. Furthermore, the total collapse of the mining industry would be a hellish embarrassment for Britain's army as well as its government.

The plan was as follows. First, they would lure the British to the far corners of the Transvaal and the Orange Free State. Then, in January or February 1901, the Boer commandos, as one, would swoop on the Witwatersrand. Dynamite would finish the job, a lot of dynamite. The mines would be reduced to rubble. By the time the British recovered from the shock, Botha, De la Rey and De Wet would be well on their way to their next assignments in Natal and the Cape Colony.

It was a stunning plan, even wilder than the one Smuts had proposed on the eve of the war. It all depended on coordination and split-second timing. Everyone would have to come into action at exactly the right moment. A pity that De Wet hadn't made it. Come to think of it, where on earth was he? The British were approaching fast. It was time to clear out of Cyferfontein.[32]

De Wet didn't have much of an excuse. Of course, he'd had a run-in with British columns, but, to be honest, he'd been asking for it and had got himself into a lot of trouble. As a result, he'd got no further than Ventersdorp, some way south of Cyferfontein. There, on 1 November 1900, he had met up with Steyn and his men again and they had ridden back to the Free State together. On 4 November they crossed the Vaal and, a day later, its tributary, the Vals. Then they set up camp in Bothaville.

By the time they got there, they had caught up on the news. De Wet reported that he had managed to organise a new commando system, but he also had a piece of bad news. Danie Theron, the commandant of the Scouts Corps, the one person who had never failed him, the man who had been his eyes and ears, was dead. He had been killed by an exploding shell at the beginning of September. It was a terrible loss. Since his death, the British had already managed to catch De Wet off guard on more than one occasion. Steyn in turn told him about Kruger's European mission and Schalk Burger's appointment as acting president. He told him too about the decisions they had taken in Cyferfontein. Botha wanted to discuss them with him again in private.

De Wet wasn't particularly enthusiastic. A new joint plan, follow-up talks with Botha? In the preceding months he'd had an uneasy feeling that the Transvaal leaders were wavering. At any rate, this was true as far as Botha was concerned. His Transvaal counterpart had hinted at peace talks more than once. De Wet wouldn't hear of it, unless independence was on the agenda. If not, he wouldn't have talks with anyone. He would rather make a plan on his own, which at least he could count on.

A letter from Barry Hertzog, the young judge who had meanwhile risen to the rank of assistant chief commandant, strengthened his view. Hertzog also suggested that the time was ripe to launch a raid on the Cape Colony, but it should be plain and simple: three units, each with 1000 Free Staters, operating independently of each other. The Transvaal could follow with another 2000 men, but it wouldn't really be necessary. 'Chief Commandant C. de Wet's name is so well known that just his presence will be enough to set the Colony ablaze,' he'd written.

That was the kind of conviction De Wet wanted to see. If he was still wavering between Botha and Smuts's plan and Hertzog's, his doubts would have been dispelled by the symbolism of the disaster that awaited him on 6 November, in Bothaville, appropriately enough. At half past six in the morning, when most of his 800 men were still asleep, the sentry corporal came to report that all was quiet. De Wet knew that the British weren't far off, and he knew who they were: Major-General Charles Knox's column, led by the 5th and 8th Mounted Infantry under the command of Colonel Philip le Gallais. But they were still on the opposite bank of the Vals, he was told, probably making for Kroonstad.

This wasn't correct. Barely were the words out of the corporal's mouth when De Wet heard shots. Someone slaughtering animals, he thought. But the firing continued. The sound came from the direction of the sentries' quarters, and suddenly the British were there, uncomfortably close, and they were coming in droves. They had caught the sentries off guard—Steyn later called it 'criminal negligence'—and now they were storming the Boer camp. The men, still drowsy with sleep, were caught unawares. Some had the presence of mind to take cover and return the fire, but most of them panicked, scrambled for their horses and made a break for it, many leaving their saddles behind, anything to get away from the bullets and shells.

De Wet was powerless to stop them. Nothing helped. 'I had never seen anything like it in my life. I had often heard about terror, but then I understood what it really meant.' Screaming and brandishing his sjambok, he went after the fugitives. Steyn, at least, had to be taken to safety, along with the state treasury and official documents. This he managed to do, but he couldn't round up his men. Most of them got away. Only a handful remained to put up a fight, too few to repel the British. They managed to stop some of them, including Le Gallais, but they were overwhelmingly outnumbered. Around 11 o'clock the remaining fighters, more than 100 of them, surrendered. Another 17 Boers were killed, and six guns—their last—were lost.

The Bothaville debacle taught De Wet a painful lesson. Danie Theron, his master scout, was no longer alive. Only now did De Wet begin to grasp the full implications of his predicament. There was no one he could trust. Sleeping sentries, panic-stricken men, fainthearted allies. He could only rely on himself. He had never really thought much of Botha and Smuts's plan, but now he was firmly against it. In any case, without artillery there wasn't much they could do to the Rand.

The following day, 7 November 1900, De Wet reached a decision. He forwarded Hertzog's letter to Botha, adding his own views on the subject. The time had come for 'our commandos to invade the Cape Colony'. He would have liked to confer with Botha and De la Rey before leaving, but 'in the circumstances that would take up too much precious time and I am already on my way'.[33]

Foreign territory

Warmbaths, November 1900

Deneys Reitz enjoyed his time in the bush. He loved the rugged terrain and the wild animals, and when he and his brother Joubert finally found General Beyers's unit at the end of their meanderings, a pleasant surprise awaited them. The Afrikander Cavalry Corps, their Free State unit, had survived after all. After their last meeting and its tragic ending at Middelburg four months earlier, their old comrades had gone north to join Beyers's unit. And now they were reunited, here in Warmbaths. Malan had been succeeded by a young commandant, Lodi Krause, who invited them to join the unit. Deneys and Joubert agreed without a moment's hesitation. They were back with the Afrikander Cavalry.

The reunion was complete when Arend turned up as well, at the end of November. After recovering his health, he had found Lydenburg dull. Their father had agreed to him going in search of his two elder brothers. They were pleased to see him fit and well again. The three of them built a reed hut to serve as a shelter. They spent their days hunting in the bush and occasionally rode out on patrol to Pienaars River, 40 kilometres south, where the British had set up a camp. Once, having ventured too close, they were spotted. They made a dash for it, with bullets whistling past their ears, and managed to escape without a scratch.

The only drawback in Warmbaths was their commandant. Christiaan Beyers was a brave man and Reitz respected him for that, but he was also deeply religious, a zealot, Deneys and his brothers thought. He and the dominee, Abraham Kriel, missed no opportunity to hold a prayer meeting. 'Come rain or wind, at midnight or under the blazing sun, whenever we unsaddled our horses we paused for prayer, and in time that grew tedious.' Young men on commando like themselves were required to attend Bible study sessions when they were out in the bush, but the three brothers unaccustomed to 'intolerance in matters of faith', refused to take part. They met with reprimands from Kriel and threats from Beyers. Were they trying to get themselves thrown out of the commando?

The storm blew over and in early December the interlude of relative peace came to an end. Beyers received orders from Botha to move south and engage in guerrilla operations. He left for the Magaliesberg with 800 men, leaving 200 behind. Deneys and Arend accompanied him. Joubert had decided he would prefer to be with the artillery. His brothers tried to dissuade him, but he had made up his mind.

Within a few days they found themselves in a valley at the foot of the mountain range which separated the bush country and the highveld. There they had a lucky break. At the beginning of the Ou Wapad, a path through one of the mountain passes, they came upon a convoy of 50 or 60 British supply wagons, which had been ambushed. Some were still ablaze, others were smouldering. It could only mean one thing: Koos de la Rey was in the vicinity. There would be action and they were looking forward to it.[34]

Kruger's reception in Marseilles was promising. At nine o'clock on the morning of Thursday 22 November 1900, the Dutch warship *Gelderland* sailed into port. The exiled president had been taken on board in Lourenço Marques a month earlier. This diplomatic coup on the part of the Dutch government was the brainchild of the minister of the navy, J.A. Röell, and a credit to Queen Wilhelmina. Before doing anything else, The Hague had obtained London's approval. Leyds had then discussed the matter with the French government to decide on the most suitable port of arrival for the start of Kruger's European mission.

Now the big moment had come. As soon as it moored in the port of Marseilles, the *Gelderland* was surrounded by ships and pleasure yachts carrying crowds of excited supporters. But they still had to wait. First a tender sailed out to the armoured cruiser; on board were Leyds, the three members of the Transvaal delegation, Fischer, Wessels and Wolmarans, and the Groningen professor of theology and French language and literature, A.G. van Hamel, whom Leyds had engaged as an interpreter. Then there was the official leave-taking from the crew. Around 11 o'clock the tender returned, bringing the man half the city had come out to see. He was wearing a dark overcoat and a top hat with a mourning band. Just like his photos, the *New York Times* reporter thought. Far better than in the photos, said the Dutch *Algemeen Handelsblad*. They were in agreement about the tumultuous cheering on the quay. Once the cries of 'Long live Kruger' and 'Long live the Boers' had died down, the chairmen of the national and local Transvaal committees extended an official welcome to the president. Leyds did the introductions. Kruger replied, first brightly, with pleasantries, but when the subject turned to the war he was overcome with emotion.

Though tremulous, his voice was still resonant and strong. His outrage boomed over the jetty. 'The war which is being waged against the two republics has reached the utmost limits of barbarity. In my life I have had occasion many times to fight with the savage tribes of Africa, but the barbarians with whom we have now to fight are much worse than the others. They have gone so far as to arm the Kaffirs against us. They burn our farms, which we have built with so much difficulty. They hunt the women and children whose husbands and fathers have been killed or taken prisoner. They leave them without protection, without homes, often without bread.' Gesticulating angrily, he continued, 'But whatever may happen, we shall never surrender . . . Our cause is just and if the justice of men fails us, the Almighty, who is above all nations, and to whom the future belongs, will not abandon us. I can assure you that, if the Transvaal and the Orange Free State are to lose their independence, it will be because the two Boer peoples have been destroyed, with their women and children.'

A hush fell over the audience for a moment. Such passion, such determination, no one had expected from the 75-year-old, mused the reporter from the *Algemeen Handelsblad*. The *New York Times* correspondent was also astounded by Kruger's 'fighting declaration'. As Van Hamel finished translating his words, the crowd erupted in another storm of applause. The ceremony was over. A long procession of carriages made its way to the Hotel de Noailles. Along the route 'the adulation grew louder, the excitement mounted from house to house'. An estimated 150,000 people filled the streets; the cavalcade virtually came to a standstill. This 'delirium of enthusiasm' continued even after Kruger's arrival at the hotel. In response to 'a thunderous ovation', he appeared on the balcony. Standing between the flags of the Transvaal and the Orange Free State, he acknowledged the tribute. After a few minutes, Kruger reached for the French flag, which hung there as well. Visibly moved, he pressed it to his heart. Then he returned indoors.[35]

Leyds hadn't expected such an overwhelming reception. There was no lack of public support and solidarity. But the visit wasn't about processions and public appearances. Decisions were taken behind closed doors, in the meetings he had arranged for Kruger in the halls of power. Seeing him again had been a painful experience. Leyds thought his president looked 'old and tired', and in spite of his three previous visits, he displayed little 'knowledge of the situation in Europe'. In Paris he would be received as a head of state, with an official reception from the French president, Émile Loubet, which he had managed to arrange. More important, however, was the meeting he would have afterwards with the foreign minister, Delcassé. That was what really mattered.

The train journey from Marseilles to Paris was an endless triumphal procession. At the stations en route, in Lyon and Dijon, dignitaries jostled to greet him. Even when the train didn't stop, admirers and well-wishers crowded the platforms to wave as Kruger passed by. At railway crossings men doffed their hats, officers saluted. In Paris he was given a hero's welcome. The city was festooned with Transvaal flags and emblems, and supporters paraded in Boer hats. The chief of protocol, Philippe Crozier, was at the Gare de Lyon to welcome Kruger on behalf of President Loubet.

His reception at the Elysée followed soon afterwards, complete with national anthems and a guard of honour. The meeting between the two presidents amounted to little more than an exchange of pleasantries. It was only when Loubet returned the visit, at Hotel Scribe, that Kruger laid his cards on the table. He said he was gratified by the exuberant display of solidarity, to which he added, 'but it will offer little consolation, if it is not followed up by deeds'. Loubet was cordial but evasive. He recalled France's earlier efforts 'to encourage friendly intervention'. Apart from this, the future would 'show how much further it would still be possible to go'.

The message, which Leyds received through Van Hamel, was clear: Loubet couldn't do much more. Only Delcassé could provide redemption. The day for it came soon afterwards, on Tuesday 27 November 1900. Once again, Van Hamel was present to interpret. After the usual formalities, Delcassé came to the point. He brusquely referred Kruger to 'other countries whose relations with Britain are less fraught than ours'. Van Hamel saw 'something like a dull resignation spread over the tired features of that beatific face, while the gnarled fingers fumbled for the hat on the chair beside him and the bowed, faltering figure slowly raised itself to leave'.[36]

So Paris could be written off. What now? Go to The Hague? There was absolutely no one who could do anything there. Berlin, and then St Petersburg? Leyds was sceptical, but Kruger was determined to leave no stone unturned. So, on to Berlin. Leyds spoke to a few of his acquaintances in the diplomatic corps. Their replies weren't exactly discouraging, although they warned that the emperor might have other commitments. Very well, Kruger and Leyds thought, in that case they could always speak to the chancellor, Bernhard von Bülow, and the foreign minister, Oswald von Richthofen. They set off for Cologne on 1 December 1900.

Leyds regretted the decision as soon as the train pulled in at Cologne station. Nothing had been arranged for them, no reception committee, no police cordon; only a rapturous crowd which, however pleasing, became a threat to Kruger's personal safety. At one point, Leyds lost him in the crush, and was 'immensely grateful to see him back at the hotel in one piece'. The authorities were clearly happier to see Kruger leave than arrive. Leyds had apparently misinterpreted the hints from the Germans. The following day, his suspicions were confirmed. A certain Heinrich von Tschirschky und Bögendorff, chamberlain plenipotentiary to the emperor, came to their hotel. The message, which he conveyed in person, spelt it out: 'His Majesty' was unable to receive the president of the Transvaal and urged him to reconsider his plans to visit Berlin. He couldn't have been more blunt. It suddenly seemed as if the amicable telegrams the two heads of state had exchanged in earlier years were a figment of someone's imagination. There was no longer a place for Paul Kruger in Wilhelm II's scheme of things. Dried-out putty in a broken window. He had to get out of Germany.[37]

There was nothing for it but to go to Holland, the ineffectual but at least hospitable land of his forefathers. Leyds knew that Oom Paul would be welcomed with open arms, even by the political authorities. Queen Wilhelmina, Pierson, De Beaufort, they wouldn't do anything either. The queen would be frustrated, the foreign minister pedantic, but they would certainly want to see him, and spare him the humiliation of a blunt refusal.

And so on 6 December 1900 it was The Hague's turn to cheer Kruger— but not too exuberantly—and welcome him. It was a poignant occasion, the more so because everyone knew from the start that his mission was doomed to fail. Asser was 'among those assembled in the station forecourt and was deeply moved by the warm reception. It was hard to fight back my tears,' he confided to Leyds. The forlorn old hero held a place in everyone's heart, but no one was able to help him. Their sense of impotence pervaded the crowded reception held a week later: Kruger seated in the midst of his entourage as a procession of 'Dutch people from all walks of life' filed past. According to the *Algemeen Handelsblad*, it was 'impossible to enumerate all the organisations and associations concerned with religion, science, art, labour, etc. whose spokesmen sought to convey their sympathy for the long-suffering old man in a few hasty but heartfelt words'. They proceeded to do so, nevertheless, row upon row: the Leiden Students' Association, the Committee for Clothing and Food for South Africa, the Cecilia Royal Choir, the Board of the Union of Exiled Officials of the Netherlands-South African Railway Company ('We were deported from your country but we hope to see you back there'), the young ladies and gentlemen of the Academy of Drawing, a delegation of the 3rd Section of the Hasselt Cross, average age 89.5. The list went on and on. Everyone was deeply affected by the plight of the Boers, everyone was moved to tears by Oom Paul, but no one was in a position to help him. A note on the admission card for the reception unwittingly expressed their helpless longing to reach out: 'Please refrain from touching the President.'[38]

The timing was perfect. Major Pond, his American agent, had worked wonders. Churchill revelled in these auspicious quirks of fate. It was half past eight on the evening of 12 December 1900, a year to the minute—

disregarding the time difference—since his escape from prison in Pretoria. And what a splendid venue! The Grand Ballroom of the Waldorf Astoria in New York, haunt of 'the rich and famous'. He couldn't have wished for a better start to his American lecture tour. Even so, he was more nervous than usual. He felt perfectly at home in high society, but this time he was being introduced by no less a luminary than Mark Twain. It was a tremendous honour and the presence of the world-famous author had undoubtedly been good for the box office. It was just that it gave Churchill cold feet. Twain was known to be staunchly opposed to imperialism, both American and British, and at his age—65, with a shock of unruly white hair—he was free to speak his mind. It could turn into a difficult evening.

He wasn't worried about delivering the speech. That he could do in his sleep. With the help of a magic lantern, he had told the story of his escape and other exploits in South Africa exactly 29 times before, in every large city in Britain. He had started right after the elections, on 30 October, in St James's Hall in London, and since then, evening after evening—except Sundays—he had addressed large, packed halls. He also had big names to introduce him, starting with Commander-in-Chief Lord Wolseley in London, and subsequently a string of prominent politicians, like Lord Rosebery in Edinburgh and Lord Derby in Liverpool.

He had made a tidy sum out of the lectures, which was precisely the idea. At the time members of parliament received no remuneration. His new seat in the Commons was only going to put him out of pocket. If he intended to devote himself to politics in the coming years, he would have to start building up a financial reserve. He had already put aside about £4000 from his income from the *Morning Post* and the royalties from his books. Now was the time to cash in on his reputation as a successful war correspondent, while the memories were still fresh. His agent, Gerald Christie, had arranged the bookings. By the end of November Churchill had more than doubled his savings—and he had won acclaim wherever he went.

He wasn't so sure how he would be received in his mother's native country. The run-up to his American debut had been bedlam. Major Pond—no one knew which unit he had been in—had included the names of a committee of recommendation in the invitations. Some committee members hadn't been aware of it, while others—pro-Boer—were furious about being publicly associated with the event. The ensuing chaos was good for ticket sales, but not for Churchill's peace of mind.

Twain's opening words did little to put him at ease. Personally, said the famous 'man in white', he opposed the war in South Africa, as he opposed his own country's war in the Philippines. He had always sought to promote ties of friendship between the two countries. After all, 'England and America . . . [were] kin in almost everything'. But 'now they are kin in sin'. So his sympathies were with the Boers. That didn't stop him from giving Churchill a warm welcome. He introduced him as 'a blend of America and England which makes a perfect match'.

Churchill received a vigorous round of applause, though his nervousness at the beginning didn't escape the notice of the *New York Times* reporter. Gradually the tension subsided, and in the end he gave 'a clear recital', interspersed with humour to enliven his story. Here, too, the colourful details of his escape went down well. Things were more difficult during the discussion afterwards. At one point Churchill repeated the adage 'my country right or wrong', to which Twain snapped back, 'When the poor country is fighting for its life, I agree. But this was not your case.'

It was a useful lesson, from which Churchill benefited on the rest of his overseas tour. The pro-Boer movement in the United States was far stronger than he had realised. His best recourse was humour. It came to his rescue in an incident in Chicago. The audience included a large contingent of Irish Americans, who jeered loudly. Churchill got by only with witty, self-deprecating remarks and praise for the Boers' courage and humanity. Still, he was relieved that his last lectures would be in Canada. His audiences there were unstintingly appreciative—just as they had been at home. He could speak his mind again. 'The first thing to be done, of course, is to crush De Wet and the guerrilla bands.'

He returned to England early in February 1901, richer in experience and his stash of dollars. Converted into pounds, his earnings came to another £1500. This brought his total savings up to £10,000. He had earned it all himself, within a year and a half, thanks to the war in South Africa. He was high and dry for a few years to come. Now he could devote himself to his career in parliament.[39]

Nature seemed to be conspiring against him: a sign from above that invading the Cape Colony, as Christiaan de Wet planned, might not be such a good idea after all. The drought had lasted until the end of November 1900. There was virtually no grazing, the horses were growing weaker by the day. If they didn't recover, they would have to be replaced. Otherwise the whole venture was doomed. The spring rains fell at the beginning of December—and didn't stop falling. Now there was far too much water. The veld became a swamp, and bubbling brooks turned into raging rivers.

On the last stretch to the Cape, De Wet and his men faced the hazards of two of these torrents. At the Caledon River it was raining cats and dogs, but they managed to trudge across. Now there was still the Orange, and beyond that the Cape. On 4 December De Wet's scouts reported that the drift at Odendaalstroom was passable, at least it was at that moment. But their hopes were dashed the following morning. It was obvious as soon as they reached the bank of the river. The water had risen overnight and they wouldn't be able to cross it. Worse still, there was a British army camp on the other side. Their invasion of the Cape Colony had failed before it began.

At least, this was De Wet's conclusion. Waiting for the water to subside wasn't an option. Approaching from the west was a British column under Major-General Knox, the commander who had caught him off guard at Bothaville and had been pursuing him across the Free State ever since. De Wet had to decide whether to go north, braving the Caledon again, or east, through officially neutral but traditionally hostile Basutoland: an unpredictable river or an unpredictable enemy. He opted for the river. But he left 300 men behind—with their best horses—led by Pieter Kritzinger and Captain Gideon Scheepers. They were to wait for an opportunity to cross the Orange to carry out at least part of the invasion plan.

They succeeded in mid-December 1900, just as Hertzog and his 1200 men were entering the Cape 150 kilometres downstream. But all De Wet could do was turn back—with Knox still at his heels. To make faster progress and delay his pursuer, he decided to release the 400 British prisoners he had taken after the capture of Dewetsdorp two weeks earlier. On 7 December he was back at the Caledon. They could still cross it at Kommissiedrift, but there they ran into British troops that had dug in. They had better luck at Lubbesdrift, a few kilometres further north.

On the other side of the river, he still had Knox to contend with. Knox had lost his trail for a while, but the skirmish at Kommissiedrift put him back on track. He resumed the pursuit, assisted by other columns, which were coming in from all sides. For a week these combined forces went after De Wet, leaving him no choice but to retreat further north. He had no opportunity to make a detour and head back to the Cape. His escape route in the north wasn't safe either. To shake off his pursuers once and for all—well, for as long as it lasted—he would have to break through a British defence line at Springhaansnek, a pass with a fort on each side. But now fortune was with him. Reinforcements from the Bethlehem and Winburg commandos, under Michael Prinsloo and Sarel Haasbroek, arrived in the nick of time. They were well equipped and their horses were fresh. With their help he forced a way through Springhaansnek on 14 December and managed to escape again.

His elusiveness dismayed Lord Kitchener, who had succeeded Lord Roberts as commander-in-chief of the British troops in South Africa on 29 November. 'As long as De Wet is out, I can see no end to the war,' he wrote to London in late December 1900. But it was also to the relief of Louis Botha, who hoped this would finally lead to a meeting with him 'to discuss matters thoroughly and make sure we understand one another correctly'. The invitation was delivered to President Steyn on 8 December by one of Botha's adjutants in person. De Wet must have seen it fairly soon afterwards.[40]

Emily Hobhouse had been in Cape Town for more than a week when she received an invitation from Sir Alfred Milner for lunch at Government House on 8 January 1901. The letter of introduction from her aunt Mary, Lady Hobhouse, and her cousin Henry, the member of parliament for Somerset East, had yielded results. She was dreading the meeting. Would she be able to persuade Milner? Only once she had got to the Cape had she heard the worst reports, about Boer refugees and about British soldiers, the countless farms that had been burned down. News of these atrocities had already reached Britain, but all those camps, 'refugee camps' they called them, for heaven's sake: that was news to her. In the train, travelling from the suburb where she was staying, her heart pounded wildly. To calm herself she turned to the letters she had just received. There was one from the Courtneys, the couple who had won her over to the Boer cause. Kate had written it, Leonard—most unusual because he had been blind for several years—had added a few words at the end: 'Be prudent, be calm.' That helped.

She trusted Leonard Courtney. He was a seasoned politician, an independent, liberal-minded thinker with a social conscience. And he had been a member of parliament for the past 25 years, in spite of his disability. In January 1900, as president of the South African Conciliation Committee, he had invited Hobhouse to become secretary of the women's branch. She had taken on the job with heart and soul. She knew all there was to know about dedication. For 15 years she had looked after her ailing father. At 35, the only romantic relationship of her life had come to an end. From then on, she devoted herself to campaigning against social injustice, to the cause of British miners who had emigrated to America, to women and children working in factories and, since the outbreak of the war in South Africa, to the plight of the Boers, initially because of the unspeakable wrongs they had suffered and, later, in sympathy with their uprooted and displaced families.

Hobhouse had first spoken out publicly about her concerns for Boer women and children on 13 June 1900, at a protest rally organised by the women's division of the Conciliation Committee at the Queen's Hall in London. Resolutions were passed against the government's policies, against efforts to silence political opposition, and against the impending annihilation of a nation of kinsmen and brothers in faith. To these Hobhouse added a fourth resolution, an expression of solidarity with the women of the Transvaal and the Orange Free State. She assured them that thousands of British women were sympathetic to their cause and deplored the actions of the British government.

The response went beyond expressions of sympathy. The second half of 1900 saw an ominous increase in reports of systematic destruction by the British army in the Boer republics. The involvement of other anti-war activists like the Liberal parliamentarian John Morley strengthened Hobhouse's resolve to take more vigorous action. 'Daily British homes were darkened by death and Boer homes by destruction and desolation.' A relief fund was needed. She would see to it, and indeed she did. The South African Women and Children's Distress Fund was established in September 1900. It was a purely benevolent, non-political organisation in support of women and children of all colours and creeds throughout the country. Its purpose was to provide food, clothing and shelter to all who had suffered because of the war in South Africa. Within two months the fund had collected £300, enough for two railway trucks of aid. Hobhouse was going to deliver it herself.

Her uncle and aunt, Lord and Lady Hobhouse, her brother and relatives and friends advised her against it. Was it wise? All on her own in a war zone, all those diseases, that gossip and backbiting, and what did she think she could achieve? But she wouldn't listen to reason. She had made up her mind. The idea turned into a plan, the plan into a mission. She was 40 and this became her calling in life. She was going to save the women and children of South Africa.

At Government House, her lunch companions took the wind out of her sails. She was the only woman in a party of eight. Milner broached the subject, but she felt uncomfortable among so many strangers and requested a private interview. He agreed. Fifteen minutes in the drawing room, which turned into more than an hour, and everything came out into the open. The high commissioner was reason itself. Yes, he agreed that burning down farms wasn't right. And no, he had no objection to Hobhouse visiting the camps to distribute aid. There was just one thing. He would have to consult the new commander-in-chief and obtain his approval.

Now it was a matter of waiting for Lord Kitchener. In the meantime,

Hobhouse came to realise just how much the Boers' recent incursion into the Cape Colony was troubling the authorities—Milner, that is. Martial law had been declared in areas where Hertzog and the other Boer commandants were about to break through. The line demarcating those areas was rapidly moving south. Milner did his best to accommodate her, but the consequences were becoming increasingly clear, even in Cape Town itself. He demanded the immediate surrender of all civilian arms, guns were installed in strategic positions, with barbed wire around them, and trenches were dug around important buildings. Cycling and riding were prohibited beyond the confines of the city. A 9.30 curfew came into effect. At 10.30, all lights were to be extinguished. But there were no Boer commandos—to Hobhouse's regret—anywhere to be seen.

On 17 January 1901 Kitchener's reply came by telegram. He agreed in principle, but imposed two restrictions. She wasn't to go beyond Bloemfontein, and he felt that it wouldn't be necessary to have a 'Dutch lady' accompany her, as she had requested. The reply was better than nothing, Hobhouse concluded, and she decided to go. Her two railway trucks were less than half full: the prices here had astonished her. The consignment came to a total of six tonnes, half clothing, half foodstuffs. On 22 January 1901 she set off for Bloemfontein. On her arrival, she heard that Queen Victoria was dead.[41]

Guilty landscape

Naauwpoort, December 1900

Three days had passed, but Deneys Reitz was still distraught. It was 16 December 1900, Dingane's Day, the commemoration of the Boer triumph over the Zulus at Blood River. At last there was something to celebrate. They had won a victory at Nooitgedacht, but he was still tormented by the image of a British soldier with half of his head blown off. The memory continued to haunt him. It had been *his* bullet, his dum-dum. In Warmbaths he had put a few of them in a separate slot in his cartridge belt to use for shooting game. But this had slipped his mind, and in the heat of battle he had unwittingly loaded one. And this was exactly where General Beyers and Dominee Kriel were intending to erect a new monument. Everyone was to lay a single stone to form a large cairn of remembrance, like the one in Paardekraal, which Roberts had later removed. Reitz didn't care for the idea.

The victory at Nooitgedacht had been a memorable one. The Boers had launched an attack for the first time in almost a year. While they had been unsuccessful at Platrand, south of Ladysmith, on 6 January 1900, this time they pressed on. Beyers's commando, among them Reitz and the rest of the Afrikander Cavalry, had forced the decision. It had been uphill, on top of it, in the half-light of dawn, storming the entrenched Northumberland Fusiliers, screaming and shooting, deflecting bayonets with the butts of their rifles. They suffered heavy casualties, around 20 dead and 60 wounded. The British lost almost 100, with the same number captured.

After seizing the British fortifications, Beyers had sent Krause and his Afrikander Cavalry to comb the mountain ridge. Reitz had been with them, of course. They had run into a division of Imperial Yeomanry making their way up, and wiped out the entire unit of 20 or 30 men—including that solitary soldier, who had suddenly appeared a short distance away.

Then they had returned to the top. It was seven o'clock in the morning, the battle at Nooitgedacht was as good as decided. Beforehand, the generals in charge—De la Rey, Smuts and Beyers—had planned to launch surprise attacks on the British army camp at the foot of the mountain and the reinforced positions on the slopes simultaneously. They had failed at the camp, because the Boers' advance guard had been detected too soon, but the success of Beyers and his men had made up for it. Having eliminated their adversaries, they now opened fire on the army camp below, leaving the officer in command, Major-General R.A.P. Clements, no option but to beat a hasty retreat.

At that point, Beyers's men began to descend as well. On the way down, Reitz came upon the soldier he had shot at close range. Only then did he see the damage his bullet had caused. He was speechless with horror. He grabbed his cartridge belt, found a few more dum-dums and flung them into the river. It was red with blood. He turned and fled downhill.

On his path he met two wounded British officers. It was like stepping onto another planet. They casually struck up a conversation with him. Did he speak English? Good. Then could he explain why the Boers were still fighting the war when it was clear that they would lose? As if he had rehearsed it, a passage from *David Copperfield* flashed through Reitz's mind. 'Oh, well, you see, we're like Mr. Micawber, we are waiting for something to turn up.' The officers laughed heartily. 'Didn't I tell you this is a funny country, and now here's your typical young Boer quoting Dickens.'

The British army camp offered more distractions. Beyers had ordered his commandos to pursue Clements's retreating troops, but they thought otherwise. The spoils were better than anything they had seen in a long time and the temptation was too great. Besides, what were they to do with even more prisoners? They were in any case always released after a few days. Reitz saw no harm in plundering; it was pure necessity, they had to replenish their provisions. Both he and his brother Arend found plenty among the camp's abundant supplies: two extra horses with saddles and halters, a new Lee-Metford rifle each, with ammunition, to replace their battered Mausers, as well as tea, coffee, salt, sugar, food, clothing and books, all of which had become luxuries.

Still, his conscience was troubling him. Reitz decided not to attend the ceremony on Dingane's Day. De la Rey, Smuts and Beyers addressed the gathering of burghers. The first two recalled the Battle of Blood River in 1838 and the Voortrekkers' pledge before their victory over the Zulus. Beyers talked about the importance of commemorating the event, especially now, when the Boers were being put to the test and it was all too easy to succumb to weakness. The pledge was repeated in a ceremony led by Dominee Kriel, and everyone laid stones to form a cairn.

Except Deneys Reitz. How could he have stood there and quoted Dickens as if nothing was wrong? He had thought long and hard about what he had done. It hadn't been intentional, but he needed to justify it.

What difference did it make if you shot someone with an explosive bullet or blew them to smithereens with a lyddite shell, as people were doing all the time in this war? Dead is dead, Master Copperfield. Even so, he wouldn't feel comfortable laying a stone.[42]

Piet de Wet thought it was time to do more. It was 11 December 1900, more than four months had passed since he surrendered, and the situation had only deteriorated. There was wholesale destruction, complete districts had been razed, the country was falling to pieces. The guerrilla raids had to stop. From Durban, where he had been living in self-imposed exile, he requested and obtained Kitchener's permission to return to Kroonstad. He had an idea for a peace initiative. On the way, he stopped off in Johannesburg. It had come to his knowledge that his sister-in-law Cornelia was staying there. Perhaps he could reason with her and she could persuade Christiaan to abandon the struggle. The very thought was naive. Cornelia showed him the door and asked the military commandant to order her brother-in-law to 'refrain from further visits in the future'. In that case, he would have to deal with the problem himself head-on.

Piet de Wet wasn't the only one who wanted to see the war over and done with. Many others had tried to intervene in the preceding months, and in December 1900 they began to form organised groups. In several towns and cities prominent *hensoppers*, including former members of the Volksraad, were forming peace committees. Piet de Wet became the chairman of the local committee in Kroonstad. Meyer de Kock was the leading light in the Transvaal Colony. Kitchener refused to negotiate with them. Britain had no intention of abandoning the struggle and there was no chance of foreign intervention: that's what they could tell the Boer fighters in the field. And they did. In late December the committees sent out scores of representatives to try to persuade them to lay down their arms.[43]

They spread the same message through newspapers and pamphlets. Piet de Wet, for instance, wrote to his brother Christiaan on 11 January 1901. Soon afterwards, his letter appeared in the *Bloemfontein Post,* and subsequently as a pamphlet called *Brother to Brother*. The introduction said it all. 'Dear Brother, I have heard that you are angry and would kill me because you believe me to be guilty of treason.' He proceeded to discuss the accusation that he had been bought off by the British, and replied quite simply, 'God will judge righteously.' But he also had something to say in reply. If his brother and Steyn continued the war, the people would be 'impoverished, as many already are'. They would ultimately become 'the country's labouring class and disappear as a nation'. And what for?

'Are you blind?' Was Christiaan really unable to see that he was 'being deceived by the Transvaal generals and burghers'? They had not 'fought a tenth of the battle that we Free Staters are fighting. The Transvaal is nowhere near as ravaged as the Free State.' And the Transvaal generals had long been wanting to surrender, 'but are waiting to see what you do. They will give up the moment you surrender, fall or are captured. I beg you to consider this all before you go any further.'[44]

His heartfelt appeal didn't have the effect he had hoped for. Christiaan de Wet ignored the letter, in any event publicly. He is said to have threatened to shoot his younger brother if he came anywhere near him. Piet de Wet didn't lose hope. He directed his efforts to like-minded people in the Cape Colony. The high commissioner, Milner, expected little to come of them, but gave his consent. In February 1901 De Wet went to Cape Town, accompanied by members of several other peace committees in the Orange River Colony. First he spoke to T.P. Theron, the president of the Afrikaner Bond, and subsequently to influential church ministers, but all to no avail.

The party also visited the prisoner-of-war camp in Green Point, an encounter that did bear fruit. For one thing, it sowed unrest among the Boer prisoners. Some reviled Piet de Wet and his companions, others were more receptive to their message of peace. At any rate, that is how it seemed, though few dared to speak openly. Moreover, De Wet noted, there were Boers among them who had voluntarily laid down their arms and who could therefore not be deemed prisoners of war. After the visit he urged Milner to establish a second camp in order to separate the 'good' prisoners from the 'bad'. Milner was in favour and proceeded to do so, notwithstanding Kitchener's reservation. A 'peace camp' was opened in Simonstown in March 1901, to which 800 prisoners—those who had accepted British rule—were transferred. Those who refused to do so could be sent to camps overseas.[45]

So Piet de Wet did achieve something, which was more than the other peacemakers could say. Even the venerable Marthinus Pretorius had got nowhere. The 81-year-old former president of both republics, and founder (in 1855) of Pretoria (named after his Voortrekker father, Andries), visited Louis Botha in January 1901, at his own initiative, according to Kitchener. He left empty-handed, with the message that Botha wasn't prepared to talk to intermediaries. If Kitchener had something to say, he should say it himself, in writing.

But at least the elderly Pretorius returned safely from his mission. A few others were less fortunate. Johannes Morgendaal and his father-in-law, Andries Wessels, were prosperous Free State Boers. Morgendaal was a justice of the peace and a scribe for the Nederduits Gereformeerde Kerk.

Wessels was a member of the Volksraad. These were men of standing in Kroonstad and its environs. Having lost faith in further resistance, they set off for Christiaan de Wet's camp towards the end of December 1900. On the way, they were arrested and tried. A court martial under General Stoffel Froneman referred their case to a higher court. Pending their hearing, they were taken along with Christiaan de Wet's commando, as prisoners. Froneman had been instructed to keep them under close watch.

On 9 January 1901 things went wrong. Early in the morning a scout reported—mistakenly, as it later transpired—that the British were approaching. Froneman ordered Morgendaal to help span the oxen. Morgendaal took no notice. 'I'm not a Hottentot,' he said. Froneman set on him with his sjambok. Morgendaal managed to wrest the whip from his hands and a fight ensued. Christiaan de Wet, watching from a distance, yelled 'Shoot the motherfucker', or words to that effect. Froneman fired, and fatally wounded Morgendaal. The following day the court martial convened to try his father-in-law. The 15 officers, chaired by De Wet, pronounced Wessels guilty of treason and sentenced him to death. He owed his life to President Steyn, who commuted the penalty.

Schalk Burger, the acting president of the Transvaal, was less lenient in the case of Meyer de Kock, who was arrested on 23 January 1901 and brought to trial a week later. He was tried on four counts: evasion of commando duties and surrendering arms to the enemy, conspiring with the enemy, possession of incriminating documents belonging to the peace committee he chaired, and attempting to incite civilians to surrender. He, too, was found guilty of treason. The difference was that Burger refused to grant clemency and signed the court judgment. On 12 February De Kock was executed by firing squad.[46]

Methodical. If there was one quality by which Lord Kitchener of Khartoum, the British commander-in-chief in South Africa, wanted to distinguish himself from his predecessor, it was his rigorous pursuit of his objectives. Obsessively rigorous, critics said, and ultimately self-defeating, as when, on a previous occasion, he had centralised the transport system and earned himself the nickname K of Chaos.[47]

Kitchener saw things differently. The problem was the way orders were being carried out, and that could only be solved by more stringent measures. The same applied to the way they were dealing with guerrilla fighters. This, too, needed to be more systematic. Lord Roberts had issued one proclamation after another and provided for appropriate reprisals, but it had still ended up in random acts of terror. It all had to be more efficient, like clockwork.

On 7 December 1900, at the end of his first week in office, he gave the first sign of what was to come. He issued a memorandum with new instructions for columns crossing the highveld. It wasn't about destroying farms or other property so much as 'denuding the country of supplies and livestock'. This served two purposes. It enabled the columns to provide for their needs and it deprived the enemy of all means of subsistence. So the first step was to remove or destroy livestock and food supplies.

Two weeks later Kitchener announced the second step: people. On 21 December he sent a confidential circular to all high-ranking officers. In order to end the guerrilla war all non-combatant civilians were to be removed from areas where Boer commandos were active. This would prevent anyone from assisting or communicating with the fighting men, whether by choice or under coercion. They would be left to fend for themselves, without logistical or moral support.

The uprooted communities were to be housed in camps in their own district, in the vicinity of a railway line to facilitate supply transports. In the process, they were to be divided into two categories: firstly, those who had voluntarily laid down their arms, along with their families, and secondly, the families of men who were still active in the struggle. It went without saying that the first category were to receive preferential treatment in the camps. Their property rights were to be respected and they were to be given priority, if necessary, when it came to accommodation and rations: better tents and more food.

A separate section of the circular dealt with the black population. The aim was not 'to clear kaffir locations' as such. But Africans living on Boer properties, as servants or otherwise, were also to be removed, along with their livestock. They could keep their possessions, if at all practicable. In the camps they were to be given adequate protection. They could also be employed to perform any necessary work, at the prevailing 'tariff for natives'.[48]

This was all to be carried out systematically: depopulating the region by obliterating all signs of life and returning the earth to a state of barren wilderness. This was Kitchener's policy resolution for the year 1901, his Christmas greeting for the twentieth century. The operation began in the eastern Transvaal at the end of January. Eight columns, more than 20,000 troops, set off under Major-General French to flush out Botha and his commandos and strip the whole region of humans, animals and crops. The commanding officers were to keep records of the 'proceeds', or what Kitchener called 'bags'.

Deneys Reitz was still serving with General Beyers's commando but they had left the Magaliesberg and were heading east. Botha had summoned them to Ermelo. One day he saw the assembled British columns approaching, filling the horizon as far as the eye could see. It came as a terrible shock. Beyers divided his men into two groups. The first went off to locate the enemy's left flank. The other, which included Deneys and his brother Arend, were to delay their advance.

They saw at once how the British went about their task. Pillars of smoke rose up behind them. From fleeing women he heard that the British were destroying everything in their path and arresting everyone they encountered. Crops too rain-sodden to burn were trampled by cattle. The following day brought a stampede of people fleeing from the columns. 'The plain was alive with wagons, carts, and vehicles of all descriptions, laden with women and children.' Horses, cattle and sheep were being 'hurried onward by native herdboys', with farms and haystacks burning behind them. Botha directed the refugees to Swaziland, across the border, to escape from the British.

In the meantime, the Boer fighters were recovering from their initial shock. They noticed that the British were unable to maintain a continuous front. 'The troops were left groping about after the elusive Boer forces, which easily evaded the lumbering columns plodding through the mud far in the rear.' The army's new strategy of obliterating everything in their path did little to dent the morale of the Boers in the field, Deneys Reitz noted. On the contrary, it only strengthened their resolve to keep fighting.[49]

Emily Hobhouse enjoyed the train journey through the Karoo more than Willem and Louise Leyds had done in their day, or Winston Churchill just over a year before.[50] And this in spite of its not being the best time of year. Sandstorms and thunderstorms followed one another in a seemingly endless cycle. The sandstorms were the worst. Even with the doors and windows closed, her coupé was covered in a layer of red dust. It penetrated her eyes, her ears, her hair; it covered everything like a tablecloth. Yet there was something extraordinary about this pristine wilderness—the wide open spaces, the flowing lines, the infinite sky. The following stretch, from Colesberg, was bleaker. Formerly the Orange Free State, it was now the Orange River Colony. Well, this really was a desolate, depressing landscape. It had once flourished, as anyone could see, but now it was deserted and lifeless, strewn with the corpses of horses and cattle, burned and abandoned farms, litter everywhere, no one tending the land. And no Boer commandos to be seen, unfortunately. There wasn't a soul on the entire journey except bored British soldiers, cadging for newspapers and books.

The soldiers were everywhere. She had found them disquieting when she arrived in Bloemfontein on 24 January 1901. You couldn't move an inch without their permission; identity checks were carried out on every street corner. It was oppressive and she could imagine how the locals must have felt. It was a good thing that she had the letter of introduction from Milner. The town's military governor, Major-General G.T. Pretyman, knew she was coming and granted her permission to visit the women's camp whenever it suited her.

Hobhouse couldn't wait. The next day she was standing at the entrance. It was a tent camp only a few kilometres from Bloemfontein, out in the veld, just like that. Not a tree, no shade at all anywhere for the 2000 women and children, plus a handful of men—*hensoppers*. Where to begin? The sister of a woman she had met in Cape Town was said to be here, a Mrs Botha. She would look her up first. She found her sweltering in one of the thin canvas tents, with her five children and a native servant. Each had a blanket, nothing more, no beds, no chairs, no table, only a small chest to store food.

Other women came to the tent, with more shocking details. When it rained, the tents flooded. Many children were ill. There was a separate tent for people with measles. More and more were dying. As they were speaking, Hobhouse noticed a snake slither into the tent, a puffadder, the women said, quite poisonous. While they went for help, Hobhouse attacked it with her parasol. Just imagine that happening at night, when everyone was asleep on the ground. Hobhouse wasn't able to drive it away, but the women returned with a man, who killed the snake with a hammer.

Hobhouse had seen and heard enough to form a first impression. What a disgrace! She would talk to the person in charge of the camps, Major R.B. Cray. As they spoke, their roles were reversed and in the end it was Cray who complained to her. He had no resources: no money, no equipment, no transport. He was at his wits' end. Perhaps she had connections who would be willing to help. She did at least have her trucks half-filled with food supplies and clothing. But it was a drop in the ocean. Far more was needed. In the first place, a separate tent for the deceased awaiting burial, who at present were left in their living quarters. More clean water—the water obtained from the Modder River contained typhoid bacteria. Insufficient wood was available to boil it. Milk and soap were in short supply. Schooling for the hundreds of children in the camp. Protection for the women: many soldiers were present in the camp. A bilingual woman director.

Cray appreciated her recommendations. However, he took ill a few days later, leaving the camp without a commander. His temporary replacement, Captain Hume, was indifferent to the suffering of his charges. He was not the kind of man Hobhouse could work with.

Hobhouse described the conditions in a lengthy letter to her aunt Mary, which was delivered by an acquaintance in order to bypass the censors. The camps were 'murder to the children'. Fifty people, mostly children, had died in the preceding six or seven weeks. If nothing was done, the mortality rate would increase. And this was only one of the camps. As far as she knew, tens of thousands of Boer women and children were incarcerated. And they weren't refugees who were there for their own safety, as the authorities claimed. They were prisoners, she said, detained against their will. Indeed, the whole of Bloemfontein was a prison of sorts. She had seen Mrs Steyn, the president's wife, in the street on several occasions, always tailed by a soldier with a bayonet on his rifle. She had also heard about a separate camp for Africans, which evidently held about 500 prisoners.

Couldn't her aunt write a letter to *The Times*? Lord Hobhouse, a member of the Judicial Committee of the Privy Council, was a man of high standing and Lady Hobhouse was influential in her own right. Could they make an appeal to the conscience of the British people? The lives of women and children were at stake. Word had it that Kitchener was intending to denude the whole of the highveld. They had already started in the Transvaal. Many more women and children would be sent to the camps as a result. Whether it was true or not, she couldn't say. Nor could she confirm the rumour that Christiaan de Wet, apparently heading south with 4000 men, had passed within 25 kilometres of Bloemfontein on the night of 31 January 1901. In any event, 7000 soldiers had been sent to pursue them. Hopefully he would escape this time, too.[51]

De Wet was indeed on his way to the Cape Colony again, not with 4000 but 3000 men. The rest of the account was true. It was also true that the British columns were close on his heels, as usual, and as usual they had arrived just too late. He had gone his own way again, regardless of Botha and Smuts's plans. They had wanted to discuss the possibility of a joint action with De Wet, but he hadn't responded to their invitation. He had more faith in the letters that had come in from his own officers. Assistant Chief Commandant Hertzog, Commandant Kritzinger and Captain Scheepers had been operating in the Cape since December 1900 and were optimistic about the mood among the Afrikaners. De Wet just needed to appear in person, they said, to unleash a mass uprising. In addition, the recent wave of destruction carried out by British troops demanded some form of reprisal, and President Steyn would like to see something done on or around 14 February 1901, exactly a year after Roberts's invasion of the Orange Free State.

This encouraged De Wet to try again. The main problem was that the British knew about his plan and were desperate to stop him. Kitchener had even withdrawn two columns from his 'dragnet operation' in the eastern Transvaal to go after him, while extra troops were being transferred by train to the border area in order to apprehend him there. His only advantage was that no one knew *where* he was planning to cross the Orange, whether he was on the east or the west side of the Bloemfontein–Cape Town railway line. He had made his previous attempt in the east, in November 1900, and he was heading in the same direction again. Or, rather, he had sent out his generals, Froneman and Fourie, with large contingents of men to give the British that impression. The ruse was successful. De Wet and a smaller unit, which included Steyn and the rest of the government, set off in the opposite direction. On 10 February 1901 they crossed the Orange at Sand Drift, about 60 kilometres west of the railway. He had finally reached the Cape Colony.

But what to do now? They had covered more than 400 kilometres since leaving the northern Orange Free State and the journey had taken its toll. Hundreds of men, afraid of what was to come, had dropped out on the way. All told, there weren't many more than 2000 men left. They had lost some of their horses, and those that remained were worn out. And good grazing turned out to be scarce in the Cape. Locusts had eaten the grass. It rained incessantly, but that didn't solve the problem. In the circumstances, De Wet decided it would be wise to wait for those who had remained behind, particularly Fourie's men.

It was a huge gamble, because the area they were in was cut off by railway lines on three sides. If the British acted quickly, they could destroy the advantage that De Wet's diversionary tactic had given them. And that is exactly what happened. Combat troops brought in by train blocked De Wet's route. He couldn't continue south and penetrate deeper into the Cape Colony. Only a small contingent of about 50 men led by Lieutenant Wynand Malan managed to get through. De Wet and his main force had no option but to go west. There, too, a railway line obstructed their path, but they managed to cross it under cover of darkness. It meant riding or, more accurately, struggling all through the night: the last stretch was marshland. It was hard enough to negotiate in normal conditions, but after the downpours of the preceding few days it was gruelling. The water came up to their saddles, the mud to their knees. Their horses were exhausted and could hardly move. The men had to dismount and lead them by their reins—and leave behind the many that collapsed. Getting the wagons through was almost impossible. They managed to transport the few guns they had with them, using up to 50 oxen for each one. The wagons with munitions and maize meal were, however, hopelessly stranded. Even the invincible De Wet was close to despair. He left Fourie behind with 100 men to make a last attempt to save their supplies. If they didn't succeed, they were to blow them up before the British arrived. He and his main force continued on their way.

By first light—it was 15 February—they crossed the railway line. A few kilometres further, they found grass for the horses and sheep for the men to slaughter. It was a relief after their ordeal in the night. But it hadn't really been worthwhile. Covered in mud, the men looked like scarecrows. More than 200 horses had died, and they had heard gunfire in the distance. They had lost their wagons and supplies as well. There was little time to catch their breath. The British were on their way. The following day De Wet decided to press on, leaving the 300 men on foot to make their way back to the Free State on their own. However, their pursuers were approaching rapidly, so they continued walking with the rest, carrying their rifles, saddles and blankets over their shoulders. The route south was still obstructed, so De Wet veered off to the north-west.

On 19 February he found himself back at the Orange, at the point where the Brak River joins it from the south. He had been in a similar situation before. They would have to cross the Brak to go further into the Cape, or the Orange in order to return. But the torrential rains had swollen both rivers and flooded the drifts, and the British were right behind him. The fact was inescapable: De Wet was marooned. With a heavy heart, he decided to call off the mission and at least try to save their lives. Under cover of darkness he followed the Orange upstream, leading his men past their British pursuers, hoping to find an opportunity to cross the river to the Orange Free State.

It was almost impossible. All the drifts they passed were still too deep. They spent more than a week trudging along the south bank of the Orange. Even Sand Drift, where they had entered the Cape Colony, was impassable. There, however, they met both Fourie's and Hertzog's commandos, which had been active in the western Cape since mid-December. The reinforcement was welcome, as the British had not yet given up hope of surrounding De Wet. On 16 February Kitchener had come to De Aar in person, to coordinate the operation. No fewer than 12 columns had assembled in the vicinity of Colesberg. But De Wet was in luck. The fifteenth drift they reached—Botha's Drift—was shallow enough for them to cross. This time the name was auspicious. On 28 February 1901 the Free State commandos crossed the Orange. The men were overjoyed to be back on their own territory. The British troops continued to hunt them down, driven by frustration more than by anything else. On 11 March they were forced to acknowledge that they had failed yet again. For the third time, Christiaan de Wet had eluded a massive manhunt.

Another miraculous escape earned him a reputation as the elusive Boer Pimpernel—and rightly so. De Wet was a brilliant tactician, a master of the unexpected manoeuvre, a wizard at taking his adversaries by surprise. As a strategist, he was a loose cannon. His actions had done nothing to improve the chances of the Boers successfully invading the Cape Colony and a subsequent uprising among the Afrikaners living there. On the contrary, through his wilfulness, his impatience and his failure to make adequate preparations, he not only shot himself in the foot, but Botha and Smuts as well.

This is not to say that a joint action by Transvalers and Free Staters—the Cyferfontein variant, carefully planned and executed—would have accomplished what they wanted. But it would definitely have made things more difficult for the British. The way things had gone now, their limited incursions had given the British ample opportunity to take precautions. By declaring martial law and requisitioning arms, munitions, horses and food supplies in the sensitive regions, the British had deprived the invading Boers and their potential supporters of vital resources. The uprising in the Cape Colony, the great ambition for the Boers and the worst nightmare for the British, had been forestalled for the time being.[52]

Dead horse

Ou Wapad, February 1901

Deneys Reitz was intending to set off early that morning, but he was concerned about his brother's chestnut. As he was untying its fetters, the animal had savaged his arm. It had never behaved like that before. He saddled up all the same and rode off, following the oxwagon on which Arend was travelling. They would be several kilometres ahead by now. Some time later he realised that all was not well. The horse was foaming at the mouth and nostrils, which he knew to be a symptom of African horsesickness. He led the animal to an abandoned farm a little further along and put him in the shade. That was his only hope. He knew he was clutching at straws, but one could never tell. An hour later, the horse was dead.

This was his third horse to die of the dreaded disease within the space of a few weeks. He had been devastated the first time. He was still in the eastern Transvaal, at the time, in the vicinity of Ermelo, with Beyers's commando. One morning his roan had come limping back from where it had been grazing. He had known at once. 'Nosing against me he seemed to appeal for help', but there was nothing he could do. 'In less than an hour, with a final plunge, he fell dead at my feet.' The loss of his 'dear old roan' affected him deeply. 'A close bond had grown up between us in the long months since the war started, during which he had carried me so well.'

There had been other partings in that time, as well. Botha had remained in the Transvaal. Beyers and his men had gone north, to the Waterberg, where most of them came from. The Afrikander Cavalry had no ties with any particular town. Their new commander, Jan Nagel, had decided to return to the western Transvaal, to join De la Rey, and the Reitz brothers had accompanied him. Arend had given Deneys one of his two horses, a spirited animal called Malperd, which allowed only the two brothers to ride it.

After returning safe and sound to the Johannesburg area, they had spent a week in the Skurweberg, which was a serious mistake. In the rainy season it was tempting fate. The region was infested with mosquitoes carrying the horsesickness virus and the consequences were disastrous. They lost more than half their horses, including Malperd. Deneys reluctantly became part of the growing group of 'foot soldiers'. They

324

weren't much use as commandos. At that point Nagel had decided to have a word with De la Rey: he might have horses for them. Half the men accompanied him, but the rest thought it futile. They had gone north, over the Magaliesberg and into the bush. So that was the end of the Afrikander Cavalry Corps.

Deneys and Arend had also gone north, but with a different destination in mind. Their father was probably still in the vicinity of Lydenburg and they assumed he would be able to arrange horses for them. It was another interminable journey, 500 kilometres, with one horse between the two of them, but there was nothing else to be done. Before long, they had a lucky break. They came upon an outspanned oxwagon, which belonged to a woman whose husband was fighting with De la Rey. When the British were approaching she had fled with her children and a black servant, preferring the hardship of the bush to confinement in a camp. All she possessed were the belongings she had been able to carry on the oxwagon. If Deneys and Arend would lend a hand, they were welcome to join her. It was a foregone conclusion.

They had travelled some distance when Deneys suddenly realised he had forgotten something. He no longer had a horse, but he still possessed saddlebags, and he had left them at the campfire that morning. They were valuable, particularly as they contained a supply of salt that he had managed to obtain a week earlier. He couldn't just leave them behind. So it was agreed that he would borrow Arend's chestnut and go back to retrieve his possessions. He would catch up with the oxwagon the following day.

His saddlebags were still there, but the next morning the horse died. He had no option but to follow the oxwagon on foot. As the sun was blazing down, he decided to rest until it grew cooler. Looking for shade, he went into the deserted farmhouse. The floor was littered with cigarette butts, matches and other debris. The British had apparently been here, too. He also found a bundle of newspapers, eight or nine months old, and settled down to read. There was a war in China, Queen Victoria was dead, Roberts had been replaced by Kitchener—he hadn't known about any of this.

But what interested him most were the reports about Boer commandos in the Cape. He was riveted. The English papers spoke of rebels, desperadoes, bandits. To Deneys Reitz they were romantic heroes: Kritzinger, Malan and Gideon Scheepers, at 22, barely older than himself. He could picture it all. And he resolved to be part of it. No more fighting on these sad, wasted plains, no more struggling with 'sore-hoofed, unshod horses—empty stomach—naked body'. There would be enough food and whatever else one needed to show that 'you can't make a Boer turn back, if he wants to go forward'—even all the way to the ocean. He had once boasted about this to his father. Now he was going to prove it.

He had no horse, his boots were worn out, but he had made up his mind. He wouldn't go north with Arend. He wouldn't ask his father for a horse. He was going south, in search of adventure.[53]

One man's heroes were another's desperadoes. There were two schools of thought about the Boer commandos invading the Cape Colony. Seen from the Transvaal and the Orange Free State, they were freedom fighters who kept alive the hope of an uprising that would change the course of the war. To the British military authorities they were lawless marauders, criminals, saboteurs, terrorists. The Cape's civilian population was also of two minds. The Afrikaners were sympathetic and supportive. Hundreds joined them, and became known pejoratively as 'Cape rebels' by their English-speaking compatriots.

The split between the whites occurred along predictable lines. The indigenous population was virtually unanimous. The vast majority of the coloured and African people[54] were vehemently opposed to the commandos. A handful, like John Tengo Jabavu, the editor-in-chief of the influential newspaper *Imvo Zabantsundu*, protested on principle against the British undermining the independence of the Boer republics. But men like him were few and far between. By far the majority of Africans and coloureds took the side of the British against the Boers.

This isn't surprising. The non-white population of the Cape Colony stood to lose a great deal—as they did wherever the Boer commandos came to power: freedom, a decent livelihood, the basic conditions for survival. The coloured and African communities had had a taste of Boer government soon after the war broke out in November 1899. Free State commando units had invaded many parts of the Cape Colony. They not only behaved like a military invading force, brandishing Mausers to seize whatever they wanted, but they also imposed a new social order, using the sjambok to enforce it. They regarded the districts over which they took control as annexed territory, and accordingly introduced the administrative structures they were accustomed to in their own republics: their laws, their rules, their newly appointed landdrosts and their systematic subordination of coloureds and Africans. Both groups were disenfranchised, compelled to carry passes and to work on Afrikaner farms. Any form of resistance was brutally suppressed.

It wasn't difficult for black people to choose between the Boers and the British. They were more than willing to lend their support to the fight against the intruders from the north. The high commissioner,

Milner, and others were soon talking about arming them, but that was a sensitive issue for the Afrikaner Bond. The Cape prime minister, William Schreiner, depended on the support of the Afrikaners and was anxious not to antagonise them, if only out of fear of inciting an uprising. The outcome was a reluctant compromise. Small auxiliary corps of coloureds and Africans were formed in regions under threat. Schreiner took cover behind the local military commanders, over whom he had no control, but that didn't help him. He resigned in June 1900 over a dispute about sanctions against the Cape rebels.

By that time, all Boer commandos had disappeared from the Cape. Roberts's incursions into the Orange Free State and the Transvaal had demanded their attention. But they returned after December 1900, still wielding the rifle and the whip: military campaigns combined with administrative reorganisation and the oppression of the African and coloured populations. They operated in the sparsely populated and predominantly Afrikaner north-east and north-west of the Cape, steering clear of the eastern region, which had the largest black population and the most militant black auxiliary corps.[55]

Boer commando raids were not confined to the border areas. Barry Hertzog and his men, for instance, advanced deep into the colony. They ventured as far as the Hantam mountains, 600 or 700 kilometres from the Free State border, and the last range before the Atlantic Ocean. One of the places they occupied was Calvinia, a small farming town with a few thousand Khoikhoi and San inhabitants, and a few hundred Afrikaners. There was nothing remarkable about this occupation, other than that it exemplified the way the Boer commandos operated in hostile territory, intentionally and unintentionally.

On 12 January 1901 Commandant Charles Niewoudt proclaimed himself landdrost and swiftly issued a warrant for the arrest of 14 'suspects'. He had got their names from Afrikaners living in the area. Nine of the detainees were coloureds, one being the local blacksmith, Abraham Esau, the undisputed leader of the coloured community. Esau had been educated at an English mission school. He felt and lived like a 'Coloured Englishman'. For months he had been trying to mount resistance against the Boers and, unsuccessfully, to secure arms for his community. As far as Niewoudt was concerned, the case was cut and dried: a coloured who thought he was an Englishman, and a troublemaker to boot. He would teach him a lesson.

On 15 January Esau was tried by Field Cornet Carl van der Merwe. The hearing didn't take long. He was convicted of slander against the Boers and of arming coloureds, and sentenced to 25 lashes. He was tied to a eucalyptus tree. Van der Merwe administered the punishment. After 17 lashes Esau lost consciousness. He was untied, held upright and beaten between the eyes with a stick. When he fell to the ground, he was kicked from all sides.

That wasn't the end of it. He was tortured for several weeks. Finally, on 5 February, on Van der Merwe's orders, Esau was shackled, bound between two horses and dragged a few kilometres outside the village. There, Stephanus Strydom shot and killed him. The Boer commando left Calvinia the following day. A British column was approaching.[56]

Abraham Esau's death caused an uproar. In Calvinia, a mob of angry protesters threatened the Boer fighters, who fired warning shots to disperse them. The English press, in the colony and overseas, was scandalised. Politicians, especially in Cape Town, were furious. Milner had known Esau, or was at least aware of his insistent requests for the coloured community to be armed, and considered him 'a most respectable, and for his class in life (a village blacksmith) superior man—far more civilised than the average Boer farmer'. Milner saw a pattern in it all: after Morgendaal and De Kock, now Esau. Murderous barbarians, those Boers.

In London these incidents had the effect of polarising political opinion. Salisbury had reorganised his Cabinet after the Khaki election of October 1900. At 70, he was no longer coping adequately with the combined offices of prime minister and secretary of state for foreign affairs. At any rate, this was his associates' opinion. He resigned as foreign secretary, appointing Lansdowne to replace him. Lansdowne's position as war secretary went to St John Brodrick, who had been under-secretary in the same department and at the Foreign Office. Soon afterwards, the British army came under a new commander-in-chief as well, when in January 1901 Roberts succeeded Wolseley. Joe Chamberlain remained as state secretary for the colonies, gaining increasing influence on foreign policy.

What didn't change, in spite of Roberts's pledges to the contrary, was the military reality in South Africa. The war was far from over. No sooner had Kitchener taken command than he asked Brodrick for reinforcements, ideally troops from the overseas territories, mounted troops from British India who, unlike their own bunch, 'forget their stomachs and go for the enemy'. But Brodrick rejected the proposal. This was still supposed to be 'a white man's war', at least in the eyes of the world. Even before Roberts returned to England, the new Cabinet had agreed to send 30,000 reinforcements—and as many horses—including new contingents from Australia and New Zealand.

This decision was grist to the mill of the Liberal Opposition, particularly to principled critics of the war like David Lloyd George. On 18 February 1901 the matter was tabled in the House of Commons. It was the first parliamentary debate on South Africa in the twentieth century, and the first under the new sovereign, King Edward VII. Lloyd George delivered a fiery speech. After all the disturbing reports about burning down farms, they wanted to send more troops? What better proof of the military and moral bankruptcy of the government's policies? He had an axe to grind with one man in particular, General Bruce Hamilton, who had been responsible for the destruction of an entire village, the community of Ventersburg in the Orange Free State. 'Brute' Hamilton would be a more appropriate name, he suggested. 'This man is . . . a disgrace to the uniform he wears.'[57]

After Lloyd George it was the turn of a Conservative member, someone who had witnessed the war at close range and could speak from experience. The Conservative speakers before him had opted for a counter-attack, drawing attention to the wrongdoings of the Boers. 'Being loyal to the British Crown': that and that alone had cost the lives of well-disposed citizens like Morgendaal, De Kock and, recently, Abraham Esau. The House was in suspense to hear what the next speaker would come up with. Young though he was, he was already known to be an independent thinker. At 26, he was a national and—since his recent lecture tour of the United States—international celebrity. But this was the House of Commons, the real thing. And this was his maiden speech.

Winston Churchill didn't launch a counter-attack. He just stood there, rigid with fear. A fellow Conservative, a seasoned veteran, finally whispered a prompt, a swipe at Lloyd George. Then he was on his own. As usual, he had memorised the whole speech. His tone was moderate, his argument sensitive. Instead of attacking, he presented a defence in the form of an extraordinary trilogy.

First of all, he came to the defence of the discredited British generals: people he had come to know personally. There were few men, he assured the House, 'with better feeling, more kindness of heart, or with higher courage than General Bruce Hamilton'. Churchill didn't dwell on the specific allegations of farm burnings. Lapses, he said, are inevitable in any war, especially those in which a civilian population took part. What about the famine deliberately inflicted on Paris in the Franco-Prussian War, 30 years earlier? He could mention many more precedents, and on those grounds the British military authorities were within their rights. In his experience, the war in South Africa stood out for its unusual humanity and generosity.

But he had words of redemption for the enemy as well. 'The Boer is a curious combination of the squire and the peasant.' Under the rough clothing of the farmer there were often noble instincts. He could also understand what impelled them to take up arms. 'If I were a Boer I hope I should be fighting in the field.' Chamberlain took exception to that remark. 'That's the way to throw away seats,' he whispered to the person beside him, but Churchill only heard about it later. He continued by expressing the hope that the Boers could look forward to an honourable settlement.

But not at any price. They would have to come to terms, he made that perfectly clear. If they weren't open to reason, it should be made 'painful and perilous' for them to continue. He wholeheartedly supported the government's decision to deploy 30,000 mounted reinforcements. More than that, he proposed a British combat force in South Africa comprising 250,000 men, with casualties and troops otherwise unable to fight being automatically replaced. The next step was to augment that number at regular intervals, by another 2000 to 3000 men a month, so that the Boers 'will not only be exposed to the beating of the waves, but to the force of the rising tide'.[58]

Deneys Reitz had met men of all kinds in his time, but his new companions were in a class of their own. They were conservative backveld Boers from Rustenburg,[59] wary of his strange city ways. But they were 'brave, unspoilt men', and they got on well together.

The hardships they endured together forged a bond between them. Reitz had met them—50 horseless men hoping to meet up with De la Rey—soon after he had decided to go to the Cape. They had spent eight days together, hiding out in the Magaliesberg, taking refuge from the incessant downpour and a division of British troops. The soldiers had made themselves warm and comfortable in houses in the valley, while they had shivered under their shelter of overhanging rocks, without even dry kindling to build a fire. For eight days they had survived on biltong.

When the rain stopped, the British moved on and they descended to the valley. Reitz's boots were ruined. He had to scramble down the sharp slope on bare feet, which were badly cut and blistered. Incapacitated, he spent a fortnight lying in a tobacco shed, where the Rustenburg men nursed him. One kind soul actually walked 30 kilometres to fetch a piece of rawhide to make him a new pair of shoes. Once he had recovered, Reitz was faced with a choice. Most of his companions decided to remain where they were, rather than take the risk of crossing the exposed plains of the highveld on foot. A few decided to continue south to join De la Rey, carrying their saddles and other possessions on their shoulders. Reitz wanted to head south as well. Thirteen of them, including himself, set off together.

Fate was on their side. They passed the spot where De la Rey had set

fire to a British supply convoy in early December 1900.[60] The wreckage
was still there and Reitz thought they might be able to improvise a
serviceable oxwagon from the undamaged remnants. They succeeded. The
question of transport animals was just as easily solved. A few kilometres
on, they found a large herd of trek oxen grazing in a kloof. It was De
la Rey's reserve supply. The herdsmen allowed them to take 12, and the
Rustenburgers, who were born cattlemen, selected the best. They hewed
yokes, wove straps and rope, and a few days later the party set off in high
spirits, pleased with their ingenuity and the fruits of their handiwork.

But their mood gradually grew sombre. The land was a barren wilderness.
Reitz had seen the same devastation in the eastern Transvaal: charred ruins,
trampled crops, dead animals—the aftermath of a drive to denude the veld.
For several days they trudged through a silent wasteland without seeming
to move. Thirteen men on a life raft adrift on a smouldering sea.

They saw the first sign of life five days later, when they met a Boer
woman who had taken shelter in a gorge with her children and a native
servant. She told them that De la Rey was camped nearby, at a place called
Tafelkop. They found him the following day, in a sullen mood. There had
been an incident, a false alarm as it turned out, but his men had fled in
panic and he was angry. He was worried, too. Besides his 1000 fighters,
200 refugees had congregated around his laager with all their wagons
and possessions, and he was finding them burdensome. Reitz and his
Rustenburg comrades were welcome all the same, but he was unable to
provide them with horses. He had sent patrols to the Orange Free State for
a new consignment and was still waiting for them to return. They would
just have to be patient.

Reitz took the opportunity to explore the camp and become better
acquainted with De la Rey. Like President Kruger on his veranda in
Pretoria, De la Rey held daily meetings around his wagon to talk to his
people. He was often in the company of an eccentric man with a long
flowing beard and wild, fanatical eyes. Van Rensburg was said to be a
prophet and a visionary. De la Rey trusted him implicitly.

Reitz was sceptical by nature, but an incident that occurred a few days
later gave him pause for thought. Van Rensburg had dreamed about a
fight to the death between a black bull and a red bull. The red bull was
gored and lay dying, which Van Rensburg interpreted to mean that the
British would suffer the same fate. Almost before he had finished speaking,
with outstretched arms and eyes ablaze, he cried out, 'See who comes!'
Everyone turned to look. In the distance they saw a horseman galloping
towards them from the east. He was a courier, exhausted and covered in
dust, bringing a letter from Louis Botha. De la Rey read it at once. His

face lit up and, in a voice trembling with emotion, he announced, 'Men, believe me; the proud enemy is humbled.' The British had proposed peace talks. Botha was going to meet Kitchener. Everyone was amazed, Deneys Reitz, too, in spite of a sneaking suspicion that Van Rensburg had stage-managed the melodramatic finale. Even so, it was impressive.[61]

Contrary to Van Rensburg's account, the red bull was not at death's door. It was attempting to lure the black bull away from the herd. Or, more prosaically, Kitchener had produced the bait and Louis Botha had agreed to talk to him. In mid-February Botha's wife, Annie, brought the two men together after Kitchener had allowed her to visit her husband. The meeting would take place on 28 February 1901 in Middelburg, halfway between Pretoria and Botha's temporary quarters in the eastern Transvaal. The date was carefully chosen. The hawks, De Wet and Steyn, were hundreds of kilometres away, hunting—and being hunted—in the Cape Colony. With luck, they would be captured before the meeting and Botha would be more amenable as a result.

Botha's motives weren't entirely clear. He was a strategic thinker from both a political and a military point of view. Kitchener had taken over as commander-in-chief, Brodrick as war secretary, Edward VII the new head of state: who knows, they might come up with something new. The best way to find out was by talking to them. At least Botha would hear what the options were, and he could always think things over. Acting President Schalk Burger and the state secretary, Reitz, approved the meeting. Still, there was something about it. A private get-together with the man who was hunting down his two closest allies.

The meeting in Middelburg—on the day that De Wet and Steyn were at Botha's Drift, making their way back home—was relaxed and had an astonishing outcome. After irreconcilable opening statements—annexation or independence—and a volley of reproaches back and forth, about the camps, the deployment of coloureds and Africans and suchlike, the conversation turned to the matter of terms for a peace settlement. Five hours later, they had a plan on the table. Of course, it was subject to the approval of London and the Transvaal and Free State governments, but there it was, in black and white.

The draft peace agreement contained ten provisions: amnesty for all 'bona fide' acts of war, including those carried out by 'Cape and Natal rebels'; the immediate return of all exiled prisoners of war; a transitional period as Crown colonies, followed as soon as possible by self-government in both territories; the use of English and Dutch in schools and law courts;

respect for church property; taking over the national debt to a maximum of £1 million; compensation for the loss of horses; no further reparations; firearm licences on application; enfranchisement of non-whites to be negotiable only after the transition to self-government.

The first person Kitchener had to talk to was Milner. The high commissioner had recently been charged with the civil administration of the two new colonies and—one could call it coincidence—on the same day, 28 February, he boarded a train in Cape Town, heading north. On the journey, he received a telegram from Middelburg, reporting on the outcome of the talks. He wasn't pleased. Unlike Kitchener—and his predecessor, Roberts—Milner was soft in wartime and tough in peace. His ultimate goal was a united and anglicised South Africa and every step had to lead in that direction. This peace plan failed to do so.

Kitchener and Milner met in Bloemfontein on 2 March 1901. Milner had pleasant memories of the railway station, where less than two years earlier he had driven Kruger to despair.[62] But Kitchener was holding a stronger hand than the Boer leader had back then; or he was better at bluffing. Whatever the case, he conjured up a spectre of doom and disaster if the peace plan failed to go through. The British soldiers were fed up, he claimed, their morale was at a low ebb after their constant, futile pursuits of elusive Boer commandos. The war had to be brought to an end, if only (although he didn't say so) because his eye had fallen on the position of commander-in-chief in British India, which would soon become available.

Milner grudgingly agreed. Kitchener had a firm reputation and was popular back home. It would be foolish to ruffle his feathers. The only condition Milner categorically rejected was amnesty for the rebels in the colonies. He demanded that they be brought to justice. And with that, the agreement was submitted to London.

The British government's response came within a couple of days. A few amendments had been made to the text, mainly at Chamberlain's insistence. The most substantial changes related to the first and last points. Milner got his way in the matter of amnesty. The rebels would be tried under the law of the land. As for enfranchisement, a clause was added to the document. Pending the introduction of voting rights for 'Kaffirs'— which were to be 'limited', incidentally, in such a way 'as to secure the just predominance of the white race'—'coloured persons' were to be given the same legal status as their counterparts in the Cape Colony.

Kitchener was disappointed, Milner relieved. Botha probably wouldn't accept this, let alone the *bittereinders*, the diehards among the Boer leaders. He was right. On 7 March 1901 the proposal, now official, was forwarded to Botha, who discussed it at length with Burger and Reitz. His reply came on 15 March: out of the question. The black bull had returned to the herd.[63]

Winter of famine

Tafelkop, April 1901

It was an incredibly stupid accident. Deneys Reitz had been on commando for a year and a half; he'd often been under fire, but never harmed. A few days earlier, on 3 April, they had sat down to dinner to celebrate his nineteenth birthday, when he had yet another narrow escape. A surprise attack by the British. Shrouded in mist, the Boer fighters had managed to slip away from the column, trotting alongside their oxen. And now this. All they were doing was building a campfire. Trying to smash a log for fuel, he had thrown a large stone at it. The wood was hard and resilient, and the stone ricocheted 'like a shot from a catapult' and struck his right leg. He had an open wound, which exposed the fractured shin bone. Fortunately, one of his comrades was able to help him, and the British left them in peace for a while.

But he wasn't having much luck. Shortly before the accident 200 wild horses had been delivered from the Orange Free State. To share them among 300 men, De la Rey decided to raffle them. Reitz's companions hadn't done badly; nine of the 12 Rustenburg men had won a new horse, but he had drawn a blank. His only solace was the pleasure of watching the horses being broken in.

A few weeks later, Reitz was hobbling around the laager with his leg in a splint. He still had no horse. Winter was approaching, no more horses would be brought in, and he was afraid of becoming 'a permanent camp dweller'. His fortunes changed. One morning, a group of Germans led by Field Cornet Mayer arrived at the camp. They had a few spare horses; Reitz was there like a shot. If he wanted to join them, they would give him a small grey mare. His leg hadn't healed completely, but he agreed without a moment's hesitation. An opportunity like this wouldn't come his way again. He took leave of his comrades and set off with the Germans, in search of De la Rey.

The going was worse than he had expected. His leg throbbed and ached with every step the horse took, and the weather had taken a turn for the worse. It hadn't troubled him in the shelter of the laager, but out here, on the plains, they were exposed to the bitter cold, to piercing winds and suffocating clouds of dust. At night he lay shivering under a threadbare blanket, listening to the crackle of ice in the pools.

Three days later they met De la Rey's commandos at Hartbeespoort. There was also a large British force in the area and an encounter was inevitable. Reitz didn't take part. De la Rey had come by while one of the Germans was attending to his leg. On seeing it, he had sent Reitz to the field hospital, which had been set up in a deserted farmhouse. The doctor, a young Dutchman, prescribed a few days' rest. One morning, Reitz was awoken by the sound of gunfire. The British were approaching, and even the sick and wounded were forced to flee. He rejoined the Germans, but it didn't come to a serious clash. The Boers were too heavily outnumbered and decided to withdraw.

De la Rey seemed unconcerned. In the afternoon he called a halt in a wood, and addressed his men. Dry humour with a serious undertone, that was his style, and it worked like a charm. There wasn't a murmur when he announced that they would have to ride through the night. Even Reitz could cope. The rest had done him good and his leg was not as painful. It was a clear night, affording a good view of a comet that had been visible in the sky for some time. Its tail was in the form of the letter V. The prophet Van Rensburg was explaining that it stood for *vrede*, the Afrikaans word for peace, when suddenly, a voice called out of the dark: No, Mr van Rensburg, 'it means *Vlug* [retreat].' The night was filled with half-suppressed chuckles. The oracle said no more.[64]

Flee again or settle for peace? Neither Botha nor the other Transvaal leaders had made up their minds. They had rejected Kitchener's proposals out of hand, but in their hearts they were still troubled. The situation seemed to be deteriorating by the day, winter was setting in, and they had no idea whether they could still expect anything of Europe. They hadn't heard from Kruger, officially still their president, since his departure in September 1900. Nor had there been news from the delegation or from Leyds. By the same token, they probably had no idea what was happening in the Transvaal. They kept sending couriers to Lourenço Marques, but they had presumably been intercepted. In any event, none had returned. They had to find some other way to communicate.

Desperate times called for desperate measures. On 14 March 1901 Botha sent for Johan Bierens de Haan, the surgeon and head of the first Dutch ambulance.[65] The two men met in Ermelo, where Botha made an astonishing request, the more so considering the shortage of physicians in the field. Would Bierens de Haan be willing to return to the Netherlands? It was vital for President Kruger to be informed about the situation, and the Red Cross doctor would not only be a trustworthy emissary, but also above suspicion. Bierens de Haan was reluctant to abandon the sick and wounded Boer fighters, but Botha managed to convince him that the mission was of paramount importance.

To ensure that the Red Cross was not compromised, he wouldn't take any documents with him. He was given a briefing by Botha, Burger and Reitz and access to confidential information in the war files, which had been unearthed for his benefit. On that basis he compiled a summary of the relevant facts, committed them to memory and burned his papers before reaching the British front. On arrival in Lourenço Marques, on 24 April, he wrote it all out again so as to convey the information to Kruger and the others as accurately as possible.

It was a depressing account. The Boers were running out of weapons, ammunition, food, clothing, horses, money, everything. Could supplies be sent from Europe, through German South West Africa perhaps? Moreover, there were 20,000 men, at most, who were still carrying arms, two-thirds in the Transvaal and a third in the Orange Free State. The black population was becoming increasingly hostile towards the commandos and more threatening towards their women and children. The British were strengthening their reinforcements, particularly around the railways, and deploying more coloureds and Africans as scouts and guards. They were arming them as well. The Boer fighters were 'disconsolate' about the plight of their families. They were either abandoned among the ruins of their farms, with no means of subsistence, or transported in open trucks to camps where they were mistreated by the *hensoppers* and deprived of food and drink. Many children were dying. Could they send emergency relief from Europe? With winter around the corner, Burger, Reitz and Botha were 'pessimistic about the future'. They were still intending to 'keep up the fight to the end', but if nothing changed, they would probably be 'compelled to lay down their arms'.[66]

Botha wisely kept this conclusion to himself when he finally met Christiaan de Wet again, in late March 1901. They had arranged to meet in Vrede, in the northern Orange Free State, to reconcile their differences and restore a basis of trust. Both had some explaining to do: De Wet about his unauthorised incursions into the Cape Colony, Botha about his unilateral decision to negotiate with Kitchener. Both of those projects had led nowhere. They would do better working together. In any event, this was the understanding on which the military leaders of the Transvaal and the Orange Free State parted company: continue the struggle.[67]

But winter set in. There was no change for the better. April passed. Bierens de Haan had only recently left the country. The Transvaal leaders were again overcome with despair. On 10 May 1901 they held a military council meeting on a farm called De Emigratie, near Ermelo. Besides Burger,

Reitz and Botha, it was attended by generals Smuts, Ben Viljoen and Chris Botha. They reached a unanimous decision. Now they needed to hear what Kruger thought of it. They assumed that the British wouldn't allow Bierens de Haan to return, in which case they would ask Kitchener, as a favour, to allow them to send official envoys back and forth. If he refused, they would request a ceasefire in order to discuss the situation with their people.

The proposal had far-reaching implications which, this time, they did discuss with their allies. Reitz wrote a letter to the Orange Free State government that same day, listing five reasons to support his case. The first two were about the loss of men and matériel. Burghers were defecting in droves, and soon there would be none left. Their supply of weapons was virtually depleted. The remaining three reasons were to do with morale. The government was losing its authority, the leaders their personal influence, and the people their trust. They couldn't 'allow things to continue as they are'. It was time 'to take decisive measures'.

President Steyn agreed, but drew a different conclusion. He had been confronted with the Transvalers' indecisiveness before—first on 1 June 1900, the day before the fall of Pretoria—and it usually threw him into a rage,[68] as it did now. On 15 May he sent two letters in reply, an official one to Reitz and a personal note to Smuts, venting his indignation. Shortages of everything, weapons, food, you name it, they had that in the Orange Free State as well; 'apathy among burghers and officers', too. But give up the struggle? The cause they had espoused for the sake of the Transvaal? Never. If the Transvalers were to desert the Free Staters and the rebels in the Cape and Natal, it would be the end of the Afrikaner nation. For the nation to survive, 'we must demonstrate that now through our perseverance and strength to fight and *suffer*'.[69]

This time, Steyn's withering reply wasn't enough to sway the Transvaal leaders. They stubbornly persisted in their plan to contact Kruger, but by other means, by sending telegrams instead of emissaries. For that, too, they needed Kitchener's consent, and again they used a Dutch intermediary.

On 22 May 1901 the consul-general of the Netherlands, F.J. Domela Nieuwenhuis, was summoned to Melrose House. British headquarters had received a request from Botha for permission to use the Dutch cipher code to communicate with Kruger by telegram. Kitchener had consented. If the Dutch consul-general agreed, the idea was to collect the telegram in Standerton, a town in the south-eastern Transvaal, between the Vaal and the railway line to Natal. Domela Nieuwenhuis thought the procedure unnecessarily complicated—couldn't Botha's representatives come to Pretoria?—but in the end he consented. On 26 May he took the train to Standerton, accompanied by the vice-consul, A.D Roosegaarde Bisschop.

The Boer representatives hadn't yet arrived, so Domela Nieuwenhuis returned, leaving his vice-consul to wait for them. Smuts only got there on 1 June, accompanied by a secretary, both of them blindfolded. Roosegaarde Bisschop received the telegram for Kruger from them and returned to Pretoria a day later. He translated the text into French and converted it into their cipher code. On 3 June the telegram was sent to The Hague.[70]

Willem Leyds was taken aback. In mid-April, not long before, someone had delivered a message from F.W. Reitz. It had been encouraging: they still had sufficient weapons and food, meat and maize meal—monotonous but adequate. Clothing was in short supply, some men were reduced to wearing sheepskins, but they were determined to carry on. They seemed to be managing.

And now this. He had received two disturbing messages, one after another, the note from Bierens de Haan and Smuts's telegram. Leyds knew that Smuts wasn't pessimistic by nature. This made it all the more worrying. 'Our circumstances are dire,' he wrote. Their weapon supplies were almost depleted. Farms and food supplies had been destroyed. Women and children were imprisoned in camps, or roaming in woods and mountains. Some had been murdered by Swazis and Zulus. 'Virtually all the kaffir tribes in the north' were rebellious. Burghers were defecting to the British side. If nothing was done, it would end in an even bigger catastrophe. In spite of it all, Smuts admitted honestly, the president of the Orange Free State wouldn't hear of giving up. He had urgently called for a conference, which was to be held as soon as a reply came from Kruger. They hadn't heard from him for the past eight months. They wanted 'a full, final statement so that we know where we stand'.[71]

This was no easy question. Leyds didn't know the answer and the delegation wasn't much help: Fischer was wary, Wessels invisible, Wolmarans a loose cannon. Nothing to be achieved there. They couldn't even agree on where Kruger should be, let alone what he should do. Montagu White, the Transvaal consul to the United States, initially thought the old Boer leader should go there, to win sympathy. But then perhaps not, because it might harm his image. Or maybe later. Wolmarans urged Kruger to settle in The Hague, close to the royal court, the nobility, the government and the diplomatic corps. Leyds thought it a terrible idea for exactly the same reason. He went to great lengths to persuade Wolmarans of the undesirable diplomatic implications, and refused to give in. In January 1901 Kruger installed himself in Hotel des Pays-Bas in Utrecht; in April he moved to a guest house, Casa Cara, in Hilversum.

That's where they held the meeting to discuss a reply to Smuts.

Leyds was best equipped to deal with the factual matters, and so he did. Intervention by one of the powers wasn't on the cards. It was impossible to get weapons through. He had tried and failed. However, judging by reports from England, the prospects in the Cape Colony weren't unfavourable. Moreover, British public opinion was shifting in favour of the Boers. Everything possible was being done to help the women and children in the camps, the prisoners of war in exile, too. Those were the facts as they stood. But the answer to the most important question had to come from the president himself. Make peace or persevere? Kruger left nothing in doubt. The two republics had started the war together, he felt; both had already made huge sacrifices 'in possessions and lives', and they should pull together to the end. Even if, 'God forbid, the situation became hopeless and further resistance impossible'. In other words, they should continue to fight together until it was no longer feasible. This was the wording of the telegram to Smuts, signed by Leyds and Fischer on Kruger's behalf. On 11 June it was coded and sent to Pretoria.[72]

The reply was received by the consul-general, Domela Nieuwenhuis, who had it deciphered and sealed in an envelope, ready to be collected. But, again, Kitchener wouldn't hear of the enemy making use of his communication lines, for security reasons. Roosegaarde Bisschop would have to go to Standerton again. Kitchener laid on a special train, this time with all due ceremony and privileges. He probably had high expectations. The train was escorted by 100 men, it stopped nowhere, the regular service was held up, and the military railway staff were 'most accommodating'. On 15 June 1901 Roosegaarde Bisschop delivered Kruger's telegram to a grateful Smuts.

The British had apparently failed to crack the Dutch cipher code (though they did later), or otherwise Kitchener wouldn't have taken the trouble to have the telegram delivered so quickly. This boosted the Transvaal leaders' morale, as did the outcome of two recent encounters on the battlefield. On 29 May, General Jan Kemp had inflicted heavy losses on a British column at Vlakfontein in the western Transvaal. And on 12 June, General Chris Muller had overpowered an Australian unit of around 350 men of the 5th Victorian Mounted Rifles at Wilmansrust, near Ermelo. Their weapons, which included pom-poms, were more than welcome, not to mention their ammunition, clothing and food.

Burger, Reitz, Botha and Smuts had regained their confidence, to the surprise of Steyn and De Wet, who on 20 June 1901 had come to the meeting in Waterval, in the vicinity of Standerton, feeling indignant and apprehensive. Hertzog, De la Rey and Viljoen were present as well. All the most important Transvaal and Free State leaders were meeting face to face for the first time since Cyferfontein, eight months earlier. It was high time they did. Little had come of the Cyferfontein resolution. Steyn opened the meeting by denouncing the Transvalers' unauthorised peace initiatives, although this hadn't come to the point where he would have to fight on alone. To his relief, he noted that their 'indecisiveness appeared to have vanished' as a result of Kruger's message. They had closed ranks again. Unanimously they reaffirmed their commitment to peace only on condition of independence for both republics. In addition, the Transvalers agreed to organise a raid on the Cape in support of the Free State men who were already operating there. De la Rey would equip the expedition, Smuts would be in command.

To inform the burghers, they published a General Notice that same day. It explained the telegrams they had exchanged with President Kruger and included a report on the 'Conference of the Governments of the Two Republics'. They claimed that the Waterval resolution had the support of 'the vast majority of our nation, women and children as well as men'. The crux of the notice was that 'no peace will be made nor terms for peace accepted which would divest us of our independence and autonomous existence as a nation, or harm the interests of our brothers in the colonies [Natal and the Cape], and that the war shall be continued with vigour'.[73]

Emily Hobhouse was excited at the prospect—although she also had misgivings that she wouldn't admit to. She would keep her vow before a full audience in the Queen's Hall. There, she would tell the British people about the suffering of the Boer women and their children. That was the mission she had sworn to accomplish. The date had been set for 24 June 1901 and 2500 people were expected. 'The musical centre of the Empire' was sold out. John Percival, the bishop of Hereford, was to chair the evening. Then it all fell apart. On government orders, the theatre cancelled the contract. Her talk was called off on account of the risk of public disturbances. An alternative venue, Westminster Chapel, rejected her application. The great public event in London failed to materialise.

Hobhouse thought it was worse for those pitiful women trapped in the war zone in South Africa, thousands of kilometres away. She felt she had let them down. They were brave, but they and their sick, undernourished children were entirely on their own. Who else would plead their cause? She had witnessed the atrocities with her own eyes. For three months, from late January to the end of April, she had visited internment camps, which were euphemistically called refugee camps. At any rate, she had seen as much as Kitchener would allow her to. And there was Milner as well. Once he had been appointed to administer the two new colonies, he had become

341

less accommodating than in the past. Besides Bloemfontein, she had visited five more camps: Norvals Pont, Aliwal North and Springfontein in the Orange River Colony, as well as those in Kimberley and Mafeking, but she had been denied access to the area north of Bloemfontein and to the whole of the Transvaal.

From what she had seen, the camps were all much of a muchness. Some were marginally less unsanitary than others, some were administered by men with at least a modicum of concern for the welfare of their charges, and here and there she met dedicated nurses. But on the whole, conditions in the overcrowded and unhygienic camps were abominable. People slept on the ground in leaky tents, deprived of sufficient food, milk, water and soap. The ablution facilities were disgraceful. No provision was made for the sick or for disposal of the bodies of the dead. Women and children were without warm clothing for the approaching winter.

The military authorities were indifferent. The camps were congested, with catastrophic consequences. While travelling back and forth between them, Hobhouse had seen transports of women and children, crowded like animals in open railway trucks, unprotected against wind and rain. As a result of her campaign, conditions at the Bloemfontein camp had started to improve when, a few weeks later, 2000 new inmates arrived, doubling the population and inevitably aggravating the problem. This, finally, had prompted her decision to return to England. She had done all she could, she had been denied access to other camps, the military regime prevented her from doing anything more. The only way forward, she believed, was to campaign in Britain, in the hope that a public outcry would compel the British government to intervene. And once this was accomplished, she would return to South Africa.[74]

Hobhouse sailed from Cape Town on the *Saxon* on 8 May 1901. As it happened, Milner was also on board. He had taken a few months' leave; Kitchener was replacing him as high commissioner during his absence. Hobhouse made several attempts to speak to Milner in private, but he seemed to be avoiding her. Only after they had passed Madeira did an opportunity present itself. In the course of their conversation she discovered the reason for his unwillingness to meet her. In the preceding months he had received 64 reports, all containing the same allegations against her. She was accused of inciting unrest in the camps and playing at politics. He himself, Milner could assure her, was nevertheless willing to allow her to return to the country, but it was ultimately for the government to decide.

The *Saxon* docked in Southampton on 24 May. The administrator and the activist parted ways. Emily Hobhouse went to her bedsit in

Chelsea. Alfred Milner was received by four Cabinet members—Salisbury, Chamberlain, Balfour and Lansdowne—and the commander-in-chief, Roberts. He was driven to Marlborough House in an open landau to appear before King Edward VII. He left Marlborough as Lord Milner, Baron of St James's and Cape Town.[75]

Hobhouse threw herself into her work, trying to gain access to politicians. She succeeded, through influential connections in Liberal circles. Her uncle and aunt, Lord and Lady Hobhouse, were also able to help her, as was Lord Ripon, Chamberlain's predecessor as secretary of state for the colonies and, as of late, president of the South African Women and Children's Distress Fund. Through them she met the Opposition leader, Campbell-Bannerman, and other prominent Liberal parliamentarians.

The war minister, Brodrick, also agreed to receive her. She went to see him on 4 June, bearing a list of recommendations. First, she demanded the release of all women and children in the camps who had relatives or friends in the Cape or who would be able to provide for themselves there, irrespective of whether their husbands were *hensoppers*, prisoners of war, deceased or still active in the field. No more women or children were to be sent to the already overcrowded camps. Every camp was to have a bilingual woman director. And finally, she asked the authorities to appoint a supervisory committee with at least six members representing philanthropic organisations. Hobhouse, of course, offered her services. In the circumstances her proposals were reasonable. Brodrick listened to her politely, agreed to consider her ideas, but promised nothing.

His indifference stood in sharp contrast to Campbell-Bannerman's outrage a week later. The Opposition leader had been trying to steer a middle course between the pro-Boer and the Liberal Imperialist factions in his party, but his meeting with Hobhouse tipped the scales. At a dinner on 14 June he delivered an uncharacteristically emotional speech to his party members. He outlined the atrocities Hobhouse had described and denounced the reign of terror against the civilian populations of the Transvaal and the Orange Free State. 'War is war,' he said, quoting Brodrick's usual laconic response to this kind of criticism, but in Campbell-Bannerman's view, this was no longer a war. 'When is a war not a war?' His reply left a lasting impression on his audience. 'When it is carried on by methods of barbarism in South Africa.'[76]

Methods of barbarism. Campbell-Bannerman had called the devil by its name. His words echoed in the press and resounded throughout the country. Normally harsh critics, like Lloyd George, expressed their indignation in even stronger terms. In a debate in the Commons three days later he grilled Brodrick about the number of women and children in the camps and the mortality rate. The figures Brodrick cited—a total of 63,000 persons in both white and black camps, and 336 deaths in the Transvaal camps in May alone—were far too low, but they were also considerably higher than those which the government had conceded previously. In response, Lloyd George accused the Cabinet of pursuing 'a policy of extermination'. Whether intentional or not, he said, this was the outcome. The military authorities had embarked on their mission to depopulate the highveld six months earlier and enough time had elapsed to bring the camps up to standard. Hundreds of children were dying each month. It was an utter disgrace.

But Brodrick stuck to his guns, arguing, as always, that the Boers and their guerrilla activities were to blame; their wives and children were sent to the camps in their own best interest. He denied allegations of neglect. They were doing all they could to improve conditions in the camps. The majority of Conservatives were satisfied. Lloyd George's no-confidence motion was defeated, with the Liberal Imperialists abstaining from voting.

The document that had caused all the upheaval was released a day later, on 18 June. The 'Report of a Visit to the Camps of Women and Children in the Cape and Orange River Colonies' held no surprises. Soon after her arrival, Hobhouse had circulated drafts of it among supporters and opponents alike. The 15-page final version described the problems and set out recommendations to improve the situation. In an appendix she reported on her interviews in the camps.

She had succeeded in drawing public attention to the suffering of Boer women and children, but what had that actually achieved? The Cabinet had brushed off the criticism like dandruff. She had been refused permission to organise a mass demonstration in London. She was invited to give talks in other parts of the country, but none of them were on the same scale as the one in the Queen's Hall.

There was another bitter disappointment. In mid-July 1901 Hobhouse received Brodrick's reply to her recommendations. A few had been adopted, certain categories of women would be allowed to leave the camps. A special commission would be appointed, but, contrary to her proposal, it would be instructed to conduct further investigations, not exercise supervision. Six women were already being considered for the job: two physicians, a nurse, a labour inspector and a general's wife. The commission would be headed by the prominent protofeminist Mrs Millicent Fawcett. Brodrick described the candidates as women who were 'removed from the suspicion of partiality to the system adopted or the reverse'—which, as he observed, did not apply to Emily Hobhouse.

Her report and lectures had generated 'much controversy'. Her presence anywhere near the camps would not be tolerated.[77]

Deneys Reitz had lost all sense of time. It was still winter, that was clear; it seemed endless this year. But was it August? Or still July? Since he had left De la Rey's camp at the end of May, one uneventful day had flowed into the next and it was hard to tell them apart. The nights, too, had all been the same; actually it was more like one long, bitterly cold night, interrupted only by the occasional gallop to warm up. Biltong, day in and day out. He could hardly remember what bread, salt, coffee, vegetables or tobacco tasted like. Nor did he have much of a plan. With Jan Kemp's commando he had dodged British columns in the western Transvaal. He had taken part in an unsuccessful raid in Bechuanaland, crisscrossed the Orange Free State with a steadily dwindling group of Germans, and finally fallen in with Jacobus Bosman, a young Afrikaner who was making his way back to the Cape. That's what Reitz was aiming for as well, and the reason why they were now travelling together.

He was despondent about what he'd seen on the way—the same 'interminable plains devoid of human life', abandoned homesteads, sheep clubbed or knifed to death, unploughed fields, 'an infinite, unpeopled wasteland . . . even the natives having fled'. Once or twice they had come across laagers occupied by women and children, scores of them, taking refuge in caves or kloofs. That, anything, rather than being imprisoned in camps.

It had also become more difficult to cross the railway line that bisected the Orange Free State. They had succeeded twice, but at Edenburg they'd been forced to abandon their third attempt. The British had been tightening up security to guard their strategic lines of communication. They had built a cordon of blockhouses at regular intervals, with barbed-wire barriers filling the gaps between them. Sentries, both black and white, were stationed at each one. In their third attempt to cross the tracks, Reitz's horse had become entangled in the barbed wire. Alerted by the ensuing noise, the sentries on duty had shot and killed it. Reitz managed to escape on a Shetland pony he had found roaming near a British camp a few days earlier.

So Reitz and Bosman were still on the west side of the railway line, but they had managed to get further south. Near Fauresmith they ran into trouble again. Three attempts were made to relieve them of their saddles and saddlebags. The first time, they had caught the thieves, but allowed them to go. The men had probably mistaken them for British spies. The second time, in Fauresmith itself, two 'forbidding guardian angels' had saved them from being robbed by a band of 'riffraff' who had been 'ejected from the fighting commandos'. On the third occasion Reitz had apprehended the thieves, and grazed the arm of one of them with a bullet 'to teach him better manners'.

Soon afterwards, they fell in with better company: General Hertzog, 'a high-cheeked man with angry eyes', who was in command of the south-western districts, and his 300 men. Reitz had known him in Bloemfontein, where he had been a judge in the old days. He and Bosman were delighted to join Hertzog. They were also hoping that some of his men would want to accompany them on their journey to the Cape. In the event, they were unable to recruit even one. Everyone had been there on commando before and they were still smarting from the ordeal and their heavy losses. It looked as if Reitz and Bosman would have to continue on their own.

One morning, however, they found luck on their side. A small group of ten young Transvalers turned up, some of whom Reitz knew from the Pretoria Commando and the Afrikander Cavalry Corps. Though weather-beaten and ragged, they still had a sense of humour. The 'Rijk Seksie' (Rich Section), they called themselves. They were making for the Cape. Things couldn't have worked out better. The 12 of them would press on together.

The following day they took leave of Hertzog and his men, and headed south-east, where people who knew the area had advised them to cross the Orange. They would find fewer British troops, more wild horses and good grazing. But it did mean they would have to cross the railway line again. They returned to Edenburg, fortunately in the company of burghers who knew their way around and could guide them safely past the blockhouses and through the barbed-wire barricade.

All went well. Near the Caledon River they came upon troops of wild horses. Each man took two, Reitz a brown mare and a roan. Within a few days they were broken in. On their fresh mounts they rode almost all the way to the Orange. Across the river lay the Cape Colony. It was the end of August 1901. Reitz had found his bearings.[78]

Banished for life

Zastron, August 1901

Deneys Reitz was in for an even bigger surprise. His ragged companions had come as a blessing. The Dirty Dozen were ready to enter the Cape Colony. The morning they were preparing to set off on the last stretch to the Orange, a large body of horsemen came riding towards them over the hills in the distance. They were Boers, as was clear from the way they rode. But who were they? An hour later the horsemen were close enough for Reitz to recognise the man at their head. It was none other than Jan Smuts. He had met him earlier in the war, right after the fall of Pretoria, in the vicinity of the First Factory.[79] At the time, Smuts had been the state attorney, a colleague of his father's, but he had since gained a reputation as a general as well. There was only one reason for him to be here: he was also on his way to the Cape. That was the biggest blessing of all.

Smuts was pleased, too, and welcomed the reinforcement. His journey from the western Transvaal to the south-east of the Orange Free State had been strenuous. The British had got wind of his plan to invade the Cape and had done their utmost to obstruct him. Smuts had escaped by moving swiftly and fighting hard, sustaining a heavy toll in casualties. He now had barely 200 men left. They were all fine young fighters from the western Transvaal, the pick of De la Rey's men, and these 12 would fit in well. He intended to deploy them as scouts.

Reitz was eager to serve under Smuts. He was also pleasantly surprised to come across a few more old acquaintances, among them his Hollander uncle, Jan Mulder, with whom he had fought in Natal almost two years earlier. According to Mulder, Smuts was probably intending to take a half-moon route to the central region of the Cape Colony and from there launch a 'flying raid'. His object was to investigate the feasibility of a large-scale invasion and, at the same time, relieve the pressure on the commandos in the north. Smuts himself said nothing about his plan, but Reitz had every confidence in him. Whatever he was doing, he wanted to be part of it.

That afternoon Smuts gave the order to set off for the Orange. Around five o'clock they could discern a dark line in the distance marking the gorge through which the river flowed. This was the border between the two territories. But there was something else on the horizon as well. British

347

soldiers were stationed along the edge of the cliff, forming a cordon to prevent them from reaching the drifts. Smuts decided to retreat and spend the night under cover, hoping to run into someone familiar with the terrain who might know of another place to cross.

The following day they had two lucky breaks. A group of 50 local burghers under Louis Wessels came to join them, and with them was an elderly man who was able to guide them to a long-forgotten drift. The footpath that led to it was steeper than the horses could manage, but it was their only chance. There were also British columns approaching from the north, and if they remained where they were, they would be surrounded the next day.

Setting off at dusk, they reached the path at three in the morning. They descended in darkness, walking their horses down the gorge. The next obstacle was the river itself. It wasn't wide, but in the turbulence of the water gushing down from the mountain it was difficult for the horses to maintain their footing. It was sunrise by the time the last man reached the other side. They had made it into the Cape Colony.[80]

These had been frustrating months for Lord Kitchener of Khartoum. February 1901 seemed promising. There were the talks with Botha in Middelburg, the third manhunt for De Wet—and Steyn—which he had coordinated personally. The war could have been over, just like that. But March had brought disappointment. De Wet and Steyn had eluded them as usual, Botha had changed his mind, and in May they had taken him for the same ride again. The Transvaal leaders' request to telegraph Kruger had given him new hope. Apparently they were still wavering. But from the reply they had received from Europe, peace was clearly not on the horizon. On the contrary, it seemed to have strengthened their resolve to keep up the fight. The tone of the General Notice they had drafted on 20 June in collaboration with the Free State authorities had been militant.

Only three weeks later did Kitchener discover just how desperate the Transvalers had been. In the early morning of 11 July 1901 a column led by General Broadwood carried out a surprise attack on the village of Reitz—named after the former president, now state secretary of the Transvaal—in the north-east of the Orange Free State. The village's name was ironic, the spoils prodigious. The British captured almost every single member of the Free State government, including 29 administrative staff, and in addition made off with more than £11,000 in cash plus all the government's official documents. Among them was the anguished letter Reitz had sent the Free Staters on behalf of the Transvaal government on 10 May, and with it Steyn's indignant reply of 15 May. It was mortifying for the Transvaal leaders, Reitz in particular, especially when Kitchener relayed the letters to London, where they were published on 19 July. The discord between the Boer leaders was out in the open.

But it was embarrassing for Kitchener, too. He had hounded the Transvaal leaders to a point where they were about to surrender, and then allowed them to slip through his fingers—like De Wet, who was always getting away at the very last minute. And Broadwood's action also fitted the mould: an excellent haul, but not quite the jackpot. One of the Boers at Reitz had been hurriedly woken by his Griqua *agterryer*, Jan Ruiter, who helped him mount his horse. Ruiter too had managed to hoodwink the British. 'Just an old Boer,' he had shouted, as his master slipped away. It was President Steyn, the soul of the Boer resistance, the man who more than once had prevented the Transvalers from capitulating. He was still riding around free.[81]

It was always nearly but not quite. The frustration must have driven him wild. Kitchener was all the more determined to tighten the screws. In May 1901 the strength of the British army in South Africa peaked at 240,000 troops—equalling the entire Boer population—a third of whom were mounted. In other words, the British had 12 times more men than the 20,000 the Boers could raise. And with 100 heavy guns, 420 field guns and 60 pom-poms, they were also superior in firepower. But it wasn't just a question of numbers. At the end of the day it was about deploying human and other resources effectively, organising the drives and filling the bags.

Kitchener had thought up a new system to achieve this. It was already being used, but in March 1901 he decided to make it more effective by applying it methodically and consistently. First, he would erect blockhouses with barbed-wire barriers running between them along both sides of every railway line, then rows of them at right angles to obstruct the enemy's movements. The idea was to divide the endless highveld into manageable plots, leaving the Boer fighters and their families with no means of escape. Mobile columns would be assigned to plots, which they would sweep clean of human life, livestock and crops. The system would work beautifully, like an iron spiderweb. The British would make their move, the enemy would be snared.

The scheme took logistics and labour. The standardised round blockhouses were initially made from bricks and mortar, later from corrugated iron. Thousands upon thousands were built. Huge quantities of building materials were needed and had to be transported and offloaded. The same applied to the thousands of kilometres of barbed wire that formed the barriers between these miniature forts. Finally, they had to be manned. Between five and 20 troops were stationed in each blockhouse;

in the end, a total of 60,000 men. Another three or four coloured or African sentries were assigned to each, that is, an additional 25,000 men. It made a considerable dent in the available manpower, but Kitchener was convinced it would work.

It certainly would, in combination with targeted individual sanctions. The Boer leaders' General Notice had given Kitchener an idea. Discipline had never been the commandos' strongest point, but those who were still fighting seemed to obey orders from their leaders. It was time to strike at those leaders personally. This had also been done before: Roberts and Buller had burned down Christiaan de Wet's and Louis Botha's farms, but the measure hadn't been applied systematically. Kitchener would take care of that.

On 7 August 1901 he published a proclamation with an ultimatum to all the Boers' political and military leaders, from commandants down to the heads of 'armed bands'. Anyone who hadn't surrendered by 15 September would be 'exiled from South Africa for life'. Moreover, those who had families in the camps would be required to pay for their maintenance. He would hit them where it hurt the most.[82]

On the other hand, perhaps South Africa should rid itself of the Boers altogether. That would actually be the best solution, Kitchener thought. He ran the idea past Brodrick, Roberts and Milner in his letters. About half the Boer population was already incarcerated—100,000 men, women and children in internment camps, 20,000 men in prisoner-of-war camps overseas, and they would undoubtedly continue to be a burden, even after the war. So why not deal with the problem now, once and for all? If they were all packed off, maybe to the Fiji islands, the whole country would be safe and there would be plenty of room for new British colonists.

Kitchener wasn't the only one who thought along these lines. The idea that the Boers should settle somewhere else cropped up from time to time. It could be in Africa—Madagascar, for instance, or German South West Africa—or perhaps another continent. Willem Leyds had heard some of these wild plans before. But the letter he received in late August 1901 was in a class of its own, if only because of the person who sent it.

The 61-year-old Hiram Maxim was an American by birth, a British subject by naturalisation and one of the last people on whom Queen Victoria bestowed a knighthood. The actual ceremony was conducted by her son the Prince of Wales. The honour was conferred for his accomplishments as an inventor. Although his claim to inventing the lightbulb was debatable, he definitely held patents on the mousetrap, the merry-go-round and—presumably the most appreciated—the machine gun. He gave his name to the Maxim gun, the fearsome pom-pom which, along with the Mauser repeating rifle, was responsible for the deluge of bullets unleashed on the South African battlefields. And they came from both sides. His invention was sold to the Boers as well as the British.

He was, as he professed at the beginning of his letter to President Kruger, well disposed to the Boers. 'The Boers are Dutch and, like all Dutchmen, are the bravest of the brave.' But bravery wasn't everything; there were also numbers to consider. That's what the British had. A few scores of thousands of soldiers more or less didn't make too much difference. That's why they would win hands down, while the Boers were doomed to lose. Maxim had thought up a plan to protect them from complete annihilation. The Boers would leave South Africa en masse to establish a new colony in the north of Mexico. The landscape and climate there were comparable to the Transvaal's for human habitation, and better for raising cattle. There was plenty of land for sale; he had made enquiries. It would take planning and there would be costs involved, but he had an answer for that as well. The owners of the gold mines and other stakeholders, who had lost so much because of the war, would be only too willing to finance the whole enterprise. And in the end, 'Mexico would become a great country completely in the control of the descendants of the Boers'.[83]

Maxim received a polite letter of thanks for his trouble, but his proposal was not taken seriously. His ulterior motives were just too obvious. He was simply putting new words to an old tune: buy out or buy off the Boer leaders. Leyds had seen and heard it all before. Earlier that month he had been approached by another luminary in the world of international business, at least, indirectly, as is the usual way.

On 6 August 1901 a certain Simon Zadoks de Moerkerk had called on the envoy in Brussels, with a letter of introduction from a Berlin lawyer with whom Leyds was on good terms. Leyds had gone to The Hague, with Zadoks hot on his heels. They spoke together a few days later. Zadoks turned out to be a Dutch national, employed in the financial sector in Paris, and he was representing the most important banker in the city. He wasn't at liberty to disclose his name. Rothschild, of course, Leyds concluded. The message Zadoks conveyed on his behalf was studded with hints and insinuations, but the gist of it was perfectly clear. The continuing state of war in South Africa was not only ruining the Boers, it was also costing the French financial world a fortune. The bankers there, 'without wishing to become involved in politics', were 'prepared to make sacrifices to compensate [the Boers] up to a point for the losses they had incurred'. Leyds knew what he was implying and cut him short, to Zadoks's obvious annoyance.

A week later, Zadoks was badgering him for another appointment.

Leyds grudgingly agreed. They settled on a meeting in Brussels, on 15 August. This time Zadoks spoke plainly, albeit with 'greasy' tact. The story was basically the same. A speedy end to the war would be best for the Boers as well as the French shareholders in the gold mines. Then he mentioned a figure. His principal in Paris would consider £400,000—and the one in London even more, he added.

Leyds had heard enough. He could either show the man the door, or bait him for more information. He placed his bets on the latter. The following day Zadoks wrote him a letter, with a separate postscript attached. The message was as good as explicit. In the event of a personal peace initiative, 'all benefits, moral and otherwise' were for him. 'And otherwise': meaning the £400,000. Again Leyds found himself in a quandary. Should he expose them? To him it was crystal clear. The Paris Rothschilds were blatantly trying to bribe him, perhaps with the knowledge of the London branch. But was that enough to convince the outside world?

After mulling it over and sounding out Fischer, he decided against. He was a good enough lawyer to know what would happen. They would deny the accusation, of course. They would argue that he had misinterpreted the note, that they had meant something entirely different. In any event, what would he gain by publishing it? The incident ended in a compromise. He didn't bring the story out into the open. He ignored Zadoks's further attempts to contact him. But what he did do was send the whole file to De Giers, his Russian counterpart in Brussels, who was still reporting directly to Tsar Nicholas II. He had to do something to let off steam.[84]

Emily Hobhouse saw publicity as the only option. In late September the war ministry had released its statistics for June to August. She was shocked. The situation had apparently deteriorated dramatically in her absence, and this was just going by the official figures. By the end of August the number of Boers in internment camps had risen to 15,000 men, 40,000 women and 50,000 children: 105,000 in all. To judge by the mortality rate, the conditions must have been horrific. In those three months alone, 4067 people had died, 3245 of them children. Hobhouse made another appeal to the war minister, Brodrick, on behalf of the people interned in the camps, this time in an open letter to *The Times* of 29 September 1901.

Three months had passed since she had initially approached him, she began, but instead of doing something he had opted for an investigation. Mrs Fawcett and her Ladies Commission had gone out to the camps, but she felt that they weren't working efficiently. For one thing, they hadn't consulted her, whereas she was the one with practical experience. A lot of time had been wasted, resulting in '3245 children who have closed their eyes for ever since last I saw you'. If things continued like that, the rest would soon follow. She urged him in the name of compassion to deal with the situation. Brodrick would surely be moved to heed 'the cry of the children'?[85]

Hobhouse's impassioned plea was understandable. Her report on conditions in the camps had opened people's eyes and hearts in Britain and subsequently on the Continent. Relief agencies were established in countries like the Netherlands, Germany and the United States to alleviate the suffering of the Boers in camps and prisons. Portugal, too, offered humanitarian aid. It took in almost a thousand refugees from the Transvaal, settling them first in Mozambique and subsequently in its home territory.[86]

But nothing practical was done, no emergency aid was provided to alleviate the misery. Nor could it be, without the cooperation of the authorities running the camps. And these were still British soldiers, who had more important priorities than the well-being of their enemies' women and children. Although Milner had been responsible for the civil administration of the two new colonies since February 1901, in practice his authority hadn't yet been extended to the management of the camps. In any case, he had been in England since early May, and his responsibilities had been transferred to Kitchener.

The commander-in-chief wasn't interested in the camps in the first place. His stock reply was that the problem had been thrust upon him because of the tactics the Boer commandos were choosing to employ. As for the high mortality rate among children, he had an answer to that as well. The Boer women, he wrote to Brodrick, were themselves to blame. Their disregard for hygiene was tantamount to 'criminal neglect'. Come to think of it, they ought to be charged with murder.

The Ladies Commission gave serious consideration to this point. As soon as they started their tour of the camps in August 1901 they came to the same conclusions as Emily Hobhouse. As far as health was concerned, the conditions were alarming, especially for children. There were frequent outbreaks of measles and other infectious diseases. However, the causes they identified differed from Hobhouse's. They enumerated three: polluted air, soil and water as a result of the continuing war, the inmates' failure to observe the elementary rules of hygiene and medical care, and—it was true—shortcomings in the management of the camps.

Those were the main findings of the report that Fawcett presented on her return to England, in December 1901. But, to Hobhouse's relief, the commission had made a number of practical recommendations before leaving South Africa. They called for regular inspections, additional qualified physicians and nurses, improved medical facilities, increased rations and the dismissal of incompetent staff.

It is hard to say whether anything would have come of the recommendations if it had been up to Kitchener and his military apparatus. But after mid-November 1901 the question didn't arise. Brodrick, the minister responsible, had never taken much notice of the criticism, nor did he bother to respond to Hobhouse's open letter in *The Times*. His experienced colleague, the colonial secretary, was more concerned about the public outcry. Chamberlain insisted that responsibility for the management of the camps be transferred to the civil authority. Milner had been back in South Africa since mid-September. He should be able to put an end to the problem. Brodrick offered little resistance. From then on, Chamberlain shouldered the political responsibility for the camps, and Milner administrative responsibility.

The difference was apparent at once. The mortality rate, which in October 1901 had risen to 3200, including 2700 children, began to decline. The improvement was slight in the first two months, but spectacular after January 1902, falling to less than 200 in May 1902.[87]

Winston Churchill had little in common with Emily Hobhouse, but he was just as critical, if not more so, of the war minister, Brodrick. Ostensibly his reasons were different, but both of them raised essentially the same objections. They felt that Brodrick was out of touch with the realities of South Africa, and as a result had little understanding of the matters for which he was responsible. But that was as far as Churchill's and Hobhouse's ideas coincided. Churchill said almost nothing about the internment camps, at least not publicly. He was mainly interested in the way the war was being fought, and there was enough wrong with that, in his immodest opinion.

In his second debate in the Commons, on 12 March 1901, a good three weeks after his maiden speech, Churchill had still stood firmly behind the minister. The issue at hand was about the dismissal of a general, something he felt Brodrick was entirely within his rights to authorise. He had argued that parliament had nothing to do with staff management. In his third speech, however, on 13 May, he played a completely different tune. Brodrick had tabled a motion to reform the army. The gist of it was that the British army should be modelled on the Continental example. In the first place, it should be bigger in order to respond more effectively to acute crisis situations, like the outbreak of war in South Africa.

Churchill thought it a bad, half-baked idea, and made no secret of his views. He said it was contrary to the nature of the British to have a larger standing army. Britain was different; it shouldn't become embroiled in

European disputes. His father, Lord Randolph, had said the same in the Commons 15 years earlier, and he endorsed his words wholeheartedly. Such an army was pointless. It would always be too small to play a significant role in the European context, it was too expensive, and it wouldn't have ended the campaign against the Boers any sooner. The problem in South Africa was not the number of British soldiers. There were other reasons for their lack of progress in the war.[88]

Churchill's attack on Brodrick met with disapproval from his fellow party members, but his conviction remained firm. In mid-July 1901 he and four other young, critical Conservatives formed a parliamentary faction known as the Hughligans, the name alluding to its leader, Lord Hugh Cecil, Lord Salisbury's youngest son. The group held weekly debates attended by prominent guests, Conservatives as well as Liberals. These debates sharpened Churchill's independent mind. He gradually moved to the left, on the issue of the war in South Africa as well, but not as regards its ultimate goal. He was and remained a 'victory-at-any-price man', standing squarely behind Chamberlain and Milner. In a debate on the financing of the war, on 17 July, he was one of the staunchest defenders of the government policy. 'Let us finish this job in style.'[89]

Britain's military policy, however, continued to trouble him. He had become closely acquainted with many senior officers during his stay in South Africa, and Churchill was a man who nurtured his friendships. He was still receiving excellent inside information about the progress of the war, which didn't please him. Things came to a head when Kitchener issued his proclamation of 7 August, with the threat of exile 'for life' to Boer leaders who failed to surrender by 15 September. This was the wrong way to go, according to Churchill's informants. The threat had no impact on Steyn, De Wet, Botha or anyone else; this much was evident from their response. It had no effect whatsoever other than to provoke another outpouring of sympathy in the European press.

In the first week of October 1901 Churchill went into action. In a series of six lectures in Conservative clubs, five of them in his constituency, Oldham, he talked about men and horses—literally, because if the British forces in South Africa were short of anything, it was 'suitable men . . . mounted on the best horses'. Men as such were there in abundance, he said. That wasn't the problem. It was about quality. They weren't deployed effectively. The Boer commandos had to be fought by their own means. This meant far better reconnaissance, more individual initiative and, most of all, real mobility, which depended on sufficient numbers of good horses. They were in short supply and the majority of those available were unsuited to heavy work. According to Brodrick, no fewer than 69 columns were active in the war zone, but Churchill had heard from a reliable source that virtually none of them had two horses per person. And that, he knew from his own experience in the cavalry, was essential not only to get the better of men like De Wet and Botha, but also to force them into submission.

Kitchener's threats, like his tendency to over-centralise, were self-defeating. What it came down to, he quipped—and this always won them over—was 'not to punish the Boers who have been caught, but to catch those who are still running about'. In Churchill's opinion the situation had deteriorated over the previous year. It wasn't safe anywhere beyond five kilometres of British positions either in the former Boer republics or in the Cape and northern Natal.

This couldn't continue. If Brodrick was unable to do anything about it, Salisbury and Balfour would have to assume responsibility and give Kitchener a nudge in the right direction. The war in South Africa was too important to be left in the hands of an ordinary minister. It needed determination and perseverance to achieve victory. Churchill would hear nothing about leniency towards the Boers, but reprisals and cruelty were not the answer either. They had to be defeated, and the nightmare had to come to an end. This was a sacred commitment, if only to the British soldiers who had fallen in the struggle. You could open a newspaper any day of the week and find the name of someone you knew—as had recently happened to Churchill with regard to his cousin R.B. Sheridan—'and learn that some bright eye known and trusted is closed for ever'.[90]

Black death

Herschel, September 1901

The men responsible for Lieutenant Sheridan's death had themselves narrowly escaped only a few weeks earlier. After crossing the Orange on the night of 3 September 1901, Smuts and his men found themselves in the Cape Colony. Formally, it was British territory, but the first inhabitants they encountered were Africans from neighbouring Basutoland. No 'European habitations' were to be seen. Deneys Reitz saw only the occasional kraal. The men separated into smaller parties and went foraging for tobacco and fodder.

Everything was fine. They thought nothing of it when a group of about 300 Sotho came riding towards them. They were armed, some with rifles, others carried battle-axes, assegais and knobkieries. Smuts ordered them to close in, that was all. The Boers continued on their way. The Sotho wouldn't contemplate attacking 'a white force equal to their own'. Reitz's group, which included his uncle, Jan Mulder, and five other men, took their time, allowing their horses to feed from 'the grain baskets to be found in any native village'. After a while, they noticed they had fallen far behind the commando. They had seen the last men disappear from view as they descended from the plateau to the plain beyond. The stragglers mounted their horses and rode on, but on reaching the edge of the plateau, they realised there was danger ahead. Their route led past a mission church with a low wall on the right. Directly opposite it, across their path, was a shelf of overhanging rock. It would be a good spot for an ambush.

The Sotho had also seen its potential. Leaving their horses on the plateau, they had taken positions on the rocks, their eyes fixed on the Boers making their way down. Their intentions were clearly hostile. Reitz's party gathered quickly to confer. They decided to descend and catch up with their force as quickly as possible. At first everything went well. Then suddenly there was a thunderous volley of rifle fire, not from the left, but the right, from inside the church. Bullets flew through the windows, bringing down showers of splintered glass. No one was hurt. Five of the men dug their spurs in and sped off. Reitz and his uncle abandoned their pack-horses and took cover behind a boulder. They had only a few seconds to reach a decision. They were being attacked from all sides and would have to make a run for it. Their only option was to continue down the path.

Under cover of the crag, they broke into a gallop and then, mustering all their courage, stormed through the hail of bullets. Keeping their heads down, they galloped on at breakneck speed. Out of the corner of his eye, Reitz saw more Sotho warriors emerge from behind the wall. Assegais and knobkieries flew past his ears. About 20 metres further, the trail took a sharp bend and fell away into the valley. That was their salvation. But there was still another obstacle to overcome. Blocking their path were some 15 to 20 Sotho men. They were squatting in a circle, engrossed in an object that lay on the ground between them. They could do little more than leap to their feet, brandishing their weapons. Reitz and Mulder galloped past in a flash. They were safe.

As soon as they were out of range of their assailants, they paused to take stock of the damage. Miraculously, they had both come out unscathed. Their horses, however, were badly wounded. Mulder's had taken two bullets to its hind legs, but the wounds looked superficial and they believed the horse would recover. Reitz's brown mare had been less fortunate. Her lower jaw had been shattered and there was nothing to be done except put the 'poor animal out of her misery'. The men continued on foot, Mulder leading their wounded horse and Reitz with his saddle slung over his shoulders. A few hours later they caught up with their commando. The only consolation was that their two pack-horses had fled and followed the group, and here they were now, with their blankets and cooking tins intact. Two of their five comrades had also escaped unharmed. No one knew what had become of the other three. They had probably been killed and 'dreadfully mutilated by the natives for medicine, in accordance with their barbarous custom'. Reitz had his suspicions about the men they had seen squatting on the trail.[91]

The attack by the Sotho wasn't as surprising as Reitz thought. The company they had run into belonged to the Herschel Mounted Police. This was an auxiliary corps of a few hundred men set up by the British expressly to prevent incursions by Boer commandos. Similar border police units, recruited from the coloured community, were operating in the north-western Cape as well, like the Border Scouts, the Bushmanland Borderers and the Namaqualand Border Scouts. As the war progressed the British were engaging increasing numbers of Africans and coloureds to perform various duties, including combat, to the Boers' consternation.

The deployment of Africans and coloureds had been a bone of contention right from the early stages of the war, particularly in the sieges of Ladysmith, Kimberley and Mafeking. The two sides accused each other of violating their unwritten agreement not to involve Africans or coloureds in the war. In the case of Mafeking the allegations were justified, as both sides recruited and armed their African allies, thereby setting the Tshidi Barolong against their rivals, the Rapulana Barolong. Elsewhere, Africans and coloureds were assigned non-combatant duties, although *agterryers* were not infrequently deployed in the trenches as well.[92]

After the fall of Pretoria the deployment practices of the two parties diverged further. The number of Boer fighters in the field declined dramatically in the guerrilla stage of the war, and the number of *agterryers* even more so, if only because of the shortages of horses, food and clothing. The majority of burghers could no longer afford to engage a servant.

The British army, by contrast, continued to expand and accordingly employed significantly more auxiliaries. Africans and coloureds were initially engaged as labourers (trench diggers, porters, herdsmen, guards, even cattle-rustlers), but they were soon performing paramilitary duties as well (scouts, couriers and the like). In the guerrilla phase they took part in drives, burning down farms and transporting Boer women and children to the camps. In 1901 the numbers employed increased dramatically, with the building of thousands of blockhouses and the erection of thousands of kilometres of barbed-wire barriers. Large numbers of Africans and coloureds were deployed to transport building materials and construct the immense metal web. Finally, to implement the blockhouse system 25,000 were engaged as sentries in addition to 60,000 white soldiers.

Another difference compared with the first stage of the war was that the British were able to recruit not only from the Cape, Natal and their own protectorates of Bechuanaland and Basutoland, but also from Swaziland, formerly a protectorate of the Transvaal, as well as from the two annexed Boer republics themselves. The Boers grew increasingly anxious. The principle of racial hierarchy, one of the basic tenets of their faith, was being undermined on their own home ground. Africans and coloureds actively engaged in the war developed a growing political awareness. Previously resigned to a condition of submission, they now ventured beyond former boundaries in their relations with Boer commandos and especially their women and children.

Of major concern to the Boers was the deployment of the Kgatla in the north-western Transvaal and the Pedi in the east. The Kgatla, from neighbouring Bechuanaland, had been overtly pro-British from the beginning of the war. Their attack on Derdepoort on 25 November 1899 had been the Boers' first (shocking) confrontation with African auxiliaries deployed in the war. The incident had been followed by a series of reprisals from both sides. On Kitchener's orders, the Kgatla chief, Lentshwe, had been encouraged to carry out raids on the Transvaal. Towards the end of 1901 the Kgatla were supplied with weapons for that purpose, and had consequently gained control of the entire region north-west of Rustenburg.[93]

As for the Pedi of the eastern Transvaal, there had been tensions between them and the Boers for decades. The Pedi had been subdued in 1879, in the period of British administration,[94] when their chief, Sekhukhune, was imprisoned, and ever since they had sought to regain independence. At the outbreak of war the Boers had sent a large armed force to maintain control of the area. This was effective, but after the fall of Pretoria in June 1900 the troops were redeployed to strengthen Botha's main force. The Pedi saw their chance. Those who had aligned themselves with the Boers were sidelined. New leaders rose to power. When the British assumed control of the region, they took advantage of the new balance of power. In April 1901 Major-General Walter Kitchener, the commander-in-chief's younger brother, reached an agreement on mutual cooperation with Sekhukhune II, Malekutu and Mpisane. Since then, the Pedi and the Boers had been in a state of open war, with both sides committing atrocities. As a result, the commandos were unable to move freely through the eastern Transvaal.[95]

The Boer force was declining and becoming increasingly white, while the British army flourished and became more ethnically mixed. This must have caused consternation among the Boers, particularly because of its implications for another sensitive issue, namely the arming of Africans and coloureds in British service. Under Roberts the instructions had been clear. Africans and coloureds were to be deployed only as 'non-combatants'. They were not to wear uniforms or bear arms, or serve as scouts or couriers.

His successor, Kitchener, adopted a more flexible approach to the 'colour line'. On taking office he asked Brodrick to send Indian cavalry regiments from British India to South Africa. The request was turned down, but London had little, if any, control over the way Kitchener deployed 'natives' under his jurisdiction. In December 1900 Africans and coloureds who possessed rifles and agreed to serve as British scouts were exempted from the requirement to surrender their arms. Their numbers in the British army subsequently escalated.

The Boers denounced this, arguing that it contravened 'the rules of civilised warfare'. The matter had been mentioned explicitly in a report for Kruger, of which Bierens de Haan received a copy in March 1901.[96] In the same month Christiaan de Wet complained to Kitchener that 'a great majority' of the British troops were African or coloured. Other Boer commandants and their political leaders made similar allegations. Schalk Burger and F.W. Reitz protested directly to Lord Salisbury against the deployment of 'these wild ruffians' who, on several occasions, had killed prisoners of war 'in a barbarous fashion'—with British troops looking on.

The strongest backlash came in July 1901 from Pieter Kritzinger, whom De Wet had since appointed assistant chief commandant of the Free State commandos in the Cape Colony. He warned that his men would execute Africans or coloureds serving in the British army, regardless of whether they were armed. A few months later he added that the same would apply to those who passed on information about the Boer commandos.

In response to Kritzinger's announcement, Kitchener, and then Brodrick and the rest of the British Cabinet, threw caution to the winds. It was no empty threat. African and coloured prisoners of war were already being subjected to summary execution. It had become routine, whether they were carrying weapons or not. They should all be armed as quickly as possible, Brodrick insisted in parliament. They should at least be in a position to defend themselves and not have to 'stand there in cold blood to be shot'.

Liberal opponents like Lloyd George warned that this was the start of a slippery slope. If they took that route, Africans and coloureds serving in other capacities would be armed as well. He was right. At any rate, it applied to blockhouse sentries, who were supplied with weapons for their own safety. Just how many Africans and coloureds were armed by the end of the war was never disclosed. Even Kitchener's superiors in London weren't informed. His stock reply to Brodrick's questioning was that 'no record could possibly be kept'. In the spring of 1902 he finally mentioned a number: 10,000 men. Britain's Liberal Opposition wasn't convinced. Lloyd George estimated the total to be around 30,000. Later assessments confirmed that this was closer to the truth.[97]

So in the second half of 1901 the war in South Africa was caught up in a spiral of violence. The British increasingly transgressed their gentlemen's agreement to wage 'a white man's war'. 'There is no such agreement,' Chamberlain bluntly declared in the Commons in August 1901. More auxiliary troops and allies entered into British service, regardless of race. The Boers retaliated by limiting their application of the 'rules of civilised warfare' to white adversaries and were ruthless towards others who supported the British war effort in any manner, even in territories beyond their own borders. In the Cape Colony, in particular, Boer commandants like Kritzinger took the law into their own hands wherever they were in control, even if only temporarily.

In the second half of 1901 the Boers made incursions into other territories again, with mixed results. In July Louis Botha sent General Tobias Smuts—no relation to Jan—and his Ermelo commando on a mission to Swaziland. Their target was Steinacker's Horse, a unit of irregular troops. It was made up of some 50 whites and 300 Africans, mainly Tsonga, led by a German adventurer, Ludwig Steinacker. The British had hired him to guard the border with the Transvaal, but he interpreted his assignment more liberally. His men plundered whatever they came across. Boers, Swazis, no one was safe, not even in adjacent Mozambique. When they captured a Swazi prince, supposedly sympathetic to the Boers, the queen regent, Labotsibeni—whose young husband, King Bhunu, had died in 1899—turned to Botha for help.[98] Smuts's commando advanced on Steinacker's headquarters in Bremersdorp and wiped out his unit. They released the prince, took horses, oxen and rifles as loot, and set fire to Bremersdorp. The action was successful apart from the burning of the town, an indiscretion for which Tobias Smuts was demoted to the rank of an ordinary burgher.[99]

Louis Botha was considerably less successful. In mid-September 1901 he made another attempt in Natal. This was what they had originally planned in Cyferfontein in October 1900, except that it was supposed to have been on a far larger scale, with 15,000 Boers who would launch a joint attack on the gold mines and then fan out to the Cape and Natal.[100] In terms of numbers Botha wasn't as wide of the mark as Jan Smuts, who charged into the Cape Colony with just 250 men. But Botha's venture was also a watered-down version of the initial plan, literally and metaphorically. The elements conspired against him, as they had against Christiaan de Wet, who had tried to invade the Cape earlier. Botha and his 2000 men entered Natal in a steady downpour of icy rain, and it was still raining 11 days later when they sloshed back to the Transvaal with their tails between their legs. Botha had won one battle and led two futile attacks against British forts that were not even particularly well defended. His return to the battlefield where he had been crowned with glory two years before was a sorry affair and best forgotten.[101]

The escalating violence in the second half of 1901 coincided with a surge in war fatalities. There was no causal relationship between the two. The majority of deaths occurred not in battle, but as a result of exhaustion, malnutrition and epidemics in the British internment camps. By September there were nearly 50 of these camps, located along the railway lines in the two annexed republics, Natal and the Cape Colony. They held a total of between 110,000 and 115,000 Boers, mostly women and children. The population remained relatively stable up to the end of the war.

Improvements in the camps' administration had some effect in reducing mortality. After peaking in October, the death rate declined gradually at first and more substantially in time. Nevertheless, the final toll—which was revealed only after the war—was shocking. A total of 27,927 Boers died in the British internment camps: 1676 men, 4177 women and 22,074 children.[102]

It wasn't only the Boers who were confined to camps. Africans and coloureds in the Transvaal and Orange Free State were held in similar conditions, with the same catastrophic results. In May 1902 their numbers matched those of the Boers: between 110,000 and 115,000 people in 66 camps. These too were located along the railway lines, mostly in the two former republics. A total of 14,154 deaths were recorded, but post-war estimates put the number closer to 20,000. In absolute terms, the mortality rate was slightly lower than among the Boers. The main difference was the duration of their internment. The African and coloured camps were established at a more advanced stage of the war, but their populations continued to increase right up to the end.

There were other differences, too. One was the level of public attention focused on the camps. Emily Hobhouse's alarming eyewitness reports generated support in Europe, including Britain, for the Boer women and children in the 'murder camps'. But almost no one campaigned on behalf of other groups. Hobhouse and the Fawcett Commission visited only the white camps. The few reports on the African camps that reached the outside world gave a relatively good impression. The inmates were said to be resigned to the circumstances and were not particularly dissatisfied.

No effort was made to bring those camps under civil administration. They were run by the military authorities until the end of the war. In June 1901 the Native Refugee Department was established for this purpose, under the direction of a Canadian, Major G.F. de Lotbinière. Military administration had one advantage in particular, because these camps differed in another respect from those to which the Boers were consigned. Unlike the Boers, African and coloured prisoners formed a labour reserve. Most of the men were employed by the British army, generally for three-month stints. In April 1902 some 13,000 men were in service, roughly two-thirds of the camps' total male population. Civilians living in the vicinity of the camps were also allowed to employ prisoners. The men were paid a shilling a day, which wasn't unreasonable, and could spend their earnings on extra comforts available in the camps like flour, sugar, tea, coffee, candles, tobacco, clothing and blankets. This was another difference between the two groups: unlike whites, Africans and coloureds were expected to support themselves as far as possible.

For the rest, all the camps were basically the same. They had been created for the same reasons and there were no significant differences in their conditions. Black prisoners, like whites, fell into two categories: refugees who had reported to the authorities voluntarily, and those who had been rounded up in Kitchener's systematic drives. His instructions applied equally to the African and coloured population of the highveld, regardless of whether they were servants of Boer families, tenants on their land, or people living in homes of their own. They were driven out in order to deprive the Boer commandos of any form of practical or moral support.

Their camps were as squalid as the Boer camps. They too were deprived of weather-resistant tents, sufficient firewood, vegetables, milk and uncontaminated water; their sanitary facilities and medical services were likewise atrocious. Here, too, the mortality rate was high, with children in particular dying from chickenpox, measles and dysentery. The mortality curve corresponded to that in the white camps, with a two-month time lapse, peaking in December 1901. The reasons were the same. The improvements in housing, nutrition and medical services, which the Fawcett Commission had recommended, were also implemented in the camps under De Lotbinière's supervision. The army did sometimes get things right.[103]

Wild fruit. It looked like a pineapple. No one knew how to prepare it. Deneys Reitz hadn't a clue either. But it was called Hottentot's bread, so one could assume it was edible, and just as well. They had reached a wild, uninhabited region on the second ridge of the Suurberg mountains, and they were famished. One of the men roasted the fruit on the campfire. It tasted good. Others followed his example, and soon half the men were eating it, Jan Smuts along with the rest.

Reitz was pleased to see him enjoy his meal. Never before had he served under a commandant of Smuts's calibre. It was late September 1901 and they had been in the Cape Colony for over three weeks. That they were still alive and free was nothing short of a miracle and they owed it all to this taciturn, sharp-featured man. Smuts had pulled them through when they were close to despair and beyond exhaustion, urging them on day after day, night after night, through sleet and over mountaintops. He had shepherded them through British columns, too many to mention, and with impeccable timing, he had launched a decisive assault. And here they were now, within 50 kilometres of Port Elizabeth. From the top of the mountain you could probably see the Indian Ocean. No, he didn't really feel like any fruit. A couple of horses had broken free. He would just go and tether them.

The first week in the Cape had been cold and wet. Once they had shaken off the Sotho they found themselves in the more hospitable environs of Lady Grey. The locals were mostly Afrikaners, their lives seemingly untouched by the war. It came as a relief after the denuded landscapes of the Boer republics. Here, one saw men working peacefully on the land, smiling women and children, who waved gaily and welcomed them. There was coffee and sugar, salt and tobacco. Clothing was in short supply, but they would make a plan. Covered in blankets to keep off the rain, they headed south: Redskins on the warpath.

Reitz's appearance was little improved when he found an empty grain bag, cut holes in it for his head and arms, and wore it as a coat. His comrades were amused at first, but they soon followed his example. And so the first week passed. It rained incessantly, the men were frozen and miserable, the horses tired and aching. They were short of ammunition, and Louis Wessels and his men were returning to the Free State. The tattered remains of their unit bore no resemblance to a fighting force which could strike fear into the hearts of the British. Two hundred scarecrows on worn-out horses.

But still the British were doing their utmost to catch them. Ahead of them, behind them, left and right, the area was crawling with columns brought in by train to pursue them, intercept them, obstruct them. At Moordenaarspoort—Murderers' Gate!—Smuts and three men on a reconnaissance mission were caught unawares by a British patrol. The three men were killed; Smuts lost his horse, but managed to escape in the dark. He arrived back at the camp on foot in the middle of the night, to the relief of his commando. Without Smuts, Reitz believed, the expedition would have failed. His two adjutants, Jacobus van Deventer and Ben Bouwer, were 'good fighting men', but neither possessed the personality or authority that was needed to save them from 'going to pieces during that difficult period.'

Smuts's inspiring leadership proved its worth again in the second week, from 10 September. It was one long nightmare, with a fantastic ending. Smuts allowed neither his men nor himself a moment's rest. The British were closing in on all sides and the only way to escape was to keep going. No sleep, no pauses, press on. They asked locals to guide them to marshes, mountain passes or other natural barriers where they could shake off their pursuers. Sixty hours non-stop. No sooner had they crossed one railway line than they came upon the next. They had to cross that, too, and get well clear, as the train would be arriving with yet another load of British troops. Dazed from exhaustion, wherever there was a delay, at 'a fence or a ditch, whole rows of men would fall asleep on their hands and knees before their horses like Mohammedans at prayer'.

And it rained mercilessly. 'The world is under water.' The advantage was that the British, with their all-important wagons and guns, made even slower progress than they did. But the sleet sliced through bone and marrow. The night of 15 September was the worst of all. Never before had Reitz suffered so badly from the cold. Around midnight the temperature fell below zero. The grain bag 'froze solid on my body like a coat of mail'. But on they went. Had they stopped, they would have frozen to death. Men who had never uttered a word of complaint were groaning in pain. At dawn they came upon a deserted farmhouse. They staggered in, tore up everything that would burn to make a fire. They warmed themselves and dried their clothing and blankets. Fourteen of their comrades were missing and were never heard from again. Fifty or 60 horses had died. The men who survived the dreadful ordeal of that night called themselves 'the Big Rain Men'.

It sounded good, but they were in a hopeless predicament. Their days as a fighting force were over. They set off again. Those who still had horses led the way, then came 'a trail of footmen' with their saddles slung over their shoulders. The wounded men, assisted by their comrades, brought up the rear. It was a pitiful sight. Who could have imagined the amazing transformation that was to take place the following day?

Early on the morning of 17 September, Smuts sent the Rich Section—at any rate, Reitz and the few others who were still mounted—to reconnoitre the area. A few kilometres further they came upon an Afrikaner. Hoarse with anxiety, he warned them that British cavalrymen were lying in wait a short distance away, at Modderfontein. There were about 200 men with two mountain guns and more than 300 horses and mules. Smuts was sent for; he took a snap decision. This was an opportunity they couldn't afford to miss. Without those horses and some ammunition, they were done for. They would attack. There wasn't a moment to lose.

They set off without delay. Fortune was on their side. After crossing a river they took cover in a grove of trees, and from there saw 15 to 20 unsuspecting soldiers cantering straight towards them. They opened fire and killed a few, while the rest galloped away. Reitz seized the rifle and ammunition belt of one of the dead soldiers, and joined in the pursuit.

In all the excitement they almost ended up in the British camp. Their proximity threw their adversaries into confusion, but their forward position wasn't safe, in any event not until the main body of the commando caught up and gave them covering fire. At that point, they gained the advantage. They managed to put the field guns out of action, or at least dispose of their crew. Now it was up to the riflemen. The two sides were within metres of each other and a grim battle ensued. It was a man-to-man fight, at such close range that, once it was over, fragments of cordite had to be removed from Reitz's face and neck. Apart from that, he was unharmed. He had fought with all his strength and shot more than his fair share of British soldiers, including a young lieutenant. After taking the bullet, the man had risen to his feet 'still trying to level his rifle at me'. But before he could do so, another commando 'shot him through the brain'.

Reitz discovered who the lieutenant was only after the Boers had overwhelmed their adversary. Thirty British soldiers had been killed, 50 wounded and another 50 taken prisoner. They had wiped out an entire squadron of the 17th Lancers and lost only one killed and six wounded. After all they had been through, it was incredible. The Battle of Modderfontein—the British called it the Battle of Elands River—was a crucial victory. The Boer fighters regained their confidence and came out of it with everything they needed so desperately: horses, saddles, rifles, ammunition and, of course, clothing. They burned whatever they didn't need and destroyed the two guns. Reitz, too, had new gear: an officer's uniform, a Lee-Metford rifle, full bandoliers and an excellent horse, 'a little grey Arab'. It had belonged to the lieutenant. His name was Sheridan, they said, and he was a cousin of Winston Churchill. Reitz also took 'a good mule for long marches and a light nimble pony for use in action'. This was the perfect combination. After turning their prisoners loose, they left the burning camp. Reitz was in the best of spirits.

After that, it had been like a holiday. The weather improved, they continued south without mishap, crossed the Winterberg, passed through verdant countryside, received warm hospitality from the Dutch-speaking community and were stoically tolerated by the English farmers they encountered on their way. They also got reinforcement. A field cornet by the name of Botha joined their company, along with 25 men. They had been hiding out in the mountains. Near Bedford they stopped off at a shop and an inn, where the men enjoyed beer and spirits for the first time in many months. Crossing the railway line from Port Elizabeth to the interior was easily done. There were no blockhouses here.

This might explain why they became over-confident. Almost by definition, a railway line meant fresh British troops, here just like anywhere else. They were being brought in again by the thousand. The Boers could see them from their hideouts. Reitz didn't know what Smuts had in mind; a raid on Port Elizabeth, perhaps. But Smuts wasn't in a hurry. Instead of heading east or west, he gave the order to go south, into the Suurberg mountains. These were a couple of parallel ranges separated by deep rugged kloofs. He believed the men would be safe there. But he was mistaken. The British came after them, field gun and all, driving them down the steep descent of the first chain and then up the equally precipitous slope of the second.

That was where they had eaten the wild fruit. Reitz was intending to try some himself when he returned from the paddock. But he was bewildered by the sight that met his eyes. Men lay on the ground, writhing in agony, Van Deventer and Bouwer among them. Smuts had almost passed out. And that wasn't all. Something else caught Reitz's eye. The British had occupied the first chain of mountains and were making their way down the kloof. Their advance guard was already starting to climb up the other side, firing at them. Hottentot's bread. Would they come to such a humiliating end?[104]

Foray

Suurberg, October 1901

Smuts and Van Deventer were completely incapacitated. Bouwer, ill as he was, managed to order every man who could still handle a rifle to take positions on the crest and return the fire. It was nearing sunset. They would have to hold their attackers off. When night fell they would reconsider their position.

They succeeded. The British turned back and after a while lights shone on the opposite side. They were probably safe until the following day. What to do now? Half the men were seriously ill—the fruit was apparently poisonous after all—and those who weren't were famished. Should they wait for the invalids to recover? They couldn't afford to lose any time. The British would almost certainly be back before daybreak, and this time they would come in overwhelming numbers. They had to get away from here, no matter how. Fortunately, most of the sick men began to rally during the night, at least sufficiently to take a few faltering steps. About 20 were still too ill to move. Smuts was one of them, but he had come round sufficiently to take command again. He ordered them to saddle up and go deeper into the mountains. This was their only chance. Those too weak to sit upright were to be tied to their saddles. He himself had to be held on his horse.

And so they set off, shuffling down the slope into the ravine and then dragging themselves up the next peak. From a distance Reitz had been keeping an eye on Smuts. Around dawn he noticed that Smuts and the two men assisting him had fallen behind and had been spotted by British scouts. Reitz galloped to their rescue and distracted the scouts, enabling Smuts to be taken up the slope by a different route. The men assembled on the crest. Everyone had come out of it alive and, to their relief, the British had abandoned the pursuit. For the time being, at least, they were safe.

Now for something to eat. They were in the depths of the mountains, far from human habitation—well, white habitation, that is. They saw smoke rising from the forest a short distance away. Perhaps it came from a kraal, where they might find food. And, indeed, they came upon a cluster of reed huts. Their occupants had fled, but left a supply of millet behind. The Boers had eaten it before and liked it. It was simple, but at least it wasn't poisonous, and there was enough to still their hunger.

Smuts remained pale and weak for a few days, but soon recovered his determination to press on. He said nothing about his plans, but from the reconnaissance missions he ordered, Reitz assumed he was still intending to raid Port Elizabeth. From the heights they could see the town in the distance. The British were apparently also expecting Smuts to head in that direction. They assembled their troops south of the Suurberg. The Boers wouldn't be able to get through; there was only one other way out, and that was north, roughly the direction they had come from, but further to the west. It would take them into the Karoo.

They left the Suurberg before daybreak on 5 October 1901. When it grew light, Smuts called his men together. He told them they had reached a turning point in the expedition. From here on, they would start heading west and make for the Atlantic Ocean. There was still a considerable distance to cover, and to be on the safe side he would divide the force in two. Half the men would go with Van Deventer, the others with him. Reitz was pleased to be assigned to Smuts's party. That afternoon they parted from Van Deventer and his men, and continued on their way.[105]

It was a daunting list. Articles 4, 5 and 7, articles 14, 15, 16, article 23 paragraphs c, d, e, f, g, article 25, and so on, plus 11 more, all of them provisions of the Laws and Customs of War on Land, which had been drawn up at the Hague Peace Conference and signed on 29 July 1899 by 26 states, including Great Britain. In the words of Willem Leyds, the Laws and Customs were 'formally sanctioned rules of war between civilised nations', and the British had violated them, one by one: mistreatment of prisoners of war, abuse of the white flag, coercive measures and systematic violence against the civilian population; the list went on and on. Leyds hadn't compiled it himself. The list—in fact, the entire text in which it appeared—had been drafted by Asser, who had helped out as a legal ghostwriter once before.[106]

This was another letter, signed by Leyds and the three members of the delegation, Fischer, Wessels and Wolmarans, now addressed not to Lord Salisbury, but to the Permanent Court of Arbitration. Like the Convention, the new court stemmed from the Peace Conference held in The Hague two years earlier. It had also been constituted there, in April 1901. Leyds seized the opportunity to make use of it. In early May he had contacted De Beaufort, president of the administrative council of the Permanent Court of Arbitration and Dutch minister of foreign affairs, requesting advice as to how the Transvaal should go about bringing an arbitration action. He received no reply. In September he tried again. By then the political landscape had changed. On 1 August Pierson's Liberal government had been succeeded by a conservative Protestant administration under Abraham Kuyper. The new foreign affairs minister, and therefore also the new president of the administrative council, was Robert Melvil, Baron van Lynden. He was an amiable man and, in his brief term of office as secretary-general of the newly established court, an authority on the subject. Perhaps an official letter might help.

On 10 September 1901 Leyds and the other three envoys, acting on behalf of the governments of the Transvaal and the Orange Free State, asked the court to hand down an 'arbitrational ruling' on 'the war being waged in South Africa'. The main questions were 'whether grounds exist for Britain's claim that the two Republics [had] acted in a manner aimed at the oppression or expulsion of British nationals in South Africa', and whether the Transvaal and the Orange Free State had committed 'any other act' which 'by international principles, would give Britain cause to deprive them of their autonomy'.

They also urgently drew the court's attention to Britain's 'persistent violations of the rules of war'. These had started at the beginning of the war and had continued ever since. A recent example was Kitchener's proclamation of 7 August threatening the Boer leaders with lifelong exile, in flagrant violation of article 20: 'After the conclusion of peace, the repatriation of prisoners of war shall take place as speedily as possible.' There were other provisions as well that had been violated. The governments of the Transvaal and the Orange Free State would gladly submit evidence in support of their claims.

If Britain refused to cooperate, one would have to conclude 'that it was reluctant to submit to the scrutiny of a scrupulous, competent and impartial court'. In that event, Britain would be responsible for 'the continuation of the terrible and unnecessary war'. Such refusal would also amount to an implicit acknowledgement that Britain's 'conduct of the war is contrary to the principles of humanity and civilisation which it had ratified'.

This was strong language, but would it achieve anything? Even Leyds had his doubts. The new court would be getting itself into hot water. It wouldn't be wise to antagonise mighty Britain right at the start. The court would probably find grounds to declare itself incompetent to hear the case. As a contingency Asser had added to the request for 'your mediation' the phrase 'or that of the Governments you represent'. Leyds made a point of mentioning this to several people he knew in the diplomatic corps. At the opening of parliament in The Hague on 17 September, for example, he spoke to the Austro-Hungarian representative on the administrative council, Alexander Okolicsányi d'Okolicsna. He seemed to be interested.[107]

A chill ran through his body. It was stupid of him, but Deneys Reitz hadn't given it a thought. For weeks he'd been strutting around in a

British cavalry uniform, as pleased as a dog with two tails. The shiny buttons, the close-cut riding breeches, the skull-and-crossbone insignia of the formidable 17th Lancers. It had belonged to Lieutenant George Crespigny Brabazon, 4th Baron Vivian of Glynn and of Truro, which made it all the more special.

But suddenly there was an alarming piece of news. They had come to a large farm late in the evening. As soon as they arrived, the farmer, a man called Le Roux, told them what had happened. Earlier that day the British had captured a Boer fighter and executed him on the spot, for no reason other than that he was wearing a British uniform. It was Reitz's friend Jack Baxter. At the end of September Kitchener had proclaimed—Le Roux produced a newspaper to show him—that 'all Boers wearing khaki uniform are to be shot after trial by a drumhead court martial'.

He could so easily have suffered the same fate. Reitz thought about how the uniform had saved him, twice, in the past week. On both occasions British patrols had taken him for a compatriot. There was also the incident of the two Boers in khaki who ran into a party of British soldiers. On the spur of the moment, they had called out, 'Don't fire, we're 17th Lancers,' and subsequently proceeded to open fire themselves, killing two men, including Captain Watson, and wounding a third. Smuts was furious. That fateful incident may have been what prompted Kitchener's proclamation.

Whatever the case, he couldn't walk around like this anymore. Not that he felt remorse—he hadn't intended to deceive anyone. It was just that his own clothes were worn to shreds. In the end he'd been reduced to wearing a grain sack. He had worn the British uniform out of sheer necessity. Anyway, now he knew it was dangerous. Le Roux, fortunately, was comfortably off and generously provided Reitz and his companions with civilian clothes.[108]

They set off the following day. There were eight of them. Delayed by their meanderings through the Karoo—to avoid British units—they had been unable to rejoin Smuts's commando. Le Roux believed Smuts was heading for the Swartberg, about 70 kilometres south. They would have to follow his tracks. Hordes of British troops were pursuing him, so they would have to be vigilant. A party as small as theirs was vulnerable.

But they were resourceful as well and managed to forage for food on the way. At one farm they were offered a meal of fried ostrich egg; at others they took what they needed. They were often not the first to arrive. Once, in the middle of the night, in a valley in the Suurberg, they had presented themselves at the home of an Englishman. 'My God!' he exclaimed. 'First come the Boers this morning and slaughter my sheep; then come the British, who kill more sheep instead of catching the Boers, and now I am hauled out of bed at this time of night by more Boers!' From which they understood that Smuts wasn't far ahead. They would soon catch up with him.

And they would have done, had it not been for the mistake they made the following day. Thinking that the British were only preoccupied with their pursuit of Smuts, they had let their guard down. They stopped for a meal in a spot from which they had no view of their surroundings. And there, Reitz had made a second mistake. Tired after a sleepless night, he had gone to rest in the shade of a thornbush, without telling his companions.

He was suddenly woken by the sound of rifle fire close by. Still dazed, he peered through the bushes just in time to see British soldiers, standing beside their horses, blazing away at his comrades. They were galloping down the valley as fast as they could. He was the only one left. The soldiers hadn't spotted him, but they certainly would. His only chance was to head in the opposite direction. He had been too tired to unsaddle his pony, which was now a blessing in disguise. He edged forward, leapt in the saddle and galloped off. He didn't get far. The British caught sight of him and, before he knew it, he was flying through the air. His pony was riddled with bullets and he himself crashed to the ground. A sharp pain shot through his hand.

With his good hand he grabbed his rifle and took to his heels. A small grove of trees on the right offered some cover. The soldiers were still firing at him and were joined by others heading in his direction. He felt something rip his boot. At a dry watercourse he hesitated for a moment while deciding whether to descend or climb higher up the slope. He glanced back to make sure his pursuers were watching him, then he sprang into the gully. Instead of turning left or right, as the soldiers would assume, he made a dash for the opposite side. He threw himself to the ground and hid among the bushes.

The ruse worked. The British split up into two groups, one heading down to the valley, the other up the mountain. Reitz lay motionless until the sun disappeared over the horizon. Then he emerged from his shelter and limped off; a bullet had torn his boot open, and a thorn, several centimetres long, had pierced the palm of his hand when he was thrown from his horse. But he was still alive and had managed to escape. Even so, he was despondent. He was tired, injured, hungry, surrounded by enemies, stumbling in the dark, alone in a foreign country and far from home. Only Providence could save him.

It did, but through its agents on earth. At first barely audible, then gathering volume, the strains of a hymn floated on the air, voices lifted in song to the accompaniment of a harmonium. Reitz knew that friends were at hand. He knocked at the door, introduced himself and was warmly welcomed into their midst. A family of Afrikaners, eager to feed him, tend his wounds and help him on his way. It would be too dangerous for him to remain there. The coloured labourers would betray him. It was the prerogative of the head of the family, a patriarch of 70, to guide Reitz on the first part of his journey. He couldn't venture far, but he knew an old wagon path that would take Reitz in the right direction. West, that's where he was sure to find Smuts.

Not that Reitz, alone and on foot, stood much chance of overtaking him, but there was nothing else to be done. He might come across his seven companions on the way. Perhaps they had made a detour to avoid the British. He was proved to be right. That very night, by the light of the moon, he picked up their spoor and even before daybreak he had found them, asleep. All were unharmed. They were amazed to see Reitz, as they had written him off.

After conferring together, they decided to stop following Smuts's tracks, or at least not as closely as they had been doing. There were too many British columns on his heels, and they themselves had only three horses among them. It would be wiser to take a different route, through less hospitable countryside, but presumably with fewer British troops around. This meant they would have to cross the Swartberg again, cover a stretch of the Karoo again, cross the Cape Town–Bloemfontein railway line, and then veer off west to Calvinia.

They endured weeks of hunger and thirst, but, as they had hoped, encountered only the occasional British patrol. In early November they met up with Smuts's main force. It was a joyful reunion. No one, not even Smuts, had expected to see Reitz alive again. But Reitz's happiness was tinged with sorrow. Little remained of the Rich Section. Only two of its men had survived unscathed. Four had been injured, the rest killed or captured. It was the end of their small reconnaissance unit. Smuts assigned the two able-bodied men to Bouwer's commando and Reitz to his own.

Reitz considered this a promotion, a reward for having overcome so many obstacles on his way. Smuts, however, probably saw it as a way to prevent the state secretary's headstrong son from getting himself into trouble again. Be that as it may, they enjoyed the first few weeks after all the hardship and deprivation they had endured. There were few British troops here, in the western Cape, far removed from the railway lines. There was the occasional garrison and, from time to time, a column, but on the whole the men were able to breathe freely. Many more bands of rebels were roaming around the area and Smuts intended to organise them into larger commandos.

On 7 November 1901 they arrived at Elandsvlei, literally an oasis of peace, with waving palm trees and an abundance of water. This was the first time since their arrival in the Cape that they had spent more than one night in the same place. In the hills nearby Reitz caught a wild mule, 'a powerful black, who squealed and bit and threw me several times before I mastered him'. Reitz was on horseback again.[109]

The foreign minister, Van Lynden, at least had the decency to break the news personally. On 22 November 1901 Willem Leyds was summoned to the ministry. He already knew what would happen. Van Lynden was friendly, but didn't mince his words. The application from Leyds and the three other Boer envoys had been turned down. The administrative council of the Permanent Court of Arbitration had declared itself not competent to hear the matter of the Boer Republics vs Great Britain. It had a mandate to hear only administrative disputes.

This didn't come as a surprise. But luckily Leyds had already sounded out the Austro-Hungarian member of the council, Okolicsányi d'Okolicsna, about the alternative he had thought up with Asser, namely, to submit their case to the signatory states directly. In particular, they had the new American president in mind. McKinley had been assassinated in September 1901 and succeeded by his vice-president, Theodore Roosevelt, who did not, like McKinley, leave the country's foreign policy entirely in the hands of the state secretary, Hay. The son of Dutch immigrants, Roosevelt made no secret of his sympathy for the Boer cause. Who knows, he might be prepared to stick his neck out.

Leyds was still pinning his hopes on official arbitration by an influential head of state. Nothing else would work. He'd heard enough well-meant but unsound proposals, mostly from shady characters with powerful connections in the realm of politics or finance. Only the day before, 21 November, a man who called himself Francis William Fox—no one had heard of him—turned up with a document which he said might serve as a framework for peace talks. It had been drafted, he explained, by 'highly influential persons'. He had already discussed it with the Dutch prime minister, Kuyper, who had intimated that he was genuinely interested. So be it, but Leyds thought it a strange story.

His old business friend Eduard Lippert had proposed something more substantial. He had mediated on a previous occasion, at the beginning of 1899, before the war, at that time in the conflict with the Randlords.[110] In the course of 1901 he had offered his services again. In July and August, on his own initiative—but with Leyds's knowledge—he had held talks with Lord Rosebery, Lord Salisbury's Liberal predecessor. One of the matters they had discussed was the possibility of granting Leyds and the members of the delegation a safe-conduct pass to South Africa to confer with the Boer leaders. The talks between Rosebery and Lippert were broken off twice, but Lippert got in touch with Leyds again in late November. Would it be a good idea to bring the matters they had discussed to the attention of the public? Lord Rosebery was about to deliver an important speech. It might be a suitable opportunity.

Leyds didn't think it a good idea at all. He trusted Lippert, but not Rosebery. He would twist things 'to suit his own party politics' and present facts out of context, which would 'give people the wrong idea about the situation'. There hadn't been any real negotiations. 'We listened to what you had to say, as a friend of our cause, expressly on that condition.' Leyds also reminded Lippert of 'the oath of confidentiality' he had taken 'regarding this matter'.

Leyds was soon proved right. Rosebery's speech to a Liberal gathering in Chesterfield on 16 December 1901 was party political through and through. He declared himself in favour of forceful action against the Boers, who had committed 'cold-blooded massacres of natives' and the 'almost unspeakable crime of flogging and murder in cold blood of an emissary of peace'. It wouldn't be tolerated and they weren't getting away with it. But this was not to say that the two republics should be completely depopulated, as Milner had recently suggested. Such a step was going too far. Peace talks would be a reasonable alternative, Rosebery suggested. Not face to face, on the spot, but through representatives of the Boers in the Netherlands. And they should be informal—nothing official. 'Some of the greatest peaces, of the greatest settlements, in the world's history have begun with an apparently casual meeting of two travellers in a neutral inn.' The travellers he had in mind were undoubtedly Lippert and himself.

Rosebery could forget it, as far as Leyds was concerned. In an interview with *The Times* he refused to comment on Rosebery's proposition. But he let fly when it came to his allegations. They were 'monstrous and absurd' and, in any case, too vague and sweeping to entertain. Except for the one specific case that Rosebery was presumably alluding to, the death of Morgendaal. It was true, Leyds conceded, that he had been shot on Christiaan de Wet's orders. But Morgendaal wasn't an emissary at all, he continued. He was a deserter and a spy. Imagine an Irish deserter doing something like that in the camp of an Irish regiment. Wouldn't a British court martial sentence him to death?[111]

All this scheming strengthened Leyds's belief in formal diplomatic procedures. Since being turned down by the administrative committee of the Court of Arbitration, he had drafted a petition addressed to the heads of government of nine countries: Russia, France, Germany, Austria-Hungary, Italy, Switzerland, the Netherlands, Belgium and—the one he had the most faith in—the United States. The letters were sent on 17 and 18 December 1901. Besides copies of his earlier application to the court, they included an impassioned humanitarian appeal for 'an end to the deplorable conditions which so many thousands of women and children have endured since the introduction of the concentration camps in South Africa'. The death toll was such that if nothing was done, 'two nations would be annihilated'.[112]

The reports Jan Smuts drew up in mid-December 1901 sounded considerably more positive. It was all a matter of perspective and information. He couldn't have known that the mortality rate in the camps had risen alarmingly since his incursion into the Cape. Nor, for that matter, was Leyds aware that the situation was in reality far worse than the official British figures led people to believe. From a military point of view the Boer commandos in the Cape Colony were doing well, at any rate in the west, where Smuts was now in command of 2000 men. Besides his own unit, he headed another 15 or so commando units from the Transvaal, the Orange Free State and the Cape Colony itself. The forces in the eastern districts were poorly coordinated, but those west of the Cape Town–Kimberley railway line had only one problem: no horses. According to Smuts, there were thousands more Afrikaners wanting to join him, but the British had done a thorough job of 'clearing' the area of horses. If not for that, he could organise the longed-for uprising in no time at all.

Deneys Reitz knew all about the shortage of horses. He had been riding a mule since the beginning of November. It was a sturdy little creature, that wasn't the problem, but its unsteady gait made it tiring to ride. And, since joining Smuts's staff, Reitz had done his fair share of riding. He was deployed primarily as a dispatch rider, which meant he was constantly on the road, riding from one commando unit to the next to deliver instructions. He had covered hundreds of kilometres.

Smuts was a man who set store by order and discipline, even from a distance. Instructions for this, instructions for that. Point by point, he put everything in writing, orders to all commandos from field cornets, assistant field cornets and corporals: furlough by permission only, on pain of flogging; consumption of alcohol, ditto; horse-feed to be dispensed sparingly; no looting before the end of a battle, and only under officers' supervision; correct treatment to be extended to all prisoners of war and civilians, including 'coloureds and British sympathisers'; no burning or destruction of private property; receipts to be issued for requisitioned or confiscated goods. 'Our aim is to win, through kindness and clemency, the support of people of all classes and stations who do not commit hostile acts against us.' This was very different from Kritzinger, Smuts's Free State counterpart in the Cape Colony, who condemned Africans and coloureds working for the British to summary execution.[113]

In between his organisational tasks, Smuts found time to draft dispatches to Botha and De la Rey as well as to Kruger, Fischer and Leyds in Europe. He could safely communicate with the latter via German South West Africa. Through the same channel, Smuts also sent a long, bewildered letter to the prominent British pro-Boer activist William Stead. 'I cannot forget that I owe my education and some of the greatest pleasures of life to England, to its great literature and its profound thinkers.' And that self-same country now seemed possessed by 'this demon of Jingoism'. He expressed the greatest admiration for Stead's courageous stand.[114]

In early January 1902, Smuts made his way to the north-west border zone to organise and coordinate the many small guerrilla bands scattered in that area. Reitz accompanied him. It was a gruelling journey over hundreds of kilometres, for the most part across desert. They travelled by night and sought shelter from the heat during the day. Kakamas, the settlement they were making for, was on the south bank of the Orange. Across the river was Bechuanaland. While Smuts went about his business, Reitz took time off to enjoy himself. There was food in abundance and he spent his days swimming in the river.

A fortnight later—it was already February—they rode back south, heading for Calvinia. On the way, at Middelpost, they came upon Van Deventer and his men, whom they had last seen in the Suurberg. There was little time for pleasantries. Van Deventer was doing battle with a British column escorting a convoy of 120 wagons. Many of the wagons were already burning, but their guards had not given up the struggle. Reitz joined in. He had arrived just in time to contribute to the victory and—just as importantly—share in the spoils. He came out of the foray with three horses, complete with saddlery. There were scores of them, enough for everyone, and Smuts approved their being taken, along with clothing, boots, ammunition and crates of horseshoes and nails.

This was an absolute windfall. Reitz was no longer a 'ragged muleteer', but better equipped than he had been at any time of the war. Everything seemed to be in their favour. In mid-February 1902, the commandos under Smuts, Van Deventer and Bouwer were reunited—with much cheering and merriment—for the first time since the Suurberg. Now the plan was to launch a joint attack on Vanrhynsdorp, which was occupied by British troops. On arriving there, they found the town deserted. The British had withdrawn to Windhoek, 15 kilometres away. That was where they would go. Reitz wasn't present when they attacked. The evening before, Smuts had sent him to deliver a message to one of the sentries in the area and by the time he returned, the following morning, the fight was over. It had been fierce. Five Boers were killed and 16 wounded. The British had lost roughly the same number, as well as 90 captured. Windhoek was back in Boer hands.

It was 25 February 1902. They were only 40 kilometres from the Atlantic Ocean. Smuts felt it was time for a break. He sent for all the men who had never seen the sea. As a boy, Reitz had been to Europe with his father, but this was an experience he didn't want to miss. Smuts took a group of 70 men to a small coastal inlet called Fishwater. It was a wonderful experience. They arrived there in the late afternoon. A hush fell over them as they approached the edge of the dunes and beheld the infinite expanse of water. Then, as one, like the Greek mercenaries in Xenophon's *Anabasis*, they surged forward, crying, 'The sea! The sea!' Soon they were on the beach. Whooping and laughing, they threw down their saddles, stripped off their clothes and, like a troop of wild centaurs, galloped bareback into the waves.[115]

Retaliation

Leliefontein, March 1902

The mission station had been razed and plundered, but the full horror struck them when they reached the rocks beyond it, where they found 20 or 30 'dead Hottentots, still clutching their antiquated muzzle-loaders'. The stench was overpowering; the bodies must have lain there for weeks. Reitz knew at once. 'This was Maritz's handiwork.' Smuts was silent, but his face was grim. 'I saw him walk past the boulders where the dead lay, and on his return he was moody and curt, as was his custom when displeased.' This was the kind of excessive brutality he had been hoping to prevent.

Everyone knew Manie Maritz, a short, swarthy man, quick-tempered and as strong as an ox. He was born in Kimberley in 1876, but had been living in the Transvaal since 1895. In combat he had cut his teeth against Jameson and his raiders. When war broke out he had initially fought in Natal, subsequently with the Zarps on the southern front, and later in Danie Theron's reconnaissance corps. As from March 1901 he had been a commandant in the Cape Colony, where he had gained a reputation as a ruthless tyrant, a zealous patriot and a born guerrilla leader.

That's how Smuts saw Maritz as well. In January 1902 he appointed him as a general. Less than a month earlier, he had been badly wounded, near Tontelbos. Reitz had seen his injuries with his own eyes: 'a terrible gash below the right armpit'. No ordinary mortal would have survived, but Maritz made a speedy recovery. He threw himself into the task to which Smuts had assigned him: an expedition to Namaqualand in the far north-west. A few British garrisons scattered in and around the Kamiesberg were the new targets. Not because the region was strategic—although it had lucrative copper mines—but to induce the British to send reinforcements from Cape Town. They would come by sea, leaving the road to the capital of the Cape Colony open. At least, that's what they assumed as they sat speculating around the campfire.

On 11 January 1902 Maritz went to the mission in Leliefontein, on the southern slopes of the Kamiesberg. His message to the Khoisan living there was short and unequivocal. Any form of collaboration with the British would be punished by death. Assistance to the Boers would be rewarded with protection, land and cattle. The offer wasn't appreciated. On 27 January Maritz returned with eight men to drive the point home.

The Khoisan also had a point to drive home. They fell upon the Boers, who only escaped by the skin of their teeth. Maritz was incensed and took revenge the following morning, with a stronger force. They killed 35 Khoisan—the rest fled in panic—and razed Leliefontein to the ground. He then made off with 1000 bags of grain, 500 head of cattle and 3000 sheep.

Smuts and his staff arrived at the mission station in early March, more than a month after the carnage. He had time to take in the grisly spectacle. They had arranged to wait there for word from other commando units, so for days they 'lived in an atmosphere of decomposing corpses'. With his senses bombarded, Smuts also found among the rubble a whetstone for the mind. Lying there was a German edition of Immanuel Kant's *Critique of Pure Reason*.[116]

There was enough for Jan Smuts to reflect on. Where, in this war, was the dividing line between legitimate retaliation and plain vengeance? Here in Leliefontein it looked as if that line had been crossed. Still, he was interested to hear Maritz's side of the story. Sometimes things weren't as straightforward as they seemed. A week earlier Smuts himself had been faced with a moral dilemma. It was about the execution of Lambert (Lem) Colyn, an Afrikaner from the Cape, a man of his own kind.

From a legal point of view it was perfectly clear. At the end of January 1902 Colyn had joined Ben Bouwer's commando in the vicinity of Vanrhynsdorp. He was a hulking man with a wild black beard. He claimed to have escaped from a British prison. They believed him. One night, after spending a fortnight with them, he suddenly disappeared. The commando had a rude awakening early the following morning, when a body of horsemen belonging to the 9th (Queen's Royal) Lancers, led by Colonel Charles Kavanagh, stormed into the Boer camp. Bouwer managed to escape with several slashes inflicted by a sabre, but his 11 men were captured. Among them were Cape colonists—'rebels'—who were now in danger of being executed by the British.

Bouwer swore to avenge Colyn's treachery. Fate was on his side. A short time later, the reunion with Smuts's and Van Deventer's units took place. They decided to hit back at once by mounting a joint attack on the British garrison, which had withdrawn from Vanrhynsdorp to Windhoek. The raid was successful. When it was over, the Boers inspected the deserted British camp, which had been set up around the homestead. Deneys Reitz was there, too. He had missed the fighting because he had gone out with Percy Wyndell, one of his old Rich Section comrades, to look for sheets and pillow-cases to use as bandages for the wounded men. In the farmhouse they discovered a man hiding in the kitchen. Reitz took him to be the farmer, but Wyndell recognised him at once. 'My God! It's Colyn!'

They dragged him outdoors, where an angry mob gathered around 'the wretched spy'. Bouwer maintained his composure and had Colyn brought before Smuts, who immediately formed a court martial. That same afternoon, Colyn was sentenced to death for espionage. To confirm the judgment, he was again brought before Smuts, who was visiting an Afrikaner friend in the vicinity. Reitz was with him. There, in Izak van Zyl's dining room and in the presence of his wife and daughters, Reitz witnessed an extraordinary scene.

Two guards escorted Colyn into the room. What should they do with him? Smuts didn't need to think long. Colyn was a spy; he had been tried and found guilty. Smuts could pardon him, if he wanted to. 'Take him out and shoot him!' The prisoner fell to his knees, begging for mercy, while the women fled from the room in tears. Smuts repeated his order.

The condemned man was given an opportunity to speak to the Reverend Abraham Kriel. Reitz knew the dominee from the time he had spent with Beyers's commando in Warmbaths 18 months earlier. Kriel's never-ending prayer meetings had driven him to distraction, but Reitz was impressed with the way he dealt with the situation now. He accompanied Colyn to the firing squad, where Andries de Wet, another member of Smuts's staff, took charge. A team of coloured labourers had dug a grave; Colyn was blindfolded and escorted to the head of it. He lifted his hands and murmured the Lord's Prayer. The shots rang out as he spoke the final 'Amen'. Colyn fell backwards into the grave and his body was covered with earth.[117]

Boer courts-martial condemned scores of people to death for treason and espionage. Taking the circumstances into account, the highest-ranking authority present would either confirm or commute these sentences. During their time in the western Transvaal, Smuts and De la Rey reviewed eight judgments handed down by the court martial in Wolmaransstad. They upheld five and commuted three. Other Boer leaders were likewise called upon to review death sentences. Steyn pardoned Morgendaal's father-in-law, Andries Wessels, but upheld several other judgments. Schalk Burger dismissed Meyer de Kock's appeal for pardon. Louis Botha's younger brother, Chris, the assistant commandant-general in the eastern Transvaal, was given an unusual sentence to review. Five brothers, Gert, Pieter, Cornelius, Okkert and Marthinus—with the ominous surname, Brits—along with their brother-in-law, Hendrik Koch, had been charged with treason. Marthinus Brits was sentenced to 20 lashes with a leather whip with a stirrup attached to it. The other five received the death penalty. Botha signed the judgments. They were executed on 26 July 1901 by a firing squad made up of 12 members of their own commando. These were all men who had grown up together.[118]

Growing resentment between the opposing parties in the later stages of the war led to more summary executions. The Boers who continued to fight in the winter of 1901 were true *bittereinders*. They were less forgiving towards former comrades who had made peace with the enemy and were now turning against their fellow countrymen in increasing numbers. Some were prominent men, like Piet de Wet in the Orange Free State and Andries Cronjé in the Transvaal, but there were many more who were now collaborating with the British and becoming increasingly active.

The National Scouts Corps, formed in early 1901, was working hand in hand with the British in the Transvaal. It acquired official status in October of that year and was incorporated into the British army. Its members wore khaki uniforms and swore loyalty to Edward VII. By the end of the war the corps was 1350 strong. Its members were deployed predominantly as patrols and scouts, but they also took part in active combat. In March 1902 Piet de Wet formed a similar but smaller corps of 450 men in the former Orange Free State. The Orange River Colony Volunteers stopped short, however, of taking up arms. Members of both corps risked life and limb if they fell into the hands of Boer commandos. A court martial wasn't always part of the process.[119]

Nor was it ever part of the process when it came to coloureds and Africans in British service. No statistics were kept but, judging from diaries and reports by witnesses and Boer fighters, the number of people executed without trial must have run into the hundreds. These were the summary executions Kritzinger had threatened them with in July 1901. And they were being carried out not only in his own territory, the eastern Cape, but all over the country, including areas where the most senior authorities—like Smuts in the western Cape—had ordered the Boers to observe the rules in their treatment of prisoners of war. He had stated explicitly that this applied to 'coloured as well as white prisoners and spies', but that hadn't stopped Maritz from inflicting a bloodbath on the Khoisan of Leliefontein. What was Smuts to do with him?[120]

It wasn't only the Boers who settled their scores by firing squad, with or without a trial. The British too, in their zeal for vengeance, came close to tipping the scales as far as the rules of war were concerned—to say nothing of their controversial measures against the civilian population. 'Cape rebels' were treated mercilessly. Treason was punished with the death penalty as a matter of course. The same applied to Boers wearing a British uniform. More than a hundred cases of this kind were recorded.

Strictly speaking, it was admissible under martial law, as were the court-martial sanctions imposed on members of their own forces and the death penalty for desertion and espionage by Africans, coloureds or whites. Nevertheless, these incidents sowed resentment among the Boers, especially when the evidence against them was inconclusive. They also objected to these executions being turned into a public spectacle. They were often carried out in the town square, to the accompaniment of bands and military parades.[121]

Three cases in particular caused a furore both locally and abroad. Two commandants, Hans Lötter and Gideon Scheepers, and a general, Pieter Kritzinger, were brought before a court martial in Graaff-Reinet, in the heart of the deeply divided Cape Colony. The charges and the validity of the proceedings were disputed in all three instances.

The case against 26-year-old Lötter revolved around a disagreement about his nationality. He was born in the Cape Colony, that much was proven, but he had also lived in the Orange Free State. In November 1899, soon after the outbreak of war, he had joined the Free State forces and subsequently fought mainly in the Cape. On the night of 4 September 1901 he had been captured in the vicinity of Graaff-Reinet. At the hearing Lötter claimed to be a citizen of the Free State. The evidence was in his saddlebag, he said, but it had disappeared at the time of his arrest. The court rejected his claim, concluding from his inclusion on the Colesberg electoral roll that he was officially a Cape Colonist. As a result, he was found guilty of treason and executed on 12 October 1901.

Scheepers's nationality was not at issue. He was born in the Transvaal in 1878 and joined the field telegraphy division of the State Artillery there at the age of 17. In 1898 he left the Transvaal to set up a similar division in the Orange Free State. He fought in the war, first under Christiaan de Wet and then from December 1900 with Kritzinger in the Cape. A few months later he was promoted to commandant. This proved to be a great success. Operating in the area around Graaff-Reinet, his unit captured 1300 British prisoners in just six months. With these feats to his name and his youthful and well-groomed appearance—he sported an elegant moustache instead of the usual scruffy Boer beard—Scheepers attracted attention, in his own circle and beyond. It was the newspaper accounts of his exploits that had inspired Deneys Reitz to join the fight in the Cape Colony.[122]

As far as his opponents were concerned, Scheepers was a scourge. In July 1901 he burned down the homes of five British sympathisers in the Cape in retaliation for Kitchener's relentless drives in the Transvaal and the Orange Free State. He was just as ruthless towards coloured and African 'spies'. When the British captured him, ill and weak, on 10

October 1901, they were understandably bent on revenge. After giving him time to recover, they brought him before a court martial on 18 December and threw the book at him. He was charged on 30 counts of murder, arson, sabotage and mistreating 'natives'. The court rejected his claim that he had been acting on the orders of his superiors, at that stage De Wet and Kritzinger. Scheepers was sentenced to death. To cover themselves, the British presented the case to Kitchener, who confirmed and signed the sentence. On 18 January 1902 Scheepers met his death before a firing squad, blindfolded and seated on a chair beside an open grave. This was only a temporary resting place. To prevent it from becoming a pilgrimage site, the British exhumed the body during the night and never revealed where they buried it subsequently.

In the meantime, Scheepers's trial had drawn international attention. The public were outraged. What right had Great Britain to execute an officer of the enemy army, who—as he himself said—was carrying out orders? And that while the war was still being fought? People demanded answers from the British government, not only the Liberal Opposition in its own country—and Churchill, whose views were shifting in that direction—but also the American Congress and other influential bodies abroad.

The storm of protest came too late for Scheepers, but it probably saved the life of General Kritzinger, the most senior of the Boer officers indicted in Graaff-Reinet. Things hadn't looked good for the Free State's assistant chief commandant on 16 December 1901, when he was severely wounded and captured. Everyone knew his name, the man who had brazenly declared that he would kill any coloureds or Africans he discovered in British service. Kritzinger was a Cape colonist by birth; he had grown up in the Orange Free State, that was a fact, but it hadn't helped Lötter or Scheepers.

After recovering, he was tried by the same court martial on charges of murdering six Africans. By then, however, it was early March 1902, and things had changed. Protests were heard on both sides of the Atlantic— even Churchill put in a word. A month later, Kritzinger was acquitted. He remained in detention as a prisoner of war.[123]

Kritzinger's case benefited from the fact that the Boers were showing their more humanitarian side. It had become routine for them to release British prisoners of war after a few days; there was nothing they could do with them anyway. But in early March they reeled in a big catch. On 7 March—as it happened, the day Kritzinger's trial began—they captured their first and last general. And this wasn't just any general. Lieutenant-General Lord Methuen was a three-time winner—at Belmont,

Graspan and Modder River, in November 1899—a mortified loser in the subsequent Black Week at Magersfontein, a serial (unsuccessful) stalker of De Wet and De la Rey, and personally responsible for burning down both their farms.[124]

He was someone with whom they had an axe to grind, or at least make a deal with: a general for a general, or something like that. But this wasn't what happened. On the contrary, the episode ended with a flourish of old-fashioned chivalry, a bolt from the blue in what had long ceased to be a white man's war, let alone a gentleman's war.

One man was behind it. Koos de la Rey was known to be someone who put compassion before justice at the end of a battle. But the generosity he extended to Methuen went beyond anything anyone had ever seen before. He was a true Samaritan. But first, De la Rey subjected his longstanding adversary to the ultimate humiliation—and reduced Kitchener to a nervous wreck for two days. Methuen's capture marked the climax of an equally old-fashioned duel.

De la Rey dealt the first blow on 25 February 1902 at Yzerspruit, 20 kilometres from Klerksdorp, where he swooped on a British convoy of 150 wagons. Many of them were empty, but he was happy with what he found: a machine gun, two cannons and a huge cache of rifles, plus a good supply of ammunition, 200 horses, 400 oxen and 1500 mules. This was just what he desperately needed. The way he gained the victory was gratifying as well. De la Rey had tried out a new strategy, which took the British by surprise. He ordered his men to storm the convoy three times, at full gallop, shooting from the saddle. The third attack broke the guards' resistance. The whole operation took barely an hour and a half. The British suffered 180 casualties, the Boers 50, and another 240 soldiers were captured.[125]

The prisoners had been released across the border in Bechuanaland when nine days later De la Rey prepared for the second blow, this time at Tweebosch, near the border, between the Great Harts and Little Harts rivers. The British were out to settle the score for the debacle at Yzerspruit, and called in their forces from all directions. One of them was led by Methuen. It wasn't an elite unit, but, to be honest, more of a ragbag of relatively inexperienced Yeomanry, irregular colonial troops and the Cape Coloured Special Police. It comprised 1300 men, only half of them mounted, equipped with four guns, two Maxims and 85 wagons. With so few cavalrymen and a force with so little field experience, Methuen should have been wary, especially after the warning he had received on 6 March. It took nothing more than a scuffle between a few Boers and his rearguard to cause instant panic.

In the evening he set up his camp at Tweebosch. In spite of the ominous signs, he was determined to continue north early the following morning. He was going to block De la Rey, no matter what it took. Some of his men, white and coloured colonists, went on the rampage on a neighbouring farm, which belonged to the Schutte family. They destroyed property, harassed the women and were about to set the whole place on fire, when Methuen stepped in.

In the Boer camp on the opposite bank of the Little Harts, De la Rey was preparing to attack. He had 750 hardened warriors, all eager to try out their Yzerspruit tactic again. The prophet Van Rensburg's dreams were auspicious. He had seen another red bull. This time it was thundering down a hill, but it reached the bottom with broken horns and a broken leg. The meaning was obvious to anyone with eyes in their head: a signed and sealed victory for the Boers, first-rate loot and a wounded British general.

And that's exactly how things turned out the following morning. A detachment of Methuen's column set off at three o'clock, followed by the main body an hour later. Behind them, another hour later, came their endless, cumbersome convoy, forming a perfect target for the Boers galloping in from all sides. Their new strategy, the mounted assault, took the British completely by surprise. Only their gunners sprang into action, and once they had been dealt with, by around ten o'clock, the fight was over. The Boers lost eight dead and 26 wounded. The British lost 68 killed, 872 captured, including 121 wounded, along with their artillery, wagons and around 500 horses.

But the greatest trophy, of course, was Lord Methuen. He had suffered a complex injury, a bullet wound and a fractured bone. After he had been shot in the thigh, his horse fell on his leg, putting him at the mercy of the man who was the bane of his life. What would De la Rey do?

De la Rey's men were rarely surprised by anything their general did anymore, but what he came up with now went beyond anything they could have imagined. It was one thing for him to visit Methuen personally after the battle and introduce him to his entire staff—with the help of an interpreter, as De la Rey spoke no English. Nor did it seem strange that he arranged for the wounded on both sides to be nursed together. That was nothing new. But they were thunderstruck a day later, when his wife, Nonnie, turned up (after their farm was destroyed, she and her children had been roaming around in an oxwagon) and without batting an eyelid presented Methuen with a bowl of chicken legs. After that, De la Rey put their prize prisoner in his own wagon and sent him to the garrison in Klerksdorp, where he would get better medical treatment.

Methuen was well on his way when the riot broke out. De la Rey's men forced him to reverse his decision. He tried to reason with them even after couriers had been sent to convey a message to that effect. Precisely this kind of humane gesture would benefit their cause most, he said. In the end, his men relented. Methuen was allowed to continue his journey to Klerksdorp. On arriving there, he sent the wagon back, filled with provisions. In return, De la Rey sent a warm telegram to Lady Methuen. The two men became friends for life.

But the 'Lion of the Western Transvaal' also had a less chivalrous side, which he revealed on hearing about the violent incidents on Schutte's farm the evening before the fight. Among the prisoners of war were eight Cape coloureds who were alleged to have been involved in the disturbance. De la Rey lost no sleep over them. They were made to dig a mass grave, they were blindfolded and then shot.[126]

Reitz was glad that Manie Maritz was still around. At times like this he was worth his weight in gold. No one else could have done what he did. He was an acrobat and shot-putter in one. He had tied three dynamite bombs together to make a ten-kilogram missile. Balancing on someone's shoulders, he carefully estimated the distance from the rock on which they were standing to the blockhouse. He lit the fuse, paused for a moment and then hurled the bomb with all his might. It landed right on the roof. The fuse hissed for two seconds, and soon there came a thunderous explosion as rocks and sandbags went flying through the air. Then silence. They crawled through the coils of barbed wire and stormed the entrance. As they approached, they heard groans and a choked voice whimpering, 'Stop throwing, stop throwing.' The interior of the blockhouse was reduced to rubble and the roof had collapsed. The soldiers were dead, wounded or stunned.

In the end Smuts had given Maritz the benefit of the doubt. Maritz said he had had no alternative; it was a matter of life and death. The Khoisan in Leliefontein had attacked him without warning and he had barely escaped with his life. He had retaliated the following day. In other words, a premeditated matter of life and death. But it didn't take a brilliant lawyer like Smuts to know that there is no such thing. Still, he had left it at that. Maritz's men wouldn't be pleased to see their leader hauled over the coals, and the bottom line was that Smuts couldn't really do without him.

Smuts was reminded of this during his attack on the three mining towns in the northern Kamiesberg. Everyone knew he wasn't interested in Springbok, Concordia or O'Okiep as such. They were bait to lure the British. The authorities in Cape Town couldn't simply abandon the local garrisons to their fate. Moreover, they had an obligation to the Cape Copper Mining Company to conduct a rescue operation. This left them no option but to send reinforcements. The more serious the threat, the larger the force they would dispatch from Cape Town. The Boers had to launch an assault that would make them stand up and take notice.

Their improvised dynamite bombs were a good start. A few Irishmen had made them (there were ample supplies of dynamite and fuses in the mining district) and they had done the job well. On 1 April 1902 Smuts with 400 commandos attacked Springbok, which was defended by a medium-sized garrison of 120, mostly coloured men. The Boer rifles were all but useless against their three forts, although Reitz managed to fire into the loopholes and shoot two of the guards in the head. The hand grenades they had cobbled together were more effective. Maritz turned out to be a master of his art. They destroyed and captured two forts on the first night of the attack. The guards defending the third one held out until the following night, but were forced to surrender when their water supply ran out.

At the second town, Concordia, just the threat of a raid was enough. Like Springbok, it was defended by about 120 men, but their commander was more open to persuasion. On 4 April Smuts sent a letter urging him to surrender. It was in everyone's best interests, he said. Captain Francis Phillips promptly agreed, on condition that all private property and property belonging to the mines was left intact. Smuts consented.

The third nut was the hardest to crack. O'Okiep was a real stronghold. It consisted of a central fort with reinforcements on two sides. These were surrounded by a ring of 15 blockhouses with coils of barbed wire forming barricades between them. The garrison was manned by more than 900 soldiers, three-quarters of them coloureds. Again, Smuts initially tried intimidation. He sent out two messengers—one of whom was Reitz—under the protection of a white flag. Their demand that the garrison surrender met with expletives from officers and men alike. 'Surrender! Surrender be damned; we're Brummagem boys, we're waiting for you.' Their commanding officer, Lieutenant-Colonel W. Shelton, expressed himself more colourfully, but basically to the same effect.

If that's what they wanted, Smuts concluded, it would have to be a siege, if only to be convincing. This meant laying in another supply of dynamite bombs. On the night of 10 April they mounted their first serious assault on the blockhouses at either end. They easily disposed of one, but the other somehow withstood the onslaught of explosives. Their attempt to breach it the following night was no more successful. Reitz was exasperated and Smuts was starting to feel sheepish. It was time to bring in Maritz.

Third time lucky. Reitz was present again, now as an admiring witness of Maritz's skilful delivery, which brought the second blockhouse crashing down. Thirteen to go, plus the main fort. But Smuts felt it was too dangerous to attack them. They stood on open ground, at too great a distance even for his master pitcher, Maritz. Instead, he proposed that they content themselves with cutting off access to O'Okiep. He and his staff installed themselves in Concordia. Reitz shared a room with his friends Edgar Duncker and Nicolaas Swart. 'Several Hottentot prisoners' cooked for them and looked after their horses, there were plenty of animals for slaughter, they slept in real beds and there was even a library. It was pleasant enough. They just had to wait for the British relief expedition to show up. The opportunity to invade Cape Town was imminent.[127]

The bitter end

Concordia, April 1902

It didn't work out that way. One day in the last week of April Reitz, Duncker and Swart had been sniping at the British posts in O'Okiep. On their way back to Concordia they saw a wagon with a white flag over the hood in the distance. Inside were two British officers who had come to deliver a dispatch from Lord Kitchener to Smuts. They didn't know what it was about, or so they said. Reitz had his own thoughts on the matter.

Smuts received the officers in his quarters in Concordia. After a while he emerged, looking subdued. He walked out into the veld, lost in thought. That evening he spoke to Reitz about it. As he had suspected, it was indeed a communication from Kitchener, the British commander-in-chief. He had held talks with the Boer leaders. Peace talks. The outcome would be discussed at a conference in Vereeniging on 15 May. All Boer commandos that were still active were to send representatives. The Transvaal government also wanted Smuts to attend, as their legal adviser. A safe-conduct pass for the journey was enclosed. By train to Port Nolloth, from there by sea to Cape Town, and on to Vereeniging by train.

It was a crushing blow for the men who had stolen into the Cape Colony eight months earlier, looking like scarecrows, who had endured peril and hardship, and finally gained control of almost the entire western Cape. And now this, when they were just about to achieve a spectacular coup. Was the situation in the Transvaal and the Orange Free State really so bad? What else could they conclude? Smuts was depressed, but he had no choice, he would have to go.

Reitz was bitterly disappointed too, but his spirits lifted on hearing that Smuts had a safe-conduct pass for a secretary and an orderly as well. He would accompany Smuts—he could choose in which capacity—and it would give him an opportunity to see his father again. The prospect revived his spirit of adventure. In spite of the dark clouds gathering on the horizon, this would be a unique journey. He wasn't sure what an orderly was, but he thought it was some kind of aide-de-camp, so that was what he chose. Smuts's brother-in-law, Tottie Krige, would go along as secretary.

The hardest part was taking leave of the men who were staying behind: Reitz's friends Edgar Duncker and Nicolaas Swart, and all the companions with whom he had shared so many experiences. Smuts summoned them all and told them about the peace talks, hinting gently that the outcome might not be what they were hoping for. But they responded only with cheers and encouragement, unable to entertain any thought other than that Britain had lost the war and that the conference had been convened 'to give us our country back'. The parting was joyous. Smuts left it at that.

Escorted by a patrol, they rode to the British lines in O'Okiep. There, their patrol relieved them of their horses, sang the commando anthem for the last time, and galloped away, firing a farewell volley. A British carriage took them to the railway at Port Nolloth. Once on the train, Reitz discovered his mistake. An orderly was a servant, not an officer. He was packed into a cattle truck, with ordinary soldiers, including a group of coloureds, while Smuts and Krige were ceremoniously ushered into a first-class compartment. Reitz was out of sorts and had an altercation with one of the coloureds. Fortunately, he was soon promoted. Over dinner Smuts mentioned that his orderly was the son of the state secretary of the Transvaal, whereupon he was plucked out of his cattle truck and invited to join the distinguished party at table.

When they reached Port Nolloth their steamer, the *Lake Eerie*, was ready to leave. A boat was sent to fetch them. Waiting on the quay, all three fell silent, each lost in his own thoughts. Reitz wondered whether Smuts and Krige were also reminiscing about campfires on mountain slopes and wide open plains, marches under the stars, the ordeals of cold, hunger and rain, and, most of all, 'the good men and splendid horses that were dead'.[128]

In the end it was Abraham Kuyper who had set the flywheel in motion. On 25 January 1902 the British foreign secretary, Lord Lansdowne, was handed a memorandum drawn up by the Dutch prime minister. It was in French, the language of diplomacy, but the gist of it, in typically Dutch style, was forthright. The government in The Hague offered its services to negotiate '*un traité de paix*', a peace treaty, between the British and the Boers. They had already worked out a scenario. First, the three members of the Boer delegation, who were still in the Netherlands, would return to South Africa to confer with the Boer leaders. They were to return with an authorisation to conduct peace talks somewhere in the Netherlands. The Dutch government would willingly provide 'the accommodation required'.

Lansdowne replied, just as bluntly, on 29 January. The British government appreciated the humanitarian considerations that inspired the offer, but on principle declined the intervention of foreign powers in the South African war. In any event, London saw no benefit to be derived from a delegation that was accredited only in the Netherlands.

Steyn and Burger were the Boers' highest-ranking authorities. If they wished to negotiate, they should contact the British commander-in-chief in South Africa.[129]

Leyds only heard about this from the newspapers—it was debated in the British parliament—and he was not amused. Apparently that Fox fellow who had approached him in November 1901 hadn't been bluffing about Prime Minister Kuyper's interest in mediating. But Kuyper hadn't taken the trouble to inform him or Fischer or Kruger about his proposal. The only person he contacted was Wolmarans, as it transpired later, and he had kept it to himself.[130]

This certainly wasn't what Leyds had understood by mediation. The Dutch memorandum didn't call on the British Cabinet to put an end to a legally and morally reprehensible war. On the contrary, it implicitly urged the Boer leaders to give up a hopeless cause. Leyds was afraid the British would use this to their advantage. He received bad news from America at almost exactly the same time. President Roosevelt's response to the Boer representatives' appeal of mid-December 1901, though sympathetic and kind, was unhelpful. Roosevelt pointed out that his predecessor, McKinley, had previously offered his services as a mediator, which was more than any other head of state had done. London had refused categorically, and would undoubtedly do so again.

A month later, towards the end of February 1902, a negative reply came from Switzerland as well. But the other government heads they had written to didn't stoop to send so much as a word of acknowledgement, not even the Russian foreign minister, Lamsdorff, in spite of an accompanying letter from his own envoy, De Giers, in support of their cause. Leyds had exhausted his diplomatic options.[131]

March was a month poised between hope and fear. On the one hand, Leyds waited in suspense to see whether the British would try to exploit Kuyper's peace initiative and, if so, how. At the same time, he was excited about De la Rey's resounding success at Tweebosch on 7 March, and his capture and astonishing release of Lord Methuen. The fact that the Boers were still capable of such a great military success, and such a noble gesture besides, was restoring the confidence of their supporters in Europe.

Leyds's hopes revived even further when four couriers arrived from South Africa towards the end of March 1902. They had come via German South West Africa, bringing news from Smuts—fantastic news. In a series of reports dating from December and January, Smuts sketched a rosy picture of the current situation in the western Cape. It made Leyds profoundly homesick. He wrote to his wife, Louise, 'I would so dearly love us to be in the open veld in South Africa. Having spent much of my

time with the couriers over the past few days, I so enjoyed savouring the
air that it was almost unbearable to be here.'[132]

It would have been a terrible disappointment. The South African veld
was becoming more oppressive by the day. Discord hung in the air. In the
course of February 1902 Milner and Kitchener had been sent the texts of
Kuyper's memorandum and Lansdowne's dismissive reply. In early March
Kitchener had figured out how best to use the correspondence. He thought
carefully about what he wanted to achieve. With the briefest possible
accompanying note he sent the two communications to Schalk Burger, the
deputy president of the Transvaal—and purposely not to his Free State
counterpart, the unshakeable Marthinus Steyn.

The effect the note had on Burger surpassed his highest expectations.
Burger replied on 10 March, saying he was 'eager and willing' to 'propose
terms for a peace'. But first he would have to confer with Steyn. Would
Kitchener be willing to provide him and the other members of the
government with a safe-conduct pass to cross the British lines? Kitchener
couldn't agree quickly enough. But where was Steyn? Burger didn't know.
Nor did Kitchener. He had last been spotted somewhere near Kroonstad.
At Kitchener's suggestion, Burger and the other Transvaal leaders decided
to head that way.

Steyn was finally tracked down on 26 March. He turned out to be
somewhere else, in the western Transvaal. His eyes had been troubling
him for weeks and he was being treated by De la Rey's physician. Steyn
proposed a meeting somewhere nearby, in Potchefstroom or Klerksdorp.
Kitchener took the decision: it would be Klerksdorp. Besides the political
leaders, the top military authorities also received an invitation and a safe-
conduct pass. By 9 April everyone had arrived. There were ten Transvalers,
including Burger, Reitz, Botha and De la Rey, and seven Free Staters, most
importantly Steyn, De Wet and Hertzog.

Almost ten months had passed since the Boer leaders had all met
together. Back then, in Waterval on 20 June 1901, they had confirmed that
they were all in agreement, or rather, they had reached a consensus again
after arguing for months about the best course to follow. In any event,
they had adopted a unanimous and final resolution: no peace without
independence.[133]

In Klerksdorp it soon transpired that some were more steadfast than
others. As before, it wasn't the Free Staters who had misgivings. De Wet
made his position clear. 'I would rather be banished for ever than sacrifice
one iota of our independence.' Steyn and Hertzog echoed that sentiment.
De la Rey, too—with Tweebosch in mind—was in favour of 'continuing

the war'. That made him the only Transvaler to take an unambiguous stand. All the rest had reservations, Burger and Botha in particular. Burger didn't mince his words. 'Our position is getting weaker by the day.' Winter was on its way, which meant that 'many burghers will have no choice but to give in to the enemy. Our nation has always had its share of stalwarts and cowards.' Of course, they could fight on and perhaps accomplish what they wanted in the end. But at what cost? They would probably end up concluding that 'our nation has been annihilated. Then for whom will we have fought?'

Botha made no secret of his concerns, either. There were differences between the regions under his direct authority, but the overall picture was discouraging. The countless drives by the British columns and the strangling network of blockhouses had taken their toll. In the space of a year the number of men he could raise had almost halved, from 9570 to 5200, of whom 400 were unmounted. Food was scarce. There were almost no slaughter-cattle left. He was on the verge of surrendering parts of the Transvaal which had been rendered uninhabitable; even their commandos were struggling to survive. Communications with, and traffic to and from, the outside world had been blocked. He was encountering armed Zulus with increasing frequency. Nothing much could be expected of the Cape Colony either. The number of Boer fighters there had risen only slightly over the preceding year, from 2000 to 2600 men. 'It's too late for a rebellion of any significance.' All told, only 15,000 to 16,000 Boers were still active in the field. In spite of it all, the men were still in good spirits. That wasn't the problem. 'But what about the people?' As their representatives, they could choose 'to persist and die like men or until we are banished to far-off islands . . . but we have a duty towards the people'.

Peace, agreed, and gladly, but at what price? The opinions expressed in Klerksdorp differed radically. A future as an independent nation or physical survival? That's what the difference between the Free State leaders and most of the Transvalers boiled down to. On one point they all agreed. They had to determine what the British would be prepared to concede. Only then could they decide what to do. This meant talking to Kitchener. On 10 April Steyn and Burger made it known that they wanted to speak to him personally. They were more than welcome. A day later they boarded the train to Pretoria. The following day, Saturday 12 April, they sat at the table with the British commander-in-chief at his headquarters in Melrose House.

The two Boer presidents—Kruger was out of the picture—were accompanied by the last remnants of their governments. So Reitz senior and Hertzog—as legal counsel—were present as well. Kitchener was alone when they arrived. Two days later Milner joined them. The set of hidden agendas was complete. Each of the four protagonists had a different objective. Steyn wanted independence, Burger an honourable peace, Kitchener a knockout victory, Milner an unconditional surrender. But not all of them were as explicit as Steyn: 'The people must not lose their self-respect.'

Naturally, they failed to reach agreement. But to Kitchener's credit, no one walked out. Milner thought Steyn was being ridiculous and wanted the talks to break down, but that didn't happen. Kitchener made uncharacteristically tactful use of the telegraph connection with London to put pressure on the Boers, without scaring them off. The British Cabinet's indirect contributions were straightforward. Independence for the former Boer republics was out of the question. The only acceptable scenario was an unconditional surrender on the terms Kitchener had proposed to Botha just over a year earlier, in March 1901, after their talks in Middelburg. Or something along those lines.[134]

The British standpoint was unequivocal. They categorically refused to reverse the annexation of the two Boer republics. Everything else was open to discussion. Burger—and undoubtedly Botha—would have signed there and then, particularly in view of the bad news coming in from the front. In De la Rey's absence, his commandos had suffered a painful defeat against Ian Hamilton's assembled columns at Roodewal on 11 April. The magic of Tweebosch had melted away.

But Steyn held his ground and steered his Transvaal counterpart to the last line of defence. Under the constitution, they argued, neither of the Boer governments was authorised to surrender their independence without consulting their people. For that there had to be a ceasefire, and they would also want a member of the delegation to come out from Europe.

Kitchener refused the latter immediately, an official ceasefire too. But he would allow them to organise and hold a referendum. In addition, Milner suggested that Boer prisoners of war should also be consulted, to which Steyn quipped back, 'How can the prisoners-of-war be consulted? They are civilly dead.' Imagine if they voted to continue the war, and the Boer fighters wanted to stop: 'What then?' Both Milner and Kitchener saw the irony. Thirty delegates from each of the former republics would be elected from among commandos who were still active in the field. The referendum was to be held in the border village of Vereeniging, on the banks of the Vaal, on 15 May 1902.[135]

He had no proof, but Deneys Reitz was convinced that their journey had been delayed on purpose. He thought the British might have wanted to prevent Smuts from raising the Transvalers' hopes with reports of his success in the Cape. Whatever the case, it had taken a long time. Five days sailing to Cape Town, in the greatest comfort, it must be said, with his own cabin, a soft bed, a steward who served morning coffee and ran his bath, and better food than anything he remembered. They had a few days' wait in Cape Town, on board the battleship *Monarch*, there too with every convenience.

At length, they took the train north. At the first stop, Matjesfontein, on the edge of the Karoo, they were paid a visit by the cavalry general, French, who had been one of their adversaries right from the start. It seemed to be a social visit, but the conversation was awkward. Smuts felt that his questions were indiscreet and answered evasively. French gloated about his narrow escape from them in September 1901, soon after their incursion into the Cape. He had been in a train, he said, which they had evidently allowed to proceed so as not to attract attention to themselves.

After Matjesfontein Smuts's party had travelled only at night. In front of their carriage was an armoured locomotive with a powerful headlight. They spent the days in a siding, so their progress was slow. It took the better part of a week to reach Kroonstad. They finally pulled in there on 4 May 1902. Kitchener came to meet them. 'He rode up to the station on a magnificent black charger, followed by a numerous suite, including turbaned Pathans, in Eastern costume with gold-mounted scimitars.' In their compartment Kitchener and Smuts politely exchanged irreconcilable views on the hopelessness of the Boers' struggle, the execution of 'Cape rebels' and Boer fighters in khaki uniforms. Kitchener also mentioned British assistance in rebuilding the country. Before leaving, he told Smuts to continue on to the eastern Transvaal to meet Botha. From there they could travel to Vereeniging together.

That night they were back in the Transvaal, after a long absence. In Johannesburg their train switched to the eastern line to Natal. Their train journey ended in Standerton the following day. After covering a short distance by wagon, they were met by a party of burghers, who had brought horses for them. From there it was a two-day ride to Botha's camp, through barren, deserted plains.

Reitz was appalled by the sight that met his eyes when they arrived there. The 300 delegates, clad in skins or sacking, were starving and ragged, their skin covered with sores. He had probably looked no different in the first weeks of their raid on the Cape, but conditions had gradually improved. If these dispossessed men were the pick of the Transvaal commandos, the war was irretrievably lost.

He also received good news of a personal nature. Botha told him that his father was somewhere up north and would undoubtedly come to Vereeniging. He had no news of his brothers, but from the men Reitz learned that both Hjalmar and Joubert had been captured. No one knew anything about Arend.

Elections were held the following day to choose delegates for Vereeniging. Even in those circumstances 'the Boers' predilection for speeches and wordy wrangling asserted itself', and occupied much of the day. By evening, they had chosen their delegates. They left early the next morning with Botha and Smuts, on horseback to Standerton and from there by train to Vereeniging.

One of the first people Reitz came upon was his father, 'shaggy and unkempt, but strong and well'. Not having seen each other for more than 18 months, since October 1900,[136] their reunion was warm and heartfelt. His father had just heard that Arend, too, was doing well. He had been fighting under Christiaan de Wet for the past year and was safe and well. Three members of their family were free men, two were prisoners of war. But they were all still alive and therefore better off than most: the majority of families were 'mourning their dead'.[137]

Sixty men who were to decide over war or peace, 30 Transvalers and 30 Free Staters, chosen by and from the midst of the 15,000 Boers who were still fighting for their cause. In those circumstances, it was a shining example of democratic decision-making. The venue was a large tent, surrounded by an overwhelming number of Brits. The scene couldn't have been more fitting. This was the conclusion to an unequal struggle which had been extraordinary from beginning to end: an armed civilian population pitted against a professional war machine. Bickering to the bitter end.

The opening of the meeting in Vereeniging, on Thursday 15 May 1902, was similar to that in Klerksdorp more than a month earlier, with one momentous difference. Steyn's health had deteriorated. He was barely able to take part in the proceedings; as a result the Boer leaders' opening statements were significantly less uncompromising. De Wet and De la Rey held their ground but spoke only a few words. Burger and Botha, by contrast, dwelt at length on the hopelessness of the situation. Botha impressed on them that 'the Kaffir question was becoming more serious by the day'. They were now in open war with the Zulus. At Holkrans, just recently, 65 burghers had been 'murdered by Kaffirs who came from the English lines'. The lives and honour of Boer women were in danger in the south-eastern Transvaal. 'Many were attacked and raped by Kaffirs. Truly, the plight of these women is more distressing than anything I have encountered in this war.'

Botha's speech struck a chord, though many of the delegates who subsequently addressed the conference were vehemently against giving up. The Free Staters, in particular, who reported on conditions in their region, dug their heels in. Echoing the words of their chief commandant, they declared that they were willing and able to hold out for another year.

Then it was Smuts's turn. Everyone had been waiting to hear him. What were the prospects in the Cape Colony? Smuts soon came to the point. Almost 3300 Boer fighters were active in the Cape and controlled large parts of the colony, notably the western region. The majority of Afrikaners were on their side. They could persist in the struggle without difficulty for some time. However, the uprising they had hoped for would not materialise, for two reasons. The first was the shortage of horses and grass. The British had seized or slaughtered the horses, and grass simply didn't grow there. 'The veld over the entire Cape Colony is overgrown with bushes.' Without horses the commandos couldn't operate. Secondly, the harsh punishment the British inflicted on colonial rebels was proving an effective deterrent. His conclusion was straightforward: continuing the war depended more on the situation in the Transvaal and the Orange Free State than on the Cape Colony.

Smuts's sobering report marked a turning point. Few Free Staters addressed the meeting after him. Most of the later speakers were Transvalers, who painted a far more dismal picture of the conditions in their districts. The tenor of the following day's talks was the same. In the course of that Friday afternoon the state secretary, F.W. Reitz, put forward a concrete suggestion aimed at retaining their internal independence. What about conceding the Witwatersrand and (their protectorate over) Swaziland? Pulling out of foreign politics? The motion was carried. It was decided that Smuts and Hertzog, working together with the two presidents, would draft a proposal.

At the evening meeting the delegates invited Botha, De Wet and De la Rey to address the conference again. Botha delivered a lengthy, emotional speech, reiterating his arguments and adding Smuts's findings. Everything pointed in the same direction, he said. 'If we wish to negotiate, now is the time. If the Lord God wills it, then, however bitter, we must come to terms . . . It has been said that we must fight "to the bitter end", but no one tells us where that bitter end is. Is it when everyone is in his grave or banished?'

De la Rey took less time, but he had something important to say. Once again he told them he had come to Vereeniging with no intention of giving up. But having heard about the desperation and misery in many other parts, 'I can empathise with their reasons for not wanting to continue the war.' De la Rey was finally convinced. He agreed that the time had come to negotiate with the enemy.

All eyes were now fixed on De Wet. Would he capitulate, too? They should have known better. He respected Botha, he assured the delegates, but he was of a different opinion nevertheless. He believed the Transvaal commandant-general implicitly and was aware of the dire conditions he had described. However, 'I do not deal in facts. The entire war is a matter of faith.' It is one and the same thing 'if we go to our grave or dig the grave of our nation'.

The following day, Saturday 17 May, the representatives of the people of the two republics adopted the peace proposal drafted by Smuts and Hertzog. They wished to retain self-government as British colonies; they would concede independence in foreign relations and concede part of their territory. These were the terms to be presented to the British, not by Steyn and Burger this time, but by their long-suffering military leaders, Botha, De la Rey and De Wet, with Smuts and Hertzog as legal advisers. Before nightfall they were in Pretoria.[138]

On the morning of Monday 19 May 1902, they were received by Kitchener and Milner, who were glad to be relieved of the uncompromising Steyn, but instead had five new negotiators to deal with. It could make things more complicated, but it also held out new prospects. Who would succeed in playing the adversaries off against each other? The two British negotiators had totally different objectives. Milner wanted to see the Boers begging on their knees, Kitchener was prepared to concede an honourable defeat. But they responded as one to the Boers' opening proposal: out of the question. This bore no resemblance to the British government's terms for a settlement, namely, the Middelburg proposals.

After much toing and froing, adjournments and deliberations in subcommittees, the Boers acquiesced. Smuts and Hertzog, together with Kitchener, prepared an amended proposal. It differed from the version of a year earlier in only a few, though significant, respects—in the Boers' favour. Although they would have to recognise Edward VII as their lawful sovereign, they would be officially recognised as representatives of the governments of the South African Republic and the Orange Free State, regardless of Roberts's proclaimed annexations. In addition, the Boers would receive reparations of £3 million instead of £1 million. The enfranchisement of coloureds and Africans would not be decided before the introduction of self-government.[139]

On 21 May the draft was telegraphed to London. Privately, Milner followed it up with a confidential note to Chamberlain. He would have no regrets, he said, if the British Cabinet rejected or radically amended the proposals. They had become far too generous towards the Boers. He thought Kitchener's judgment may have been clouded by his desire to bring the war to an early end.

And perhaps by his personal sympathy for the Boer leaders, Milner might have added. No matter how relentlessly they had fought on the battlefield, the military men at the negotiating table soon found themselves on common ground. Even Ian Hamilton, Kitchener's chief of staff, who had inflicted the last serious Boer defeat just over a month before, warmed to his opponents. On 24 May he had attended a dinner held to celebrate Smuts's 32nd birthday. He wrote a cheerful letter about it to Churchill, explaining that he had sat between Botha and De la Rey, with De Wet on Botha's right, and Smuts on De la Rey's left. They had swapped anecdotes about all their escapes. He'd had a splendid evening, 'and never wish to eat my dinner in better company'.[140]

The reply from London came on 27 May. With just a few editorial amendments, the British Cabinet accepted the new terms. Chamberlain had ignored Milner's advice. The treaty contained ten points. The Boers would lay down their arms and acknowledge the sovereignty of the British monarch. Prisoners of war would be allowed to return home on the same condition. Their personal liberty and property rights would be respected. With a few exceptions—three, to be precise—no legal proceedings would be taken against them. The Dutch language would be allowed in schools and courts of law. Possession of licensed weapons for personal protection would be permitted. Military administration would be replaced by civilian government as soon as possible, leading up to self-government. Only at that stage would the matter of the 'Native Franchise' be addressed. No war tax would be levied. Special commissions would be appointed to organise the population's return and the reconstruction of the country, for which £3 million would be made available in reparations and loans on 'liberal terms'.

The document was submitted to the Boers on 28 May. Their questions were few. Would the delegates in Vereeniging be able to propose amendments? No, they wouldn't, Milner snapped back. They had to decide now, 'yes or no'. He read out another document, drawn up in London, concerning the rebels in the Cape Colony and Natal. They were to be disenfranchised, initially for life; the penalty was later commuted to five years. Their leaders would be brought to trial, but none would receive the death penalty. That was that. At nine in the evening, the five

Boer leaders set off for Vereeniging. They had arranged to be back in Pretoria by 31 May.

They had a lot of explaining to do to the delegates the following day. And they did, or at least Botha, De la Rey and Smuts did. All three went to great lengths to explain why they had returned with a proposal so different from the one they had been sent to deliver. The British government simply wasn't prepared to accept anything else. Breaking off the talks wasn't an option. They were in dire straits. The information that had trickled through to Botha in Pretoria—some from British sources, some from Boer informants—was even worse than he had thought. Only 15,000 of the 60,000 armed civilians who had joined the struggle at the start were still in the field; 3800 had died and 31,400 were in captivity. He didn't account for the discrepancy, but everyone understood that the remaining 10,000 were the *hensoppers* and 'joiners'. In addition, there was the horrific death total of women and children in the concentration camps, 20,000 in all. In other words, he could see no advantage in 'the further prosecution of the war . . . [It] would mean the destruction of our national existence.'

Smuts stood firmly behind Botha, and De la Rey urged the delegates to adopt the proposal. However, the two Free State negotiators held different opinions. Hertzog was wavering. But De Wet wasn't wavering yet. He urged them to reject the proposal. 'Let us persist in this bitter struggle and say with one voice: We will persevere, no matter how long, until we secure our independence.'

Then it was the delegates' turn. They spent two days, Thursday 29 and Friday 30 May, mulling over the arguments for and against. The majority of Transvalers supported Botha's view, while the Free Staters who got up to speak—again, far fewer of them—stood behind De Wet. Moreover, De Wet gained an advantage when ill health forced Steyn to resign as president. With little ado, De Wet was nominated to replace him. It was therefore all the more important for Botha and the other Transvaal leaders to win him over.

Early on Saturday morning, before the meeting, Botha and De la Rey went round to De Wet's tent. Could they at least agree on procedure? All the pros and cons had been discussed. It was 31 May, the day they would have to take a decision. Perhaps Smuts and Hertzog could compile a list of all the arguments. They could submit this to the delegates and leave the final decision to them. De Wet agreed, and announced the idea at the meeting.

Smuts and Hertzog got down to work. They set out the reasons in favour of accepting the British proposal: the complete ruin of the two republics and the destruction of all means of subsistence; the suffering and deaths of women and children in concentration camps; the increasingly active and aggressive participation of coloureds and Africans in the war; the mass confiscation of private property; the dwindling numbers of active Boer fighters, the sacrifices they were called upon to make and the hardships they were forced to endure. All things considered, there was 'no justification . . . in proceeding with the war, since that can only lead to the social and material ruin, not only of ourselves, but also of future generations'.

At two o'clock that afternoon the document was presented to the delegates. The outcome was almost an anticlimax. The proposal was adopted by an overwhelming majority of 54 to six—three Transvalers and three Free Staters. Burger delivered a last solemn word. Dominee J.D. Kestell led the closing prayer. Then Kitchener's representatives were called in. A deathly silence fell as Botha announced that the meeting had adopted the British government's peace proposal.

Hurried preparations were made for the official signing. Burger, Reitz, Botha, De la Rey and the two members of the Executive Council, L.J. Meyer and J.C. Krogh, signed on behalf of the Transvaal. De Wet, Hertzog and the two members of the government, W.J.C. Brebner and C.H. Olivier, signed for the Orange Free State. Just before 11 that evening their train pulled in at Pretoria. Kitchener and Milner were waiting for them in Melrose House. The formalities were over in five minutes. Burger signed first, Milner last. The Boer War had officially come to an end. The silence was unearthly. Kitchener was the first to speak. 'We are good friends now.'[141]

Epilogue
Winners and losers
Bloemfontein, 6 July 2012

Today is the closing date. If no objections have come in, the decision will be final. In future, Paul Kruger Avenue in Bloemfontein will be known as OR Tambo Street. The street signs will be replaced. 'Oom Paul' will disappear to make way for 'OR'. The Boer leader who started the war against the British has been superseded by the ANC leader who fought against the apartheid regime.[1]

This is nothing unusual. Streets, cities and countries are renamed after a change of regime. In South Africa the process has actually been relatively slow: 18 years have passed since the ANC came to power. But now it is being implemented more vigorously, and not just in Bloemfontein but throughout the country; in Durban and Cape Town by the score.[2]

The whole procedure has stirred unrest, notably in Pretoria, the country's administrative capital, where the name of the city itself is at issue. A resolution to rename it Tshwane has touched a raw nerve in the Afrikaner community. Pretoria has been the bastion of Afrikanerdom since it was founded in 1855 by Marthinus Pretorius, who named it after his father. Even today, its inhabitants are predominantly Afrikaners and 75 per cent are white.[3]

The change touches a nerve because the new name is as emotionally charged as the one it replaces. Tshwane was a legendary chief of the Ndebele, hence an ancestor of Mzilikazi and Lobengula. He is said to have ruled the area where Pretoria is now situated in the eighteenth century, long before the Voortrekkers arrived. The evidence consists of information transmitted orally from one generation to the next. In 2006 a six-metre bronze sculpture of Chief Tshwane was erected in the square outside the City Hall, opposite the existing statues of Pretorius and his father.

The symbolism is unmistakable. A city's name, the sculptures in its streets: this is about defining public space. It is a political test of strength, with the historical dimension of competing invented traditions. Pretoria and Tshwane stand for disparate narratives of South Africa's history, and different answers to questions like 'Which tribe was here first, the Ndebele or the Voortrekkers?' or 'Who developed this country, the whites or the blacks?' The answers to these questions have far-reaching implications. Ultimately they shape the paramount social debate in South Africa today: 'Who does this country belong to?'[4]

The ANC centenary, celebrated on 8 January 2012, appears to have heightened its leaders' awareness of the importance of historical claims. The church in Bloemfontein where the ANC was founded was spruced up in time for the celebrations. Claims to the past are not going to stop there. The government recently identified an additional 28 heritage projects which, in President Zuma's words, will help 'to correct the legacies of a colonial and apartheid past'.[5]

So it would seem that the ANC has finally gained the upper hand. Things looked very different a century ago. In terms of legal status, the African and coloured populations were in fact the real losers of the Boer War.

The Peace of Vereeniging, which ended the war on 31 May 1902, dealt a blow to African leaders like Sol Plaatje. All their sacrifices had been in vain. Their support of the British was rewarded with betrayal. Article 8 of the peace treaty may have seemed innocuous, but it extinguished all hope. 'The question of granting the Franchise to Natives will not be decided until after the introduction of Self-Government.' In other words, it wasn't going to happen at all. The Boers would never have accepted it. The British yielded to the demands of their vanquished adversaries. The whites had settled their differences on a piece of paper and excluded the rest of the population.

They excluded coloureds and Africans and the immigrants from British India represented by Mohandas Gandhi, whose loyalty during the war, whose ambulance corps on Spion Kop and other battlefields, counted for nothing. Gandhi was faced with the same truth as Plaatje and every other leader of every non-white community.

This applied not only in the two former Boer republics but in the Cape Colony and Natal as well. Article 8 was just the beginning. In the following years, the Boers and the British throughout South Africa shared a common view of the destiny of their African and coloured compatriots. Their only future was as a labour force for the mines and the agricultural sector, and for that they had no need of the vote or any other civil right. What they needed was passes, by the handful, to prevent them from coming and going as they pleased.

Only one more attempt was made to put up a show of organised resistance against white rule. In Natal in 1906, a local chief, Bambatha, rebelled against the introduction of a new tax. The British colonial administration responded with an iron fist and the Bambatha uprising was brutally suppressed. Thousands of Africans were killed and thousands more imprisoned or flogged.

Gandhi reacted by making one last attempt. Again, he offered the colonial regime the services of the Indian community, initially in the form of a combat unit, subsequently as an ambulance corps. Their second offer was accepted, but that too failed to achieve its ulterior objective. The colour bar couldn't be crossed by his people, either. Disillusioned, he abandoned his struggle for acceptance by the whites and turned to a new strategy, *satyagraha*, nonviolent resistance.

Black leaders like Sol Plaatje also reached a breaking point. They too had spent years fruitlessly pinning their hopes on those among the British who supported their cause. The ultimate instrument of oppression was the Natives Land Act of 1913, which denied Africans and coloureds the right to own land except in a few designated areas, which amounted to seven per cent of the land surface. Other black leaders around the country had responded to the growing discontent by establishing the (South) African (Native) National Congress.[6]

On a very different, less existential level, the Netherlands was also one of the losers of the Boer War. The Peace of Vereeniging allowed the use of Dutch in schools and law courts, but apart from that the old motherland's role had played out. The strategic bastions of Dutchness that President Kruger had painstakingly constructed in the Transvaal had disintegrated during the war. The Netherlands-South African Railway Company, the proud flagship, had been nationalised and its staff deported by the British.

Willem Leyds personified the demise—and originally the creation—of the 'Dutch connection'. For him the Peace of Vereeniging was a threefold defeat. The Boers had lost. The Netherlands' input in South Africa was at an end. And on a personal level the peace came as a shock. Up to the end he had clung to the belief that things would come right. All of a sudden he had to face up to reality, not just the country's, but his own as well. In a single stroke he was unemployed and stateless. He was 43 years old, young enough to make a fresh start, but did he actually want to?

A few days later he knew the answer. The Boer cause had become too great a part of his life. He couldn't shake off the 18 years he had spent living in and working for the Transvaal. In early June 1902 he wrote to his brother, saying, 'I won't give up hope.' He firmly believed that 'the Boer element in South Africa will triumph in the end'. Leyds dedicated the rest of his life to that aspiration. Not that he wasn't in demand. He could have held a chair at the university in Leiden, he could have been consul-general in Teheran, but he chose The Hague—once more as a Dutch national and still for the cause célèbre which had come his way on the brink of his career as a lawyer. After returning to the Netherlands he devoted himself to writing historical works with pregnant titles like 'The Containment of the Boer Republics'.

Leyds was rarely to return to South Africa. In 1904 he escorted the recently deceased former President Kruger to his last resting place. After that, he seldom accepted invitations, preferring the solitude of his study. He felt that public life in South Africa had become 'completely politicised' and refused to become embroiled in the feud between the Afrikaners. He spent his time writing and rewriting the history he had been instrumental in shaping. For him too, Paul Kruger was the hero and Britain the source of all evil.

But history didn't stand still. It almost brought an ironic end to Leyds's life. In early May 1940, amid fears of a German invasion, the 81-year-old Leyds decided to flee from the Netherlands. The only place left that he could go to was England. What could be more incongruous than for him to seek refuge in the country he had been castigating for years? But fate intervened. He took ill while preparing for the journey and died in hospital in The Hague on 14 May 1940.[7]

Great Britain may have emerged as the winner of the Boer War, but its losses were staggering. Over 22,000 soldiers killed, more than half by disease, 400,000 horses and mules slaughtered, £217 million squandered. Not to mention the incalculable damage to the country's prestige. Its reputation as a military power was tarnished, its moral authority in shreds, its diplomatic status undermined, and the nation's self-confidence shaken as a result. Against this background it wasn't surprising that London had had enough of the war, and that in May 1902 it was prepared to make more concessions to the Boers than a year earlier.

To Winston Churchill the Peace of Vereeniging didn't come as a surprise. Through well-connected acquaintances like Ian Hamilton he was kept informed about everything—including his friend's growing sympathy with the Boer generals. They ranked higher in Hamilton's estimation than the 'Cape loyalists' or the Uitlanders. Churchill agreed. He, too, was in favour of assisting the Boers to recover as quickly as possible. They were 'the rock' on which the British would build in South Africa.[8]

Once peace was restored, Milner busied himself with the aim of totally anglicising the two old and the two new colonies. But he met with resistance from the Afrikaners as well as the English-speaking community. Forgive, forget and join hands with the Boers. This was the groundswell of opinion among the British, in London as in Cape Town and Durban. Besides the promised £3 million in reparations, ten times more was provided in loans to rebuild the ravaged country.

In 1905 the process of reconciliation was given an extra boost. In Cape Town Milner was replaced by the more amenable Lord Selborne. In London the Liberals superseded the Conservatives, and Churchill, whose politics had become more progressive, was appointed secretary for the colonies in the new Cabinet. In this capacity he made a substantial contribution to South Africa's transition to self-government. Finally, on 31 May 1910 the four colonies were united to form the Union of South Africa, as a dominion of the British Empire.

The First World War was the litmus test for the new state. The South African government suppressed an uprising by former Boer commandos and opted to give Great Britain its active support. Thousands of troops were deployed against the German colonies in Africa and subsequently in Europe as well. For many it meant rubbing shoulders again with their old enemies from the Boer War, but this time they were on the same side. One of their comrades-in-arms was Winston Churchill. In the meantime he had risen to the heights of political office and also taken a hard fall. Hoping to restore his reputation, he returned to the trenches near Arras in 1916, now as lieutenant-colonel of the 6th Battalion of the Royal Scots Fusiliers. In early 1917 the 1st Battalion came to relieve them. Among them was a South African major, a man called Reitz.[9]

Many Boers were in shock after the Peace of Vereeniging. Their losses were horrific. 34,000 people had died, 6000 in battle, 28,000 in the camps, mostly children; millions of cows, sheep and horses had been lost, thousands of farmhouses ruined, all their property and possessions had gone up in smoke, their land lay barren. And these were only the visible scars.[10]

Deneys Reitz bore witness to their bewilderment. The proceedings at Vereeniging in May 1902 cut him to the quick. The 60 Boer fighters assembled there were 'the pick of our nation—all brave fighters and tough as nails'. Now they lay in their tents, 'weeping like children at the grave of their freedom'. His father was devastated. He had signed the ultimatum that unleashed the war, and now the peace treaty that ended it. Unable to endure any more, he went to the Netherlands to join his wife and youngest children. Deneys stood by him, but chose his own exile. He settled in Madagascar, where he eked out a living by conveying goods.[11]

Yet, the Reitz family had been fortunate to survive it all. Most Boer families were in mourning, for a vanished past, for the loss of those who had died or for those who had made the 'wrong' choice and disappeared from their lives for ever. The lost war gouged a rift between *bittereinders* and *hensoppers* in Afrikaner society which remained long after peace was restored. Divided, they were unable to grieve as a nation and come to terms with their loss. This was the real tragedy and its effects were felt for decades.

On the face of it, however, the Boers seemed to have recovered from their defeat in no time at all. Deneys Reitz was a good example. In December 1903 he was back in Pretoria, penniless and half dead with malaria. Jan Smuts and his wife took him into their home and nursed him back to health. He went on to study, became a lawyer, and witnessed the country's economic revival and the political success of Louis Botha's South African Party, which espoused a policy of appeasement with Great Britain. In 1910 Botha became the first prime minister of the Union of South Africa. Four years later Barry Hertzog formed the anti-British National Party in opposition to the government.

The First World War also confronted Reitz with difficult decisions. His old commando comrade Manie Maritz, the Leliefontein avenger, the hurler of bombs at O'Okiep, led a rebellion, backed by thousands of *bittereinders*, including Christiaan de Wet. But Reitz sided with Botha and, in particular, Smuts, under whose leadership he helped to suppress the rebellion and conquer the territories of German South West Africa and German East Africa. He subsequently enlisted on the European front. Thanks to Smuts, who had become a member of the Imperial War Cabinet, he was assigned to the Royal Scots Fusiliers, and served in the trenches of Arras, following in Churchill's footsteps.

In later years Reitz remained loyal to Smuts, now in the realm of politics. Smuts succeeded Louis Botha as prime minister of the country until he was superseded by Hertzog in 1924. The 1930s saw a remarkable intermezzo in Afrikaner politics. The South African Party, led by Smuts, and Hertzog's National Party reconciled their differences and formed the United Party, a move that met with disapproval from nationalist extremists.

The Second World War brought an end to the alliance. Anti-British sentiment, which had been dormant, flared up again. Hertzog chose the path of neutrality but was outvoted by Smuts, who took the country to the war on Britain's side. Like Smuts, Reitz supported Great Britain unconditionally. His last public office was that of high commissioner in London. His official residence was South Africa House, not far from the Cabinet War Rooms, where Churchill, now prime minister, was supervising the British war effort.[12]

The Voortrekker Monument, on the outskirts of Pretoria, is an ambiguous piece of architecture. It falters between two ideas, strange as that description may be for a monolithic 40-square-metre building surrounded by a circle of 64 granite oxwagons. But it's precisely this paradox that intrigues. What does it mean? That the Boers have established themselves so firmly in this country that they'll be here forever? Or the opposite? That they could break up their laager any moment and move on to a new Promised Land?

The architect, Gerard Moerdijk, had the former idea in mind. He wanted his building to stand for the next thousand years as a testimony to the historic importance of the Great Trek. In 1949 the monument was inaugurated by the new prime minister, D.F. Malan, the 'purified' nationalist who had won the election from Smuts a year earlier. The National Party was back in power. Racial segregation became more firmly entrenched as an official policy. Twelve years later, on 31 May 1961, the Afrikaners cut themselves off from the outside world when South Africa severed its ties with Great Britain and became a republic. Fifty-nine years, to the day, after the Peace of Vereeniging, the *bittereinders* had prevailed. The Boers were now boss in the whole of South Africa.

But not for a thousand years. Thirty years later, under the pressure of internal resistance and protest from abroad, the apartheid regime was forced to back down. President F.W. de Klerk took the first step in 1990. The African National Congress was unbanned and Nelson Mandela was released from prison. In the first non-racial general election, in 1994, the ANC won 63 per cent of the vote. Mandela was elected president. The land of apartheid became the Rainbow Nation. In 2009 the ANC still gained a two-thirds majority.

The Voortrekker Monument still stands today. Moreover, it has recently become the first Afrikaner monument to be declared a national heritage site under the new dispensation. Announcing this on 16 March 2012, the arts and culture minister, Paul Mashatile, described the nomination as a step towards reconciliation and an acknowledgement of the monument's 'deep historical significance to the Afrikaner community'. But it meant different things to different people, he added. 'Part of our history is painful. It is a history of exclusion, suppression, domination of one by another and a history of division. However, we cannot wish away this history.'

What the ANC *can* do, and does liberally, is present an alternative narrative of the past. Placing the sculpture of Tshwane opposite the two Pretoriuses is a good example. In the same speech Mashatile announced plans to enlarge Freedom Park, since 2007 the counterpart of the Voortrekker Monument. This is an elaborate theme park, just a few kilometres away—the location has been chosen carefully—which illustrates South Africa's diverse history from prehistoric times up to the present.

Instead of looking a thousand years into the future, Freedom Park looks back on hundreds of thousands of years in the past. It answers unequivocally the question of who has the oldest rights in southern Africa. And it clearly isn't the Afrikaners. They have been there for three and a half centuries, which is nothing compared to millennia of human habitation in the region. If the balance of power between the races in South Africa is to be determined by the right of first settlement—as the younger generation of ANC leaders insists—it won't stop at street names and statues. The real issue will be the redistribution of wealth and, in the near future, the redistribution of land and natural resources. Only when this hurdle has been crossed will it be possible to draw up a new profit and loss account for the Boer War.[13]

Notes

Prologue

1 http://mg.co.za/article/2011-03-11-ancs-r15million-heritage-house-ripoff; http://m. news24.com/citypress/South Africa/News/The-panel-beater-shop-with-a-multimillion -rand-price-tag-20110813.

2 www.anglo-boer.co.za/virtual tour/; Albert Grundlingh, 'The National Women's Monument: The Making and Mutation of Meaning in Afrikaner Memory of the South African War', www.celat.ulaval.ca/histoire.memoire/histoire/capeI/grundlingh.htm.

3 Martin Bossenbroek, *Holland op zijn breedst. Indië en Zuid-Afrika in de Nederlandse cultuur omstreeks 1900,* Amsterdam, 1996.

4 Peter Warwick, *Black People and the South African War, 1899–1902* (Cambridge, 1983). Cf. also Bill Nasson, *Abraham Esau's War: A Black South African War in the Cape, 1899–1902* (Cambridge, 1991); Johan Wassermann,'"Sowing the Seeds of Rebellion": Chief Bhambatha kaMancinza and the Anglo-Boer War, 1899–1902', *African Historical Review* 39, 2 (2007), 91–106.

5 Speech Thabo Mbeki, www.info.gov.za/speeches/1999/9910111133a1008.htm; speech Jacob Zuma, www.info.gov.za/speeches/1999/9910111133a1004.htm.

6 See also his web page www.willemboshoff.com/documents/artworks/32000.htm.

7 Fransjohan Pretorius, *Historical Dictionary of the Anglo-Boer War* (Plymouth, 2007), 107–108; cf. www.measuringworth.com/calculators/ukcompare/relativevalue.php; Martin Meredith, *Diamonds, Gold and War: The Making of South Africa* (London, 2007); Thomas Pakenham, *The Boer War* (London, 1979); H.L. Wesseling, *Verdeel en heers. De deling van Afrika, 1880–1914* (Amsterdam, 1991).

8 Keith Wilson, ed., *The International Impact of the Boer War* (Chesham, 2001).

9 André van Deventer, 'Gebruik van rolprent as 'n massa-medium tydens die ABO', lecture Anglo-Boereoorlog Museum, 24 September 2011; Stephen Badsey, 'The Boer War as a Media War', in Peter Dennis and Jeffrey Gredy, eds., *The Boer War: Army, Nation and Empire* (Canberra, 2000), 70–83; Stephen Bottomore, *Filming, Faking and Propaganda: The Origins of the War Film, 1897–1902* (Utrecht 2007); Vincent Kuitenbrouwer, *A War of Words: Dutch Pro-Boer Propaganda and the South African War (1899–1902)* (Amsterdam, 2010); Kenneth O. Morgan, 'The Boer War and the Media (1899–1902)', *Twentieth Century British History* 13 (2002), 1–16.

10 S.B. Spies, *Methods of Barbarism? Roberts and Kitchener and Civilians in the Boer Republics: January 1900–May 1902* (Cape Town, 1977).

11 Greg Cuthbertson and A.M. Grundlingh, eds., *Writing a Wider War: Rethinking Gender, Race, and Identity in the South African War, 1899–1902* (Athens, 2002); Hermann Giliomee, *The Afrikaners: Biography of a People* (London, 2011); Alwin de Jong, *Wil de ware Afrikaner opstaan? De Boerenoorlog als ijkpunt van nationalisme in Zuid-Afrika (1815–1925),* Bachelor's thesis, University of Utrecht, 2012; Lindie Koorts, *D.F. Malan: A Political Biography* (Cape Town, 2010); Peter Limb, *The ANC's Early Years: Nation, Class and Place in South Africa before 1940* (Pretoria, 2010); Shula Marks and Stanley Trapido, eds., *The Politics of Race, Class and Nationalism in Twentieth-Century South Africa* (London, 1987); David Omissi and Andrew S. Thompson, eds., *The Impact of the South African War* (Basingstoke, 2002); Hans Erik Stolten, ed., *History Making and Present Day Politics: The Meaning of Collective*

412

Memory in South Africa (Uppsala, 2007); Christi van der Westhuizen, *White Power: The Rise and Fall of the National Party* (Cape Town, 2007); Nigel Worden, *The Making of Modern South Africa: Conquest, Apartheid, Democracy* (Oxford, 2012).

12 Bill Nasson, *The War for South Africa: The Anglo-Boer War (1899–1902)* (Cape Town, 2010); Pakenham, *The Boer War*; Wesseling, *Verdeel en heers*.

13 See below, p. 119–120.

14 P.J. van Winter, *Onder Krugers Hollanders. Geschiedenis van de Nederlandsche Zuid-Afrikaansche Spoorweg-Maatschappij* (Amsterdam, 1937); B.J.H. de Graaff, *De mythe van de stamverwantschap. Nederland en de Afrikaners 1902–1930* (Amsterdam, 1993); Chris A.J. van Koppen, *De geuzen van de negentiende eeuw. Abraham Kuyper en Zuid-Afrika* (Maarssen, 1992); R. Kuiper, *Zelfbeelden wêreldbeeld. Antirevolutionairen en het buitenland, 1848–1905* (Kampen, 1992); M. Kuitenbrouwer, *Nederland en de opkomst van het modern imperialisme* (Amsterdam, 1985); G.J. Schutte, *De Boerenoorlog na honderd jaar. Opstellen over het veranderende beeld van de Anglo-Boerenoorlog (1899–1902)* (Amsterdam, 1997); G.J. Schutte, *Nederland en de Afrikaners. Adhesie en Aversie: Over Stamverwantschap, Boerenvrienden, Hollanderhaat, Calvinisme en Apartheid* (Franeker, 1986).

Part I: For a good cause

1 Martin Bossenbroek, 'Geschiedschrijving als hoger beroep. Willem Johannes Leyds, advocaat van de Boeren (1859–1940)', in M.Ph. Bossenbroek, M.E.H.N. Mout and C. Musterd, eds., *Historici in de politiek* (Leiden, 1996), 191–211, 192–194; Kees van Hoek, *Kruger Days: Reminiscences of Dr. W.J. Leyds* (London, 1939), 2–4; F. Netscher, 'Dr. W.J. Leyds', in Netscher, *Karakters* (Haarlem, 1899), 112–138, 129–133; L.E. van Niekerk, *Kruger se regterhand. Biografie van dr. W.J. Leyds* (Pretoria, 1985), 11–19.

2 Van Koppen, *Geuzen*, 26–28; Schutte, *Nederland*, 9–24.

3 F. Lion Cachet, *De worstelstrijd der Transvalers aan het volk van Nederland verhaald* (Amsterdam, 1882), 561; see also Bossenbroek, *Holland*, 66–67, 259–260; Van Koppen, *Geuzen*, 69–103; Kuiper, *Zelfbeeld*, 124–133; Kuitenbrouwer, *Nederland*, 118–121; Kuitenbrouwer, *War of Lords*, 24–34; Schutte, *Nederland*, 24–29.

4 W.J. Leyds, *De eerste annexatie van de Transvaal* (Amsterdam, 1906), 366–382; Nasson, *The War*, 42–44; Wesseling, *Verdeel en heers*, 345–348.

5 Stuart Cloete, *African Portraits: A Biography of Paul Kruger, Cecil Rhodes and Lobengula, Last King of the Matabele* (London, 1946), 159–161; Leyds, *Eerste annexatie*, 402–403; Nasson, *The War*, 44.

6 *De Standaard*, 14 November 1883, cited in Van Koppen, *Geuzen*, 116–132.

7 Bossenbroek, *Holland*, 175–177, 323; Van Koppen, *Geuzen*, 116–132.

8 Van Winter, *Onder Krugers Hollanders* I, 48–80.

9 Van Koppen, *Geuzen*, 110–114; Van Niekerk, *Kruger se regterhand*, 16–17; Van Winter, *Onder Krugers Hollanders* I, 65–66.

10 Bossenbroek, 'Geschiedschrijving', 194; Van Hoek, *Kruger Days*, 3–4; W.J. Leyds, *Onze eerste jaren in Zuid-Afrika 1884–1889. Intieme correspondentie van mevrouw Louise W.S. Leyds-Roeff en dr. W.J. Leyds, bestemd voor familie en belangstellenden* ('s-Gravenhage, 1938), 1–2; Netscher, 'Dr. W.J. Leyds', 129–132; Van Niekerk, *Kruger se regterhand*, 17–19.

11 Leyds, *Onze eerste jaren*, 22–25.

12 Leyds, *Onze eerste jaren*, 3–4, 25, 60; Wesseling, *Verdeel en heers*, 144–146.

13 Leyds, *Onze eerste jaren*, 6–9, 25, 58.

14 Leyds, *Onze eerste jaren*, 9–25, 60–63.

15 Leyds, *Onze eerste jaren*, 25–29.

16 Van Hoek, *Kruger Days*, 5–7; Leyds, *Onze eerste jaren*, 25–29; C.J. van der Loo, *De geschiedenis der Zuid-Afrikaansche Republiek (Transvaal) aan het volk verteld*

413

(Zwolle, 1896), 78–80, 167–190; Van Niekerk, *Kruger se regterhand*, 31–33.

17 Giliomee, *Afrikaners,* 215–223; Van Koppen, *Geuzen,* 92–94, 135–137; Leyds, *Onze eerste jaren,* 25–29; Van Niekerk, *Kruger se regterhand,* 31–33.

18 Giliomee, *Afrikaners,* 228, 231; Van Hoek, *Kruger Days, 5–6;* Leyds, *Onze eerste jaren,* 17, 25–30; Lion Cachet, *Worstelstrijd,* 349–351, 399–404; Meredith, *Diamonds,* 74–78; Antony Preston, *Geïllustreerde geschiedenis van Zuid-Afrika* (Alphen aan den Rijn, 1995), 63.

19 Cloete, *African Portraits,* 25–84; Leyds, *Onze eerste jaren,* 30–32; Van Niekerk, *Kruger se regterhand,* 5–15, 50–54.

20 Cloete, *African Portraits,* 162–167; Leyds, *Onze eerste jaren,* 30–32; W.J. Leyds, *Het insluiten van de Boeren-Republieken* (Amsterdam, 1914), passim; S.M. Molema, *The Bantu Past and Present* (Cape Town, 1963), 43–54; Van Niekerk, *Kruger se regterhand,* 50–54; Wesseling, *Verdeel en heers,* 348–349.

21 J.A. Heese, *Die herkoms van die Afrikaner 1657–1867* (Cape Town, 1971); Molema, *Bantu Past and Present,* 35–60; Robert Ross, *A Concise History of South Africa* (Cambridge, 2008), 5–37.

22 Ross, *A Concise History,* 37–58; John J. Stephens, *Fuelling the Empire: South Africa's Gold and the Road to War* (Chichester, 2003), 54–86.

23 Meredith, *Diamonds,* 22–59; Ross, *A Concise History,* 59–67; Wesseling, *Verdeel en heers,* 333–335.

24 Meredith, *Diamonds,* 63–104; Ross, *A Concise History,* 64–70; Wesseling, *Verdeel en heers,* 334–341.

25 Leyds, *Onze eerste jaren,* 74–76, 79, 91.

26 Meredith, *Diamonds,* 173–181; Stephens, *Fuelling the Empire,* 157–160.

27 Cloete, *African Portraits,* 128–139; Meredith, *Diamonds,* 153–163; Stephens, *Fuelling the Empire,* 157–160.

28 It was named after surveyor general Johann Rissik and mines inspector Christiaan Johannes Joubert; see Pretorius, *Historical Dictionary,* 197.

29 Leyds, *Onze eerste jaren,* 91–96.

30 Charles van Onselen, *Studies in the Social and Economic History of the Witwatersrand 1886–1914,* 2 parts (Johannesburg, 1982), passim.

31 Cloete, *African Portraits,* 136.

32 Meredith, *Diamonds,* 186–193, 293; Ross, *A Concise History,* 70–74; Stephens, *Fuelling the Empire,* 170–181; Wesseling, *Verdeel en heers,* 356–359.

33 Leyds, *Onze eerste jaren,* 128–129; Van Niekerk, *Kruger se regterhand,* 34, 48–50.

34 Leyds, *Onze eerste jaren,* 76, 80–84.

35 Van Hoek, *Kruger days,* 7.

36 Leyds, *Onze eerste jaren,* 85; Van Niekerk, *Kruger se regterhand,* 60.

37 Meredith, *Diamonds,* 170–171.

38 Leyds, *Onze eerste jaren,* 86–90.

39 Meredith, *Diamonds,* 184–185.

40 Leyds, *Onze eerste jaren,* 111–112; Van Niekerk, *Kruger se regterhand,* 59–60.

41 Leyds, *Onze eerste jaren,* 94–94, 98–99, 102, 104–105; Van Niekerk, *Kruger se regterhand,* 44–45; R.C. de Jong, G.M. van der Waal and D.H. Heydenrych, *NZASM 100, 1987–1899: The Buildings, Steam Engines and Structures of the Netherlands South African Railway Company* (Pretoria, 1988), 36; *In memoriam NZASM* (Amsterdam, 1910), 8–9; Stephens, *Fuelling the Empire,* 193–194; Van Winter, *Onder Krugers Hollanders* I, 161–166.

42 Van Niekerk, *Kruger se regterhand,* 424–45.

43 J.P. FitzPatrick, *The Transvaal from Within: A Private Record of Public Affairs* (London, 1899), 62–65.

44 Meredith, *Diamonds,* 169–171; Stephens, *Fuelling the Empire,* 145–148; Stanley Trapido, 'Imperialism, Settler Identities and Colonial Capitalism: The Hundred Year Origins of the

1899 South African War', *Historia* 53, 1 (2008), 59–61; Stanley Trapido, 'Reflections on Land, Office and Wealth in the South African Republic, 1850–1900,' *Historia* 53 (2008), 36–37; Van Winter, *Onder Krugers Hollanders* I, 115–116; II, 33–42.

45 Meredith, *Diamonds*, 296–301; Stephens, *Fuelling the Empire*, 145–148; Trapido, 'Reflections', 36–37; Van Winter, *Onder Krugers Hollanders* I, 115–116; II, 33–42.

46 Van Niekerk, *Kruger se regterhand*, 128.

47 FitzPatrick, *The Transvaal from Within*, 62–72; *In memoriam NZASM*, 8–9; De Jong et al., *NZASM*, 31–37; Van Niekerk, *Kruger se regterhand*, 44–45; Van Winter, *Onder Krugers Hollanders* I, 115–116; II, 33–42.

48 Luke 11: 15–17; see also Matthew 9: 34, 12: 24–25; Mark 3: 22–25.

49 Leyds, *Onze eerste jaren*, 131, 187.

50 De Jong et al., *NZASM*, 37–39; Van Niekerk, *Kruger se regterhand*, 46–47; Van Winter, *Onder Krugers Hollanders* I, 172–175, 220–134.

51 Leyds, *Onze eerste jaren*, 176; Van Niekerk, *Kruger se regterhand*, 63–66.

52 Leyds, *Onze eerste jaren*, 156; Van Winter, *Onder Krugers Hollanders* I, 220–234.

53 Leyds, *Onze eerste jaren*, 172–184, 190–191.

54 Leyds, *Onze eerste jaren*, 186, 192; Van Niekerk, *Kruger se regterhand*, 101–102.

55 Leyds, *Onze eerste jaren*, 194–203.

56 Leyds, *Onze eerste jaren*, 202, 203, 213–215.

57 Van Niekerk, *Kruger se regterhand*, 110–113.

58 Bossenbroek, *Holland*, 95, 102, 112.

59 Bossenbroek, *Holland*, 206–207; Van Koppen, *Geuzen*, 137–140; Kuitenbrouwer, *War of Words*, 29–30; Schutte, *Nederland*, 101–117.

60 Leyds, *Onze eerste jaren*, 221–228.

61 Leyds, *Onze eerste jaren*, 172–203.

62 Van Niekerk, *Kruger se regterhand*, 144–177; Schutte, *Nederland*, 131–133.

63 Kuitenbrouwer, *War of Words*, 34–36; C.G.S. Sandberg, *Twintig jaren onder Krugers Boeren in voor- en tegenspoed* (Amsterdam, 1943), 61; Schutte, *Nederland*, 117–128; Van Winter, *Onder Krugers Hollanders* II, 73–78.

64 Schutte, *Nederland*, 103–108.

65 Kuitenbrouwer, *War of Words*, 36–37; Sandberg, *Twintig Jaren*, 61; Schutte, *Nederland*, 114–117; Van Winter, *Onder Krugers Hollanders*, 247–250.

66 Van Winter, *Onder Krugers Hollanders* I, 247–289.

67 Van Niekerk, *Kruger se regterhand*, 100–102; Van Winter, *Onder Krugers Hollanders* II, 117–120.

68 Meredith, *Diamonds*, passim; Preston, *Geïllustreerde geschiedenis*, 84–87; Wesseling, *Verdeel en heers*, 359–364.

69 De Jong et al., *NZASM*, 44–47; Van Koppen, *De Geuzen*, 34–37; Van Niekerk, *Kruger se regterhand*, 92–95; Schutte, *Nederland*, 134–138; Van Winter, *Onder Krugers Hollanders* II, 124–149.

70 J. Cooper-Chadwick, *Three Years with Lobengula, and Experiences in South Africa* (London, 1894), passim; Leyds, *Het insluiten* II, 195–306; Meredith, *Diamonds*, 207–237; Gustav S. Preller, *Lobengula: The Tragedy of a Matabele King* (Johannesburg, 1963), passim; Wesseling, *Verdeel en heers*, 359–376.

71 Leyds to Beelaerts van Blokland, 11–4–1899, in Leyds Collection 30.

72 Leyds, *Het insluiten* II, 66–101; Meredith, *Diamonds*, 207–237.

73 Cooper-Chadwick, *Three Years with Lobengula*, passim; Ruth First and Ann Scott, *Olive Schreiner: A Biography* (New York, 1980), 225; Leyds, *Het insluiten* II, 243–206; Meredith, *Diamonds*, 207–237; Preller, *Lobengula*, passim; Wesseling, *Verdeel en heers*, 359–376.

74 Leyds, *Het insluiten* II, 102–168, quotation 148; Meredith, *Diamonds*, 238–243.

75 Van Winter, *Onder Krugers Hollanders* II, 136–149.

76 De Jong et al., *NZASM*, 47–49; Van Niekerk, *Kruger se regterhand*, 95–99; Van

Winter, *Onder Krugers Hollanders* II, 150–189, 223–251.

77 Leyds to acting state secretary Van Boeschoten, 26–1–84, in Leyds Collection 31; Van Niekerk, *Kruger se regterhand*, 99–100.

78 Cloete, *African Portraits*, 261; Wilson, *International Impact*, 27; Van Winter, *Onder Krugers Hollanders* II, 248.

79 Leyds to Beelaerts van Blokland, 21–7–1895, in Leyds Collection 31; Van Winter, *Onder Krugers Hollanders* II, 248.

80 Leyds to Beelaerts van Blokland, 21–7–1895, in Leyds Collection 31.

81 *Jaarverslagen NZASM*, 1894 and 1895; in: Archive NZASM; *In Memoriam NZASM*, 66–68.

82 Lady Sarah Wilson, *South African Memories: Social, Warlike and Sporting, from Diaries Written at the Time* (London, 1909), 23; First and Scott, *Olive Schreiner*, 234.

83 Van Hoek, *Kruger Days*, 20–22.

84 Meredith, *Diamonds*, 291–308; Nasson, *The War*, 45–49; Van Niekerk, *Kruger se regterhand*, 129–132; Stephens, *Fuelling the Empire*, 198–216; Wesseling, *Verdeel en heers*, 377–379.

85 Van Niekerk, *Kruger se regterhand*, 124–126; Stephens, *Fuelling the Empire*, 216–218.

86 See map on pp. xx–xxi. Map of the railway network in South Africa, in *Jaarverslagen NZASM*, 1889; Van Winter, *Onder Krugers Hollanders* II, 190–222.

87 Meredith, *Diamonds*, 317–322; Van Niekerk, *Kruger se regterhand*, 103–106; Van Winter, *Onder Krugers Hollanders* II, 190–222.

88 Leyds to acting secretary Van Boeschoten, 17–10–1895, 31–10–1895, 6–11–1895, in Leyds Collection 31.

89 Leyds to Moltzer, 3–2–1895, 19–5–1895, in Leyds Collection 31.

90 Leyds in diary to Louise Leyds, 26–7–1895; Louise Leyds to Leyds, 7–8–1895; Leyds to Moltzer, 13–9–1895, in Leyds Collection 31.

91 Leyds to Van Boeschoten, 17–11–1895 (twice), in Leyds Collection 31.

92 Leyds to Moltzer, 10–11–1895, in Leyds Collection 31; Leyds's telegram to Beelaerts van Blokland, 18–12–1895, in Leyds Collection 46; Leyds to Moltzer, 25–12–2895, in Leyds Collection 89.

93 Leyds to Louise Leyds, 31–12–1895, 1–1–1896, in Leyds Collection 31.

94 Van Niekerk, *Kruger se regterhand*, 130–140.

95 Cloete, *African Portraits*, 288–235; Meredith, *Diamonds*, 311–344; Nasson, *The War*, 50–51; Pakenham, *The Boer War*, 1–5; Wesseling, *Verdeel en heers*, 379–385; Van Winter, *Onder Krugers Hollanders* II, 252–268.

96 Leyds to Louise Leyds, 5–1–1896, in Leyds Collection 31; Van Niekerk *Kruger se regterhand*, 139–141.

97 Leyds to Louise Leyds, 5–1–1896, in Leyds Collection 31; Van Niekerk, *Kruger se regterhand*, 139–141.

98 Leyds to Louise Leyds, 29–1–1986, in Leyds Collection 31; Van Niekerk, *Kruger se regterhand*, 142–143.

99 Leyds to Louise Leyds, 8–2–1896, in Leyds Collection 31; Van Hoek, *Kruger Days*, 17–20; Van Niekerk, *Kruger se regterhand*, 144–145.

100 Meredith, *Diamonds*, 340–350; Van Niekerk, *Kruger se regterhand*, 147–148.

101 Leyds to the Duke of Mecklenburg, 30–5–1896, in Leyds Collection 31; Roy Mack, 'The Great Africa Cattle Plague Epidemic of the 1980s', *Tropical Animal Health and Production* (1970) 4, 210–219.

102 *Staats-almanak voor de Zuid-Afrikaansche Republiek* (1893) 56, (1897) 39, (1898) 39; *Jaarverslagen NZASM*, 1895, 1896; FitzPatrick, *The Transvaal from Within*, 71–72.

103 Van Boeschoten to Leyds, 4–6–1896; Leyds to Kempner, 12–7–1896, in Leyds Collection 31; J.H. Breytenbach, *Die geskiedenis van die Tweede Vryheidsoorlog in Suid-Afrika, 1899–1902* (Pretoria, 1969), I, 77–89.

104 Breytenbach, *Die geskiedenis* I, 77–89; Van Niekerk, *Kruger se regterhand*, 148–148;

Van Winter, *Onder Krugers Hollanders*, 258–259.

105 Meredith, *Diamonds*, 348–349.

106 Cloete, *African Portraits*, 339–349; First and Scott, *Olive Schreiner*, 225–231; Meredith, *Diamonds*, 354–361.

107 Peter J. Cain, *Hobson and Imperialism: Radicalism, New Liberalism, and Finance 1887–1938* (Oxford, 2002), 59–63; Meredith, *Diamonds*, 349.

108 Meredith, *Diamonds*, 349–353; Pakenham, *The Boer War*, 25–31; Wesseling, *Verdeel en heers*, 382–385.

109 Lippert to Van Boeschoten, 2–6–1896, in Leyds Collection 31; Meredith, *Diamonds*, 349–353; Van Niekerk, *Kruger se regterhand*, 145–147.

110 Leyds to Moltzer, 16–8–1896; Moltzer to Kruger, 12–9–1896, in Leyds Collection 31.

111 Leyds in diary to Louise Leyds, 16–2–1897, 22–2–1897, 22–2–1897, 27–2–1897, 2–3–1897, 5–3–1897, in Leyds Collection 32.

112 Chamberlain to Leyds, 10–5–1897; Leyds to Chamberlain, 11–5–1897; Leyds to Van Boeschoten, 21–5–1897; Chamberlain to Sir W. Harcourt, 15–5–1897; Leyds to Chamberlain, 18–5–1897; Chamberlain to Leyds, 22–5–1897, in Leyds Collection 32.

113 Leyds in diary to Louise Leyds, 17–3–1897, First draft preface to the Collection 1897, in Leyds Collection 32.

114 Leyds to Van Boeschoten, 22–4–1897 and 30–4–1897, in Leyds Collection 32.

115 Leyds to Van Boeschoten, 30–4–1897, in Leyds Collection 32; Van Niekerk, *Kruger se regterhand*, 153–154.

116 Van Niekerk, *Kruger se regterhand*, 134–135.

117 Lord Rothschild to Leyds, 10–5–1897; Leyds to Van Boeschoten, 15–5–1897, in Leyds Collection 32.

118 Chamberlain to Leyds, 10–5–1897, in Leyds Collection 32.

119 Leyds to acting state secretary Van Boeschoten, 21–5–1897, in Leyds Collection 32.

120 Leyds to Van Boeschoten, private, 21–5–1897, in Leyds Collection 32.

121 Leyds to Van Boeschoten, 2–7–1897, in Leyds Collection 32.

122 Chamberlain to Leyds, 22–5–1897, 7–6–1897; Leyds to Van Boeschoten, 21–7–1897; Leyds, First draft preface to the Collection 1897, in Leyds Collection 32.

123 Leyds to Chamberlain, 14–6–1897; Leyds to Van Boeschoten, 2–7–1897, in Leyds Collection 32.

124 Leyds to the Pretoria government, 25–5–1897; Leyds to the acting state secretary, 28–5–1897; Leyds to the acting state secretary, 3–6–1897, in Leyds Collection 32.

125 Leyds to Van Boeschoten, 1–6–1897, in Leyds Collection 32.

126 Leyds to the consuls of the ZAR, 27–5–1897; Leyds to Quarles, 27–5–1897; Leyds to Van Boeschoten, 1–6–1897, in Leyds Collection 32; Van Niekerk, *Kruger se regterhand*, 182–183.

127 H. Andreas to Leyds, 10–5–1897; telegram Leyds to government in Pretoria, 14–6–1897, in Leyds Collection 32.

128 Leyds to Van Boeschoten, 1–6–1897, in Leyds Collection 32.

129 Telegram government in Pretoria to Leyds, 12–6–1897; Leyds to Chamberlain, 14–6–1897, in Leyds Collection 32.

130 Chamberlain to Leyds, 17–6–1897, in Leyds Collection 32.

131 Leyds to Van Boeschoten, 2–7–1897, in Leyds Collection 32.

132 Leyds to Van Boeschoten, 15–7–1897, in Leyds Collection 32; Van Niekerk, *Kruger se regterhand*, 162–164.

133 Leyds to government in Pretoria, 3–8–1897; Montagu White to Leyds, 5–8–1897, in Leyds Collection 32.

134 Leyds in diary to Louise Leyds, 27–2–1898, in Leyds Collection 35.

135 NZASM's tariff reductions, compiled by the foreign affairs ministry in Pretoria for the Transvaal consul in Frankfurt, 17–11–1898, in Leyds Collection 34; Van Niekerk, *Kruger se regterhand*, 135–137.

136 Leyds to Louise Leyds, 24–3–98, in Leyds Collection 35.

137 W.J. Leyds, *Eenige correspondentie uit 1899* (The Hague, 1919), 200–206; Van Niekerk, *Kruger se regterhand*, 165–167.

138 Leyds in diary to Louise Leyds, 8–3–1898, 12–3–1898, 5–4–1898, 10–4–1898, 14–4–1898, in Leyds Collection 35; Van Niekerk, *Kruger se regterhand*, 191–195.

139 Van Niekerk, *Kruger se regterhand*, 183, 194.

140 John Darwin, *The Empire Project: The Rise and Fall of the British World-System 1830–1970* (Cambridge, 2009), 234–235; Meredith, *Diamonds*, 365–373; Wesseling, *Verdeel en heers*, 387–389.

141 Meredith, *Diamonds*, 374–375; W. Basil Worsfold, *Lord Milner's Work in South Africa* (London, 1906), 107–114.

142 Darwin, *The Empire Project*, 236–238, 243–245; Meredith, *Diamonds*, 378–385.

143 Leyds, *Eenige correspondentie*, 1–2; Van Niekerk, *Kruger se regterhand*, 184–185, 202–203.

144 Leyds, memorandum 'Voor de intimi', 1898; Leyds to his brother Reinier, 9–7–1898; Leyds to Reitz, 26–8–98; Leyds to Grobler, 14–10–1898, in Leyds Collection 35; Leyds, *Eenige correspondentie*, 231–235; Van Niekerk, *Kruger se regterhand*, 195–2000.

145 Leyds to Reitz, 8–7–1898; Leyds to Reitz, 19–8–1898; Leyds to Reitz, 4–11–1898, in Leyds Collection 35; Van Niekerk, *Kruger se regterhand*, 205–210.

146 Leyds, memorandum 'Voor de intimi', 1898; Leyds to Reitz, 16–12–1898 (twice); Leyds to his mother, 16–12–1898, in Leyds Collection 35; Van Niekerk, *Kruger se regterhand*, 198–102.

147 Van Niekerk, *Kruger se regterhand*, 155–157.

148 Van Niekerk, *Kruger se regterhand*, 199.

149 Wesseling, *Verdeel en heers*, 391–392; Wilson, *International Impact*, 28–30, 146–148.

150 Wesseling, *Verdeel en heers*, 301–322; Wilson, *International Impact*, 72–75.

151 Smuts to Leyds, 30–4–1899, and Grobler to Leyds, 30–4–1899, in Leyds Collection 36; Leyds, *Eenige correspondentie*, ix, 1, 11–13, 198–200; Darwin, *The Empire Project*, 238–241; Meredith, *Diamonds*, 387–399; Van Niekerk, *Kruger se regterhand*, 168–170; Pakenham, *The Boer War*, 52–56; Wesseling, *Verdeel en heers*, 392–396.

152 Leyds, *Eenige correspondentie*, vi, 2–8, 200–211.

153 *Staats-almanak voor de Zuid-Afrikaansche Republiek* (1899), 36, 51, 53.

154 Darwin, *The Empire Project*, 238–238; Leyds, *Eenige Correspondentie*, 38–43; Darwin, *The Empire Project*, 389–409; Meredith, *Diamonds*, 389–409; Pakenham, *The Boer War*, 46–70; Wesseling, *Verdeel en heers*, 396–399.

155 Leyds, *Eenige correspondentie*, 2–3, 200–211.

156 FitzPatrick, *The Transvaal from Within*, passim; Leyds, *Eenige correspondentie*, 222–225; Pakenham, *The Boer War*, 71–88.

157 Leyds, *Eenige correspondentie*, 112–115; Meredith, *Diamonds*, 409–415; Pakenham, *The Boer War*, 89–92.

158 Meredith, *Diamonds*, 409–415; Pakenham, *The Boer War*, 92–94.

159 Meredith, *Diamonds*, 402.

160 W.K. Hancock and Jean van der Poel, eds., *Selections from the Smuts Papers: Volume I, June 1886—May 1902* (Cambridge, 1966), 313–322; Pakenham, *The Boer War*, 102; S.B. Spies and Gail Nattrass, eds., *Jan Smuts: Memoirs of the Boer War* (Johannesburg, 1994), 24.

161 The pamphlet was first published under the name of state secretary F.W. Reitz. See F.W. Reitz, *Een eeuw van onrecht*, 2nd impression (Dordrecht, 1900), passim.

162 Leyds to P.G.W. Grobler, 17–8–1899, and Leyds to F.V. Engelenburg, 18–8–1899, in Leyds, *Eenige correspondentie*, 106–109; Van Niekerk, *Kruger se regterhand*, 172.

163 Leyds, *Eenige correspondentie*, 2–3, 31–32, 200–211.

164 Ibid., 16–19, 158–159.

165 Ibid., 109–112, 118–123, 126–130, 150, 155–158, 175.

166 Ibid., 79, 81, 171.

167 Ibid., 30; Wilson, *International Impact*, 66–68.

168 Bossenbroek, *Holland*, 256–257; Van Koppen, *Geuzen*, 150–161.

169 Leyds, *Eenige correspondentie*, 25–26, 33, 216–218.

170 Leyds, *Eenige correspondentie*, 60–66, 83–85.

171 Ibid., 83–89, 132–149, 165–166, 172–173.

172 Ibid., 172–173, 179, 185–186; Leyds to Lippert, 10–10–1899, in Leyds Collection, 36; cf. J.P. de Valk and M. van Faassen, eds., *Dagboeken en aantekeningen van Willem Hendrik de Beaufort 1874–1918* (The Hague, 1993), 1, 34–49, 67–68.

Part II: Like a boys' adventure story

1 Winston S. Churchill, *My Early Life, 1874–1904; with an Introduction by William Manchester* (New York, 1996), 74–230; Roy Jenkins, *Churchill* (London, 2002), 22–50; Brian Roberts, *Churchills in Africa* (London, 1970); Celia Sandys, *Churchill: Wanted Dead or Alive* (London, 2005), 9–20.

2 Winston S. Churchill, *The Boer War: London to Ladysmith via Pretoria and Ian Hamilton's March* (London, 2002), 1–2; Churchill, *My Early Life*, 230–235; Omissi and Thompson, *Impact*, 100–105; Pakenham, *Boer War*, 113; Roberts, *Churchills*, 139; Sandys, *Churchill*, 21–23.

3 See p. 119.

4 Churchill, *My Early Life*, 230–235; Pieter G. Cloete, *The Anglo-Boer War: A Chronology* (Pretoria, 2000), 34–35; Nasson, *War*, 88–90; Pakenham, *Boer War*, 71, 76, 93, 96–98, 103, 107, 110–113; Wesseling, *Verdeel en heers*, 399–402.

5 Churchill, *My Early Life*, 230–233; Roberts, *Churchills*, 138–139; Sandys, *Churchill*, 10–18.

6 Jenkins, *Churchill*, 51; Roberts, *Churchills*, 138–139; Sandys, *Churchill*, 13, 16, 22.

7 Churchill, *Boer War*, 1–6; Churchill, *My Early Life*, 234–238; Jenkins, *Churchill*, 51; Pakenham, *Boer War*, 156–157; Roberts, *Churchills*, 138–10; Sandys, *Churchill*, 22–26.

8 J.E.H. Grobler, *The War Reporter: The Anglo-Boer War through the Eyes of the Burghers* (Johannesburg, 2011), 1–10; Pakenham, *Boer War*, 157–160.

9 Churchill, *Boer War*, 7–12; Churchill, *My Early Life*, 239–240; Pakenham, *Boer War*, 166; Roberts, *Churchills*, 140–141; Sandys, *Churchill*, 22–26.

10 Hancock and Van der Poel, *Selections*, 313–322.

11 Leopold Scholtz, *Waarom die Boere die oorlog verloor het* (Pretoria, 1999), 28–45.

12 Breytenbach, *Geskiedenis* I, 26–31, 75–76, 105–106, 153–155; Cloete, *Anglo-Boer War*, 48; Grobler, *War Reporter*, 2; Hancock and Van der Poel, *Selections*, 562; Pretorius, *Historical Dictionary*, 204–205, 445–447; Sandberg, *Twintig jaren*, 228; Schutte, *Boerenoorlog*, 40; Scholtz, *Waarom*, 28–43; Wesseling, *Verdeel en heers*, 400–404.

13 Breytenbach, *Geskiedenis* I, 26–31, 75–76, 105–106, 146–178; Cloete, *Anglo-Boer War, 39, 48, 339–340*; Nasson, *War*, 74–84; Pakenham, *Boer War*, 125–127; Pretorius, *Historical Dictionary*, 445–446.

14 Breytenbach, *Geskiedenis* I, 141–146; Pakenham, *Boer War*, 125–127; Pretorius, *Historical Dictionary*, 448–449; Wesseling, *Verdeel en heers*, 399–400.

15 See above, pp. 12–13.

16 Churchill, *Boer War*, 13–21; Churchill, *My Early Life*, 240–243; Roberts, *Churchills*, 140–142; Sandys, *Churchill*, 28–31.

17 Breytenbach, *Geskiedenis* I, 237–263; Cloete, *Anglo-Boer War*, 44–45; Grobler, *War Reporter*, 7; Pakenham, *Boer War*, 133–141; Pretorius, *Historical Dictionary*, 137–138, 220–221; Scholtz, *Waarom*, 47–55.

18 Breytenbach, *Geskiedenis* I, 62–68; Hans Jannasch, *Onder Boeren, Britten en Bantoes* (Amsterdam, 1942), 190–207; J.W. Meijer, *Dr H.J. Coster, 1865–1899* (Pretoria, 1883), passim; Pretorius, *Historical Dictionary*, 108, 480–481; Sandberg, *Twintig jaren*, 215–227; G.J. Schutte, ed., *Beste ouders. Brieven uit de Transvaal van Karel van den Berg 1896–1900* (Amsterdam, 1999), 5–31; G. Vissering, *Een Hollander in Zuid-Afrika* (Amsterdam, 1900), 5–31.

19 Churchill, *Boer War*, 22–34; Churchill, *My Early Life*, 243–244; Jenkins, *Churchill*, 52; Roberts, *Churchills*, 52; Sandys, *Churchill*, 30–31.

20 Churchill, *Boer War*, 24, 35–36; Churchill, *My Early Life*, 243–244; Jenkins, *Churchill*, 52; Roberts, *Churchills*, 162–166; Sandys, *Churchill*, 43–46.

21 Churchill, *Boer War*, 22–26; Churchill, *My Early Life*, 243; Roberts, *Churchills*, 162–164; Sandys, *Churchill*, 32–34, 37–43.

22 Breytenbach, *Geskiedenis* I, 303–342; Cloete, *Anglo-Boer War*, 448–49; Grobler, *War Reporter*, 9; Pakenham, *Boer War*, 142–155; Pretorius, *Historical Dictionary*, 231–236, 490–491; Scholtz, *Waarom*, 47–55; M.C.E. van Schoor, *Christiaan Rudolph de Wet. Krygsman en volksman* (Pretoria, 2007), 68–69.

23 Churchill, *Boer War*, 26–27, 31–34; Sandys, *Churchill*, 32–33, 39–41.

24 Churchill, *Boer War*, 36–44; Churchill, *My Early Life*, 244–253; Jenkins, *Churchill*, 53; Roberts, *Churchills*, 166–169; Sandys, *Churchill*, 47–55.

25 Churchill, *Boer War*, 45–79; Churchill, *My Early Life*, 253–262; Jenkins, *Churchill*, 53–55; Roberts, *Churchills*, 169–180; Sandys, *Churchill*, 58–59; Frederick Woods, ed., *Young Winston's Wars: The Original Despatches of Winston S. Churchill, War Correspondent 1897–1900* (London, 1972), 173–179.

26 Churchill, *Boer War*, 43–79; Cloete, *Anglo-Boer War*, 46–65; Grobler, *War Reporter*, 11–19; Pretorius, *Historical Dictionary*, 116–117; Roberts, *Churchills*, 173, 202–203.

27 W.J. Leyds, *Tweede verzameling (correspondentie 1899–1900)* ('s-Gravenhage, 1930), I, xii–xiii, 78, 175–178; L.E. van Niekerk, *Dr. W.J. Leyds as gesant van die Zuid-Afrikaansche Republiek* (Pretoria, 1980), 143–179, 230–256; Wilson, *International Impact*, 43–64.

28 Leyds, *Tweede verzameling* I, xi; II, 57–59; Ulrich Kröll, *Die internationale Buren-Agitation 1899–1902* (Munster, 1973), 67–122, 197–206; Van Niekerk, *Leyds as gesant*, 144–148, 230–256; Wilson, *International Impact*, 25–42, 65–78.

29 Bossenbroek, *Holland*, 252–253; Kuitenbrouwer, *War of Words*, 129–164; Leyds, *Tweede verzameling* I, 81–82.

30 Bossenbroek, *Holland*, 351 and passim; Leyds, *Tweede verzameling* I, xi–xii, 69–70, 126–134, 142, 207–209, 223–224.

31 Leyds, *Tweede verzameling* I, 183–184; Van Niekerk, *Leyds as gesant*, 288.

32 Leyds, *Tweede verzameling* I, ix–x, 94–98, 160–161, 176, 186–187; Van Niekerk, *Leyds as gesant*, 286–287; Wilson, *International Impact*, 197–122.

33 First and Scott, *Olive Schreiner*, 236–238; Leyds, *Tweede verzameling* I, 140–141, 156–157; Pretorius, *Historical Dictionary*, 430–431; William T. Stead, *Shall I Slay My Brother Boer? An Appeal to the Conscience of Britain* (London, 1899), 61–63 and passim.

34 Bernard Porter, *The Absent-Minded Imperialists: Empire, Society, and Culture in Britain* (Oxford, 2004), 176–180; Roberts, *Churchills*, 174–175.

35 Churchill, *Boer War*, 77–83; Churchill, *My Early Life*, 261–271; Jenkins, *Churchill*, 55–60; Roberts, *Churchills*, 204–210; Sandys, *Churchill*, 89–98; Andrew Thompson, 'Imperial Propaganda during the South African War', in Cuthbertson, *Writing*, 303–328.

36 Churchill, *Boer War*, 88–91; Churchill, *My Early Life*, 271–286; Jackie Grobler, ed., *The War Diary of Johanna Brandt* (Pretoria, 2007), 37–38; Jenkins, *Churchill*, 56–61; Roberts, *Churchills*, 208–215, 235–242; Sandys, *Churchill*, 99–125.

37 *In memoriam NZASM*, 97–107; De Jong et al., *NZASM 100*, 223–231; Van Winter,

Onder Krugers Hollanders I, 270–271; II, 337–347.

38 Breytenbach, *Geskiedenis* I, 127–130; Diana Cammack, *The Rand at War, 1899–1902: The Witwatersrand and the Anglo-Boer War* (London, 1990), 38–82; *In memoriam NZASM*, 105–106.

39 Cammack, *Rand*, 50–54, 83–100; Warwick, *Black People*, 127–137.

40 Jenkins, *Churchill*, 60–61; Roberts, *Churchills*, 235–241; Sandys, *Churchill*, 99–115.

41 Churchill, *My Early Life*, 288–295; Jenkins, *Churchill*, 61–62; Roberts, *Churchills*, 247–254; Sandys, *Churchill*, 142–143.

42 Churchill, *Boer War*, 91–95; Churchill, *My Early Life*, 295–300; Jenkins, *Churchill*, 61–62; Roberts, *Churchills*, 247–254; Sandys, *Churchill*, 131–140, 142–143.

43 Breytenbach, *Geskiedenis* I, 364–366; Nasson, *War*, 124, 132–134; Pakenham, *Boer War*, 160–165; Pretorius, *Historical Dictionary*, 62–64.

44 Breytenbach, I, 396–399, II, 99–166; Cloete, *Anglo-Boer War*, 59–69; Grobler, *War Reporter*, 15, 17, 22; Nasson, *War*, 135–138, 143–147; Pakenham, *Boer War*, 188–206; Pretorius, *Historical Dictionary*, 32, 164, 285–288, 259–262.

45 Breytenbach, *Geskiedenis* I, 296–225; Cloete, *Anglo-Boer War*, 66; Grobler, *War Reporter*, 14–21; Nasson, *War*, 139–142; Pakenham, *Boer War*, 214–215; Pretorius, *Historical Dictionary*, 434–436.

46 Breytenbach, *Geskiedenis* I, 226–337; Cloete, *Anglo-Boer War*, 57–58; Grobler, *War Reporter*, 57–58, 60, 70–73; Nasson, *War*, 147–153; Pakenham, *Boer War*, 215–218, 224–241; Pretorius, *Historical Dictionary*, 90–92, 493–494.

47 Roberts, *Churchills*, 216–234; Sandys, *Churchill*, 28–29.

48 Breytenbach, *Geskiedenis* I, 286–394, 411–413, 459–461; Nasson, *War*, 11–116; Pretorius, *Historical Dictionary*, 255–258; Warwick, *Black People*, 28–38.

49 See Part I, p. 25.

50 Breytenbach, *Geskiedenis* II, 392–404; Cloete, *Anglo-Boer War*, 41, 46–47, 50–52, 54–56, 60, 62; Grobler, *War Reporter*, 6–7, 12, 14–15, 19; Nasson, *War*, 116–122; Pakenham, *Boer War*, 181–190; Pretorius, *Historical Dictionary*, 212–214; Warwick, *Black People*, 129–130.

51 Breytenbach, *Geskiedenis* II, 333–349; Nasson, *War*, 106–110; Pakenham, *Boer War*, 238–241; Pretorius, *Historical Dictionary*, 236–238.

52 Churchill, *Boer War*, 95–105; Churchill, *My Early Life*, 301–306; Jenkins, *Churchill*, 61–62; Sandys, *Churchill*, 138–148.

53 Churchill, *Boer War*, 135–138; Churchill, *My Early Life*, 305–306, 311–312; Cloete, *Anglo-Boer War*, 86–89; Grobler, *War Reporter*, 34–35; Pakenham, *Boer War*, 284–304; Roberts, *Churchill*, 280–281; Sandys, *Churchill*, 158, 162–163.

54 Breytenbach, *Geskiedenis* III, 1–61; Cloete, *Anglo-Boer War*, 75, 79–81; Grobler, *War Reporter*, 25–30; Pretorius, *Historical Dictionary*, 117, 210, 256, 332–335.

55 Churchill, *Boer War*, 106–112.

56 See above, pp. 19–20.

57 Breytenbach, *Geskiedenis* III, 62–106; Churchill, *Boer War*, 112–126; Cloete, *Anglo-Boer War*, 82–86; Grobler, *War Reporter*, 31–33; Nasson, *War*, 154–155; Pakenham, *Boer War*, 277–284; Pretorius, *Historical Dictionary*, 486–487.

58 Breytenbach, *Geskiedenis* III, 113–167; Churchill, *Boer War*, 127–131; Churchill, *My Early Life*, 307–308; Cloete, *Anglo-Boer War*, 82–86; Sandys, *Churchill*, 149–154.

59 Breytenbach, *Geskiedenis* III, 168–219; Churchill, *Boer War*, 137–139; Churchill, *My Early Life*, 311–312; Pakenham, *Boer War*, 288–305; Pretorius, *Historical Dictionary*, 426–428, 501–502; Sandys, *Churchill*, 161–163.

60 Breytenbach, *Geskiedenis* III, 219–230; Churchill, *Boer War*, 139–140; Churchill, *My Early Life*, 312–314.

61 Breytenbach, *Geskiedenis* III, 230–236; Churchill, *Boer War*, 140, 150–151; Churchill, *My Early Life*, 314; Pretorius, *Historical Dictionary*, 325–428.

62 See above, p. 187.

63 Breytenbach, *Geskiedenis* III, 237–437; Churchill, *Boer War*, 156–178; Churchill, *My Early Life*, 314–322; Cloete, *Anglo-Boer War*, 91–94, 101, 103–104; Grobler, *War Reporter*, 39–40, 42, 44; Nasson, *War*, 161–165; Pakenham, *Boer War*, 344–349; Pretorius, *Historical Dictionary*, 325, 468–469; Roberts, *Churchill*, 283–286; Sandys, *Churchill*, 167, 170–173.

64 Breytenbach, *Geskiedenis* IV, 101–231; Cloete, *Anglo-Boer War*, 91, 95–97; Grobler, *War Reporter*, 29, 41; Nasson, *War*, 167–171; Pakenham, *Boer War*, 314–320, 327–328; Pretorius, *Historical Dictionary*, 388–389.

65 Cloete, *Anglo-Boer War*, 98; Steve Lunderstedt, ed., *Summer of 1899: The Siege of Kimberley 14 October 1899 to 15 February 1900* (Kimberley, 1999), 220–228; Pakenham, *Boer War*, 321–328; Pretorius, *Historical Dictionary*, 212–215; Brian Roberts, *Kimberley: Turbulent City* (Cape Town, 1985), 313–333.

66 Breytenbach, *Geskiedenis* III, 359–371; Grobler, *War Reporter*, 37.

67 Breytenbach, *Geskiedenis* III, 444–525; Churchill, *Boer War*, 179–194; Churchill, *My Early Life*, 322–324; Cloete, *Anglo-Boer War*, 104–110; Grobler, *War Reporter*, 46; Pakenham, *Boer War*, 356–361; Pretorius, *Historical Dictionary*, 325–327; Roberts, *Churchills*, 286; Sandys, *Churchill*, 173–174.

68 Breytenbach, *Geskiedenis* IV, 232–239; Pakenham, *Boer War*, 318–320.

69 Breytenbach, *Geskiedenis* IV, 232–430; Cloete, *Anglo-Boer War*, 104–111; Grobler, *War Reporter*, 43–45; Nasson, *War*, 172–178; Pakenham, *Boer War*, 331–342; Pretorius, *Historical Dictionary*, 110–11, 309–315, 388–389.

70 See above, p. 161.

71 Breytenbach, *Geskiedenis* III, 526–572; Churchill, *Boer War*, 195–210; Churchill, *My Early Life*, 324–326; Cloete, *Anglo-Boer War*, 111–112; Grobler, *War Reporter*, 46; Nasson, *War*, 156–161; Pakenham, *Boer War*, 356–368; Pretorius, *Historical Dictionary*, 327–329; Roberts, *Churchills*, 286–287; Sandys, *Churchill*, 174–178.

72 Roberts, *Churchills*, 286–291; Sandys, *Churchill*, 169–170, 182–184.

73 Joseph J. Doke, ed., *M.K. Gandhi: An Indian Patriot in South Africa* (London, 1909), 52–57; Eric Itzkin, 'The Indian War Memorial: National Memory and Selective Forgetting', *Historia* 54, 1 (2009), 147–158; Shula Marks, 'British Nursing and the South African War', in Greg Cuthbertson et al., eds., *Writing a Wider War*, 159–185; Russell Miller, *The Adventures of Arthur Conan Doyle* (London, 2008), 204–219; Stephen M. Miller, *Volunteers on the Veld: Britain's Citizen-Soldiers and the South African War, 1899–1902* (Norman, 2007), 55–76.

74 Breytenbach, *Geskiedenis* III, 568–572; Churchill, *Boer War*, 211–224; Pakenham, *Boer War*, 224–225, 237–238, 293, 347, 352–355; Pretorius, *Historical Dictionary*, 274–278; J.C. de Villiers, *Healers, Helpers and Hospitals: A History of Military Medicine in the Anglo-Boer War* (Pretoria, 2008), I, 127–163, 309–333; II, 13–117.

75 Zuster Hellemans, *Met het Roode Kruis mee in den Boeren-Vrijheidsoorlog* (Amsterdam, 1901), 47–120; De Villiers, *Healers*, I, 426–432.

76 Pretorius, *Historical Dictionary*, 275–276; De Villiers, *Healers*, 340–374.

77 Van Niekerk, *Leyds as gesant*, 125–132; Pretorius, *Historical Dictionary*, 275–276; De Villiers, *Healers*, 413–556.

78 Leyds, *Tweede verzameling* I, 516–523.

79 Leyds, *Tweede verzameling*, 302–303, 383–384, 445, 454–455.

80 See above, pp. 164–166; Leyds, *Tweede verzameling* I, 385, 402–403, 439–440, 447–467; W.J. Leyds, *Derde verzameling (correspondentie 1900)* (The Hague, 1931) I, 115–117; Van Niekerk, *Leyds as gesant*, 144–149.

81 Leyds, *Tweede verzameling* I, 308–309, 356–359, 369–372.

82 See above, pp. 161–163; Leyds, *Tweede verzameling* I, 416-417, 464–465 and II, 175.

83 Breytenbach, *Geskiedenis* V, 32–26, 557–563; Leyds, *Tweede verzameling* I, 413, 416–427, 468–469, 476–477, 494–496; II, 175–189.

84 Breytenbach, *Geskiedenis* V, 285–288; Pakenham, *Boer War*, 381–385; De Villiers,

Healers, I, 287–293; II, 105–112.

85 Churchill, *Boer War*, 225–236; Churchill, *My Early Life*, 327–334; Roberts, *Churchills*, 309–312; Sandys, *Churchill*, 184–189; Woods, *Young Winston's Wars*, 138.

86 Churchill, *Boer War*, 5, 237–240; Vincent J. Cirillo, *Bullets and Bacilli: The Spanish-American War and Military Medicine* (Piscataway, 1999), 138–145; Miller, *Adventures*, 212–217; Pretorius, *Historical Dictionary*, 276–277; Sandys, *Churchill*, 189–191; De Villiers, *Healers*, I, 287–293, II, 105–112.

87 Breytenbach, *Geskiedenis* V, 3–4, 107, 123–125; Churchill, *Boer War*, 237–245; Churchill, *My Early Life*, 335–336; Cloete, *Anglo-Boer War*, 118, 120, 121, 136; Grobler, *War Reporter*, 51, 61; Pakenham, *Boer War*, 375–380; Pretorius, *Historical Dictionary*, 337; Roberts, *Churchills*, 312–314; Sandys, *Churchill*, 192–194.

88 Breytenbach, *Geskiedenis* V, 156–171; Cloete, *Anglo-Boer War*, 119–120, 122–125, 129–136; Grobler, *War Reporter*, 51–52, 59–61; Pakenham, *Boer War*, 386–389; C.R. de Wet, *De strijd tusschen Boer en Brit. De herinnering van den Boeren-Generaal C.R. de Wet* (Amsterdam and Pretoria, 1902), 80.

89 Breytenbach, *Geskiedenis* V, 156–171; Cloete, *Anglo-Boer War*, 119–120, 122–125, 129–136; Grobler, *War Reporter*, 51–52, 59–61; Pakenham, *Boer War*, 390–394; Pretorius, *Historical Dictionary*, 292–293, 400–402; De Wet, *Strijd*, 88–112.

90 Breytenbach, *Geskiedenis* V, 156–158, 171–172, 418–419; Cloete, *Anglo-Boer War*, 118; Grobler, *War Reporter*, 166; Leyds, *Tweede verzameling* I, xviii, 501–506; II, 178–179; Leyds, *Derde verzameling*, vii–xii, 8–19, 25–40, 47, 50–51.

91 Churchill, *Boer War*, 244–272; Churchill, *My Early Life*, 335–341; Roberts, *Churchills*, 312–315; Sandys, *Churchill*, 192–197.

92 Breytenbach, *Geskiedenis* V, 506; Churchill, *Boer War*, 290–316; Churchill, *My Early Life*, 341–344; Roberts, *Churchills*, 316–317; Sandys, *Churchill*, 198–200.

93 See above, pp. 18–21.

94 Hellemans, *Met het Roode Kruis mee*, 143–164.

95 Cloete, *Anglo-Boer War*, 142–145; Grobler, *War Reporter*, 67–68; Pretorius, *Historical Dictionary*, 141–142, 255–258.

96 John L. Comaroff, ed., *The Boer War Diary of Sol T. Plaatje: An African at Mafeking* (Johannesburg, 1973), 11–159; Pat Hopkins and Heather Dugmore, *The Boy: Baden-Powell and the Siege of Mafeking* (Rivonia, 1999), xv–xviii, 167–175; Pakenham, *Boer War*, 396–419; Pretorius, *Historical Dictionary*, 22–24, 255–258, 331–332; Roberts, *Churchills*, 292–308; Warwick, *Black People*, 30–38.

97 Cloete, *Anglo-Boer War*, 142–145; Pakenham, *Boer War*, 414–418; Porter, *Absent-Minded Imperialists*, 52–53, 194–196; Pretorius, *Historical Dictionary*, 22–24, 255–258; Roberts, *Churchills*, 304–308.

98 See above, p. 149.

99 Cammack, *Rand*, 101–109; Cloete, *Anglo-Boer War*, 147–148; Grobler, *War Reporter*, 63; Leyds, *Tweede verzameling* II, 202–203; Leyds, *Derde verzameling* II, 34–38.

100 Breytenbach, *Geskiedenis* V, 515–549; Churchill, *Boer War*, 328–350; Churchill, *My Early Life*, 344–349; Cloete, *Anglo-Boer War*, 150–152; Pakenham, *Boer War*, 419–433; Pretorius, *Historical Dictionary*, 128–129; Roberts, *Churchills*, 316–320; Sandys, *Churchill*, 198–203.

101 Breytenbach, *Geskiedenis* V, 542–556; Churchill, *Boer War*, 351–356, 387–390; Churchill, *My Early Life*, 349–352; Cloete, *Anglo-Boer War*, 151–157; Grobler, *War Reporter*, 71–76; Nasson, *War*, 199–203; Pakenham, *Boer War*, 431–434; Roberts, *Churchills*, 320–322.

102 Breytenbach, *Geskiedenis* V, 535–556; Cloete, *Anglo-Boer War*, 153–157; Grobler, *War Reporter*, 71–76; Hancock and Van der Poel, *Selections*, 537–553; Pretorius, *Historical Dictionary*, 396–397.

103 Churchill, *Boer War*, 389–401; Cloete, *Anglo-Boer War*, 158–160; Grobler, *War Reporter*, 77; Hancock and Van der Poel, *Selections*, 547–561; Pakenham, *Boer War*,

434; Pretorius, *Historical Dictionary,* 122–123; Roberts, *Churchills,* 328–329; Sandys, *Churchill,* 204–208.

104 Leyds, *Derde verzameling,* I, xvi–xvii, 134–135, 146–147.

105 Leyds, *Derde verzameling,* I, x–xii, 150–155; II, 65–70.

106 Leyds, *Derde verzameling,* I, 107, 113–115.

107 Leyds, *Derde verzameling,* I, xx–xxiii; II, 49–64.

108 *Het Nieuws van den Dag,* 12–06–1900, source for the translated quotes.

109 Churchill, *Boer War,* 400–401; Churchill, *My Early Life,* 353–354; Roberts, *Churchills,* 323–331; Sandys, *Churchill,* 204–209.

Part III: Death and destruction

1 Deneys Reitz described his experiences in the Anglo-Boer War in Dutch and English in his unpublished memoirs, 'Herinneringen', now in the Brenthurst Library in Johannesburg, which he used later for his *Commando: A Boer Journal of the Boer War* (London, 1929) and the Afrikaans translation *Kommando. 'n Boere-dagboek uit die Engelse Oorlog* (Bloemfontein, 1929). The passages quoted in the present publication are from *Commando: A Boer Journal of the Boer War* (London 1948). See also his biography by G.J. Calitz, *Deneys Reitz (1822–1944). Krygsman, avonturier en politikus* (Pretoria, 2008).

2 Calitz, *Deneys Reitz,* 78; Grobler, *War Reporter,* 71–75, 78; Nasson, *War,* 197; Pakenham, *Boer War,* 430–431; Pretorius, *Historical Dictionary,* 371–372; F.W. Reitz, *Outobiografie en 62 gedigte* (Cape Town, 1978), 43–44; Reitz, *Kommando,* 103–110.

3 J. Ploeger, *Die lotgevalle van die burgerlike bevolking gedurende die Anglo-Boereoorlog, 1899–1902,* 5 vols. (Pretoria, 1990), ch. 13: 5–14.

4 Cloete, *Anglo-Boer War,* 155–163; Grobler, *War Reporter,* 75, 79, 81; A.M. Grundlingh, *Die 'Hendsoppers' en 'Joiners'. Die rasionaal en verskynsel van verraad* (Pretoria, 1979), 7–44, 58–62; Leyds, *Vierde verzameling* II, 93–96; Ploeger, *Lotgevalle,* ch. 13: 13–24; Pretorius, *Historical Dictionary,* 388–391; S.B. Spies, *Methods of Barbarism? Roberts and Kitchener and Civilians in the Boer Republics: January 1900—May 1902* (Cape Town, 1977), 90–95, 101–117.

5 W.L. von R. Scholtz, *Generaal Christiaan de Wet as veldheer* (Leiden, 1978), 183; M.C.E. van Schoor, *Christiaan Rudolph de Wet. Krygsman en volksman* (Pretoria, 2007), 107–108.

6 Grundlingh, *'Hendsoppers',* 20–25; Ploeger, *Lotgevalle,* ch. 11: 10, 16, 18, 20; ch. 14: 13–16; Pretorius, *Historical Dictionary,* 108–110, 406–407.

7 Leyds, *Derde verzameling* II, 89; Ploeger, *Lotgevalle,* ch. 13: 11, 14.

8 Cloete, *Anglo-Boer War,* 154–163; Grobler, *War Reporter,* 78–86; Nasson, *War,* 199–205; Ploeger, *Lotgevalle,* ch. 11: 45, 11–13, 20, 23, 25, 26-43; ch. 12: 1–3; ch. 13: 19–23.

9 Calitz, *Deneys Reitz,* 92–93; Reitz, *Outobiografie,* 43–45; Reitz, *Kommando,* 110–115.

10 Albert Blake, *Boereverraaier. Teregstellings tydens die Anglo-Boereoorlog* (Cape Town, 2010), 59–62; Cloete, *Anglo-Boer War,* 171, 174; Mark Coghlan, 'The Other De Wet: Piet de Wet and the Boer "Hendsoppers in the Anglo-Boer War"', http://samilitaryhistory. org/vol116mc.html; Grobler, *War Reporter,* 89; Grundlingh, *'Hendsoppers',* 241–251; Pretorius, *Historical Dictionary,* 121–122, 244–246; Pieter le Roux, 'Verraaier of held. Verdere gedagtes oor Genl Piet de Wet', *Knapzak 21,* 2 (October 2009); Scholtz, *De Wet,* 194–195; Van Schoor, *De Wet,* 109–118; C.W.L. de Souza, *No Charge for Delivery* (Cape Town, 1969), 134–135; De Wet, *Strijd,* 166–168, 184.

11 Calitz, *Deneys Reitz,* 92–93; Cloete, *Anglo-Boer War,* 127–176; Grobler, *War Reporter,* 90; Reitz, *Kommando,* 115–117.

12 Cloete, *Anglo-Boer War,* 171–181; Grobler, *War Reporter,* 87, 90; Spies, *Methods,*

128–127.

13 Cloete, *Anglo-Boer War*, 171–181; Emily Hobhouse, *The Brunt of the War and Where It Fell* (London, 1902), 22–28; Pakenham, *Boer War*, 451–455; Ploeger, *Lotgevalle*, ch. 13: 36–40; ch. 28: 10–14, 22–40; Pretorius, *Historical Dictionary*, 104; Spies, *Methods*, 43–44, 128–137.

14 Cloete, *Anglo-Boer War*, 171–181; Grobler, *War Reporter*, 87, 90; Pakenham, *Boer War*, 438–445; Pretorius, *Historical Dictionary*, 57–58, 333–335.

15 Cloete, *Anglo-Boer War*, 171–181; Grobler, *War Reporter*, 89–93; Pakenham, *Boer War*, 451–455; Pretorius, *Historical Dictionary*, 120–121; Von Scholtz, *De Wet*, 221–246; De Wet, *Strijd*, 176–179.

16 Leyds, *Derde verzameling* I, ix–x, 195–196, 235–236, 238, 256–260, 90–93.

17 Leyds, *Derde verzameling* I, 184–187, 192–193, 197–198.

18 See above, p. 108.

19 Leyds, *Derde verzameling* I, 264–273, 280; II, 94–101.

20 Cloete, *Anglo-Boer War*, 181–185; Grobler, *War Reporter*, 93, 95; Pakenham, *Boer War*, 451, 454–456; Pretorius, *Historical Dictionary*, 33–36; Reitz, *Kommando*, 117–119.

21 Cloete, *Anglo-Boer War*, 287–188; Grobler, *War Reporter*, 95; Pretorius, *Historical Dictionary*, 36, 228.

22 Cloete, *Anglo-Boer War*, 186–187; Grobler, *War Reporter*, 96; Reitz, *Kommando*, 117–123.

23 Calitz, *Deneys Reitz*, 93–94; Reitz, *Kommando*, 124–126.

24 http://www.tokencoins.com/oompaul.htm.

25 See above, pp. 36–38.

26 Grobler, *War Reporter*, 95; Spies, *Methods*, 116–124.

27 Spies, *Methods*, 124–127.

28 Cloete, *Anglo-Boer War*, 188–193; Grobler, *War Reporter*, 95; Grundlingh, 'Hendsoppers', 54–58; Ploeger, *Lotgevalle*, ch. 14: 21–26; ch. 29: 15–18; Pretorius, *Historical Dictionary*, 104–105; Spies, *Methods*, 143–145.

29 See above, p. 174. Churchill, *My Early Life*, 355–356; Sandys, *Churchill*, 209–211.

30 See above, pp. 222–223.

31 Churchill, *My Early Life*, 355–361; Robert Rhodes James, ed., *Winston S. Churchill: His Complete Speeches 1897–1963, volume 1: 1897–1908* (New York, 1974), 53–61; Jenkins, *Churchill*, 64–66; Sandys, *Churchill*, 211–215; http://en.wikipedia.org/wiki/United_Kingdom_general_election_1900.

32 Hancock and Van der Poel, *Smuts Papers* I, 340–342; Pakenham, *Boer War*, 470–472; Von Scholtz, *De Wet*, 287–293; S.B. Spies and Gail Nattrass, eds., *Jan Smuts: Memoirs of the Boer War* (Johannesburg, 1994), 110–133.

33 Pakenham, *Boer War*, 470–476; Pretorius, *Historical Dictionary*, 54; Von Scholtz, *De Wet*, 276–293; De Wet, *Strijd*, 226–230.

34 Calitz, *Deneys Reitz*, 94–97; Reitz, *Kommando*, 126–129.

35 *Algemeen Handelsblad*, 23 November 1900; *New York Times*, 23 November 1900.

36 *Algemeen Handelsblad*, 24–25 November 1900; Leyds, *Vierde verzameling* II, 1–7.

37 Leyds, *Vierde verzameling* II, 7–14; *cf.* above, pp. 65–69, 81, 87.

38 *Algemeen Handelsblad*, 14 December 1900; Bossenbroek, *Holland*, 343–344; Leyds, *Vierde verzameling* I, 25; II, 15–22.

39 Churchill, *My Early Life*, 363; Rhodes James, *Churchill: His Complete Speeches* I, 62–62; Jenkins, *Churchill*, 68–71; Sandys, *Churchill*, 212–213; *New York Times*, 13 December 1900.

40 Cloete, *Anglo-Boer War*, 199–207; Von Scholtz, *De Wet*, 293–314; De Wet, *Strijd*, 232–256.

41 Jennifer Hobhouse Balme, *To Love One's Enemies: The Work and Life of Emily Hobhouse* (Cobble Hill, 1994), 1–84; Pakenham, *Boer War*, 501–503; Rykie van

Reenen, ed., *Emily Hobhouse: Boer War Letters* (Cape Town, 1984), 1–46.

42 Calitz, *Deneys Reitz*, 97–101; Cloete, *Anglo-Boer War*, 205–206; Grobler, *War Reporter*, 101; Pakenham, *Boer War*, 476–481; Pretorius, *Historical Dictionary*, 303–304; Reitz, *Kommando*, 130–141; Spies and Nattrass, *Jan Smuts*, 146–157.

43 Grundlingh, 'Hendsoppers', 82–95, 248; Ploeger, *Lotgevalle*, ch. 14: 32–37; Spies, *Methods*, 205–206.

44 Grundlingh, 'Hendsoppers', 107; *Nieuwe Tilburgsche Courant*, 13 February 1901; Spies, *Methods*, 205–206.

45 Grundlingh, 'Hendsoppers', 109–117; Spies, *Methods*, 205–206.

46 Blake, *Boereverraaier*, 142–156; Grundlingh, 'Hendsoppers', 95–96, 101–104; Spies, *Methods*, 203–206.

47 See above, p. 227.

48 Ploeger, *Lotgevalle*, ch. 30: 34–38; Spies, *Methods*, 170–190.

49 Calitz, *Deneys Reitz*, 102–103; Cloete, *Anglo-Boer War*, 208, 218–219; Grobler, *War Reporter*, 105; Pakenham, *Boer War*, 496–499; Reitz, *Kommando*, 142–148.

50 See above, pp. 11 and 147.

51 Hobhouse, *Brunt*, 116–120; Hobhouse Balme, *To Love*, 85–98; Ploeger, *Lotgevalle*, ch. 41: 26–27, 36–38; ch. 43: 3–4, 6; Pretorius, *Historical Dictionary*, 102–106; Van Reenen, *Emily Hobhouse*, 46–57; Spies, *Methods*, 190–210.

52 Cloete, *Anglo-Boer War*, 218–229; Grobler, *War Reporter*, 110; Von Scholtz, *De Wet*, 321–370; De Wet, *Strijd*, 264–290.

53 Calitz, *Deneys Reitz*, 103–105; Reitz, *Kommando*, 149–154.

54 See above, p. 22.

55 Warwick, *Black People*, 110–124.

56 Nasson, *Abraham Esau's War*, 120–141.

57 Pakenham, *Boer War*, 468–469, 496, 501–505.

58 Churchill, *My Early Life*, 364–367; Rhodes James, *Churchill: His Complete Speeches* I, 65–67.

59 See above, p. 17.

60 See above, p. 302.

61 Reitz, *Kommando*, 154–160.

62 See above, pp. 115–116.

63 George Arthur, *Life of Lord Kitchener* (London, 1920) II, 18–26; Cloete, *Anglo-Boer War*, 226; Grobler, *War Reporter*, 109, 112; J.D. Kestell and D.E. van Velden, *Die vredesonderhandelinge tussen die regerings van die twee Suid-Afrikaanse Republieke en die verteenwoordigers van die Britse regering wat uitgeloop het op die vrede wat op 31 Mei 1902 op Vereeniging gesluit is* (Cape Town, 1982), 123; Nasson, *War*, 223–224; Pakenham, *Boer War*, 487–491, 499–500, 504; Pretorius, *Historical Dictionary*, 282; Von Scholtz, *De Wet*, 371–372; De Wet, *Strijd*, 294–297.

64 Reitz, *Kommando*, 161–169.

65 See above, pp. 220–222.

66 Leyds, *Vierde verzameling* II, 103–104.

67 Cloete, *Anglo-Boer War*, 232; Eric Rosenthal, *General De Wet: A Biography* (Cape Town, 1946), 84–85; De Wet, *Strijd*, 296.

68 See above, pp. 253–254.

69 Cloete, *Anglo-Boer War*, 238; Grobler, *War Reporter*, 115; Grundlingh, 'Hendsoppers', 152–153; Hancock and Van der Poel, *Selections* I, 389–391; Rosenthal, *General De Wet*, 85–87; De Wet, *Strijd*, 300–304.

70 Leyds, *Vierde verzameling* II, 84–88; Pakenham, *Boer War*, 513.

71 Hancock and Van der Poel, *Selections* I, 395–396; Leyds, *Vierde verzameling* I, xxviii, 186, 248–249.

72 Hancock and Van der Poel, *Selections* I, 397–399; Leyds, *Vierde verzameling* I, xxii, 252–254.

73 Cloete, *Anglo-Boer War*, 241–245; Grobler, *War Reporter*, 116, 118; Grundlingh, 'Hendsoppers', 153; Hancock and Van der Poel, *Selections*, 400–402; Leyds, *Vierde verzameling* II, 86–87, 89–92; Pakenham, *Boer War*, 520–521; De Wet, *Strijd*, 304–309.

74 Cloete, *Anglo-Boer War*, 236; Hobhouse, *Brunt*, 114–125; Emily Hobhouse, *Report of a Visit to the Camps of Women and Children in the Cape and Orange River Colonies* (London, 1901), 5–12; Pakenham, *Boer War*, 506–507; Van Reenen, *Emily Hobhouse*, 123.

75 Cloete, *Anglo-Boer War*, 240; Pakenham, *Boer War*, 501–503; Van Reenen, *Emily Hobhouse*, 115–116, 121.

76 Cloete, *Anglo-Boer War*, 242, 244; Hobhouse, *Report*, 14–15; Pakenham, *Boer War*, 503–504, 508; Van Reenen, *Emily Hobhouse*, 121–123, 125–126; W.T. Stead, *Methods of Barbarism: 'War is War' and 'War is Hell?' The Case for Intervention* (London, 1901).

77 Cloete, *Anglo-Boer War*, 244–245; Hobhouse, *Brunt*, 126–137; Hobhouse, *Report*, 13–14; Pakenham, *Boer War*, 504–510; Van Reenen, *Emily Hobhouse*, 115–116, 121.

78 Reitz, *Kommando*, 170–196.

79 See above, p. 271.

80 Reitz, *Kommando*, 197–200.

81 Cloete, *Anglo-Boer War*, 242, 246–247, 252; Pakenham, *Boer War*, 513; Pretorius, *Historical Dictionary*, 432–433.

82 Cloete, *Anglo-Boer War*, 256–258; Grobler, *War Reporter*, 121; Pakenham, *Boer War*, 499, 522, 529, 535–538; Pretorius, *Historical Dictionary*, 27–28, 46–47; Spies, *Methods*, 233–239.

83 Cloete, *Anglo-Boer War*, 245–246; Leyds, *Vierde verzameling* I, xxxviii–xxxix, 363–365; II, 125–128, 184–189.

84 Leyds, *Vierde verzameling* I, xl, 304; II, 114–124.

85 Hobhouse, *Brunt*, 145–140; Hobhouse Balme, *To Love*, 277–328.

86 Leyds, *Vierde verzameling* I, xxiv–xxvi, 122–123, 152, 154–158, 164–165, 265–265, 179–280, 342, 356–359, 459–460.

87 Hobhouse, *Brunt*, 319–346; Ploeger, *Lotgevalle*, chs. 41 and 42; Pretorius, *Historical Dictionary*, 104–106, 145–146, 184–185; Spies, *Methods*, 221–227, 252–269.

88 Churchill, *My Early Life*, 367–370; Rhodes James, *Churchill: His Complete Speeches* I, 70–86.

89 Rhodes James, *Churchill: His Complete Speeches* I, 87–90.

90 Rhodes James, *Churchill: His Complete Speeches* I, 95–109.

91 Calitz, *Deneys Reitz*, 108–109; Hancock and Van der Poel, *Smuts Papers* I, 430–431; Reitz, *Kommando*, 200–201.

92 See above, p. 190.

93 See above, p. 164; Pretorius, *Historical Dictionary*, 210–211; Warwick, *Black People*, 45–46.

94 See above, p. 27.

95 Nasson, *Abraham Esau's War*, 19–21; Pretorius, *Historical Dictionary*, 29–31, 42–44, 210–211, 317–318, 443–444; Warwick, *Black People*, 63–74, 87–90, 96–109, 119–122.

96 See above, p. 336–337.

97 Cloete, *Anglo-Boer War*, 247, 255–256; Warwick, *Black People*, 19–25.

98 See above, p. 62.

99 Cloete, *Anglo-Boer War*, 254–256; Pretorius, *Historical Dictionary*, 421, 444; Warwick, *Black People*, 100–101, 107.

100 See above, pp. 297–298.

101 Pakenham, *Boer War*, 528–532.

102 See above, p. 354.

103 Cloete, *Anglo-Boer War*, 344; Ploeger, *Lotgevalle*, ch. 43; Pretorius, *Historical Dictionary*, 102–106; Warwick, *Black People*, 145–157.

104 Calitz, *Deneys Reitz*, 109–116; Cloete, *Anglo-Boer War*, 266; Hancock and Van der Poel, *Smuts Papers* I, 410–412, 422–427; Reitz, *Kommando*, 205–236.

105 Calitz, *Deneys Reitz*, 115–116; Hancock and Van der Poel, *Smuts Papers* I, 412–413; Reitz, *Kommando*, 236–244.

106 See above, pp. 286–287.

107 Leyds, *Vierde verzameling* I, xxxiv–xxxvi, 378–379, 392–393, 450–451; II, 135–141; http://avalon.law.yale.edu/19th_century/hague02.asp.

108 Calitz, *Deneys Reitz*, 116–117; Pretorius, *Historical Dictionary*, 464–465; Reitz, *Kommando*, 246–255.

109 Calitz, *Deneys Reitz*, 116–119; Hancock and Van der Poel, *Smuts Papers* I, 419–428; Reitz, *Commando*, 250, 264–265; Reitz, *Kommando*, 255–274.

110 See above, p. 112.

111 See above, pp. 315–316.

112 Leyds, *Vierde verzameling* I, xxxvi, xl–xl, xlv–xlvi, 448–450, 462-465; II, 153–155, 158, 161–162; Wilson, *International Impact*, 110–112.

113 See above, pp. 360–361.

114 Hancock and Van der Poel, *Smuts Papers* I, 437–505.

115 Calitz, *Deneys Reitz*, 120–123; Reitz, *Kommando*, 227–293.

116 Cloete, *Anglo-Boer War*, 296; Hancock and Van der Poel, *Smuts Papers* I, 513; Nasson, *Abraham Esau's War*, 108–114; Pretorius, *Historical Dictionary*, 240–241, 265–266; Reitz, *Kommando*, 288–290; Warwick, *Black People*, 122.

117 Blake, *Boereverraaier*, 230–238; Pretorius, *Historical Dictionary*, 95; Reitz, *Kommando*, 288–290; see above, pp. 294–295.

118 See above, p. 315–316; Blake Boereverraaier, 30–44, 84–115, 158–175.

119 Blake, *Boereverraaier*, 45–62, 202–204; Grundlingh, 'Hendsoppers', 198–230; Pretorius, *Historical Dictionary*, 200–202.

120 Blake, *Boereverraaier*, 68–72, 284–285; Hancock and Van der Poel, *Smuts Papers* I, 446.

121 Blake, *Boereverraaier*, 64–67.

122 See above, p. 325.

123 Churchill, *My Early Life*, 368; Cloete, *Anglo-Boer War*, 294–295, 310, 317; Grobler, *War Reporter*, 133; Leyds, *Vierde verzameling* I, 603–604; Pretorius, *Historical Dictionary*, 224–225, 249, 404–406.

124 See above pp. 183–185, 238, 272, 284–286.

125 Cloete, *Anglo-Boer War*, 304–305; Grobler, *War Reporter*, 137; Pakenham, *Boer War*, 549, 556; Pretorius, *Historical Dictionary*, 503–504.

126 Cloete, *Anglo-Boer War*, 308–311; Grobler, *War Reporter*, 139; Pakenham, *Boer War*, 549, 556; Pretorius, *Historical Dictionary*, 280–281, 461–462.

127 Calitz, *Deneys Reitz*, 124–130; Cloete, *Anglo-Boer War*, 316–317; Reitz, *Commando*, 298–313; Reitz, *Kommando*, 294–309.

128 Reitz, *Kommando*, 310–314.

129 Kestell and Van Velden, *Vredesonderhandelinge*, 15–20; Leyds, *Vierde verzameling* II, 177–183.

130 See above, p. 375; Leyds, *Vierde verzameling* I, xlvii–l.

131 Leyds, *Vierde verzameling* I, 155–157.

132 Leyds, *Vierde verzameling* I, 672.

133 See above, p. 340.

134 See above, pp. 332–334.

135 Arthur, *Life of Lord Kitchener* II, 86–94; Cloete, *Anglo-Boer War*, 321–324; Kestell and Van Velden, *Vredesonderhandelinge*, 15–20; Pakenham, *Boer War*, 551–554.

136 See above, p. 293.

137 Calitz, *Deneys Reitz*, 131–134; Reitz, *Kommando*, 314–318.

138 Cloete, *Anglo-Boer War*, 326–328; Kestell and Van Velden, *Vredesonderhandelinge*, 51–91.

139 Cloete, *Anglo-Boer War*, 328; Kestell and Van Velden, *Vredesonderhandelinge*, 90–116; see above, pp. 332–334.

140 Pakenham, *Boer War*, 561.

141 Cloete, *Anglo-Boer War*, 329–332; Kestell and Van Velden, *Vredesonderhandelinge*, 116–175; Pakenham, *Boer War*, 564–570.

Epilogue

1 www.bloemfontein.co.za/renaming-big.jpg.

2 dailymaverick.co.za/article/2012–0329-south-africa-the-returnof-the-namechanging-cliffhanger.

3 www.afriforum.co.za/t-hemde-tee-naamsveranderinge.

4 See above, pp. 22–24, 60–62. Cf. also the recent commotion surrounding the historically inspired so-called 'white' and 'black' songs, the most striking examples being, on the one hand, the popular Afrikaans song *'De la Rey'* by Bok van Blerk and, on the other hand, the struggle song *'Awudubhule ibhunu'* (Shoot the Boer), revived by the ANC Youth League. Albert Grundlingh, 'Die historiese in die hede. Dinamika van die De la Rey-fenomeen in Afrikanerkringe, 2006–2007', *New Contree* 53 (2007), 135–154.

5 www.info.gov.za/speech/DynamicAction?pageid=461andsid=27620andtid= 69127; www.info.gov.za/speech/DynamicAction?pageid=461andsid= 28766andtid=74709.

6 Lake and Reynolds, *Drawing*; Nasson, *War*; Warwick, *Black People*, passim.

7 Leyds, *Vierde verzameling* I, xlix–li, 756–757; Bossenbroek, 'Geschiedschrijving', 209–210; Van Niekerk, *Kruger se regterhand*, 356.

8 Pakenham, *Boer War*, 561–562.

9 Jenkins, *Churchill*, passim; Pretorius, *Historical Dictionary*, 80, 107–108, 374–376; Deneys Reitz, *Trekking On* (London, 1933), 122–123, 149–150.

10 Cloete, *Anglo-Boer War*; Nasson, *War*; Pakenham, *Boer War*; Pretorius, *Historical Dictionary*, passim.

11 Calitz, *Deneys Reitz*, 135–137; Reitz, *Kommando*, 319–321.

12 Deneys Reitz, *No Outspan* (London, 1943), passim.

13 See above, pp. 404–406; Marc Howard Ross, *Cultural Contestation in Ethnic Conflict* (Cambridge, 2007), 240–250; www.info.gov.za/ speech/ DynamicAction?pageid=461andid=25951andtid=60804; www.freedompark.co.za/ cms/index.php?option=com_contentandvie=articleandid=29 andItemid=35andphpMyAdmin=17b79oef73ob81dao 9aI3c43cI2692b2.

Bibliography

Archive material used for this book—the Leyds Collection and the archives of the Nederlandsche Zuid-Afrikaansche Spoorweg-Maatschappij (Netherlands-South African Railway Company)—are in the National Archives of the Netherlands in The Hague and South Africa House in Amsterdam. Most of the literature listed below can be found at the African Studies Centre in Leiden and South Africa House in Amsterdam. I am grateful to the staff of both, and to the staff of the War Museum of the Boer Republics in Bloemfontein, for their kind assistance. I would also like to thank students of the history faculty at Utrecht University for their inspiring enthusiasm.

Alberts, Paul, ed., *Die smarte van oorlog. Verontregting van Boerevroue en -kinders tydens die Anglo-Boereoorlog 1899–1902*, Brandfort, 2005

Arthur, George, *Life of Lord Kitchener*, London, 1920

Badsey, Stephen, 'The Boer War as a Media War,' in Peter Dennis and Jeffrey Gredy, eds., *The Boer War: Army, Nation and Empire*, Canberra, 2000, 70–83

Blake, Albert, *Boereverraaier. Teregstellings tydens die Anglo-Boereoorlog*, Cape Town 2010

Boje, John and Fransjohan Pretorius, '"Kent gij dat volk?" The Anglo-Boer War and Afrikaner Identity in Postmodern Perspective', *Historia* 56 (2012), 59–72

Bossenbroek, Martin, 'Geschiedschrijving als hoger beroep. Willem Johannes Leyds, Advocaat van de Boeren (1859–1940)', in M.Ph. Bossenbroek, M.E.H.N. Mout and C. Musterd, eds., *Historici in de politiek*, Leiden, 1996, 191–211

Bossenbroek, Martin, *Holland op zijn breedst. Indië en Zuid-Afrika in de Nederlandse cultuur omstreeks 1900*, Amsterdam, 1996

Bossenbroek, Martin, 'The Netherlands and the Boer War. Their Wildest Dreams: The Representation of South Africa in Culture, Imperialism and Nationalism at the Turn of the Century', in K.M. Wilson, ed., *The International Impact of the Boer War*, Leeds, 2001, 123–139

Bottomore, Stephen, *Filming, Faking and Propaganda: The Origins of the War Film, 1897–1902*, Utrecht, 2007

Brandt, Johanna, *Die Kappie Kommando of Boerevrouwen in geheime dienst*, Cape Town, 1913

Breytenbach, J.H., *Die geskiedenis van die Tweede Vryheidsoorlog in Suid-Afrika, 1899–1902*, 6 vols., Pretoria, 1969

Cain, P.J., *Hobson and Imperialism: Radicalism, New Liberalism, and Finance 1887–1938*, Oxford, 2002

Calitz, G.J., *Deneys Reitz (1882–1944). Krygsman, avonturier en politikus*, Pretoria, 2008

Cammack, Diana, *The Rand at War 1899–1902: The Witwatersrand and the Anglo-Boer War*, London, 1990

Changuion, Louis, Frik Jacobs and Paul Alberts, *Suffering of War: A Photographic Portrayal of the Suffering in the Anglo-Boer War*, Bloemfontein, 2003

Churchill, Winston S., *My Early Life, 1874–1904; with an introduction by William Manchester*, New York, 1996

Churchill, Winston S., *The Boer War: London to Ladysmith via Pretoria and Ian Hamilton's March*, London, 2002

Cirillo, Vincent J., *Bullets and Bacilli: The Spanish-American War and Military Medicine*, Piscataway, 1999

Cloete, Pieter G., *The Anglo-Boer War: A Chronology*, Pretoria, 2000

Cloete, Stuart, *African Portraits: A Biography of Paul Kruger, Cecil Rhodes and Lobengula, Last King of the Matabele*, London, 1946

Comaroff, John L., ed., *The Boer War Diary of Sol T Plaatje: An African at Mafeking*, Johannesburg, 1973

Conan Doyle, Arthur, *The War in South Africa, Its Cause and Conduct*, New York, 1902

Cooper-Chadwick, J., *Three Years with Lobengula, and Experiences in South Africa*, London, 1894

Cuthbertson, Greg and A.M. Grundlingh, eds., *Writing a Wider War: Rethinking Gender, Race, and Identity in the South African War, 1899–1902*, Athens, 2002

Darwin, John, *The Empire Project: The Rise and Fall of the British World-System 1830–1970*, Cambridge, 2009

De Graaff, B.J.H., *De mythe van de stamverwantschap. Nederland en de Afrikaners 1902–1930*, Amsterdam, 1993

De Jong, Alwin, *Wil de ware Afrikaner opstaan? De Boerenoorlog als ijkpunt van nationalisme in Zuid-Afrika (1815–1925)*, Bachelor's thesis, University of Utrecht, 2012

De Jong, R.C., G.M. van der Waal and D.H. Heydenrych, *NZASM 100: 1887–1899: The Buildings, Steam Engines and Structures of the Netherlands South African Railway Company*, Pretoria, 1988

De Souza, C.W.L., *No Charge for Delivery*, Cape Town, 1969

De Valk, J.P. and M. van Faassen, eds., *Dagboeken en aantekeningen van Willem Hendrik de Beaufort 1874–1918*, 2 vols., The Hague, 1993

De Villiers, J.C., *Healers, Helpers and Hospitals: A History of Military Medicine in the Anglo-Boer War*, 2 vols., Pretoria, 2008

De Wet, Christiaan, *De strijd tussen Boer en Brit. De herinnering van den Boeren-generaal C.R. de Wet*, Amsterdam and Pretoria, 1902

Doke, Joseph J., ed., *M.K. Gandhi: An Indian Patriot in South Africa*, London, 1909

Du Preez, Max, *Of Warriors, Lovers, and Prophets: Unusual Stories from South Africa's Past*, Cape Town, 2004

Ferreira, Jeanette, ed., *Boereoorlogstories. 34 verhale oor die oorlog van 1899–1902*, 2nd edition, Cape Town, 2011

First, Ruth and Ann Scott, *Olive Schreiner: A Biography*, New York, 1980

FitzPatrick, J.P., *The Transvaal from Within: A Private Record of Public Affairs*, London, 1899

Giliomee, Hermann, *The Afrikaners: Biography of a People*, Cape Town, 2010

Godby, Michael, 'Confronting Horror: Emily Hobhouse and the Concentration Camp Photographs of the South African War', *Kronos* 32 (2006), 34–48

Grobler, Jackie, ed., *The War Diary of Johanna Brandt*, Pretoria, 2007

Grobler, Jackie, *The War Reporter: The Anglo-Boer War through the Eyes of the Burghers*, Johannesburg, 2011

Grundlingh, Albert, 'Die historiese in die hede. Dinamika van die De la Rey-fenomeen in Afrikanerkringe, 2006–2007', *New Contree* 53 (2007), 135–154

Grundlingh, Albert, 'Reframing Remembrance: The Politics of the Centenary Commemoration of the South African War of 1899–1902', *Journal of Southern African Studies* 30, 2 (2004), 359–375

Grundlingh, Albert, *The Dynamics of Treason: Boer Collaboration in the South African War of 1899–1902*, Pretoria, 2006

Grundlingh, Albert, 'The National Women's Monument: The Making and Mutation of Meaning in Afrikaner Memory of the South African War', www.celat.ulaval.ca/histoire.memoire/histoire/cape/grundlingh.htm

Grundlingh, A.M., *Die 'Hendsoppers' en 'Joiners'. Die rasionaal en verskynsel van verraad*, Cape Town, 1979

Hancock, W.K. and Jean van der Poel, eds., *Selections from the Smuts Papers. Volume I: June 1886–1902*, Cambridge, 1966

Heese, J.A., *Die herkoms van die Afrikaner 1657–1867*, Cape Town, 1971

Hellemans, Zuster, *Met het Roode Kruis mee in den Boeren-Vrijheidsoorlog*, Amsterdam, 1901

Hobhouse, Emily, *Report of a Visit to the Camps of Women and Children in the Cape and Orange River Colonies*, London, 1901

Hobhouse, Emily, *The Brunt of the War, and Where It Fell*, London, 1902

Hobhouse Balme, Jennifer, ed., *To Love One's Enemies: The Work and Life of Emily Hobhouse*, Cobble Hill, 1994

Hopkins, Pat and Heather Dugmore, *The Boy: Baden-Powell and the Siege of Mafeking*, Rivonia, 1999

Ingham, Kenneth, *Jan Christian Smuts: The Conscience of a South African*, London, 1986

In memoriam NZASM, Amsterdam, 1910

Itzkin, Eric, 'The Indian War Memorial: National Memory and Selective Forgetting', *Historia* 54, 1 (2009), 147–158

Jaarverslagen NZASM, 1895–1898

James, Robert Rhodes, ed., *Winston S. Churchill: His Complete Speeches 1897–1963, vol. I: 1897–1908*, London, 1974

Jannash, Hans, *Onder Boeren, Britten en Bantoes*, Amsterdam, 1942

Jansen, Ena and Wilfred Jonckheere, eds., *Boer en Brit. Ooggetuigen en schrijvers over de Anglo-Boerenoorlog in Zuid-Afrika*, Amsterdam, 2006

Jenkins, Roy, *Churchill*, London, 2002

Kapp, Pieter, '31 Mei 1902–31 Mei 2002. Twee vredes, twee visies, een toekoms. Die betekenis van die Anglo-Boereoorlog vir vandag en môre', *Tydskrif vir Geesteswetenskappe* 42, 4 (2002), 273–281

Kestell, J.D., *Met de Boeren-commando's. Mijne ervaringen als veldprediker*, Amsterdam and Pretoria, 1902

Kestell, J.D. and D.E. van Velden, *Die vredesonderhandelinge tussen die regerings van die twee Suid-Afrikaanse Republieke en die verteenwoordigers van die Britse regering wat uitgeloop het op die vrede wat op 31 Mei 1902 op Vereeniging gesluit is*, Cape Town, 1982

Korf, Lindie, *D.F. Malan: A Political Biography*, Cape Town, 2010

Krebs, Paula M., *Gender, Race, and the Writing of Empire: Public Discourse and the Boer War*, Cambridge, 1999

Kröll, Ulrich, *Die internationale Buren-Agitation 1899–1902*, Munster, 1973

Kuiper, R., *Zelfbeeld en wêreldbeeld. Antirevolutionairen en het buitenland, 1848–1905*, Kampen, 1992

Kuitenbrouwer, M. *Nederland en de opkomst van het moderne imperialisme*, Amsterdam, 1985

Kuitenbrouwer, Vincent, *A War of Words: Dutch Pro-Boer Propaganda and the South African War (1899–1902)*, Amsterdam, 2010

Lake, Marilyn and Henry Reynolds, *Drawing the Global Colour Line: White Men's Countries and the International Challenge of Racial Equality*, Cambridge, 2008

Le Roux, Pieter, 'Verraaier of held. Verdere gedagtes oor Genl Piet de Wet', *Knapzak* 17, 3 (November 2005), 18–22

Lester, Alan, *From Colonization to Democracy: A New Historical Geography of South Africa*, London, 1996

Lester, Alan, *Imperial Networks: Creating Identities in Nineteenth-Century South Africa and Britain*, London, 2001

Leyds, W.J., *De eerste annexatie van de Transvaal*, Amsterdam, 1906

Leyds, W.J., *Eenige correspondentie uit 1899*, The Hague, 1919

Leyds, W.J., *Het insluiten van de Boeren-Republieken*, 2 vols., Amsterdam, 1914

Leyds, W.J., *Onze eerste jaren in Zuid-Afrika 1884–1889. Intieme correspondentie van mevrouw Louise W.S Leyds-Roeff en dr. W.J. Leyds, bestemd voor familie en belangstellenden*, The Hague, 1938

Leyds, W.J., *Tweede, derde en vierde verzameling (correspondentie 1899–1902)*, 8 vols., The Hague, 1930–1934

Limb, Peter, *The ANC's Early Years: Nation, Class and Place in South Africa before 1940*, Pretoria, 2010

Lion Cachet, F., *De worstelstrijd der Transvalers aan het volk van Nederland verhaald*, Amsterdam, 1882

Lunderstedt, Steve, ed., *Summer of 1899: The Siege of Kimberley 14 October to 15 February 1900*, Kimberley, 1999

Mack, Roy, 'The Great Africa Cattle Plague Epidemic of the 1890s', *Tropical Animal Health and Production* (1970)

Magubane, Zine, *Bringing the Empire Home: Race, Class, and Gender in Britain and Colonial South Africa*, Chicago, 2004

Marks, Shula and Stanley Trapido, eds., *The Politics of Race, Class and Nationalism in Twentieth-Century South Africa*, London, 1987

Medalie, David, 'A Century Later: New Fictional Representations of the Boer War', *Journal of Southern African Studies* 30, 2 (2004), 377–392

Meijer, J.W., *Dr. H.J. Coster, 1865–1899*, Pretoria, 1983

Meredith, Martin, *Diamonds, Gold and War: The Making of South Africa*, Johannesburg, 2007

Miller, Russell, *The Adventures of Arthur Conan Doyle*, London, 2008

Miller, Stephen M., *Volunteers on the Veld: Britain's Citizen-Soldiers and the South African War, 1899–1902*, Norman, 2007

Molema, S.M., *The Bantu Past and Present*, Cape Town, 1963

Morgan, Kenneth O., 'The Boer War and the Media (1899–1902)', *Twentieth Century British History* 13 (2002), 1–16

Muller, H.P.N., *Zuid-Afrika. Reisherinneringen*, Leiden, 1889

Nasson, Bill, *Abraham Esau's War: A Black South African War in the Cape, 1899–1902*, Cambridge, 1991

Nasson, Bill, 'Commemorating the Anglo-Boer War in Post-Apartheid South Africa', in Daniel J. Walkowitz and Lisa Maya Knauer, eds., *Memory and the Impact of Political Transformation in Public Space*, Durham, 2004, 277–294

Nasson, Bill, *The War for South Africa: the Anglo-Boer War (1899–1902)*, Cape Town, 2010

Nederland–Zuid-Afrika. Gedenkboek uitgegeven door de Nederlandsch Zuid-Afrikaansche Vereeniging, bij gelegenheid van haar vijftig-jarig bestaan, 1881–1931, Amsterdam, 1931

Netscher, F., 'Dr. W.J. Leyds', in L.E. van Netscher, *Karakters*, Haarlem, 1899, 112–138

Omissi, David and Andrew S. Thompson, eds., *The Impact of the South African War*, Basingstoke, 2002

Pakenham, Thomas, *The Boer War*, London, 1979

Penning, L., *De verkenner van Christiaan de Wet. Een verhaal uit den Engels-Zuid-Afrikaanschen Oorlog 1899–1902*, The Hague, 1902

Pienaar, Philip, *Met Steyn en De Wet. Belangrijke mededeelingen en persoonlijke ervaringen*, Middelburg, 1902

Plaatje, Solomon Tshekisho, *Native Life in South Africa: Before and since the European War and the Boer Rebellion*, New York, 1916

Ploeger, J., *Die lotgevalle van die burgerlike bevolking gedurende die Anglo-Boereoorlog 1899–1902*, 5 vols., Pretoria, 1990

Porter, Bernard, *The Absent-Minded Imperialists: Empire, Society, and Culture in Britain*, Oxford, 2004

Preller, Gustav S., *Lobengula: The Tragedy of a Matabele King*, Johannesburg, 1963

Preston, Antony, *Geïllustreerde geschiedenis van Zuid-Afrika*, Alphen aan de Rijn, 1995

Pretorius, Fransjohan, *Historical Dictionary of the Anglo-Boer War*, Plymouth, 2009

Pretorius, Fransjohan, *Kommandolewe tydens die Anglo-Boereoorlog 1899–1902*, Cape Town, 1991

Pretorius, Fransjohan, Stephan Hofstatter and Wilhelm Snyman, *The Great Escape of the Boer Pimpernel: Christiaan de Wet—The Making of a Legend*, Pietermaritzburg, 2001

Raath, A.W.G. and R.M. Louws, eds., *Die konsentrasiekamp te Bethulie gedurende die Anglo-Boereoorlog*, Bloemfontein, 1991

Raath, A.W.G. and R.M. Louw, eds., *Vroueleed. Die lotgevalle van die vroue en knders buite die konsentrasiekampe 1899–1902*, Bloemfontein, 1993

Reitz, Deneys, *Commando: A Boer Journal of the Boer War*, London, 1929

Reitz, Deneys, *Kommando. 'n Boere-dagboek uit die Engelse Oorlog*, Bloemfontein, 1929

Reitz, Deneys, *No Outspan*, London, 1943

Reitz, Deneys, *Trekking On*, London, 1933

Reitz, F.W., *Outobiografie en 62 gedigte*, Tafelberg, 1978

Reitz, F.W., J. de Villiers Roos and J.C. Smuts, *Een eeuw van onrecht*, Pretoria, 1899

Roberts, Brian, *Churchills in Africa*, London, 1970

Roberts, Brian, *Kimberley: Turbulent City*, Cape Town, 1985

Rosenthal, Eric, *General De Wet: A Biography*, Cape Town, 1946

Ross, Marc Howard, *Cultural Contestation in Ethnic Conflict*, Cambridge, 2007

Ross, Robert, *A Concise History of South Africa*, 2nd edition, Cambridge, 2008

Sandberg, C.G.S., *Twintig jaren onder Krugers Boeren in voor- en tegenspoed*, Amsterdam, 1943

Sandys, Celia, *Churchill Wanted Dead or Alive*, London, 2005

Schmidl, Erwin A., 'The Anglo-Boer War in a Century of Peace', *Historia* 52, 1 (2007), 155–171

Schoeman, Karel, *In liefde en trou. Die lewe van pres. en mev. M.T. Steyn*, Cape Town, 1983

Schoeman, Karel, ed., *Witnesses to War: Personal Documents of the Anglo-Boer War from the Collections of the South African Library*, Cape Town, 1998

Scholtz, Leopold, *Waarom die Boere die oorlog verloor het*, Pretoria, 1999

Scholtz, Leopold and Ingrid Scholtz, 'Regverdige oorlog. 'n Verkennende historiese studie oor die bruikbaarheid van die begrip, deel 1, deel 2', *Tydskrif vir Geesteswetenskappe* 41, 4 (2001),
243–257 and 42, 1 (2002) 14–26

Scholtz, W.L. von R., *Generaal Christiaan de Wet as veldheer*, Leiden, 1978

Schutte, G.J., *De Boerenoorlog na honderd jaar. Opstellen over het veranderende beeld van de Anglo-Boerenoorlog (1899–1902)*, Amsterdam, 1997

Schutte, G.J., *Nederland en de Afrikaners. Adhesie en aversie: Over stamverwantschap, Boerenvrienden, Hollanderhaat, Calvinisme en apartheid*, Franeker, 1986

Schutte, G.J., 'Nederland en de Eerste Transvaalse Vrijheidsoorlog, 1880–1881', *Tijdschrift voor Geschiedenis* 94 (1981), 565–594

Schutte, G.J., 'Willem Johannes Leyds', in J. Charité and A.J.C.M. Gabriels, eds., *Biografisch woordenboek van Nederland 4*, The Hague, 1994, 292–294

Spiers, Edward M., 'The Learning Curve in the South African War: Soldiers' Perspectives', *Historia* 55, 1 (2010), 1–17

Spies, S.B., *Methods of Barbarism? Roberts and Kitchener and Civilians in the Boer Republics: January 1900–May 1902*, Cape Town, 1977

Spies, S.B. and Gail Nattrass, eds., *Jan Smuts: Memoirs of the Boer War*, Johannesburg, 1994

Staats-almanak voor de Zuid-Afrikaansche Republiek, Pretoria 1894, 1897, 1898, 1899

Stanley, Liz, '"A Strange Thing is Memory": Emily Hobhouse, Memory Work, Moral Life and the "Concentration System"', *South African Historica Journal* 52 (2005), 60–81

Stanley, Liz, *Mourning Becomes: Post/memory and Commemoration of the Concentration Camps of the South Africa War,* Manchester, 2006

Stanley, Liz and Helen Dampier, 'Cultural Entrepreneurs, Proto-nationalism and Women's Testimony Writings from the South African War, *Journal of Southern African Studies* 33, 3 (2007), 501–519

Stead, W.T., *Methods of Barbarism: 'War is War' and 'War is Hell?' The Case for Intervention,* London, 1901

Stead, W.T., *Shall I Slay My Brother Boer? An Appeal to the Conscience of Britain,* London, 1899

Stephens, John J., *Fuelling the Empire: South Africa's Gold and the Road to War,* Chichester, 2003

Stolten, Hans Erik, ed., *History Making and Present Day Politics: The Meaning of Collective Memory in South Africa,* Uppsala, 2007

Trapido, Stanley, 'Imperialism, Settler Identities and Colonial Capitalism: The Hundred Year Origins of the 1899 South African War', *Historia* 53, 1 (2008), 46–75

Trapido, Stanley, 'Reflections on Land, Office and Wealth in the South African Republic, 1850–1900', *Historia* 53, 1 (2008), 26–44 [originally 'The South African Republic: Class Formation and the State, 1850–1900', *Societies of Southern Africa in the 19th and 20th Centuries* (1973), 53–65]

Unger, Frederic William, *With 'Bobs' and Kruger: Experiences and Observations by an American Boer War Correspondent in the Field with Both Armies,* Philadelphia, 1901 (reprint Cape Town, 1977)

Van den Berg, Karel, foreword G.J. Schutte, *Beste ouders. Brieven uit de Transvaal van Karel van den Berg 1896–1900,* Amsterdam, 1999

Van der Loo, C.J., *De geschiedenis der Zuid-Afrikaansche Republiek (Transvaal) aan het volk verteld,* Zwolle, 1896

Van der Westhuizen, Christi, *White Power: The Rise and Fall of the National Party,* Cape Town, 2007

Van Heyningen, Elizabeth, 'Costly Mythologies: The Concentration Camps of the South African War in Afrikaner Historiography', *Journal of Southern African Studies* 34, 3 (2008), 495–513

Van Hoek, Kees, *Kruger Days: Reminiscences of Dr. W.J. Leyds,* London, 1939

Van Koppen, Chris A.J., *De geuzen van de negentiende eeuw. Abraham Kuyper en Zuid-Afrika,* Maarssen, 1992

Van Niekerk, L.E., *Dr. W.J. Leyds as gesant van die Zuid-Afrikaansche Republiek,* Pretoria, 1980

Van Niekerk, L.E., *Kruger se regterhand. Biografie van dr. W.J. Leyds,* Pretoria, 1985

Van Onselen, Charles, *Studies in the Social and Economic History of the Witwatersrand 1886–1914, vol. 1: New Babylon, vol. 2: New Nineveh,* Johannesburg, 1982

Van Reenen, Rykie, ed., *Emily Hobhouse: Boer War Letters,* Cape Town, 1984

Van Schoor, M.C.E., *Christiaan Rudolph de Wet. Krygsman en volksman,* Pretoria, 2007

Van Winter, P.J., *Onder Krugers Hollanders. Geschiedenis van de Nederlandsche Zuid-Afrikaansche Spoorweg-Maatschappij,* 2 vols., Amsterdam, 1937

Van Winter, P.J., 'Dr. Leyds en Zuid-Afrika', *Jaarboek van de Maatschappij der Nederlandse Letterkunde* (1942), 13–36

Verloren van Themaat, H., *Twee jaren in den Boerenoorlog,* Haarlem, 1903

Vermeulen, Bram, *Help, ik ben blank geworden. Bekentenissen van een Afrika-correspondent,* Amsterdam, 2009

Viljoen, B.J., *Mijn herinneringen uit den Anglo-Boeren-Oorlog,* Amsterdam, 1902

Vissering, G., *Een Hollander in Zuid-Afrika,* Amsterdam, 1900

Wagenaar, H.D., *Nederlandse onderwijzers in Zuid-Afrika. Een analyse van brieven en postkaarten van Nederlandse onderwijzers ten tijde van de Anglo-Boerenoorlog (1899–1902)*, Rotterdam, 2008

Warner, Philip, *Kitchener: The Man behind the Legend*, London, 1985

Warwick, Peter, *Black People and the South African War, 1899–1902*, Cambridge, 1983

Wassermann, Johan, '"Sowing the Seeds of Rebellion": Chief Bhambatha ka-Mancinza and the Anglo-Boer War, 1899–1902', *African Historical Review* 39, 2 (2007), 91–106

Wesseling, H.L., *Verdeel en heers. De deling van Afrika, 1880–1914*, Amsterdam, 1991

Wessels, André, 'Trauma tydens en na afloop van die Anglo-Boereoorlog van 1899 tot 1902. Enkele historiese perspektiewe', *Knapzak* 21, 2 (October 2009), 143–58

Wessels, André and Anna-Karin Evaldsson, 'Die herdenking van historiese gebeurtenisse', *Werkwinkel* 1, 1 (2006), 147–165

Wessels, André and Annette Wohlberg, 'Black People and Race Relations in the Largest Anglo-Boer War Concentration Camp: Merebank, 1901–1902', *New Contree* 49 (2005), 33–47

Wilson, Keith, ed., *The International Impact of the Boer War*, Chesham, 2001

Wilson, Lady Sarah, *South African Memories: Social, Warlike and Sporting, from Diaries Written at the Time*, London, 1909

Woods, Frederick, ed., *Young Winston's Wars: The Original Despatches of Winston S. Churchill, War Correspondent from 1897 to 1900*, London, 1972

Worden, Nigel, *The Making of Modern South Africa: Conquest, Apartheid, Democracy*, Oxford, 2012

Worsfold, W. Basil, *Lord Milner's Work in South Africa*, London, 1906

Zweers, Louis, *De Boerenoorlog. Nederlandse fotografen aan het front*, The Hague, 1999

Index